HITLER

HITLER

THE PATH TO POWER

Charles Bracelen Flood

HOUGHTON MIFFLIN COMPANY · BOSTON

1989

For information about permission to reproduce selections from this
book, write to Permissions, Houghton Mifflin Company, 2 Park
Street, Boston, Massachusetts 02108.

Library of Congress Cataloging-in-Publication Data
Flood, Charles Bracelen.
Hitler, the path to power / Charles Bracelen Flood.
p.   cm.
Bibliography: p.
Includes index.
ISBN 0-395-35312-2
1. Hitler, Adolf, 1889–1945. 2. Germany — Politics and
government — 1918–1933. 3. Heads of state — Germany — Biography.
I. Title.
DD247.H5F54   1989
943.086'092'4 — dc 19   88-39547
[B]   CIP

Printed in the United States of America

V 10 9 8 7 6 5 4 3 2 1

Specfic excerpts from *Unheard Witness* by Ernst Hanfstaengl. Copy-
right 1957 by Ernst F. Sedgwick Hanfstaengl. Reprinted by permis-
sion of Harper & Row, Publishers, Inc.
Specific excerpts from *Munich 1923: The Story of Hitler's First
Grab for Power* by John Dornberg. Copyright © 1982 by John
Dornberg. Reprinted by permission of Sterling Lord Literistic, Inc.

Every effort has been made to obtain permission to reprint the photographs of Rudolf Hess and Hans von Seeckt. If necessary, credits
will be added in future printings.

This book is dedicated to my children, Caperton, Lucy, and Curtis, in the hope that they will always think for themselves.

ACKNOWLEDGMENTS

Most authors thank everyone else before saying a few kind words about the role that their spouses have played in sustaining their work. I wish to reverse the process, and thank my wife, Katherine Burnam Flood, for her remarkably cheerful and steadfast support during this long and complicated project. In the face of ever-receding dates for the manuscript's completion, she has skillfully managed our family affairs and offered me constant and much-needed encouragement. Her affectionate help has been beyond all praise.

Sylvia Burkhart, professor of German at Eastern Kentucky University, rendered into English for the first time scores of significant passages from the pertinent original sources. Working on my behalf both in Munich and in the United States, she combined the skills of a gifted translator and the instincts of a detective, and played a singularly important role in bringing this story to life.

Dagmar Fischer of Gelnhausen, Federal Republic of Germany, contributed many fine translations to this work, and her efforts were successfully followed by those of Marion Sinsel, also of Gelnhausen. Dagmar Fliedner of Hamburg produced many extremely effective translations for me. Jean C. Surplus of Richmond, Kentucky, translated a lengthy document concerning Hermann Goering's flight from Munich following the Beer Hall Putsch in November of 1923.

In the Federal Republic, others who were of assistance include Frau Elisabeth Heidt of the Süddeutscher Verlag Bilderdienst in Munich and Frau Christel Sembach-Krone of Munich's famous circus company, the Zirkus Krone. Professor Burkhart's research inquiries on my behalf in Munich were greatly expedited through the cooperation of the staffs of the Institut für Zeitgeschichte and the Munich City Archives.

Here in the United States, John Toland answered questions about photographs, and offered suggestions concerning assistance in doing research in Munich. In an exchange of letters in 1983, Agnes F. Peterson of the Hoover Institution was most helpful in regard to the microfilmed documents known as Collection NSDAP Hauptarchiv. Also during 1983, John E. Taylor of the Military Archives Division of the National Archives offered many useful suggestions concerning the holdings of the National Archives. During the same period of research, Raymond Teichman and Mark Renovitch of the Franklin D. Roosevelt Library at Hyde Park, New York, facilitated my use of the John Toland Papers.

A special word of thanks is due Milan Hauner, author of *Hitler, The Chronology of His Life and Time*, for making available to me the page proofs of that exceedingly useful work prior to its publication by the Macmillan Press. Access to this day-to-day record of Hitler's life came at a most opportune time, and I am truly grateful.

Among the libraries on whose resources I drew were the Manuscript Division of the Library of Congress, the New York Public Library, the library of the New-York Historical Society, and the Washington and Lee University Library.

Closer to home, I am much indebted to a number of people at Eastern Kentucky University. Theodor Langenbruch, professor of German and chairman of the Department of Foreign Languages, led me to translators, answered many questions raised by my research, and offered many valuable observations. Ursel Boyd, professor of German, shared with me a number of fascinating experiences stemming from her childhood in Berlin during the later years of the Weimar Republic. Joseph A. Biesinger, professor of social science, offered many useful comments based on his study of conditions in Munich during the early Weimar period, and Glenn O. Carey, professor of English, contributed insightful evaluations. Glen Kleine, professor of journalism, brought additional sources to my attention.

Thanks and praise are due my friend Dean Ernest E. Weyhrauch, director of libraries and learning resources at Eastern Kentucky University, and his able and conscientious staff. Whether initiating interlibrary loans or making available their microfilm copies of the

Völkischer Beobachter, these dedicated librarians could not have been more helpful. Paul A. Willis, director of libraries at the University of Kentucky, kindly placed his library's services at my disposal, and I am also indebted to Brad Grissom of the university staff for his loan to me of personal materials helpful in reconstructing the events of the Beer Hall Putsch. The library of Berea College was a valuable source, and I thank Barbara Power, circulation librarian, for her cheerful and never-failing assistance.

Several friends offered indispensable help. Jill Halcomb, author of *The SA: A Historical Perspective*, was tremendously helpful in my selection and organization of the illustrations for this book. Thomas Parrish, a walking encyclopedia of the antecedents of World War II, frequently interrupted his work on his book about the relationship between President Franklin D. Roosevelt and General George C. Marshall to answer questions and offer his opinion on matters large and small, and I am deeply grateful for his patient and often unique aid. Thomas Fleming offered sound and badly needed advice concerning the total organization of a project of this length. Helen Poz made valuable suggestions. Mrs. Athey R. Lutz of Parkersburg, West Virginia, wrote me an exceptionally interesting letter about her travels in Germany between the wars, and similar information was furnished me by Marion Chaffee of Farmington, Connecticut.

As always, my agent, Sterling Lord, represented my interests most constructively. He spent considerable time reading this book at an earlier stage, and was extremely encouraging during a long period of work. I thank him for his help with this and earlier books. At Houghton Mifflin, I have benefited from the strong support and fine editorial suggestions of Austin Olney, whose retirement removes from the scene one of the nation's first-rate editors. Helena Bentz, as Houghton Mifflin's managing editor, was a fount of excellent professional help and encouragement — and a delightful telephone conversationist. I also very much appreciate the impressive manner in which John Sterling has taken over as my editor.

Superb manuscript editors seldom receive their well-deserved praise. Both in *Lee — The Last Years* and in this work, I was fortunate in having Frances Apt give me the benefit of her eagle eye, sense of humor, and fine feeling for the small detail and the project as a whole. The final line editing was done most thoroughly and effectively by Gerry Morse. I thank these two for their attention to both facts and style. I also wish to thank Rebecca Saikia-Wilson, Liz Duvall, and Marie B. Morris for expediting this project. In this Lee-Hitler continuum at Houghton Mifflin, Stella Easland was most helpful in keeping track of matters large and small, and I am grateful to her for it, and for being a friend as well.

Last, but never least, are those who provide the indispensable secretarial assistance. In my case, this has involved correspondence on research, as well as the typing and retyping involved in a project of this size. This book would have been an indecipherable mass of filing cards, rough drafts, and dictation tapes without the friendly, professional, endlessly conscientious work of the following: Debbie L. Angle, Mary Ellen Shuntich (now of the Development Office at the University of North Carolina at Charlotte), and Diana E. Miller. Their efforts were ably complemented at various times by Wendy Ashcraft, Felicia May, and Pam Ruchka.

Nothing is more dangerous in political
life than the abandonment of reason. The
intellect must remain the controlling,
regulating force in human affairs.
— KURT SONTHEIMER

Wherever they burn books, they will
also, in the end, burn people.
— HEINRICH HEINE

Thank God, I've always avoided
persecuting my enemies.
— ADOLF HITLER

HITLER

HITLER

CHAPTER

1

PROFESSOR KARL ALEXANDER VON MÜLLER, a thirty-six-year-old Bavarian historian of conservative political convictions, was nearing the end of his two-hour lecture on post-Reformation German history. On this June morning in 1919, seven months after Germany's defeat in the First World War, an unusual group of students sat in a lecture hall at the University of Munich. They were selected officers and enlisted men of the German army, some of whom were career soldiers hoping to remain in the forces that had been so drastically reduced since the Armistice; most were officers waiting to be demobilized.

The object of the lectures, an army-organized indoctrination course, was to equip these men to deliver propaganda lectures to units throughout Bavaria. A high priority was assigned to arguments against Bolshevism. In Munich the postwar chaos had given German communists the opportunity to seize power and create the short-lived Bavarian Soviet Republic, which had come to its bloody end a month earlier. Some of the students in field grey uniforms had been in the columns that fought their way back into Munich and killed other Germans who wore red armbands. The changes of recent months were dizzying — military defeat, the Kaiser's abdication and flight to Holland, a new form of government in Berlin led by socialists, violent uprisings by communists, and a crushing peace treaty about to be signed at Versailles. That, and shortages of food and clothing, unemployment, inflation, and the continuing struggle between millions of adherents of both left and right, were making Germans ask questions and seek answers as they had never done before. In setting up this course, the army wished to stress the ideal of a conservative, tradition-respecting society dedicated to rebuilding the nation's power. To that end it was enlisting the services of such men as Müller, an aristocrat who in happier days had studied at Oriel College, Oxford, as one of Germany's first group of Rhodes Scholars.[1]

Professor von Müller ended his lecture, and a lively discussion period ensued. When at last the men finished their questions and observations, the professor stepped down from the platform and started out of the large room. He found his way obstructed by a group that was "standing spellbound around a man who was vehemently haranguing them in a strangely guttural voice, and with mounting passion. I had the peculiar feeling," Müller wrote, "that the man was feeding on the excitement which he himself had whipped up. I saw a pale, thin face, and hair hanging down the forehead in unmilitary fashion. He had a close-cropped mustache, and his strikingly large, pale blue eyes shone with a cold fanatical light."[2]

The next morning Müller gave his other lecture in this course, a talk on the political history of the war. After his lecture, but before the men left, he chatted with a former classmate, Captain Karl Mayr of the General Staff. In this volatile postwar situation in Bavaria, Mayr was one of the army's important men, and a busy one. As commander of the propaganda section of army headquarters in Munich, he monitored the activities of local political parties, using army funds to support right-wing organizations and publishing firms. To gather political intelligence, he had a group of enlisted men who were designated as *Vertrauensmänner*, undercover agents. Mayr had organized this course and chosen those who were to attend, including a number of his agents who were slated to give propaganda lectures to their fellow soldiers.

"Do you know," Müller asked Mayr, "that you have a natural wonder of an orator among your instructors? Once he gets started, he just keeps going."

"Where is he sitting?"

Müller pointed to the man he had noticed the day before.

"Oh, that's Hitler of the List Regiment. You, Hitler, come up here."

As Müller recounted it, "He came obediently, with clumsy movements, advancing to the podium with a sort of defiant embarrassment." The professor tried to draw him out, but "the conversation proved unproductive."[3]

This thirty-year-old *Gefreiter*, a rank equivalent to lance corporal or private first class, had served throughout the war as a notably brave and reliable regimental headquarters runner who carried messages forward under fire, but his recent usefulness to his superiors had been as an informer, a military stool pigeon. When the communists took over Munich, Hitler's regiment had remained, without leadership, in the Maximilian II Barracks on the city's outskirts. Some of the troops enthusiastically joined the Reds, while the rest, presumably including Adolf Hitler, wore red armbands as protection. Hitler's activities during this period never became clear, but when Munich was recaptured, he started working for the military Commission of Inquiry that brought to trial those soldiers who were accused of fighting beside the armed workers of the communist councils. His job was to testify against these men, and he threw himself into it; a contemporary said that Hitler's evidence was "mercilessly exact."[4] Men began dying in front of firing squads as a result. Hitler's superiors saw him not only as an exemplary soldier who had won the Iron Cross, First Class, a medal rarely awarded to enlisted men, but as a patriot who had proved his willingness and ability to support them in their postwar battles against the Marxists. At the moment his only duties were to attend these lectures, but he, too, was carried on Captain Mayr's roster as an undercover agent.

The city through which this solitary bachelor soldier walked during off-duty hours was a place of great contrasts in the spring of 1919. There was always the Munich sky, shifting from sultry grey to shimmering blue and white above a city that had views of the Alps, just twenty-five miles to the south. The Isar River flowed beside pastel-shaded buildings and churches whose cupolas and domed "onion" towers spoke not of Gothic Germany, but of Italy and even the minarets of the East. Munich was more than two hundred miles from the Western Front, on which Hitler had served, but its houses were pocked by gunfire from *der Krieg nach dem Kriege* — the war after the war.

A few steps down from a cobblestoned street brought one into a cavernous cellar, one of the hundreds of beer halls in this city of six hundred thousand. The mountain sky vanished, and with it the statues, the fountains, the view of the opera house and the cathedral, the aboveground Munich that reflected centuries of artistic activity. A returning prewar visitor recognized the fat waitresses in dirndl skirts, the oomp-pah-pah music, the men in lederhosen eating Munich's special sausages and sliced white radishes, but in these huge cellars something new was happening: a fight was taking place for the German soul.

As soon as the Western Front fell silent and the various forms of revolution began, these underground halls began to echo with the speeches of agitators who realized that the way to win over the man in the street was to follow him into the cellar where he drank. Everything was new: before the war, German political speeches had been like long lectures. Now impassioned young orators flung their calls for action to Bavarians who had seen their comfortable lives vanish and their society collapse. A speaker in these new arenas had to compete with hundreds of conversations already in progress, the clinking of beer steins, and the constant movement of waitresses through the blue-grey pipe smoke. If he were so fortunate as to attract attention, he had to be ready for bitter heckling from a war-disillusioned crowd. Only those speakers who loudly caught and held their audiences had a chance of finishing what they had to say.

The new conditions favored the orator who spoke to the emotions of those for whom the old answers had failed. In the first flush of leftist influence and power, this was exemplified by Ernst Toller, the twenty-six-year-old Jewish playwright, poet, and veteran of the trenches. A man who listened to the revolutionary leader denounce those who led Germany into war described it: "He cried out his feelings heatedly, ecstatically, and with wild gesticulations and a distorted face. . . . He carried everyone along with him. Single women wept or became completely wild." A student at the university said of Toller's Marxism, selective pacifism, and calls for revolution, "He carried the people by the force of his own convictions. . . . They wanted a mission in life; Toller supplied them with one."[5]

The extreme left was now gone in Munich; Toller was in prison, and many of his fellow leaders dead. Right-wingers of every type had flocked into the normally easygoing city, but in the beer halls there was still a wide range of views to be heard. The speaker who persisted found an audience desperate for an explanation of Germany's plight. Racists provided scapegoats; monarchists urged that Bavaria restore its royal House of Wittelsbach. A witness to all this subsequently wrote, "There was nothing so stupid that it would not have found thousands of willing believers in Munich," and the American foreign correspondent Ben Hecht, later to achieve fame as co-author of the play The Front Page, cabled his managing editor in Chicago: "Germany is having a nervous breakdown. There is nothing sane to report."[6]

A few days after completing the indoctrination course, Gefreiter Hitler was temporarily assigned to a regiment stationed in Munich, to give propaganda lectures to the troops. He found the soldiers still far below wartime standards of discipline. In the army's effort to combat leftist influences, "the men were now expected," Hitler said, "to learn to feel and think in a national and patriotic way."

Hitler was ready to do his part. "I started out with the greatest enthusiasm and love. For all at once I was offered an opportunity of speaking before a larger audience; and the thing that I had always presumed from pure feeling without knowing it was now corroborated: I could 'speak.' "[7]

2

ADOLF HITLER had been getting ready to "speak" for a long time.
Born on Easter Sunday, April 20, 1889, in the small Austrian town
of Braunau on the Inn River, which separated what was then the
Austro-Hungarian Empire and the German Empire, he and the other
German-speaking Austrian boys with whom he grew up in a succession
of border-area towns considered Germany to be their cultural and
spiritual home.

Adolf's father, Alois Hitler, was a self-made man, a customs inspector whose civil service rank assured him a degree of local prominence.
Although he went through a legitimation proceeding at the age of
thirty-nine, Alois was illegitimately born, and his mother had gone to
her grave without revealing the name of his father. Thus it was that
Adolf Hitler, living in communities where gossip was the great cottage
industry, would never know who his paternal grandfather was.

In his relations with women, Hitler's father was a small-town Henry
VIII. Alois's freewheeling bachelor ways had already produced an
illegitimate daughter before his marriage, at the age of thirty-six, to
a widow, fourteen years his senior, who soon became an invalid. After
seven years of her husband's infidelities, the lady sued for a legal
separation from Alois, who was having an affair with a nineteen-year-
old kitchen maid in the hotel where he and his sick wife were living.
It was rumored that he had already bought a coffin for his wife.[1] Two
years later the kitchen maid, now his common-law wife, bore him an
illegitimate son, and the following year his estranged wife died, in
time for him to go to the altar with his child's mother, who was seven
months pregnant with a daughter. The next year his second wife
conveniently died, enabling Alois Hitler to marry his children's nurse-

maid, Klara Pölzl, a sweet and quiet country girl twenty-three years younger than Alois and pregnant by him.

Four years later, after the death of this child and two more, Klara gave birth to Adolf. In ways different from those the various women had experienced, he was to have just as harsh a time with his father. Alois had a capacity for violence. According to Adolf's illegitimate older half-brother, Alois Jr., their father "often beat the dog until the dog would cringe and wet the floor." When the paternal attention made one of its frequent shifts to the older boy, he was beaten "unmercifully with a hippopotamus whip," and was on one occasion choked until he lost consciousness.[2] Alois Jr. ran away at the age of fourteen, leaving seven-year-old Adolf and his father on a collision course. Paula Hitler, Adolf's sister, two years younger than he, said that Adolf "challenged my father to extreme harshness," and as a result "got his sound thrashing every day."

The physical side of this confrontation ended one day when Adolf was eleven and read in an adventure story that those who are truly brave experience pain without flinching. "I then resolved never again to cry when my father whipped me." As his mother cowered on one side of the room, helpless to stop what was going on, Hitler's father kept beating him with a stick, determined to produce the usual cries. "I counted silently the blows of the stick which lashed my rear end." After thirty-two lashes his father stopped; Hitler said his father never tried to beat him again.[3] Three years later Alois died of a pleural hemorrhage at the age of sixty-five, leaving a hideous legacy. He had created in his son the classic desire of a whipped child: the need for revenge, the still-unformulated search for an enemy to punish and destroy. In young Adolf this marched beside his Pan-Germanism, the romantic dream of an ever-greater Germany that was so dear to these Austrian boys who were determined to be more German than the Germans, and a notion of a Nordic racial ideal that impelled him to tell one of his friends, "You are not a *Germane*," the term for the ancient Teutonic tribes, because his friend had brown eyes instead of blue ones like Adolf's.[4] In Linz, the large town of fity thousand to which Klara Hitler moved with her children two years after her husband's death, anti-Semitism was not nearly as strong as in Vienna, which at that time was governed by an elected municipal council made up almost entirely of members of a specifically anti-Semitic political party. Nonetheless, the prejudice was present. "We didn't like them," a classmate of Hitler's later said of the Jewish boys in their school, "but we never interfered with them. Once Adolf shouted at another boy, 'You dirty Jewish pig!' "[5] August Kubizek, Hitler's only close friend, remembered that during a walk along the Bethlehemstrasse, as they passed the town's one small synagogue, Hitler said, "This shouldn't be here."[6]

By 1919, when he was at last ready to "speak," that youth was a hate-filled and self-centered man of thirty. Back in Linz, a succession of frustrations and sorrows had slowly begun to unfold for him. His schooling stopped after the ninth grade; at the age of sixteen, his formal education was over. One of his teachers spoke of his being "distinctly talented," but his grades were poor, and he had demonstrated that he was both "fiery-tempered" and absolutely unwilling to do any kind of work that did not interest him.[7] To complete his secondary education, he would have had to go on to three years of *Oberrealschule*, but it is unlikely that he would have been admitted, and in any case he did not want to go. He sat around at home, enjoying the meals cooked for him by his doting mother and staying up all night absorbing endless books on art, history, and military matters, as well as the wildly inaccurate tales of cowboys and Indians written by Karl May, a German who had never crossed the Atlantic.

Hitler had a flair for drawing; filling the apartment at 31 Humboldtstrasse with his sketches, he dreamed of becoming a great painter. His friend Kubizek never found him dull. Adolf was constantly thinking up grandiose schemes, including an idea, far ahead of its time, to turn nearby Wildberg Castle into a living museum filled with men and women in medieval costume demonstrating their crafts and trades. One night after they had seen Wagner's opera *Rienzi*, based on the life of the Roman commoner who became a dictator and sought to restore the ancient greatness of Rome, Hitler burst into rapturous eloquence. His eyes "feverish with excitement," he spoke in a transported way of a future day when he would be entrusted with a special mission and would receive a mandate from his people to lead them out of bondage.[8]

His troubles began when Adolf confidently went off to Vienna at the age of eighteen to take the entrance examinations for the General School of Painting at the Academy of Fine Arts. His precise but lifeless drawings failed to gain him admission. "When I received my rejection," he wrote, "it struck me as a bolt from the blue."[9] A revised dream of becoming a great architect collided with reality when the Architectural School informed him that he was ineligible for consideration because of his incomplete education. On top of these rejections came the death of his mother, the one person in his life whom Hitler indisputably loved. The doctor who attended Klara Hitler and signed her death certificate said, "In all my forty odd years of practice I had never seen a young man so broken by grief and bowed down by suffering as young Adolf Hitler was on that day."[10]

Then came six strange and dismal years, the first five of them in Vienna, where he had been living when he was called home for his mother's final illness. August Kubizek soon arrived in Vienna to pursue his musical studies at the conservatory; they shared a rented room. Kubizek knew his friend's extraordinary range of ideas and moods, but now he saw something more: "Altogether, in these early days in Vienna, I had the impression that Adolf had become unbalanced. He would fly into a temper at the slightest thing. . . . Choking with his catalogue of hates, he would pour his fury over everything, against mankind in general who did not understand him, who did not appreciate him and by whom he was persecuted." When Hitler stopped pretending to his friend that he was attending art classes and admitted that the academy "rejected me, they threw me out, they turned me down," he launched into a tirade during which "his face was livid, the mouth quite small, the lips almost white. But the eyes glittered. There was something sinister about them. As if all the hate of which he was capable lay in those glowing eyes!"[11]

Greater humiliation lay some distance ahead. Although he lived simply, Hitler was using up the money left him by his father and mother. It took a year and a half for it to run out, eighteen months during which he made virtually no effort to find a suitable job. He continued the life of a student without a school; his wide self-assigned reading included each month's issue of *Ostara*, a magazine that explained the world in terms of a superior Aryan race mortally in danger of sexual seduction and mongrelizaton by swarthy ape-men. His long walks around Vienna took him to the Reichsrat, the magnificent Austrian parliament building. Because Hitler still clung to the idea of becoming a self-taught architect, his initial purpose may have been to study the details of this building as he had those of so many others, but at the age of nineteen he stepped into the Strangers' Gallery of the House of Deputies. According to Hitler, "I had always hated parliament, but not as an institution in itself." His anger was stirred by the knowledge that the representatives of the German-speaking population of this western half of the Austro-Hungarian Empire were outnumbered by the total of legislators representing Czechs, Slovenes, and Austrian Poland, threatening what Hitler called "my instinct of national self-preservation." Nonetheless, "in consequence of my extensive newspaper reading, I had, without myself realizing it, been inoculated with a certain admiration for the British Parliament. . . . Could a people have any more exalted form of self-government?"[12]

On the House floor, an important economic measure was under debate. Hitler described what he saw:

> A wildly gesticulating mass screaming all at once in every different key, presided over by a good-natured old uncle who was striving in the sweat of his brow to revive the dignity of the House by violently ringing his bell and alternating gentle reproofs with grave admonitions.
> I couldn't help laughing.

A few weeks later, Hitler returned to see the lawmakers.

> The picture was changed beyond recognition. The hall was absolutely empty. Down below everybody was asleep. A few deputies were in their places, yawning at one another; one was "speaking." A vice-president of the House was present, looking into the hall with obvious boredom.
> The first misgivings arose in me.[13]

In mid-September of 1909 Hitler ran out of money. A year earlier, while Kubizek was on vacation, he had moved out; too proud to admit even to his one close friend that he had to seek cheaper lodgings, he left no forwarding address. Now, in the autumn of his twentieth year, having moved an additional time to even worse quarters, he slipped out of Room 21 at Sechshauserstrasse 58 without telling his landlord, presumably because he could not pay the rent. All he had left to sustain him was a government orphan's pension of twenty-five kronen a month. He became a vagrant, sleeping for three cold autumn months in coffee houses, in the cheapest flophouses, and on park benches.

Shortly before Christmas, Adolf Hitler took his place in a long, shuffling line of Vienna's poorest tramps, waiting for a night's free shelter in the *Obdachlosenheim,* a vast barracks for the homeless. Hitler's overcoat was gone, probably for cash at a pawn shop. His checked blue suit was filthy, and his body was weakened. He was taken in and given a shower while his clothes were deloused. Then he was given a bowl of soup and some bread, and assigned a wire-spring cot with two faded brown sheets.[14]

Assisted by professional tramps, he began a slow upward climb. He earned a few coins in tips he received from travelers whose bags he carried at a train station. Within two months he was a resident in the *Männerheim,* a relatively comfortable charitable institution for homeless men, where he had a cubicle and a bed with two clean white sheets. Having swallowed his pride to the extent of writing his aunt Johanna, who sent him fifty kronen, he was able to buy some art supplies and go into an odd little business with another vagrant, Reinhold Hanisch. In a corner of the reading room of the Männerheim, Hitler started painting postcards, watercolors that were copies of pictures of Vienna street scenes, and Hanisch took them around to taverns and sold them to tourists. Soon they found a more lucrative market: Adolf Hitler, who had dreamed of entering the Academy of Fine Arts and becoming a great painter, started doing larger watercolors and oil paintings for frame makers who found that their frames sold more readily when there were pictures of some sort already in them.

For the next three years Hitler continued this strange existence in the men's home, with free accommodations, working space, and an income pieced together from his pension, his paintings, and presents of money from his aunt Johanna. Six months after they began their partnership, Hitler had the police arrest Hanisch on the charge that he had cheated him of his share of the sale of a painting; the merits of the case were never adjudged by the court, but thereafter Hitler was his own salesman. He hated going around to these dealers in frames, tipping his hat and displaying his latest batch of pictures for them to choose from, but he did it, making sure that his hair was cut and his threadbare clothes neat. The dealers greeted him politely and paid him fairly, and Hitler never ceased to feel ashamed of what his dream of being a painter had become.

On this low rung of society, he became a respected figure among the long-term residents of the shelter. He learned to budget and saved a small amount of money. In many respects his life was spartan; it was womanless, which did not appear to bother him, and he touched no alcohol and rarely smoked. He had ample time to read; his favorite of the newspapers he pored over in workingmen's cafés was the *Deutsches Volksblatt,* an anti-Semitic sheet. Always there was time for frequently heated political debate with the other residents, one of whom called him a "reactionary swine" for his ideas.[15]

Hitler loved music and knew a considerable amount about it. A small sum bought him standing room at the performances of Wagner at the Vienna Opera, then at its zenith. For Hitler, Wagner's operas were not only a supreme musical experience, but the throbbing center of his vision of a romantic mythological Germany, glorious in the past and destined to be even greater in the future. It was the era of half-digested Darwinist interpretation, the idea that might makes right, and Wagner struck every kind of chord in the seeking Hitler. There was Wagner's life, the triumph of initially unappreciated genius over lesser men of conventional tastes, the premonition even in humiliated hours that greatness lay ahead; Wagner's ideas, the belief that emotion and intuition are superior to reason, that genius has all rights and mediocrity none; Wagner's racism, Valhalla for Nordic warriors falling in splendid battle, and his anti-Semitic summation: "I hold the Jewish race to be the born enemy of pure humanity and everything noble in man."[16]

II

These six years of institutionalized failure and selective self-instruction led to the cruelest of examinations, the trench warfare of 1914–1918. Its outbreak found Hitler living in Munich, to which he had moved in 1913 to escape conscription into the army of the Austro-Hungarian Empire, an army serving "the Habsburg regime which I so hated," a monarchy that Hitler saw as a "sorry dynasty" reigning over a multilingual "impossible state" that was bent upon "the gradual Slavization of the German element" within it.[17]

Hitler volunteered on the day Germany declared war on France, petitioning to be allowed to serve in the Bavarian forces although he was an Austrian citizen. He received just eight weeks of training before being sent to the Western Front as a rifleman in the Sixteenth Bavarian Infantry Reserve Regiment, also known as the Regiment List, for its commander, Colonel Wilhelm von List.

At twenty-five, Private Adolf Hitler was headed for Ypres, a town near the North Sea in the part of Belgium known as West Flanders. The slaughter starting there would in time leave Ypres within a vast ring of forty cemeteries. As for how Hitler might stand the rigors of the front, Hans Mend, an enlisted man who was responsible for some of his brief training, asked himself the first time he saw Private Hitler, "What is this slender man going to do, if he has to carry a pack on active service?"[18] Mend was not the first to have such doubts; when the Austrian military authorities had finally caught up to Hitler six months before the war and ordered him to come from Munich to Salzburg for a physical examination, Hitler was rejected with the notation "Too weak for armed or auxiliary service, unfit to bear arms."[19] His five-foot-nine-inch body was somewhat above the average height of those in the German army, but he looked frail, and his skin was so sallow that Mend spoke of his "slim yellow face."

Other than long and seemingly compulsive walks, Hitler had engaged in neither exercise nor sports in civilian life, and had experienced a number of illnesses. He did not drink and no longer smoked even an infrequent cigarette, but for years he had eaten skimpy meals at odd hours; the food was nutritionally poor, and his friend Kubizek had joked about his craving for the sweetest pastries. His sleep habits were worse than his diet. Yet, despite the recruit's yellow color, Mend was struck by Hitler's "energetic face," which at this time had a wide, full mustache, and also by a "dynamic glance" from Hitler's startling light blue eyes, which he described as having a "lively shine."

On the second day of training Mend saw Hitler handling his newly issued rifle. "He looked at it with delight, as a woman looks at her jewelry, which made me laugh secretly."[20]

At Ypres, Hitler received the bloodiest possible baptism of fire. At seven o'clock in the morning of October 29, 1914, the Bavarians moved forward through thick fog toward the line held by the British between Gheluvelt and Becelaere, five miles east of Ypres. They had already come under some random fire, but now British machine guns opened up on them. "Suddenly men were saying that Stöwer, our platoon commander, was wounded. Good God, I thought, that's a fine beginning."[21]

Something far worse was about to happen. The men of the Regiment List were wearing caps that looked like those of the British. In the fog, the German regiments coming through the mists behind the Bavarians, Württembergers on one side of them and Saxons on the other, opened fire at what they thought was a surprise counterattack. Private Ernst Schmidt was lying beside Hitler under a hedge, trying to escape this murderous crossfire, when an officer appeared through the fog. He asked them to volunteer to go back the way they had come, across terrain where other Germans would be shooting at them. They must find regimental headquarters and report what was happening.

Realizing that the caps were the problem, Hitler threw his away. He and Schmidt both made it back to headquarters; even then, it was half an hour before the firing from their own side could be stopped. Private Ignaz Westenkirchner, who served with Hitler throughout the war, said of their first hour on the Western Front, "The losses among the Sixteenth Regiment were enormous."[22]

Hitler rejoined his company, and by ten in the morning had experienced an eternity of combat. At one point he lay at the edge of a wood, jolted by incoming British artillery shells, which he saw "sending up fountains of stones, earth, and sand, tearing enormous trees out by their roots and smothering everything in a stinking yellow-green smoke."[23] By now his company commander, all the lieutenants, and all but one sergeant were dead or wounded; the major commanding the battalion appeared through the smoke and led them in a final dash to an enemy trench. Hitler leapt in and, wondering why he landed so softly, realized that under his feet was a carpet of "dead and wounded English soldiers." At last the German artillery was heard from, smashing a British trench 250 meters on their left front until the British started "swarming out like ants out of an ant-heap and then we charged. We were across the fields in a flash and after some bloody hand-to-hand fighting we cleared one trench after another. A lot of the enemy put their hands up. Those that didn't were slaughtered."[24]

It was still before noon. Hitler's company had lost not only its officers and all the sergeants except one, but most of the corporals as well. The major reappeared, "calmly smoking and cool," accompanied by his adjutant, a second lieutenant, and told them to prepare to attack again. On their own initiative, Hitler and some others scoured the battlefield, hunting up knots of leaderless soldiers, some from other regiments, and brought them forward as replacements.

> When I came back for the second time after rounding up a party of Württembergers, the major was lying on the ground with a gaping hole in his chest, round him a pile of corpses. Now only one officer was left, his adjutant. We were boiling with rage. "Lead us into the attack, sir!" we all shouted at him. . . . Four times we tried and each time we had to withdraw. Of my whole section, only I and one other remained and soon there was only me. My right sleeve was ripped off by a bullet but miraculously I was not even grazed. Finally at 2 o'clock we launched our fifth attack and this time were able to occupy the edge of the wood and the farm buildings.[25]

At the end of this day, regimental headquarters remembered the two men who had reported that the forward elements were under fire from their own side. Hitler and the taciturn Schmidt were unofficially attached to headquarters as runners, messengers who carried dispatches to and from the units of the regiment in the front-line trenches, or in the open, moving forward. On his second day in his new job, a few hours after Colonel von List had been killed, Hitler was lying on the battlefield close to List's deputy when that lieutenant colonel was seriously wounded. Under heavy fire, Hitler pulled him back to a place where he found a combat medical orderly; then he and Schmidt carried the officer to a dressing station. The next day, Hitler was promoted to Gefreiter.

On November 3, the survivors of Hitler's regiment were pulled off the front for three days of rest and reorganization, after which they were sent back to battle at Messines, six miles to the southwest. Hitler, Schmidt, and Westenkirchner were now officially assigned to regimental headquarters as messengers. They therefore lived in better conditions, slightly behind the line, and ate better food, but it was no sinecure: on the first day of their next action — an attack on the French at Wytschaete, two miles north of Messines — three of the regimental staff's eight messengers were killed and a fourth was severely wounded.

North of Wytschaete, in an attack on a woods that the British had nicknamed "Shrewsbury Forest," the regiment's second battalion ran into such deadly resistance that it was soon being commanded by a lieutenant, who himself was killed before the day was out. Trying to get a grip on the situation, the new regimental commander, Lieutenant Colonel Philipp Engelhardt, a man whom Hitler said they all "worshipped," went forward on a personal reconnaissance, accompanied by Hitler and another runner.[26] Arriving at a position from which he could overlook the wooded area through which his men were moving, Engelhardt stepped from behind some bushes to get a better view of the action. Instantly bullets snapped at him from British rifles and machine guns. Hitler and the other runner pounced on him, shielding him with their bodies and shoving him back into a ditch. As they lay there, both privates lectured their commander to the effect that they did not want to lose him. He silently shook hands with them.[27]

The next day, in the combination of tent and dugout that was serving as regimental headquarters, Hitler was inside, along with the colonel and the rest of the headquarters staff, while the list was being composed of the first men in the regiment who had been recommended for the Iron Cross; Hitler's name was on it. Four company commanders came into the crowded command post to discuss those recommended for the honor; to make room for them Hitler and the other three messengers who had survived Wytschaete went outside. "We had not been out there more than five minutes," Hitler wrote, "when a shell hit the tent, severely wounding Lt-Col. Engelhardt and either killing or wounding the rest of the headquarters staff."[28]

On December 2, 1914, Hitler received the Iron Cross, Second Class. Westenkirchner knew him well enough by then to understand what was happening. "He had now found that for which he had been longing for many years, a real home and recognition. The Regiment List had given it to him."[29] Though it subjected you to constant risk of your life, here was an institution that did not reject you, but instead pinned a medal on your chest. Here was a figure of authority that did not lash you with a stick, but shook hands with you. Writing to his landlord back in Munich two days after he received his Iron Cross, Hitler told him, "It was the happiest day of my life."[30] He was later to say "I passionately loved soldiering," and he referred to the war as "the greatest and most unforgettable time of my earthly existence," an experience "equivalent to thirty years' university training in regard to life's problems."[31] Another soldier said of him, "The Austrian never relaxes. He always acts as if we'd lose the war if he weren't on the job every minute."[32] While the other runners were discussing whose turn it was to take a message forward to a command post under fire, Hitler would put the message into the pouch on his belt and be gone.

Hans Mend had been assigned to headquarters as a mounted courier riding to and from the rear areas with dispatches. "As soon as serious firing would begin on the front," he said, "Hitler acted like a racehorse before it has to start. He had the habit of walking around restlessly, buckling on his equipment. This often got on the nerves of the others."[33] The situation during a British smash at the German lines in northwestern France was described by a telephone operator at headquarters: "Well, it was the day when the Tommy attacked and we no longer had any communications to the front. No telephone functioned, the heavy fire had torn all cables, courier dogs and messenger pigeons no longer returned, everything failed, so Adolf had to dare it and carry a message out in danger of his life. We all said to each other — he won't come back! — but he came back in good condition and could give the regiment important information about everything."[34]

III

After the first bloody days of combat in 1914, the men at headquarters began to know one another better. Hitler's comrades called him Adi, and noticed the peculiarities about him that men living in close quarters see — the way Hitler walked a bit stooped forward, his head held slightly to the left, and the fact that he had big feet. Westenkirchner saw that Hitler liked to keep his hands in his pockets; the hands themselves were beautifully proportioned, with long, gracefully shaped fingers.

"He was always hungry," said Ernst Schmidt, the silent man who was his closest comrade. "He always had an unbelievable hunger."[35] Hitler liked to load up his mug of tea with the artificial honey issued to the troops and was famous around headquarters for the amount of marmalade he could pile on a single piece of bread. The slang word for stealing from the food supplies was "organize": Hitler "organized" flour, but his great coup involved a supply of zwieback. Taking his turn standing guard at night over the staff living quarters, he found nearby a few large boxes that proved to be filled with the sweet biscuits. He devised a way of opening the boxes from the bottom; taking some for himself and the other runners each night he was on guard, he was able to keep the continuing pilferage undetected. When meat ran short later in the war, no one was better than Hitler at finding dogs and cats for the cooking pot, despite his fondness for a pet dog that was stolen from him in 1917.

Although they laughed when he mimicked one of the officers or read aloud in deadpan fashion a singularly stupid housekeeping regulation that had been posted in their dugout, Hitler's comrades were aware that here was a man aloof and different from themselves. While they chatted, he would sit among them, lost in thought for long periods; suddenly he would begin speaking in an animated and authoritative fashion. "There is almost no subject," Westenkirchner said, "about which he did not talk. He mastered each theme and spoke fluently. We simple fellows were very much impressed, and we liked it. His favorite subject was art. He wanted to become a great architect."[36] When the subject of politics arose, Mend noted that "it was as if we were at the Reichstag," the German parliament. "Hitler was the spokesman." As for the effect of all this, Mend's estimate was that "almost no one could withdraw himself from Adolf Hitler's strong personality, and his opinions were accepted by most of us."[37] Westenkirchner observed that Hitler did not demand deference within their group, but such "a special position naturally arose by itself."[38]

Hitler was offered a promotion from lance corporal to corporal, but acceptance would have meant leaving headquarters and returning to his original company. There was no provision for promoting a regimental runner above the rank of Gefreiter; by choosing to remain where he was, Hitler stopped his own advancement, although his lack of formal education and eccentric behavior would in any case have made it virtually impossible for him to rise past the rank of sergeant to become an officer. He continued as a messenger, and his dedicated performance on the battlefield was matched by a singular set of off-duty attitudes. When at Christmas of 1914 there was discussion about visiting with British soldiers in the no man's land between the opposing trenches during a truce, "Adolf Hitler was a bitter opponent of such an idea," a comrade said. "Such a thing should not happen during wartime."[39]

On the other hand, Hitler made a point of attending the funerals of British pilots whose planes crashed inside German lines; he spoke admiringly of the courage of the British airmen he saw in action, and he approved of full military honors for those who fell. Mend found him "always extremely thoughtful in his treatment of wounded prisoners and in his dealings with the civilians who were within the battle area." Regarding Hitler and women, Mend said, "He never approached the French girls and never had any flirtations. We always called him 'the woman hater.' Sometimes he looked at me inquiringly if I talked with a French girl, and I often had to take some remarks from him about it."[40]

A baptized Catholic, Hitler in his adult civilian life had never attended church and had no discernible religious faith, but at the front, despite many opportunities to avoid it, he attended church parade because it was in the regulations.[41] Other men lived for the chance to go home on leave; during fifty-two months of wartime service, Hitler availed himself of only a fraction of the time due him, taking two leaves of fourteen days each.[42] "The trenches around Fromelles were his world," Mend said, referring to the site of a terrible battle in the summer of 1915, "and what lay behind them didn't exist for him."[43]

This was brought into high relief when Hitler was finally wounded on the Somme in October of 1916, a shell fragment slashing his upper left thigh. Men were praying for such flesh wounds, injuries that would not cripple them but would keep them away from the lines for several months. "It isn't so bad, Lieutenant, right?" Hitler said from his stretcher to his immediate superior, Fritz Wiedemann, the regimental adjutant, as they were readying him for the ambulance to the field hospital. "I can still stay with you, I mean, stay with the regiment! Can't I?"[44] Soon after Hitler was released from a hospital near Berlin and assigned to the regiment's replacement battalion in Munich, he wrote to Wiedemann, asking him to expedite his return to the front, and Wiedemann obliged, sending a telegram requesting the immediate shipment of Hitler to his unit.

That was the Hitler his comrades saw. As the cannon blasted and the machine guns chattered, private processes were at work, some of which occasionally became visible. During the first two and a half years of the war, until his leather picture case was stolen, Hitler kept up some of his sketching and painting, producing scenes of little streets in Belgian and French towns, some ruined, some intact, and a memorable impressionistic watercolor of a sunken lane at Wytschaete along which 192 German soldiers were killed or wounded in a single day.[45] Hans Mend said, "With great talent, he made cartoons of Jewish types in Vienna."[46] Lieutenant Wiedemann heard no anti-Semitic comments from Hitler, and the same was true of Ernst Schmidt. Westenkirchner noted, "When he talked about Vienna, then he also spoke about the great influence of the Jews, but without spitefulness."[47] Hans Mend had a different experience, in a town behind the German lines.

> According to military discipline, Hitler behaved himself correctly in regard to Jewish officers, but he hated them. . . . During a morning in December I met Hitler on the street. . . .
> While we were talking, we saw our Jewish adjutant G. coming along and because Hitler did not want to salute him he jumped behind a tree. However, the officer had recognized him, and demanded an explanation of why he jumped away, but Hitler just looked at him.

The officer rode off with the threat that he would report Hitler for what was known as a "respect violation," and Hitler turned to Mend and said, "This Jew I can acknowledge only when he is on the battlefield. Here he can be arrogant, but if he really had to go to the front line, then he would hide himself in a mousehole, and would not worry about a salute."[48]

This case was a complicated and ironic one. Among the officers of Hitler's regiment were two Jews who received high decorations for valor, but this lieutenant, Assistant Adjutant Hugo Gutmann, "was not esteemed or liked among the messengers," according to Westen-kirchner, because "he was more careful than brave."[49] The irony was that, later in the war, it was Gutmann who made a special effort to put through the paperwork that resulted in Hitler's receiving the highly esteemed Iron Cross, First Class.

"Every free minute he used to read," a comrade recalled. "Even at his battle station he sat in a corner, his ammunition bag around his middle, rifle in his arms, and read. He once borrowed a book from me; it was Nietzsche, as far as I can remember."[50] Hitler had several books in his military baggage, including a well-worn copy of Scho-penhauer's *The World as Will and Idea*. His reading was intense, but by his own statement it bore no resemblance to that of those who read for pleasure or to acquire knowledge for its own sake; reading "should provide the tools and building materials which the individual needs for his life's work," and it should be used to support and strengthen one's Weltanschauung, one's view of life. Reading was ammunition; without the right arguments and examples, an advocate of an idea "will find neither grounds for reinforcing his own contentions nor any for confuting those of his adversary."[51]

This called for reading selectively, and discarding everything that could not help one in the battle of life. There was more to Nietzsche than his belief that a decadent Western Christian civilization must be swept away in favor of a new type of self-willed heroic superman who would be far above the common herd, far above conventional morality, and entitled to rule the world, but for Hitler this meshed with what he chose to extract from the life and ideas of Wagner. Hitler took from Schopenhauer principally the idea of will as force, which was a profound misperception of the man who wished in the last analysis a Buddhistic renunciation of worldly desires and the transformation of the planet into Nirvana, but in Schopenhauer Hitler had found a man who read as he did, noting with approval whatever confirmed his own convictions.

Hitler's Weltanschauung had Hitler at its center, but the foil for all his thought was his imaginary Germany, a superior Nordic race whose march to glory was blocked and threatened by Slavs, Jews, Englishmen, Marxists, and the French. He was by nature suspicious; Hitler was certain that there was more to Germany's suffering than met the eye, but he had yet to draw his final conclusions. In January of 1915, after nine weeks at the front, he wrote to an acquaintance in Munich. Using "we" as if he were empowered to speak for every German at the front, he said that all the German troops were not only determined to win on the battlefield, "cost what it may," but they also hoped, "if we're lucky enough to get home again, to find it cleaner, and cleansed of foreign elements." The foreign elements were not specified. He closed by saying, "As for Austria, things will turn out as I've always said they would."[52] Although he did not expand on it here, Westenkirchner had heard his view: "He was convinced that with the victorious end of the war, all Germans in Austria would join a great German Reich."[53]

Hitler did yet another kind of reading: he studied the propaganda leaflets that were dropped from British planes. As the Germans captured Allied prisoners and advanced into and remained in Belgian and French territory, he became aware of the propaganda that the Allies were using to motivate their own troops and civilian populations. His conclusion was that "the war propaganda of the English and Americans was psychologically sound. By representing the Germans to their own people as barbarians and Huns, they prepared the individual soldier for the terrors of war, and thus helped to preserve him from disappointments. After this, the most terrible weapon that was used against him seemed only to confirm what his propagandists had told him."[54] By contrast, at the outset of the war, Hitler said, the German newspapers had portrayed the English as "unbelievably cowardly. . . . I remember well my comrades' looks of astonishment when we faced the Tommies in person in Flanders. After the very first days of battle the conviction dawned on each and every one of them that these Scotsmen did not exactly jibe with the pictures they had seen fit to give us in the humor magazines and press dispatches."[55]

In broader terms, Hitler scorned what he termed "the inner ambiguity" of German propaganda; whereas the British bombarded their own public and the Germans with endless repetition of the idea that Germany was solely responsible for the war, the German line was that Germany might be partly responsible for the conflagration, but no more than anyone else. The English approach succeeded with the German public: "At first the claims of the propaganda were so impudent that people thought it insane; later, it got on people's nerves; and in the end, it was believed."

Quickly convinced of the uncompromising nature of warfare, Hitler studied this psychological weapon as if he were stripping down a machine gun. "Its effect," he decided, "for the most part must be aimed at the emotions and only to a very limited degree at the so-called intellect." The target was "the primitive sentiments of the broad masses." Selectivity and repetition were everything: "It must confine itself to a few points and repeat them over and over." Reassembling the machine gun, Hitler outlined its operation:

> The receptivity of the great masses is very limited, their intelligence is small, but their power of forgetting is enormous. In consequence of these facts, all effective propaganda must be limited to a very few points and must harp on these in slogans until the last member of the public understands what you want him to understand by your slogan.[56]

Like his hero Wagner, Lance Corporal Hitler believed in his star, although at times he was moving in broad daylight through powder smoke so thick that he could not see ten meters ahead. Shortly before Christmas of 1915, Hans Mend noted, "he said that we would hear much about him. We should just wait until his time had arrived."[57]

A different side to Hitler was shown in a poem he wrote in the spring of 1916. In the surviving manuscript there is this combination of title and note by Hitler: "It was in the Thicket of the Forest at Artois. . . . Based on a true event."

It was in the thicket of the Artois Wood.
Deep in the trees, on blood-soaked ground,
Lay stretched a wounded German warrior,
And his cries rang out in the night.
In vain . . . no echo answered his plea . . .
Will he bleed to death like a beast,
That shot in the gut dies alone?

Then suddenly . . .
Heavy steps approach from the right
He hears how they stamp on the forest floor . . .
And new hope springs from his soul.
And now from the left . . .
And now from both sides . . .

Two men approach his miserable bed
A German it is, and a Frenchman.
And each watches the other with distrustful glance,
And threateningly they aim their weapons.
The German warrior asks:
"What do you do here?"
"I was touched by the needy one's call for help."

"It's your enemy!"
"It is a man who suffers."

And both, wordless, lowered their weapons.
Then entwined their hands
And, with muscles tensed, carefully lifted
The wounded warrior, as if on a stretcher,
And carried him through the woods,
'Til they came to the German outposts.
"Now it's over. He will get good care."
And the Frenchman turns back toward the woods.
But the German grasps for his hand,
Looks, moved, into sorrow-dimmed eyes
And says to him with earnest foreboding:

"I know not what fate holds for us,
Which inscrutably rules in the stars.
Perhaps I shall fall, a victim of your bullet.
Maybe mine will fell you on the sand —
For indifferent is the chance of battles.
Yet, however it may be and whatever may come:
We lived these sacred hours,
Where man found himself in a man . . .
And now, farewell! And God be with you!"[58]

IV

According to Ernst Schmidt, it was not until 1918, when the German
military effort began to falter, that Hitler started to talk about politics
in a consuming fashion. Even before 1918, when German soldiers
were angry they cursed the war as a "swindle," but now, Schmidt
said, the term was used in "bloody seriousness." The new and earnest
defeatist talk at the front infuriated Hitler, and he soon found a focus
for his generalized anger. Another division, the Tenth Bavarian, had
been so badly mauled that it was in effect dissolved, and part of one
of its units, the Sixth Franconian Infantry Regiment from Nuremburg,
was attached to Hitler's regiment, with some personnel assigned to
headquarters. These new men had lost all hope of victory and openly
expressed the view, not long before Germany's de facto wartime leader
General Erich Ludendorff reached the same conclusion, that further
resistance was pointless. When any of these men ventured such opinions in Hitler's presence, according to Schmidt, he "became very

furious and shouted in a terrible voice about the pacifists and shirkers, who would ultimately lose the war." This led to a fistfight with a corporal from Nuremberg; Hitler took a lot of punches, Schmidt said, "but finally he won. From this day on the new ones did not like him anymore, but we old comrades liked him just that much more."[59]

Gefreiter Hitler went on trying to win the war. Many Allied soldiers of all ranks later spoke with admiration of the tenacity and valor with which many German units and individual soldiers fought to the end; one of these men was Adolf Hitler. The vagrant who had been deloused at public expense at the Obdachlosenheim, the failure who had carried travelers' bags for tips at a train station, was a success, in a way that had always meant a great deal to Germans. His superiors and his fellow runners saw him as a brave soldier of great endurance, and as a man who was exceptionally good at transmitting oral orders. Unlike the other messengers, he studied the headquarters maps, learning the safest route to go forward and frequently making accurate predictions about the course of battles and campaigns. By 1918, this combination of qualities and abilities had made an extraordinary impression on the professional soldiers who led his regiment. Lieutenant Colonel Engelhardt, the first of his regimental commanders who knew him, called Hitler "an exceptionally brave, effective, and conscientious soldier," and his last commander, Lieutenant Colonal Maximilian Baligand, spoke of him as a "courageous and outstanding soldier and comrade."[60] Other regimental commanders and senior officers under whom he served used such phrases as "exceptional courage," "shining example," "admirable unpretentiousness," "profound love of country," and "altogether upright and honorable nature." One lieutenant colonel summed it up: "Hitler never let us down."[61]

Hitler had yet another experience awaiting him. Carrying a message for a battalion that had broken through the first line of French defenses in one of the final German offensives, he could not find the unit and started walking through a forest, looking for its rear elements. Seeing something that looked like a French helmet at a man's height within a section of trench, Hitler pulled out the pistol he had been given to replace the rifle that a runner formerly carried. Moving cautiously to the edge of the trench, he found ten or twelve French soldiers in it, still armed but dazed by the German attack that had overrun the forest and cut them off.

Hitler shouted at them, aiming his pistol and ordering them to surrender. Although he had the draw on them, the Frenchmen were reluctant to put down their rifles, until he fired a shot into the trench;

then they dropped their weapons and raised their hands. Hitler pointed to the rear with his pistol and marched off behind them.

When his group of French prisoners came to the edge of the forest and realized that they had not yet seen another German, they slowed down and began to discuss ways to overpower Hitler. Just at this moment he saw some men of the headquarters staff of the battalion for which he had been looking, and hastily called them over. Hitler delivered his message and borrowed a man with a rifle. Together they marched his prisoners back to regimental headquarters, where he personally delivered them to his colonel, who had expected him to return alone as usual. By coincidence, it was only a short time later that he received his Iron Cross, First Class. It was given him not for this feat, but for his entire performance since 1914. The recommendation for the medal, signed by yet another of his regimental commanders, said in part:

> As a runner his coolness and dash in both trench and open warfare have been exemplary, and invariably he has shown himself ready to volunteer for tasks in the most difficult situations and at danger to himself. Whenever communications have been disrupted at a critical moment in battle, it has been thanks to Hitler's unflagging and devoted efforts that important messages continued to get through despite every difficulty.[62]

Although he could not know it, Hitler's role in the war was soon to end. He had distinguished himself within a regiment that spent forty-five months in the front lines, being shuttled from one sector to another and fighting in thirty-six major battles. A total of 3,754 men of the Regiment List died during the war. Death surrounded Hitler for more than a thousand days, and the ways in which he avoided it were uncanny.

> I was eating my dinner in a trench with several comrades. Suddenly a voice seemed to be saying to me, "Get up and go over there." It was so clear and insistent that I obeyed mechanically, as if it had been a military order. I rose at once to my feet and walked twenty yards along the trench, carrying my dinner in its tin-can with me. Then I sat down to go on eating, my mind being once more at rest. Hardly had I done so when a flash and a deafening report came from the part of the trench I had just left. A stray shell had burst over the group in which I had been sitting, and every member of it was killed.[63]

Hans Mend once said to him, after Hitler reappeared through the smoke of a battlefield where thousands were dying, "For you there is no bullet!" Mend remembered that Hitler did not reply: "A grin was his answer."[64]

<h1 style="text-align:center">V</h1>

In October of 1918, Hitler's regiment was back in position on the Ypres battlefield, four miles from where he had first gone into action on a foggy October morning in 1914. Half a million men had died there in the intervening forty-eight months; the British still held Ypres, as on that first day, and the Germans were still to the south and east of it.

On the evening of October 13, the regimental runners who were not on duty and some of the telephone operators went to pick up their rations at a field kitchen that had been set up in an unoccupied gun position on a hill near the village of Wervicq. As the food was being handed out, English high explosive shells started coming in; before Hitler and the others realized what was happening, shells containing chlorine gas also landed in the area. By the time they got their gas masks on, most of them had breathed in some of the poison. "As early as midnight," Hitler said, "a number of us passed out, a few of our comrades forever." In the next hours some found they could not speak or see. Toward morning Hitler was in pain, and his eyes were afire.

When Hitler wrote about this, he portrayed himself as completing a mission in the line of duty, struggling through to headquarters: "I stumbled and tottered back with burning eyes, taking with me my last report of the War."[65] In fact, he joined a line of men who were partly or totally gas-blinded. One said, "In order not to get lost we held on to the coattails of the man ahead, and so we went in single file to Linnselle, where we got first aid."[66]

Within a few hours, Hitler's agony was complete: "My eyes had turned into glowing coals; it had grown dark around me."[67] He was sent to a hospital in Pasewalk, in Germany. Hitler's days on the Western Front were at an end.

CHAPTER

3

T HE HOSPITAL at Pasewalk was seventeen miles south of the inlets of the Baltic Sea, in the flat and scrubby northern lands of the Prussian maritime province of Pomerania. A special team of doctors treated gas-blinded patients there, with considerable success; Hitler found that "the piercing pain in my eye sockets was diminishing; slowly I succeeded in distinguishing the broad outlines of the things about me."

Early in November, truckloads of sailors waving red banners suddenly arrived in this place of quiet suffering. They "proclaimed the Revolution," Hitler said, making speeches that demanded an immediate German surrender, the removal of the Kaiser, and the creation of an ill-defined new government of the left. Shouting slogans about peace and freedom, the mutinous sailors roared off in their trucks.[1]

Unable to read newspapers, unwilling to believe rumors, Hitler had this reaction: "My first hope was that this high treason was only a more or less local affair."[2] It had in fact been local for a few days, but at the time Hitler caught his shadowy glimpse of red flags and clenched fists, revolutionary action was spreading across Germany.

For four years, until he was gassed, Hitler had been, in a sense, at the center of Germany's hour-by-hour history. The conflict was total; opposing nations pitted themselves against each other at the front. Now everything in Germany was changing faster than any individual could comprehend. For months to come, Hitler would be on the sidelines, at times not even a spectator, but the events that were unfolding, and the manner in which they were interpreted and misinterpreted by Germans, would have the profoundest effect on his future.

*

The uprising these sailors were heralding had begun in the last days of October at Kiel, the Baltic port that was the German imperial navy's largest base. At a time when the new chancellor, Prince Max of Baden, was corresponding with Woodrow Wilson about preconditions for an armistice, the proud and defiant Navy High Command unilaterally decided to send out the High Seas Fleet in hopes of engaging the British Grand Fleet in a final great battle. The mission was suicidal; there could be no question that the far stronger British fleet, which had kept the German battleships and cruisers penned up since the Battle of Jutland in 1916, would sink them all. To the diehard German officers, this was preferable to running up the white flag in port and having to steam in disgrace under guard to Scapa Flow, which was indeed the fate the Allies were planning for them. "Better an honorable death than a shameful peace," the naval officers were saying to each other.[3]

The enlisted men aboard the battleships saw the matter differently and refused to put to sea. On November 3, 1918, a crowd of twenty thousand men gathered at the exercise field on the outskirts of Kiel. Sailors from the battleships and cruisers and dockyard workers, they were there to protest the arrest of 180 men of the battleship *Markgraf*. There were speeches by Karl Altelt, a naval stoker, and Arthur Popp, a civilian, who belonged to the Independent Socialist Party, a radical group positioned between the Majority Socialists, who wanted liberal reforms but were opposed to violence, and the small and fanatical Spartacist Bund, communists who wanted to start duplicating the Russian Revolution of the year before.

The impassioned speeches were both accurate and prophetic. Stoker Altelt cried out that he should not be considered a mutineer, because he and the others who refused to get up steam for battle were acting in line with the policy of the transition government in Berlin. Insofar as Prince Max was concerned, that was true; the chancellor had already ordered the U-boats to cease hostilities and return to their bases as part of the truce conditions demanded by Woodrow Wilson, and he was appalled when he learned of the navy's last-minute folly. Altelt and Popp went on to declare that the Kaiser and the officer class had brought Germany to ruin. The Kaiser must go and the power of the officers must be reduced. A peace must be concluded swiftly, and a "workers' and sailors' council" must be formed to usher in the new era at Kiel.

The immediate concern was the release of the 180 sailors who were in the naval prison on charges of mutiny. By now it was dark; carrying torches, singing, and shouting, the crowd set off in the direction of the prison. As they started up the sloping Feldstrasse, they could see bayonets awaiting them in the dim lights at the top of the street. There stood a company of highly disciplined sailors, under the command of a Lieutenant Steinhauser. These men were from the destroyer force; many were volunteers, and they had seen more combat than the men of the battleships, who had spent much of the war in port and were now engaging in mutiny. They did not think much of the battleship sailors, or of the way that some of them were coming up the slope singing "Die Internationale."

Steinhauser's orders were to disperse the mob. He commanded his men to fire a warning volley over the heads of the advancing crowd of sailors and dockyard workers, and they did. The demonstrators came on. Steinhauser ordered his men to fire into the torch-shadowed crowd. They fired. The crowd vanished into the night, leaving twenty men lying dead or wounded. After four years of killing their nation's enemies, Germans had killed Germans. The mutineers began breaking into arms lockers, aship and ashore. The outnumbered men of the destroyer force boarded their ships and sailed into the Baltic.[4]

II

By the time Hitler witnessed the truckloads of sailors pulling into the hospital at Pasewalk, armed insurrection was taking place in city after city. There was little resistance; the German population was mortally sick of the war, and the overwhelming impulse was to go along with whatever seemed to promise an immediate peace. For the moment, the lethal Kiel confrontation was not repeated; even the most trusted military and police units refused to fire on other Germans. By default, control passed bloodlessly into the hands of hastily improvised councils whose titles represented every combination of the soldiers, sailors, workers, and peasants who composed them. Despite the speed with which the traditional organs of authority were immobilized, it was all spontaneous. The Spartacists and Independent Socialists were trying to take advantage of every development, but this was no Moscow-directed conspiracy coming to fruition; soldiers in cities tore the epaulettes of rank from the shoulders of officers they encountered, because they represented a system that had led them through hardship, terror, and slaughter — for naught.

Only at the front was there still self-sacrifice and discipline. Despite the hundreds of thousands of American troops aggressively pushing through the Argonne Forest, brave and expert German machine gunners continued to die in their assigned positions as the rear guard of a skillful withdrawal. The German army was at the point of collapse, but it was still intact and fighting, not on German soil, but on that of France and Belgium.

In Berlin, the able Prince Max had been performing necessary political surgery since his sudden appointment as chancellor on October 3. Summoned to Berlin from Baden, he had been told in confidence information that stupefied him. General Erich Ludendorff, who since 1916 had been acting as a dictator, scorning civilian advice and speaking only in terms of victory, had suddenly gone into a panic and was demanding that an immediate armistice be produced. That was why Prince Max, known to the Allied leaders as a liberal, was asked by the Kaiser to become chancellor and negotiate the best possible terms for Germany.

Although Prince Max had known that the nation could not sustain its effort on the Western Front indefinitely, he, like the German public, had no idea that things had come to this pass. The German public had been led to believe that victory lay ahead, if only everyone would keep on working and fighting and trusting the Kaiser, General Ludendorff, and Field Marshal Paul von Hindenburg. The average authority-conscious German was able to think that this was true: Russia had been knocked out of the war, many divisions had been transferred from the east to the Western Front, and German forces continued to fight well inside enemy territory. German towns and cities bore no scars of war.

Acceding to Ludendorff's request, Prince Max had opened his correspondence with Woodrow Wilson. When Wilson's notes awoke Ludendorff and Hindenburg to the severity of the terms the Allies intended to impose, they tried to backtrack on their intention to surrender, but Prince Max forced Ludendorff's ouster. Reacting to Wilson's message that the United States would not conclude an armistice if it had to "deal with the military masters and monarchical autocrats of Germany," Prince Max began working on the Kaiser to abdicate.[5]

This ending of the Prussian Hohenzollern dynasty was finally accomplished by Prince Max on November 9, the day when a general strike began in Berlin and other cities, with huge hostile crowds converging on the Chancellery at the center of Berlin. To forestall an explosion that would have dwarfed the Kiel mutiny, Prince Max announced the abdication of Wilhelm II at 11:30 A.M., even though the Kaiser, at the army's Supreme Command headquarters at Spa, in Belgium, had not yet reached the inevitable decision. Thirty minutes later Prince Max was called on by five leaders of the Majority Socialists, the name taken by the Social Democratic Party in 1916, when its radical wing became the Independent Socialists.[6]

The meeting took place in the Chancellery library; everyone remained standing, but the conversation was polite and to the point. This delegation was not concerned about bringing the fighting on the Western Front to an end, because they knew that Prince Max had already dispatched an armistice commission to meet with the Allied representatives in the Forest of Compiègne. With the Kaiser gone, it was obvious that the chancellor he had appointed must soon resign, and these men had come to ask that one of their number, Friedrich Ebert, be named as his replacement. They were asking to become the new leaders of Germany.

There was no hint of triumph or gloating among these grave Majority Socialists. As Social Democrats, their party had opposed the monarchy for decades; the Kaiser was gone now, but they were Germans, in a defeated Germany. They were dazed and wary. In the last month, partly as a sop to the Allies and partly because of his own beliefs, Prince Max had brought about greater constitutional reforms than had been gained in the previous four decades. As part of this process he invited two Majority Socialist leaders to join the cabinet he had formed on taking office. Some of the party leadership questioned the wisdom of joining this last-ditch government led by the prince, because they feared that they would receive part or all of the blame for a defeat that was the result of men and policies entirely different from their own.

Prince Max knew that these were the logical men to take over whatever power the government might have. The Majority Socialists were far enough to the left to satisfy many, although far from all, of those wavers of flags and brandishers of rifles. On the other hand, they had not the slightest intention of repeating the purges and destruction of the Russian Revolution. As for the transfer of power, the constitutional procedure called for the Kaiser to ask the man of his choice to serve, but the prince had just announced the Kaiser's abdication. With a few words, Prince Max simply told Friedrich Ebert that he was chancellor of Germany, wished him luck, and left.

*

Within an hour, Prince Max was vindicated in his assessment of the nonrevolutionary tendencies of Friedrich Ebert. When Ebert made his way over to the Reichstag after frigidly telling an Independent Socialist delegation that he would allot them only a few government positions in which to practice their radical socialism, he found the legislature in an uproar. It appeared that his colleague Philipp Scheidemann, who had been at the meeting with Prince Max, was eating a bowl of soup in the Reichstag restaurant when he was told that there was a crowd outside, wanting to know the latest developments. Scheidemann had risen from the table, gone to a window overlooking the crowd, and announced Ebert's appointment as chancellor, closing his few words with a suddenly inspired "Long live the German Republic!" Then he had gone back to his soup.

When Ebert heard that the morning's empire had been transformed into a republic just because Scheidemann decided to end a speech with a flourish, he was furious. Ebert had already decided that, when there was sufficient order and stability, the nation must go to the polls to elect representatives who would meet in a constituent assembly that would define Germany's political character. "You have no right to proclaim a republic!" he angrily told Scheidemann. "What Germany is to be — a republic or anything else — is for the Constituent Assembly to decide!"[7]

It was too late. Everyone had taken up the name, and embassies and press agencies were cabling the news around the world that Germany was a republic.

Late in the evening of November 9, Friedrich Ebert was pacing around his new office, desperately aware of his inadequacies and his government's vulnerability. The Majority Socialists were an opposition party; the reality of government administration was outside their experience. The portly forty-seven-year-old Ebert was a former saddlemaker and a longtime party worker and partisan political leader; now he was the head of state of a nation of seventy million people. He was a man who loved Germany and had lost two sons in the war. He was trying to get a consensus for governing, and the view both to his right and left was bleak. Hostilities on the Western Front would be stopping within a very few days; it was apparent that the army would come marching back intact. If its leaders chose to do so, they could literally blast Friedrich Ebert and his Majority Socialists out of office within an hour.

in the magnanimity of our previous enemies — I could stand it
no longer. It became impossible for me to sit still one minute
more. Again everything went black before my eyes; I tottered
and groped my way back to the ward, threw myself on my bunk,
and dug my burning head into my blanket and pillow.

He was sobbing. "Since the day when I had stood at my mother's
grave, I had not wept. . . . And so it had all been in vain. In vain all
the sacrifices and privations; in vain the hunger and thirst of months
which were often endless; in vain the hours in which, with mortal fear
clutching our hearts, we nevertheless did our duty; and in vain the
death of two millions who died."[10]

CHAPTER

4

O N THE FOLLOWING DAY, the Armistice went into effect on the
Western Front. Ten days later, on November 21, Hitler's treatment at the hospital was finished. He could read newspaper headlines,
and his eyesight was continuing to improve. Ordered to report to the
replacement battalion of his regiment at Munich, Hitler headed there
gladly, believing that the Bavarians would never succumb to the revolutionary fervor that had swept so much of Germany.

He could not have been more in error. Munich had moved faster
than Berlin. Two days before the Kaiser's abdication, a workers' and
soldiers' council had authorized the formation of a "Bavarian Republic." That sounded as if it was a separate nation, and in many ways it
was. For eight centuries prior to Bismarck's unification of the twenty-
five German-speaking kingdoms, duchies, principalities, and free cities into an empire in 1871, Bavaria had been the domain of the royal
House of Wittelsbach. Second in size and power only to the northern
colossus of Prussia and its Hohenzollern dynasty, the Bavarian kingdom had been required to accept the primacy of the Prussian Kaiser,
but had retained its Wittelsbach monarchy and its postal service and
railway system. Acting independently of the ambassadors whom Berlin
sent to foreign capitals to represent the German Empire, Bavaria had
its own embassies in Vienna, at the Vatican, and in prewar Russia.
The army in which Hitler had served was the Bavarian Army; although
it had been fully incorporated into the forces directed by Berlin, the
oath of loyalty he had taken at the war's outset was not to the Kaiser,
but to Ludwig III of Bavaria. It was the Prussians who were imbued
with militarism, but the Bavarian Army had mobilized as swiftly as
the Prussian forces, had fought as well, and had received an equal
number of medals for bravery. Berlin was in Prussia; in the Bavarian

psyche there was always a resentment of the condescending northern view of Munich beer drinkers as quaint rustic types who could not be counted on to accomplish anything much. Bavaria had been part of the German Empire for forty-seven years, and now there was no empire. The Kaiser had abdicated and was in exile in Holland; in Bavaria, Ludwig III had fled, to take up private life in the country. In the minds of many, it might be better to go on as the separate nation they once had been, no matter what it was to be called.

The man who had bloodlessly strolled into power in Catholic Bavaria, Kurt Eisner, could have become minister-president only at a time of fluidity and confusion. He was a fifty-one-year-old Jew who was born in Berlin and spent most of his life in Prussia. A gifted satirical journalist whose target was the Prussian aristocracy, at the age of thirty he had written an article ridiculing the Kaiser. That earned him nine months in a Prussian prison, brought him to the attention of prominent socialists, and led to his holding important positions on *Vorwärts*, Germany's most influential socialist newspaper, published in Berlin. At forty, he was forced off the paper in a factional fight; deserting his wife and five children, he went to Bavaria, eventually rising to the position of political editor of the Social Democrats' *Münchener Post*.[1]

Although Eisner had a lively interest in reporting the German political scene and in urging liberal reforms, during the prewar years in Munich his fellow socialists in Bavaria had no interest in advancing him within the Social Democratic Party. They saw him as a bohemian, a man who also served the *Münchener Post* as its drama critic, a writer of literary essays who was living with a woman journalist. Eisner was truly at home in the artists' cafés of Munich's Schwabing district; with his long wispy grey beard, his big black hat, thick steel-rimmed glasses, and seedy suits, the birdlike little man, complete with Berlin accent and Jewish religion, was not the leadership material with which the socialists hoped to win over Bavaria's Catholic workingmen.

It was only his early opposition to the war that began to make a special place for Kurt Eisner in the Bavarian political scene. His collisions with wartime military press censorship left him unemployed and poor, and gave him ample time to initiate a transformation from political commentator to political activist. Demonstrating unsuspected strength and determination, in 1917 he founded the Bavarian branch of the Independent Socialists and was one of the organizers of a strike for peace, in January of 1918, that put him in prison for eight months. Fresh from his cell and with a reputation as an antiwar martyr, he appeared at two in the afternoon on November 7 at the west side of the Theresienwiese, the immense field that is the center of Munich's annual Oktoberfest. There was a huge crowd listening to various socialist leaders; the sometime drama critic upstaged them all by shouting: "Scatter throughout the city, occupy the barracks, seize weapons and ammunition, win over the rest of the troops, and make yourselves masters of the government!"[2]

The crowd did as it was told, and just after midnight Eisner and his followers walked into the hastily opened Bavarian parliament building and formally assumed power. Eisner managed to effect the revolution in Bavaria without a single wounding or death, but his troubles were only beginning. Not surprisingly, it developed that he had no idea of how to run a state with a population of seven million. He had a good word for all the soldiers' and workers' councils, but his real love was the Council of Intellectual Workers, composed of his Schwabing coffee house cronies. Like Ebert in Berlin, he wanted peace and stability, and had no interest in moving the revolution further to the left. His fellow socialists were astounded to hear him say, after concluding that Bavaria's industries were virtually inoperative, "There can be no socialization when there is scarcely anything to be socialized."[3] Misreading the extent of the Bavarian desire for independence, on November 26, in the wake of an argument with Ebert about documents Eisner had published that placed the full blame for starting the war on Prussia, he broke diplomatic relations with Berlin, only to find that most Bavarians wanted parity with Prussia rather than secession from the German Republic. Within three weeks, the people's hero of November 7 was not only receiving abuse and threats from the right, but was hearing a dissatisfied rumble from almost every segment of the left.

This was the rudderless Munich, hung with red flags, to which Adolf Hitler returned at the end of November. Signing into the Turkenstrasse barracks, he found that enlisted men no longer saluted officers and that the only discipline in effect was something called "voluntary obedience."[4] The millions of men who had moved back into Germany on Hindenburg's orders were being demobilized with great speed; within another three weeks Ebert could find only two nearby army units totaling eighteen hundred soldiers when he needed to defuse a government confrontaton with the far-left People's Naval Division of three thousand men in the center of Berlin. The soldiers who hung around barracks such as the one into which Hitler moved either hoped to go on serving in the skeleton force or dropped in to eat and sleep there because they could find no civilian jobs and had nowhere to go.

Adolf Hitler was in this latter category. He had been a splendid combat soldier, but at the age of twenty-nine he had no desire to stay in the army and work his way up from lance corporal. Although the army had been his home for fifty-two months, he was in a sense singularly homeless. His sister Paula and stepsister Angela, neither of whom he cared much about, were in Austria, a country to which he did not want to return. Despite his four years in the trenches and his medals and wounds, he had not gained German citizenship. Nobody intended to deport him, but he was in effect a stateless person whose only success in life had been on the Western Front, now silent.

In the barracks, Hitler found Ernst Schmidt. Bored, and disgusted by what they saw of the soldiers' councils that appeared to be running both the army and segments of the civilian government, Hitler and Schmidt volunteered for duty guarding Russian and British prisoners of war who had not yet been repatriated, at a prison camp at Traunstein, sixty miles east of Munich, near the Austrian border. It was monotonous, but they had rifles in their hands and a job to do.

II

Elsewhere in Germany, things were not at all boring during these months. The Spartacists had nearly wrecked the National Congress of Workers' and Soldiers' Councils that Ebert had organized in Berlin in mid-December. Their tactics had ranged from picketing the Prussian Landtag building within which the Majority Socialists were trying to decipher every sort of socialist rhetoric, to sending rifle-waving squads of the People's Naval Division running up and down the aisles with mud on their faces, shouting that this convention should abandon its plans to hold a constituent assembly in January. One of the Spartacists' Independent Socialist colleagues pushed through a resolution that required all insignia of rank to be abolished in the army, and for officers to be elected by the enlisted men.

When Hindenburg heard about this at the army's new headquarters outside Kassel, he and other generals exploded. Hindenburg said, "I shall not allow my epaulettes or my sword to be taken from me," and Ebert was informed that Hindenburg and General Groener would fight "to the last ditch" against the subversions of the army's traditional structure.[5] Within twenty-four hours Ebert indicated that these and other anti-army resolutions were not going to become government policy; at a time when the economy was at the point of collapse and a worldwide influenza epidemic was killing thousands throughout Germany, Friedrich Ebert had to defend himself against charges that he was pro-epaulette.

As 1918 ended, it was obvious to Ebert that the German revolution, remarkably bloodless in comparison with the Russian Revolution that had begun the year before, was apparently about to scatter corpses through the streets. The Spartacist Bund, which had added to its title the designation of German Communist Party, wanted no part of a watered-down leftist coalition and intended to make a military attack upon the government in Berlin. It was all very well to have Hindenburg and scores of high-ranking officers on duty at Kassel. But when Ebert had needed soldiers to restore order at a time of crisis, they had been able to send him only eighteen hundred men.

On the afternoon of January 4, 1919, while the Spartacists were rioting and striking all over Berlin, Ebert and his minister of defense, Gustav Noske, climbed into a car and were driven thirty-five miles southwest of Berlin to Zossen, a town with an army camp. Noske was a man of politically liberal persuasion who had performed a near miracle when Ebert sent him to Kiel, where he had hammered out a compromise between the admirals and the mutinous sailors. Since then Noske had found it impossible to come to any accommodation with the self-styled Red Guards, who were interested not in defending the government, but in overthrowing it. Having served as a noncommissioned officer in the regular army in years well before the war, Noske discovered that he and the generals at Spa could talk the same language.

They were driving to Zossen that day because a little-known general, Ludwig Maercker, had asked them to come out to see a voluntary force of recently discharged soldiers who he said were available to serve the government. At this point, with the garrison actually stationed in Berlin consisting of only 150 enlisted men, Ebert and Noske were interested in seeing any force at all that was loyal to the government, but their expectations were limited. The great army that had acquitted itself so memorably on the Western Front had dissolved and was only a memory, at just the moment when a few crack divisions were what was needed to stabilize the deteriorating situation.

Greeted by rigid salutes from Maercker and the trim professional officers of his staff, Ebert and Noske were escorted to the parade ground, which was covered with snow. In a short time they heard a band thumping out one of the regular army's marches, and then long grey columns of helmeted soldiers with fixed bayonets on their rifles strode onto the field, marching with perfect military bearing. Ebert observed with satisfaction that these were "real soldiers"; it was like seeing the ghosts of Hindenburg's disbanded divisions come to life.[6] Noske was busy noting that each infantry company included a machine gun detachment, accompanied by men with flame throwers. Behind the infantry there rolled well-oiled cannon, the impassive artillerymen on the caissons riding with their arms stiffly folded across their chests. There were armored cars, perfectly suited for dispersing mobs. Maercker mentioned that the men were going through intensive training in house-to-house fighting. For field operations, he was organizing both tanks and airplanes. In all, four thousand soldiers passed in review, saluting Ebert and Noske.

After Maercker had seen them off, cordially assuring them that the entire brigade could be moved into action on short notice, Noske clapped Ebert on the back as they drove along, and said, "You can relax now. Everything is going to be all right."[7]

What the leaders of Germany's shaky government had witnessed was a *Freikorps*, a privately raised unit that took orders from its *Führer*, or leader. Just as the armed bands of the revolution had sprung up overnight without directions from Moscow, so these units of the counterrevolution were coming into being without orders from Berlin or army headquarters at Kassel. Ebert and Noske had just seen one of the first, largest, and best-organized of these freelance fighting organizations, but they were being formed spontaneously throughout Germany. The gemlike little army at Zossen had been entirely Maercker's idea; the generals at Kassel approved his plan and placed some army funds at his disposal, but Maercker had the responsibility of finding uniforms and supplies. Weapons were no problem; as the leftists had demonstrated, piles of recently discarded rifles were lying all over Germany.

Although the ranks of these Freikorps were composed almost entirely of men of right-wing persuasion, the men who flocked to these leaders were doing so not because of political conviction. Most of the German army's combat veterans had accepted their discharges with relief and gone home to melt into the civilian population, but, as the Freikorps recruiters were discovering, the war had aroused in a quarter of a million young soldiers a blood lust that could not be extinguished by the signing of a document at Compiègne. Many of these young men had entered the trenches as boys of eighteen; now in their early twenties, all they had known during these formative years were the iron bonds of discipline, shared fear, pride of unit, and male comradeship in what the French writer Jules Romains called "a monastery with walls of fire."[8] To ask them to stop fighting now was like asking them to stop eating; they had to fight someone, somewhere, and the sooner they resumed firing their weapons in earnest, the happier they would be. As for the officers and sergeants, they were professional soldiers for whom there was no place in the suddenly shrunken regular army. As other men needed their families or money or success in their chosen fields, they needed men to command and hills to storm.

Some of these units were already in action. As the Allied delegates at the Paris Peace Conference worked on the complex problem of fixing the boundaries of newly independent Poland, Polish nationalist forces were making sorties into territory that Germany was not certain it would have to cede. Vicious fighting was starting there, and would spread into the political vacuum along the Baltic, where Russia's new Red Army was trying to stamp out Latvia's claim to be an independent state. The Allies would turn a deaf ear to the sounds of firing heard daily by the British Royal Navy's Baltic Squadron; with their own expeditionary forces at Archangel and Murmansk to support the White Russian forces who were still fighting the Red Army, the Allies saw no harm in having skillful German warriors shed some blood to keep the Reds out of the Baltic provinces that they intended to confirm as independent nations.[9] No one thought so far ahead as to consider that when these men returned to Germany after their postwar graduate studies in killing and looting, they would require a constant diet of violence.

And so, greatly cheered, Ebert and Noske returned to Berlin, confident that they had just seen the solution to their problems. The size of the official German army could be kept as low as the Allies wanted it, and the Freikorps could take up the slack, defending Germany's eastern borders and patrolling its troubled streets. Noske would see to it that more of these units were recruited, and that the men were paid. As Ebert and Noske saw it, they were acting out of necessity; from necessity, they were establishing the precedent that anyone could create a private army and march it around Germany, or keep detachments in a hundred cities and towns.

III

While Hitler was in bleak Traunstein guarding prisoners of war, one day on guard duty and one day off, his eyes had improved to the point where he could read two-day-old newspaper accounts of Germany's turmoil. The day after Ebert and Noske saw Maercker's force at Zossen, the Spartacists and Independent Socialists held an enormous demonstration on Berlin's Alexanderplatz, in front of the police headquarters they had held since November. The following morning they began a general strike, with two hundred thousand workers, many of them armed, participating in a gigantic parade through Berlin. Behind the scenes there was a meeting of the leaders of the Spartacists, Independent Socialists, and Revolutionary Shop Stewards. Many of them had doubts about the wisdom of starting a full-scale uprising, but Karl Liebknecht's passionate pleas convinced them. If the government buildings could be taken over, he told them, if Berlin were in Red hands, all of Germany would follow suit. By a vote of sixty-five to six, the meeting agreed to fight. When Rosa Luxemburg, working at the *Red Flag* office, heard of this total disregard of her warning that the time was not ripe, she went to Liebknecht and exclaimed, "Karl, how could you? What about our program?"[10] The next day armed men with red armbands took over the railroad stations. Riflemen atop the Brandenburg Gate covered the main avenues at the center of the city.

On the night of January 9, Freikorps units began to enter the city, singing the marching song "Germany, High in Honor." The next morning Berliners had a vivid demonstration of professional military ability as well as ruthlessness. Three hundred fifty armed revolutionaries had taken over the building in which the Majority Socialist newspaper *Vorwärts* was published. Men of the Freikorps Regiment Potsdam, composed of veterans of the elite Guards Regiments, opened their attack by blowing the roof off with shells from trench mortars. Moments later, machine guns on rooftops across the street fired into the upper windows.

Two cannon were rolled into the square in front of the *Vorwärts* offices and began blasting holes in the front wall. A tank appeared and battered down the barricaded front doors. Armored cars drove up and fired through the first-floor windows. By now the defenders were waving white flags, but the infantry had not yet had its chance. As helmeted foot soldiers threw stick grenades through the windows before rushing in, another detachment with a flame thrower burned a fence behind the building and smashed through from the rear. Fifty of the defenders were dead; the rest were marched off, and several of them were shot shortly afterward.

It took a few days to put down all the armed resistance in the turbulent capital. Four days after the Freikorps marched in, the Revolutionary Shop Stewards announced that their general strike was over. Within another forty-eight hours the streets of Berlin were silent at night, while slowly moving armored cars pointed their searchlights along the doorways of houses in the working-class districts. Foot patrols made their way through every quarter of the city. A few nights later, one of these squads, acting on a tip, captured Karl Liebknecht and Rosa Luxemburg. They had been hiding in an apartment near the Eden Hotel, which the regular army's Horse Guards Division was using as its headquarters during the mopping-up operation. As Liebknecht was being led out of the Eden after questioning, ostensibly for transfer to the Moabit prison, a strapping mustachioed private, Otto Runge, carried out his orders. On duty as a sentry at the hotel door, he raised his rifle and smashed its butt against Liebknecht's head. The dazed and bleeding Liebknecht was shoved into a car filled with Freikorps officers, who took him to the Tiergarten Park and killed him with a pistol shot to the back of the neck. The officers who murdered him delivered his body to a first-aid station in the zoological gardens, where it was tagged "Unknown Spartacist."

Rosa Luxemburg was escorted from the hotel a few minutes later. Again Private Runge carried out his orders; he was getting the hang of it, and this time his small victim was unconscious as they threw her into the back of a car. After they drove off, a Lieutenant Vogel fired a bullet into her brain as she lay on the seat. He supervised the wrapping of her body in wires to which stones were attached, and she was dropped into the Landwehr Canal, where her decomposed remains were discovered four and a half months later. Vogel returned to the Eden Hotel, displaying to his fellow officers a tiny woman's shoe, one of the more unusual battle trophies of "the war after the war."[11]

Ebert was aghast when he heard of these murders. He ordered an investigation, which Freikorps leaders were able to turn into a farce: Private Runge spent several months in prison for "attempted manslaughter," and Lieutenant Vogel, convicted of negligence in not reporting a death and for unlawfully disposing of a corpse, was spirited off to Holland and eventually returned to Germany without serving a day in jail.

The communist world had two new martyrs; Rosa Luxemburg would haunt the government's efforts to come to any sort of accommodation with the parties to the left of the Majority Socialist position. Equally significant, the kill-or-be-killed thinking of the trenches was transforming politics: Ebert's party associate Philipp Scheidemann shrugged off the manner of the deaths with the statement that Liebknecht and Luxemburg had "now become the victims of their own bloody terroristic tactics," and Minister of Defense Noske, agreeing that it was regrettable that no working-class military genius had appeared among the enlisted men who supported the government, wrote: "I was obliged, therefore, to fall back on the officers. It is quite true that many of them are monarchists, but when you want to reconstruct you must fall back on the men whose profession it is."[12] Germany was reaping a strange harvest of war. Men who on the battlefield had impersonally killed, without process of law, Frenchmen whom they did not know, because they were told these men threatened the Fatherland, were equally ready to do the same to Germans on the streets of German cities. In war, one fought with every weapon at one's command. The demarcation lines between war, revolution, political struggle, and murder were disappearing. Assassination as a political statement was becoming a part of German life.

CHAPTER

5

As FEBRUARY BEGAN, Adolf Hitler, still at Traunstein, brooded over what he had witnessed in Munich and was reading in the newspapers. He had recently written two poems. The first, "It Must Not Be!" — an angry lament for Germany's plight — pictured the goddess Germania as maddened with grief, pouring ashes on her head as "her locks flew about uncontrolled!" Hitler, her guardian, was beside himself at what he saw happening to her.

> Invincible — powerful queen of peoples,
> are you seated like a widow on the ground,
> beating your breast?
>
> Why do I continue to breathe?
> I, your warrior, the scorned one![1]

The other poem, "Marxerei," was filled with contempt for the German people's willingness to believe that Marxism held answers for Germany.[2] It also expressed a returning veteran's anger toward the leftists who, because of their disillusionment with the war, were not showing what he felt was the proper respect to wounded veterans or orphans and widows. Hitler wanted to help Germany in this crisis, but, as he later said of himself at this moment, "The end of every meditation was the sober realization that I, nameless as I was, did not possess the least basis for any useful action."[3]

In "Marxerei," whose title was coined by Hitler to allude to a futile failure for pompously worded Marxist plans, Hitler expressed his hatred for the way in which the communists were trying to incite class warfare in Germany. Germans should be Germans first, Hitler believed, and doctors and army officers and grocers and miners second. He did not want the workers of the world to unite; he wanted Germans to unite, far to the right of the Majority Socialists.

As for Ebert and his government, on January 19 they had held a national election to choose representatives who would draft the new constitution by which Germany would be governed. It was an election notable for the fact that women voted, at a time when French, British, and American women did not yet have the right to do so, and also for the support shown for Ebert and his government. Of thirty-five million persons eligible to vote, thirty million had gone to the polls, giving the future National Assembly the clearest possible mandate to proceed with its business. The Majority Socialists received 39 percent of the vote, far more than that given any other party, and would have 163 of the assembly's 423 seats.

The delegates convened on February 6, 1919, at Weimar, a small central German city of slightly more than forty thousand inhabitants, located on the river Ilm, 130 miles southwest of Berlin. This quiet place, with its winding medieval streets, was chosen to avoid the massive demonstrations this meeting would have produced had it been held in Berlin, but the selection of Weimar was also an effort to remind the world, and Germans themselves, of the "other Germany," that glorious galaxy of artistic genius and scholarship that had nothing to do with heavy industry and war. In the grand ducal vault in the cemetery, Germany's greatest poet, Goethe, lay buried beside the poet, dramatist, and philosopher Schiller. Bach had served here as concertmaster to the duke of Weimar. Under the later duke Charles Augustus and his successors, Weimar became a center of German liberalism in the nineteenth century.

The assembly produced a constitution that was a model for ensuring widespread popular representation. Indeed, the document founding the government that became known as the Weimar Republic was too democratic for the situation in which Germany found herself. It encouraged the proliferation of political parties, all of which would have blocs of seats in the Reichstag, making it almost impossible for any government to get rapid and decisive action on issues of great and pressing importance. The assembly itself, fair-minded and colorless, lacked the show of authority for which many Germans were yearning. The Kaiser had ridden a white horse; their emperor was gone, and many Germans wanted a clear symbol of power who would tell them what to do. One of the Freikorps riflemen on guard outside the National Theater watched the delegates come and go, and wrote: "Lots of belly and long beard. Here were no saviors of Germany in her hour of need."[4]

II

Bavaria had also held an election, on January 12, to choose the representatives who would serve in the Bavarian legislature, the Landtag. The election had in effect been a public referendum on Kurt Eisner and his Independent Socialists, who in the first flush of revolution had been able to gain the support of most of the Majority Socialists. Bavarian voters sent Eisner an insulting message; after watching his whimsical statecraft for two months, they gave him only 86,000 votes, as compared with 1,124,000 for the Majority Socialists.[5] Stripped of effectiveness but not yet required to step down, Eisner survived in office for a few more weeks by putting together various coalitions. But on the morning of February 21, he left his office at the Foreign Ministry and walked toward the Landtag to announce his resignation as minister-president of Bavaria. In his pocket was a speech, a brief review and defense of his administration, including a favorable and accurate contrast between the events in Berlin and his own nonviolent coup in November and the relative calm in Bavaria since then: "Just as the revolution itself was achieved without bloodshed, so has Bavaria until now been preserved from serious and lasting internal convulsions."[6]

The uneasy truce between left and right in Bavaria was about to end. As Eisner turned into the Promenadestrasse, accompanied by his secretary and an armed sailor, a uniformed Bavarian Army lieutenant, Count Arco-Valley, drew his pistol and killed Eisner with two shots to the head. A moment later Arco-Valley was also lying on the pavement, severely wounded by three shots fired from the pistol of Eisner's security guard. Only the frantic intervention of Eisner's secretary stopped some Spartacists who had been loitering nearby from beating Arco-Valley to death. The count was taken by the police to a Munich surgeon, who was able to keep him alive. This assassin, an Austrian by birth, was another of those Austrians who felt a more mystical bond with Germany than did the Germans themselves. He survived to say, succinctly, that he had perceived Eisner as "the grave-digger of Germany," and added that "I despised and hated him from my heart."[7] But the count had yet another reason for proving to himself, and to others, that he was a German patriot: although he had been decorated for bravery in the fighting against the Russians earlier in the war, he had recently been refused membership by the Thule Society, an ultra-rightist, nationalist, anti-Semitic Bavarian organization, because his mother was Jewish.

The killing had taken place at 9:45 in the morning. Munich was first stunned by the news, but it did not take leftists long to launch their revenge. An hour later, the shocked and bewildered Landtag was listening to an eloquent eulogy of Eisner, given by his principal and bitter political opponent, Erhard Auer. Amidst the confusion, one of Eisner's devoted followers, a butcher's apprentice named Alois Lindner, managed to walk right to the area immediately beneath the podium, carrying a Browning rifle. While the entire legislature, suddenly realizing what was happening, watched in horrified silence, he aimed at Auer and fired twice, severely wounding him.[8] As Auer fell, the assassin marched out of the chamber, killing an army major who tried to disarm him. Just as the stunned legislators began turning to each other with gestures and exclamations, a volley of shots from the visitors' gallery killed one of their number. In panic, the demoralized Landtag dissolved.

Bavaria plunged into anarchy. Priests were forced at gunpoint to toll the bells of Munich's churches for days on end in mourning for Eisner. The various councils of workers decreed a three-day general strike; as a deterrent against any right-wing attempt to seize power, scores of Bavarian aristocrats were taken hostage and placed in prison. Leftist crowds broke into the offices of conservative newspapers; throwing hundreds of bundles of papers into the streets, they stacked them in pyramids, set them afire, and danced wildly amidst the flames. The Majority Socialists claimed that they were the rightful dispensers of power in post-Eisner Bavaria, but that claim was forcefully disputed by the Independent Socialists and by the communists. Huge demonstrations filled Munich's streets, squares, and beer halls.

After more than three weeks of a vacuum at the seat of government, the Landtag reconvened just long enough to adopt an enabling act that placed authority in the hands of a cabinet led by Johannes Hoffmann, a Majority Socialist. In assuming office as minister-president, Hoffmann made a prophetic statement: "Every revolution has two enemies. One stands to the right, the other to the left."[9] Hoffmann had no forces adequate to put down an attack from either direction. Unlike the Majority Socialists in Berlin, who had just used the Freikorps to smash a second Spartacist-Communist uprising, Hoffmann had no paid right-wing mercenaries to keep his socialist government in power, because Eisner had forbidden the recruiting of such units in Bavaria. Constantly aware of Independent Socialist and Communist Party plots against his shaky regime, Hoffmann tried to govern at a time of persistent crisis. The Central Labor Bureau estimated that there were forty thousand unemployed in Munich; in addition to this social and economic dislocation, there was a calamitous coal shortage during an exceptionally severe winter. There was a thriving black market, and an erosion of the mark through inflation. As early as the day of the Armistice on November 11, Munich had begun printing its own emergency currency; now, ominously, Bavaria's government officials had so lost confidence in the economy that most offices in Munich were refusing to accept payments made in the city's own money.

This was the Bavaria to which Lance Corporals Adolf Hitler and Ernst Schmidt returned in March after the prisoners at Traunstein had all been repatriated. In the barracks, Hitler and Schmidt found that no one bothered them, but there was literally nothing to do. They found a supply officer and volunteered to do any work that needed to be done. He gave them a task that was a classic among useless military chores. A warehouse held many thousands of gas masks, which would never be used again. Nonetheless, procedures required that they be sorted into those which worked and those which did not. All day long, week after week, as the political fate of Bavaria hung in the balance, Hitler and Schmidt unscrewed the mouthpieces of gas masks, examined them to see whether they appeared to be in working order, screwed the mouthpieces back on, and tagged them appropriately. The supply officer gave them 3 marks a day, the equivalent of 50 cents in the American currency of 1919. Their food and lodging were provided at the barracks, so this represented spending money for them. Despite the chaos in Munich, the opera was still performing on schedule, and Hitler went to the opera house every night, sometimes with Schmidt. They sat in the cheapest seats, and Schmidt was struck by the intensity of Hitler's absorption in the music.

III

Within days of Hoffmann's taking office on March 18, there was news that jolted all of Bavaria, and further energized the radical leftists who wished to unseat the new minister-president. In the postwar dissolution of the Austro-Hungarian Empire, Hungary had suddenly emerged as a genuine communist state, the Hungarian Soviet Republic. German right-wingers were mistaken in thinking that the Ebert government in Berlin, or the Eisner government in Munich, was the result of agents sent from Moscow, but the Hungarian coup had been precisely that. The central figure was Béla Kun, a thirty-three-year-old Hungarian Jew from the eastern domain of Transylvania who had served in the Austro-Hungarian army until he was captured by the Russians in 1916. Taken to a prisoner-of-war camp at Tomsk, he had become a convert to communism after the Russian Revolution in November of 1917. He was assigned the mission of converting other Hungarian prisoners to Marxism; his successful results brought him to the attention of Lenin, who had lengthy talks with him and decided that this was the man to capture postwar Hungary for Marxism.

The method by which this was accomplished was a form of communist Trojan horse. Béla Kun and a large and highly trained revolutionary cadre entered Hungary on a mission of mercy from the Russian Red Cross. Using the huge bankroll he had brought with him to Budapest, Béla Kun organized a Hungarian Communist Party, started a newspaper, and sent skilled agitators throughout Hungary and nearby nations. He received constant radio messages directly from Lenin.

The tottering Károlyi government in Hungary briefly imprisoned him and then released him, and overnight Hungary was a true communist dictatorship, with no legislature, just Béla Kun and eleven commissars. European communists were enchanted; here was proof that the communist revolution was not unique to Russia, but was toppling and replacing capitalist societies in the prophesied fashion.

In Bavaria, the effects of all this meshed with other factors. Hoffmann was already in trouble with the Bavarian People's Party, which represented the traditionally conservative Catholic vote and the views of the Catholic hierarchy; having no cushion of support to his right, Hoffmann was doubly vulnerable to the accelerated machinations of those on his left who wished to overthrow him and follow the Hungarian example.

Even nature itself seemed to be against Hoffmann's government of Majority Socialists, who were once again calling themselves by their earlier name, Social Democratic Party. During the last two days of March, twenty inches of snow fell on Munich — an astonishing amount for Bavaria at that season, and one that led the authorities to categorize conditions in Bavaria's paralyzed capital as "catastrophic."[10] Persons of every political persuasion were frustrated, frightened, and angry; resentment focused on the Hoffmann regime.

Seizing on these events, the leaders of the workers councils, those ad hoc bodies spawned by the revolution which were being denied a share of power by Hoffmann, met in the Bavarian city of Augsburg, thirty miles northwest of Munich. There they declared an intention to create a Bavarian Soviet Republic. This was to be an independent state, and one of its highest priorities was the formation of alliances with the Hungarian Soviet Republic and the Soviet Union itself. Even this program was considerably more moderate than what had recently been demanded by an excited crowd of three thousand radical leftist war veterans meeting in the Löwenbräu, one of Munich's beer halls. That group had asked for full Communist Party control of the workers councils, and the immediate creation of a Red Army. An even more specific threat to the Hoffmann regime was voiced by an organization of the unemployed, whose members met in another of the big beer halls, the Kindlkeller. Protesting the increase in utility rates and street-car fares, they issued an ultimatum: if their demands were not met, their statement said, "the unemployed of Munich will be forced to help themselves."[11]

The Augsburg meeting took place on Thursday, April 3. At its con-clusion, the assembly called for a general strike to begin the next day and appointed a delegation to take its demands to the Hoffmann gov-ernment in Munich. Learning of this in the late afternoon, Hoffmann decided that his position in Munich was untenable. Boarding the evening train for Berlin, he next appeared in the northern Bavarian city of Nuremberg, as head of what he claimed was still the lawful government of Bavaria. In the meantime, on April 7, a coalition of the radical leftist parties and groups proclaimed the Bavarian Soviet Republic.

Bloodlessly, a second Bavarian revolution had occurred, moving the stated course of Bavaria further to the left and creating greater disorder than anything seen since the Armistice. As Adolf Hitler and Ernst Schmidt spent their days sorting through the mountain of gas masks, what became known as the "Pseudo Soviet Republic," led by a group that was caustically referred to as the "Coffee House Anarchists," tried to function. The chairman of the *Zentralrat*, the body representing the various revolutionary councils, was Ernst Toller. The twenty-six-year-old Jewish combat veteran was an idealistic playwright who could inflame crowds with his passionate oratory, but he knew nothing of governing. At a time when Bavaria was facing a food shortage, in part because of the blockade of Germany that the Allies were only now changing to a policy of sending food, Toller's first speech as Bavaria's leader expressed the hope that new forms would be found in architecture, painting, sculpture, and drama — forms that would enable humanity to express itself more fully. Gustav Landauer, a theater critic and lecturer who was known throughout Germany as a published scholar, sent a friend a postcard describing his role in the new regime: "I am now the commissar for propaganda, education, science, art, and a few other things. If I am allowed a few weeks' time, I hope to accomplish something."[12]

Landauer announced the educational reforms that he intended to make at the University of Munich. Anyone over eighteen could become a full-time student, regardless of previous academic record. The university would be run by a "Students' Soviet," and there would be no more examinations or conferring of degrees. Speaking to a foreign correspondent, Landauer put it in a nutshell: "Every Bavarian child at the age of ten is going to know Walt Whitman by heart. That is the cornerstone of my educational program!"[13]

Other appointments and performances were equally interesting. An unknown, Georg Paulukun, as commissar, was entrusted with responsibility for Bavaria's railways, road system, and river transport; apparently his qualification for the appointment was that he had occasionally held jobs repairing railroad tracks. A man who had been a waiter in a restaurant was given the portfolio of military affairs. The pièce de résistance was Dr. Franz Lipp, a little man whose beard was so large that all that could be seen of his face was his nose poking through the beard and his eyes above it. He had twice been treated in mental institutions. Named as commissar for foreign affairs, Lipp may in fact have been joking, rather than demented, when he answered a cable from Lenin, "Please give us details about the revolution in Bavaria. . . . We know nothing," by wiring back, "The proletariat of Bavaria happily united . . . [but] the fugitive Hoffmann has taken with him the key to my ministry toilet."[14] Whatever Dr. Lipp's mood, he was unable to perform his job.

All this was being watched impatiently by two fervent German Communist Party members who were on the scene in Munich. Only the Bavarian revolution could have produced the coincidence of two names as nearly alike as Levien and Leviné, joined with the fact that Leviné had been sent to Bavaria by Paul Levi, the new German Communist Party leader in Berlin. Max Levien and Eugen Leviné, each in his mid-thirties, were Russian Jews who had spent much of their lives in Germany. Both had been active in the revolution in Berlin at the war's end, but neither was an agent sent from Moscow.

While Toller made speeches extolling the freedom that the masses would experience under the red banner, Levien and Leviné shook up the Communist Party leadership in Bavaria, hardened the hearts of their extremist followers, and waited for the moment when a true communist dictatorship could be locked in place.

The chance for which they were looking came on Palm Sunday, April 13, when an uprising of republican security guards loyal to the exiled Hoffmann government was put down by armed workers. This attempted takeover served as proof of the need for a revolutionary regime with greater strength, and by nightfall a meeting of workers councils — again deliberating in a beer hall — named Eugen Leviné, who had arrived in Bavaria only five weeks before, as the chief executive of the Bavarian Soviet Republic.

The second revolution, that of the Coffee House Anarchists, had lasted only six days, and now the Communist Party had indeed captured the Bavarian revolution. A Bavarian Red Army was formed by the one Bavarian in the entire revolutionary leadership, Rudolf Egelhofer, a twenty-six-year-old sailor who had participated in the Kiel mutiny. Egelhofer knew how to treat his troops; a private's pay was eight times what Hitler and Schmidt were getting for checking gas masks, and these Marxist warriors had free liquor and free prostitutes. Their ranks soon grew to twenty thousand men.

The Coffee House Anarchists were not purged, but merely elbowed back into the second rank, while Levien, Leviné, and their closest comrades worked on their version of a dictatorship of the proletariat. There was a sense of starting society all over again. The schools were closed until it could be decided what should be taught. Newspapers could print only one approved Communist Party line. The Frauenkirche, the Catholic cathedral, received a form of communist deconsecration; presided over by a woman dressed as the Goddess of Reason, a ceremony proclaimed the cathedral to be a "revolutionary temple." Squads of armed men broke into citizens' houses, confiscating food and taking money and valuables for the coffers of the revolution. A curfew came into effect at sunset; the nights were filled with the sound of Red Army trucks patrolling and shots fired by trigger-happy communist militia.

Adolf Hitler was no longer reading about the revolution in newspapers at Traunstein; here it was. Soldiers he knew had thrown in their lot with the Red Army. He later claimed to have kept some men of his barracks from going over to the Reds, and he also claimed to have grabbed a carbine and faced down three Red Army men who came to arrest him as a known anticommunist. There was never any verification of this; Ernst Schmidt said, "He hadn't much to say about the revolution, but it was plain enough to see how bitter he felt"; this was the middle ground taken by many men in the barracks.[15] Their officers had fled; surrounded by twenty thousand weapons-carrying Red Army troops who were given to firing at shadows, men like Hitler wore their obligatory red armbands and tried to stay out of the way, waiting for something to happen.

For a time it seemed in Munich as if the Reds might make good on their revolution. There were rumors that powerful Russian and Hungarian forces were on the way to reinforce their position. From Nuremberg, a column of militia loyal to Hoffmann marched south to retake Munich and were routed at Dachau, a market town ten miles north of the city. This time Hoffmann's retreating forces did not stop at Nuremberg; they fled past to Bamberg in the Bavarian province of Upper Franconia.

The picture was about to change dramatically. When he and his cabinet first left Munich for Nuremberg, Hoffmann had declined to ask Berlin for help. Bad as things were in Munich, Hoffmann's socialist followers at first felt that this was a Bavarian struggle that ought to be won by Bavarians. They detested the idea of being rescued by Prussian right-wing columns, and they did not like the idea of Prussian soldiery loose among Bavarian civilians. As soon as they changed their minds and asked Minister of Defense Noske for aid, a force of thirty thousand men was assembled. The operational commander and his staff were from the Reichswehr, as the postwar German army was known, and the fighting columns were Freikorps troops, including many recruited in northern Bavaria. One unit had quickly achieved a reputation as particularly fearsome and successful fighters. This was the Second Naval Brigade, composed of sailors like those who had fired on the marching nighttime demonstrators during the Kiel mutiny. Known as the Ehrhardt Brigade, from the name of its commander, Lieutenant Commander Hermann Ehrhardt, it had just taken part in putting down a leftist uprising in Brunswick. Its members had adopted the army's helmets, and on each man's helmet was now painted a swastika, the hook-ended rotary cross whose design was to be found in many ancient civilizations. In German mythology it was the "fire whisk," which twirled the earth into existence at its creation; in the late nineteenth century it had been adopted as a symbol by German nationalists and racists, and the design was often found in the pages of *Ostara,* the anti-Semitic magazine Hitler read in Vienna.

Near the end of April these forces came pouring across the Bavarian border. Other than encountering sniper fire, they were unopposed until they reached the outlying Munich suburbs on April 29, when some Red Army units put up stiff but unsuccessful resistance. On April 30, Dachau fell; by afternoon Munich was encircled by forces that were superior in number, organization, weapons, leadership, and experience. The Red commanders were in terrified disarray, most of them cursing Levien and Leviné for bringing them to disaster in the name of acting out class warfare.[16]

Later that evening, Rudolf Egelhofer gave the order for a brutal act that was to discredit the left in Bavaria for years to come. In a school building known as the Luitpold Gymnasium there were a number of hostages from upper-class and rightist elements, as well as captured Freikorps soldiers. Among them were several members of the ultra-nationalist Thule Society, including its pretty thirty-two-year-old secretary, Countess Heila von Westarp. Egelhofer told the man in charge of the hostages to start killing them, and, two by two, they were taken out, put against a wall, and shot or killed by having their heads smashed in with rifle butts. It was a senseless crime; the hostages did not figure in negotiations and were being murdered in retaliation for casualties suffered by the Red Army's First Infantry Regiment at Dachau earlier in the day. As soon as Toller discovered what was going on, he had it stopped, but ten persons were dead, including three Freikorps men, the young countess, and Prince Gustav von Thurn und Taxis, who was from a noted European family.

The next day was May Day. In Moscow, Lenin said to a cheering crowd in Red Square, "The working class, which has liberated itself, now celebrates its day freely and openly not only in Soviet Russia but also in Soviet Bavaria."[17] The Freikorps units surrounding the city were under orders not to attack that day, presumably to avoid giving the communists a group of martyrs who had died for their cause on May Day. With dawn, however, the news of the murder of their captured comrades, and a countess and a prince, had reached the besieging regiments. Responding to the rage of their men, a number of commanders unleashed their columns. In the next thirty-six hours Munich saw several faces of war. Parts of the city came under artillery bombardment. Rightist sympathizers who had been inside the city engaged in guerrilla skirmishes with Red militia. Freikorps men used flame throwers in house-to-house fighting. With the center of the city secured, a parade was staged, with Freikorps troops goose-stepping as they passed the Feldherrnhalle, the monument to Bavaria's victorious generals of the past. A mass of thanksgiving was celebrated in front of the cathedral, which was no longer a revolutionary temple. During the final roundups, Gustav Landauer was beaten to death by Freikorps men, and Rudolf Egelhofer was similarly murdered by a Munich mob. With Red Army men throwing down their arms and melting into the civilian population, or sneaking through quiet districts to hide in the countryside, the fighting was over by May 3.

During the next six days the victors settled their accounts with the vanquished. Right-wing bloodletting vastly exceeded anything done by the left during its control of Munich. The Freikorps approach to hunting down leftists was expressed by a Major Schulz of the Lützow Free Corps in addressing his officers on May 4, the day after all armed resistance had ended.

> Gentlemen! Anyone who doesn't now understand that there is a
> lot of hard work to be done here or whose conscience bothers
> him had better get out. It is a lot better to kill a few innocent
> people than to let one guilty person escape. . . . You know how
> to handle it. . . . Shoot them and report that they attacked you
> or tried to escape.[18]

It was now that Adolf Hitler took his modest part in this retribution. The officers of the regiment to which he was attached had returned to Munich with the attackers and were back in authority, and they wanted to know which of their men had been among the Reds firing at them as they entered the city. Repeatedly appearing as a witness before the military Commission of Inquiry, Hitler energetically supplied the testimony that was used at the courts-martial of the accused. These proceedings were not the summary executions being dealt out by the Freikorps, who in one instance killed twenty-one members of a Catholic youth group before they realized that these were not the fugitives they sought; nonetheless, men killed through courts-martial were just as dead as men shot in an alley. As a result of testimony by Gefreiter Hitler, several soldiers, perhaps as many as ten, were executed by a firing squad.[19]

CHAPTER

6

O N MAY 9, just when the first men of the victorious Freikorps were beginning to leave Munich for the north, the German public learned the contents of the 440 non-negotiable stipulations in the completed draft of the peace treaty that had just been handed to the shocked German delegation at Versailles. "If I were a German," Woodrow Wilson said to his secretary of war, Newton D. Baker, "I think I should never sign it." Wilson's secretary of state, Robert Lansing, read the finished product and dictated a memorandum for posterity that said, "The terms of peace appear immeasurably harsh and humiliating."[1]

This was a dictated peace; the German government was invited to make "observations" on the document before signing it, but there was no pretense that anything would be changed in the list of requirements that the Allies had hammered out. Germany's alternatives were to sign the treaty, which at least permitted its continued existence as an independent nation, or to face the continuing vindictive wrath of Premier Georges Clemenceau of France, who could order Marshal Ferdinand Foch to march the largest army in Europe all the way to Berlin and rule Germany with bayonets from there.

The many idealistic utterances of Woodrow Wilson had led the German leaders and public to think that the abdication of the Kaiser, the transfer of the government to men of lifelong liberal persuasion, and the adoption of an eminently democratic constitution would work in favor of a reasonable postwar settlement. The infant Weimar government had nothing to do with past Prussian military adventurism, and was trying to clean up a mess that was not of its making. The rhetoric used by many of the peacemakers in Paris had suggested the vision of a humane postwar world in which all nations' mistakes of the past would be forgiven, a new "order of world peace" that had no place for punishment or inflexible demands.

In their wishful thinking, there were things the Germans had forgotten, or never felt to their marrow. Because the war in the west had been fought on French and Belgian soil, and never inside Germany, it was the French and Belgians who could still see destroyed cities and towns, shattered churches and schools, and remember miles-long columns of refugees fleeing their burned or enemy-occupied homes. The Germans had also forgotten the Treaty of Brest-Litovsk, and the terms that Germany had imposed on the Russians after their victory in the east. Russia had been forced to cede three hundred thousand square miles of its territory to Germany and its allies; fifty-six million Russian subjects, a third of the population, were to come under control of the victors, and huge sums were demanded as compensation for wartime losses. The German defeat by the Allies canceled all this, but the Germans had themselves set a precedent for harsh dealing with a vanquished foe.

The news from Versailles was stunning. With a nationwide gasp, Germans saw that they had been living in a dream. Germany was to give up her colonies in Africa and the Pacific, without discussion or appeal. At home she was to lose substantial territory along all her land borders; 13 percent of prewar Germany would slip behind the boundaries of other nations. Regarding the new Polish frontiers, the victors were giving themselves the right to take more German soil even after the treaty was signed: "The boundaries of Poland not laid down in the present Treaty will be subsequently determined by the Principal Allied and Associated Powers."[2] What had already been decided was that Prussia would be cut in two by the creation of a Polish Corridor, which would give Poland access to the Baltic at the seaport of Danzig. The Allies were giving themselves not only territorial but financial blank checks; reparations for war damages to be paid by Germany would be fixed at sums determined by the victors as they went along. Within this arrangement was a punitive tax on future prosperity: if the German economy should gather strength despite what was being done to it at Versailles, a sliding scale would transfer profits to the Allies. In the meantime, large amounts of Germany's coal and timber were to be sent directly to the victors, with Germany paying the costs of freight. Every merchant vessel of appreciable size was confiscated, and German shipyards were ordered to start building 200,000 tons a year of new shipping for the Allies.

There was a seemingly endless list of exactions, many of which struck

Secretary of State Lansing as "impossible of performance."[3] Such terms shocked and terrified Germans of every class and occupation, but what enraged them were the "guilt clauses," in which Germany was to accept responsibility for starting the war, and hence for causing all loss and damage resulting from it. These clauses were preceded by Articles 228 through 230, in which Germany agreed to hand over for trial by Allied military courts all Germans "accused of having committed acts in violation of the laws and customs of war."[4]

Over Germany there arose a cry of humiliated pain and anger. Ebert had been named president of the republic under the new constitution; his colleague Philipp Scheidemann was now chancellor. Waving a copy of the treaty before the National Assembly at a special meeting in the Great Hall of the University of Berlin, Scheidemann spoke in a cold rage, denouncing the treaty as "unacceptable," and adding, "What hand would not wither that binds itself and us in these fetters?"[5] In Munich, one of Germany's greatest men of letters was equally indignant. At the desk in his house where he was writing *The Magic Mountain*, Thomas Mann penned this to Philipp Witkop, poet and professor of modern German literature at the University of Freiburg: "The blindness of the victors is revealed — whom the gods would destroy . . ." Showing an elegant little touch of German racism, Mann went on to say of Clemenceau, "The venomous old man who concocted this peace in the insomniac nights of old age has *slant* eyes. Perhaps he has a right to dig the grave of Western culture and bring on *Kirghisdom*."[6] The most sober reaction may have been that of Count Harry Kessler, a socialist sympathizer, publisher of beautifully printed books, and man-about-Europe, who wrote, "A terrible era begins for Europe, like the gathering of clouds before a storm, and it will end in an explosion probably still more terrible than that of the World War."[7]

Germans raged and wept and growled, Philipp Scheidemann resigned as chancellor rather than be part of a government that would sign such a treaty, the foreign minister, Count Ulrich Brockdorff-Rantzau, resigned, but everyone knew that Germany had to sign, and on June 28, Germany did.

Reading about the Versailles Treaty completed a process that had been accelerating within Adolf Hitler during recent months. In his view the treaty was "this instrument of boundless extortion and abject humiliation" and an "unprecedented pillaging of our people," but he was also beginning to see a pattern in everything that had happened to Germany.[8] By the time Germany signed the treaty, Hitler had been appointed a *Vertrauensmann*, one of the cadre of soldiers who were to act as the low-level political agents of the Bavarian command, gathering political information as well as giving right-wing patriotic talks to assembled troops. As he began this work after attending the course in political indoctrination, Hitler brought to the task some rock-hard conclusions. Some of what he thought was shared by most Germans, some of his ideas were beliefs held only by the right, but the passionate way in which he clung to his tunnel-vision deductions was unique to Hitler.

When Prince Max had gone back to his native Baden after the Kaiser's abdication, he had said nothing of the backstage reasons that had caused his sudden appointment as chancellor. Virtually no one in Germany knew that it was General Erich Ludendorff who had suddenly begged the civilians in government to stop the fighting. Certainly Ludendorff was giving no hint that this had been so. Hitler and many millions of Germans took at face value his self-characterization as a simple soldier who had fought on until a leftist government suddenly had seized power, betraying Germany with a needless surrender that led to this crippling and shameful peace. Indeed, Ludendorff was prepared to go further than that. According to his wartime subordinate Wilhelm Breucker, who became a trusted and supportive friend during the postwar period, it was during the early summer of 1919 that Ludendorff had a fateful conversation with General Neill Malcolm, leader of the British Military Mission in Berlin. In Breucker's account, Ludendorff told Malcolm that the German army would never have been defeated if it had not been subverted by politicians on the home front, causing the British general to ask, "You mean that you were stabbed in the back?"

"That's it exactly," Ludendorff replied. "We were stabbed in the back — stabbed in the back."[9] Ludendorff's wartime partner Field Marshal Paul von Hindenburg was to state, at a governmental inquiry into the conduct of the war, "An English general has said, with justice: 'The German Army was stabbed in the back.' "[10] Whatever its origins, the idea of a *Dolchstoss*, a stab in the back, embedded itself in the German consciousness: millions of people with more moderate views than Adolf Hitler's, and far more education, believed that in November of 1918 Germany had been the victim of a widespread and carefully engineered civilian Marxist plot to win at home a victory that the enemy could never have gained at the front.

This conjured up shadows of a conspiracy running from Kiel to Versailles, and in a paranoid crystallization Hitler suddenly understood it all. For an anti-Semite with a desire to find a scapegoat, there was a simple explanation. It was all the fault of the Jews. In Moscow, Trotsky the Jew directing revolution with his Jewish fellow communist leaders Zinoviev and Kamenev. In Hungary, Béla Kun the Jew setting up his Soviet Republic with Jews serving as eight of his eleven commissars. In Berlin, Rosa Luxemburg and Karl Liebknecht. In Munich, where he had seen the revolution at first hand, Eisner, Toller, Landauer, Leviné, and Levien. Jews, Jews. They were the ones. All Marxists. Jews were Marxists, and Marxists were Jews. The left, which had stabbed in the back the brave men fighting at the front, was an international Jewish conspiracy, started by the Jew Karl Marx, whom Germany had foolishly nurtured and educated. It had all been done by Jews.

Here was selectivity again. Never mind that the leaders at Kiel were Gentiles, as were Prince Max of Baden, Ebert, Noske, and all the Allied leaders who had just finished pulverizing Germany at Versailles. Hitler had his culprits. Here were the people who had stabbed Germany and were sucking her blood through the treaty they had somehow arranged at Versailles. Here were the ones who deserved the humiliating and painful lashes his father had wrongly given him. There had to be an explanation for Germany's plight, and now he had it.

It had been a long and complicated road for Adolf Hitler, from his childhood through his defiant and disappointing performance at school, his rejection by the Academy of Fine Arts, his strange years of marginal existence in Vienna, and his endless brave service on the Western Front. When he said of his new assignment after the course at the University of Munich, the posting to a Munich regiment to give propaganda lectures to the troops, that "the thing that I had always presumed from pure feeling without knowing it was now corroborated: I could 'speak,' " he was being imprecise.[11] He had always possessed a passionate eloquence that held his friend August Kubizek and his comrades at the front. What happened during this violent first half of 1919 was that he had seen the outlines of what he was going to say. From now on there was going to be less rambling talk about architecture and painting and music. The subject thrust upon him by events, the subject erupting from his lifelong Germanic mythological fantasy, could be only one thing: Germany and her enemies.

a religion. They were a race: "There lives among us a non-German, alien race." The mere presence of that race, with its different and more materialistic values, resulted in systematic corruption of the German people and produced "a race tuberculosis."

In his summation, Hitler explained that pogroms were too easy a solution, simply a transient persecution arising from the emotions. "Racial anti-Semitism must be directed toward a methodical legal struggle against them. . . . The final aim must be the deliberate removal of the Jews." This would be possible only with "a government of national strength, not with a government of national impotence." As for what Germany really needed, it was "the ruthless intervention of national personalities possessing leadership and profound inner feelings of responsibility."[5]

II

The army and police listed more than fifty different political parties and associations as functioning in Munich in September of 1919, and all of them, right and left, were subject to periodic surveillance. On September 12, Hitler was told to attend a meeting of a tiny splinter group with forty members known as the German Workers' Party. Despite its leftist sound, it was nationalist in sympathy, but had the notion, novel for the snobbish and conservative right, of weaning the workers away from Marxism.

As evening came, Hitler walked toward the place of the meeting, the beer-serving back room of the Sternecker brewery. The weather was described by Thomas Mann in his diary: "Short, hot days. The sun is fierce, but night falls before seven."[6] Hitler was wearing a dark blue suit and had recently clipped his full wartime mustache into a dark little bush that was narrower than the width of his lips. Although he was in civilian clothes, he was not trying to hide his military affiliation to any great extent; at the guest register near the door, he signed into this public meeting as "Gefreiter München 2. I. Rgt.," a lance corporal of the Second Infantry Regiment, to which he was attached.[7]

In the smoky room there were forty-four men and one woman, the daughter of a district judge. Among others who had signed in were a doctor, four businessmen, a chemist, two bank employees, two engineers, a writer, sixteen skilled laborers, six soldiers, and five students — a small gathering, but representing far more of a cross section of society than could usually be found at the meetings of the larger partisan political gatherings in Munich.[8]

The speaker was Gottfried Feder, an olive-skinned, intense man. His family had acted as advisers to the Prince Otto of Bavaria who was later the first king of Greece; an engineer by training and profession, the thirty-six-year-old Feder had developed his own construction company in Munich, and was the brother-in-law of the historian Karl Alexander von Müller. Since the close of the war he had thrown himself wholly into right-wing politics, his specialty being the presentation of his views on economics, a field in which he had no formal training; a fellow right-winger characterized him as "a financial crank."[9]

Feder spoke on the topic "How and By What Means Can One Abolish Capitalism?"[10] His was an extraordinary solution. There were two kinds of capital, he said. The good kind was tangible — mines, railroads, factories, machines. The bad kind was money when it was used for loans, which created "interest slavery." The worst kind of banking capital was international finance, which he categorized as being an enterprise created and run by Jews, who should be excluded from all legal and educational positions in Germany, although they should be permitted to send representatives to the Reichstag in proportion to their numbers. As for land, the state should own the great majority of the nation's acreage, and prohibit private sales of land.

In some of what he was saying, Feder had a large though unacknowledged debt to Karl Marx; his own touches involved the anti-Semitism and his desire to keep his particular German socialism untainted by any other. Feder had no hesitation in seeing himself as a socialist, as long as it was understood that he was a nationalist, anti-communist, anti-Semitic socialist.

Hitler listened to the talk with interest, although he had heard Feder say much of this at the indoctrination course he had attended, but his assigned task was to listen to the discussion afterward, during which the real character and possibilities of the party might become apparent. Captain Mayr's office was empowered to assist right-wing groups. This one had not yet received any money; perhaps it should.

Hitler's job was to listen, not speak, but during the discussion period a Professor Baumann rose and advocated that Bavaria not only should secede from Germany, a common enough view in Munich, but that Bavaria should then form a union with Austria.

This was intolerable to Hitler, whose Pan-German instincts were to bring Austria into a great German Reich, but never to allow Germany to lose part of its territory. "I could not help demanding the floor," he said of this moment, "and giving the learned gentleman my opinion on this point."[11] He did so, overwhelmingly, for fifteen minutes; on the platform, Anton Drexler, the railway yard toolmaker who had founded this party with some right-wing encouragement, turned to the party committee member next to him and said in a low voice, "This one has a big mouth! We could use him."[12]

Hitler routed the professor, who, "even before I was finished, left the hall like a wet poodle." He had had the last word of the evening, and as the meeting broke up, Drexler came after him and pressed into his hand a pink-jacketed forty-page pamphlet. It was Drexler's own story, *My Political Awakening*, and he gave it to Hitler "with the urgent request that I read it."[13]

Very early the next morning, in the barracks, Hitler did.

I had gotten in the habit of putting a few left-overs of crusts of bread on the floor for the mice which amused themselves in my room, and watching the droll little beasts chasing around after these choice morsels. I had known so much poverty in my life that I was well able to imagine the hunger, and hence also the pleasure, of these little creatures.

At about five o'clock in the morning after this meeting, I thus lay awake in my cot, watching the chase and hustle. Since I could no longer fall asleep, I suddenly remembered the past evening and my mind fell on the booklet which the worker had given me. I began to read.[14]

Subtitled "From the Diary of a German Socialist Worker," the tract demonstrated a hostile fear of both Freemasonry and the Jews, the latter, according to Drexler, having "almost made themselves masters of the world."[15] Its author showed a surprising independence of intellect in other areas when recounting his own experiences and conclusions as a workingman dealing with unions, management, and the rest of society. Now thirty-six, Drexler at the age of eighteen had lost a job in Berlin because of his refusal to join a union. Although he presently belonged to the Independent Union of Railwaymen and inveighed against "the systematic strangulation of the manual worker by the railways," he totally rejected the Marxist portrait of workers around the world as being a united nationless class, engaged in righteous class warfare within their respective countries. Drexler felt that much must be gained by the German worker, but it must come from a peaceful evolution within Germany that would involve the cooperation of all classes, and would have nothing to do with conditions in any other nation.

The key was the attitude of the worker, who must think of the good of the nation as a whole and realize that constant union wage demands would result in "the destruction by the working class of the middle class, the independent worker, and the national culture."[16] Drexler's vision was of proud, conscientious, self-reliant workmen like himself, millions upon millions of them, rising into the middle class until there was no lower class, no working class, but only a "National Union of Citizens." The manual laborers and artisans would be allied with the farmer, the shopkeeper, the office worker, and even the intellectuals and those in the professions.

At first glance, the liberal government in Berlin might have seemed to offer Drexler a reasonable prospect for achieving precisely these ends, but this champion of the skilled laborer did not want democracy; the workers' rise was to take place within a benevolent but authoritarian German state. An anti-Semite and an ardent wartime supporter of the Kaiser and his generals, Drexler shared the rightist view that the postwar government was made up of traitorous Bolshevik Jews.

Drexler had a name for the type of German government and society he desired: national socialism. Neither the term nor the concept was his own; the idea of a nationally and ethnically based socialism, to be achieved by a more moderate reordering of society than that proposed by the Marxists, had been a minor facet of European political thought since the turn of the century. In the Austro-Hungarian Empire, national socialism had been one of the barricades behind which German-speaking workers stood, attempting to repel the incursions of lower-paid Czech workers into German-populated areas. Along with this Pan-German desire to establish ethnic superiority and to be absorbed within new and extended German borders, there had been a substantial measure of anti-Semitism.[17]

Hitler found Drexler's pamphlet somewhat stimulating and in accord with some of his ideas, but he was not greatly impressed. A few days later he received a postcard telling him that he had been "accepted" for membership in the German Workers' Party, although he had shown no interest in joining. "I was requested to express myself on the subject." He should appear on the coming Wednesday at the next committee meeting, which was to be held at the Altes Rosenbad, a tavern in the Herrenstrasse.

"I must admit that I was astonished at this way of 'winning' members and I didn't know whether to be angry or to laugh." Hitler's indignation revealed the height of his self-esteem; asked after one appearance to join a tiny but nonetheless identifiable political party, this lance corporal felt that "what they asked of me was presumptuous and out of the question."[18] At first he thought of writing them a pointed letter of rejection; then "curiosity won out and I decided to appear as requested to explain my reasons in person."[19]

CHAPTER

8

THE ALTES ROSENBAD was, Hitler said, "a very run-down place that no one seemed to stray into more than once in a blue moon." It was evening. He entered and looked around.

I went through the dining room in which not a soul was sitting, opened the door to the back room, and the "session" was before me. In the dim light of a broken-down gas lamp four young people sat at a table, among them the author of the little pamphlet, who at once greeted me most joyfully and bade me welcome as a new member of the German Workers' Party.

Hitler had come intending to berate the group for assuming that he would become a member, but, "as I was now informed that the actual 'national chairman' had not yet arrived, I decided to wait with my declaration." After a time, the leader appeared; he was Karl Harrer, a shabbily dressed sportswriter, who moved in an ungainly fashion because he had a club foot. Harrer was on the staff of the right-wing *Münchener-Augsburger Abendzeitung*.

The meeting began, with Hitler still not having delivered his scathing speech of rejection. The minutes of the last meeting were read, and the secretary was given a vote of confidence. This was followed by the treasurer's report of a balance of 7 marks, 50 pfennigs — not enough to buy a good hat. The treasurer was given a vote of confidence.

Next came the reading of replies sent to a letter from Kiel, one from Düsseldorf, and one from Berlin, followed by a report that there were now three new letters to be answered: one from Düsseldorf, one from Berlin, and one from Kiel.

This growing correspondence was interpreted as the best and most visible sign of the spreading importance of the German Workers' Party, and then — then there was a long deliberation with regard to the answers to be made.

Terrible, terrible! This was club life of the worst manner and sort. Was I to join this organization?

After more business, Hitler had the opportunity to ask a few questions, "but, aside from a few directives, there was nothing, no program, no leaflet, no printed matter at all, no membership cards, not even a miserable rubber stamp, only obvious good faith and good intentions."[1]

Hitler walked back to his barracks through the darkness in a pensive mood. He had not told them to go on their way without him; he had not told them anything. To a veteran of four years at the front, tonight's imitation of action could only be farcical, but "I had stopped smiling, for what was this if not a typical sign of the complete helplessness and total despair of all existing parties, their programs, their purposes, and their activity?" Ineffectual though Drexler and Harrer and their colleagues might be, Hitler nonetheless believed that they were expressing a yearning for a better Germany.

That night the question stalked him, a question that he had not for a moment expected to have to face: Should he join the German Workers' Party? "Reason could advise me only to decline, but my feeling left me no rest, and as often as I tried to remember the absurdity of this whole club, my feeling argued for it."

For days Hitler debated the question. During the war he had come to understand his capacity for single-minded devotion to a cause. "I knew that for me a decision would be for good, with no turning back. For me it was no passing game, but grim earnest."

In the midst of his restlessness, "fate itself now seemed to give me a hint. . . . This absurd little organization with its few members seemed to me to possess the one advantage that it had not frozen into an 'organization,' but left the individual an opportunity for real personal activity."

In short, he could become a leader; "the smaller the movement, the more readily it could be put into the proper form." Like many an impatient combat veteran of both right and left, Hitler wanted to reform the political scene with bold strokes: "It was a new philosophy and not a new election slogan that had to be proclaimed."[2]

II

The party that Hitler decided to join considered itself to be on the left side of the political spectrum in its concern for the welfare of the worker, but its self-styled patriotism and anti-Semitism placed it within the orbit of the right-wing *völkisch,* or nationalist-racist, groups. Drexler might think of himself as being primarily interested in politics, and Feder might fancy himself an economist, but Harrer represented the murky, troubled half-world of groups that were unequivocally racist.[3]

These associations, and the psychology and views they represented, were a peculiar part of postwar German political life. There was no organic connection between the German Workers' Party and the secretive Thule Society, but Harrer had come to Drexler as Thule's emissary, a few days after Germany's defeat, to suggest the formation of the Political Workers' Circle, which was the forerunner of the party that Hitler was about to join. It was in organizations such as Thule that the full racist message flourished. Couched in visceral terms, it spoke of a morally and physically superior Aryan-Nordic race, warrior-guardians of German racial purity and national honor. The völkisch postwar vision was predictable: a noble German people, stabbed in the back by treacherous Jews, had lost its warrior king-emperor the Kaiser, and was being defiled by evil lesser races intent upon its permanent enslavement. In such extremity, the racist message said, conventional laws did not apply, and true Germans would not hesitate to use any weapons and tactics to win the battle for survival. All these influences reached into rightist political parties that called themselves nationalist, or "national-minded," terms that connoted something beyond conventional patriotism. Permeating the spectrum of the right were varying degrees of belief in a racist pseudoscience whose absurdity was sometimes starkly revealed. Thule itself derived from the semisecret *Germanen Orden,* the Teutonic Order. This group's activities ranged from placing a seemingly innocuous advertisement aimed at "German-blooded, serious men of pure character," who might be interested in joining a "Germanic lodge," to providing an application form in which the prospective member was asked the amount of hair on various parts of his body, and to provide "if possible an imprint of the sole of the foot on a sheet of paper."[4] Both Thule and the Teutonic Order used the swastika as their symbol.

Although the wartime Thule members had been elitist in outlook, somewhere in the society there had existed the notion that Germany's working class should be given a völkisch alternative to the Marxism that was sweeping Eastern Europe. The problem was that nobody knew any manual laborers to whom these views could be imparted. With Germany's defeat and the convulsive politicization of Bavaria, someone, probably Thule's leader Rudolf von Sebottendorff, assigned Karl Harrer to find some workers and start promoting the racist brand of German nationalism as a counterweight to communist internationalism.[5]

Within a few days, Harrer had found Drexler, who had not yet written the pink pamphlet that ten months later he pressed into Hitler's hands. They decided to form the Political Workers' Circle. The object would be to hold frequent discussions for the dissemination of ideas acceptable to patriotic workers who were anticommunist.

Thinking in terms of large numbers of workers, Drexler agreed, only to find that, under Harrer's direction, the circle was more like a secret society. Harrer restricted the membership to seven, although guests could be invited. Harrer would present a talk — "Germany's Greatest Foe: The Jew" or "Who Is Responsible for the World War?" — and those attending would then discuss his ideas. Drexler became restive; he wanted to reach a wider audience at a time when Munich was seething with political action. Harrer resisted, but the handful of members backed Drexler's thrust to expand. The Circle would continue in existence, but something larger was to be created.[6]

On the evening of January 5, two dozen men gathered at a third-rate Munich hotel, the Fürstenfelder Hof, to found the German Workers' Party.[7] There were friends of Drexler's from the railway machine shops, members of the Circle, and some who had belonged to a back-the-Kaiser wartime group of workers founded and led by Drexler. There was forthright handling of Drexler's form of German nationalist socialism; it was agreed that the worker must not regard himself as a proletarian, but as a member of the middle class, and that room for the workers to enter the middle class and prosper must be achieved "at the cost of big capitalism." The anti-Semitism was expressed in code words; the new party wanted a nation that was "to be ruled by Germans," and "religious teachings contrary to the moral and ethical laws of Germany should not be supported by the state."

A few days later, the members of the German Workers' Party gathered at the Thule Society's headquarters at the Hotel Vier Jahreszeiten, Munich's best, to organize themselves formally. Harrer suggested himself as national chairman; Drexler was named second, or deputy, chairman. While the Red regime held sway in Munich, the new party conducted its meetings in clandestine fashion: "We could do little but discuss and study," Drexler recalled.[8]

With the fall of the Bavarian Soviet Republic, the party was able to meet openly, but it remained a discussion group, with members inviting their friends to the talks. The membership climbed slowly from twenty-four to forty, and the attendance lists of the members' occupations showed that, in microcosm, Drexler was starting to attract his classless society; his machine shop workers were being joined by men from other, and in several cases more intellectual, occupations. There was also an addition of a handful of soldiers, representing the single most powerful force in Bavaria, whose leaders were eager to protect and encourage any group that wanted to lead the rank and file away from international communism. By August the party was able to present two of the most prominent Bavarian right-wing speakers, Dietrich Eckart, a poet, journalist, and translator whose work ranged from substantial accomplishment to racist drivel, and Gottfried Feder.

This, then, was the party that Hitler decided to join: minute and malleable. Sent once more by Captain Mayr to attend and report on a German Workers' Party meeting held October 3, on the following day Hitler concluded his brief summary: "I request the Captain's permission to join this association or party, because these men are giving voice to the thoughts of combat veterans."[9] Hitler may even at this point have already involved himself somewhat with the party's few activities, but in any case Captain Mayr's permission was readily forthcoming; Gefreiter Hitler, while still a soldier, living in barracks and paid and fed by the army, began to devote all his time to the German Workers' Party. For the moment he did not trouble himself with the group's ideology but threw himself into the job of attracting more of an audience to party gatherings. Attendance was still by invitation, "written," Hitler said, "on the typewriter and sometimes by hand on slips of paper and the first few times were distributed, or handed out, by us personally. Each one of us turned to the circle of his friends, and tried to induce someone or other to attend one of these affairs. . . . I still remember how I myself in this first period once distributed about eighty of these slips of paper."

In terms of attendance, Hitler added, "the result was miserable."

The party had no home; a cigar box, carried to meetings, contained the few banknotes of low denomination that made up the party funds, and the same box contained a few stamps, envelopes, and sheets of paper to carry on the correspondence with like-minded souls in other cities. Hitler prevailed upon a friend who was a sergeant to provide a temporary place for the party's few records in the barracks office where he worked. Organizationally, the party had a first and second chairman — Harrer and Drexler — a first and second secretary, and a first and second treasurer. These six were the executive committee. There were no other titles or positions. In practice, the party did not deal with finances. No one was paid. There were no membership dues. The expenses of meetings were paid by the organizers and by voluntary contributions.

"We changed over to having the invitation slips written on a machine and mimeographed in a Munich stationery store. The result at the next meeting was a few more listeners." Near mid-October the decision was made to cease relying solely on invitations and to go directly to the public. A meeting was set for Thursday, October 16, and "by little collections among us poor devils the funds were raised with which at last to advertise the meeting by notices in the then independent *Münchener Beobachter* in Munich."

The evening of this first fully public meeting came. "We had organized the meeting in the Munich Hofbräuhauskeller (not to be confused with the Munich Hofbräuhaus-Festsaal), a little room with a capacity of barely 130 people. To me personally the room seemed like a big hall and each of us was worried whether we would succeed in filling this 'mighty' edifice with people."

The main speaker was to be Dr. Erich Kühn, the editor and co-publisher of the right-wing magazine *Deutschlands Erneuerung*, Germany's Renewal. He was to talk about "The Jewish Problem — A German Problem," and was to be followed by Hitler, who was scheduled to speak for twenty minutes, endorsing and emphasizing some of the guest speaker's remarks. "In the eyes of Herr Harrer, then first chairman of the party," Hitler said, "the affair seemed a great adventure. This gentleman, who was certainly otherwise honest, just happened to be convinced that I might be capable of doing certain things, but not of speaking."[10]

At seven o'clock, 111 people had gathered, more than twice as many as the party had previously attracted. Kühn spoke at length, and then Hitler arose. Although he had spoken to the troops at Camp Lechfeld, and had at his first party meeting attacked the professor who advocated a Bavarian-Austrian state, this was Hitler's first scheduled appearance before a cross section of the German public. A reporter from the *Münchener Beobachter* was present; his story read in part: "Herr Hitler of the German Workers' Party used inflammatory words in urging the necessity for concerted action against the common enemy of all nations, and he particularly stressed support for a true German press, so that the people can learn what is suppressed by the Jewish-controlled newspapers."[11]

Hitler also saw himself as "inflammatory" — "After thirty minutes the people in the small room were electrified and the enthusiasm was first expressed by the fact that my appeal to the self-sacrifice of those present led to the donation of three hundred marks."[12]

Hitler sat down as a different quantity in the party from what he had been half an hour before. Harrer still could not see Hitler's passionate rhetoric as being effective, but he was alone in this. Hitler had upstaged the main speaker, had carried the audience with him, and had just brought in forty times the amount of money that the party's treasury had possessed when he attended its executive meeting less than a month earlier.

III

Three days after this personal victory, Hitler at last officially applied for party membership. His letter of October 19 said in part, "I'm a salesman" — an inexplicable and seemingly unnecessary misrepresentation — "but I'd like to become a propaganda speaker; I'm said to have the talent for that."[13]

All this was of course a formality. Hitler was already spending every Wednesday evening at the Café Gasteig, a coffee house that reserved a corner table for the weekly meeting of the six officers of the party and their enthusiastic new member. "When we were assembled . . . how did we look? Forbidding. Military pants, dyed coats, hats of undefinable shapes but shiny from wear, our feet in remodeled war boots." It was part of the larger scene: "1919 in Munich was a sad time," Hitler remembered. "Little light, lots of dirt, unrest, poorly dressed people, impoverished soldiers."[14]

But at the table in the café there was hope. The 300 marks brought in by Hitler made it possible to think in terms of advertising another of these new, larger meetings. This time there would be four speakers: three guest speakers and the party's own Herr Hitler. Into this mood of faintly stirring confidence Hitler introduced an idea that was entirely new on the Bavarian political scene. They would charge admission to this next meeting: 50 pfennigs; half a mark.

National Chairman Harrer could scarcely believe what was happening. He did not like the term "party" as it was being used to describe this association. What he wanted was to play a role in a conspiratorial right-wing network. If there had to be public meetings, he still thought Hitler's oratorical vehemence to be a most unsuitable way of getting across any sort of idea. Drexler and the other executive committee members were committed to the idea of moving the party further into the public arena, but were worried about overreaching themselves. One hundred eleven had attended this last meeting, but it was free, as all political meetings in Munich had been until then. People were poor, and there were more than fifty other political parties that charged no admission to their gatherings. Reluctantly, the committee members allowed themselves to be persuaded by Hitler.

On November 13, 129 persons spent 50 pfennigs each to enter the Eberlbräukeller. Advertising had in a sense paid off, but among those spending their half mark were some leftists who intended to heckle these anti-Semitic, anticommunist speakers. Hitler was their prime target, and little wonder; his talk was heavily and repetitiously anti-Semitic. The written cues from which Hitler spoke included: "The Spartacist uprising in Berlin," "The Jews Liebknecht, Luxemburg, and Radek," and "Who were the leaders of the bloody Soviet government in Bavaria? The Jew Mühsam, the Jew Landauer, the Jew Levien, the Jew Leviné, the Russian Jew Axelrod, also Eisner was a Jew."[15]

The hecklers stood up and started shouting. Hitler had asked a number of his soldier friends from a trench mortar company to be on hand for just such a contingency, and they swung into action. "The disturbers flew down the stairs with gashed heads."[16]

Hitler was supposed to speak for fifteen to twenty minutes; in fact he spoke for an hour and a half, and his audience would not have wished it shorter. A police officer whose job was to report on the content and reception of the speeches made no mention of the violent ejection of the hecklers, but wrote that Hitler was "masterful" and that his words produced "tumultuous applause." Hitler chose his facts so selectively that they bore little resemblance to the complicated postwar reality, and he slammed the same few points home again and again. Britain's post-Armistice naval blockade had starved Germany into accepting the monstrous and humiliating Versailles Treaty; as for France, what could be expected from a nation whose leader Clemenceau had said that there were twenty million too many Germans in the world? As those in the room stood up and cheered, he closed with: "We must stand up and fight for the idea that things cannot go on this way! German misery must be broken by German iron! This day must come!"[17]

The excited crowd filed out. The reporter noted that Hitler was surely on his way to becoming "a professional propaganda speaker."[18]

By now, National Chairman Harrer had no choice but to admit Hitler into the party's inner sanctum. The one entity over which Harrer had kept full control was the Political Workers' Circle, from which the expanded party had developed. Although there was some duplication of these men and the party's executive committee, this group had gone on meeting dutifully to hear and discuss Harrer's private little talks. Harrer considered the Circle to be the keepers of the flame, the thinkers who pondered the future of German society. Three days after Hitler's success at the Eberlbräukeller, he was brought into this group; with Drexler also present, the minutes of the meeting noted, "Introduction of Herr Hitler into the spirit of the circle, by Herr Harrer."[19] The principal business that evening was to begin evolving a full statement of the hopes and beliefs of the German Workers' Party. A committee to draft this party platform was named; Hitler was to serve on it, with Harrer, Drexler, Feder, and one other. A week later, at another Circle meeting, Hitler was appointed the party's *Werbeobmann*, propaganda chief, and agreed to become director of a program, possibly suggested by him, to train more speakers.

Hitler spoke twice more; the first speech drew 170 listeners, but attendance fell off to 140 at the second. The executive committee felt that the party was trying to have too many speechmaking evenings, and that the public would become bored with what some committee members called "demonstrations." Hitler saw it differently: "There were violent arguments in which I upheld the view that a city of seven hundred thousand inhabitants could stand not one meeting every two weeks, but ten every week, that we must not let ourselves be misled by failures, that the road we had taken was the right one, and that sooner or later, with steady perseverance, success was bound to come."

The day after the disappointing lower attendance, Hitler started

78 ▪

some party infighting. He had accurately identified an inconsistency: the German Workers' Party was totally opposed to the democratic ideals and practices of the government in Berlin, yet the party itself was totally democratic in its internal procedures. The executive committee, Hitler later wrote, "was exactly what it was trying to combat, a parliament on a small scale. Here, too, the vote ruled; if big parliaments yelled their throats hoarse for months at a time, it was at least about something important, but in this little circle the answer to a safely arrived letter let loose an interminable argument!"[20]

Hitler's solution to this was a document he had written, which he now submitted to the executive committee. Entitled "Organization of the Munich Branch and Its Standing Orders," it was in effect an attack on Harrer and the Circle. The executive committee should be elected by the members of the party at a public meeting — something that had really not been done when Harrer and Drexler suggested themselves as first and second chairman at the long-ago organizational meeting in the Thule headquarters — and the executive committee should then have power to make all decisions for the party, without referring issues back to the membership. The sole check on "the activities of the committee" should be the party program, which Hitler was working on with Drexler. Specifically excluded was "any form of control by either a higher or a subsidiary body, be it a circle or a lodge" — the clearest possible reference to Harrer's Circle. The proposed reorganization plan closed with a thinly veiled invitation to Harrer to assess his role and influence: "By strictly following [the evolving party program] each member of the committee should obtain a feeling for his own value and usefulness for the movement."[21]

It was a bold, rude move; too bold, and perhaps too rude, for the executive committee. It did not accept Hitler's proposal, yet this initiative of his showed a realistic appraisal of what was necessary if the group was to be more than a völkisch forum. Thus far, initially through Drexler, the party had moved from being a closed discussion group to an entity that proclaimed its ideas to growing audiences. As things stood, the German Workers' Party hired halls, presented speakers, whipped up audiences, and let them walk into the night. That was all: the socialist government in Berlin was denounced, the Jews and Marxism were attacked, the Versailles Treaty was reviled. Other parties were shouting the same indictments. Hitler wanted to move from rhetoric to action. More than anyone on the executive committee, he believed in propaganda; unlike the others, he understood that political speeches were for the purpose of gaining political power.

IV

As Christmas approached, Hitler scouted around Munich on his own, looking for a cheap place that the party could rent as an office. He found it on the premises of the Sterneckerbräu, the brewery in whose back room he had attended his first party meeting. It was a small former taproom, a cellar room with a vaulted ceiling: the one window faced a narrow sunless alley, and the landlord was in the process of removing the wood paneling, leaving it, Hitler said, looking more like "a funeral vault than an office."[22] The rent was only 50 marks a month, light and heat extra, and Captain Mayr was willing to use some army discretionary funds to give this ideologically acceptable group a home.[23]

A bemused party executive committee hesitantly went along with this; as one of the signers of the lease, Hitler again avoided identifying himself as a soldier, and gave his occupation as *Maler*, artist. The party's empty headquarters room was not even furnished with electricity; Hitler had electric light installed, along with a telephone. Soon there was a table, some borrowed chairs, an open bookcase, and two cupboards. An old Adler typewriter appeared at the new headquarters, and Hitler ordered three rubber stamps with the party's name on them. Hitler acquired a safe; this meant that the party records being kept at the barracks by his friend Sergeant Rudolf Schüssler could be brought there, and Hitler decided that the sergeant should come along with them.[24] Schüssler, described by Hitler as "upright and absolutely honest," was about to leave the army; Hitler arranged that, with the coming New Year of 1920, Schüssler would be hired as the party's business manager — its first paid employee.[25]

National Chairman Harrer, who still worked at his full-time job as a sportswriter, watched these developments and said that Hitler was a "megalomaniac."[26] Harrer was not a man who could check Hitler's surge of activity, and he knew it; he resigned, leaving the leadership to Drexler, who was worried by Hitler but thought the crowd-pleasing orator represented the party's best hope for gaining greater attention.[27]

In the last days of 1919, Hitler spent many hours with Drexler, working on revisions of Drexler's initial drafts of the party program. Sometimes they stayed up long past midnight at a bare table in a workers' canteen, discussing, writing, and rewriting their theses of national socialism.[28] On other evenings, Hitler would take the trolley out to the Nymphenburg district, where Drexler lived. The two men would become so engrossed in their drafting and revisions that Drexler's wife would have to tell them several times that supper was ready. Drexler recalled that "my little girl used to climb on Hitler's knee. She knew she was always welcome." The child called Hitler "Uncle Adolf."[29]

The manifesto being hammered out by Drexler and Hitler finally emerged as twenty-five points, each a short statement of what the party wanted, or believed. In Drexler's earlier drafts the language was gentler in tone; one of Hitler's last pieces of editing, made in February of 1920, was to begin thirteen of these statements with the abrupt "*Wir forden*," we demand.

In essence, the program contained four elements. The first was the cry of revenge for Versailles, a demand that the treaty be abolished. That in itself was standard rhetoric among völkisch parties; what was interesting was that even in the hour of abject defeat, there was this thrust for territorial expansion: "We demand land and territories [colonies] for the nourishment of our people and for settling our excess population."

A second area was devoted to Gottfried Feder's Marxian-derived views. Unearned income had to be abolished, large industries nationalized, and there had to be land reform.

The eight anti-Semitic provisions displayed a certain ingenuity. Using the term "members of the nation" to mean Gentiles, the drafters' restrictions on Jews proceeded from this: "None but members of the nation may be citizens of the state."[30] Hence, Jews could not be citizens and could live in Germany "only as guests and must be subject to laws for aliens."[31] This meant that they could not hold office and was linked with a statement that they must not be allowed to work on the editorial staff of newspapers or have any share in their ownership. "If it should not be possible to feed the whole population, aliens (non-citizens) must be expelled."[32]

Finally, there was a line of authoritarian thought, meant to apply to all in Germany. "Bodily efficiency" was to be increased "by obligatory gymnastics and sports laid down by law." Hitler's awareness of the power of words was reflected in this: "It must be forbidden to publish newspapers which do not conduce to the national welfare. We demand legal prosecution of all tendencies in art and literature of a kind likely to disintegrate our life as a nation."[33] As for individual civil rights, out of a thousand words, among the few set down in capital letters were COMMON GOOD BEFORE INDIVIDUAL GOOD.[34]

*

For Lance Corporal Hitler, 1919 had been quite a year. In its first days he had been at Traunstein, a rifle slung on his shoulder — a recently gas-blinded soldier guarding enemy prisoners. Now hundreds applauded him at political meetings. As the new year began, he was scheduled to appear with Professor Karl Alexander von Müller and other lecturers in an army-run indoctrination course like the one he himself had attended six months earlier.

When Hitler came to write of these months in the German Workers' Party, he belittled Harrer and Drexler and made it sound as if, overnight, he had moved in, taken over the party, formulated its philosophy, and written its program. This was not true: the executive committee had rejected his self-serving reorganization plan, and it would do so again. Drexler still controlled the executive committee, and he and its other members had already been moving away from Harrer, and toward public activity, before Hitler appeared. The party's program, sketched out by Drexler before Hitler first saw a draft of it, took its substance from sources ranging from Karl Marx to German völkisch demagogues. Hitler's contribution was to infuse the language with a tone of adamant resolve.

While Hitler's Cinderella story, as told by him, overstated the role he played during his first months in the party, he had given its members something more than his undoubted accomplishments: he had presented them with himself. Hitler was to write that at this moment the party needed men who were able "not only to bear in their hearts fanatical faith in the victory of a movement, but also with indomitable energy and will, and if necessary with brutal ruthlessness, to sweep aside any obstacles which might stand in the path of the rising new idea."[35]

And what was this rising new idea? For all its fulminations and vague promises, the party program in its twenty-five points pictured a single-minded classless society of German Gentiles, intensely anti-Semitic and anticommunist, working under an authoritarian regime to raise the standard of living, avenge Versailles, and acquire new lands. On one of the last nights of 1919, Hitler and Drexler sat up until dawn with a draft of the program, "boiling it down," as Drexler put it, to make it as pointedly expressive as possible. "We cracked our brains over it, I can tell you!" There was light at the window when they finished. Hitler leapt to his feet, stared into Drexler's bloodshot eyes, banged his fist on the table, and shouted, "These points of ours are going to rival Luther's placard on the doors of Wittenberg!"[36]

CHAPTER

9

As 1920 OPENED, the world presented a curious mosaic of bright beginnings and bitter unfinished business. To the east of Germany, the Soviet Red Army was still fighting, and destroying, the various White Russian forces that vainly hoped to negate the Revolution. Greek and Turkish units were clashing in Asia Minor, and there would soon be a full-scale war between their nations. In their eastern areas, the Turks were starting yet another of their periodic slaughters of the Armenians, while in India Mahatma Gandhi moved toward his proclamation of a campaign of "non-violent non-cooperation" against British rule.

Air travel was in its infancy, with only thirty-two hundred miles of regularly scheduled routes to serve the entire globe, but within a few months this figure would triple and soar from there. During the year's early weeks, the British public first heard music through the airwaves, broadcast to their headset radios from the Marconi Company's transmitter at Chelmsford, and in Berlin Albert Einstein continued the work on theoretical physics that would win him a Nobel Prize.

Across the Atlantic, a young American named Scott Fitzgerald nervously awaited the publication of his first novel, *This Side of Paradise*. Jack Dempsey was the new heavyweight boxing champion, Babe Ruth was baseball's home run king, and a reddish chestnut stallion named Man o' War was in the process of winning twenty of twenty-one starts. Sinclair Lewis would see his novel *Main Street* published in October, and Charlie Chaplin had in production *The Kid*, the first of his major films. The world's first traffic light went into operation at Forty-second Street and Fifth Avenue.

In Washington, Woodrow Wilson had in a sense become the war's final casualty. A year before, he had traveled to Paris for the Peace

Conference, arriving in a firestorm of adulation. Millions throughout Europe hailed him as a savior, the champion of idealism who in his own person guaranteed a just and permanent peace.

Until he sat down with the other victorious Allied leaders, Wilson shared the European public's estimate of the omnipotent role that he was about to play in the negotiations. The others around the table understood something that those who cheered the American president in the streets did not: Wilson's Democratic Party was in a minority in the Senate, and the chairman of the Senate Foreign Relations Committee, Henry Cabot Lodge, was a powerful isolationist who hated Wilson and intended to minimize American postwar involvement in European affairs. Parisian crowds might go into what one newspaper called "an ecstasy of abandonment" as Wilson rode past in an open carriage flanked by a mounted guard of honor, but Georges Clemenceau and David Lloyd George knew that they were dealing with an empty symbol, a man whose wartime mandate to govern had since eroded to a point just short of repudiation by his own people.[1] Insofar as Wilson represented anything at Paris, it was a nation that was enthusiastically shipping tens of thousands of its soldiers out of Europe every day, and discharging them as soon as they got home.

To those at the Paris Peace Conference, it soon became clear that Wilson lacked bargaining chips, and was a hopeless card player. By the time he returned to the United States, he had won only one hand — European agreement to create and participate in a League of Nations — but was unable to deliver his own country's agreement to join that new body. It was while he was frantically touring the West Coast, belatedly urging support for league membership, that he collapsed and subsequently suffered a stroke. Incapacitated, as 1920 began he was still the nation's chief executive, communicating with his own cabinet by means of oral messages brought from a screened-off White House sickroom by his wife.

The League of Nations, without American participation, came into being on January 10, 1920. Ironically, it was Germany, which was not permitted to be a member, that officially activated the league. By ratifying the Treaty of Versailles on that date, the Reichstag deputies brought the previously signed document into binding force, and among its provisions was the establishment of this organization. Thus it was that Europe possessed, in Geneva, an entity designed to subordinate national self-interest to the collective interest of a community of nations seeking to live in peace.

To many Germans, this was all a bad joke. Prince Max had been brought in as chancellor at the war's end because it was felt that his reputation as a liberal would smooth the path between Germany and Woodrow Wilson, to whom the initial requests for peace terms had been addressed. As far as Germany was concerned, Wilson was gone, the other victors had made a mockery of his Fourteen Points, on which Germany had initially relied in approaching him, and now neither the United States nor Germany belonged to Wilson's league.

Seemingly inexplicable events nonetheless required explanations. After a year of government by the Social Democrats, Germany remained politically and emotionally fragmented. To the left, the Communist Party and the Independent Socialists relentlessly attacked the Berlin government as being fake socialists who were the tools of conservative interests; on the right, the völkisch parties, the monarchists, and the conservatives all continued to view that same government as a collection of Jewish communists who had betrayed Germany and must be driven from power. Some of the same generals whose despairing 1918 battlefield reports had led Ludendorff and Hindenburg to insist on an immediate truce now believed that they could have fought on successfully if leftist traitors had not seized power and sold them out. Large segments of the German population were demonstrating that a totally inaccurate perception, believed and acted upon by enough people, can carry as much weight as if it were true.

The government plodded into 1920, tepidly accepted by millions who simply wanted to get on with their lives, but this sane, democratic Weimar Republic found little popular support among Germans. During the last year of the war Thomas Mann had written, "I don't want the trafficking of parliament and parties that leads to the infection of the whole body of the nation with the virus of politics. . . . I don't want politics. I want impartiality, order, and propriety."[2]

Mann was voicing an old German prejudice against politics: worthy public service was not to be found in unseemly debate, but in straightforward military or civil careers. Prior to the close of 1918, Germany had experienced only a minimal, constricted form of democracy; now the nation had an eminently democratic constitution, and many thinking persons found that they mistrusted both the system and those who were supposed to make it work. Floating about was the half-expressed thought that democracy was a bit of a bore, compared with Bismarck's "blood and iron" and the march to and through the war. There was a haunting feeling that by adopting democracy, Germany had somehow given up its soul. Writing in his diary on January 21, Mann reported a near riot during a lecture at the University of Munich, which came about when the pioneering sociologist Max Weber ventured to criticize the imprisoned Count Arco-Valley. For doing so, Mann wrote, Professor Weber "was booed out of the hall, and when he reappeared he was greeted with such an uproar that the rector, since called in, had to cancel the class." Mann's reaction to this offered a revealing look into the German cultural aristocracy: "The antirevolutionary, nationalistic mood of the students is basically gratifying to me, although Arco is a fool and the individual proponents of that mood are boors."[3]

II

During January, the German Workers' Party compiled a list of its new strength of 190 members. The average age was thirty-one, and there were nineteen women, occupations not given.

Of the 171 men, only four in this "workers' party" were unskilled manual laborers. The largest group consisted of fifty-six skilled workers, most of them machinists from the shops at the railroad yards. These were friends of Drexler's who shared his view that they were not proletarians, but aspiring members of the middle class whose destiny lay in a powerful Germany rather than in an international movement of workers. Their support for Drexler guaranteed that Hitler could not then push through his reorganization plan.

The middle class itself was represented by small shopkeepers, salesmen, and office workers, and in the category of "academic professions" there were doctors, engineers, a number of teachers and minor civil servants, and a writer — the völkisch propagandist Dietrich Eckart, the playwright and poet who published *Auf gut Deutsch*, a racist sheet that was about to come out with 120,000 copies of an issue entitled "In the New Germany." Completing the more educated segment of the party was a group of twelve university students.[4]

Twenty-two soldiers had joined, some recruited by Hitler and some sent along by sympathetic Reichswehr commanders. Four of these were officers, including an exceptionally able captain named Ernst Röhm, a brave, pudgy latent homosexual whose wartime wounds included a deep puncture in his left cheek, a diagonal furrow in his chin, and the shot-away bridge of his nose. His current assignment was to equip units of the Civil Guard and Temporary Volunteer Corps with weapons, ammunition, and supplies, and Röhm was using this opportunity to create a right-wing Bavarian paramilitary fiefdom, with himself as its key figure.

These 190 individuals were being asked to pay party dues of 50 pfennigs a month.[5] They had the little headquarters which they could drop into, and on a table there they could usually find a copy of the *Völkischer Beobachter*. This was the new name, meaning Nationalist-Racist Observer, of the *Münchener Beobachter*, as that anti-Semitic newspaper had been known when it rejected Hitler's offer to write for it the previous summer. The *Beobachter*, still owned by the fading Thule Society, was published twice a week and cost 40 pfennigs. Its first issue of the year, published on January 3, got right down to business with a poem, "The Times Will Change," which ended with the exhortation "You must make a supreme effort, and bury the Jew!" Near it was an article by Rudolf Jung, the leading theorist among the national socialists of the Sudetenland, as the German-speaking portion of newly created Czechoslovakia was known. Although the six hundred thousand Jews in Germany made up slightly less than one percent of the population, Jung was yet another proponent of the völkisch belief that Jews had a limitless capacity for acquiring power; his article was entitled "On the Way to World Domination."[6]

In the next issue, January 7, there was an advertisement that began

TAKE THE JEWS INTO PROTECTIVE CUSTODY,
THEN THERE WILL BE PEACE IN OUR COUNTRY

This was followed by a list of indictments, including "Jews are Spartacist agitators," "Jews agitate the People," "Jews prevent Germans from communicating with each other," and "Jews force their way to the top in every field." Then, in boldface:

LET'S GET RID OF THE JEWISH ACTIVISTS
AND AGITATORS![7]

The advertisement was paid for by the Schutz-und Trutzbund, the League for Defense and Attack. This was an umbrella organization of the far right; founded during the political polarization of 1919, it was much the largest of the völkisch associations, with a membership climbing toward 250,000. Its anti-Semitic activities included economic boycott; when the Karlsruhe branch, in Baden, was established in November of 1919, the group's first act was to distribute leaflets identifying the shops in town that were owned by Jews.[8]

The völkisch swastika symbol appeared several times in these pages; indeed, at the bottom of page 6 was the advertisement of Theodor Strumpf, whose jewelry store in northwest Berlin offered for sale various items for ladies, ranging from a sterling silver swastika brooch at 800 marks to gold-plated swastika pendants and necklaces for 3 marks, 50 pfennigs. There was also a round enamel tie pin for men, a swastika at its center, for 3 marks.[9]

On the evening of the day that this issue of the *Beobachter* appeared, Hitler led the discussion, at the Kindkeller, after another speaker's talk on "The Jewish Question." He was getting a reputation as a *Rednerkanone*, a speaker like a cannon.[10] As the party's propaganda chief, Hitler was working with Drexler and others on the party's first propaganda leaflet, "Why Did the German Workers' Party Come into Being? What Does It Want?"[11] In terms of political theory, the party had only an assortment of largely illogical ideas derived from outside sources, but this leaflet represented yet another effort to redirect the workers' energy and impulses. The struggle must not be a class struggle; German society must be viewed not as a battleground between exploiters and exploited, but as an innocent and worthy body of "Aryan" Germans who were constantly being betrayed and manipulated by Jews who could speak the language but were racially and culturally "alien." There was still a need, however, to appease various other prejudices in the völkisch mentality, so the party in this leaflet also attacked the Freemasons, whom some völkisch thinkers believed to be the dupes of international Jewish interests, and "Anti-Jesuitism" was added to the slogans.

To this point, the German Workers' Party had made itself known in Bavarian völkisch circles, but otherwise had attracted little attention. Its only press coverage had been a few lines in the *Beobachter*; among Munich's more than half a million citizens, the man in the street was unaware of the party's existence. There had been the few leftist hecklers at meetings, but Bavaria's leftist movement was largely unaware of this group with its 190 members.

The propaganda chief was about to change that. Despite some executive committee hesitation, with which Hitler was now familiar, much larger meetings were planned, and to announce these Hitler decided to put on the streets of Munich huge posters that could not be ignored. The paper on which they were printed was *knallrot* — glaring red, the left's own color. "We used red on principle," Hitler said, referring not to political principles, but to the principle of attracting attention by every possible means. "It is the most exciting and provocative color."[12]

It excited the left, particularly when Munich's communists and Independent Socialists began reading the few pungent lines of anti-Marxist, anti-Semitic text that were printed on the color they considered ideologically sacred. Hitler correctly anticipated the sharp influx of leftist hecklers this would bring to February's meetings, along with the increase in attendance by those who found that the slogans on the big placards had aroused their curiosity and interest. To keep order in these larger crowds, Hitler ceased relying on a random collection of his more muscular army friends; instead, using some of the same individuals as well as some additional volunteers, he formed an *Ordnertruppe*, a steward's troop, or, as Hitler put it, a "monitor service," to act as ushers, bouncers, and bodyguards for the speakers during the meetings.[13] Almost any political party's leadership might have been expected to view this little group purely in terms of a security force to be used to protect its gatherings, but Hitler, still a soldier and constantly thinking of politics in terms of the uncompromising nature of warfare, saw them as infantrymen going into the field against dogmatic and brutal communist opponents. Writing later of these young "monitors," Hitler described their indoctrination:

> From the very outset [they] were instructed and trained in the viewpoint that terror can only be broken by terror; that on this earth success has always gone to the courageous, determined man. . . . They were imbued with the doctrine that, as long as reason was silent and violence had the last word, the best weapon of defense lay in attack; and that our monitor troop must be preceded by the reputation of not being a debating club, but a combat group determined to go to any length.[14]

Although this unit was to act the role set for it by the violence-dreaming Hitler, its debut was peaceful. On February 5 the party held its first truly large meeting, in the biggest hall available at Zum Deutschen Reich. Two thousand people, fifty times the number that had attended Hitler's first meeting five months earlier, jammed in to hear the brilliant and burly fifty-one-year-old Dietrich Eckart. On this occasion Drexler read the crowd the text of "Why Did the German Workers' Party Come into Being?" Stirred by Eckart's eloquence and attracted by the text of the leaflet as read by Drexler, forty people joined the party that night.[15]

The party was gaining momentum, and events were assisting the efforts of Eckart, Drexler, Hitler, and their colleagues. In his diary entry of January 21, Thomas Mann wrote that his wife, Katia, "reported a depressing air of crisis in town. The price of bread had doubled, the value of the mark is down to eight centimes, and a silver mark coin fetches eight paper marks."[16] The postwar political unrest had never really ended, and inflation was making many Germans feel frantic. Now there was about to be a sharp kick from outside.

CHAPTER

10

O N FEBRUARY 4, 1920, the Allied powers delivered to the German government's representative in Paris a note demanding that nearly nine hundred German soldiers and civilians be handed over for trial as war criminals. The Kaiser and his three sons were on the list, as were Ludendorff, Admiral Alfred von Tirpitz, Hindenburg and three other field marshals, Crown Prince Rupprecht of Bavaria, and two wartime chancellors, Theobold von Bethmann-Hollweg and Georg Michaelis. In addition to scores of generals and prominent civilian leaders, the list included the names of hundreds of lower-ranking military officers and enlisted men who were accused of specific atrocities involving Allied soldiers or French and Belgian civilians.

The extradition of all these people for trial outside Germany was being demanded under Articles 227–230 of the Versailles Treaty, which the Reichstag had ratified just twenty-four days earlier. In practice, Germany had been complying with most of the Allied stipulations ever since the treaty was signed at Versailles on June 28 of the previous year, but the Allies had hesitated to enforce these articles until Germany's legislators gave the treaty their bitterly reluctant acceptance. The demand for the surrender of Germany's wartime leadership closed with the statement that the Allies reserved the right to add names to the list.

Germany howled. Nine months earlier, when the German public had first learned what the treaty would impose, the anger had been tempered with a measure of shock and fear, but the Germany of 1920 reacted with a defiance born of desperation. In the past months Germans had seen what all those treaty terms really meant. Article 45 meant that France was operating all the coal mines in Germany's Saar Basin; it meant that not a single cubic yard of coal from the Saar was available for German industry or for heating German houses in the winter. Threadbare out-of-work Germans stood beside the railroad tracks, watching endless trains carrying German coal to France and muttering *"Ententekohlen, Ententekohlen,"* Allied coal.[1]

Only a small portion of Germany was under Allied military occupation, but the reports from there had become almost insupportable for a proud people. At the war's close, the French, British, Belgian, and American armies had taken over certain bridgehead areas across the Rhine; Article 428 had confirmed them in possession of these, along with a stipulation that all German territory west of the Rhine would be occupied for fifteen years, unless Germany worked off its treaty obligations sooner than that. In the American zone, all was calm; the troops, known to the populace as "Sammies," Uncle Sam's nephews, were generally considered free-spending inoffensive fellows whose government was trying to disentangle itself from Europe and would probably send them home before long. The British were severe but generally "correct"; certainly so by the standards the Germans had imposed in their wartime occupation of Allied territory.

German men hated the requirement that they take their hats off to British officers, and great numbers of them began going bareheaded in all weather. In the British zone there was strict press censorship, and private mail was routinely opened for examination. All telephones were disconnected, and owners of cars could use them only by special permission. British military policemen in red caps directed traffic. All Germans had to be in their houses by seven o'clock at night, and stay there until morning. British soldiers were billeted in houses whose owners had to provide light, heat, dishes, linen, and maid service. Travel to other parts of Germany was by special permission only. In cities such as Cologne, the time was changed from Central European time to Greenwich mean time, a little reminder of who was in charge, and one that was more deeply resented than any other regulation.

In the French zone, things were different. The men of the occupying force had experienced the destruction of a third of their own nation, and crimes of rape, theft, and assault were more frequent than in the British and American zones. It was commonplace for French officers to use their riding crops to lash civilians who did not step off the pavement into the street to let them pass. German civil servants were routinely jailed for failing to show the proper enthusiasm for the occupation. The French were so detested that when they set up a brothel that was intended to serve a brigade of two thousand men, only two German prostitutes could be found who were willing to work there.

Administrative pettiness eclipsed the British regulations: persons wishing to repair or repaint their houses could do so only if the French authorities approved their plans and colors of paint. On the average of once every nine days, a newspaper in the French zone was ordered to suspend publication, and there was a list of 180 books that Germans were forbidden to read. Although the Weimar Republic's new flag consisted of broad stripes of red, gold, and black, inevitably there were many objects that still bore the old imperial colors of red, white, and black. Aware that the nationalist movement was using the old colors, the French outlawed everything colored red, white, and black, no matter what its historical associations. Lapel ladges of sports clubs were ripped from civilians in the streets, and in Landau a French major impounded a furniture van that happened to be painted in those colors. As in the other zones of occupation, the best restaurants and railway cars had signs saying, "Allied Troops Only" and "No Germans Allowed Here."[2]

Towering above all other things that Germans found infuriating was the presence in the French zone of twenty-five thousand colonial troops from France's African possessions. These tribesmen ranged in appearance from olive- and brown-skinned Moroccans to black Senegalese. Illiterate, speaking no European language, and recognizing only the authority of their French officers, these men came from societies in which women were either cloistered or treated as little more than beasts of burden.

The French authorities maintained that stationing Malagasy and Algerians and other dark-skinned soldiers in the Rhineland was not meant as a humiliation. According to this explanation, priority was being given to the demobilization of metropolitan Frenchmen who wanted to be reunited with their families, and to make this possible, colonial troops were being used as occupation forces. In fact, the French had other white troops they could have used in Germany, and, even when they saw the enraged German reaction, they kept the African regiments in place.

Inevitably, there were cases of rape. The German press exploded with a campaign against the "black shame" being imposed by France, and reaction in the United States prompted the secretary of state to cable a request that the commander of the American occupation forces make an inquiry into the situation. Relying on French statistics, the report sent to Washington included figures totaling sixty-eight alleged rapes, with a disposition of twenty-eight convictions, eleven acquittals, twenty-three cases in progress, and six cases in which the accused could not be found. "These cases have been occasional and in restricted numbers," the report said in its conclusions, "not general or widespread. The French military authorities have repressed them severely in most cases and have made a very serious effort to stamp the evil out."[3]

Some knowledgeable Germans were later to admit that there had been widespread exaggeration in the stories of rape, and some accounts were apparently complete fabrications, invented as propaganda.[4] Rapes had occurred, however, and the impact of these African troops on the German psyche was overwhelming. Germans everywhere believed that the French had deliberately turned loose a savage horde of blacks who were raping blond Fräulein every hour. One thing was clear: the garrisoning of these troops on German soil was a priceless gift to the nationalist-racist groups throughout Germany.

It was into this year-long German experience with the victors that the Allied note of February 4 fell. The German representative in Paris refused to accept the note, resigning rather than having to transmit it to his government, and Premier Alexandre Millerand of France was obliged to send it to Berlin by his own courier. Only the Spartacist-Communists and Independent Socialists refrained from the nationwide condemnation of what was rightly seen as a principally French-inspired act of revenge. Thomas Mann noted in his diary, "Massive patriotic demonstrations in Germany," and Otto Braun, the Social Democratic prime minister of Prussia, spoke for the nation when he attacked this "senseless claim for the surrender of the Kaiser and over eight hundred so-called 'war criminals.' "[5] Holland, where the Kaiser was in exile, had already stated that it would not turn over the former German emperor to anyone for trial, but almost all the others that the Allies wanted were still on German soil, and the government was now plunged into crisis. It would be literal suicide for President Ebert, Chancellor Gustav Bauer, and Defense Minister Noske to comply with the Allied demands; only a few days before this, there had been a bungled rightist assassination attempt upon the life of Matthias Erzberger, who had signed the Armistice agreement in November of 1918. Not a German soldier would lift his hand to protect officials who showed even the slightest willingness to turn Ludendorff and Hindenburg over to the Allies, and mobs of Social Democrats as well as rightists would have the government leadership hanging by their necks from the Chancellery windows within an hour.

The government decided to stall, and the army evolved a position of its own. Six days after the Allied note was received, a meeting of the Reichswehr's staff officers and departmental chiefs was called by Colonel General Hans von Seeckt, the brilliantly able chief of staff. Seeckt said that German honor required that the government be stopped from handing over a single person wanted by the Allies. On the other hand, if the government should refuse the Allied demands and the Allies invaded Germany to enforce their ultimatum, the army would fight. Seeckt did not think that the Allies would go so far, but he proceeded to set forth an entire war plan that had some extraordinarily imaginative aspects. In the west, German forces would fall back to prepared defensive positions behind the Weser and Elbe rivers, but in the east the plan called for attacking one side of Poland while the Soviet Red Army attacked the other. Having crushed Poland, which was proving to be a thorn in the side of both Germany and the new Soviet Republic, Germans and Russians would then fight side by side against the British and French forces. Soviet participation in such a scheme was a possibility; Britain, France, and the United States had all sent expeditionary forces to Russian soil after the war to assist the White Russians who were battling the Reds, and the Red Army had some scores to settle with the capitalist Allies.[6]

Seeckt was talking strategy on a grand scale, but within the officer corps there had for some months been another idea brewing: stage a coup in Berlin, throw out this "Jewish Republic" government, and either bring back the Kaiser or put into power some conservatives who would repudiate the Versailles Treaty, rearm Germany, and run the country the right way. Many had flirted with the idea, but the few who had seriously considered making such a Putsch now had their hands greatly strengthened by additional Allied actions. As if they were determined to destabilize the fragile Weimar government, an Inter-Allied Military Control Commission sent a force composed principally of French troops to occupy the eastern German province of Upper Silesia, on the Polish border. This, too, was being done under the terms of Versailles; the rich industrial area, which before the war had supplied Germany with 20 percent of its coal, was also claimed by Poland. At the peace conference, France had wanted to give Upper Silesia to Poland without further discussion; one of the few points Woodrow Wilson gained, besides the creation of the League of Nations, was an agreement that Upper Silesia's fate should ultimately be determined by a plebiscite. Ostensibly, the French were now marching in to neutralize the area until the day of that future vote, but Germans were quite right in thinking that the French intended to support and strengthen the Polish nationalist movement in the area, in hopes of splitting it permanently from the Reich. To underscore their intentions, the French were concluding an alliance with Poland that specified that if Poland were attacked, France would fight on her side.

Coupled with these moves were Allied pressures that were less obvious to the German public, but were guaranteed to enrage various segments of the officer corps. Under the treaty, the army had to be reduced to 100,000 men by the end of 1920. At this point there were fewer than 290,000 left, but the significance of the reductions was different from that of the enormous demobilization soon after the Armistice, when a force of five million men was reduced to 490,000 within four months. That had been the end of the wartime army, and most of the 4.5 million men released had been glad to get out.

The cuts made since that time were a different matter. Across the past year 15,000 officers who desperately wanted to make a career of the military had been forced to leave the army for a civilian life in which there was widespread unemployment. There were 9,000 officers left, and another 5,000 would have to leave before the Provisional Reichswehr, as the army was then known, would be down to its treaty strength of 4,000 officers.[7] The men who were being forced out, and those who feared that they would be, focused their resentment upon the government in Berlin. As they saw it, this leftist government had stabbed the old imperial army in the back when it capitulated to the Allies; then the "Jewish Republic" had kept them on its payroll as long as it needed protection from its domestic enemies, and was now dropping them under Allied pressure. The officers of the Freikorps felt the same way. Many of them had in fifteen months made a first transition from the imperial army to being freelance officers who were unofficially fighting the government's battles along the Baltic and on the Polish border; in a second transition, they and their men had become semiassimilated units of the Reichswehr. Now the Inter-Allied Military Control Commission ordered Defense Minister Noske to abolish the Freikorps; the leaders of these proud and independent combat columns felt that they were the intended victims of a second Social Democrat "stab in the back," and they were in a mood to do some stabbing of their own.[8] The anger of the Freikorps leaders was matched by the graduates of Haupt-Kadetten-Anstallt, the famous military academy that was often referred to as Gross Lichterfelde, the name of the Berlin suburb in which it was located. Although it was a private institution, it was to Germany what West Point, Sandhurst and Woolwich, and St. Cyr were to the Allied nations. Its graduates were, as one of them put it, "a caste within a caste."[9] Now it was to be closed down.

II

For the moment, the government survived. The deliberate delay in answering the Allied note baffled the victors. As days passed and the Allies made no move, Thomas Mann gleefully noted in his diary, "The impotence of the Entente in the extradition matter is glaring."[10] The government finally offered the Allies a compromise: certain individuals on the list — the implication was that they had best be the most obscure of the nine hundred — would be tried for alleged wartime wrongdoing, but by German judges in German courts.

The Allies assented, and sixteen cases were eventually tried, resulting in six convictions. The immediate crisis had been averted, but, far from being regarded as a government victory, the entire matter increased the widespread dissatisfaction with what was seen as a spineless and ineffective administration. In Munich, Hitler had recently given a speech entitled "Against the Destroyers of the Reich and the Frenchlings," the "Destroyers" once again being Jews, leftists, and particularly the Social Democrats, who were barely clinging to power.[11] Hitler was able to convince his listeners, despite the evidence to the contrary, that the government was encouraging the French to demand the trial of Germany's wartime leaders. Privately, Hitler was delighted with the propaganda value of recent events. He saw the strict enforcement of the Versailles *Diktat*, as it was being called, and the Allied statements on the "war guilt" question, as "a precondition for the success of our movement in the future."[12]

On February 20, the German Workers' Party renamed itself; it was now the National Socialist German Workers' Party. The executive committee was copying, with only one change in word order, the title of the German National Socialist Workers' Party, the Pan-German group founded years earlier in the Austro-Hungarian Empire. The second of the party's large meetings was scheduled to be held in just four days; Hitler was not to be the principal speaker, but he had been selected to read the party's twenty-five-point program for the first time in public. The new name of the party was to be announced at the same time. Hitler did not like the addition of "Socialist" to the party's name, but had agreed only for whatever value it might have in attracting workers from the left. In German the new title was

Nationalsozialistische Deutsche Arbeiterpartei. The pronunciation of the first word contributed to the name Nazi, by which the party came to be known.

Heading toward its most important public meeting at a time of great public unrest, the party really represented the lunatic fringe of the right, yet its concept of National Socialism was about to get an implied endorsement from a thinker far more prominent than anyone in the active völkisch ranks. He was Oswald Spengler, a former high school history teacher who had already stunned the German intellectual world with the first volume of his massive and multifaceted *Decline of the West*. Published at the war's end, Spengler's "philosophy of the future" prophesied an imminent descent into cultural and political impotence and degeneracy — a trend that could be reversed only by the reordering of society into a better-disciplined and cohesive body that rejected mass democracy and was obedient to the state. Spengler's ideas were in good part derived from Nietzsche, but many of Germany's best minds initially responded with enthusiasm to Spengler's world view, which drew unexpected parallels between what was provable in mathematics, physics, and natural history, on the one hand, and the cultural accomplishments of various historical cycles on the other. Thomas Mann, who later saw his fellow citizen of Munich in an entirely different light, found himself "dazzled" by Spengler's work; placing him on a par with Schopenhauer, he wrote that "Spengler's book may mark an epoch in my life in somewhat the same way that I was affected twenty years ago by *The World as Will and Idea*," and added that the erudite assemblage of concepts "elicits my astonishment and admiration."[13]

Now, between publication of the first and second volumes of *Decline of the West*, Spengler published a political pamphlet, "Preussentum und Sozialismus," The Prussian Spirit and Socialism. It was in the first instance an intellectually snobbish attack upon the Weimar Republic and its people's legislature — "The revolution of stupidity was followed by the revolution of vulgarity" — but what followed was a unique analysis of socialism. Karl Marx was identified as being in essence an English liberal, which in Spengler's view meant that Marx was materialistic, sophisticated, and filled with sentimental idealism.[14] Socialism was undoubtedly the next step in the world's political and societal development, so the immediate challenge was "to liberate German socialism from Marx."[15] German socialism must be made of sterner stuff and not waste its time with class struggle. What was needed was a blend of Prussian leadership and discipline, and the loyalty of the natural leaders among the anti-Marxist workingmen. The German people would instinctively respond to this "Prussian socialism." That would end the foolish German flirtation with democracy: "Together, Prussianism and socialism stand against the England within us, against the world view which has penetrated the whole existence of our people, paralyzed it, and robbed it of its soul."[16] At the successful close of the "conservative revolution" that Spengler wanted, the natural configuration of the German nation would stand revealed. It was to be an authoritarian state: "Everyone is given his place. There are commands and obedience."[17]

Oswald Spengler had never heard of Anton Drexler, yet Spengler's widely read tract was in effect a thunderous amplification of Drexler's *My Political Awakening*. Although the anti-Semitism was missing, as it always would be in Spengler's thought, his intellectual adventure with "Prussianism" pointed in the same direction as Lance Corporal Adolf Hitler's kill-or-be-killed view of the world. These words, addressed to a wide audience, might well have been shaped to whisper in Hitler's ear:

> When ideas press for decision they disguise themselves as states, nations, or parties. They want to be fought out with weapons, not words. . . . One usually fights for one's ideas. War has always been a higher form of human existence. States exist for the sake of war; they signify readiness for war.[18]

Spengler and his right-wing German socialism conferred an important measure of respectability upon the parallel concept of National Socialism, but a more immediate reason for the size of the crowds turning out for the party's gatherings was that they were getting the reputation of being exciting events. Many who came were true völkisch believers, but others, from housewives to students, were searching for something they could understand, believe, and even enjoy. In contrast to Hitler's Rednerkanone performances, the meetings held by the Social Democrats were surpassingly dull. Violet Markham, an Englishwoman who had been living in Germany since the Armistice and was writing a book, *A Woman's Watch on the Rhine*, described how members of an audience would enter a hall to find the Social Democratic speakers all seated in their places behind a table on the platform, chatting, making notes, and looking at their watches. The program would consist of "very tepid" lectures by self-styled political theorists who read their talks from the sheafs of papers they held in their hands, going on in a monotone and seldom looking up from their meticulously prepared texts.[19] At the end of the speeches, hecklers were invited to come forward, mount the platform, and turn to the audience to voice their criticisms. They were given as much time as they wanted, so that they, too, ended up giving long and boring speeches. In her chapter "Some Electioneering Impressions," Violet Markham recounted her experience at a more forceful meeting of a conservative party, the Deutsche Volkspartei, and concluded with some thoughts that had escaped many European statesmen. The speaker was "a distinguished professor from Berlin" who proceeded to attack the Allies and blame the Social Democrats for accepting the Versailles Treaty.

> Now for an Englishwoman sitting unperceived and unrecognised among a German audience this speech was not pleasant hearing. Naturally, the speaker glided easily over the rotten ice of Germany's responsibility for the war. He had nothing to say as to the original crime of German militarism, the real starting point of his tale of woe. For him history began with the Peace, an indefensible position. Nevertheless, all that he had to say on that subject drove home every doubt people like myself have felt as to the scrapping by the Peace of the fundamental principles for which we fought the war. The speech was a practical illustration of how the Treaty itself has played straight into the hands of the German reactionaries, how it has brought democratic professions into utter contempt, how it has made the lot of a German democratic government practically impossible.[20]

III

On February 24, 1920, the party held its most important meeting. According to Drexler, Hitler was not in favor of this particular meeting. The reason was not hard to find: a communist was threatening to shoot Hitler, and also whoever was the principal speaker. The atmosphere was electric, and the decision was made to go ahead, despite the certainty of strong and possibly lethal opposition.[21]

The meeting had evolved in the following fashion. Financially, the gathering was facilitated because a gift to the party of 300 marks was presented by a Frau Dornberg, one of the increasing number of women who were becoming interested.[22] This contribution, supplemented by party funds, made it possible to rent, for 700 marks, the large Festival Hall of the Hofbräuhaus. Looking for a principal speaker,

Drexler approached Dr. Johannes Dingfelder, a prominent völkisch figure who contributed articles to popular journals under the pseudonym Germanus Agricola. Dingfelder had in the 1890s been one of the founders of the recently revived German Socialist Party, another rightist group with a leftist-sounding name, and one that held many of Drexler's views. Dingfelder had never heard of Drexler, who handed him a copy of the party program, and, without mentioning the communist's death threat, said that he was asking him to make the main speech because no one else was willing to face what was expected to be a partly hostile crowd.

Dingfelder accepted, and the party printed huge brilliant red posters, addressed to "The Suffering Public" and announcing that Dr. Johannes Dingfelder would speak on the topic "What We Need." Hitler's name appeared nowhere on the poster nor on handbills that the party distributed in the streets.[23] When Dingfelder arrived on the appointed evening, he found two thousand people already jammed into the Festival Hall. He was informed that Drexler, who was supposed to chair the meeting, had suffered a nervous collapse, and that there were at least four hundred Red opponents present.

Because the acoustics were better when one spoke from the side of the hall, Dingfelder mounted a table beside an enormous tiled stove. His speech was a model of tact, considering that he had to make anticommunist and anti-Semitic remarks in front of leftists who revered the memory of the Jewish leaders of the revolution in Bavaria, and who just three days earlier had attended mass meetings on the anniversary of the assassination of Kurt Eisner.

With considerable eloquence, Dingfelder began by stressing the need for order in the world, quoting both Shakespeare and Schiller in praising the harmony of nature and the ideal of a peaceful society. If there were wars and unrest, he believed, nature itself would cease to produce, and might do so at any time. "Work alone creates real value," Dingfelder told the crowd. "The salvation of the fatherland lies in order, work and sacrifice."[24] As examples of the breakdown of order, he cited Munich's own postwar experience, the murder of the Thule hostages, and the ravages of the revolution. Bolshevism had been brought to Bavaria by "people of a foreign race." This was an unmistakable reference to Jews, but the hall remained quiet; apparently only the word "Jew" was going to trigger an outburst. "I am a communist too," Dingfelder said, "but in the *Christian* sense." Still no noise from the leftists, who were perhaps still appraising the husky young men of the Ordnertruppe, who were very much in evidence.

What was needed were "selfless leaders," not the present government leaders, who were "spiritually blind" and stood "under the influence of foreign races." Everything was still quiet. Dingfelder praised Ludendorff and Hindenburg, and said that if Germany would only return to the right völkisch views, "the world will — must — at last find health through the German spirit!"[25]

Near the end of Dingfelder's speech there was suddenly a shouted chorus, not against him, but a chant of "Out with the Jews!" — a demonstration quite possibly planned by Hitler, who was to speak next.[26] Dingfelder closed with some religious thoughts, reiterated the need for strong völkisch leadership, and said, "For us too a savior is approaching!"[27] He stepped down from the table, receiving what the *Völkischer Beobachter* called "raging applause."[28]

Then Hitler walked to the front of the hall. Dingfelder had never seen him before; his impression was of "a thin man with a small moustache."[29] Hitler's job was to read the twenty-five points, but he had no intention of doing that without a bit of a warm-up. He started in on the Versailles Treaty, the weak and cowardly government in Berlin, and the miseries of the millions of poor and unemployed. He lashed out at the "leeches," war profiteers, and accused the government of taking bribes to protect those who hoarded goods on a large scale, whom he identified as being Jews, while prosecuting only the small Gentile hoarders.[30] This shot against the Jews finally brought an angry roar from the Reds, but Hitler pressed on, attacking the Eastern European Jewish refugees who had been pouring into Germany since the war, and the shouts of the völkisch majority in the hall drowned out the leftists. There were cries of "Down with the Jewish press!" — another outburst probably orchestrated by Hitler.[31]

In the audience was a twenty-year-old named Hans Frank, who had served in the Freikorps and was soon to join the party. "The first thing you felt," he said of his initial sight of Hitler, "was that there was a man who spoke honestly about how he felt and was not trying to put across something of which he was not honestly convinced." Frank felt that this thin man in the worn blue suit "went to the core of things" and "made things understandable even to the foggiest brain." Insecure, romantic, searching for belief, and responsive to the self-righteous violence he sensed in the thirty-year-old combat veteran who was speaking with such conviction, Frank concluded that "if anyone could master the fate of Germany, Hitler was that man."[32]

Hitler paused, and the chairman said to the audience, "Herr Hitler will now set forth the program."[33] As Hitler read each point, he stopped and asked if the crowd endorsed that position. This brought shouts from the opposition, countered by cries of "Get out!" from the party members and their supporters. The Munich police reporter who was making copious notes of the meeting jotted down his own reaction that he thought a huge free-for-all could erupt any time.

Hitler finished reading the program and stepped down. The real furor began when a party member made a motion that the meeting express itself as being opposed to letting the Jewish community of Munich share in a relief shipment of wheat flour. Leftists leapt on the tables and chairs to condemn this, while the völkisch majority continued to scream "Get out!"[34] The majority so successfully threatened the leftists in the hall that none of them dared to vote against the motion, and one of the party members was able to speak for a few minutes. Then an Independent Socialist got the floor and accused the party's members of being enemies of the unemployed poor. This provoked more shouting, but another party speaker was able to address the audience. The final unscheduled speaker was a leftist who rose to say that he had served at the front for forty-two months, was as much of a German patriot as anyone in the room, and wanted Germany governed by a communist dictatorship.[35]

That last provocative remark released such an uproar that Hitler's efforts to conclude the meeting with a few words of his own were drowned out. The meeting broke up, with about a hundred Communist-Spartacists and Independent Socialists marching to the gate of the city hall, cheering for the Soviet Republic and the Communist International, and shouting, "Down with Hindenburg, Ludendorff and the German Nationalists!"[36]

That was the evening as it occurred. The next day forty-seven persons joined the party.[37] The *Beobachter* said that here was a movement "that will force its way through under all circumstances," but its entire mention of "Herr Hitler" was that he had "presented some striking political points, which evoked spirited applause, but also aroused numerous already prejudiced opponents present to contradiction; and he gave a survey of the party's program, which in its features comes close to that of the Deutsch-Sozialistische Partei."[38] The politically middle-of-the-road newspapers concentrated on Dingfelder; all Hitler got from the next morning's *Münchener Zeitung* was "The Committee member Hitler presented, following the lecture, the program, which among other things stands for Greater Germany, opposes the Jews, and demands the breaking of interest slavery."[39]

Hitler's version of the evening is a masterpiece of omission, although not without extraordinary embellishments. Eckart's speech three weeks earlier, to a crowd of similar size, is expunged; this is "the movement's first large mass meeting." Dingfelder is referred to once, not by name but as "the first speaker," with the implication that he was readying the crowd for Hitler. Rather than the steady flow of objections to the successive points of the party program as they were read, there is this tour de force:

> From minute to minute the interruptions were increasingly drowned out by shouts of applause. And when I finally submitted the twenty-five theses, point for point, to the masses and asked them personally to pronounce judgment upon them, one after another was accepted with steadily mounting joy, unanimously and again unanimously, and when the last thesis had found its way to the heart of the masses, there stood before me a hall full of people united by a new conviction, a new faith, a new will.[40]

11

Events in Berlin were reaching a superheated condition. Soon there would be an explosion that would, among other things, give Adolf Hitler his first airplane ride, bring General Erich Ludendorff to live just outside Munich, and provide the Nazi Party with a manpower pool drawn from Germany's most experienced killers.

On February 29, five days after Hitler announced the party's twenty-five points, the decision was reached in Berlin to disband, effective immediately, two of the three Freikorps known as the Naval Brigades. The most famous of these, the Ehrhardt Brigade, was stationed at the army depot at Döberitz, fifteen miles west of Berlin. Originally formed from naval personnel and led by Lieutenant Commander Hermann Ehrhardt, this force had become a type of marine corps, and was the most effective fighting unit in Germany. These mercenaries had fought the Reds in Brunswick, acted as the spearhead of the attack that destroyed the communist regime in Munich, and had then campaigned extensively in the east against the Polish nationalist forces that were disputing the border areas. Although they had not fought along the Baltic, the earlier dissolution of the Freikorps grouping known as the Iron Division had brought an influx of these Baltikumers into their ranks.

Several of these veterans had become something less than fully human. Ernst von Salomon, all of eighteen years old and destined to become a famous author and writer of screenplays, had participated in the retreat from Latvia, a desperate withdrawal in the face of superior forces, and one in which he and his comrades had the embittering knowledge that the Berlin government was at one moment aiding and abetting them, and at the next was cutting off their supplies and claiming that their activities were unauthorized. Falling back through the same Lett villages in which they had at times been quietly billeted, Salomon and his comrades engaged in wanton frustrated behavior that he described:

> We roared our songs into the air and threw hand grenades after them. . . . We no longer had anything of human decency in our hearts. The land where we had lived groaned with destruction. Where once peaceful villages stood, was now only soot, ashes and burning embers after we had passed. We kindled a funeral pyre and more than dead material burned there — there burned our hopes, our longings; there burned the *bürgerlich* tablets, the laws and values of the civilized world; there burned everything. . . . And so we came back, swaggering, drunken, laden with plunder.[1]

That was the temper of the twenty-five hundred men stationed at Döberitz, many of whom had been fighting since 1914. Insofar as they had political attitudes, they were reflected in their passwords and countersigns, the first having to do with the Republican colors.

> Black and gold: Incredible
> League of Nations: Nonsense
> Poles: Smash them[2]

On hearing of the decision to put his brigade out of existence, Lieutenant Commander Ehrhardt jumped into a staff car and had himself driven to Berlin. There he was ushered into the presence of the third-ranking officer of the Provisional Reichswehr, General Baron Walther von Lüttwitz, a small, handsome, dapper man, a monarchist who was described by a fellow general as being the ideal "old Prussian officer . . . a royalist nobleman from top to toe."[3] Because of the uncertain nature of the postwar army's command structure, Lüttwitz was commander of the Reich's field forces, ranking just beneath General Walther Reinhardt, the largely nominal chief of the High Command, and General von Seeckt, the brilliant and energetic chief of staff. The result of this amorphous situation was that Lüttwitz saw himself as the army's real commander, and his view was shared by numerous other officers. He was in any event the de facto commanding officer of all forces in the Berlin area.[4]

Ehrhardt angrily, and truthfully, told Lüttwitz that he was having trouble restraining his men from marching on Berlin, and asked him what he ought to do about it.

LÜTTWITZ: Don't do a thing and keep quiet. I will not permit
             the troops to be disbanded.

EHRHARDT: But the order has already gone out.

LÜTTWITZ: That is my worry.[5]

Ehrhardt went back to camp and, when the men asked him if they
were about to be discharged, grinned and said, "Shut up and get back
to duty." Ehrhardt observed that "the men were as happy as children."[6]

As for Lüttwitz, for months he had been trying to interest various
high-ranking officers in a Putsch. The only man whose enthusiasm
matched his own was not a soldier, but a sixty-two-year-old civilian
named Wolfgang Kapp. Born in the United States, the son of one of
the German revolutionaries of 1848 who had emigrated, Kapp had
returned to Germany at thirteen, and had eventually entered the civil
service and risen to be the head of the East Prussian land office. Later
elected to the Reichstag as a Conservative Party deputy, during the
war he had become nationally known as the cofounder of the Fatherland Party; it was his initiative in the ultraconservative attack on
the "slackness" of Chancellor Bethmann-Hollweg which drove that
leader from office. As a monarchist, he was appalled at the revolution
in Germany, and this exhausted, limited civil servant went about trying
to do what he could to promote a counterrevolution.

One of the places where Kapp and Lüttwitz kept running into each
other was the drawing room of General Erich Ludendorff, who was
on retired status but was at the center of a buzzing hive of military
and civilian right-wingers, a salon that included a number of women
whose interest in the general struck Frau Ludendorff as being more
than political in nature. Since his startling demand for an immediate
armistice, a demand made when the "man of steel" was under the
care of a psychiatrist who was in attendance on him at headquarters,
Ludendorff's behavior and role had been singular. He had fled the
country five days after the Armistice, wearing civilian clothes, a fake
beard, and blue spectacles as he boarded a train for Denmark. Once
safe in that neutral country, he went on to Sweden. From there he
wrote to his wife, who had remained in Germany, "My nerves are too
much on edge and sometimes my speech gets out of control. There
is no help for it, my nerves have simply gone to pieces!"[7]

Returning to Germany at the end of February 1919, Ludendorff
seemed to have regained his composure. During the war he had in

effect run Germany, insisting on and exercising an absolute authority unknown since Frederick the Great: "I ought never to have let myself be dismissed," he now said to his sycophantic circle. "It would have been better if, while the war was still in progress, I had snatched the Dictatorship for myself."[8] As for the Weimar Republic, he told his wife, "The greatest blunder of the revolutionaries was to leave us all alive. If I once get back to power, there'll be no quarter. I should hang up Ebert, Scheidemann and the comrades with a clear conscience and watch them dangle!"[9]

Had the right-wingers fully understood the record of the man they looked to for leadership and example in this stormy period, even they might have restrained their praise. It was Ludendorff who had sent Lenin through Germany in a sealed railroad car on his way to torch a revolution that had indeed knocked Germany's enemy Russia out of the war, but had also given impetus to the revolution in Germany that the nationalists so detested. Britain's minister for war and air minister, a rising forty-five-year-old politician named Winston Churchill, believed that Ludendorff's mid-1918 offensive, rather than Allied attacks, had wrecked the German army and left it too weak to resist the final Allied push in the autumn. Having bled the army to death, Ludendorff left the resulting chaos in the hands of civilians whose authority he had usurped and weakened, and then made his famous "stab in the back" accusation against those who moved into the vacuum he had created.

This was the man the right wing referred to as the "national commander." For one with such a ponderous appearance — under his *Pickelhaube*, the spiked helmet, he looked like a German Colonel Blimp, with bushy eyebrows, pomegranate cheeks, and a double chin — Ludendorff was able to walk the tightrope with surprising skill when asked if he favored an armed uprising against the Ebert government. None of the many intriguing nationalists heard him indicate a specific desire to head a new government, and yet there was the national commander every afternoon in the spacious drawing room of his apartment on the Viktoriastrasse, charming the ladies and making remarks about President Ebert that sounded like the sighs of Henry II wishing his knights could somehow arrange to have Thomas à Becket vanish from the scene.

Kapp and Lüttwitz saw that, although they had Ludendorff's patronage and encouragement, they must strike the blow themselves, leaving in abeyance the role that Ludendorff might play if presented with a fait accompli. All their recent plotting had been based on the assumption that Ehrhardt's brigade would be available to march in from Döberitz at night — the brigade had practiced this march several times, without being given reasons for the exercise — and blast aside any opposition and take over the government buildings. Kapp felt the need to work out more details concerning civilian operation of a newly seized bureaucracy, but suddenly, with the order that the brigade be disbanded, there was little time left if they were to use Ehrhardt's fearsome troops. As for Lüttwitz, he lived in a dream of past martial splendor, and was moving with a sense of destiny. His disdain for politics was complete. When two right-wing politicians asked him what his immediate plans were, because they wanted to ask for a new national election that they felt would repudiate the present government, Lüttwitz replied, "I prefer to rely on my battalions."[10]

Feeling against the French continued to run high, and in the first week of March the powder-keg possibilities of this hatred were demonstrated by an incident at Berlin's best hotel, the Adlon. Prince Joachim, an officer cadet who was a relative of the Kaiser's, was in uniform, dining there with several friends. A violinist was playing, and after dinner the prince ordered him to play "Deutschland, Deutschland, über alles." Half the people in the hotel dining room stood up, but two French officers in uniform sat quietly at their table. The prince asked them to stand, and when the Frenchmen indicated that they were not going to rise, Prince Joachim and his friends began throwing wine glasses at them. One of the Frenchmen was hit in the head and fell from his chair. The police arrived and arrested the prince.[11]

The hatred of the French in Berlin was perhaps surpassed in Munich. On March 8, Thomas Mann entered in his diary: "Anger at the French is very strong among the populace. The people are saying, 'In the next war we won't take any prisoners.' "[12]

For professional military men, there was soon to be a final humiliating agony. On March 10, the military academy at Gross Lichterfelde held its farewell parade before closing down in compliance with Allied orders. Ludendorff was among the graduates present. A British general stationed in Berlin gave this account:

> Sitting in my room in the deepening twilight I suddenly heard the stirring music of "Fridericus Rex." I went to the window and below I saw the cadets marching in columns of four across the Potsdamer Platz in their blue trousers and Pickelhauben. . . . At

the head of the column marched the older generation of alumni, generals and colonels who had gone gray in the service, in a uniform representing the flower of the army in dissolution and of regiments doomed to disappear — Guards, Cuirassiers, Foot Guards, Death's Head Hussars, Foot Artillery, Uhlans — like a parade of ghosts. . . .

The cadets marched at parade step in perfect time. . . . As they kept their eyes fixed straight on the colors of their corps, their young faces seemed strangely expressionless and immobile as though they mastered some emotion too deep for tears. At a corner of the square, a German general mounted on a gray horse took their salute and as their eyes turned toward him it seemed as though a mighty cry went up from a thousand hearts.[13]

At the time of the parade, reports were filtering into the Chancellery that there might be an attempt against the government. Hard upon this news came a request from General von Lüttwitz for a meeting with President Ebert. When Lüttwitz was shown in, he found Gustav Noske also present and immediately demanded of the defense minister that the demobilization of the Freikorps be stopped, and that General Reinhardt, the army's chief, be replaced by a general of Lüttwitz's choosing.

Noske rejected these demands with the remark that he would immediately remove from command any general who was disloyal. With this, Lüttwitz turned angrily to Ebert and set forth a political agenda: Ebert must call for new Reichstag elections, a presidential election, and the appointment of a new cabinet composed of economic experts rather than politicians. President Ebert began to discuss these points in a noncommittal way, and Lüttwitz, who had not consulted with Kapp before asking for this meeting, began to feel out of his depth. When he attempted to regain the initiative, Noske stopped him with, "Matters have gone far enough. The time has come when you either obey orders or resign. You are mistaken if you think you have the whole Reichswehr behind you. If you use force, we shall proclaim a general strike."[14]

General von Lüttwitz strode out, leaving Noske to ponder the actual strengths and weaknesses of the government's position. He did not underestimate the independence of the Ehrhardt Brigade — instead of the government's red, gold, and black colors, they carried the white and black battle flags of the Kaiser's army, and wore on the front of their helmets a black untilted swastika painted on a white circle —

but as a prewar noncommissioned officer in the army, he placed great faith in the chain of command. General Reinhardt was unequivocally in favor of supporting Germany's government, and his orders to that effect would go right down the line. If the Ehrhardt Brigade was so foolish as to march into Berlin, Noske was sure that Reinhardt could confront them with larger numbers of soldiers who had amply tested professional skills in handling their Mauser rifles and Maxim machine guns.

Germany's minister of defense continued to think that way until the evening of March 12, when there were confirmed reports that the Ehrhardt Brigade had left its barracks at Döberitz and was marching to Berlin. Noske called a council of war: among the generals present were his two senior officers, Reinhardt and Seeckt. Within minutes it became clear that only Reinhardt and one staff major were committed to supporting the government and challenging the Ehrhardt Brigade. Among the other Reichswehr leaders there was no support for Lüttwitz, but a great fear that the army was on the eve of destroying itself. Addressing Noske, General von Seeckt said, "Troops do not fire upon troops! Do you, Herr Minister, have the intention of countenancing a battle . . . between troops who have fought side by side against the enemy?"

Noske heatedly replied that Seeckt was protecting a force that was on its way to Berlin to bring down the government.

"Not so," Seeckt said, "but I know the tragic consequences. . . . If Reichswehr clubs down Reichswehr, then all comradeship in the Officer Corps is at an end. When that occurs, then the true catastrophe, which was avoided with so much difficulty on November 9, 1918, will really occur."

At that moment the scales fell from Noske's eyes. He was being told that the army was much more interested in preserving itself than in defending the government. "Then I will mobilize the police," Noske said.

In a tone verging on contempt, Seeckt said quietly that Berlin's regular police and security police had committed themselves to the putschists.

Noske shouted, "Everyone has deserted me! Nothing remains but suicide!" Seeckt remained silent. Noske composed himself and said matter-of-factly, "The session is closed."[15]

General von Seeckt went home, and conveyed to the government his offer to resign from the army. As he was therefore on an indefinite leave of absence, pending action on his resignation, he had ample reason to believe that, whichever side prevailed in the next days, neither would ever again ask him to wear a uniform.

Trying to pick up the pieces, Defense Minister Noske asked President Ebert to call a cabinet meeting in the early hours of March 13, as the Ehrhardt Brigade made its way through the night to Berlin. The only general present was Reinhardt, and Noske had the final bitter experience of hearing the chief of the High Command say that this insurrection should be opposed and that he was willing to lead the fight, but that the officers and men of the Berlin garrison would put up little if any resistance. The decision was made to order the Reichswehr troops in Berlin to remain in their barracks and stay there, whatever happened; then the cabinet voted to leave the capital and look for a city that would provide a secure base from which to organize nationwide opposition to the impending Putsch.

If Gustav Noske had been naïve about the generals who had until now flattered him because he was the only game in town, there was equal naïveté among the putschists. Lüttwitz assumed that if he could only put the Ehrhardt Brigade into possession of the government buildings, then Seeckt and the more than a quarter of a million Reichswehr soldiers throughout Germany would simply switch allegiance to a new government whose philosophy would be far more to their taste. Under Reichswehr protection, the government would continue to run the country, but would lead it with better policies. It was as simple as that. Despite his autocratic character and record, Ludendorff had some little-known anticapitalist views; he and a few of the backstage conspirators had convinced themselves that millions of German workers would see that a new regime would work to their benefit. Here was yet another variation on the idea of National Socialism: the leftist government must be deposed, and then the military and the workers would make a new, noncapitalistic, anticommunist government.[16] As for Kapp, he was to be the first head of state, with the possibility that Ludendorff would have some prominent title and role. As a bureaucrat, Kapp assumed that with the government buildings in his hands and a new government proclaimed, all the government's functions and paperwork would continue to flow smoothly; it was, after all, simply a change in management.

Throughout the internecine plotting and planning, no one seemed to have given much thought to what the Allied reaction might be. Members of the Allied control commission in Berlin had gotten wind of the impending moves and were conveying their strong disapproval to every rightist they could find. Ludendorff, who had fought the French for four years, had only to read newspapers to know that they were ready to use any pretext to increase the amount of German territory they occupied. The French already had the Saar and their share of the Rhineland, and a month earlier had marched into Upper Silesia. The Versailles Treaty stipulated that both the German and French armies must stay out of the Ruhr, Germany's richest industrial area, and that law and order there was to be maintained by German police. The French were keeping within the letter of the agreement, but coveted the vast productive facilities of Germany's great steel industry. The Ruhr was populated by factory workers of strong leftist leanings who could not possibly be expected to welcome a government symbolized by the rightist National Commander Ludendorff or his associates. Widespread unrest in the Ruhr would give the French the perfect excuse to take over; ever since the Armistice, their well-trained regiments had been ready to do just that.

II

During the early days of March, few intimations of the imminent Putsch in Berlin reached anyone in Munich. Bavaria was indeed a separate world; on the first of March, Drexler and Hitler had written a letter to Dr. Walter Riehl, the head of the Austrian party whose name they had just adopted, rejecting Riehl's suggestion that they "fight against Berlin" and make Bavaria an officially separate state.[17] From the outset, Drexler had seen his party as having something to offer all of Germany; even when there were only twenty-four members, all living in Munich, there had been a "National Chairman," and the activities in Munich had been known as the "Munich branch" or "Munich local" of something that was larger. Now a new local came into being, at Rosenheim, in the foothills of the Bavarian Alps thirty-five miles southeast of Munich. In Munich itself, after the meeting of February 24, the local had been divided into four sections, corresponding to four of the city's districts. These had no offices, and the real purpose of dividing the city in this fashion was to give to party members living in each district the responsibility of conducting propaganda work in their own areas.

This idea was probably Hitler's; in any case, as propaganda chief, he chose the section leaders from each of the city's districts. On Monday nights these four men would come to the party's little office, each of them accompanied by others from his district who were willing to take special responsibilities in spreading the party's message. Hitler would preside over the indoctrination session, setting the topic that was to be discussed and coaching the small corps of speakers, teaching them what to say and how to say it effectively. After studying under Hitler on Monday night, these fledgling propagandists spoke to small groups in their own locals on Tuesday and Wednesday nights.[18]

In starting this program, Hitler at last had a power-acquiring activity that was his alone. Unfettered by the executive committee, he picked the top Nazi in each of four districts of a city of more than half a million; for these men, and the enthusiasts who came with them to the weekly training sessions, Hitler was their point of contact with the party, the man who told them what to say and encouraged them in their efforts to say it.

For the reinforcement, in another medium, of what his speakers were saying throughout the city, Hitler could not have asked for more than what was being printed in the *Beobachter*. Inflation, unemployment, and the feeling against the French had created the crisis atmosphere that breeds intolerance and the search for scapegoats. On March 10, the same day that the Gross Lichterfelde cadets who would never graduate were marching in the school's farewell parade, the *Beobachter*'s banner headline read CLEAN OUT THE JEWS ONCE AND FOR ALL! In "sweeping out the Jewish vermin with an iron broom," the paper demanded that all Jews who had entered Germany after the war began in 1914 should immediately be deported. All Jews who worked in government posts, or for newspapers, or were active in the theater or any part of the movie industry, were immediately to be removed from their positions. Special "collection camps" must be organized to receive them, and the "most ruthless measures" must be taken to ensure the *Endziel*, the final goal — their elimination from German life.[19]

The propaganda war of course had two sides, and on March 3 the leftist press had finally awakened to the fact that there was a party whose initials in German were NSDAP, and that the NSDAP was no friend to communists. On that date the Independent Socialist newspaper, *Der Kampf*, called the Nazi Party "the handymen of the Prussian aristocrats and militarists."[20] In fact, the Bavarian-based party was totally out of touch with the Prussian aristocrats and militarists such as General von Lüttwitz, so Hitler, Drexler, Eckart, and even army captain Röhm were unprepared for the electrifying news that reached Munich on the afternoon of Saturday, March 13. Thomas Mann wrote in his diary all that Munich learned that day.

> In Berlin a counterrevolutionary overthrow without a struggle. Kapp proclaimed "dictator" and Lüttwitz minister of the Reichswehr. The former government has fled, the National Assembly and the Prussian Diet are dissolved. . . . Noske's troops were unwilling to fire on the advancing forces and were withdrawn.

Mann interjected a remark that summed up the reaction of millions of essentially apolitical, right-of-center Germans: "I do not care for Kapp at all; but doubtless it is true that the previous government had already made too much of a mess of things."[21]

Here was a great moment for the völkisch movement in Bavaria, but in what happened next Lance Corporal Hitler was left totally aside as men of higher rank moved, and moved swiftly. The Bavarian Reichswehr commander was General Arnold Ritter von Möhl, who, as soon as he heard the news from Berlin, declared his continuing loyalty to the Ebert government, which consisted of a long string of cars looking for a friendly city in which to stop, take stock of the situation, and try to rally its many millions of leftist adherents. Möhl had no affection for Ebert and his cabinet, but, like a number of the key commanders around the nation, he noted that Seeckt and the Reichswehr high command were not endorsing the new regime, and it seemed best to reaffirm his allegiance to duly constituted authority, wherever it might be driving around at the moment.

Möhl's decision brought down on his head the openly expressed criticism of many of his pro-Kapp subordinates, as well as the threat that such organizations as the Freikorps Oberland might start taking matters into their own hands in Bavaria. A compromise was implicitly reached, and the victim of that compromise was Bavaria's minister-president, Johannes Hoffmann, a Social Democrat. Hoffmann's government had fled Munich just a year earlier, retiring to Bamberg when the communists set up their Bavarian Soviet Republic. Rescued and restored to power by the Reichswehr and the Freikorps, Hoffmann and his cabinet had governed as a well-behaved anachronism, an administration that was to the left of the Bavarian people, had never had a true parliamentary majority, and was doomed to eventual extinction by the growing rightist majority in the Bavarian Landtag.

Having agreed to finish Hoffmann off, Möhl called on him and politely explained that, to avoid uprisings of either right or left pending clarification of the situation in Berlin, the Reichswehr would have to assume full governmental powers during this emergency.

With equal politeness, Hoffmann said that such an arrangement was not acceptable to him. The rest of Hoffmann's cabinet were more impressed by the power that Möhl represented, and voted to accept his terms. The government collapsed, and the archconservative Gustav von Kahr, a Protestant whose family had for generations been advisers to the Catholic kings of Bavaria, soon consented to form a new government. Overnight, Bavaria had ratified its de facto position as Germany's rightist headquarters, but at the same moment the workers of Bavaria had a chance to demonstrate their power. As the Ebert government rolled into Stuttgart, it had issued a call for a national general strike, to protest and bring down the Kapp dictatorship.[22] In Munich, there was no public transportation and there were no newspapers; the schools closed. This situation paled beside the news from Berlin, where all the stores were closed, the factories were shut, the railroads in and out of the city were stopped, the garbage was piling up, and there was no electric light and no running water.

As all that was going on, Dietrich Eckart came to Hitler with an interesting piece of information. Dr. Gottfried Grandel, an industrialist from the nearby city of Augsburg and a supporter of völkisch activities, had offered to put a plane at their disposal so that they could fly to Berlin, find out what was going on there, and see what sort of relationship might be established with the putschists.[23]

Hitler was impressed. Eckart moved in a world where such things happened, where even in a poverty-stricken nation some people had planes and pilots and chauffeurs and racehorses. The colorful older man had befriended Hitler, taking him to better restaurants than he had ever been in, introducing him to new and influential circles, and giving him a trench coat, which he wore constantly. Eckart believed in Hitler, saying, "There is the coming man of Germany of whom the world will someday speak."[24] An early guest speaker for the party, he had joined it not long after Hitler did.

There had to be consultations as to whom they were to see in Berlin, and what was to be asked and answered. They talked with Röhm, who quickly had them sitting down with his immediate superior, Colonel Franz Ritter von Epp, the man furthest to the right among the top echelon of the military in Bavaria. At some point they discussed contingency plans for their little mission. Different parts of the country were declaring for or against Kapp; in some cases neighboring towns had different loyalties. The plane could not get to Berlin on one load of fuel, so they would have to set down somewhere to take on more gasoline. No one could be certain of what the political sympathies of those in charge at a given airfield might be, so Eckart and Hitler were each furnished with two sets of passes, one to get them in and out of a Red-held airfield and the other to show to Kappist sympathizers.[25] If they were detained by the Reds and questioned, Eckart intended to say that he was a paper manufacturer flying to Berlin on business, and that Hitler was his accountant.

On the morning of Wednesday, March 17, four days after the Putsch began, Eckart and Hitler walked out to an open-cockpit plane on the field at Augsburg. Their pilot was Lieutenant Robert von Greim, who during the war had won the Pour le Mérite, Germany's highest decoration. There was little chance that anyone at an airfield far from Munich would recognize Hitler, but he was carrying a fake goatee to snap on his chin when they landed. Off they went, and Hitler became airsick and started vomiting.[26]

CHAPTER

12

H ITLER SOON had the chance to don his disguise. Lieutenant von Greim landed to refuel at Jüterborg, which was in the hands of militant leftists. The cover story worked; the pass acceptable to the workers was produced, and on the strength of it they were able to get enough gasoline to fly on to Berlin, with Hitler throwing up all the way.[1]

They arrived at Tempelhof Airfield to find that, after four and a half days, the Putsch was collapsing. Once in the center of the city, Eckart and Hitler soon learned the outlines of what had happened. The soldiers of the Reichswehr's Berlin garrison had indeed remained in their barracks, and the Freikorps troops of the Ehrhardt Brigade had marched into Berlin unopposed. Halting at the Brandenburg Gate at dawn on Saturday, they were met by General von Lüttwitz, and by Kapp and the designated civilian leaders of the new government, who had turned out in top hats, morning coats, striped pants, and spats. Ludendorff appeared; he was later to claim that he was out for a stroll and happened "by chance" to encounter these thirty-five hundred soldiers at the break of day.[2] With everyone assembled, at precisely seven o'clock orders rang out, and a band began to play "Deutschland über alles." Led by Ludendorff, Lüttwitz, and Kapp, the goose-stepping troops marched through the Brandenburg Gate and down a short stretch of Unter den Linden, turning right into the Wilhelmstrasse. With the white and black battle flags of the old imperial army at the head of the principal units, and the untilted swastika on the front of their helmets, the troops ended their parade in front of the deserted Chancellery. Other units swiftly occupied the Ministry of Justice, the Interior Ministry, the Reichstag, and other government office buildings.

By seven-thirty in the morning, the seat of government was in right-wing hands, without a shot having been fired.

That moment proved to be the high-water mark of the Kapp venture into government. Having marched down the Wilhelmstrasse, Ludendorff went home to see how things turned out. The Berlin garrison stayed on in their barracks, neither opposing the putschists nor offering them any sign of support. General von Seeckt remained at home, in civilian clothes, supposedly on leave of absence but constantly telephoning his office to find out what was happening. Several generals declared for the Kappists, along with scores of more junior officers, but the majority of the army's officers and enlisted men maintained a tepid and confused loyalty to the government of President Ebert. In many instances, commanders were receiving orders from Noske and Lüttwitz that contradicted each other, and were unable to determine which ones to obey. Even the commanders supporting the government were most reluctant to start any real fighting, and the result was that the Reichswehr became something of a military vacuum.[3]

For the moment, Wolfgang Kapp had a free hand, but could start nothing. Because the date of the Putsch had been shoved forward by the impasse concerning the demobilization of the Ehrhardt and Baltic brigades, Kapp and his fellow civilian conspirators had not completed their sketchy plans for taking power, and proved to be babes in the administrative woods. The lawyer from Naumburg who was writing the new constitution and legal code had neither project ready to present to the nation. Dr. Kapp's daughter was hastily assigned the task of typing up a ringing proclamation of the objectives and policies of the new regime, but when she arrived at the Chancellery, it took so long for her to find a typewriter that she completed the manifesto after the deadline for the next day's newspapers.[4]

In the meantime, Wolfgang Kapp was sitting at a desk, riffling through memoranda that meant nothing to him, and being interrupted by office seekers who hoped to get in on the ground floor of the new regime. From time to time he would run through the halls crying, "Where is Schnitzler? Where is Schnitzler? I cannot govern without Schnitzler!" The indispensable "Doctor Schnitzler" was a freelance journalist from Ingolstadt whose real name was Handke, a dentist who had received his degree from a correspondence school and had spent much time since the war ingratiating himself with the second echelon of right-wingers.[5] He was one of the two conspirators whom the Ebert regime had actually detected and jailed, but the "action plan" for the

Putsch that the police had found in his house was still on some minor official's desk when the Ehrhardt Brigade marched in. While Kapp was demanding that his "chief adviser" Schnitzler be produced, Schnitzler, who had been freed by police officials sympathetic to the right-wing coup, was trying with no success to talk his way past the Freikorps sentries who were guarding the Chancellery.

Thus the debut of the Kapp regime. Kapp dissolved the Prussian Diet on Saturday, and canceled his action on Monday. After arresting the members of the Prussian cabinet, he released them. When the most effective general strike in history paralyzed Berlin, Kapp and his cabinet tried to open negotiations with the strike leaders. When their overtures were spurned, they first ordered those leaders to be arrested and executed, and all pickets shot on sight; then they rescinded the order. The civil service refused to acknowledge the authority of Kapp's new heads of ministries. Arnold Brecht, a key administrator in the Chancellery who was later to become a professor at the New School for Social Research in New York, sabotaged the Kappists by ordering the Chancellery telephone operators to take a week's paid vacation.[6] When Kapp discovered that the Reichsbank was refusing to hand over funds to pay the Ehrhardt Brigade, he told Ehrhardt to take some of his troops over there and demand Treasury funds at gunpoint. Ehrhardt, whose men had laid waste many a Polish village, replied, "Certainly not! I'm an officer, not a bank robber!"[7]

Ludendorff entered the picture directly at least three more times after his dawn march to the Chancellery at the head of the Ehrhardt Brigade. A few hours later he appeared at the offices of the Ministry of Defense and approached Colonel Wilhelm Heye, the senior member of General von Seeckt's staff.

"Well, Heye," Ludendorff said forcefully, "what do you think of our affair?"

In a mixture of diplomacy and an instinct for survival, Heye answered that he did not know what was going on, and added, "But if you intend to make a Putsch against the government, it seems strange to me that the government you want to remove hasn't been arrested yet."

The confusion of the morning may have been such that neither man knew that the government leaders had fled the capital, but in any case Ludendorff shook hands cordially with Heye, said, "We shall finish the job!" and strode out of the building.[8]

Ludendorff's second and third appearances during the Putsch occurred as the Kappists' fortunes were diminishing. Both were at meetings in the captured Chancellery. On the first occasion Ludendorff conferred with Ehrhardt, Captain Waldemar Pabst of the putschists, and Colonel Max Bauer, an important member of his wartime staff who had been deeply involved in this conspiracy. Shedding tears of frustration, Bauer begged Ludendorff to take charge of the Putsch and declare himself Germany's new leader, but Ludendorff felt the game was lost, and refused.[9] At an even later stage Ludendorff was present at an unusual meeting in the Chancellery. The assembled group included the commanders of the Reichswehr units that had remained in their barracks, as well as the putschist leaders Lüttwitz and Ehrhardt. The thrust of the discussion was that, with the exception of Ehrhardt and his men, virtually all the officers and enlisted men in the Berlin area rejected Lüttwitz's authority, and that it was time for everyone to restore unity in the military and support General von Seeckt. Only Ludendorff and one other general, as well as Ehrhardt and two leaders of minor units, continued to back Lüttwitz.[10]

Thus, as Hitler arrived at the Chancellery, the abortive rightist grab for power had already failed. The general public had shown no support for it. Ebert's socialist government, which had halted its flight at Stuttgart, refused any form of negotiation with the monarchistically inclined Kappists and was exhorting the workers to maintain their strangulation of essential services. Kapp's groundless hope that the Allies might prefer him to the socialists had been destroyed the previous day, when General Neill Malcolm of the British Military Mission gave General von Lüttwitz the message that Britain would under no circumstances recognize the Kapp regime. Even the members of the National Association of German Industries were so appalled by the putschists' incapacity that they issued a statement formally repudiating them.[11] At about the time Hitler and Eckart were climbing into their plane in Bavaria, the Security Police abandoned their position of neutrality and demanded that Kapp resign. That was the end: without the acquiescence of the Security Police, even the Ehrhardt Brigade could not maintain order in a city and suburban area whose population approached four million. Only the Reichswehr could save the putschists, and that support had evaporated.

Kapp's exit was less than Napoleonic. He announced his resignation in a preposterous communiqué that included the phrase "having completed all my aims."[12] The right-wing revolution could not at this moment produce even an automobile for his departure, and at noon a taxi was hailed in front of the Chancellery and told to wait for a minute. Out came Kapp, his coat collar up and his face buried in a scarf, with his hat pulled down over his eyes. As he entered the taxi, an aide shoved a package of papers in behind him. There had been no time to pack, so his personal effects, wrapped in a tied-up sheet, were tossed onto the luggage rack on the taxi roof. Kapp's daughter, the typist of manifestos, came out of the Chancellery in tears and got in beside her father. Exactly a hundred hours after he had seized power with the words "We will not govern according to any theory," Wolfgang Kapp was driven off to Tempelhof Airfield, where a plane was waiting to take him to exile in Sweden.[13] On the way to the airport, his taxi may have passed Hitler and Eckart, coming into the city.

Once at the Chancellery, Hitler and Eckart tried to find out more about what was happening and what might still be accomplished. During this lull between the departure of Kapp and the return to the capital of the Ebert government, some of Kapp's erstwhile officials were still on hand. Hitler and Eckart were received by a man who had at various times during the past hundred hours served as press officer and press censor. This was Ignatz Timothy Trebitsch-Lincoln, as colorful a figure as ever rode the Orient Express. Born in Hungary of Jewish parents and named Ignatz Trebitsch, the adventurer who greeted Hitler and Eckart was thirty-nine years old. In that time he had traveled widely, become converted to Christianity, lived in England first as an Anglican clergyman and then as a member of Parliament, and been arrested in the United States during the war on a charge of forgery preferred by the British government, which suspected him of being a German agent. His sensational escape from federal custody and the ensuing manhunt made nationwide headlines in the United States, and the announcement of his capture was greeted by cheering in the House of Commons. Released from prison in England and deported in August of 1919, he soon made his way to Berlin and became involved with the Kapp plotters, having a particularly close relationship with Ludendorff's associate Colonel Max Bauer.[14]

Eckart saw only a Jew, and was appalled to think that a right-wing regime should have chosen a Jew as its spokesman with the press. "Come on, Adolf," the Bavarian writer said, grabbing Hitler's arm. "We have no further business here."[15] Hitler concurred: his written report to the party said, "When I saw and spoke to the press chief of the Kapp government, I knew this could be no national revolution and that it had to remain unsuccessful, for the press chief was a Jew."[16]

*

As Hitler and Eckart came down the steps of the Chancellery, hoping to salvage something from this trip to Berlin, the Ehrhardt Brigade was preparing to march back to its barracks at Döberitz. The men in the ranks were bewildered and angry. They felt that the Ebert regime had used and betrayed them. Happy to march against the government that had ordered their disbandment, they had no notion of just what should replace it. One incident told all: when an old man came up to members of a Freikorps street patrol and asked with hope if their presence in Berlin meant that they were bringing back the Kaiser, one of the soldiers haltingly answered, "N-no, no. Not that, not that." Well then, the old man persisted, what was the point of all this military activity? What was the sense of it?

The soldier mused on the question and answered, "The sense? The sense? There is sense only in danger. Marching into uncertainty is sense enough for us, because it answers the demands of our blood."[17]

Now these hardened troops were about to march out of Berlin, past crowds of workers whose general strike had rendered their weaponry impotent. The troops felt that Kapp, whoever he was, had failed them, too. His policy of arresting his opponents and then releasing them stirred the contempt of these men of action, who thought that a few executions by firing squad would have given the new regime credibility. "Blood is the cement of revolution," one of them observed.[18]

Ludendorff may have been sincere in his hope of welding an alliance between nationalist-minded soldiers and laboring men whose strike had defeated the entire right-wing effort, but in reality there was a constant angry mistrust between those two forces. In the east, during these brief days of Kapp, four Freikorps units in Breslau had behaved in such a way that a general reported, "There is an indescribable hatred of the military among the large majority of the population."[19] Of Berlin itself, a British witness said, "The absolute vacuum of moral support in which the invading troops moved could be felt within the first few hours of their capture of the city."[20] As for the Ehrhardt Brigade, now forming ranks to move out of Berlin, one of its favorite marching songs ended with:

> Worker, worker, what's to become of you
> When the Brigade is ready to fight?
> The Ehrhardt Brigade smashes everything to bits,
> So woe, woe, woe to you, you worker son-of-a-bitch![21]

Large crowds, quiet but hostile, turned out to watch the departure of these proud troops who had been defeated by the general strike.

An English brigadier general, J. H. Morgan of the Inter-Allied Military Control Commission, was walking down the Wilhelmstrasse after lunch when he came upon the scene.

> I saw guns limbering up and teams hooked in. The "Baltic" troops, after their brief and inglorious adventure, were preparing to evacuate the city over which they had lorded it for five days. Their faces were surly and I looked for trouble. It came. They formed up in the Unter den Linden, guns in column of route, troops in column of fours.

The troops marched off, heading for the Brandenburg Gate, through which they had paraded with Ludendorff at their head five mornings earlier. Now there was no Ludendorff, no band playing, no goose-stepping.

> A dense crowd watched them in silence. A boy laughed. Two soldiers broke out of ranks, clubbed him with the butts of their rifles and kicked his inanimate body as he lay prostrate upon the ground. No one dared interfere, but the crowd hissed. At that, an officer shouted some words of command of which only the word "*rücksichtlos*" [ruthless] reached me. The troops opened fire. The crowd was an easy target. The street suddenly resounded with the "rat-tat" of machine-guns, the whistling of bullets, the crack of splintered glass, and the cries and groans of the wounded. The people ran. The rest lay where they had fallen. The stricken bodies had a strangely shrunken look. They seemed like heaps of old clothes.

General Morgan heard the command to cease fire, and then a parade ground bellow, "Quick march!"

> The troops marched out under the arch of the Brandenburger Tor in the direction of Charlottenburg, some of them occasionally breaking out of the ranks to run on to the pavement and beat an offending civilian, whose face they did not like, over the head with the tail-end of their stickbombs.[22]

What Hitler and Eckart did then is not clear. In his racist sheet, *Auf gut Deutsch*, Eckart was to write that, with the collapse of the Putsch and the imminent return of the Ebert government, he and Hitler feared arrest and returned to Munich.[23] Eckart was not one to minimize anything important that he may have achieved in Berlin, so his account has credibility. Hitler made no comment about this journey, but another version of events has Hitler and Eckart sending Greim back to Bavaria with the airplane while they remained in Berlin for some days, establishing contact with various right-wing groups.[24]

According to this account, Eckart introduced Hitler to General Ludendorff in Berlin. If this happened, Eckart must have moved swiftly on the afternoon that the Ehrhardt Brigade made its bloody exit from the city. For the second time in two years, Ludendorff was on the run; frightened by what the returning Ebert government might do to him for his role in the Putsch, Ludendorff wore civilian clothes and the same fake beard and blue spectacles he had used as his disguise when he fled to Sweden. Using the name Herr Lange, he took the evening train for Munich, where a right-wing friend gave him refuge in a Bavarian castle on a hill above the Inn Valley.[25]

Wherever he had been in the meantime, Hitler was conspicuously in view twelve days later. On the evening of March 29, at a party *Sprechabend*, a discussion meeting, he began what the party called "a full-scale speech." It was indeed full scale, requiring three separate evening sessions to present. Ranging from the 1848 Revolution to the current state of affairs in the Balkans, its theme reflected Drexler's vision of a unified German society, achieved by weaving together the efforts and ideals of the manual workers and those engaged in more intellectual occupations. With recent events in Berlin burned into his mind, Hitler told the party members: "The military can never be a tool of revolution, or the basic support of the government. It can only support the will of the people."[26]

By the time Hitler spoke, some results of the Kapp Putsch were bloodily apparent. During the week after Kapp first seized the Chancellery, many leftists had taken up arms in the belief that they were supporting the Social Democratic government that had been driven from Berlin and was calling for a general strike. The German Communist Party, however, saw this as the great opportunity to take over the demilitarized Ruhr and use it as the base from which to launch a nationwide offensive. The purpose of the attack would be to destroy both the forces of the right and the power of the Social Democrats, whom the communists saw as bourgeois betrayers of true socialism. The objective was to establish a communist regime in Berlin.

The German Communist Party knew exactly what it wanted, but others were not so clear in their understanding. At least one Reichswehr arsenal was opened up by a commander who thought he was handing out rifles in accordance with the government's wish that the Kapp Putsch be opposed, but in any event there was soon a "Red

Army of the Ruhr" of fifty thousand armed workers. Led by noncommissioned officers, they quickly occupied the Ruhr industrial cities of Remscheid, Dortmund, Hagen, and Düsseldorf. In taking the industrial capital of Essen, they killed three hundred, many of them policemen, and the largest of the Krupp munitions factories soon had red flags waving from their chimneys. As the Red columns gained complete control of this area from which both Allied and German troops were excluded by the Treaty of Versailles, the *Ruhr Echo* trumpeted: "There can be only one salvation for the German people. The red flag must wave victoriously over the whole of Germany."[27]

The Ebert government, installed once more in Berlin, looked at all this and saw only enemies who had to be put down. If anything more was needed to make the Freikorps troops politically cynical, or to earn the Social Democrats the undying hatred of large segments of the left, it now happened: the government that had ordered the Ehrhardt Brigade dissolved, the government that had fled Berlin at the brigade's approach, that same government rehired the brigade and ordered it to fight the leftist uprising. Defense Minister Noske went further; the Kapp regime had promised Ehrhardt's men a bonus if they succeeded in ousting the Ebert government, and, to keep the troops pointed in the right direction, the Ebert government paid them the sums promised by Kapp.[28] The same pragmatic approach taken to acquire riflemen was in evidence at the level of high command: General Hans von Seeckt, who had refused to protect the Social Democratic government when the Ehrhardt Brigade marched on Berlin, was installed as the Reichswehr's leader, because this time there was an enemy he was willing to fight.

Twenty-one different Freikorps columns struck into the Ruhr on April 3. In five days they obliterated the workers' makeshift army. The victory was a replica of the capture of Munich the previous year. Hundreds of workers were shot after they had surrendered. "Anyone who falls into our hands first gets the rifle butt and then is finished off with a bullet," a young member of the Freikorps von Epp wrote home to his family from Wischerhöfen. "We even shot ten Red Cross nurses on sight because they were carrying pistols. We shot those little ladies with pleasure — how they cried and pleaded with us to save their lives. Nothing doing! Anybody with a gun is our enemy."[29]

The finale at Essen on Easter Sunday morning had a surreal quality: well-dressed middle-class churchgoers, accompanied by their children who were hugging stuffed Easter bunnies, stopped to watch Freikorps troops attacking workers making their last stand in a red brick water tower. Two teen-age sisters, dressed for church, left their parents and served as nurses for the wounded workers. They saw the Freikorps slaughter the workers who were taken prisoner. Walter Duranty of the *New York Times* interviewed the two shocked girls in their blood-stained finery, and the younger sister wept as she said, "I think all soldiers ought to be put in front of their own machine guns and shot till there are none of them left."[30]

Eager to occupy more of Germany on any pretext, the French on April 6 marched their troops into the cities of Frankfurt, Darmstadt, and Hanau, outside the Ruhr. The move was accompanied by the statement that the soldiers would return to France as soon as Germany got its soldiery out of the demilitarized Ruhr. The Germans were able to do so within a week; on April 17 the French marched out again, but during their stay they shot seven youths who protested when the French flag was hoisted.

The tremors of the Kapp Putsch were also felt in bloodless ways. Endorsing the conclusions of investigations conducted by special commissions composed of civilians, General von Seeckt dismissed 180 Reichswehr officers.[31] In varying degrees, these men, including twelve generals, had supported the Putsch. For Seeckt, the issue was not one of politics — he held many right-wing ideas himself — but of insubordination. As Seeckt saw his own actions, it had been necessary to neutralize the Reichswehr at the outset of the Putsch in order to prevent fratricidal combat and the disintegration of the officer corps, but he had remained ready to serve the government, and indeed had soon been asked to lead the army. Those who actively supported the Putsch had broken their oath to serve Germany's government, whatever its political coloration might be, and Seeckt now made them pay. His message to the Reichswehr was twofold: the army must be depoliticized, and action and policy would henceforth be determined by only one man, whose name was General Hans von Seeckt.

Gustav Noske resigned as minister of defense; he later summed up his sixteen turbulent months in that office in his book *From Kiel to Kapp*. Widespread dissatisfaction with the government's handling of the recent threats from both right and left brought about the resignation of Chancellor Gustav Bauer, who was replaced by another Social Democrat, Hermann Müller. A new Social Democratic cabinet did not satisfy the angry, frightened German public; in the general elections of June 6, the Social Democrats lost fifty Reichstag seats and decided to relinquish their control of government and become an opposition party. The Weimar coalition was replaced by a political configuration in which both right and left were stronger, and the moderates correspondingly weaker. Konstantin Fehrenbach of the Center Party became chancellor; the parties represented in his cabinet controlled only 176 votes out of the 466 seats in the Reichstag, so his was a minority government, unable to ask for the customary vote of confidence as it took office.

On balance, power had moved to the right, with right and left further apart than ever. The Kapp Putsch had produced yet another, somewhat less visible result: its failure signaled the extreme right that the public was not interested in a restoration of the old order. The soldiers of the Freikorps went further; for them, the spring of 1920 was the end of their tolerance of any form of civilian government, no matter what its objectives. They were finished with politicians of the traditional type, and they were none too pleased with what they had seen of the Reichswehr generals who sat on the sidelines. The collapse of the Putsch, wrote a Freikorps veteran, "meant that for the first time the road was now completely open to the young men's own political thinking."[32]

That thinking was inevitably warlike; political power was something to be seized and held by force. "Everything would have been all right," a lieutenant of the Ehrhardt Brigade said in looking back at the Kapp fiasco, "if we had just shot more people."[33] The troops were ready to try again, but now they would do so only for leaders whom they perceived to be as uncompromising and decisive as themselves. Writing in the *Weltbühne*, an influential leftist journal that frequently indulged itself in the dangerous luxury of making fun of the responsible moderates who were trying to run Germany, the brilliant journalist Kurt Tucholsky wrote: "The Kapp Putsch was an unsuccessful dress rehearsal. Opening night has been postponed."[34]

II

During this momentous spring came the day for Lance Corporal Adolf Hitler to be discharged from the army. On March 31, 1920, he signed the payroll for the last time and received 50 marks plus an issue of clothing to take him into civilian life: cap, coat, jacket, pants, underwear, a shirt, socks, and shoes.[35]

It was a milestone in Hitler's life. He had been a soldier for nearly six years. It was in the army that he had snapped together as a functioning person; it was in the army that he had first achieved success and known admiration. He would no longer wear a grey uniform, but in essence he remained a *Frontkämpfer*, a front-line fighter who imposed his will upon problems and objectives with the desperate emotions of hand-to-hand combat in the trenches. It was the war's legacy, bequeathed to a man with no sense of guilt, a supremely self-centered man who referred his ideas of right and wrong to no judge other than himself. The war had resolved the impasse between a violent nature and the *bürgerlich* inhibitions of a provincial official's son. The Western Front had revealed the violent nature to itself, and in Hitler's eyes had legitimated violence and even ennobled it. In his exhortations to his völkisch audiences, "ruthless" was an oft-recurring word.

For sixty-seven months he had lived in dugouts or barracks; now he rented an odd pair of rooms in a middle-class district near the Isar River, a neighborhood of narrow residential buildings with shops and offices on their ground floors. His new home was at 41 Thierchstrasse, around the corner from the offices of the *Völkischer Beobachter*. Located opposite a fruit store, the rundown house had a little niche in its front in which there was a weatherbeaten Madonna. Hitler's lodgings were reached by two flights of a creaking stairway. A visitor described what he found:

> He lived there like a down-at-heels clerk. He had one room
> and the use of a quite large entrance hall as a subtenant of a
> woman named Reichert. . . . The room itself was tiny. I doubt if
> it was nine feet wide. The bed was too wide for its corner and
> the head projected over the single narrow window. The floor was
> covered with cheap, worn linoleum with a couple of threadbare
> rugs, and on the wall opposite the bed there was a makeshift
> bookshelf, apart from a chair and rough table, the only other
> piece of furniture in the room.

In this setting, the visitor said, "Hitler used to walk around in carpet slippers, frequently with no collar to his shirt and wearing suspenders. There were quite a lot of illustrations and drawings hanging on the wall."[36]

And what did Frau Reichert think of her subtenant? "He is such a nice man, but he has the most extraordinary moods. Sometimes weeks go by when he seems to be sulking and does not say a word to us. He looks through us as if we were not there. He always pays his rent punctually in advance, but he is a real bohemian type."[37]

This "real bohemian type" stayed up until all hours reading or making notes, and was late for appointments during the day, but he was always on time for his speeches, and there were many of them. At the public meetings his audiences were invariably large, averaging eighteen hundred, and he repeatedly served up the Jews as scapegoats.[38] On April 6, in a non sequitur that sailed past his enthusiastic audience, he declared, "We don't want to encourage a pogrom, but we are very much determined to get the evil at its roots and to exterminate it completely." According to the reporter making notes for the Munich police, this elicited "lively applause," and Hitler continued, to further applause, "In order to reach our goal we have to use every means, even if we must work with the Devil!"[39] Four speeches later, on April 27, he told a cheering crowd, "We need a dictator who is a genius if we want to rise again," and added, "As soon as we assume power, then we will work like buffaloes."[40] The party whose assumption of power in Germany Hitler was confidently predicting numbered 353 members that evening, although some of his appearances were bringing as many as two thousand völkisch enthusiasts into the Festival Hall of the Hofbräuhaus.[41]

Among these audiences was a twenty-seven-year-old man who was becoming influential in the party because Hitler valued his astigmatic views on Jews and the communist revolutions in the east. He was Alfred Rosenberg, a protégé of Dietrich Eckart's who frequently published anti-Semitic articles in *Auf gut Deutsch*. His manner, one party member said, was as "cold as the tip of a dog's nose," and another described him as "a sallow untidy fellow" who had the "infuriating habit of whistling through his teeth when I talked to him."[42] A refugee from the Baltic, one of the German community there who had fled an impending invasion by Soviet Russian forces, Rosenberg had arrived in Munich at the time of the leftist takeover in November 1918.

In his meager baggage was a copy of a pamphlet, then available only in Russian: *The Protocols of the Elders of Zion*. This document, purporting to be the text of a plot by Jewish leaders of different nations to topple the existing world order, was based on a piece of fiction. In 1868 there had appeared the first volume of *Biarritz*, a novel by the reactionary German writer Hermann Goedsche, who used the pen name Sir John Retcliffe. It contained a scene in which the Wandering Jew and the latter-day representatives of the Twelve Tribes of Israel were overheard as they conferred in Prague's Jewish cemetery. In Goedsche's fantasy, this meeting in 1860 was the latest in a series of meetings, held once a century, in which the Jewish hierarchy schemes to destabilize society by controlling international finance and by backing the radical causes of the left.[43]

The baseless tale next appeared in the early 1900s as a fabricated document apparently put in circulation by the czarist secret police in an effort to discredit the Russian Jewish intellectuals who were striving for liberal reform. That hoax had been disavowed by the czar himself, and for nearly two decades the forgery remained an obscure and insignificant tract.

Now in 1920, with much of Western Europe and the United States frightened by communist and socialist successes and seeking an explanation for them, this supposedly authentic account of a secret conference was appearing in translations from the Russian, and received widespread attention on the grounds that it represented the key to a Jewish-communist conspiracy. It was not only being taken at face value by racists; it frequently deceived those who should have seen through it. Although the *Times* of London would, a year later, do the definitive job of disproving its authenticity, in May of 1920 the newspaper published a long article stating that the *Protocols* appeared to be genuine and should be viewed in that light.[44]

As far as is known, Alfred Rosenberg had no knowledge of the novel published in German in 1868. His Russian was excellent, and in due course he became an expert on the two German translations of the version concocted by the czarist police, and may have made a third translation of this scurrilous work. A text of the *Protocols* began appearing in the *Völkischer Beobachter* on February 25, 1920, the morning after the meeting at which Hitler had first set forth the party's program. Hitler loved it, and later said that it "incomparably" demonstrated "to what an extent the whole existence of this people is based on a continuous lie."[45] Rosenberg accompanied the publication with numerous commentaries on the *Protocols*, appearing in article and pamphlet form, and also published two books of his own composition, *The Tracks of the Jew Through the Ages* and *Immorality in the Talmud*.

In Hitler's eyes, these were credentials of the highest order, so in company with Eckart and the "interest slavery" economist Gottfried Feder, Rosenberg completed the small circle of those whom Hitler considered the party's thinkers. With the *Protocols*, Rosenberg was riding a real wave of public feeling; if the victors in England could take this fraud seriously, how much more so the vanquished, who were looking for more dimensions to the Dolchstoss, the stab in the back, in which they already believed. A Jewish reporter was shocked by the seemingly sensible and respectable people who were ready to believe these things.

> In Berlin I attended several meetings which were entirely devoted to the Protocols. The speaker was usually a professor, a teacher, an editor, a lawyer or someone of that kind. The audience consisted of members of the educated class, civil servants, tradesmen, former officers, ladies, above all students, students of all faculties and years of seniority. . . . Passions were whipped up to the boiling point.[46]

It was just such an audience that elicited a similar reaction in a reporter for *Der Kampf,* the Independent Socialists' Munich newspaper, when he attended a Nazi Party meeting on June 24. Specifically identifying the audience as "middle class," he said that when Hitler appeared on the platform, he was greeted with "fanatic jubilation" that was *"minutenlang,"* one or more minutes in duration. "Demand after demand for the murder of the Jews followed and each time there had to be a pause because the bourgeois mob needed to respond to every such crudity by sustained shouting."[47] The Munich police reporter said of this same meeting that when Hitler shouted, "Out with the Jews who are poisoning our people!" there was "sustained, wild applause."[48] The socialist *Münchener Post* reported of another Hitler appearance, "When the speaker threw out the question as to how one should defend oneself against the Jews, there were shouts from the audience — a model audience, the speaker called it — Hang them! Beat them to death!"[49] Speaking at a meeting organized by the newly formed party local in the town of Rosenheim, Hitler closed with his adaptation of the communist slogan "Workers of the world, unite!" Hitler shouted, "Anti-Semites of the world, unite!"[50] This produced "wild applause," according to the Rosenheim *Tagblatt,* which noted that the largest beer hall in town could not accommodate all, "friends as well as foes," who wished to enter.[51]

By now the Munich newspapers were fully aware of the four hundred members of the Nazi Party and the extraordinary speeches being given by its propaganda chief. The *Münchner Neueste Nachrichten,* the city's largest middle-class paper, contented itself by saying that the Nazis "insulted the Jews, the Socialists, and the press," but the journals with leftist leanings were after Hitler and did not know quite what tone to take.[52] The *Post* started by saying that the Nazis had just announced "two lectures of popular science for this week."[53] It was a point perhaps too subtly made, but one that was devastatingly accurate: all of Hitler's speeches were laden with statistics and historical allusions that clothed hatred in the trappings of anthropology, sociology, and economics. Germans did indeed love lectures — it was said that if there were two doors, one marked "Heaven" and the other "Lecture on Heaven," Germans would throng through the second door — and Hitler was presenting his audiences with false premises that he frequently argued with airtight logic. He enabled listeners to sanction their own aggressions in the name of reason and patriotism.

The *Post* went on to be a bit more blunt, but still avoided dignifying Hitler with serious description. At a time when the violence of the anti-Semitism in the *Völkischer Beobachter* caused the Munich police to close down that paper for six days, the *Post* first likened Hitler to a comedian, and soon after said, "He's the most artful and cunning of the rabble-rousers now spreading their poison around Munich."[54] Finally, in June, the *Post* stopped mincing words and told its readers, "The swastika is an incitement to race murder."[55]

As for the swastika, Hitler was at just this time devoting many hours to a consideration of what colors and design would most effectively present the ancient symbol whose name is a Sanskrit word meaning "All is well." The party did not yet have a flag; now it was to have one. Designing it, Hitler said, "occupied us intensely. . . . From all sides came suggestions, which for the most part it must be admitted were more well-intended than successful."[56] Most ideas centered on the swastika, but a white flag was suggested, a black flag was suggested, a blue and white flag was suggested.

A dentist from the Bavarian town of Starnberg, Friedrich Krohn, had designed a flag, since lost, that was used at the founding meeting of the party local there in May of 1920. It placed a black swastika on a white disk against a red background.[57] Once again, there were two versions of events, one being that Hitler adopted the design just as it was and later claimed to have revised it, and Hitler's account, which stated:

> Actually, a dentist from Starnberg did deliver a design that was not bad at all and, incidentally, was quite close to my own, having only the one fault that a swastika with curved legs was composed into a white disk.[58]

In the Hitler version, "In the meantime, after endless attempts, I had come up with the final design; a flag that also had a red background with a white disk in the center of which was a black swastika. After long experimentation I also found a fixed relationship between the size of the flag and the size of the disk, as well as the shape and thickness of the swastika."[59]

Whatever the truth, Hitler was enthusiastic about the result.

> It was excellently suited to our new movement. It was young and new, like the movement itself. No one had seen it before; it had the effect of a burning torch. We ourselves experienced an almost childlike joy when a faithful woman party comrade for the first time executed the design and delivered the flag.[60]

The use of red, white, and black brought before the German public the colors of the imperial flag, presented in a design entirely different from the three broad horizontal stripes of that banner. "This color combination," Hitler said, "stands high above all the others. It is the most brilliant harmony in existence."[61]

Now that he had the motif, the party's propaganda chief wanted a pin that all party members were supposed to buy and wear at all times, the women on their blouses or dresses, the men in the lapels of their jackets or on the left breast of their shirts. "A Munich goldsmith named Füss furnished the first usable design, which was kept."[62]

At the same time, Hitler ordered red swastika armbands that were to be worn at meetings by the men of the Ordnertruppen, the "monitor detachments" that alternately cheered the speakers and ejected leftist hecklers.[63] Their numbers had grown, and they were undergoing an important change. Although the government had used the Freikorps to put down the uprisings in the Ruhr, in May the last of them were ordered out of existence, and the government ceased to pay them. This decision was made partly to comply with Allied pressure, and partly because General von Seeckt felt that these elite units were entirely too good at overthrowing governments. The epitaph of their official existence could have been the remark made by the commander of the Iron Division to his chief of staff a year before, when his unit's brilliant capture of the Latvian capital of Riga frightened everyone: the inhabitants, the Berlin government, and the Allies. "My God," General Rudiger Graf von der Goltz said, "we've killed ourselves with victory!"[64]

With the dissolution of the Freikorps, there began the creation of a large and complicated paramilitary underground. Although some units were absorbed in their entirety into the Reichswehr, the Ehrhardt Brigade was too notoriously independent to be considered for such an incorporation. By the same token, it was far too independent an organization to allow itself to be destroyed by the stroke of a pen. The Association of Former Ehrhardt Officers was immediately formed, and soon was operating out of an office in Munich.[65] Ehrhardt himself found a haven in Bavaria, and moved at the center of clandestine activities that would eventually result in political murders. Some of his enlisted men also gravitated to Bavaria. In eastern Prussia, Freikorps veterans found that right-wing employers, including the aristocratic proprietors of large agricultural estates, would give them preference for jobs. Some Freikorps men found jobs that kept them outdoors and shooting, as gamekeepers.

After working hours, these men brought a new and militant tone to the Einwohnerwehr, the Civil Guard, which was in itself a controversial organization, with 267,000 enrolled in Bavaria alone.[66] To the Allies, the Germans pictured these local militia units as being semi-social clubs in the category of volunteer fire departments, and hence far removed from the Versailles Treaty stipulation that German armed forces be reduced to one hundred thousand men.[67] In fact, the Civil Guard units had served as a nationwide reserve for the Freikorps; they were armed and regularly drilled by Reichswehr officers. Now, with the dissolution of the Freikorps, the influx from the hardened regiments into the Civil Guard made the Allies that much more suspicious and the Einwohnerwehr that much more important to General von Seeckt and a government that knew its need for emergency-service soldiers had not ended.

Although they were only a few at first, these Freikorps–Civil Guard types began appearing at Nazi Party meetings as Ordnertruppe members, with the new red armband on the left sleeve of their civilian clothes. Many of them were truly völkisch in thought; all of them loved a fight. The party had originally relied on Hitler's army friends from Mortar Company Number 19, but in the wake of the Kapp Putsch the Bavarian Reichswehr, sympathetic to the right though it was, could not have its soldiers in uniform acting as bouncers and bodyguards at meetings that denounced the government in Berlin. Although the Ordnertruppen wore civilian clothes, the "monitor detachments" had enrolled some of history's most skilled and heartless killers.

If anything more was needed to make these Freikorps veterans, and all right-wingers, feel that they could act with some impunity, it came with the last official actions related to the Kapp Putsch. The Ebert government charged 705 people with high treason for their varying roles in the affair, and their cases were then examined by officials of the Ministry of Justice. It became apparent that the German judiciary was in effect an extension of the nation's right-wing network: 412 cases were amnestied wholesale, 108 were eventually dismissed, and 185 were simply not brought to trial. Kapp and Lüttwitz were tried and acquitted of all charges. Ludendorff was never charged; he remained untouched. Only one man, Traugott A. von Jagow, who had served as the Kapp regime's minister of interior, received a sentence. The five years he was ordered to serve stood in contrast to the total of 615 years' imprisonment meted out to the leftist leaders who had supported the Bavarian Soviet Republic the previous year.[68]

So it was that in the end Wolfgang Kapp's tragicomic Putsch failed but set the stage for terrible dramas to be played out in Bavaria. The actors kept arriving, and none was more firmly fixed in the national consciousness than General Ludendorff, who was again zigzagging between secretive and highly public activity. After moving from his refuge in a castle above the Inn River to successive hideaways in Stefanskirchen and Augsburg, he was soon to take up residence in Ludwigshöhe, a village just outside Munich. With his wife Margarethe, who had come from Berlin to join him, he lived in a villa surrounded by high walls that were patrolled around the clock by some of Ehrhardt's newly arrived troopers.[69] From this seclusion he sallied forth to become the central figure at a review of right-wing veterans' organizations held in Munich.[70] All that was known of his thinking at this moment was that he had lost faith in what he termed "the upper ten thousand" — the generals, industrialists, and higher-echelon civil servants who had failed to support the Putsch.[71] For the right, he was still the "national commander"; his role in the Kapp fiasco was seen as that of a martyr, forced to flee to the hospitable völkisch climate of Bavaria. Houston Stewart Chamberlain, the English-born racist writer who had married Richard Wagner's daughter Eva and lived at what was virtually a Wagner shrine at Bayreuth in Bavaria, admired Ludendorff profoundly. The author of the widely read *The Foundations of the Nineteenth Century* referred to the general as "the splendid Ludendorff."[72]

The left took a different view. Count Harry Kessler, the liberal-thinking aristocratic book publisher who had prophesied, as soon as he learned of the Versailles Treaty terms, "A terrible era begins for Europe," gave his opinion of the general whom so many millions admired and saw as a man who could still deliver Germany from its postwar agony. Writing in his diary some days after reading the first accounts of the Kapp Putsch, Kessler said:

Unfortunately there seems to be no doubt about Ludendorff's participation. How shattering that from 1916 to 1918, the most frightful moment in German history, a man with such atrocious lack of political judgment should have been in dictatorial control of our destiny.

Kessler summed up:

We have been the victims of political imbeciles and adventurers, not of great though unfortunate soldiers. This stunt of theirs stains our history retroactively. Ludendorff sinks to the level of an idiotic professional genius who was also a ruthless gambler.[73]

CHAPTER

13

WHILE MILLIONS of Germans were wondering what Ludendorff might do next, the Nazi Party picked up an obscure recruit named Rudolf Hess, who joined, along with three other new members, on July 1, 1920.[1] Tall, lantern-jawed, and looking perpetually in need of a shave, the twenty-six-year-old veteran had buck teeth and shy good manners that concealed an intense nature.

Like Hitler and Rosenberg, Hess was one more of those Germans, born outside the Fatherland, who were determined to be more German than the Germans. The son of a prosperous wholesale merchant, Fritz Hess, he lived in the Egyptian city of Alexandria until he was sent to Germany at the age of twelve to attend a boarding school in the town of Godesberg, just south of Bonn. The other students promptly nicknamed the black-haired youth "the Egyptian," a designation he vehemently resented.[2]

Two years after graduating, Rudolf Hess had ample opportunity to demonstrate his patriotism. The outbreak of war found him in a dull business apprenticeship in an office in Hamburg. Like Hitler, Hess had a warped relationship with a tyrannical father and a passive, adoring mother; vastly to the surprise of his father, who ordered him to stay on his job until he was conscripted, he rebelled for the first time in his life. "Now it's not merchants, but soldiers who are giving the orders!" he informed his dumbstruck father, and traveled to his ancestral homeland of Bavaria, where he was promptly accepted for army service on August 7, 1914, four days after Germany declared war on France.

Again like Hitler, Private Rudolf Hess received his baptism of fire at Ypres, entering that terrible battle as a foot soldier six days after Hitler did. For two years he knew the same trench warfare, rising slowly to corporal and receiving the Iron Cross, Second Class, for bravery at Arras in successfully defending a position in hand-to-hand combat.[3] Then he entered a battle worse than any Hitler saw: Verdun. Wounded in the left hand and upper arm in June of 1916 during the fighting for Fort Douamont, he passed through two hospitals and into the reserve, and was next committed to battle on the Eastern Front against the Rumanians as a vice-sergeant and acting platoon leader. Although he was wounded again in the upper arm, he remained with his unit until a rifle bullet tore into his left lung in August of 1917 at the storming of Ungureana. After four months in hospitals and two months of convalescent leave, Hess was pronounced unfit for the hardships of infantry service and informed that an application he had made to enter pilot training would be granted.

There was, however, one chore to carry out before he left the infantry, and that was to take charge of a company of replacements in Munich, and deliver them to the Regiment List on the Western Front. While reporting to Lieutenant Colonel Freiherr von Tuboeuf at regimental headquarters, Hess was struck by something about the appearance and manner of a slender lance corporal standing next to the colonel. The lance corporal was Hitler, and, although he had seen an endless number of sergeants during his four years at the front, something about Sergeant Hess also stayed with Hitler. The two men looked at each other, did not speak, and in a few minutes Hess had signed over his replacements and was on his way back to Bavaria and flight training.[4] Commissioned a lieutenant and posted to Fighter Squadron 35 on the Western Front, he flew in combat for only a week before the war ended.[5] After the Armistice Hess hoped to find a place as one of the few pilots flying in support of Freikorps units, but by February of 1919 he was studying economics at the University of Munich. His father's company in Egypt had been confiscated by the British, so to support himself he took a job as a salesman for a furniture company.

Two days after Hess started that job, his employer took him to a meeting of the Thule Society in its rooms at the Hotel Vier Jahreszeiten.[6] At this moment in his life, Rudolf Hess was an impoverished, confused veteran seeking reasons for Germany's defeat and the presence of the leftist regime in power in Munich. He was exceptionally impressionable, an able man, a follower who wanted to be told what to think and what to do. In the Thule rooms he met men who had no self-doubt in them: the Thule leader Rudolf von Sebottendorff, Eckart, Feder. Until then Hess had been indifferent to Jews; he knew a few of them and was aware that even the Kaiser had Jewish friends. Now in the middle of a revolution, Hess heard, and suddenly believed, such things as Sebottendorff's "Democracy is Jewish. All democratic revolution is Jewish."[7]

As if his postwar marching orders had been handed to him, Rudolf Hess started working for the Thule Society. Well-spoken, polite, persistent, he was an ideal völkisch fund raiser, meeting with right-wing citizens who recognized him as the son of an eminently respectable, although recently expatriated, Bavarian family. He acquired money for Thule, and weapons. He recruited young men for Freikorps Oberland, which had been started by Sebottendorff, and distributed the counterfeit travel documents that got them past the Red Guards at the railroad stations. He led sabotage squads in raids against the army of the Bavarian Soviet Republic, on one occasion putting a fleet of cars out of commission by exchanging the magnetos in their engines.

On the afternoon that the Red Guards seized the Thule rooms and took the hostages who were soon executed, Hess was distributing falsified travel passes; hearing the news that his headquarters was gone, he used one of these passes to reach the Freikorps Regensburg. In action with the Freikorps columns that recaptured Munich, he was again wounded, this time in the leg.[8]

Through all this, the self-effacing Hess wanted no credit for himself, but wished only to play an effective, inconspicuous role in doing what he thought was right. By the beginning of 1920, he was attending not only the meetings of the dwindling Thule Society, but also those of the vigorous semisecret organization known as the Iron Fist, a group of reactionary young army officers. It was here that he met Ernst Röhm, who was no public speaker but voiced such sentiments as "The primacy in the government belongs to the soldier!" — a concept in which Hess now believed.[9] On other evenings Hess sometimes sat quietly at Dietrich Eckart's table in the Weinstubbe Brennessel in Schwabing, appreciatively listening to the writer's witty, tipsy monologues.

On May 10 Hess attended a Monday evening Sprechabend at the Sterneckerbräu. Chairman Anton Drexler of the Nazi Party greeted the group and turned things over to the speaker for the evening, "our member and propaganda chief, the painter Herr Hitler."[10]

Hess saw the slender Gefreiter of the List Regiment field headquarters rise and begin speaking. There was a lot of dandruff on the collar and shoulders of his worn dark blue suit. Hitler's topic was "The Worker and the Jew," but he also spoke about the growing strength of the party, its new locals that were coming into being in Bavaria, and he conjured up a relentless march into the future, a great cause, a great movement, a great pure German destiny.[11]

Hess was mesmerized. Everything Hitler said seemed so clear, so logical, so important, so right. There was hope for Germany after all, because Adolf Hitler said there was. When the meeting was over Hess ran home through the streets, laughing and sobbing, "The man! The man!"[12] The next night Hitler addressed a large crowd in the Festsaal of the Hofbräuhaus on "What We Want." Hess was there, with a spoiled young girl he had recently met, who after a long courtship would become his wife: Ilse Pröhl, daughter of the former chief medical officer in the most feudal unit in the Kaiser's army, the First Regiment of Foot Guards.

Hitler started by saying that "international Jewish high finance and the docile press" were responsible for the French occupation of Frankfurt during the battle between the Reds and the Freikorps in the Ruhr. He bemoaned the lack of any true *Nationalpolitik*, a consensus that would save Germany. As usual, the Jews were Germany's overriding problem: "The Jewish question cannot be avoided; it must be solved. There can only be one course of action." At this point, the police reporter noted "lively applause," but the reaction to Hitler's closing words challenged his powers of description. Hitler shouted, "The day will come, when it will come true: 'The people rise up, the storm breaks loose!' " This brought on "lengthy repeated waves of stormy applause."[13]

Hess was at peace. The born disciple had found his master. A week later Dietrich Eckart introduced Hess to Hitler, who immediately liked the quiet, earnest veteran who was five years younger than himself. Hess attended every party discussion evening, every speech to the public, and began doing small chores for the party: putting up placards, distributing sheets of propaganda on the streets. Occasionally he was invited to join Hitler for one-sided conversations at coffee houses and cafés. With Dietrich Eckart paying, the abstemious Hitler and the equally abstemious Hess would nurse a drink all evening long at the Fledermaus Bar. Hitler loved movies; on occasion Hess was allowed to accompany him, and sometimes visited Hitler in his dingy Thierchstrasse lodgings. There were those who thought that Hitler felt most at home with coarse, jocular Bavarian types who were serious about their brawling and their beer, but the son of a customs official and the son of a businessman, both sons of gentle mothers, got on well together. Hitler respected the lengthy war record of this decorated, wounded veteran, and saw in him a discreet, efficient, adoringly loyal lieutenant. "The Egyptian" had found his emotional home.

II

The party that Rudolf Hess had just joined, and all the forces of the right, were about to be handed some ammunition by the actions of the Allies. At this moment, the postwar economic, political, and emotional relationships between Germany and her recent foes had spun such a web that there was no such thing as a purely domestic German political issue. Everything, real or imagined, was influenced by German perceptions of outside pressures. What now happened demonstrated the speed with which matters could move to a flashpoint.

Since the signing of the Versailles Treaty the previous year, two matters uppermost in the minds of the Allies were German disarmament and German payment of reparations to the victors. General von Seeckt's reduction of the Reichswehr was behind schedule, and the Allies had good reason to be suspicious of the network of camouflaged military organizations that spanned Germany. During the Kapp-triggered general strike and the workers' rebellion in the Ruhr, Germany had fallen behind in its treaty-stipulated shipments of coal.

The Allies decided that the way to deal with these inflammatory subjects, the disarmament and coal-delivery clauses of the Treaty of Versailles, was to discuss both of them in a single conference with the Germans. For the first time since the Armistice, the Germans were invited, rather than summoned, to a meeting with the Allies for negotiations to be conducted on a formal basis of equality. The Germans accepted, and the Allies selected as the place for these sessions the Belgian town of Spa, whose famed mineral waters had caused its name to become a synonym for "health resort."

The principal delegations arrived with differing objectives. The British were in a conciliatory mood. Faced with a large and bloody rebellion in Ireland, and impressed by Germany's difficulties in keeping internal order, the British wanted to avoid a situation in which they might have to reinforce their army of occupation in the Rhineland. On economic matters the British were even more in a mood to negotiate; their thinking had been much affected by *The Economic Consequences of the Peace*, a book by a brilliant thirty-seven-year-old economist, John Maynard Keynes, who had been the British Treasury's chief representative at the Paris Peace Conference. Keynes had resigned from the British delegation at Paris when his suggestions concerning the financial and reparations clauses of the treaty were rejected, and had swiftly written his book, which argued that the deliberate wrecking of the German economy would postpone all of Europe's postwar recovery. Other scholars were to disagree with Keynes's contentions, maintaining that German industrial compliance with the treaty could equally well act as pump-priming for the German economy, but for the moment Keynes's thinking was parallel to that of Prime Minister Lloyd George, who believed that the time had come to ease the restrictions on Germany, and to move from a stringent post-Armistice structure to a real peace.

The French set off for Spa in a punitive frame of mind. For them there was no English Channel; at enormous cost in blood and treasure, they had finally penned the Hun behind the Rhine. In 1870 German troops had besieged Paris during the Franco-Prussian War; in 1871 the victors had proclaimed Wilhelm of Prussia as emperor of Germany in the Hall of Mirrors at Versailles; in 1918 German siege guns had indiscriminately fired a two-hundred-pound artillery shell into Paris every twenty minutes for 139 days. The French intended to keep Germany's army small. France needed German coal, because German soldiers had destroyed the coal mines of France. In 1871 the Germans had demanded that France pay an indemnity, the equivalent of a billion dollars, within three years, and France had paid, on time. As the French saw the events of 1914–1918, the Boches had waged war on French soil, had been defeated, and had signed a treaty. *Alors*, let them pay.

For the German delegation, there was the opportunity for an exercise of true diplomatic skill. What was needed was to avoid unnecessarily reminding the French of German militarism, listen politely to all that was said, and quietly play off the English against the French, forcing the French to make some sort of compromise in order to get anything signed.

On the morning of July 5, 1920, in this town that had been the last wartime headquarters of the Kaiser's army, General Hans von Seeckt and several of his staff strode into the conference room wearing their uniforms and medals.[14] The German minister of defense, Otto Gessler, had already told the assembled international press that Germany really could not be expected to reduce its army to the figure of one hundred thousand required by the Versailles Treaty. Gessler and Seeckt then sat down and demanded that the Versailles Treaty provision be revised to permit Germany an army of two hundred thousand.

With one stroke, the Germans had shoved Lloyd George into the French position; the British prime minister pointed out that the Germans had not surrendered the quantities of arms stipulated under the treaty, and that having millions of unaccounted-for weapons throughout Germany was a threat both to German governmental stability and to the nations bordering Germany. Just offstage was the fighting that had broken out between Russia and Poland; France wanted its ally Poland to prevail, but Seeckt, while on the one hand encouraging the Allies to think of Germany as a "wall against Bolshevism," in fact wanted Russia to bleed the newly reconstituted state on Germany's eastern border.[15]

Confronted by Germany's demand for a larger army, Britain and France decided that the time had come to supplant negotiation with dictation. The Germans were asked to sign a document that gave them until the treaty-allowed date of January 1, 1921, to bring the army down to one hundred thousand; the document also threatened further Allied occupation of German regions, possibly including the industrial Ruhr, if that deadline was not met.

The Germans refused to sign an agreement containing a threat that was greater than any in the Versailles Treaty. The Allies then forced them to sign a protocol that was in accord with the treaty, in which they agreed to disarm the Civil Guard and complete the long-promised surrender of weapons.

All this was of course being sent back to German newspapers, and, although what was signed was simply a repetition of terms accepted at Versailles, it was perceived as another embittering German defeat. The threat of further Allied occupation could only fuel the völkisch forces who had no day-to-day responsibility for running Germany, and had never accepted the Versailles terms as binding. Two evenings after the Spa Conference began, the Nazi Party began capitalizing on it. With Drexler in the chair, Hitler launched into a speech on "The Shameful Peace of Versailles," addressing an audience of twenty-four hundred, the largest the party had yet attracted. One reason for the crowd's size was the presence of many communists and Independent Socialists as hecklers. "Stormily greeted," Hitler promptly attacked the middle-of-the-road *Münchner Neueste Nachrichten* for its "crawling and obsequious" refusal to become indignant over the events at Spa.

As for the German government willing to knuckle under to the Allies all over again, it "must learn that for us, there cannot be any answer at Spa: never — at any time!" To "put an end to all this rotten business" Germans should refuse to pay their taxes.

When Hitler inevitably brought the Jews into the conspiracy against Germany being practiced at Spa, leftist hecklers shouted, in the Jews' defense, "Human rights!" Hitler shot back, "The Jew should look for them where he ought to go, where he belongs, in his own state of Palestine." This produced "fervent applause." Notes of the meeting went on to record, "Turmoil, verging on attacks." Afterward, "Groups formed in the street, and there were passionate arguments until almost midnight."[16]

Those at Spa who had assumed that the military clauses would produce the greatest difficulties were soon to learn otherwise. As the generals left and the wary delegations turned to the subject of coal shipments, Germany's most successful businessman appeared in the conference room as a member of the German negotiating team. He was the legendary Hugo Stinnes, who could indeed claim to know something about coal and its shipment.[17] The fifty-year-old multimillionaire had started a small coal business for himself twenty-eight years earlier, armed with a degree as a mining engineer and a capital of 50,000 marks. He had parlayed these assets into the acquisition of mines, barges, river steamers, and a fleet of freighters that operated in waters extending from Scandinavia to Egypt. He built iron and steel mills, and during the war had been one of Germany's leading industrialists, owning among other things the Rhine Westphalian Electric Company, the principal source of electricity for the Ruhr. It was during the post-Armistice inflation, however, that Hugo Stinnes eclipsed all other German entrepreneurs. No one was as good at acquiring new properties with borrowed marks that could be repaid with their inflated successors. Stinnes was raking in what would eventually total more than nine hundred companies, including, in Germany and elsewhere, fifty-seven banks and insurance companies, thirty-seven oil fields and refineries, numerous hotels, forests and paper mills, sixty-nine construction companies, assorted chemical plants and sugar refineries, and 150 newspapers and magazines whose editors learned to present his conservative viewpoint if they wished to keep their jobs.

This was the man who had come to Spa to straighten things out.

With supremely false modesty, he referred to himself as a simple "merchant in Mülheim," the city in which he had begun his career.[18] Wearing ill-fitting suits and scoffing at the recreational pursuits of the rich, he had a face and beard that made him look like a Byzantine potentate who had rushed into the wrong century.

Despite his immersion in business, Hugo Stinnes heard yet another and fateful siren song: the sweet music of political power. During the war he had acted as an intermediary in an early effort to arrange a separate peace with Russia. The venture was unsuccessful, but it had given Stinnes a taste for attempting to change the behavior of nations. He had a seat in the postwar Reichstag, representing the right-of-center Volkspartei, but he yearned for a larger role in directing Germany's destiny. With the assurance of one of the century's great self-made men, he was certain that what he saw as the proper German stance at an international conference would indeed benefit Germany.

To this point in the conference, all the delegates, including the now-departed German generals, had made their remarks and responses while seated across the table from their counterparts. Hugo Stinnes stood up, saying, "I rise in order to be able to look the hostile delegates straight in the eyes." He then began lecturing the representatives of England and France as if they were stupid middle-management executives who needed to have their selfish inefficiencies pointed out to them before being fired. He spoke scornfully of "our insane conquerors." The German Foreign Ministry had included him in the delegation as a technical expert, not as a formulator of foreign policy, but now Stinnes linked the earlier protocol on disarmament with the subject of coal shipments, and single-handedly issued the Allies an ultimatum: if they dared to occupy the Ruhr, Germany would never send them another ounce of coal.

"The Allied delegates were pale with anger and surprise," said Lord d'Abernon, who was the British ambassador to Germany and a man who sincerely wished for an improvement in relations.[19]

The Allies had an answer for Hugo Stinnes, and for Germany. If within seventy-two hours the Germans did not signify their willingness to make up the deficits in their coal shipments, the French and British armies would march into the Ruhr. Marshal Ferdinand Foch, who had been ready to do just that for twenty months, was summoned to prepare plans for the Allied march. Field Marshal Sir Henry Wilson, chief of the imperial General Staff, swiftly crossed the channel to Spa.

At last the Germans bethought themselves of diplomacy. Foreign

Minister Walter Simons quickly closeted himself with Professor Julius Moritz Bonn, who was with the delegation as Chancellor Konstantin Fehrenbach's adviser on reparations, and had some friends in the British delegation. Simons and Bonn went, hats in hand, to see Lloyd George, and found that he was no more interested in starting a new war than they were. After further difficult but substantive negotiations the Germans signed an Allied-prepared protocol establishing quotas for coal deliveries for the next six months.[20]

So the Spa Conference ended, and who should emerge from it as a German hero? Hugo Stinnes, who was doing his best to devalue the mark in his own dealings, and would recommend that the government step up its printing of paper money. It was to be expected that the right-wing press should hail Stinnes as a patriot who had bravely challenged the Allies, but on the floor of the Reichstag the usually rational historian Otto Hoetzsch accused everyone in the Spa delegation, except Stinnes, of dishonoring Germany. Even Gustav Stresemann, a political figure of some stature, felt compelled to thank his fellow Volkspartei member Stinnes for his contribution at Spa.

It was all grist for Adolf Hitler's mill. On July 15, the evening before the conference at Spa ended, he had addressed a crowd of twelve hundred at the Hofbräuhaus, saying that the German people should not lose courage, and that "the hour of vengeance tolls."[21] During the discussion period, a Jewish woman identified as Frau Sara Moser said, "The peace treaty must be honestly fulfilled."[22] This produced shouts from the audience: "She is sick! Take her to Eglfing [a local mental hospital]! The ambulance is right outside!" Notes of the meeting reported, "[Moser] cannot be heard over the noise; chairman cuts her off in order to restore order."[23]

Amidst general agreement, although there were some other critics in the hall, Hitler summed it up: "The present government cannot bring about peace and order." That unleashed cries of "Bring it down!" Hitler went on, "The National Socialist German Workers' Party is the only party. Join it. Then internal peace will come to our land. We cannot fulfill the peace treaty, and if we try, the German people will only sink lower and lower. It is not possible, just not possible."[24]

This less strident tone — "It is not possible, just not possible" — was something Hitler used in counterpoint to his transports of denunciation. "Hitler had caught the casual camaraderie of the trenches," an early party member recalled, "and without stooping to slang, except for special effects, managed to talk like a member of the audience." The man, who was in these crowds, added:

In describing the difficulties of the housewife without enough money to buy the food her family needed in the Viktualien Markt he would produce just the phrases she would have used herself if she had been able to formulate them. . . . He had this priceless gift of expressing exactly their own thoughts. He also had the good sense, or instinct, to appeal to the women in his audience. . . . Many a time I have seen him face a hall plentifully sprinkled with opponents ready to heckle and interrupt, and in his search for his first body of support, make a remark about food shortages or domestic difficulties or the sound instinct of his women listeners, which would produce the first bravos. And time and again these came from women. That would break the ice.[25]

As for his personal relationship with women, sexually oriented friendships or encounters were notable by their absence. Hermann Esser, a rising young Nazi who was proving to be the party's second best speaker, later spoke of the "Austrian politeness he showed to every woman," but the wife of an early follower said to her husband, "I tell you he is a neuter."[26] Every sort of tale was to be told of Hitler, including an undocumented story that he had caught a venereal disease from a Jewish prostitute during his prewar days in Vienna, but in Munich, at the age of thirty-one, his behavior was that of a man who displayed no sexual interest in women.

They, on the other hand, flocked to see the pale, thin young combat veteran with his earnest manner and compelling voice. "As a speaker he fascinated them," Alfred Rosenberg recalled, while another early party member said, "The women were crazy about him."[27] One spectator at a Hitler speech was struck by the sight of a young woman whose face, as she listened to Hitler, seemed to be in sexual throes. Hitler himself likened an audience to a woman who has to be wooed and won, saying, "The mass, the people, is for me a woman."[28] The oratorical experience, which left him sweating and pale, physically spent, and emotionally calm at the end of the final crashing words of his long speeches, may have been a sexual substitute, a sublimation; one woman who was not carried away by his rhetoric said that the atmosphere of shouted hatred and violent response at a Hitler speech made her feel that she had witnessed a sexual ax murder.

Here, then, was another of the inconsistencies presented by the man. The essence of his speeches was empathy; for his audience, a speech by Hitler was an electric hour in which he and they shared the hardships and humiliations of daily German life, and vented their frustrations upon the targets he placed in front of them. Speaker and listeners were one, yet the same man who could achieve this intimate emotional communion with each of thousands of individuals was not able, or willing, to give himself fully to any other human being. Supreme among his inconsistencies was that the same psyche housed brutal attitudes in many areas but considerable sensitivity in others. The same man who preached merciless vengeance could sit down and write a drippingly sentimental poem, "Consider This!" which was published in Munich's Sunday *Morgenpost*. An appeal for patience and kindness toward one's aged mother, it began, "When your mother has grown older,"

> When her dear, faithful eyes
> No longer see life as they once did
> When her feet, grown tired,
> No longer want to carry her as she walks,
> Then lend her your arm in support,
> Escort her with happy pleasure —
> The hour will come when, weeping, you
> Must accompany her on her final walk.
> And if she asks you something, then give her an answer,
> And if she asks again, then speak!
> And if she asks yet again, respond to her,
> Not impatiently but with gentle calm.
> And if she cannot understand you properly,
> Explain all to her happily.
> The hour will come, the bitter hour,
> When her mouth asks for nothing more.[29]

Buried here was the emotional youth of the days before the flophouses in Vienna and the trenches at Arras, the adolescent who worshiped from afar a young beauty in Linz named Stefanie, adoring her from such a distance that she was later in life startled to learn that he had even seen her pass by. Hitler's early confidence in his future had in no measure extended to the girls of Linz or Vienna. The same ferocious pride and bottomless vulnerability that led him to pretend to August Kubizek that he was attending class each day at the academy was incapable of risking rejection at the hands of a flesh-and-blood woman. His comrades of the List Regiment had noted that Hitler not only disapproved of their associating with French girls, but did not go out with German girls, either, when the rest of them were.

Now, in Munich, the driven, stupendously ambitious son of a minor provincial official was painfully aware of the awkward figure he cut in the socially superior circles to which Dietrich Eckart was gradually introducing him. Hitler knew just enough to bow and kiss the hand of a lady when he was presented to her, and knew all too well that he did it clumsily. He preferred the motherly attentions of Frau Carola Hoffmann, an elderly admirer of his who was the widow of a high school principal. Pretty, dignified, and small, Frau Hoffmann loved attending Hitler's speeches and was undismayed by the brawls with hecklers that she witnessed.[30] Hitler was a frequent visitor at her house in the suburb of Solln, where she fussed over him, fed him cakes and cream, did his laundry, gave him lectures on what to wear and how to behave, and sent him home with packages of cookies for the sweet tooth his wartime comrades remembered. Hitler referred to her as "my beloved and devoted *Mütterchen*," or little mother, while some of the less reverent party stalwarts referred to her as "Hitler-Mutti," Hitler's mommy.[31]

And what would Adolf like as a present from his Mütterchen? A nice rhinoceros-hide dog whip, like the one his father had beaten him with when he was a boy. Eventually Hitler was to have three of these whips, made from either rhinoceros or hippopotamus skin, each a present from an older woman who was taking an interest in his career.[32] He liked to carry one, to brandish it, and to smack it against his thigh or into the palm of his hand.

These were some of the outward signs and behavior of this enigmatic young orator-politician. Another war veteran, shaking hands with him for the first time, spoke of "his soft palm gripping mine firmly enough. I noticed then, as in the future, that his palm was clammy and moist, which is probably a sign of his inner nervous tension and emotional excitability."[33] A reporter wrote of a speech made at the time, "Herr Hitler . . . flew into a fury and screamed so that not much could be understood at the back."[34] The obsessive hatred and repetitive violent language of the speeches bespoke a sick mind; a warped libido may well have been part of this disturbed psyche, but for the moment all that could be seen was a womanless bachelor, consumed by his self-set presumptuous task of creating a new Germany.

Hermann Esser would describe Hitler as "a very affable man," and another early follower described evenings in beer gardens when "the play of humor, especially Eckart's, was contagious. Hitler liked to be amused, to laugh, and showed his utter contentment by slapping his knee."[35] Yet at evening's end he went home to his shabby lodgings by himself. Klara Hitler, the mother he adored, dead for thirteen years, had said to August Kubizek, "He goes his way, just as if he were alone in the world."[36]

CHAPTER

14

HITLER had not left Germany since fighting in Belgium and France during the war; now, in August of 1920, he and party chairman Anton Drexler traveled to Austria for a meeting of the National Socialist groups of Czechoslovakia, Germany, and Austria itself, where the idea of National Socialism had first found adherents nearly two decades earlier. The Austrian Nazi Party was far better established than the group in Munich; although it had failed to get anyone into a high office, its candidates had received as many as thirty-four thousand votes in a national election.[1]

The trip from Munich to the congress in Salzburg was an uneventful seventy-mile train ride through beautiful alpine country, but for Hitler it was an immensely symbolic return to the land of his birth, youth, and young manhood. Seven years earlier he had left Austria as a vagrant avoiding conscription into the army of the Austro-Hungarian Empire. On this journey the train stopped at Traunstein, where, twenty months earlier, he had been a lance corporal guarding prisoners of war. Now Hitler was returning to Austria as one of two official delegates representing a political party that had recently grown to a strength of 725 members.

The meeting that was called to order on August 7 amidst the picturesque towers and squares of Salzburg lacked immediate political potency — of the fifty National Socialist delegates attending, none held elected office in his or her respective nation — but the concerns of these Pan-German men and women paralleled those of millions of Germans, inside and outside the borders of Germany. To those who wished to expand the borders of Germany to include additional German-speaking areas, recent Allied actions that further dismembered Germany were an agony. Just the previous month, despite a plebiscite

■ 151

in which a large majority in the disputed areas of Allenstein and Marienwerder voted to remain German, the Allies had handed over most of West Prussia to Poland to create the Polish Corridor, an avenue varying from twenty-two to seventy miles in width that gave Poland the access to the Baltic Sea that had been promised her at Versailles. Danzig, the former capital of West Prussia, which sat squarely in the middle of this new Polish coastline, had a population that was 96 percent German; it was given the special status of Free City and placed under the protection of the League of Nations, to which Germany was not allowed to belong.

The National Socialists in Salzburg had an entirely different idea of how the map of Europe should be redrawn. As a result of the redistribution of the former Austro-Hungarian Empire at Versailles, Austria was only a quarter its former size, but, without its non-German-speaking provinces, 95 percent of the remaining population spoke German. Most of the lands that constituted the new Austrian republic had been part of Germany from the middle of the tenth century until the middle of the nineteenth. For decades a substantial number of the German-Austrians had yearned for *Anschluss*, a union with Germany, and this objective was at the core of the program of the Austrian Nazis whom Hitler was meeting. The Germans from the Sudetenland also desired to become one with Germany, politically and geographically. Those from the disputed German province of Upper Silesia, soon to face a plebiscite to determine whether their land was to continue within Germany or be given to Poland, passionately shared these concerns.

Many National Socialists, including Hitler's companion Anton Drexler, felt that the thrust of their gathering should be to create a single unified party, with a headquarters in Berlin. The new party should be democratic in spirit, and reach its decisions through parliamentary debate.

This was not at all what Hitler wanted.[2] While he felt that the desire for inclusion within Germany's borders was eminently commendable, he did not wish to subordinate the Munich-based Nazi Party to any other entity. As for democracy, that was what was wrong with postwar Germany.

Hitler was scheduled to give a speech; how was he to handle the question? Like a good politician, he handled it by avoiding it. "Fellow Germans!" he began. "I am thoroughly ashamed that the same movement which began in German-Austria in 1904 is only now catching hold in Germany after so many years."

Immediately he moved to the results of the war, a common grievance, and something that had nothing to do with establishing an office in Berlin. "It is sad that the great misfortune that has struck us was necessary in order to show our people that, first and foremost, personal interests must be put aside, that the class distinction between proletariat and nonproletariat must cease, and that there must at last be a distinction between fellow Germans who work honestly and the drones and scoundrels."

Applause. Time to whip the Allies. "It is impossible to achieve anything for our people as long as they are nothing but . . . the slave of foreign countries. This is the first requirement that we demand and must demand; that our people be freed, that the chains be broken, that Germany again become her own master, and control her own history" — now it was time to play to the Austrians and Sudeten Czechs — "including that of all those who want to join Germany."

More applause. All the National Socialists were völkisch, which meant that they were anti-Semitic in varying degrees.

> For us it is a problem that decides whether our people become
> internally healthy again, that decides whether the Jewish spirit
> will really disappear. Don't think that you can battle a disease
> without killing the virus, without annihilating the bacillus, and
> don't think that you can battle racial tuberculosis without seeing
> to it that the people are freed from the virus which causes racial
> tuberculosis. Jewish influence will never disappear, and the poi-
> soning of the people will not end, as long as the virus, the Jew,
> has not been removed from our midst.[3]

More applause, but none of it deceived Anton Drexler, who knew that his propaganda chief was trying to undermine every effort to weld these National Socialist groups. He knew that Hitler disliked the democratic voting procedures that still governed the actions of the party's executive committee in Munich; Hitler's two written proposals for a smaller "action committee," both rejected by the executive committee, were still fresh in his mind. Hitler was the party's greatest asset, but Drexler had watched Hitler drive National Chairman Harrer right out of the party, and he was well aware that such close Hitler associates as Eckart and Rosenberg, though not holding party offices, were becoming a sort of shadow leadership.

Drexler still held cards; Hitler might attract most of the party's new members, but Drexler's friends controlled the executive committee. Hitler might give a popular speech at Salzburg, but when it came time for photographs, twenty-one people, three of them women, were asked to pose for a picture of the National Socialist movement's leadership; Hitler was not among them. Drexler was seated next to Dr. Walter Riehl, head of the Austrian Nazis, who was in the center of the front row. Hitler appeared only in a picture of the entire congress, staring glumly from the third row.

The trip back to Munich differed in spirit from the trip over. Hitler and Drexler were for the first time clearly in opposition. By contrast, Drexler and Dr. Riehl had all sorts of plans for coordination between their parties, though the idea of having a headquarters in Berlin appeared to have been abandoned.

Within twenty-four hours after returning from Austria, Hitler was once again in form. One of the Sudeten Czech delegates who had been at Salzburg, Dr. Alexander Schilling from Moravia, had come to Munich, and he gave a lecture at the Hofbräuhaus on "The Germans in Czechoslovakia." During the discussion that followed, Otto Ballerstedt, president of the Bayernbund, rose to his feet. Ballerstedt's Bavarian League believed that Bavaria should secede from Germany and become part of a Danubian Confederation that would include Austria, Czechoslovakia, and Hungary.

For Hitler, this was the same kind of separatist talk that had triggered his scornful eloquence when a professor had spoken in this vein the evening Hitler attended his first meeting of the German Workers' Party. Germany must have more territory, not less. France was constantly whittling at the edges of Germany; French agents were encouraging every German border state to go its own way; and the French, in defiance of the Weimar Constitution, had just established a special diplomatic mission in Munich to further this end.

In a moment Hitler was on his feet, attacking Ballerstedt, shouting him down. "Better to have a Greater Germany under the Bolsheviks than a Southern German State dependent upon the Czechs and the French!"[4]

There was pandemonium in the beer hall, and in the uproar Ballerstedt was beaten up and thrown out. It was the beginning of a feud that was to have many episodes; Otto Ballerstedt was the only private citizen ever to succeed in getting Adolf Hitler put in jail.

Things were not dull to begin with in August of 1920, but a chain of events brought a real face-off between Bavaria and Berlin. Implementing a protocol signed at the Spa Conference, the Reichstag had passed legislation known as the Disarmament Law. This was a serious effort to disarm the nation's Civil Guard units, into which so many

Freikorps veterans had gone when their regiments were disbanded. If Berlin had needed more warning that the right-wing paramilitary units were getting out of hand, the summer had provided two striking examples of the threat. The first had been Prussia's discovery that Bavaria was exporting illegal military activity, in the form of Bavarian Civil Guard leaders who were secretly traveling about organizing a nationwide armed force known as the Orgesch, which described itself as a "White army against the Red army."[5] Right on top of this came sensational disclosures from Saxony, where it was found that a Spy Central existed in Magdeburg. This armed group of conspiratorial freelancers had ties not only to Orgesch but to the Reichswehr, and its stated purpose was "to overthrow the existing government."[6]

It was against this background — Allied pressure, and the realization that the Civil Guards might succeed where the Kapp Putsch had failed — that on August 11, 1920, the national Disarmament Law took effect, requiring that Bavaria disband its Civil Guard forthwith.

For the first time since Bismarck united Germany, a German state flatly refused to comply with a law enacted by the national legislature. There was a certain robust alpine independence about the Bavarian stance; the Bavarian government allowed its 267,000-man Civil Guard to hold a huge "Bavarian Shooting Match" and announce to the world that it would be an annual event.[7]

The Allies observed this impasse with growing wonder. Berlin did nothing; Bavaria went about its business. The French hoped that this would lead to Bavaria's secession; as far as France was concerned, the Bavarian monarchists could bring back the House of Wittelsbach if they liked, as long as it fragmented Germany. Lloyd George felt that the Germans were simply not playing the game, and was to say that it was apparent that either "the German government does not intend to carry out its treaty obligations, or that it has not the strength to insist, in the face of selfish and shortsighted opposition."[8] The Allies thought and thought, and decided that perhaps another conference might be a good idea.

During this summer of 1920, Hitler was developing some foreign policy ideas of his own. Under the influence of Rosenberg, he began to think about eastward expansion. In a speech at Rosenheim he said that the völkisch movement had no quarrel with the Bolshevik-exploited Russian workers, but only with what he characterized as Russia's Jewish communist leaders who were "the greatest enemies of nationally conscious Russians."[9] In another speech he even spoke of an alliance with Russia, saying on one occasion that such a thing would be possible if the Jews in Russia were "deposed."[10] According to the *Bayerische Volkszeitung*, he told yet another crowd that in order to get rid of the shameful burden of the Versailles Treaty, "he would be prepared to ally himself not only with Bolshevism, but even with the devil, against France!"[11]

Like the infinitely more influential General von Seeckt, Hitler was instinctively looking for new relationships that could be used to break the Allied grip on Germany. Seeckt had not the slightest use for the Soviet Union's communism, but he saw Germany and Russia as Europe's pariahs, both excluded from the League of Nations and hence not bound by it, and sensed that in some combination they might checkmate the Allies. Hitler saw yet another potential friend in a recent enemy, Italy. Addressing a meeting of the League of German War Veterans in Nuremberg, Hitler told them not to cause too much of a stir about the 180,000 Germans of the South Tyrol who had been annexed into Italy as a result of the peace settlement — a startling contrast to his views on any other German-speaking area.[12]

Beneath all his views, however, was his obsessive anti-Semitism, always at hand to explain what was wrong with Germany and the world. All his speeches were laden with hatred for the Jews, but now he composed a three-hour lecture that truly deserved the *Münchener Post*'s earlier apellation "popular science." "Why Are We Anti-Semites?" was his first attempt to talk about the subject comprehensively since the letter he had written to a former *Vertrauensmann* at Captain Mayr's request a year earlier.[13] Delivered to a crowd at the Hofbräuhaus, the speech was interrupted by applause fifty-eight times, but its most striking feature was the complete absence of factual validity. Among other things, Hitler characterized Judaism as lacking a spiritual dimension, and cited a few Old Testament references to "the curse of labor" as proof that Jews had an aversion to hard work and were therefore destined to be parasites on others. As for the heroic Aryans, they were responsible for the greatness of Egypt, Persia, and Greece, and, "with the exception of these states, no cultural states at all were founded on this earth" — a statement that might have surprised the Chinese, among others.

Hitler's thesis was that the Nordic race, evolving under harsh conditions in cold climates, had developed a moral sense of duty, a profound spiritual life, and an instinctive code of behavior in which noble cultural and political values were inextricably woven. All this was, of course, accompanied by "pure racial breeding," in which only the fittest survived the hardships of the northern climes. Jewry, by contrast, had faced no such race-improving challenges, and in its decadent parasitism had been enabled to subvert the noble Germanic "culture state" by means of interest slavery. Everything followed from that; as Hitler saw it, the Jews had captured German painting, music, poetry, the theater, movies, the press, and, indeed, the national legislature itself. There could be only one appropriate response: "Entfernung der Juden aus unserem Volk," the removal of the Jews from our people.

These ideas outraged some of the non-völkisch individuals who came, for whatever reasons, to hear Hitler. In a Reichswehr informant's report of a meeting at which Hitler combined his anti-Semitism with a call for compulsory military service to strengthen Germany against the Allies, there was this note: "A gentleman who called Herr Hitler a monkey was calmly thrown out."[14] As far as Hitler was concerned, the important thing was that the party was getting attention.

II

In October, the season that Munich reserves for its carefree beer-drinking festival, there was a demonstration of how sharply Germans could differ on the subject of loyalty. Marie Sandmeier, a servant girl, was dismissed from her job at a manor house in Upper Bavaria and went to Munich to find work. In her walks around the city, she saw placards that had been put up by the Allied control commission, ordering that all privately owned weapons and ammunition be turned in to the authorities.

Marie remembered that on her former employer's estate there was a secret storage place for large numbers of just such contraband weapons. Wanting to retaliate against her employer for firing her, she went to report him, but instead of telling the Allied control commission, which would have taken action, or the police, who probably would have decided to forget it, she gave her information at the shop where the posters were printed.

A day or so later, a man appeared at Marie's address in Munich and said he was from the Allied control commission. He asked her to accompany him to the commission's offices. She went off with him.

The next morning the body of Marie Sandmeier was found at the base of a tree in Forstenrieder Park. She had been strangled. On the tree was a note from her killers. "You vile bitch," it read, "you have betrayed your Fatherland."

Soon after, a waiter named Hartung, who was having some differences with the Civil Guard, was heard boasting that he intended to take a truck and steal the weapons in a right-wing arms cache whose whereabouts he knew. The next day Hartung's body, with eleven bullets in it, was found in a river. An investigation placed a Civil Guard truck and two officers at the scene of the crime, and the same two officers were implicated in the death of Marie Sandmeier. Just as the police were about to arrest them, Munich police commissioner Ernst Pöhner reassigned the case to another bureau in the department, giving the suspects time to escape from Bavaria.[15]

The full range of affiliations of the two men was never uncovered, but these killings were only the first of hundreds that followed the influx of disbanded Freikorps men into Bavaria. The Association of Former Ehrhardt Officers was rapidly evolving into an underground network, highly selective in its membership, known as Organization Consul.[16] A simple measure of its values was that it considered the outlawed Orgesch to be inhibited, squeamish, and effete. The name Consul was taken by the group because Consul Eichmann was one of the aliases used by Lieutenant Commander Ehrhardt in avoiding the Berlin government. Like the Orgesch, O.C., as it was known to initiates, had as its objective the destruction of the Weimar Republic. Both chose the strategy of provoking a leftist uprising, which could then be suppressed in a climactic version of the Freikorps captures of Munich and the Ruhr, to be followed by the installation of a völkisch dictatorship in Berlin.

There, however, the similarities between the two right-wing groups ended. The Orgesch believed that a leftist uprising could be provoked by having sympathetic right-wing producers of food and goods hold them off the market long enough to start riots by leftist consumers, but Organization Consul felt that the way to get the left to take up weapons again was to start killing its leaders.[17]

O.C. had a secret oath and bylaws that included explicit objectives, referred to as spiritual and material goals. Under the spiritual heading were "warfare against Jewry, Social Democracy, and leftist radicalism; fomentation of internal unrest in order to attain the overthrow of the antinationalist Weimar Constitution."[18]

In the category of material goals were "the suppression of internal unrest . . . the establishment of a nationalist government; creation of local shock troops for breaking up meetings of an antinationalist nature; the maintenance of arms and military capability, and the education of youth in the use of arms."[19]

The O.C. soon began killing; although it had already targeted some nationally known figures, the earliest murders were on the order of those of Hartung and Marie Sandmeier, and may have included them.

A politician approached Police Commissioner Pöhner and whispered, "Herr Police Commissioner, are you aware that there are political murders being committed in Bavaria?"

The tall man looked through his pince-nez and replied, "So, so, aber zu wenig!" — Yes, yes, but too few![20]

CHAPTER

15

HITLER was not in Munich at the time Marie Sandmeier was killed in October of 1920; he was once again in Austria, this time on a two-week speaking tour to support Austrian Nazis who were running for seats in the Austrian National Assembly in an election scheduled for October 16. Although he had left the Salzburg National Socialist congress that past summer under a bit of a cloud, Hitler, not Drexler, was now receiving the Austrians' attention. Drexler still had to report for work every day at his job in the Munich railroad yards, but the frugal Hitler had limitless time for party activities. On September 29 he gave his first speech of the Austrian election campaign at Innsbruck. "His party is firmly determined to solve the *Jewish question* with well-known German thoroughness," the *Innsbrucker Nachrichten* reported to its readers. "The National Socialists . . . support with all their energy the joining of *all Germans* in one *state territory* and will not give up until this goal is reached."[1]

Hitler spoke in Salzburg, in Hallein, and in his birthplace, the border town of Braunau on the Inn River. After the first of his two appearances in Vienna, that city's *Deutsche Arbeiter-Presse* said, "The Bavarian National Socialistic proletarian leader talked for two hours about Germany's fate — and we could have listened to him for days."[2]

During the time Hitler was away from Munich, an extraordinary confrontation took place at a party speechmaking evening at the Hof-bräuhaus. The Nazi speaker was an attorney-at-law named Ludwig Ruetz; the poster advertising the meeting had vilified the Talmud, claiming that the written basis for the religious authority of traditional Judaism was the source of "the Jews' hatred and contempt for everything that is human."[3]

This was the first time that the party had announced a speech that was to be an attack on a specific part of the Jewish religion, and a rabbi, Dr. Leo Bärwald, went to the meeting with five men from his temple. The anti-Semitic Ruetz launched into his talk, saying that none of the world's religions was as mean spirited as Judaism, and that the Talmud ordered Jews to swindle, steal from, and betray the Gentiles. The Talmud, Ruetz said, ordered Jews to remain in rear areas in time of war, and added that the Talmud's attitude toward sex was "impossible and shamelessly immoral." The Jews as a people were "the dregs of society."

After the speech, there was a short intermission before the discussion period, and Rabbi Bärwald and his five companions moved through the crowd toward the speaker's platform. The rabbi explained politely to the Nazi officials that he had been taking notes during the past hour, and that he would appreciate the opportunity to address the audience and correct some of what had been said.

One of the men who was with the rabbi recounted what happened next. "The notes that Dr. Bärwald had written down were taken away from him with the explanation that it was forbidden to write notes at the meeting, since the notes would only be misused." Then, while the rabbi was left standing unharmed before the rostrum, "we five Jews (in a crowd of 1,500 people) were pushed out of the hall and kicked down the stairs while being beaten and mistreated. I'd like to stress that we hadn't disturbed the meeting at all by our behavior."

That left Rabbi Bärwald surrounded by Nazis. Someone, probably Drexler, who was chairman of the meeting, told the crowd that a rabbi was asking to give his views, and asked for a vote on whether he should be allowed to do so. The crowd voted that he be allowed to speak.

Rabbi Bärwald turned to face the audience, and began by saying that he was proud to be a Jew, but equally proud to be a German. The Talmud, he pointed out, was available in the National Library for anyone to read, and he could prove, and they could confirm, that its views and commandments were uplifting to humanity as a whole. At this there were shouts throughout the audience, demanding whether the things that Ruetz had said were in the Talmud were there or not.

The rabbi replied that everything Ruetz had told them "was untrue and lies." At this point, the noise of the crowd kept Bärwald from continuing. Ruetz stepped forward and, according to notes of the meeting, "said that he could prove everything. . . . He was herewith publicly stating that Dr. Leo Bärwald is a common liar and that he was thereby giving him the opportunity to sue him so that he could provide proof. He requested that Dr. Bärwald be allowed to leave unmolested. (The latter was then escorted out.)"

The Nazis found themselves unsettled by this encounter, and determined that nothing like it should happen again. The announcement in the *Völkischer Beobachter* of a forthcoming speech by Hitler said, in part:

> Jews are not allowed at this meeting as well as at all future ones. The leaders of the party want to point out that from now on they will resolutely remove these creatures from the hall immediately, as the latest events unquestionably prove that a group of Jewish provocateurs and people employed by Jews only go to the meetings of the NSDAP in order to provoke trouble, and thus try to portray the party as a brutal rapist of "harmless" participants.[4]

When the poster for the next meeting hit the streets of Munich, at its bottom, reading left to right, were these three items: Admission 1 mark; War invalids free; Jews not admitted.[5] The same prohibition against Jews was to be on every subsequent poster. At a meeting soon after this one, when Hitler said, "We do not deal with Jews at all," one or more racists shouted, "Negroes!" meaning that blacks, too, should not be dealt with. Without missing a beat, Hitler said, to applause, "I would rather have one hundred Negroes in the hall than one Jew."[6]

As for Dr. Bärwald and the courageous men who had accompanied him, they decided not to sue, but to tell their story to the people of Munich. The *Münchner Neueste Nachrichten* gave them space in its pages to recount what had happened. Their account closed with these words:

> We are appealing to the public out of the conviction that the great majority of our Christian fellow-citizens regrets these riots and condemns them. If they have been quiet so far we can only explain that by assuming that they are not yet aware of the great danger not only for the Jews but also for the authority of the state and the safety of all its inhabitants.[7]

II

During December 1920, Hitler found himself in the first crisis of his short political career. On the surface, there were no threats in view;

he was surrounded by evidence of the Nazi Party's growth and activity and of his role in its expansion. Within the preceding twelve months membership in Munich had risen from 190 to 1,512, and the ten locals that had been formed in other Bavarian towns, as well as one outside Bavaria, brought NSDAP membership to approximately two thousand.[8]

The party's forty-nine public meetings in Munich in 1920 drew an attendance of sixty-two thousand; Hitler was the featured speaker at twenty-one of these large gatherings, and he led the post-speech discussions at seven others.[9] He had been the dominant figure at the party's Monday night discussion evenings, often using them as rehearsals for his large public speeches.

As the party's propaganda chief, he had also employed these occasions to develop and coach a cadre of lesser speakers and speaker-instructors who viewed him as the party's voice. During the year he had made an additional twenty public speeches: seven in Austria, seven before the party's locals in other Bavarian towns, and six, in his private capacity and for pay, to veterans' groups and the völkisch association known as the Schutz-und Trutzbund. He had also given six talks at a Reichswehr course similar to that in which his own speaking talents had been noticed.

Thus, as December began, thirty-one-year-old Adolf Hitler was by all odds the party's most visible figure, but he was far from having a clear-cut leadership role. Although he was a de facto participant in the discussions of the party executive committee, his name was not among the six appearing as its official *Vorstand*, or board of directors, when the party had in October acquired legal status by incorporating.[10] On paper, at least, Hitler was not a member of the principal policy-making group, which had twice rejected his proposal for the action committee. Chairman Anton Drexler was no match for Hitler in terms of ability and energy, but he was holding his own in the party infighting and continued to keep the loyalty of his original adherents, five of whom served with him on the six-man board of directors.

Of itself, this would not have forced Hitler to an open confrontation with the party leadership, which was giving him a free hand with his enthusiastically received speechmaking activities. What troubled Hitler was the party leadership's continuing tendency to explore alliances and even formal mergers with other right-wing groups. It was Drexler's enthusiasm for organizational unity with the Austrian Nazis that had put him at odds with Hitler in Salzburg the previous summer; as Hitler saw it, creation of one large Pan-German National Socialist Party, complete with Sudeten Czechs, would eclipse the growing young party in Munich, robbing it, and its propaganda chief, of their freedom of action.

Now there was an immediate threat. The executive committee was considering marriage with the DSP, the völkisch group that had the Nazis' identical objective of weaning the workers from communism, and had set forth that objective years before Harrer, Drexler, and Hitler came upon the scene.[11] The DSP was slightly larger than the Nazi Party, and had locals in thirty-five towns.

As Hitler was contemplating the setback he might receive if he were buried in such a merger, he became aware of another situation that could do him harm or good. The *Völkischer Beobachter*, which was in effect the newspaper of record for the twenty right-wing organizations operating in Bavaria, was for sale. Ownership of the paper would greatly strengthen whatever group could afford to buy it. By the same token, if a group competing with the Nazis should emerge as the new owner, the *Beobachter*'s pages might cease to carry news of the Nazi Party — and of its leading orator.

There was considerable backstage maneuvering under way, and here the plot grew thicker.[12] The paper's editorial staff was dominated by members of the DSP, which had particularly close ties to the remnants of the Thule Society. This was significant because nearly 50 percent of the *Beobachter*'s stock was in the hands of two women — the mistress and the sister of Thule's founder, Rudolf von Sebottendorff. Of the eight shareholders, the Sebottendorff ladies were the ones who wanted to sell out of an enterprise that was 250,000 marks in debt and would require additional funds to keep operating. Presumably these women would prefer to sell to their friends of the DSP, but of course if the DSP and the Nazis merged, the paper would belong to the new combined party.

All this was repugnant to Hitler, who wanted the Nazi Party to acquire the *Beobachter* as sole owner, something the party treasury could not cover. He realized that purchase might not be possible, but he decided to strike his strongest blow against merger with the DSP, no matter what the fate of the newspaper. He took a calculated risk and threatened to reduce his activity for the party drastically, thereby accepting the chance that his bluff might be called and his prominent role in the party ended. On December 9 he wrote to Chairman Drexler, "I declare herewith in writing once and for all my withdrawal from the Party Committee . . . and from 15 December my resignation

164 ▪

from the Press Committee."[13] In short, they could find themselves a new propaganda chief.

There is no record of a written reply from Drexler or the executive committee, but Hitler's gamble must have paid off: the talk of mergers temporarily ceased, and he continued his full range of activities. As events were about to demonstrate, Drexler and Hitler were able to put aside their differences when they both saw something greater at stake.

On Thursday, December 16, Hitler heard of an entirely new offer to buy the *Beobachter*. Gottfried Feder, the high priest of interest slavery, had a one-twelfth interest in the paper: combined with the shares of the Sebottendorff faction, that would guarantee a controlling interest. On the face of it, that might have seemed good news for the Nazis, because Feder had often spoken at their meetings and selectively espoused their positions, but Feder was essentially a single-issue man. His great interest was not National Socialism, but his own idiosyncratic economic theories, and he was willing to work with any right-wing group that furthered them. His partner in the pending offer for the *Beobachter* was Count Karl von Bothmer, a Bavarian monarchist who was under serious suspicion of being supported by French money in his effort to separate Bavaria from the rest of Germany.[14]

Hitler was aghast; it would be bad enough for the party to lose out to the DSP, but to have Bavaria's one well-known right-wing newspaper get into the hands of a man who not only wanted to bring back the Wittelsbachs and make Bavaria a separate kingdom, but who was also *financed by the French* — that was insupportable.

At two o'clock the next morning Dietrich Eckart answered the noise at his door, and in rushed Hitler and Drexler, accompanied by party speechmaker Hermann Esser and Oskar Körner, an ardent Nazi who owned a toy store. All four were in a state; Hitler told Eckart that the party simply had to have the *Beobachter*, immediately. The purchase price was 120,000 marks — approximately nine times an average German worker's yearly wages. The paper's creditors would allow the new owners to sign a contract for future payment of the 250,000 marks in debts, but the purchase price would have to be raised in a matter of hours to forestall the competition.

The heavyset Eckart moved quickly; he and Hitler turned first to Dr. Gottfried Grandel, the Augsburg industrialist who had provided the plane and pilot that took them to Berlin during the Kapp Putsch. Grandel came forward with 56,500 marks, and Eckart arranged for contributions of another 3,500, possibly putting in some himself.

Impressive as it was to have raised half the needed money in a few hours, an additional 60,000 marks had to be found somewhere, quickly. There was no hope of obtaining a conventional loan; not a bank in Germany could have justified making a substantial loan to buy a hate-mongering little twice-weekly newspaper that was a quarter of a million marks in debt. Eckart headed in an entirely different direction; the climax of his day came when Colonel Franz Ritter von Epp, the most right-wing of Bavaria's higher Reichswehr officers, lent him 60,000 marks. Although it was in the form of a personal loan from Epp to Eckart, the assumption was that it came from secret Reichswehr funds, not unlike those which had been made available on a far smaller scale to enable the Nazi Party to move into its first headquarters. The debt was never repaid, and no one seemed to expect repayment; in 1922, when the *Münchener Post* got hold of the story that the army had subsidized the Nazi Party's purchase of its newspaper, it became a scandal that received national attention.[15]

So in one day the Nazi Party had acquired the only Bavarian news-paper that invariably publicized the activities of all the entities of the extreme right: the Schutz-und Trutzbund, the coalition known as the National Students' Organizations, the Pan-Germans of Austria and Czechoslovakia, the extremist veterans' organizations, and various völkisch political parties. For some of these groups, December 17, 1920, marked the end of the guaranteed sympathetic coverage they had been receiving in the *Völkischer Beobachter*. In the Nazi Party's ad hoc organizational structure, Hitler's position as propaganda chief put the paper under his direct control, and he had no intention of allowing it to advance the cause of competing right-wing parties.[16] The DSP men on the editorial board were sent packing, leaving in a dead heat with Feder's man, who had been editor.

Hitler was close to ecstatic about the purchase; the day after Eckart's coup, he sent him a grateful letter that closed, "I am so devoted to the Movement body and soul, you could scarcely believe how happy I am as a result of reaching this much desired goal, and I cannot refrain from expressing my heartfelt thanks for this present good fortune."[17]

Apart from the *Beobachter*'s record and reputation as a völkisch sheet, what in fact had the Nazi Party acquired? In terms of circulation the *Beobachter* was small potatoes, with a press run of eleven thousand copies.[18] In its twice-weekly appearances the paper appeared with six and sometimes four or eight small pages, twelve inches high and eight inches wide, with three columns of print on each page. Like most newspapers of 1920, it carried no photographs but was able to reproduce drawings; the issue of December 12, the last before the Nazi takeover, featured a front-page cartoon in which an angry crowd of Gentiles in Munich's Marienplatz are looking up and shaking their fists at three Jews — a gigantic rabbi who is standing in a dominant position atop Munich's New Town Hall and two similarly out-of-proportion bankers in silk top hats who perch on the twin towers of the Frauenkirche, the cathedral. One banker is saying to the other, "There are getting to be fewer stupid people in Germany — we have to watch our step," while the crowd below shouts, "The people's will shall live!" Most of the columns of reportage and comment were written in a primitive sort of German, in a sense suitable to the crudity of their content: the issue of November 28 contained a front-page box in which the editors proudly announced that "one single canvasser brought us a petition with no fewer than 20,000 signatures endorsing the initiative to introduce capital punishment for usury." Beneath this the editors had the single word *"Heil!"*

The advertisers did nothing to elevate the *Beobachter*'s intellectual level. For 46 marks, readers were informed, they could buy Karl Georg Zchaetzsch's new 527-page book, *Origin and History of the Aryan Race*. "This work contains *29,500 years of Aryan history*."[19] The paper carried columns of anticommunist vituperation by some of Munich's postwar White Russian colony, many of them Alfred Rosenberg's friends, who sent the paper financial contributions as well as their prose.

On Christmas Day 1920, the paper appeared for the first time since its purchase. The new management announced, "The National Socialist German Workers' Party has, with greatest sacrifice, taken over the *Völkischer Beobachter* in order to develop it into a relentless weapon for Germanism against all hostile, un-German efforts." Whatever "sacrifice" was involved had been confined to the German army and the industrialist Grandel; the one party member who had to suffer a little was Gottfried Feder, who had lost his chance at ownership of the paper and was now asked by the party to accept a delay in his payment of 10,000 marks for his shares in the enterprise.[20]

For the moment, it was Christmas, the time, in Germany as elsewhere, for peace on earth and good will toward men. The Nazi Party's Christmas message to its readers was on the front page:

Germans!

Buy your Christmas presents at German stores, but not from Jews or in Jewish stores.[21]

CHAPTER

16

As 1921 BEGAN, Hitler threw himself into writing articles for the newly acquired *Beobachter*. He believed that speeches were far more effective than the printed word, but with the new party organ he could, twice a week, reach eleven thousand readers — more than had attended all the party's public meetings during any given month in 1920. On New Year's Day Hitler led off with "The Nationalist Idea and the Party," blaming Germany's ills on two causes: the Jews and the fact that the nation was composed of different classes that mistrusted and opposed each other. The reader was assured that the NSDAP could solve both problems.

Two mornings later the paper was out again, this time with Hitler's "Stupidity or Crime," flaying the Berlin government for its acquiescence in the terms of the Versailles Treaty — a particularly sore point with Germans that month, since the Allies were meeting among themselves in Paris to fix a new formula for German payment of reparations. The following evening Hitler used his article as the basis for a talk to a crowd of two thousand at the Kindlkeller.[1] Thus, with a newspaper, Hitler was able to enlarge and reinforce his extraordinary ability to see and exploit the propaganda possibilities of the turbulent times and conditions in which all Germans lived. Speaking of the party's propaganda activities, including the swift printing of leaflets and posters, Hitler said, "Its aim was to enable us to take a position on current questions in the form of mass meetings within twenty-four hours," and the *Beobachter* was now used for similar swift response and commentary.[2]

Despite his frantic activity, in the first month of 1921 Adolf Hitler was still an unknown in the larger world of German politics. Even the great majority of Müncheners had never heard of this busy young

Austrian racist who was living among them. With its small circulation, the *Beobachter* was reaching only a tiny percentage of the six hundred thousand residents of Munich. Hitler might fill a beer hall, but the really large crowds in Munich were to be found at the vast railroad station on Sunday morning, queuing up even before seven o'clock, knapsacks on their backs, buying tickets for trains that would take them for a day of tramping in the mountains — men in lederhosen and Tyrolean hats, women in either the full-skirted Bavarian national costume, or more modern skirts, jackets, and hiking shoes. Indeed, as Hitler rode on Munich's blue and white trolleys, or walked across the Marienplatz on clear days when a flag atop the New City Hall signaled the populace that they could climb its tower to view the Alps, he was seldom noticed as the man who could hypnotize a thousand listeners.

One of his followers said, "when I met him in the early 'twenties he was a minor provincial political agitator, a frustrated ex-serviceman, awkward in a blue serge suit. He looked like a suburban hairdresser on his day off."[3] A somewhat different but no more flattering picture came from a party member who approached Hitler on the street just after one of his speeches and found him "still perspiring, dishevelled in his dirty trench-coat, his hair plastered against his brow, his nostrils distended." Hitler, this supporter added, had an "obvious indifference to his personal appearance," but "the whole man was concentrated in his eyes, his clear, straightforward, domineering, bright blue eyes."[4] A woman who met him differed as to the shade of those eyes, but not their effect: "Hitler's eyes were startling and unforgettable — they seemed pale blue in color, were intense, unwavering, hypnotic."[5]

Aesthetically, Hitler and Munich fitted each other badly. Thin, sallow, preoccupied, Hitler slipped like a ghost through the red-cheeked families strolling with their dachshunds beneath the tall old trees of the city park known as the English Garden. Even his habits of eating and drinking in no way resembled what Thomas Mann called "the Munich of peasant sensuality and the baroque."[6] In the world's greatest beer-drinking city, Hitler would place a stein of beer beside him on the rostrum and, studiedly, take a swallow of it at some point during his speech, to show that he, too, was a Münchener. His taste was for sweeter things; often they were not sweet enough. A party member who invited Hitler to his house poured him a glass of white wine. "I was called out of the room to the telephone," the host recalled, "and as I came back caught him putting a heaping spoonful of sugar in the glass. I pretended I had not seen and he drank the concoction with evident relish."[7] This was eclipsed by the experience of the little daughters of a family Hitler was visiting, who saw him put seven spoonfuls of sugar into a cup of tea.[8]

So nondescript on Munich's streets — one follower said that he looked "like a waiter in a railway station restaurant" — Hitler suddenly came into focus when he mounted a stage to address a crowd.[9] A man attending his first Hitler speech was struck by a sudden lifelong impression of the orator's "small, pleading hands."[10] And there was the voice. One Nazi with a nearly professional knowledge of music reacted to a speech by Hitler as if he were writing a review of a recital: "A mellowness and resonance about his baritone and he could bring gutturals into play which sent a shiver down one's spine . . . subtleties of tone that were extraordinarily impressive."[11]

Always there was the audience, and always the speeches. In a sense, the chronic postwar stress and suspicion were making possible the career of this strange young fanatical anti-Semite, but the constant interaction between Hitler and his audiences was caused only in part by his selective use of each day's headlines to illustrate his preconceived views. Hitler needed rising inflation and new Allied demands, but he was also being made possible by a continuing postwar vacuum. With the exception of the monarchists and some of the clergy, in every walk of life there was a recognition that the old institutions and certainties were gone. On that point, dissimilar voices agreed, often in almost the same words. Ludendorff commented on the year 1920:

> We look into nothingness. Self-deception, empty words, the practice of trusting to others or to phantoms, lip courage, meaning vain promises for the future and weakness in the present. . . . Something else is needed.[12]

Walter Gropius, the architect whose Bauhaus in Weimar was revolutionizing contemporary design, reflected on the postwar scene:

> Today's artist lives in an era of dissolution, without guidance. He stands alone. The old forms are in ruins, the benumbed world is shaken up, the old human spirit is invalidated and in flux toward a new form. We float in space and cannot yet perceive the new order.[13]

A third of the myriad available voices was that of the writer Hermann Hesse, whose essay "The Brothers Karamazov, or the Decline of Europe" portrayed "cultural Bolshevism" in a Europe swept by "the spirit of the Karamazovs."[14] All the old verities were gone, he said: there would have to be a new good and a new evil, new values, new ethics, a new aesthetic that might entirely reevaluate what was beautiful and what was ugly.

Many German expeditions were pushing into this moral and societal terra incognita. Ever since native German efficiency had rapidly assimilated the mass mechanization of the later nineteenth century, German creative artists, philosophers, and social critics had been troubled by the resulting bureaucratized bourgeois society. There was a longing for some sort of restoration of the pre-industrial community, a glorification of the agricultural village with its communal values, even a wistful look back at the Nordic tribes hunting in the forest. Bürgerlich German society was seen as a mistaken soulless detour in the historical development of a great people. With the bloodletting of the war it seemed as if society had purged itself of its previous obligations.

In part, Hitler had his small place in Bavarian life at the beginning of 1921 because he represented a new violence and irrationality that was attractive to many Germans who would not have seen the relationship between their intellectual questing and Hitler's demagogic speeches. Professors who would not have dreamed of attending an anti-Semitic rally were nonetheless flirting with the notion of a new postwar Nietzschean man, hardened in battle and ready to deal with life in its Darwinian reality. Many German thinkers decided that the fullest life was visceral, not cerebral. Instincts, attachment to earth, the joy of the hunt, the natural comfort of preferring those of one's own tribe — all became celebrated as the values of a popularized overreaction to earlier German pedantry and rationalism. There was much talk about "listening to one's blood." The individual and collective "will" were admired in a way that was tantamount to applauding stubbornness for its own sake.

The war and its humiliating aftermath were suddenly seen as revealing certain truths. The critical faculty had been of no use in hand-to-hand combat in the trenches; who was to say that the intellect was relevant to the realities of life's biologically determined struggle? An exaggerated *Lebensphilosophie*, the idea that life itself would tell you all you needed to know about life and how it should be lived, made great strides in the German academic community.[15] Few called it anti-intellectualism, but a reputable ethnologist was studying the behavior of Stone Age men for help in ridding modern society of its corruption, while a leading political scientist concluded that German foreign policy should be based on a simple premise: Let them hate us, as long as they fear us.[16] There was a desire for Wagnerian greatness, the heroes of the Nordic sagas. At just this moment Oswald Spengler published his lengthy essay, "Pessimism?" which made this contribution to German culture:

> I shall come right out and say it — let those who wish cry out in protest: The historical significance of art and abstract thought is seriously overrated. . . . It was Nietzsche who questioned the validity of science. It is high time that we asked the same questions about art.[17]

What was wanted were leaders, heroes, men of iron: "Hardness, Roman hardness is taking over now." Spengler closed his essay with, "We Germans will never again produce a Goethe, but certainly a Caesar."[18]

Parallel to this path of intellectual vandalism there ran a wider and perhaps deeper avenue of expression. Twenty-six months after the guns stopped their slaughter on the Western Front, many men were beginning to forget what war had really been like. A certain nostalgia and sentimentality were creeping into the national memory. Those who had served in honorable terror were starting to see the war as the great comradely test of manhood, and those who had truly enjoyed it were able to convince others that killing in combat had a unique spiritual legitimacy. While many outside Germany were appreciating German cultural achievements such as the recently released film *The Cabinet of Doctor Caligari,* or reading about the newly opened astrophysical institute at Potsdam known as the Einstein Tower, the German public was responding strongly to a book called *Storm of Steel.* It was an astonishing literary debut, of the sort calculated to make an educated humane reader despair, for it was brilliantly written, and it glorified war. The gifted young author was Ernst Jünger, an officer from Prussia who was still serving happily in the Reichswehr. In fact, Jünger had not always loved war. As an idealistic young volunteer he had been nauseated by the sight of blood, and on a beautiful April day in 1915 the nineteen-year-old lieutenant wrote in his diary:

> Surely this day that God has given
> Was meant for better uses than to kill.[19]

Jünger may have been one of those sensitive men who must throw themselves into the violence or go mad; in any case, in the next two years he was wounded more than fifteen times, won the Pour le Mérite, and rose to command a battalion of the special trench raiders known as Shock, or Storm, Troops. Looking back on it in *Storm of*

Steel, he wrote things like, "The overpowering desire to kill gave me wings. . . . Only the spell of primaeval instinct remained."[20] As Jünger presented it to the German public, war was not just one part of the human drama: it was the ultimate human experience, life in its most real and heightened form. It was no more unnatural than a tornado; war was inevitable, to be accepted as one must accept the weather and the seasons. Here was its product, as Jünger articulated it in a later work:

> This is the New Man, the Storm soldier, the elite of *Mitteleuropa*. A completely new race, cunning, strong, and packed with purpose. What made its appearance openly in the war will be the axis around which life will whirl faster and faster. . . . This war is not the end. It is only the call to power. It is the forge in which the world will be beaten into new shapes and new associations. New forms must be molded with blood, and power must be seized with a hard fist.[21]

Every word of that might have been said by Hitler's friend and military supporter, Captain Ernst Röhm, who was also still on active service in the Reichswehr, or by Hitler himself. As for patriotism, Jünger required no less than this:

> A belief in the Volk and the Fatherland which with demon-like power flares up from all classes of society; everybody who feels differently must be branded with the mark of the heretic and exterminated. We cannot possibly be nationalist enough. . . . The merging of all Germans into the great empire of a hundred millions which the future will bring — that is an aim for which it is worth while to die and to beat down all opposition.[22]

There were of course other German reactions — artists such as George Grosz and Otto Dix were savage in their satirization of Prussian militarists and devastating in their renderings of mutilated veterans, while in Munich itself Bertolt Brecht was writing *Drums in the Night*, a play whose returning-veteran protagonist indicts society for transforming him into a killer. Millions of Germans simply put the recent horror out of their minds and went about their business and pleasure.

The left took a pacifist stance, but in other countries, too, there were versions of Jünger's response to war: Marinetti and some of the Italian Futurists were claiming that life was not truly comprehensible to any artist who had not served at the front. "We want to sing the love of danger," their manifesto declared.[23] In England, where a constant sobering note was supplied by the casualty lists from the guerrilla warfare in Ireland, even such an eminently civilized man as Maurice Baring felt compelled to say a good word for mortal combat. A member of one of England's richest banking families, this perceptive writer had at the age of forty-one volunteered for the Royal Flying Corps and spent the entire war in France as an able and compassionate staff officer who watched innumerable young pilots and gunners climb into planes that failed to return. As 1921 began he was working on his book *The Puppet Show of Memory,* in which he stated, "War is to man what motherhood is to woman — a burden, a source of untold suffering, and yet a glory."[24]

All these valedictorians might well have listened in respectful silence to a voice beyond the grave. It belonged, interestingly enough, to Ludendorff's stepson Franz, as brave a soldier as any. The teen-age graduate of the harsh elite military school at Gross Lichterfelde had reached the Western Front with the first regiments in the summer of 1914, and by mid-September was lying in a hospital with his head full of grenade fragments. Marked unfit for further infantry service, he had asked for his stepfather's assistance in being accepted for pilot training and had survived for close to two years as a fighter pilot, flying on both the Eastern and Western fronts before being shot down in a dogfight with a British plane over the English Channel in September of 1917. His body was washed up on the Dutch coast weeks later; in the meantime, his mother had ample time to read and reread this, in one of his last letters home:

> Mother, you can't imagine what a heavenly feeling it is when all the day's fighting is successfully over, to lie in bed and say to oneself before going to sleep, "Thank God! you have another 12 hours to live."[25]

Mothers were still grieving over a Franz or Johann or Willi, but Germany was starting a classic process of the vanquished, earlier exemplified in the American South: having lost the war in the field, it was imperative for the defeated to extract meaning from the disaster by celebrating and enshrining the valor of those who fought and fell. The victors, too, had their cemeteries and monuments, but only in Germany were there great crowds turning out as the drums beat and the long columns marched in the parades of the right-wing veterans' organization known as the Stahlhelm, the Steel Helmet. While the Allies also had their memorial services, and the French tried ceaselessly to make certain that the German giant would remain prostrate, only in

Germany did the sound of drums bring out people on whose faces was the vengeful expression of those who felt they had unfinished business.

II

The year 1921 was scarcely under way before it became apparent that Hitler and the Nazi Party were redefining themselves. Both were moving from aggressive statements to aggressive action. Thus far, Hitler and the party had claimed only an absolute right to conduct their meetings as they pleased, barring Jews, ejecting hecklers, and criticizing reporters from the non-völkisch newspapers — "He also denounced the press," an account noted, saying that Hitler had commented that "at the last meeting one of those dirty journalists wrote everything down."[26] Now, "to wild, sustained applause," Hitler told a crowd of two thousand in the Kindlkeller that in the future the National Socialist movement in Munich would "ruthlessly prevent — by force, if necessary — all meetings and lectures intended to have an undermining effect on our already sick fellow Germans."[27]

What Hitler and the more militant wing of the party meant by this soon became clear. The Munich theatergoing public was flocking to see one of the erotic comedies of manners written by the Austrian Jewish playwright Arthur Schnitzler, whose work vividly depicted extramarital affairs in the frothy Vienna of his youth. A sizable group of Nazi men bought tickets for a performance. Soon after the play began, they stood up in their scattered locations throughout the theater and started shouting, keeping it up until the management rang down the curtain and the house emptied. When the play's producers sought substantial police protection to prevent a recurrence of the incident, the police ordered the play closed, stating:

> The police are not in the position, without neglecting more important tasks, to place such a large contingent at the constant disposal of the business directors [of the theater], in order to insure the undisturbed performance of a play that mocks all healthy sensitivities of the people, and that therefore has rightly awakened heavy protests in wide circles.[28]

The implications of this victory were not lost on the Nazis, who soon discovered that even the threat of picketing outside a controversial play would serve the Munich police as a pretext for closing down, in the guise of preventing riots, a production that police officials disliked. This new de facto right-wing censorship was instantly apparent to the creative artists of Schwabing, a district once second only to the Left Bank of Paris as a center of artistic ferment and free expression. Bertolt Brecht would in time decide that Munich was no place for a playwright, and leave for Berlin.

The muscular Nazis who were taking their fight into new arenas were no random assortment of the rank and file. "As far back as the middle of the summer of 1920," Hitler said, "the organization of the monitor troop took shape, little by little."[29] During the autumn of 1920, the groups of beer hall bouncers known as Ordnertruppen had been reorganized under the cover name Sports Section, *Sportabteilung*, referred to by the initials SA. They were led by Emil Maurice, one of Hitler's circle who was a watchmaker by trade and a wartime and Freikorps veteran. Though there was no money to buy distinctive uniforms, many of these brawlers wore their wartime grey; the left arm of every man displayed the red, white, and black swastika armband. Under the tutelage of some of their greatly experienced members, they were learning to march and maneuver in squads and larger units. Many carried concealed knives, brass knuckles, blackjacks, and pistols.

Hitler was also going on the offensive, in less physical form. In the pages of the *Völkischer Beobachter* he again attacked Otto Ballerstedt, the leading advocate of Bavarian secession, and Ballerstedt promptly brought charges of criminal defamation.[30] Hitler appeared in court at the end of January and repeated all his charges, calling Ballerstedt's Bavarian Bund "raving separatists" who were "breaking up and destroying the Reich . . . following the same goal that the French have followed for three hundred years." The court reporter noted that Hitler went on to say that the Nazi Party was "rejecting, for the present, all monarchies, and was also opposed to all dictatorship by force, but that of course it would prefer a Ludendorff dictatorship" in contrast to anything Ballerstedt might have to offer.[31] Hitler's "testimony" turned into a passionate speech lasting two and a half hours, during which he set forth his views and the program of the NSDAP. Unlike his beer hall speeches, his remarks were received in silence by the crowd in the courtroom, until, as the *Münchener Post* reported, "when Herr Hitler explained with unnecessary vocal exertion that his gatherings always proceeded in completely orderly form, he was rewarded with loud laughter."[32]

The court appearance was something of a propaganda victory for Hitler and the party, but Hitler had done much of the court's work for it by slandering Ballerstedt while under oath on the witness stand; at the end of a three-day hearing, Hitler was pronounced guilty, and sentenced to serve a prison term of one hundred days, or pay a fine of 1,000 marks. Hitler chose the latter; where he got the money was never known.

In the meantime, the Nazi Party held its first general membership meeting on January 21, 1921. Among other actions voted on by the 411 members who attended was the adoption of this resolution: "A woman can never be admitted into the leadership of the party and into the executive committee."[33] With one stroke, the party added male domination to the redefinition that now included a small private armed force, the SA, and Hitler's call for physical attacks on gatherings and events that were unacceptable to the Nazis. The decision to restrict women to a minor and subservient role came at a time when one of every seven members was a woman, and women were donating more money per capita than were the men.[34] Frau Andrea Ellendt, a German who spent most of her time in Mexico, had recently addressed a crowd of 350 at a party meeting in the Mathildensaal, resulting in immediate applications for membership by twelve of her listeners.[35]

Nonetheless, the policy was certainly in keeping with the views of Adolf Hitler, who might smile at the ladies and awkwardly kiss a few hands, but who had spoken to August Kubizek about "the senselessness of women studying."[36] Hitler knew how to appeal to the housewives in his audience, but, while wanting them as supporters, he was to say of the party's view of their role in life, "Our aims encourage women to marry and stay home."[37] Of Woman, generically, he said, "Her intellect is of no great consequence."[38]

It was becoming evident that Hitler and his militant faction within the party wanted the masses to support unquestioningly a "movement" — a self-sanctioned, male-dominated, weapons-bearing crusade that had no relation to the political parties of the past. Just as Hitler had previously tried to destroy the essentially democratic governance of the party, replacing all debate and voting by a three-man action committee, so he wanted political carte blanche from a public that he could not trust to make the judgments and decisions that he believed to be necessary.

As the two-day party meeting was adjourning, having again elected Anton Drexler as first chairman, with Hitler still not gaining a place in the six-man Vorstand, the Allies announced the results of their meeting in Paris concerning German reparations. Scrapping a more reasonable formula for payments that had been worked out in a meeting with the Germans at Brussels in December, the Allies unilaterally set forth a staggering schedule of sums that Germany was to continue paying until 1963. The total came to 216 billion gold marks. In addition to the fixed sums for annual payments, Germany was to give the Allies 12 percent of her exports for forty-two years. An American historian, aware of the food shortages that caused riots throughout Germany in early 1921, characterized the entire scheme as "palpably impossible."[39]

Indignation about the increased demands swept Germany. In Munich a coalition of völkisch organizations wanted to organize a huge protest meeting, but Hitler soon became aware of what he called "hesitation and delay in carrying out decisions that had been taken. First there was talk of a demonstration on the Königsplatz, but this was abandoned for fear that it would be broken up by the Reds." Two more sites were discussed, but days passed, "and the action committee could not make up its mind to set a definite date."[40] Twice more, on successive days, Hitler pressed for an answer as to when and where this great völkisch gathering was to take place. On Wednesday, February 2, he received a reply.

> The answer was again indefinite and evasive; I was told that they "intended" to call a demonstration for the following Wednesday.[41]
> With this my patience was at an end, and I decided to carry out the demonstration of protest on my own. . . . I dictated the poster to a typist in ten minutes and at the same time had the Zirkus Krone rented for the following day.[42]

That was audacity indeed; the Zirkus Krone was the largest auditorium in Munich, capable of seating an audience of six thousand. The party had never drawn an audience greater than thirty-five hundred for any gathering, and even those crowds had come as the result of substantial advance publicity. Now Hitler proposed to attract six thousand or more, on a winter's night, with twenty-four hours' notice. There was, first, the danger that a light attendance would be seen as a significant party failure — Hitler said, "A thousand persons made the Hofbräuhaus seem very well filled, while they were simply swallowed up by the Zirkus Krone" — and there was also the possibility that such a large hall could offer Ballerstedt's vindictive followers, as well as newly resurgent leftist opponents who were sometimes armed, a better opportunity to break up the meeting.[43] "Any failure," Hitler stated, "could throw us back for a long time to come."[44] In fact, a failure like this, which could be attributed entirely to Hitler's impulsive grandiose act, would have been welcomed by Drexler and the party's old guard, whose opposition to their firebrand propaganda chief was steadily hardening.

Hitler made his rash decision at noon on Wednesday; on Thursday morning, with less than twelve hours until the eight o'clock "mass meeting," some posters were up around the city, but Hitler was looking out at rain that seemed destined to turn to snow by evening: "The fear seemed founded that under such circumstances many people would prefer to stay home, instead of hurrying through the rain and snow to a meeting at which there might possibly be murder and homicide."[45] He dictated the text for a printing of twenty thousand leaflets advertising the meeting, but was told that they could not come off the press until afternoon.[46] By the time they were ready, Hitler had hired two trucks; they "were swathed in as much *red* as possible, some of our banners were attached to them, and each truck was manned with fifteen or twenty party comrades; the order was given to drive through as many streets as possible, throwing out leaflets."[47]

Prior to this raw, wet afternoon, it was only the Marxists who used red-draped trucks to go though the city, shouting their slogans. The bourgeoisie looked at these Nazi propaganda trucks, Hitler said, and "thought of a revival of the Spartacist revolution: they were not able to conceive that there could be wide differences between Red and Red. The Reds, who saw things a little more clearly, were beside themselves with fury at this trespass on their domains."[48] In the working-class sections of Munich, Hitler said, "numerous clenched fists arose" as the Nazi trucks cruised past, scattering their leaflets.[49]

At the huge auditorium, only fifty or sixty of the party's organized strong-arm men had shown up by early evening, but there was no opposition to worry about, no crowd to watch or control; the hall was empty. It was snowing; evidently even the most ardent völkisch adherents did not feel like lining up at the box office to pay one mark apiece to protest the Allied demands on Germany.

The meeting was set for eight. "At seven in the evening the Zirkus was not yet well filled. I was kept informed by telephone every ten minutes, and I personally was rather worried; for at seven or a quarter after seven the other halls had usually been already half filled, sometimes even filled."[50] If the crowds were staying away, it was not because of any blandness in the advertising. Hitler's topic was "Future or Ruin," which Germans understood meant a future for them or ruin at the hands of the Allies. In the text of the poster, England was castigated as a colonial power that "with methodical diabolism hunts Ireland's people to death" and exploited India's masses, while France dragged Africans to European trenches to die as soldier-serfs, using the survivors to enforce a cruel occupation of the Rhineland: "Who is so crazy as to believe that from slave drivers, anything but slavery can be expected?" The public was urged to protest to gain at least one thing, "the respect which is denied him who kisses the whip that beats him."[51]

At seven-thirty the telephone call from the Zirkus was much more optimistic, and "at a quarter to eight word came that the hall was three-quarters full and that large crowds were standing outside the box office windows."[52]

Hitler arrived in front of the Zirkus at two minutes past eight. There was still a crowd in front of the building, many of them Hitler's opponents. Others were simply curious to see what might unfold; some were afraid to enter an arena where there might be violence.

A year earlier, the conservatives in the party had thought Hitler mad when he rented the Festival Hall of the Höfbrauhaus for the party's first large public meeting. Now, he had a greater experience in the far larger Zirkus Krone:

> As I entered the mighty hall, the same joy seized me as a year
> previous in the first meeting at the Munich Hofbräuhaus Fest-
> saal. But only after I had pushed my way through the wall of peo-
> ple and had reached the high stage, did I see the success in all
> its magnitude. Like a gigantic shell the hall lay before my eyes,
> filled with thousands and thousands of people.[53]

Even the standing room areas were "black with people." Sixty-five hundred people had come out on this bitter February night; certain groups did not have to pay admission, such as the monitor detachments, wounded veterans, and those who could prove that they were students, but fifty-six hundred of the audience had spent money to hear what Adolf Hitler had to say.

> I began to speak, and spoke for about two and a half hours;
> and my feeling told me after the first half hour that the meeting
> would be a great success. Contact with all these thousands of in-
> dividuals had been established. After the first hour the applause
> began to interrupt me in greater and greater spontaneous out-
> bursts, ebbing off after two hours into the solemn silence. . . .
> Then you could hardly hear more than the breathing of this
> gigantic crowd, and only when I had spoken the last word did

the applause roar forth to find its consummation in a passionate singing of the *Deutschland* song.

Sweating, still breathing hard, Hitler "stayed to watch as the gigantic hall slowly began to empty and for nearly twenty minutes a colossal ocean of human beings forced its way through the enormous center exit."[54] Then he left to go home by himself to his dingy lodgings. His appraisal of what had happened on this night was accurate: "We had for the first time overstepped the bounds of an ordinary party of the day. We could no longer be ignored."[55] Eager to prove that the success of the party's first mass meeting was not a fluke, Hitler scheduled two more mass meetings at the Zirkus Krone in the next weeks, and both were resounding successes. Driven to despair by Germany's plight, genuinely distinguished individuals began to appear in the audience, not committing themselves to the party, but listening nonetheless. Professor Max von Gruber, president of the Bavarian Academy of Sciences, was among those who went and listened carefully. He left the Zirkus Krone perturbed by Hitler and unconvinced about much of what he had said, but fascinated by both the orator and the audience.

"He controlled the many-thousand-headed audience completely," Gruber wrote of the evening. "I found it strange that those groups of the population who were completely enamored of democratic and socialist dreams a year or a year and a half ago, were now again enthusiastic about nationalism, and sang 'Deutschland über alles' and 'Die Wacht am Rhein.'" In terms of substance, "what Hitler said about the November Revolution, the war, enemies, the importance of the mother-country, were to the point." On the negative side, "what he said about shaking off the hostile yoke was quite illusory, and his economic program was childish." Gruber's conclusion about Hitler was that he would "create immense damage through senseless behavior."[56]

CHAPTER

17

WITH SPRING'S APPROACH, Hitler was immersed in two kinds of mounting tension. The hostile crescendo between the Allies and Germany provided material for his speeches and *Beobachter* articles, but he was also entering a crucial phase of his private war with the party's old guard.

On the larger scene, far from Munich, the European nations that had been allied against Germany during the war left nothing to be desired in their Hitler-cast role as villains. Even the bit parts were brilliantly played: when the Allies asked the Germans to meet with them in London to negotiate further on reparations, the first official German delegation to go to England since the war found that the porters would not carry their luggage.[1] Offstage, and never to be outdone in this type of drama, the French added a neat touch in the cemeteries in which German soldiers lay buried in French soil. The crosses marking the German dead were painted black, while the French dead lay beneath white markers.

In London, everything went swiftly from bad to worse. Dr. Walter Simons, the German foreign minister, unveiled the German counteroffer to the Allied demand for payments totaling 216 billion gold marks. The German scheme had merits, because it was based on present value, excluding the interest rates the Allies expected to be paid for forty-two years, and also deducted the value of cash, coal, timber, mines, and so forth, that had already been handed over to the Allies. However, the German counteroffer of only 30 billion gold marks, arrived at after devious deductions like the worth of the captured German battle fleet that German sailors had succeeded in scuttling under the noses of the British guard at Scapa Flow in 1919, convinced the Allies that the Germans would negotiate seriously only if force were applied.[2] On March 8, 1921, in an illegal occupation nowhere sanctioned by the Versailles Treaty, French, British, and Belgian troops marched into the Rhine ports of Düsseldorf, Duisburg, and Ruhrort.

The Germans left London, and on March 23 announced their inability to raise the smaller sums that were required to be paid under the treaty by May 1. On the following day, the British Reparation Recovery Act imposed a duty of 50 percent on German goods, thereby halting German exports to Britain and its empire. Germany was in an uproar — in Munich, Hitler had filled the Zirkus Krone on March 6 as he urged rejection of the Allied demands in a speech, "London and Us" — but, as with the original acceptance of the Versailles Treaty, someone had to knuckle under to an Allied pressure that could have been increased to the point that it would literally dismember the country.

In a desperate move, the German foreign minister had appealed to the new American president, Warren G. Harding, who had succeeded Woodrow Wilson on March 4. The United States was, step by step, disassociating itself from the policies and actions of its wartime allies, and Foreign Minister Simons asked President Harding to act as referee in the entire reparations question, assuring him in advance that Germany would unconditionally accept any settlement he set forth.[3]

From the German viewpoint, this was a stratagem that appeared to have at least some possibilities. France, Belgium, and Britain were all deeply in debt to the United States as a result of wartime loans and could not afford to disregard American financial recommendations. American leverage also included the presence of its occupation forces on the Rhine; although small in number, these troops represented a politically significant commitment that the other victors did not wish to see ended.

Among the nations that had defeated Germany, the United States was in a unique and delicate position. Because the Congress had refused to ratify the Versailles Treaty, the nation was not a signatory to the postwar settlement, but shared in many of the rights and arrangements stipulated in its provisions. Until this time, having signed no peace treaty between them, the United States and Germany were still technically at war, with shooting suspended under the Armistice agreement of November 11, 1918 — an ironic situation, considering the good relations existing between American soldiers and German civilians in the American zone on the Rhine, and the strong sentiment for isolationism in the United States.[5] Just at the time the French, British, and Belgians were applying the financial screws to Germany, the United States was preparing its own separate peace treaty, to be signed at Berlin later in the year.

President Harding had taken the German appeal for economic clemency under consideration, saying that he would not act as referee, but would send on to the Allies anything new and appropriate the Germans might wish to offer. Such a transmittal by the American president would inevitably have carried some weight with his debtors, but it quickly became apparent that the Germans were simply rehashing their previous bargaining positions. On May 3 the United States announced that in its view the German proposals added nothing that would further negotiations and that there was no point in transmitting them. The United States was still in general accord with its European allies on the subject of reparations.[6]

That was the end of the weak government of Chancellor Konstantin Fehrenbach. He and his cabinet resigned on the following day, and on May 11 the new government formed by Joseph Wirth of the Center Party informed the Allies that it would accept the scaled-down demand of 132 billion gold marks contained in what became known as the London Ultimatum.

An integral part of these negotiations was that their terms were enumerated in gold marks, rather than in the unstable German paper currency of 1921. The gold marks that Germany was agreeing to pay were not gold. They were what one historian called "an abstraction," an effort to create a unit of constant value in the postwar inflationary situation.[7] The Allies had decided that a gold mark was a prewar German paper mark, which in the exchange rates of early 1914 had been quoted at four to the dollar.

The nonexistent gold mark, then, was in effect an American quarter. To furnish the Allies with verifiable equivalencies, Germany had to operate in terms of the dollar, which was then backed by gold. With the actual 1921 German paper mark fluctuating between forty and sixty to the dollar, the Allied demand in May for an immediate good-faith payment of a billion gold marks meant that Germany had to buy 250 million American dollars on the foreign currency exchanges. To do this at the time it was demanded, the German government had to come up with 15 billion paper marks, which it did not have on hand. Complying with the Allies' condition that the payment be made within twenty-five days, the Germans started printing great numbers of new marks, and this further weakened the German currency.[8] Allied critics were to accuse Germany of creating domestic inflation to pay off her international debts with ever-cheaper marks, and the Germans were to say that they were forced to take special measures because of Allied demands that were impossible to fulfill in any other way. This was only a part of the German inflationary spiral, but it played its role in destabilizing the mark.

Running parallel to the reparations crisis were two others. In late March there was an armed communist uprising in central Germany, which was smashed by a combination of Reichswehr artillery and efficient Prussian state police units. Transcending that, however, was the profound crisis in the eastern German province of Upper Silesia, which was also home to a large number of Poles. The postwar fighting between the Freikorps and Polish volunteers in this contested area had resulted in Allied occupation of the region in February 1920. Now, on March 21, 1921, the long-awaited plebiscite mandated by the Versailles Treaty was held to determine the province's future, and 717,122 voted to remain German, while 483,514 voted to join Poland. The immediate result was that Germans felt the entire province should remain within the borders of Germany, while the Allies were confronted with the problem of trying to draw a boundary, also required by the treaty, that reflected the majority vote in each of the province's districts. On May 1, the Allied Plebiscite Commission announced that it would soon fix the boundary line that would run through this area of mixed population, and two days later Polish volunteer forces poured into Upper Silesia in an effort to take by force what they had not been able to win at the ballot box.

Although the Polish move was a flagrant affront to the Allied occupation, the French regiments remained in their barracks, demonstrating the French hope that Upper Silesia could in some way be detached from Germany. To forestall any German attempt to send in the Reichswehr, the French repeated their favorite threat of occupying the Ruhr. Checkmated on the official level, but unwilling to see Upper Silesia become Polish by default, the German government once again looked the other way as the banned Freikorps units came to life and resumed their bloody campaigning on the Polish border.[9]

It was against this volcanic background that Hitler fought his own smaller war with the old guard of the NSDAP. Stung by criticism from party members who said that he was irresponsibly inciting the public to violence, Hitler struck back with this letter to the executive committee:

Registered Party member Adolf Hitler No. 55 herewith requests that his membership be expunged from the records.
I have neither violated the statutes nor did I make the remark
that "the masses want to see — and should see — blood."
Request acknowledgment.

Adolf Hitler[10]

In fact, Hitler's correspondence, and the nearly verbatim police
reports of his speeches, revealed no use of the statement he was accused of making, although it was entirely in keeping with his willingness to use violence. Faced once again with the prospect of losing their
ever-more-prominent orator, Chairman Drexler and his pre-Hitler
colleagues drew back from a final rupture and Hitler continued to
have a virtually free hand as propaganda chief. In other areas, however,
the old guard had no intention of relinquishing its very real constitutional power within the party. Although many in the NSDAP looked
to Hitler as their real leader, the policymaking function was still vested
in the executive committee.

Over Hitler's vehement opposition, at the close of March Drexler
went to the German city of Zeitz, in Thuringia, for a meeting of the
same Pan-German organizations that Hitler had observed, with Drexler, in Salzburg the previous summer.[11] While Hitler fumed in Munich, Drexler added the NSDAP's endorsement to a plan to organize
a unified nationalist party, representing German, Austrian, and Czech
National Socialists. In addition to the possibility of submerging the
Munich Nazis in a larger organization in which Hitler would have less
power, the resolution specifically provided that Berlin be the seat of
the new united party. This was putting salt in Hitler's wounds, for his
constituency was entirely Bavarian, and he was quite correct in arguing
that Bavaria offered the most hospitable climate for militant right-wing
activity.

On April 14, 1921, two weeks after Drexler got back from Zeitz,
the party's executive committee met in Munich with representatives
of the DSP to begin another round of negotiations for a merger with
this group that had such a similar platform and objectives.[12] The DSP's
postwar success was in a sense a repudiation of Hitler: with no one
to match him as an orator and propagandist, the DSP had nonetheless experienced a comparable growth, giving ammunition to those
who wished to believe that it was the appeal of nationalist-racist ideas
that drew new members, rather than the performance of a particular
speaker. In the April 14 negotiations, Drexler and his committee indicated a willingness to establish the headquarters of the merged party

in Berlin. Although there were logical reasons for establishing any political headquarters in the city that was the seat of the national government, it was probable that Drexler and the executive committee once again wished to detach Hitler from his Bavarian power base.

This was too much for Hitler. He appeared before the executive committee and entered the talks, opposing the merger with the full force of his personality. For the moment he forestalled a marriage that for months had been considered by members of both parties. Hitler's true frame of mind was hard to fathom; while it was blindingly clear that he wished the Nazi Party to remain independent and based in Munich, and equally clear that he would tolerate no criticism or infringement of his propaganda leadership, there was some question as to whether he really wanted to wrest the position of first chairman from Anton Drexler. Some of the executive committee members felt that Hitler was so immersed in his speechmaking and his articles for the *Beobachter* that, when it came to the less glamorous realities of running a political party, he regarded himself as "above and beyond the situation."[13] The committee members later claimed that they had on several occasions offered Hitler some approximation of the three-man action committee he had long wished for, and that he had declined to serve as its chairman, a position that would have put all power in his hands.[14]

Drexler's mind-set in this spring of 1921 seemed equally ambiguous. While using his position to negotiate on behalf of the party, taking positions that Drexler knew infuriated Hitler, he wrote, in answer to a letter from Gottfried Feder, "Every revolutionary movement must have its dictatorial head, and for that reason I consider that our Hitler is the most suitable one for our movement, without me having to be shoved into the background."[15] Hitler was at about the same time privately saying that Drexler was "without character," "a son of a bitch [*gemeiner Hund*]," and "an idiot."[16]

As for the party rank and file, many of them seemed content with the current balance, in which Drexler's name appeared as "Summoner for the Party" on Hitler-written posters advertising speeches by Hitler. Drexler would preside over the meeting, opening and closing it, and Hitler would carry the audience into near hysteria. In both the *Beobachter* and in party memoranda, the term Führer was used to refer to Drexler as well as Hitler, and both were sometimes referred to jointly as *unsere Führer*, our leaders.[17]

*

While the friction between Hitler and the old guard continued to build, he was adding dimensions to his persona. Julius Streicher of Nuremberg, the DSP's leading orator, reported after a trip to Munich that Hitler was seen being driven through the city "with smoking ladies" — fast company for 1921, when it was considered scandalous for a woman to smoke in public.[18] Although Hitler retained most of his spartan bachelor habits, he was not averse to an occasional evening of relative elegance, during which he was never paired off with any one woman, but was frequently surrounded by female admirers.

He was becoming known in some circles as "the King of Munich," a title he showed no inclination to disavow. For some time he had been carrying a pistol, not without reason, and to the double-breasted military raincoat given him by Dietrich Eckart he added a wide-brimmed black velour hat. With a dog whip hanging from its loop over his wrist, and shoes and long woolen stockings that completed a daytime outfit with knickers, he looked like a mixture of Montparnasse artist, soldier, and Tyrolean hiker. One of Hitler's admirers had sent him a young wolfhound; Ernst Schmidt, who was living in Munich and had joined the party, said, "Hitler fell in love with him, and they became inseparable companions."[19] Hitler rented his modest lodgings as a subtenant of a Frau Reichert, but the building belonged to a Herr Erlanger, who often encountered Hitler and his dog on the steps or at the door. The dog he described as "a lovely wolfhound"; as for Hitler, "he was generally scribbling something in a notebook."[20]

Dog lover, Jew hater, sugar addict, music lover, Hitler moved through Munich like a magnet picking up metal filings, large and small. He saw Dietrich Eckart and Rudolf Hess nearly every day, and often spoke with Alfred Rosenberg. Also in his immediate entourage was Hermann Esser, the handsome young former left-wing journalist, now a party speechmaker, who was said to live off one or more women, and Hitler was frequently accompanied by the party's SA commander, Emil Maurice, whose mustache was very much like Hitler's own.

There were in addition two men who served as bodyguards. The first, Ulrich Graf, a former butcher, was a minor employee in the city council. A better-educated Nazi than Graf said that his "exquisite sturdy head had all the quality of a Hans Memling portrait."[21] With a pistol in his pocket, Graf was never more than a few feet away from Hitler during a speech, and he had heard endless applause for Hitler; to his surprise, when Graf delivered his charge safely home to his lodgings at 41 Thierchstrasse, Hitler would pace back and forth bewailing his failings as an orator. "If I could only speak!" Hitler would

shout as he turned against the dingy wall. "If I could only speak!"[22]
The other principal bodyguard was Christian Weber, who usually
carried a whip. An early party member gave this description of him:

> A former horse-trader, a typical Munich roughneck, good-
> hearted and naive, but of colossal strength and nerve in the Nazi
> cause. . . . He was an immense mountain of a man, almost
> broader than tall, an extraordinary sight when he wore leather
> shorts and a Tyrolean hat sporting a dashing chamois tuft.
> His face was adorned by an immense Kaiser moustache and he
> fancied himself as a lady-killer. But his social life consisted
> chiefly in drinking endless seidels of beer.[23]

There were moments when members of this rougher element were
carefully hidden from view. One such came on May 14, when the
Bavarian minister-president, Gustav von Kahr, for the first time received a delegation of the NSDAP leadership, including Hitler. Such
recognition from the head of Bavaria's government was in one sense
an accolade of respectability, but it was also a measure of the clutching-
at-straws mentality that was to be found even among educated Germans. Kahr's family had for generations served as ranking governmental ministers who implemented the wishes and orders of the kings
of Bavaria; a few years earlier, Kahr would have thought it inconceivable that men like the toolmaker Drexler and the failed artist and
lance corporal Hitler could become a force in Bavarian politics. Now,
in a month that had seen Germany's bitter acceptance of the London
Ultimatum, the resumption of fighting in Upper Silesia, the resignation of Chancellor Fehrenbach, and the coming to power of Joseph
Wirth, the reactionary monarchist Kahr was ready to shake the hands
of these political parvenus of the radical right. Kahr privately referred
to Hitler as the "raging Austrian," but the minister-president was
himself no paragon of constructive rectitude; defending the right,
whatever its behavior, he could come up with nothing better than,
"If there were no radical anti-national leftists there would obviously
be no need for radical right-wing nationalists."[24]

It was a strange meeting — the squat, dark Kahr, his big head
pushed forward between hunched shoulders, his small dark eyes looking through heavy, horn-rimmed glasses as his long, bony fingers
reached forward to shake the strong craftsman's hand of Anton Drexler.
Then Hitler, very polite, bowing, turning on his charm, with no indication that he and Drexler were on a collision course. Finally the
tall, beetle-browed Rudolf Hess, twenty-seven, earnest and gentle in

manner, a Nazi with whom Kahr could relax, since he came from a Bavarian family that was known to him. Sensing that his words might carry some weight with the minister-president, Hess wrote a letter to him three days after this brief formal meeting.

I personally know Herr Hitler very well, since I speak with him almost every day and since I'm very close to him emotionally. He is an unusually decent, honest character, full of deep kindness of heart, religious, a good Catholic. He has only one aim: the well-being of his country. Therefore he is sacrificing himself unselfishly, without getting a penny of profit from the movement. He lives on the money he gets for speeches he sometimes makes to other groups.

Hess went on to review Hitler's war record, and in closing said, "Your Excellency can unconditionally trust Hitler."[25]

II

In June, Hitler and Dietrich Eckart traveled to Berlin to raise money for the financially ailing *Beobachter*. They were to remain there for nearly six weeks, meeting with potential donors to the party and a variety of völkisch political figures. The trip ended with the final clash between Hitler and the party's old guard, who thought they saw the opportunity to stage a political elopement with the DSP while he was gone.

The Adolf Hitler who set off for Berlin in the early summer of 1921 was glacially frozen, in some parts of his personality and thought, while showing a skewed but expanded development of other ideas. The anti-Semitism was a granitic constant, possibly a mirror of self-hatred; the child whipped by his father courted the hatred of his enemies in his speeches, asking for their rage to strike him, and promising revenge in the same coin: "We will pour hate, burning hate into the souls of the millions of our fellow countrymen, until one day a flame of wrath flares up which will take revenge upon the corrupters of our people."[26] Hitler had his own twisted view of what constituted acceptable anti-Semitism; it was good "only if it is no longer used opportunistically by unscrupulous political candidates to get their seats, but if it is really seriously represented as the condition for the inner recovery of our people. Electoral anti-Semitism is immoral."[27]

Accompanying the incessant, obsessive anti-Semitism was Hitler's vision of future German greatness, which would require the acquisition of new lands. Hitler explained to a crowd in the Hofbräuhaus, shortly before he set off for Berlin, that Germany had in the past tried four methods of stabilizing its population and economic needs: birth control, overseas colonization, emigration, and industrial exports. All had failed: there were more Germans and less German land. The new empire must be acquired by expanding to the east, right through Poland and the other Eastern European nations, and into Russia itself.[28] The nation strong enough to do that, Hitler became convinced at this point in his thinking, had to have compulsory military service, a strong centralized government, and "abolition of the freedom of the press."[29] Although revenge against the French must not cease, the real enemy was the "Fool's Government" in Berlin, which insisted on practicing democracy: "More than ever it is our duty to instruct our people about the destructiveness of parliamentarianism."[30]

That was the mosaic of thought in Adolf Hitler's head as he arrived in Berlin. He was occasionally to refer to himself as a *Trommler*, a mere drummer, "a very small sort of Saint John" who was preparing the way for a great and yet unknown leader, but in Berlin as elsewhere his prevailing attitude appeared to be one of limitless confidence.[31] This was in no way undermined by Dietrich Eckart, who introduced him as "Germany's young Messiah" to their hostess in Berlin, Frau Helene Bechstein.[32] During Eckart's earlier years as a drama critic in Berlin, he had come to know Helene and her husband, Edwin, the rich and internationally known manufacturer of pianos, and the Bechsteins had continued to keep up with Eckart through their frequent business-related trips to Munich. Both husband and wife were enthusiastic supporters of right-wing activity, and Hitler and Eckart were now their house guests in what a mutual acquaintance called "one of those hideous great houses built in the eighteen-seventies, somewhere in the center of the city. It was all very pretentious in the manner of the Berlin *haute bourgeoisie*." The same acquaintance described Helene as "sitting there wearing diamonds as big as cherries strung around her neck and wrist."[33]

After spending a few days taking Hitler around Berlin and introducing him to various influential right-wingers, Eckart returned to Munich while Hitler stayed on in the Bechstein mansion. The King of Munich, now thirty-two, was being entertained royally, dining with such völkisch figures as Count Ernst zu Reventlow and his French wife, the former Baroness d'Allemont, who in turn introduced him to the famous Freikorps leader Walther Stennes. He also met Count

Yorck von Wartenburg, whose interest was less in anti-Semitism than in finding militant right-wing movements that could act as counter-weights to communist uprisings such as the one that had occurred in central Germany just three months earlier.

The social activity still left Hitler alone for many hours with his hostess, who felt as if she had some rare but endearing wild animal under her roof. One observer noted that these Berlin women sniffed "the smell of a barbaric wildness" about Hitler that was lacking in their own men; an acquaintance of Hitler's spoke of his "long black coat and black slouch hat, which made him look like an absolute desperado."[34] Helene Bechstein started calling him *Wölfchen*, little wolf, and thought he would make an exciting husband for her daughter Lotte, who was still living at home.[35] In the meantime, a drama instructor arrived every afternoon to give Hitler elocution lessons intended to diminish his Austrian accent and improve the delivery of his speeches.[36]

When Hitler sallied forth for meetings around the city with prospective contributors to the *Beobachter*, his principal guide was Emil Gansser, another friend of Eckart's, whose outward appearance belied his true interests. An executive with the giant electrical engineering and manufacturing firm of Siemens & Halske, Dr. Gansser was described this way by a contemporary: "He wore stiff white collars and starched shirts, always dressed in a black coat and striped trousers and was a man of some substance." When the writer of this description finally called on Gansser at home, however, he "found that behind his staid exterior he was a crackpot inventor. There were tubes and retorts and presses all over the place and the bathroom looked like a scene out of *Faust*. He was apparently making some new form of bomb no bigger than a tennis ball which would blow up a house."[37] Gansser was a passionate anti-Semite; nicknamed "Pretzel" for his main source of calories, he was, Hitler said, a man who "scented traces of plots everywhere."[38] Gansser constantly wrote letters in code to Eckart concerning his fund-raising efforts for the Nazi Party in Berlin.

One day Gansser took Hitler to the National Club, whose members were as notable for their prominence in business life as for their conservative leanings. There, and the next day at the Officers' Club in the Pariser Platz, Hitler found that these elements of the Prussian establishment were not receptive to his extremist program. "They were terrified lest people should know that they had even heard of it!" The one exception was Admiral Ludwig von Schröder, described by Hitler as "a grand old bull of a man, charged with energy!" One of the real fire-eaters of the imperial navy, retired as overage when the war began, he had been recalled to duty and raised a corps of marines that he commanded in battle: "I myself saw these marines in action for the first time at the Battle of the Somme," Hitler said in praising Schröder, "and compared with them, we felt we were the rawest of recruits."

Before the end of that afternoon at the Officers' Club, Hitler had made his first convert in the higher ranks of the navy. "Old Schröder," Hitler recalled, "the most energetic of men, that uncompromising fanatic, accepted the whole thing without further ado. . . . When I discover a man like Schröder, I grab him at once."[39]

The Berlin through which Adolf Hitler moved on his fund-raising calls for the *Beobachter* was in 1921 a place of startling contrasts, many elements of which were to be paved over by a stereotypical view of Weimar-era debauchery. There was the Berlin that was the vice capital of Europe, the Berlin of George Grosz's savage drawings and the destructive nightlife described and condemned by Stefan Zweig, but there were other Berlins. Albert Einstein and his wife lived modestly in an apartment at Hufelandstrasse 5. On one of many such occasions, it had been arranged for a boy who admired the incomparable physicist to come past, shake hands, and be given an autograph. The boy remembered it half a century later.

> Mrs. Einstein opened the door and called "Albert, an autograph!" The professor appeared — a tall man with an open face and a mane that made him look like a musician — holding a sheet of paper in his hand. He smiled kindly but disappeared right after giving me the paper. . . . The great man had written: "Goodness and a strong character are better than intelligence and learning."[40]

Amidst political strife, inflation, profound social change, and strands of unredeemable decadence, Berlin wove a brilliant cultural tapestry. George Grosz was not wrong in saying that the capital's uninspired public buildings and square miles of dingy tenements resembled a "stone-gray corpse," but this was also the world's capital of theater, the city of Max Reinhardt's new Grosses Schauspielhaus, Leopold Jessner's memorable productions in his Staatstheater, and Erwin Piscator's Political Theater.[41] It was an era of memorable Berlin performances by great actresses and entertainers: Elisabeth Bergner, Tilla

Durieux, Fritzi Massary, Trude Hesterberg, Claire Waldorf. Germany's orchestras, conductors, and soloists were the world's best, and the city was the setting for triumphal concerts, operas, and recitals.[42] This was the year in which the composer Richard Strauss said to young Paul Hindemith, "Why do you write this atonal stuff? You have talent!" — a remark that elicited the reply, "Herr Professor, you make your music and I'll make mine."[43] Hindemith's élan was equaled by that of the rising Arnold Schönberg: speaking of the twelve-tone scale, he told a student at just this time, "I have discovered something that will ensure supremacy for German music for the next hundred years."[44]

Other fields were equally yeasty. On the first day of the previous year's Kapp Putsch, a group of pioneering enthusiasts had attended the first lecture given at the newly opened Berlin Psychoanalytic Institute. Of the seven disciples to whom Freud had, in Vienna, presented Greek intaglios that were to be mounted in rings, three — Karl Abraham, Hans Sachs, and Max Eitington — now worked in Berlin.[45] At Berlin University, the Gestalt school was represented in the Department of Psychology by Wolfgang Köhler, Max Wertheimer, and Kurt Lewin.[46] In other departments at the university, the liberal historian Friedrich Meinecke was developing new methods of historiography, and Max Planck, the father of quantum studies, was continuing the research in radiation that had won him a Nobel Prize in 1918.

Among those coming forward with fresh ideas and approaches, Hermann Rorschach had nearly completed his work on the psychological test named after him, based on the interpretations that individuals give to random inkblots on paper. The art historian Max Dvořák was bridging the gap to modern art with his published study that showed its antecedents in the work of El Greco and Brueghel, and Jakob von Uexküll, the initiator of environmental studies, had just published his *Theoretical Biology*.

Away from the schools and laboratories and libraries, there was a rich blend of the arts, politics, and nightlife. At the corner of Kurfürstendamm and Joachimsthaler Strasse was the Café des Westens, around whose small white marble tables and second-floor billiard and chess tables there gathered both poor aspiring writers and artists and such luminaries as "the Salon Communists" — Grosz, a living satire in an English-cut suit and a Homburg, and Rudolf Leonhard, who wore a monocle and silk shirt and carried a rhinoceros-hide cane to defend himself against any right-wingers who might identify and attack him for his artistic representation of his leftist views.[47]

Not far from the des Westens was the Allaverdi, one of the many Russian restaurants and nightclubs started after the influx of fifty thousand White Russians who had fled the Revolution. Despite the political polarity between the management and the communist regime in Moscow, a table was reserved every night for the official Soviet representatives in Germany.

One man who dined at this table many evenings was Karl Radek, Lenin's personal envoy in Berlin. Had they been present, Hitler and his Russian-speaking anti-Semitic theoretician Alfred Rosenberg would have considered the scene proof of their prophecies: Radek, a short man with curly black hair and sideburns, was not a Russian but a Polish Jew who had ridden into Russia in the sealed railroad car with Lenin at the start of the Revolution. Here he was being waited on by refugees who were minor Russian princes, Gentiles expelled from their ancestral homeland by communism.

Behind the Allaverdi's bar was a door that opened on a circular stairway leading to a basement after-hours club. The Berlin playwright Carl Zuckmayer was sampling its champagne and pickled mushrooms and violin music late one night when he had an unexpected look at the world's greatest ballerina. A new group had just come in and seated themselves; there was whispering among a crowd that contained rich and poor, adherents of right and left, and then:

> Many of the men stood up to bow in the direction of a small
> sofa in one corner. There sat an inconspicuously dressed woman
> with a silk shawl over her head. It was Pavlova. She was ob-
> viously in no way annoyed by this classless homage. On the con-
> trary, she suddenly rose and with an expressive gesture removed
> her shawl and the jacket to her suit, under which she was wear-
> ing a sleeveless white blouse.

Waiters quickly started moving the chairs and tables into an adjoining cellar room, clearing a space so that the supreme dancer could dance, and the crowd pressed back against the racks of bottles that lined the cellar club's walls.

> Pavlova whispered briefly with the violinist, who began the
> melody of *The Dying Swan*. And for five minutes, she floated
> about that narrow space like a phantom, then with a deep bow
> of her whole body sank to the stone floor. The cheers that burst
> out seemed on the point of shattering the vaulted ceiling, but
> she silenced them with another gesture of her lovely arms,

then returned to the small sofa and her companions. Thereafter, no one looked in her direction.[48]

That was the Berlin of memorable substance, so different from the sad alleys patrolled by prostitutes of all ages and both sexes, including rouged little boys and girls. Sexually, there was something in Berlin for persons of every taste and impulse, at a price. One bordello had nothing but women who were middle-aged and older; the customers were not given an exit poll, but the assumption was that they came to satisfy longings for their mothers.[49] The Topfkeller was a nightclub that catered to middle-aged homosexuals, married men who spent their days as factory hands or clerks or small shopkeepers and ate a plain supper with their wives and children before going there. Prior to the defeat in 1918 these men would never have demonstrated their sexual predilections in public, nor would the police have allowed them to do so. A bemused observer gave this description of the activities on the dance floor:

> Anyone who has not seen the *gemütlich* fifty-year-olds, salt of
> the earth, with rounded bellies and threadbare evening clothes
> (from mother's chest), wiping the foam of Pilsener from their citi-
> zenly mustaches, asking another mustache in evening dress for
> a dance, to glide across the room in a polka, can have no con-
> ception of this daredevil transgression raised on home cooking.[50]

Berlin's specialized establishments included a bathhouse featuring black male prostitutes; later, one of its ardent devotees was Hitler's friend and supporter Captain Ernst Röhm, who moved from latent to overt homosexuality when he was seduced by the noted Freikorps commander Gerhard Rossbach. Röhm wrote a friend that "the steam-bath there is, in my opinion, the epitome of all human happiness!"[51]

It seemed as if Berlin was densely populated with homosexuals; that was not true, but the capital's postwar laissez-faire attitude gave them license to be highly visible. Brigadier General J. H. Morgan, the British representative on the Inter-Allied Military Control Commission who had been an eyewitness when the Ehrhardt Brigade fired into an unarmed crowd at the close of the Kapp Putsch, said that in the late afternoon the lobby and lounges of the Adlon Hotel attracted a different clientele from the industrialists and big black market operators and German generals in civilian clothes who frequented the place at lunch: "The smart crowd was flecked with young men with painted faces hovering and darting to and fro like dragon-flies."[52]

At the Café Mikado the American journalist and playwright Ben

Hecht noted a group of German aviators in civilian clothes, "elegant fellows, perfumed and monocled and usually full of heroin or cocaine. They made love to one another, openly kissing in the café booths."[53] There was a sedate nightclub for lesbians, the Silhouette, "where most of the women, sitting on hard benches along the walls, wore men's clothes with collar and tie; but the younger girls with them wore dresses with accentuated femininity. . . . You could see women well known in German literature, society, the theater and politics."[54] The transvestite cabarets were livelier, and frequented by tourists. A young Englishman said, "At El Dorado it really was possible to mistake some of the habitués for beautiful women until you found yourself standing beside one in the pissoir."[55]

How much of this life Hitler may have glimpsed in his weeks in Berlin is not known; he was to inveigh against Berlin as "the great Babylonian whore," but a postcard he sent to a young member of the Nazi Party local in Rosenheim contained only a reference to a visit to a military museum.[56] For Hitler, Berlin was indeed a suspect land that nevertheless contained contributors for the party, but the truth about Berlin, and Weimar Germany, lay somewhere between right and left, somewhere between the devoted family life of Albert Einstein and the remark of Thomas Mann's son Klaus, who said after a trip to Berlin, "Once we had an unsurpassed army; now we have unsurpassed perversities!"[57] Henry Pachter, then a young adult in Berlin and later a professor at the New School in New York, pointed out that the increased number of prostitutes was linked to increased poverty and inflation, and that the average Berliner never set foot in a single one of the capital's fabled nightspots. Pachter wrote:

> Berlin, for those who knew it, was four million hard-working citizens endowed with a special kind of humor, half gemütlich and half ironical, addicted to a special beer, and heirs to an inimitable language which cries out for being used in slightly off-color lyrics, in a spoof on some establishment, or in self-persiflage.[58]

From the sociologist's viewpoint, this was what to watch: not the conservative elements in society nor the cultural nihilism of the Dadaists, but the millions of individuals who were functioning in a society that was in transition. Women had the vote; they were steadily progressing through the higher levels of education and entering the professions in unprecedented numbers. Eleven million women in Germany had some kind of job outside the home, and an entirely new situation existed in the nation's offices.[59]

With added independence, and personal incomes not doled out by fathers or husbands, German women were adding to their social and sexual freedom. Middle-class girls were still expected to be virgins when they married, but they no longer entered the bridal chamber as their mothers had, unaware of the details of sexual intercourse. For increasing numbers of married and single women, birth control was an available option. Contraceptives could be bought even at neighborhood grocery stores; a popular brand had as its trademark a stork whose beak was tied shut with a ribbon and a bow.[60] Alone or in groups, women could venture into much of the entertainment and sporting world of Berlin without male escorts. Berliners were crazy for such novelties as the six-day bicycle races at the Sportspalast and the automobile races at the new Avus track. The city had gone wild for dancing: there was tea dancing, there was dancing in the evening at hotels and nightclubs, there was dancing until dawn. Everyone danced to "Avalon" and "Look for the Silver Lining." Berlin's youths were particularly fascinated by new American jazz tunes, but German bands could not keep a certain oom-pah-pah beat out of the music. A cigarette lighter was the 1921 status symbol — millions of them were sold in Germany. Berlin was decking itself out in neon lights, the first European city to do so, and single women could enter telephone bars in which each table was equipped with a telephone and a prominently displayed number that enabled men at other tables to dial and ask if they might come over.

That was the Berlin, the many Berlins, from which Adolf Hitler was suddenly recalled to Bavaria in the second week of July. Both the Hitler wing and the old guard of the party had been busy in his absence. The party's strong-arm men broke up a performance of *Dichterliebe*, a song cycle in which the poems of Heinrich Heine are set to the music of Robert Schumann. The real offense of this Munich production was that the great lyric poet and satirist Heine had been a Jew. "It is terrible," the *Beobachter* told its readers after the party's Sports Section, the SA, had done its work in the theater, "that such a Jewish piece of work, which really must have a provocative effect on wide sections of the population, is in the program of a theater." The *Beobachter* sanctimoniously concluded, "We expect of the police that they stop such provocations of the German people in order to prevent further scandals."[61]

The authorities were finally fed up; this, and further thinly veiled incitations to violence, caused the police to order the *Völkischer Beo-*

bachter to suspend publication on June 26, the ban to last a month. The Nazi response was to start publishing another, exactly similar newspaper, the *National Socialist*.[62]

While Hitler's close associates continued to act just as he would have wished them to had he been there, Drexler and his followers chose Hitler's absence as the moment to go to the altar with the DSP. By the time Hitler received a warning from his party friends in Munich, the groundwork had been laid for a meeting that was to be held on July 10 in Augsburg.[63] Although the negotiations for the Nazi Party were to be conducted by its Augsburg local, Drexler and the NSDAP executive committee in Munich saw this as the final process in the creation of a new party that was to have its headquarters either in Augsburg or Berlin, but not in Munich, where Hitler had such influence with both party members and audiences. While the executive committee genuinely believed this merger to be good for the future of National Socialism, there could be no doubt that the maneuver was also intended to reduce Hitler's power permanently. Drexler and his colleagues were entitled to empower the Augsburg members to hold such negotiations on behalf of the party.[64] It may well have been that the old guard hoped that if they stayed in Munich and let the Augsburg leaders handle the matter, they could keep men like Eckart and Esser from learning what was happening.

Hitler went straight to Augsburg and rushed to what he described as "the negotiation hall."[65] There he found a leading DSP figure, Dr. Otto Dickel, author of a book entitled *Resurrection of the West*. According to Hitler, Dickel was apparently negotiating from strength:

> He demanded not only the renunciation of our name, but an abandonment of our program, its replacement by a meaningless, bloatedly vague structure, and finally the diluting, or rather the destruction of, the organization by causing ultimate control of the movement to be placed in his hands through a presumably prearranged plan which had been worked out in detail.

Hitler argued for three hours, getting nowhere with anyone; when he stormed out, "the official representatives of the Party who were present not only did not support me, but on the contrary continued the negotiations."[66] Returning to Munich, Hitler resigned from the party the next day, July 11.[67]

Two days later Dietrich Eckart brought the news that Drexler had asked him to act as an intermediary. Hitler thought he sensed victory, and on the next day, July 14, he sent the executive committee a letter in which he dictated his terms for rejoining the party. Hitler demanded that a special meeting of party members be called within a week to deal with "the following agenda," which read in part:

1. The Party committee resigns its offices; in the election of a new committee I demand the position of First Chairman with dictatorial authority to immediately establish an action committee which will carry out the ruthless cleansing of the foreign elements that have forced their way into the Party. The action committee consists of three members.
2. Inviolable affirmation of the principle that the seat of the movement is and forever remains *Munich*. . . .
3. Any additional change in the name or the program is to be avoided for a period of six years. Members who are nevertheless active in this direction and for this purpose are to be excluded from the movement.

In a fourth point, Hitler ordered that any effort to merge with the Austrian Nazis or other Pan-German National Socialist groups "is to cease in future. For the Party there can never be a union with those who want to join with us, but rather only their annexation. Concessions on our part are totally out of the question." Hitler went on to say that the choice of participants in any future negotiations "is reserved exclusively to me," and finished his demands by stating that a forthcoming National Socialist Congress in his boyhood home of Linz "is not to be attended."

Hitler summed up with a wonderfully unconvincing disavowal:

I do not make these demands because I am greedy for power, but because recent events have more than ever convinced me that without iron leadership the Party — even without an external name change — would internally cease in a short time to be what it should be.[68]

III

Hitler had thrown his demands at the executive committee; the next day, back came what on the face of it seemed to be an abject surrender.

The committee is prepared, in acknowledgment of your tremendous knowledge, your singular dedication and selfless service to the Movement, and your rare oratorical gift, to concede to you dictatorial powers, and will be most delighted if after your re-

entry you will take over the position of First Chairman. . . .
Drexler will then remain as your coadjutor in the executive committee and, if you approve, in the same position in the action
committee. If you should consider it desirable to have him completely excluded from the Movement, the next annual meeting
would have to be consulted on the matter.[69]

A somewhat closer look at the "coadjutor" role proposed for Drexler,
in which he would serve with Hitler and one other man in the new
governing action committee, revealed some rearguard fighting, coupled with a reminder to Hitler that the party rank and file still had
the power to vote on any new arrangement. In fact, the committee
could not "concede" the dictatorial powers demanded by Hitler without a majority vote at the special meeting for which Hitler had known
that he must ask, and Hitler insisted that such a meeting be called
quickly.

The executive committee seemed to be in no hurry to call the
meeting, and a possible reason soon appeared. Three thousand copies
of a leaflet entitled "Adolf Hitler, Traitor?" were circulated around
Munich; the *Münchener Post* reprinted it.[70] The executive committee
denied all knowledge of this attack upon Hitler; much later it became
known that its author was Ernst Ehrensperger, who had worked as
Hitler's immediate subordinate in the propaganda section.[71] Whatever
assistance and encouragement Ehrensperger did or did not receive,
his leaflet was clearly intended to turn the party's members against
Hitler before they were assembled to vote him dictatorial powers.
Hitler was characterized as having "a lust for power and personal
ambition"; to an anti-Semitic audience that was predisposed to believe
in conspiracies, Hitler's new demands were portrayed as "bringing
disunion and schism into our ranks by means of shadowy people behind
him, and thus to further the interests of the Jews and their friends."[72]
The pamphlet moved on to more personal attacks:

> When asked by members what he lives on and what his former
> occupation was, he always became agitated and flew into a rage.
> . . . So his conscience cannot be clear, especially since his excess
> in relations with women, to whom he has often referred to him-
> self as "King of Munich," costs a great deal of money.[73]

It concluded:

> National Socialists! Make up your minds about such characters!
> Make no mistake. Hitler is a demagogue and relies solely on his
> talents as a speaker. He believes himself capable of leading the

German people astray, and especially of filling you up with all
kinds of tales that are anything but the truth.[74]

The war was on; Hitler and the party committee members argued
face to face, with Hitler calling them names like "weak fool" and "low
hound." Eckart retained his role as moderator.[75]

As the intramural battle raged, there was a sudden and completely
unauthorized move by Hitler, who at the time was neither a member
of the party nor empowered to speak at one of its meetings unless
invited to do so. All posters advertising Nazi Party public speeches
had NATIONAL SOCIALIST GERMAN WORKERS' PARTY as their first headline. Now one appeared on the streets of Munich that began, NA-
TIONAL SOCIALISTS, MANUAL AND WHITE COLLAR WORKERS OF MU-
NICH! It advertised a speech by Herr Adolf Hitler, "Fatherland or
Colony," to be given at the Zirkus Krone on Wednesday, July 20.
Posters proclaiming sanctioned Nazi Party meetings invariably had at
the bottom the words "Summoner: For the party management," usually followed by the name Anton Drexler. This poster simply said,
"Summoner: Hermann Esser."[76] Six thousand people, summoned by
party member Esser, who had no right to act in place of the executive
committee, came to hear embattled nonmember Adolf Hitler attack
the Berlin government for allowing Germany to become a mere colony,
exploited by Jewish-Allied interest. Within twenty-four hours the executive committee announced Hermann Esser's expulsion from the
party.[77]

Through this succession of stormy days, Hitler was pressing Drexler
for both a meeting that would confirm him as the party's dictator and
for an *Ehrenerklärung*, a public statement of apology and vindication
of Hitler's character, which was to be combined with a denunciation
of the "Traitor" pamphlet.[78] On July 25, two weeks after resigning
from the party, Hitler on his own initiative called a meeting of the
party membership to be held in the public rooms of the Sterneckerbräu, the same building in which the party had its headquarters.[79]

This was too much for Anton Drexler. He went to the police and
pointed out that Hitler had resigned from the party and could not go
around announcing and conducting party meetings. The police told
Drexler that they had no jurisdiction over such a matter, and with
that, Drexler gave up.[80] The next day's sequence of events is not clear,
but at different times Hitler both rejoined the party, receiving number
3,680, and threatened that he would "no longer regard [himself] as a
member of the Party" if his demand for a defense of his character had

not been met by 1:00 P.M. of the following day. In this final ultimatum, Hitler demanded that the vindication also be publicly endorsed by Julius Streicher, the violently anti-Semitic DSP leader.[81]

By the evening of Tuesday, July 26, Adolf Hitler started to get what he wanted, in abundance. Drexler agreed to hold a large meeting on July 29; in the meantime, a "preparatory gathering," apparently thrust on the executive committee by Hitler, began with reference to internal party strife. Soon, however, the audience was witnessing the oft-seen spectacle of two bitter enemies from within the same party publicly smiling and embracing each other, for the good of the party and themselves. Drexler had never wanted to lose Hitler, but had constantly underestimated the price that Hitler would eventually exact; for his part, Hitler, three days hence, would need to have Anton Drexler's old-guard endorsement when he went before a general membership meeting. The *Beobachter* rushed to sound the right note of harmony between Hitler, who had been calling Drexler a "son of a bitch," and Drexler, who had complained to the police about Hitler. "The unshakable unity between Hitler and Drexler was once again confirmed," the party newspaper told its readers. "Hitler spoke about the essence, basis, and goal of National Socialism and received unanimous, enthusiastic approval."[82]

The last act came at the July 29 meeting, with 544 party members present. Earlier that day Drexler had accompanied Hitler to the police, to endorse and join in Hitler's libel complaint against the *Münchener Post* for reprinting "Adolf Hitler, Traitor?"[83] Now Drexler sat near Hitler on the platform as the latter began the speech that was to precede the vote confirming him as absolute ruler of the National Socialist German Workers' Party. "Fellow Germans!" he began, in what was truly an election speech. "I was a common soldier, have never quarreled about a position, on the contrary I repeatedly refused the First Chairmanship. . . . Between me and my friend Drexler there is no difference of opinion."[84]

As always, the audience was with him. Hitler spoke with the "guttural thunder" noted by a contemporary.[85] "We will proceed ruthlessly. The salvation of Germany can be brought about only by Germans, not by parliament, but by revolution. We do not want the collapse of other parties, but we want to annex them so that we retain leadership. Whoever will not join can go."[86]

Then came the vote, which first was in the form of an amendment to the party statutes, a new measure that said the party would be run on the basis of personal authority rather than by majority rule. In that moment, the Nazi Party left behind all vestiges of democracy. Then Hitler was voted in as first chairman with dictatorial powers, 553 to 1. The sole courageous holdout was an unknown librarian named Rudolf Posch, who had joined the party not long after Hitler came to it. The payoff for Drexler's last-minute cooperation was the position of honorary chairman, for life.[87]

The next day, Adolf Hitler wrote to Julius Streicher, who had evidently written him something that Hitler considered a momentarily adequate atonement for the DSP's sin of trying to merge with the NSDAP on equal terms. Hitler thanked Streicher for his expression of "nationalist sentiments" and went on to make one of his confident and prophetic assumptions: "I am glad that in the end the German-Socialist Party will find its way into the NSDAP."

Beneath that, Hitler signed his name, and then added, for the first time: der Führer der NSDAP.[88]

CHAPTER

18

THE NEWLY DESIGNATED Führer set about putting the party's central mechanism under his direct control.[1] At last Hitler had his three-man action committee; he was its head, and named the other two members. The next tier of authority consisted of six subcommittees, dealing with matters varying from finance to propaganda. Hitler named the chairmen of five of these committees, quickly elevating his closest supporters to key positions. Hermann Esser became head of propaganda, and Dietrich Eckart was appointed as director of the *Beobachter*.

One area Hitler kept to himself: the subcommittee on investigation. This group decided which applications for party membership should be accepted or rejected, and was empowered to terminate existing memberships without explanation. It was in effect an internal unit devoted to ideological purity and personal loyalty, and the Führer personally directed and reviewed its activities.

There was another subject that needed attention: the party was choking on its paperwork. "In the summer of 1921," Hitler later said, "work in the business office had become impossible. So many people kept milling around in the narrow room that organized activity was out of the question. Everybody was in everybody else's way."[2] Hitler's solution was to hire a new business manager, Max Amann, who had been a sergeant in the headquarters company of Hitler's regiment during the war. Able, direct, and forceful, Amann had a conventional business career before him when chance brought him back into contact with Hitler at the time of the July crisis within the Nazi Party. At that moment, Amann was not a member, but Hitler spotted him then, and soon asked him to run the party's office and business affairs. Amann agreed, on condition that he be responsible only to Hitler and always have direct access to him.

In tandem with the internal organization of the party there was a quickly orchestrated effort to sell the new Führer to those members who had felt more comfortable with Drexler and the deposed old guard. Dietrich Eckart had always maintained links with the more conservative wing of the party, as was demonstrated by Drexler's choice of Eckart to act as a go-between during the July crisis. On August 4 the lead article in the *Beobachter* was "The Dishonest Trick Against Hitler." In it, Eckart reviled the anonymous persons who had distributed the pamphlet calling Hitler a traitor. Eckart spared no praise of the new leader: "In my conviction, no person anywhere can serve a cause more selflessly, more self-sacrificingly, more devotedly, and more sincerely than Hitler devotes himself to ours."[3] The new stern party line, born out of the maneuvering with the DSP, was communicated to the members in a form of indoctrination. Speaking of Hitler, Eckart said that he was "not for the joining of our party to the others, but for the joining of the other parties to our party."[4] Eckart's defense and praise of Hitler was immediately echoed in the pages of the *Beobachter* by Rudolf Hess, who five months earlier had founded a National Socialist students' group at the University of Munich, following an enthusiastically received speech by Hitler. In his article "Concerning the Anti-Hitler Flyer," Hess wrote, "Are you really blind to the fact that this man has the personality of a Führer, who alone is able to carry out the battle? Do you believe that without him the masses would jam the Zirkus Krone?"[5]

In addition to this internal propaganda campaign, Hitler's closest followers instituted face-to-face meetings with the more obscure members of the Munich party cadre in an effort to make them feel comfortable with the new dictatorial forms and procedures. Although Hitler had been voted his new and sweeping powers by 553 party members, that left another two thousand in Munich and eight hundred throughout the rest of Bavaria who had not given him a specific mandate. On August 16 anad 17, less than three weeks after the fateful vote was taken, virtually all the active party workers in Munich were assembled for intensive indoctrination. Under the Nazi organizational plan for lower-level party activity within the city, Munich remained divided into four administrative sections.

Hermann Esser spent hours with the cadre from two of these four quadrants of the city, answering their questions, reassuring them, and setting forth the efficiency and integrity of purpose that could be expected from the new *Führerprinzip*, the autocratic leadership principle. It was made clear that the days of discussion and committee voting were over. As Hitler was to enunciate it to the party as a whole, "The first chairman of a local group is appointed by the next highest leader; he is the responsible leader of the local group. All committees are subordinate to him and not, conversely, he to a committee. There are no electoral committees, but only committees for work."[6] In case anyone might doubt that the former parliamentary apparatus had been streamlined, Hitler set forth his view: "The best organization is not that which inserts the greatest, but that which inserts the smallest, intermediary apparatus between the leadership of a movement and its individual adherents."[7]

While Esser was familiarizing the workers from half of Munich with the new philosophy and procedures, Oskar Körner, the toy store owner who had been part of Hitler's shadow leadership, was working on the group representing the other two administrative sections. In his efforts he had an interesting ally. Anton Drexler reappeared as a conciliatory figure. He had obviously decided that the movement, even in an altered form, was worthy of his continued support. In a move that left little to be desired in the way of irony, Hitler had recently appointed Drexler as chairman of the subcommittee on mediation. This was analogous to putting a recently maimed lion tamer back into a cage with several ferocious beasts. On paper, Drexler's position as mediator gave him the power to call a special meeting of the entire membership if he felt Hitler was taking the party down the wrong path, but both Hitler and Drexler knew that the party's former leader was only a weakened and necessarily cooperative figure — the sole survivor of the former leadership group who could claim any influence whatsoever. In this limited role, he had also been rehabilitated as the "Summoner for the Party" on posters advertising Hitler's speeches, and he served as a symbol of continuity between the parliamentary past and the dictatorial present.

In Munich, the selling of the altered party and its new leader went smoothly; Drexler spoke in a working-class district where his word carried considerable weight, winning many of the old guard rank and file over to the new view of things, and Hitler himself spoke at two of a second series of indoctrination meetings held a week after the initial appearances by Esser, Körner, and Drexler. Thus, a month after Hitler was voted party dictator by a minority of the membership, he had won the allegiance of the entire party in Munich. The locals elsewhere in Bavaria were a different story. Hitler's instinct for what was acceptable failed him; flushed with the success of his endorsement in Munich, Hitler issued a *Rundschreiben*, a circular letter to all the party's locals. In the tone of an impatient military commander chiding his subordinate officers, Hitler stated that "local groups are urgently requested to send in overdue membership fees to the party head-quarters immediately. Based on a decision of the membership of July 29, 1921, membership fees will be 2 marks per month including 50 pfennigs press tax as of August 1. Of this amount, 20% plus the entire press tax is to be forwarded to headquarters." The dictatorial tone continued, in comments on areas that had hitherto been entirely op-tional.

> The various local groups . . . are required to advocate that
> every individual member subscribe to the *Völkischer Beobachter*.
> Local groups are required to send in to the *Völkischer Beobach-*
> *ter* announcements of all their events as well as discussions of
> the results of the events. Keep the discussions short and to the
> point![8]

The response was thunderous silence from the locals. Only a distinct change in the tone of his communications, explaining the need for mutual cooperation, began to produce a small flow of the desired money, information, and subscriptions to the *Beobachter*.

Coloring these activities, both as they pertained to Munich and more rural areas, were Hitler's vagaries. On the one hand, Hitler had created an administration designed to relieve him of any detail work, thus freeing himself to write his speeches and address and promulgate matters of policy. In practice, he capriciously involved himself in the minutiae of bureaucratic details — on one day he would be found issuing instructions about the wearing of armbands and lapel pins; on the next he would be closeted with the *Beobachter*'s printer, com-plaining about costs. Having asked for decisions on a myriad of un-related details, Hitler would appear surprised when these recommen-dations and results were brought to him, and shrug them off and refer them back to the departments which normally and logically had responsibility for them.

Two devoted followers of Hitler's, writing their reminiscences in different years and in widely separated places, used an uncanny sim-ilarity of language to describe his behavior in this regard. The first wrote:

He was hopelessly unpunctual and incapable of keeping to any sort of schedule. He walked around leading a fierce Alsatian hound named Wolf and always carried a whip with a loaded handle. Ulrich Graf, his bodyguard, followed him everywhere. He would drop in after breakfast at Amann's office and then usually call in at the *Beobachter*'s office round the corner in the Schellingstrasse, and talk away with anyone who was fortunate enough to find him there.

He never stopped talking all day, committed nothing to paper, issued no orders and was the despair of his staff.[9]

The second said:

Even on ordinary days in those times it was almost impossible to keep Hitler concentrated on one point. His quick mind would run away with the talk, or his attention would be distracted by the sudden discovery of a newspaper, and he would stop to read it avidly, or he would interrupt your carefully prepared report with a long speech as though you were an audience, emphasizing his periods with the butt of his old dog-whip.[10]

II

As part of his reorganization of the party, Hitler decided to formalize and emphasize the SA. Although the former monitor detachments were already known as the Sports Section, on August 3, Hitler created within the party structure a subcommittee for "gymnastics and sports," and decreed that the units have the official designation Gymnastics and Sports Section of the NSDAP.[11] Emil Maurice began to phase out his leadership in this area; the man Hitler named to replace him was Hans Ulrich Klintzsch, who possessed unusual credentials for a gymnastics teacher. A naval lieutenant who had served in the Ehrhardt Brigade and taken part in the Kapp Putsch, this Freikorps veteran was also a member of the Organization Consul, the secret terrorist unit formed from selected Ehrhardt veterans.

On August 14, Klintzsch addressed a recruiting appeal to the membership in the pages of the *Beobachter*.

To Our German Youth!

Fellow Party members! . . . The NSDAP has formed a Gymnastics and Sports Section within its organization. It is intended that it should join together our young party members so that as an iron unit they can place their strength at the disposal of the entire movement as a battering ram. It is to be the symbol of defense of a free people. It should serve as the protective shield for the work of spreading the message that the leaders wish to accomplish.

It was an opportune time to begin the quasi-covert recruitment for the party's expanding paramilitary arm. Previous to Hitler's definitive assumption of power within the party, some of the old guard had taken a dim view of the physical force used by the monitor detachments. Now that last inhibiting influence was gone; with Hitler's full approval, Klintzsch began instilling a more aggressive attitude into the party's self-styled gladiators. Within a month the evolving force dropped the name Sports Section, and the initials SA now stood for *Sturmabteilung*, Storm, or Attack, Section.[12] The men themselves became known as Storm Troops.

Although stress was laid on getting young recruits — the stated age limits were eighteen to twenty-three — older veterans were not only accepted but welcomed. Of the first twenty-five names on the earliest list of Storm Troopers, eight were veterans, the oldest one thirty, and two of them had been wounded.[13] At the time, a particularly great number of unaffiliated warriors were in Bavaria. During the past May, the Bavarian troops of the rejuvenated Freikorps Oberland had participated in the brilliant capture of the Annaberg in the battle against Polish volunteer forces in Upper Silesia. The day after this feat the victorious Bavarians were shocked to learn that President Ebert, using the emergency powers set forth in Article 48 of the Weimar Constitution, had issued a decree making it illegal for anyone to belong to a Freikorps organization. Although it was the Allies who had thrust this decision upon Ebert, the hardened Freikorps troops saw it as one more stab in the back by the liberal government in Berlin. While many of the Oberland troops went underground as "agricultural laborers" on great estates in Upper Silesia, a good number of embittered fighters returned to Bavaria, only to find that the more conventional paramilitary forces there were also facing an Allied crackdown. The Bavarian Civil Guard was in the process of being disbanded: near the end of July more than half their 250,000 rifles were delivered to representatives of the Allied control commission.

Many of Bavaria's freelance soldiers were to continue their activities under other guises and other names — within a few months the Freikorps Oberland was to reappear as the Bund Oberland, supposedly a

Hitler as a twenty-five-year-old World War I combat infantryman, Flanders, late 1914 (Süddeutscher Verlag Bilderdienst)

General Erich Ludendorff in early 1924, while he was being tried on charges stemming from his role in the Beer Hall Putsch. A psychiatrist who treated Ludendorff during the war said, "He had never seen a flower bloom, never heard a bird sing, never watched the sun set. I used to treat him for his soul" (National Archives).

German army soldiers guarding captured armed leftists immediately after World War I (Jill Halcomb)

"German children are starving." This 1923 poster, made from a charcoal drawing by the leftist painter Käthe Kollwitz, summed up the plight of a nation (Süddeutscher Verlag Bilderdienst).

Die Patienten werden gebeten, infolge der Kohlennot zur Heizung des Wartezimmers bei jedem Besuch ein Brikett mitzubringen.
Dr. med. Wagner

Referring to the postwar lack of fuel, the sign in a doctor's office reads, "Due to the coal shortage, patients are requested to bring a coal briquette with them to help heat the waiting room" (Süddeutscher Verlag Bilderdienst).

Anton Drexler, a machinist at the Munich railroad yards, was a cofounder of the German Workers' Party, a splinter group that Hitler joined and shaped into the Nazi Party (National Archives).

Hitler in 1921, the year he won full control of the Nazi Party (Süddeutscher Verlag Bilderdienst)

Pilot-lieutenant Rudolf Hess in 1918. After first hearing Hitler speak at a Nazi meeting in 1920, Hess ran home shouting, "The man! The man!"

This photograph of a Storm Troop company was probably taken in 1921, when these Nazi units were forming but had not yet acquired uniforms. The nattily dressed man with the wing collar, third from the left in the third row, is Alfred Rosenberg (National Archives).

A unit of the Bund Oberland, a Bavarian right-wing paramilitary group that supported the Nazis (National Archives)

fraternal patriotic society — but for the moment there was a decline in the number of organizations offering an outlet for aggressive nationalist activity. Into this vacuum came Klintzsch. The results of his recruiting appeal were immediate and obvious. The time was indeed ripe for attracting members of a human "battering ram." In September, the police broke up a meeting of one hundred Storm Troops who were training secretly at night in a Munich school building. The SA men, carrying rubber truncheons, had letters of invitation to the meeting that had been signed by Emil Maurice, who remained active during the transition that put the force under Klintzsch's command. The report of this raid brought about a debate on the Nazi Party in the Munich city council. Evidence was produced to show that the SA did intensive recruiting within the party by sending personally addressed postcards to prospective Storm Troops. One such read:

> You are asked to fall into ranks with the Sturmabteilung,
> Wednesday, September 7, 1921, at 8:00 in the evening in the
> Sterneckerbräu. Bring your armband.
>
> Klintzsch[14]

This type of independent paramilitary activity, whether engaged in by the Nazi Party or such left-wing organizations as the militant Erhard Auer Guards, was of course a form of taking the law into one's own hands. Whether of the left or right, the picketers, hecklers, and brawlers always believed themselves to be striking a blow for a better Germany. There was about to be a stunning example of the lengths to which such fervor could run.

Matthias Erzberger, the Center Party politician who had signed the Armistice agreement that ended the fighting for Germany in November of 1918, was one of those men who see things so clearly that millions of their fellow citizens hate them for it. His formidable powers of analysis were coupled with the aggressive and often tactless instincts of a self-made man who was determined to prevail. Erzberger had the courage of his convictions, but no one ever called him charismatic: meeting him at a discussion on economic matters related to the Paris Peace Conference, John Maynard Keynes noted his first impression: "fat and disgusting."[15] Peering at the world through the thick lenses of a pince-nez and wearing trousers that were two inches too long, Erzberger had unbounded faith in himself and in his God; in the eyes of the right, he was guilty of holding the horrendous notion that Germany, like other nations, might sometimes be wrong. He had been elected to the Reichstag from his native Württemberg in 1903, at the exceptionally young age of twenty-eight; within two years he became nationally known through his protracted campaign against the abuses committed by the colonial administration of Germany's African possessions.[16] He exposed everything from the inequitable monopolies held by certain German landholding interests, shipping firms, and military suppliers to specific instances of officially conducted torture and murder of natives. A devout Catholic, Erzberger was genuine in his insistence that German officials treat black Africans with brotherly love — a thought that elicited reactions ranging from bemusement to indignation in a Reichstag that largely held the view that African natives were an inferior form of human life.

By the time of the war's outbreak, in 1914, Matthias Erzberger was, at the age of thirty-eight, one of the most influential politicians in Germany. To his credit there stood real though often controversial reforms in the areas of taxation, social justice, religious tolerance, parliamentary reform, and the treatment of the Polish population in Prussian Poland. He had also spoken out against the upper-class practice of dueling with swords, which he found barbaric.

The euphoria at the outbreak of war clouded Erzberger's judgment: he drafted an important policy statement that called for immensely greedy war aims. Belgium was to become permanently part of Germany, as would the French coast of the English Channel as far as Boulogne. The French city of Belfort was to become German; a similar destiny was assigned to other industrial and mining areas of France. The Belgian Congo was to belong to Germany, along with a vast French colonial area in Africa. Poland, the Baltic countries, and the Russian Ukraine were to be puppet states of Germany and Austria. Erzberger concluded his postwar shopping list by setting forth a bill for reparations that was fully comparable with that which was in fact set before Germany by the Allies at Versailles and the subsequent economic conferences.

Unlike the more stubborn and conservative members of Germany's legislative, administrative, and military apparatus, Erzberger, by 1916, saw that his nation could hope for nothing better than a resolution of the war on the basis of something approaching prewar political and territorial realities. He unsuccessfully opposed the decision for unrestricted submarine warfare, and in 1917 was instrumental in the Reichstag adoption of a resolution which stated to the world that the German legislature had given up all hope of territorial conquests and that "the Reichstag strives for a peace of understanding and permanent reconciliation of peoples."[17] His actions led to a series of showdowns from which Ludendorff emerged as the leader of the nation. When Germany's army reached the end of its strength, as Erzberger had for some time been certain it would, he was one of many, in and out of uniform, who believed that the agony must be ended as soon as possible. This feeling led to his reluctant acceptance of the position of head of the German Armistice Commission.[18] Thus, to the relief of the generals, the German public saw not a soldier, but a civilian, signing the Armistice agreement in a railroad car at Compiègne.

Far from being the traitor later portrayed by Hitler and other right-wingers, Erzberger in his personally and internationally fateful hours in that railroad car was not engaged in betraying his nation; he was in direct contact with Field Marshal von Hindenburg during the negotiations at Compiègne. Appalled at the Allied conditions for a cease-fire, Erzberger had telegraphed army headquarters at Spa for instructions. Hindenburg had answered that a number of terms must be modified or avoided if possible, but if Marshal Foch remained inflexible, "the Armistice must be signed even if those modifications cannot be attained."[19] In three hours of tenacious early-morning bargaining with enemies who had every advantage, Erzberger was able to negotiate important concessions concerning the total numbers of weapons to be surrendered, timetables for evacuation of territory, immunity from prosecution for certain individuals, and reduction in the planned Allied zones of occupation. Only then did Erzberger carry out the military's traditional responsibility for concluding a cease-fire between opposing armies in the field.

Not one German in a hundred thousand knew of the dignified and nearly defiant statement which Erzberger read to Foch in that railroad car immediately after signing the Armistice document.

> The German delegates . . . also wish to reemphasize their view that the consummation of this armistice must throw the German people into anarchy and famine. They had a right to expect conditions which, while guaranteeing the full military security of our enemies, would at least end the suffering of non-combatant women and children.

Erzberger's final words to Marshal Foch and the Allied representatives, delivered moments after he had signed an agreement that stopped Foch from marching on to Berlin, were: "The German people, who stood steadfast against a world of enemies for fifty months, will preserve their freedom and unity no matter how great the external pressure. A nation of seventy millions can suffer, but it cannot die."

Foch had looked at the fat little man who uttered these ringing words at a moment when he and his tiny delegation were literally encircled by enemy bayonets in a forest miles within French territory, and said, "Très bien."[20] When Erzberger returned to the German Supreme Headquarters at Spa, Hindenburg congratulated him for reducing the original Allied terms, and thanked him for "extremely valuable services" to the Fatherland.

This was the man who had been the subject of endless vilification by the right. Predictably, Erzberger had gone on to urge in the Reichstag that the Versailles Treaty, harsh as its terms were, be signed in order to salvage what was left of Germany. As postwar finance minister, he became involved in a personally damaging libel suit, during the course of which he was slightly wounded in an assassination attempt, and had resigned from office in the spring of 1920. By mid-August of 1921, Erzberger was cleared of every charge of unethical financial dealings in his personal affairs, the basis of the politically motivated attacks on him. He was still a member of the Reichstag, although he had not appeared in that body since his resignation under fire as finance minister more than a year earlier. Erzberger was, objectively speaking, a man who deserved better of his countrymen than the attacks by Adolf Hitler, who at various times accused him of "diplomatic grovelling toadyism," termed him "the greatest scoundrel of all," and said that "because of him, millions of Germans ended up in servitude."[21] One line of Hitler's notes for a speech called for "physical punishment" for Erzberger; at another time Hitler demanded Erzberger's death by hanging.[22] "We find it incomprehensible," Hitler had said on the evening of February 24, 1920, when he first publicly announced the Nazi Party program, "that this gentleman is not yet sitting in prison."[23]

At just the time that Hans Ulrich Klintzsch was taking over the Nazi Party's Storm Troops, Matthias Erzberger and his wife and six-year-old daughter, Gabriele, were vacationing in Baden at Bad Griesbach, a small and simple resort in the Black Forest. Even the bitterest of his political enemies had no criticism to make of Erzberger's exemplary family life. Staying in a hotel run by Catholic nuns, Erzberger and his wife and little girl took long walks up the Kniebis road, which looped up the mountain of that name. It was a world far from the battles of the Reichstag in Berlin, or the racist beer hall oratory of

Munich. A man named Heinrich Köhler, who was also staying at the hotel on the evening of August 25, noticed Erzberger and his wife and Gabriele returning at sunset from one of their walks up the mountain.

Shortly after supper a heavy thunderstorm caused a short circuit in the hotel electricity. For a moment all was dark. But the sisters who ran the hotel quickly came with candles lighted in shining silver candlesticks. They placed them on the table, the wax began to steam, and their honey-sweet smell brought a festive mood into the room. The guests became a single large family, and many began to sing, as Germans always do when they are ashamed of their emotions. Old tunes echoed through the room while there was rain, thunder and lightning outside.

The guests were singing "Today is today," an old song, sung in part by each person in turn, when Erzberger, holding his little girl's hand, entered the dining room.

He was a man who could easily enter into simple fun, and he joined the group and sang, "Today is today" as his turn came. Then Erzberger, his small daughter, and his delicate, quiet, and proud wife . . . retired for the night.[24]

The next morning, after attending mass with his wife and child, Erzberger happily greeted his friend and Center Party colleague Karl Diez, a Reichstag deputy, who had just arrived to spend some time with him.

Accompanied by his friend, Erzberger headed off on his favorite walk on Kniebis Mountain. Diez listened as Erzberger spoke animatedly about his hopes for increasing the lot of workers under an applied philosophy that was known as Christian Solidarism. In Erzberger's view, both the capitalist employer and the communist commissar were equally guilty of robbing the worker of his freedom and dignity. The former finance minister believed that 50 percent of all corporations should be owned by the workers, their equity being built up to that amount by a gradual transfer of a percentage of the company's profits into a stock-purchasing employees' treasury.

There was a light, misty rain on the mountainside; after they had been walking for an hour, Diez and Erzberger were passed by two young men, whom they barely noticed in the midst of their conversation about social justice in the Germany of the future. At about eleven o'clock in the morning the two Reichstag deputies turned their steps back down the mountain, continuing their talk.

Suddenly the two young men who had passed them minutes earlier reappeared from the side of the road. Both pulled revolvers and each fired one shot at Erzberger, the bullets striking his chest and forehead from only six inches away. Diez thrust his umbrella at the attackers and was shot in the chest. Erzberger leapt off the road and tumbled down the steep slope. Although he came to rest thirty feet away, the assassins fired three more shots into him as he tried to crawl behind a pine tree for protection. The young murderers moved quickly to where Erzberger was lying and fired three more shots into him.

Diez lost consciousness; when he sat up after a few minutes, he saw Erzberger lying at the bottom of the slope beside the road and made his way down to confirm his conviction that his friend was dead. In the distance he could see the two killers walking down the road, toward Bad Griesbach. With blood all over the front of his body, Diez made his way back to the hotel.[25]

Although the identities of the assassins were initially known only to those who planned the murder, it was immediately apparent to all of Germany that this was the work of right-wingers, taking revenge on the man who had signed the Armistice. There had been a string of political assassinations during the thirty-four months since the war ended, but the killing of a Reichstag deputy who had held a cabinet-level position in the national government aroused the nation as no previous violence had. In Baden's ancient university seat of Heidelberg, seven thousand socialist students and workers who had gathered to protest the killing went on a rampage, smashing the windows of a right-wing newspaper and ripping insignias of the former monarchy off buildings and statues.[26] At Erzberger's burial service in Biberach, the heart of the district he had represented in the nation's legislature, there was a crowd of thirty thousand. Joseph Wirth, chancellor of Germany, gave the funeral oration, calling his friend a martyr for the humane philosophy of the Weimar Republic. Wirth expressed the hope that Erzberger's sacrifice might prove a turning point in the fight for democratic ideals and Christian principles.

On the same day, August 29, 1921, Wirth announced a presidential proclamation, based on the catch-all Article 48 of the constitution. "The present plight of our country makes it doubly necessary to take severe steps against these actions of unscrupulous or misguided Germans," Wirth said as he instituted an emergency decree empowering civil authorities to ban newspapers and restrict freedoms of speech and assembly when there was evidence of agitation that might incite the population to violent action against the government.[27] In Bavaria, Gustav von Kahr refused to accept this decree; overestimating the strength of the right in Bavaria at that moment, he refused all compromise on the matter, and was forced to resign as Bavaria's minister-president when he lost the support of his legislature's executive committee.

Despite widespread public indignation, the right felt that long-overdue justice had been done and did not hesitate to celebrate Erzberger's death. The nationalist *Oletzkoer Zeitung* said on the day after the murder: "Erzberger . . . has suffered the fate which the vast majority of patriotic Germans have long desired for him."[28]

In Munich, Hitler told a crowd in the Festival Hall of the Hofbräuhaus that Erzberger had been the nation's biggest *Judentzer,* a word meaning "a lover and supporter of Jews."[29] He went on to portray the killing as a manifestation of a nationwide völkisch uprising. In the pages of the *Beobachter*, Dietrich Eckart gave Erzberger this epitaph: "He was a bum."[30]

The trail of the killers ran right past, if not directly into, the Munich headquarters of the Nazi Party. Storm Troop commander Klintzsch was held in jail as a suspect for several weeks, as were other members of the Organization Consul. The two young killers were in fact two former army officers, Heinrich Schulz and Heinrich Tillessen. Both had served in the Ehrhardt Brigade and subsequently in the Freikorps Oberland. After killing Erzberger they returned to the Organization Consul headquarters in Munich, which was operating under the cover of the offices of the fictitious Bavarian Wood Products Company. Here they immediately received assistance from right-wing sympathizers within the Bavarian police, who issued them false passports, and, while the killers fled to Hungary, obstructed the efforts of the Baden police to find them. In Hungary, which had a right-wing regime, the assassins were arrested and then released on orders from headquarters in Budapest. The Hungarian authorities refused to extradite them for trial in Germany.[31]

Hitler's reaction to the eventual release of Klintzsch was: "Even if Klint[z]sch has been in prison for suspicion of the Erzberger killing, we did not shake him off as certain other parties would have. On the contrary: when he came back we carried him through the hall on our shoulders."[32]

III

The autumn of 1921 was to provide a counterpoint that shifted from ideas to violence, and back to ideas. In the midst of the anti-right backlash caused by Erzberger's murder, there appeared a book, *Warfare and Politics*, written by none other than General Erich Ludendorff. Spending his time mainly in seclusion, the man who was far more responsible than Erzberger for plunging Germany into misery concluded that Germany's worst enemies were Judaism, Freemasonry, and Catholicism, in that order. During the war German Jews had served, been decorated, and died in the same proportion to their numbers as had German Gentiles, but Ludendorff saw them as hostile and treacherous guests: "The Jewish people wanted to rule over the people who had admitted them . . . to castrate us as men and people, so that others with a stronger national will can rule us."[33] The ponderous Ludendorff made a perfect target for Kurt Tucholsky, the leftist writer who was the finest German master of satire since Heine. In one of his frequent articles about anti-Semitism, Tucholsky created a scene in which Ludendorff, arriving at the gates of heaven, hears a solemn voice asking him to justify his dictatorial role in prolonging a war that had cost two million German lives.

"Dear God," Ludendorff answers, "it was the Jews!"[34]

While Tucholsky and Ludendorff stood at opposite ends of the political spectrum, there were interesting shifts nearer the center. Thomas Mann, who twenty months earlier had written in his diary, "The antirevolutionary, nationalistic mood of the students is basically gratifying to me," was having second thoughts about the drift of German life.[35] Although the house of Germany's greatest living writer was within two miles of the beer halls and auditoriums in which Hitler constantly harangued his thousands, there was no indication that Mann was aware of him. Not a single reference to Hitler appreared in his diaries, letters, manuscripts, or in the reminiscences of those who recalled their conversations with Mann at this period. Nonetheless, something was causing a profound unease in the man who was writing *The Magic Mountain*. The term "fascism" was not in use among Germans when they discussed the politics of their nation. The term was known only from the Italian Fascists, the party, led by Benito Mussolini, that was using street violence in its quest for power. Now Mann applied the term to the völkisch movement. In the week that Erzberger was killed, Mann finished his essay *Goethe und Tolstoi*. He wrote:

> I do not propose to dwell upon German fascism, nor upon the circumstances, the quite comprehensible circumstances of its origin. It is enough to say that it is a racial religion, with antipathy not only for international Judaism, but also, quite expressly, for Christianity, nor do its priests behave in more friendly fashion toward the humanism of our classical literature. It is a pagan folk-religion, a Wotan cult; it is, to be invidious — and I mean to be invidious — romantic barbarism.[36]

The physical side of political struggle was about to regain center stage, with Hitler at its center. Otto Ballerstedt of the separatist Bavarian League had called a meeting of his followers for the evening of Wednesday, September 14. Hitler took Ballerstedt seriously: "As an orator, Ballerstedt was my most dangerous opponent," he later said. "What a feat it was to hold my own against him! . . . He was a devilish dialectician!"[37] Ironically, Hitler was as opposed to the Berlin government as Ballerstedt was, but Hitler's dream was of a tightly unified Germany in which National Socialism prevailed, whereas Ballerstedt wanted virtual autonomy for Bavaria, and possible confederation with Austria and Czechoslovakia.

When Ballerstedt arrived at the meeting, in the hall for which his Bavarian League was paying, he found that four of every five seats near the speakers' platform were already taken by Nazi Party members. The atmosphere was electric. A non-Nazi account of the meeting was to say that, although the front rows were dominated by Nazis and there were many other Nazis in the hall, "a large section" of the audience was there to support Ballerstedt's idea of more independence for Bavaria.[38] Kahr, Justice Minister Christian Roth, and Police Commissioner Pöhner were about to be swept out of office as a result of Kahr's ill-considered opposition to the decree of national emergency that had been issued on the day of Erzberger's funeral. With these friendly political leaders about to step down, the Nazis were particularly eager to make an effective show of force somewhere, somehow. Ballerstedt had never committed himself on the "Jewish question," and the Nazis intended to force him to make a statement concerning his view of the Jews.

When Hitler strode into Ballerstedt's meeting, the predominantly Nazi audience rose to greet him with applause. Hermann Esser had already been primed to speak. In the disingenuous words of Hitler's explanation of what then happened, given in an information sheet for the benefit of those party members who were not there, "Bowing to pressure from the numerous party members who were present, Party Member Esser rose to speak and contested in a few words Herr Ballerstedt's right to set himself up as Bavaria's protector."

As Hitler modestly described it, the arranged scenario unfolded thus:

> Then Herr Esser said that the National Socialists, who were in the vast majority, demanded that Hitler speak.
>
> Amidst tumultuous applause Herr Hitler ascended the podium to give a brief explanation. The intention was to allow the gathering to vote on the proposal to give Herr Ballerstedt three-quarters of an hour to speak, and to give Herr Hitler the same amount of time. Unfortunately Party Member Hitler's explanations were prevented by continual loud disturbances which had arisen due to the fact that individual supporters of Ballerstedt were provoking the audience, which consisted in overwhelming majority of National Socialists, by means of catcalls, etc.[39]

Someone turned out the lights in an attempt to calm the crowd, many of whom were shouting, "Hitler! Hitler!"[40] When the lights came on again, Ballerstedt was at the center of the stage; he declared that anybody who tried to disrupt the meeting would be charged with disturbing the peace. Ballerstedt was to claim that his purpose in speaking was to calm the nearly hysterical audience of two opposing parties. The Nazi Party version of what happened next was:

> Instead, he screamed out into the hall that he would call the police to deal with the opponents, and have them locked up for committing breach of the peace. With that, Herr Ballerstedt had poured oil onto the fire. Herr Ballerstedt was pushed down from the podium by the enraged crowd and shoved out of the hall.[41]

Ballerstedt had indeed been "pushed down from the podium," and it was Hitler, along with Esser and Oskar Körner, accompanied by their bodyguards, who used sticks and chairs to knock him to the floor.[42] A reporter from the *Münchner Neueste Nachrichten* wrote, "Ballerstedt received a head injury which bled badly."[43] The police arrived, and Hitler, Esser, and Körner were arrested and taken to a police station. In response to further police questioning at a later date, Hitler summed up with a pragmatic and amoral reaction: "It's all right. We got what we wanted. Ballerstedt did not speak."[44]

The police interest in Hitler went well beyond questioning him about his role in breaking up Ballerstedt's meeting. Three days after that fracas, there came the resignations of Bavaria's Minister-President Kahr, Justice Minister Roth, and Police Commissioner Pöhner. They were replaced by the more moderate Count Hugo von Lerchenfeld and a more liberal cabinet. Although certain elements of the police remained intensely sympathetic to völkisch ideas — two of the first twenty-five Storm Troops were policemen — Hitler had lost his governmental shield and was placed under closer scrutiny.[45]

The authorities were genuinely worried about some form of right-inspired uprising against Lerchenfeld's new Bavarian government. During the first half of September, Munich had seen a mass distribution of anti-Semitic leaflets and other material. The tone of the pamphlets — one of them entitled "Workers' Revolution or Jewish Dictatorship?" — struck the police as intended to bring crowds into the streets.[46] The authorities, armed with the emergency decree against such inflammatory tracts, started a search for the publishers of this literature. Coupled with that was a report made to the police that "the NSDAP was planning a demonstration for the opening of the Landtag" — the meeting of the Bavarian parliament at which Lerchenfeld would officially take office as minister-president.[47]

If more were needed to worry the police about Hitler, he soon provided it. On the day that Kahr resigned, the party issued its Circular Letter Number 5, which said that party members were to wear the swastika lapel insignia at all times, and that "Jews who take offense at this are to be dealt with immediately in a ruthless manner." To this was added, "At all gatherings of the NSDAP it is to be unconditionally seen to that entrance is forbidden to Jews."[48]

On the same day, September 17, Hitler issued the party's Communiqué Number 1. This was nominally a blast against the government in Berlin, calling its members "parliamentary parasites" and "slimy filth," but the implication was that the new Bavarian government had many of the same characteristics. Hitler closed:

> We must urge our people, not to let their fate be bartered
> away by some ambitious scoundrels, but rather to show this par-
> liamentary rabble, through street demonstrations if necessary,
> that the people . . . are not a herd of sheep. If it should be nec-
> essary, then these Berlin Asians and their depraved followers
> must be pitted against the German skull and the Bavarian fist.[49]

This was enough for the police. The communiqué threatening street demonstrations had been signed by Adolf Hitler; on September 20, he was arrested, kept overnight in jail while Lerchenfeld was installed as Bavaria's leader, and questioned at some length on the following day. Hitler claimed to have no knowledge of the distribution of the anti-Semitic pamphlets and said that he certainly had not intended to call for demonstrations in the streets against the Bavarian government, because he felt that any such overt opposition would be crushed and would mean the end of the party.[50] Released after his interrogation, Hitler promptly issued Communiqué Number 2, in which he returned to the attack with an accusation that his enemies were engaging in "depraved agitation."[51]

Unable to find enough evidence to prosecute Hitler, the police closed down the *Beobachter* until the beginning of October. Hitler's reaction, in a circular letter, was "It is now necessary for all Party members to make increased propaganda for our Party organ out of this blocking of its publication. With clever work we can succeed in gaining considerable capital for the paper."[52] Allowed to resume publication on October 1, 1921, the *Beobachter* was again shut down on October 6, this time for two articles attacking the Berlin government, one of which sarcastically and contemptuously called Joseph Wirth the "Iron Chancellor." The name by which Bismarck had been known was in such obvious contrast to Wirth's belief in fulfilling Germany's Versailles obligations that it was indeed a mockery, one which the police punished with another nine days of suspended publication for the Nazi paper.[53]

In the interplay of violence and ideas, a new voice was heard. Since 1917 the papal nuncio to Bavaria had been a bishop named Eugenio Pacelli. Aside from their innate personal conservatism, the future Pope Pius XII and Thomas Mann had little in common — one, a career Vatican diplomat; the other, a novelist born into a Lutheran merchant family in the Baltic city of Lübeck. Nonetheless, both had been watching the German scene, and on October 1 the *Bayerischer Kurier* had this quotation from Pacelli for its readers:

> The Bavarian people are peace-loving. But, just as they were seduced during the revolution by alien elements — above all, Russians — into the extremes of bolshevism, so now other non-Bavarian elements of entirely opposite persuasion have likewise thought to make Bavaria their base of operation.[54]

One such non-Bavarian was soon to write a letter that would underscore Pacelli's point. From behind the walls of his villa, the Prussian Erich Ludendorff wrote to his friend and wartime subordinate Wilhelm Breucker concerning his feelings about the Jews. His anti-Semitism, he said, was not directed against any individual Jew. "For me this is a question of race. . . . I cannot hurt a single person, only the race."[55]

CHAPTER

19

IN OCTOBER OF 1921, Germany had ample domestic political and economic problems, but now the Allies sent reeling whatever stability Chancellor Wirth had been able to achieve in the aftermath of Erzberger's assassination.

Although the Allies had succeeded in bringing to an end the fighting between the Freikorps and the Polish volunteers in Upper Silesia, Britain and France had thereafter been unable to agree on a method for dividing up this industrially rich province between Germany and Poland. Under any circumstances it would have been a most complicated situation: the plebiscite of the previous spring had shown a vote of 717,122 votes for German rule and 483,514 for affiliation with Poland. The German public had of course taken this to mean that very substantial portions of the region's mineral wealth and factories would remain in German hands once the fighting was stopped and a boundary was drawn. Many Germans had even assumed that the entire province was to be awarded to whichever nation's adherents polled the most votes. Understandable though this feeling was, the Treaty of Versailles stipulated that the border be set on the basis of the votes in each district. The tabulation showed that in 664 districts there was a German majority, while the Poles had won in 597. By the end of the summer of 1921, the Allies were deadlocked among themselves concerning the fate of Upper Silesia, and handed it over to the League of Nations to decide. On October 20, the league gave Germany the greater part of the land but awarded Poland the sections containing 80 percent of the region's factories and most of its valuable coal mines. Cities such as Königshütte and Katowice, with overwhelmingly German populations, suddenly found themselves belonging to Poland.

The complications arising from this solution were to be resolved surprisingly well in practice under a special treaty that was a milestone in the effective application of international law. In the autumn of 1921, however, Germans could not imagine that the solution might work to the benefit of both nations. As they saw it, the League of Nations, to which they were not allowed to belong, had done the Allies' dirty work for them and stolen everything that was worth having in a province that once belonged entirely to Germany. Hitler had been predicting such an outcome, and now, true to his policy of commenting on public events within twenty-four hours, on the evening of Friday, October 21, he set forth his thoughts on the Upper Silesian settlement in a speech at the Zirkus Krone. Perhaps because of the short notice, the auditorium was only half filled, but he was able to lash his audience into a frenzy as he attacked the Berlin government for supinely accepting the loss of German territory. Again, Hitler held the Jews responsible: the hastily produced poster for his speech spoke of "Upper Silesia, the Victim of the Stock Exchange Parliament." Referring to recent declines in the value of the mark, the poster also said, "Complete Bankruptcy Approaches with Gigantic Steps." The situation was summed up: "Leather straps are being cut out of our people."[1]

In the vast hall, Hitler used one of his increasingly effective oratorical techniques in putting before his audience an idea that he knew they would reject. "Upper Silesia *is* lost and *will remain* lost!" he roared.

"No!" the audience screamed. "Never!"

"If you're going to say no, then you must make it happen and make the public agitate against those who are responsible for the loss!"

Among the words the crowd now screamed was "Heil!" With the Austrian Nazis it had taken on a special nationalist and Pan-German connotation; the Nazis in Munich had only recently borrowed it as a sort of party cheer, and the police reporter's note of widespread shouts of "Heil!" on this occasion was the first time that it was mentioned in any accounts of meetings, although it had appeared in the *Beobachter*. When Hitler recited the names of the leaders of the Berlin government, the crowd responded, "Hang them!"

Hitler closed with an appeal to the "youths among you," saying, "You seventeen- and eighteen-year-olds, you are not too young" to join the Storm Troops. "Strengthen the ranks of this Sturmabteilung, protect your speakers, and you have done the highest thing that youth can do!"[2]

As the crowd poured out of the auditorium, it was obvious that many of them were not going to let the evening end there. Outside, someone was holding a swastika flag, and a crowd formed behind it and started parading down the street. When they came to the offices of the *Münchener Post*, they smashed the newspaper's windows. Other acts of violence occurred that night, and four days later, in response to a summons from the headquarters of the Munich police, Hitler was once again interrogated; this time he was threatened with an entirely new form of punishment. He was told that if he and the NSDAP continued on their present course, he would have to be prepared for deportation from Germany, a nation of which he was not a citizen, back to his native Austria.

The police had struck a nerve. Literally the last thing Hitler wanted was to be exiled from Germany. The police report of the interrogation reveals a seemingly chastened man.

> Hitler explained that he could not be made responsible for all these things; in the case of the smashing of the windows at the *Münchener Post* office, it was, as far as he had learned, an act of revenge on the part of former members of the Freikorps Oberland. He had not approved the last parade with the flag after the end of the gathering in the Krone, but had instead condemned it and taken it as an occasion to dismiss from the party some who had participated in it. He promised to do everything to stop such riots before they began.[3]

II

Hitler's strategy remained unchanged, but his afternoon with the police momentarily modified his tactics. Although there was no record of his expelling anyone from the party, the evening after his interrogation he spoke to a group of sixty Storm Troops who had gathered for a meeting with him in the Restaurant Adelmann. Addressing them as "My Young Friends," Hitler told them:

> We must not get into trouble with the police. . . . Privately, they like us because they, too, hate the Jews. We mustn't, therefore, call them servants of the Jews . . . otherwise, it might come to the point that the Sturmabteilung will be banned by the police. Should this happen, all our work would be in vain. . . . I understand you, your blood runs faster . . . but you must restrain yourselves.[4]

Apparently one of Hitler's Storm Troops, who now numbered about three hundred, was a spy for the police. In any case, Hitler's remarks, in full, were soon at police headquarters. His apartment may well have been searched: speaking to another gathering of some fifty Storm Troops on November 2, and referring to their organization for the first time as the SA, Hitler said, "I'm always happy when the doorbell rings and the searchers come that I have everything in a safe place and that they find nothing." Hitler also referred to "spies and traitors who sneak into the gatherings. In the field these fellows would receive the death penalty."[5] Since these remarks were immediately transmitted to Munich police headquarters, one or more "spies" must once again have been present.

The Storm Troops were about to receive their baptism of fire. In keeping with Hitler's temporarily cautious approach, a situation arose in which, ironically, the SA were to be blooded in a defensive battle, rather than in taking their fight to an opposition gathering. The Nazi Party had announced a speech by Hitler to be given in the Festival Hall of the Hofbräuhaus on the evening of Friday, November 4. The topic was "Who Are the Murderers?"[6] Whatever Hitler's intention in giving this title to his speech, Munich's Social Democrats, Independent Socialists, and communists found it inflammatory. On October 21, the day after the partition of Upper Silesia, unknown assailants had fired shots at Erhard Auer, Bavaria's Social Democratic Party leader, as he walked home with several companions after an evening political gathering. The would-be assassins had placed themselves inside the walled South Cemetery; coming from there, the shots intended for Auer missed him and his friends. Auer, who had been severely wounded in an assassination attempt made on the floor of the Bavarian parliament in 1919, always carried a pistol; he took cover and returned the fire. Although the police were promptly informed of the exact location of the snipers, the assailants escaped, and the story immediately got about that the police had allowed them to get away. The socialists believed that the shooting was the work of the Nazi Storm Troops.

It was in this highly charged atmosphere that Hitler's speech was announced. In fact, his intention appeared to be to talk about the Jews who in his view were murdering Germany, but at this moment the mere word "murderers," coming from the Nazi first chairman, was enough to mobilize the most militant of Munich's leftists.

Hitler's speech was scheduled for eight o'clock. "Between six and seven in the evening," he later recalled, "I received the first positive news that the meeting would definitely be broken up, and that for this purpose they intended to send in great masses of workers, especially from a few Red factories."[7] These "great masses" did not amount to more than 450 men, but they had indeed been told by the Republican Schutzbund, the leftist defensive alliance that worked with the workers' councils in Munich's factories, to get to the meeting early, take places near the speaker, and let Hitler experience what Ballerstedt had endured at the hands of the Nazis in September. From the Nazis' point of view, this threat to them could not have come at a worse moment. The party was moving from its old crowded office to new quarters in Corneliusstrasse; as Hitler said, "We were out of the old one, but could not yet move into the new one because work was still going on inside. Since the telephone had already been taken out of the old one and not yet installed in the new one, a number of attempts to inform us by telephone of the intended invasion had been in vain."[8]

The infant SA had in any case not yet perfected the method of alerting its three hundred members and mobilizing them in a short space of time. "Only about forty-six men were present," Hitler said of the detachment he found on duty when he arrived at the hall at a quarter to eight.[9] "There could no longer be any doubt of the existing intention. The hall was overcrowded, and for that reason the doors had been closed by the police. The enemies who had come very early were in the hall and our supporters were for the most part outside of it."[10]

Hitler ordered the men of the Sturmabteilung to line up in military formation in the lobby, where he addressed them.

> Today for the first time you will have to be loyal to the movement in a life or death fight. None of us leaves this hall unless they carry us out as corpses. If anyone backs out in cowardly fashion, I personally will rip off his armband and remove his insignia. Remember, the best defense is to attack at the slightest attempt to break up the meeting.[11]

As Hitler remembered it, the reaction to his exhortation was "a threefold *Heil* that sounded rougher and hoarser than was usual."[12]
Hitler went into the hall.

> Now I could study the situation for myself. They were seated packed in there, and tried to drill through me with their eyes. Countless faces were turned toward me with grim hatred, while

others sneeringly contorted their faces and came out with shouts that left no doubt about their intentions. Today they would "finish us off," we would have our guts cut out, they would shut our mouths permanently, and there were other pleasantries. They were fully aware of their superior numbers and behaved accordingly.[13]

Among those in the hall was Frau Magdalena Schweyer, the old woman who ran the fruit and vegetable store across the street from Hitler's lodgings. Because of her acquaintance with Hitler as a customer who occasionally bought some fruit to munch on in his rooms, she had gone to an early Nazi meeting, heard Hitler speak, and ended up as party member 90. While the party was still in its infancy and Hitler had virtually no money, she would occasionally send him "a pot of jam, or a sack of sausage, or a handful of apples."[14] "A Herr Esser'd pop in sometimes, one of Herr Hitler's friends, and buy a couple of large white radishes for the pair of them. That was their idea of a supper."[15]

Frau Schweyer never missed a Hitler speech, but tonight she would have been well advised to do so.

> The place was pretty well full. We womenfolk were told to get well up in front: it would be safest there, far from the doors. I was too excited really to be frightened. It was plain that there'd be some trouble: half the people in the place belonged to the Reds. I found a table right in front.
> Then they came and sat another near it, and . . . Herr Esser got up on it to open the meeting. As soon as he jumped down again, Herr Hitler took his place. They greeted him with a few boos and yells, but after a bit he gripped even the enemy and was speaking without interruption.[16]

As Hitler stood atop the big table along one side of the hall, he noticed the following as he was getting well into his speech:

> In front of me, especially to the left of me, only enemies were sitting and standing. They were all robust men and young fellows, in large part from the Maffei factory, from Kustermann's, from the Isaria Meter Works, etc. Along the left wall they had pushed ahead close to my table and were beginning to collect beer mugs; that is they kept ordering beer and putting the empty mugs under the table.[17]

From where she was sitting, very near Hitler, grey-haired Frau Schweyer also became aware of what was happening to these stoneware beer mugs, which were sometimes known as pots. "The old ones were piled under the tables," she said of this collection of potential weapons being assembled by Hitler's enemies.[18]

One reason that trouble had not yet started was that Hitler was expressing great sympathy for the plight of the workingman. The "murderers" of the title proved to have nothing to do with Bavaria; they were described as the false leaders in Berlin who whipped the workers into a state of misery and deprivation, always allying themselves with the Jews who manipulated "international capitalism." Indeed, Hitler made a direct appeal to the left:

> You, Fellow German, whether you're an Independent Socialist or a Communist, you who are today fighting here for two hours a week [an improvement in working conditions] — Do you want to take upon yourself the yoke without defending yourselves, without a thought for your wife, your children, your future? . . . Do you want to be servants forever and eternally to this International Capitalism, which for the past forty years you thought you were fighting against?[19]

Although there were occasional heckling remarks, this kind of emotional appeal to the workers, by a master orator who knew how to speak their language, prevented trouble: Hitler had been speaking for an hour and a half. "It seemed almost as if I was going to be master of the situation. The leaders of the invading troops seemed to feel this themselves; for they were becoming more and more restless. They often went out, came in again, and talked to their men with visible nervousness."[20]

Suddenly everything changed. Frau Schweyer heard someone shout "Freiheit!" — the leftist battle cry, "Liberty!" — and, she said, "A beer pot went crash!"

> That was the signal for things to begin. Three, four, five heavy stone pots flew by within an inch of the speaker's head and next instant his young guards sprang forward shouting to us women to "duck down!"
> We ducked sharp enough! The row was ear splitting. Never heard anything like it in your life! Pandemonium had broken out. . . . One heard nothing but yells, crashing beer mugs, stamping and struggling, the overturning of heavy oaken tables, and the smashing up of wooden chairs.[21]

From his vantage point on the table, Hitler had a far better view than did Frau Schweyer, who was huddled on the floor.

In a few seconds the whole hall was filled with a roaring, screaming crowd, over which, like howitzer shells, flew innumerable beer mugs, and in between the cracking of chair legs, the crashing of the mugs, bawling, howling, and screaming.[22]

It was an insane uproar.[23]

From her place on the floor, Frau Schweyer looked up at the Führer of the National Socialist German Workers' Party.

Hitler stuck to his post. Never got off that table! He made no effort to shield himself at all. He was the target of it all, it's a sheer miracle how he never got hit. Them murderous heavy mugs was flying at his head all the time. I know because I got a sharp look round just between whiles: there he stuck, quiet as a statue, waiting for those boys of his to get the tumult under.[24]

The Storm Troops had gone into action. Hitler said:

Like wolves they flung themselves in packs of eight or ten again and again on their enemies, and little by little actually began to thrash them out of the hall. After only five minutes I hardly saw one of them who was not covered with blood. How many of them I only really came to know on that day; at the head my good Maurice . . . Hess, and many others, who, even though gravely injured themselves, attacked again and again as long as their legs would hold them.[25]

The hand-to-hand fighting went on for twenty minutes, and at the close of that time the majority of the opponents, Hitler said, "had for the most part been beaten out of the hall and chased down the stairs by my men numbering not even fifty."[26] Only in the left rear corner of the hall was a large group of leftists still spiritedly fighting. "Then suddenly two shots were fired from the hall entrance toward the platform, and wild shooting started. Your heart almost rejoiced at such a revival of old war experiences."[27]

The police later ascertained that the shooting had come from the platform as well as at it. The Storm Troops redoubled their efforts; looking at "the boys with the arm-bands," Frau Schweyer saw "their jackets torn half off their backs, and their faces all patched and dabbled with blood. Anyhow, they *did* get the Reds outside somehow."[28]

Hitler was still standing on the table. "The hall looked almost as if a shell had struck it," he observed.[29] As Frau Schweyer raised her head, she saw that "the room was simply wrecked. There was over four hundred smashed beer mugs lying about everywhere, and piles of broken chairs."[30] Many of the Nazis who had been in the hall were being bandaged, and others had to be taken to a hospital, but the crowd loyal to Hitler was still in place. Hermann Esser, who had acted as chairman in opening the meeting, got back up on the table beside Hitler and said, "The meeting goes on. The speaker has the floor."[31] Hitler resumed speaking.

According to Hitler, it was after the Nazis had closed the meeting that "an excited police lieutenant came dashing in, and, wildly swinging his arms, he cackled into the hall: 'The meeting is dismissed!' "[32]

Some non-Nazi accounts had it that the police had arrived somewhat earlier and had themselves cleared some of the leftists from the hall, but this *Saalschlacht,* or Battle of the Hall, promptly entered Nazi legend. There was no question that the Storm Troops had fought hard and effectively, although it was undoubtedly also true that other Nazis in the hall had assisted the outnumbered SA men. Esser's spontaneous understatement, "The meeting goes on. The speaker has the floor," had a certain cool, invincible quality that appealed to Germans, and it was widely quoted. Within the party, the episode eventually assumed heroic proportions — no one then said that there had been more than 450 opponents, but with time, printed party accounts claimed as many as 800.[33] In any event, there was no doubt that an important victory had been won. Speaking to a group of eighty-five SA men five nights after the Saalschlacht, Hitler began:

Comrades!

We have won a battle. You have withstood your baptism by fire well, in spite of the fact that our numbers were relatively speaking only small. But you are not there only to protect the gathering, but you are also to become fighters for our cause. You must protect the speaker. It is very easy to kill me with three bullets, but I do not mind; I know what I'm dying for, I'm not afraid.

There was applause, and Hitler went on to exhort the bruised and bandaged Storm Troops to do even better.

The whole thing on Friday lasted much too long. It could have been taken care of in five minutes. You must proceed in closed ranks, table by table, and hustle them out. You must not despair if you get hit now and then. Whoever goes to battle has to expect things like that.

In a final touch, Hitler reviewed the situation in such a way as to make his Storm Troops feel that they had been fighting the Jews themselves five nights earlier.

For us there are only two possibilities: either we remain German or we come under the thumb of the Jews. This latter must not occur; even if we are small, we are a force. A well-organized group can conquer a strong enemy. . . . If you stick close together and keep bringing in new people, we will be victorious over the Jews.[34]

Hitler veered back and forth in his thinking about the size of the party. At one moment he felt that he could get the best results with a relatively small but fanatical group of followers, and at others he saw the need for having as many members as possible from the public at large. Whichever way he was thinking, he was delighted with his new force of strong-arm men. In a speech to approximately 125 members of the SA on November 30, Hitler referred to them as Storm Troops for the first time, and told them to attend opposition gatherings and "harass the speaker, whoever it is, until he addresses the Jewish question and makes his views on this issue known." He also said that the NSDAP had recently been referred to as a "rough, brutal group that stops at nothing." Hitler added, "This makes me uncommonly happy because I expect that my efforts and my party will become feared and at the same time known." He went on to announce that the "master boxer Haymann" had joined the Storm Troops and would be giving boxing lessons to SA men two or three times a week. Hitler told the gathering that he planned to have a pool of sixty to eighty trained boxers available, and to enlist an additional five hundred Storm Troops, "so that dissenting political parties will tremble with fear as soon as they even hear of Hitler's Boxing and Storm Troops."[35]

Hitler felt that a reputation for violence would not only keep the public from attending the meetings of parties who were sure to become targets for Storm Troop attacks, but that the public would be attracted to an organization that would "stop at nothing" to gain its ends. "Today the Party numbers 4,500 in Munich alone. . . . I believe that, due to the work of the Storm Troop, through the breaking up of gatherings, many fellow Germans will in future come to a view that will, I hope, result in an enormous growth in our membership."[36]

And who were these future members to be? Hitler opposed the communists politically, but admired the fanaticism shown by many of them. Writing to Gustav Seifert, who had started an NSDAP local in the northern city of Hanover, he said, "What we need is to attract vigorous masses, most preferably from the far left and the far right wings."[37] Converts from communism were welcome; what was important was their need to believe ardently in something, and Hitler was ready to provide targets for their anger and a sense of participating in a supremely important crusade. As 1921 neared its end, Hitler veered back to the idea of the smaller, more militant party. In Information Sheet Number 9, issued on December 19, he said to the membership, "The strength of a movement lies not in its external size, but in its inner substance."[38]

III

As had happened previously in this postwar era, events were coming to the aid of those, Hitler among them, who fed upon economic unrest and public confusion. Inflation had been a fact of daily German life in the three years since Erzberger signed the Armistice, but during 1921 it accelerated. Although Hitler was prompt to blame the new wave of economic troubles on Allied reparations demands and the acquiescence to them by the postwar leadership in Berlin, the largest factor coming home to roost was the wartime policy of the Kaiser's ministers of finance. It was they who had decided to pay for the war by running up a string of enormous deficits, not visible to the average German, instead of using the realistic but harsher method of taxation in direct relation to the war's cost. Thus, at the war's end, Germans were suddenly brought face to face with a distinct reduction in the buying power of the mark. The average German noticed it only on a purchase-by-purchase basis, but in fact the wartime government printing presses had more than quintupled the number of marks in circulation. This fiscal policy had in part been initiated early in the war on the assumption that it would be possible to collect from Germany's vanquished enemies the same sorts of enormous sums in reparations which were now demanded of Germany itself.[39]

For those who had not concerned themselves with international trade while it was suspended during the war, by January of 1919 it had become clear that the mark, which had been pegged at 4.2 to the dollar in July of 1914, was valued at only 8.9 to the dollar. A lack of confidence on the part of Germans in their own currency contributed to the slump, and by July of 1919 it took 14 marks to buy a dollar. Six months later, the mark was pegged at 64.8 to the dollar, and so, with some improvements at various times, it had remained at this unfortunate but temporarily stabilized level until the summer of 1921.[40]

Then, starting in July, the added postwar strains on the German economy began to be dramatically reflected in the value of the mark.

234 ∎

Although the inflation had been homegrown, the Allies' May 5 demand for an immediate payment of a billion gold marks accelerated the German government's printing of paper money. Other nations were hesitant to invest their more solid currencies in a German economy that was being drained by the Allies at the same time that its own financiers, like Hugo Stinnes, were urging that the government print more money as a panacea. Running the presses was a convenient solution for those who wished to pay off their debts with less valuable marks, but it was a terrible blow to monetary stability.

In July of 1921, just when Hitler was engaging in the intraparty struggle from which he emerged as Führer, the mark fell in value to the point at which it traded at 76.7 to the dollar.[41] Foreign currencies became virtually unavailable to the German government, and by September the mark was quoted at more than 100 to the dollar. By the end of the year the mark would lose another 50 percent of its shaky value. While speculators like Stinnes were betting that the mark would continue its decline, and using all their influence to see that the government followed policies that guaranteed it would, workers on fixed incomes and those on pensions were aware only of a drastic reduction in what their money could buy.

Those who could least understand the problem were the ones who suffered the most. With the onset of cold weather, the mayor of Berlin reported on the conditions in families of poor workingmen and the unemployed:

> Very many children, even the youngest, never taste a drop of milk and come to school with no food inside them. . . . Many have no shirt or warm clothing, or else are kept away from class because they have no underwear. . . . All they can think about is the struggle against cold and hunger.[42]

The Nazi Party, too, was feeling the effects of inflation. The price of the *Beobachter* was raised from 10 to 20 pfennigs on November 15; on December 3, it was raised to 50 pfennigs. NSDAP Circular Letter Number 11, appearing on November 19, reported that jobless party members were turning to the party for help, and that local groups "are requested to announce that the central office will inform party members of job opportunities free of charge. Anybody knowing of a job possibility should report it to the office."[43]

As 1921 neared its end, the party was expanding both its services and its image of benevolence toward its rank and file. Members were invited to browse in the library that was being started at the new party headquarters, and the leadership asked for donations of books, "especially items with völkisch content."[44] A large Christmas party was planned, and the Munich sections were "requested to collect money as well as useful objects as gifts for children." At six in the evening there was to be the "distribution of gifts to children," and at eight the general celebration would start, "including regimental music and first-rate artistic talents."[45]

Behind these activities were factors that had little to do with Christmas. The *Beobachter* had always required subsidization; during the first half of 1921 the membership had been sold a total of forty thousand interest-free 10-mark loan certificates. These promissory notes were illegal, but Hitler's comment was "We presume as a matter of course that every decent Party member must be cheerfully prepared to contribute this small share to maintain the common newspaper."[46] It was at this time of financial crisis — on December 16, Germany applied to the Allies for a moratorium on reparations payments — that the term "Nazi" came into wide use in describing the party and its individual members.[47]

Hitler's contribution to the Christmas spirit was to tell a meeting of the National Club in Berlin, in answer to a question concerning how he intended "to solve the Marxist and Jewish problems in case of a nationalist takeover," that the best solution would be to put Jews and leftists into *Konzentrationslager*, concentration camps. This, Hitler told the right-wing group, would be done, as a member of the audience put it, "in order that the takeover of power could be carried out with as little bloodshed as possible."[48] The NSDAP was outlawed in Prussia, and in order to make his appearance before this influential group, Hitler had to slip in and out of Berlin to avoid being arrested by the police.

Returning to Bavaria, he finished the year in a flurry of nontraditional Christmas activity. On the same day that Chancellor Wirth's government was asking the Allies for more time to make its reparations payments, Hitler launched into a speech, "The German Woman and the Jew," before a crowd in the Festival Hall of the Hofbräuhaus, the same hall in which the Saalschlacht had occurred. Although there was never to be any documentation for the rumor that Hitler had caught a venereal disease from a Jewish prostitute during his prewar years in Vienna, there could be no doubt that he spoke of the Jews with particular ferocity when talking about sex.[49] According to the text of this speech in the *Völkischer Beobachter*, Hitler had this to say:

The Jew knows no *love*, he knows only *the body*, especially in
the area of sex life. . . . The basic difference between the . . .
Jewish and the German outlook on life is simply stated this way:
The German can give his *life* for his *love* and his *woman*; the
Jew can only purchase a woman![50]

His prewar exposure to the lurid drawings in racist magazines like
Ostara, which featured hairy cavemen attacking blond Fräulein,
emerged in this fantasy in which Jews were somehow responsible for
the French decision to include African colonial troops in their occupation forces: "He *wants* to disgrace, to ruin our German race; therefore in the Rhineland he throws the German woman to a Negro."[51]

At the year's end, Hitler was still unknown to the German public
outside Bavaria. On the international scene, he did not exist. In November, at the time of the Storm Troop debut in the Saalschlacht,
the American consulate in Munich was reopened for the first time
since the United States declared war on Germany in 1917. One of the
political officers assigned there was Robert Murphy, a twenty-seven-
year-old member of the Foreign Service, destined for later work of
the highest importance as a diplomat. To familiarize himself with
Bavaria's political scene, he attended a number of Hitler's speeches
at NSDAP gatherings. His companion was a German employee of the
consulate, Paul Drey, who was an expert on the Bavarian parties and
their prominent figures. Speaking of the Nazis, Murphy asked Drey,
"Do you think these agitators will ever get anywhere?"

"Of course not!" Drey replied. "The German people are too intelligent to be taken in by such scamps!"[52]

CHAPTER

20

THE NEW YEAR of 1922 was to add yet another strain on Europe's brittle peace. Although it would not at first have seemed related to the tensions existing among Germany, France, and England, the growing isolationism in the United States played a role in further destabilizing Europe.

For Americans, the great and bloody adventure across the Atlantic was a thing of the past. The Roaring Twenties were fully under way, and nightclub hostess Texas Guinan symbolized the Prohibition era as she sat atop a piano and greeted speakeasy patrons with "Hello, sucker!" Americans were going mad for the newly introduced ancient Chinese game of mahjong; the complicated four-handed game, played with 152 small rectangular blocks of wood faced with ivory or bone, took the nation by storm. New York's radio station WEAF started running the first paid commercials, prompting Lee De Forest, the radio pioneer, to say "What have you done with my child? You have sent him out on the street in rags of ragtime to collect money from all and sundry. You have made of him a laughingstock of intelligence."[1] The nation was looking inward, reading the first edition of Emily Post's *Etiquette* and buying the first Maytag washing machines. Everyone was singing "Chicago" and "Way Down Yonder in New Orleans." The really big news was automobiles: Ford acquired the Lincoln Motor Company, Chevrolet was overtaking Ford's Model T in sales, and Deusenberg's luxury cars had the first hydraulic brakes. The nation loved speed, and the annihilation of distance; a young U.S. Army pilot named Jimmy Doolittle flew from Florida to California in twenty-one hours and twenty-eight minutes.

The domestic scene was yeasty, but there were two pieces of troublesome unfinished business. America's wartime European allies had received loans and credits totaling nearly $11 billion, and were not even paying interest on these enormous debts. There was also the matter of the American occupation forces still stationed in Germany. The number of soldiers on duty in the Rhineland was small — just under nine thousand men — but in the tinderbox atmosphere existing between the French and the Germans, there was a fear that American troops might become embroiled in a resumption of fighting over issues that seemed distant and irrelevant to the realities of American life in 1922.[2]

The $11 billion did not seem irrelevant, however. President Harding informed Belgium, France, Great Britain, and Italy that the United States was not prepared to write off the immense loans, which, like the introduction of the American Expeditionary Forces, had played a pivotal part in reversing the tide of events and ensuring victory.

Lord Balfour, Britain's foreign secretary, in a statement primarily intended for French consumption, reacted to the American position in diplomatic language that nonetheless had a sharp edge to it. Britain owed huge sums to the United States, but it had made vast loans to France, and under the reparations agreement was due many millions from Germany. What Britain owed America amounted to a sum that was one-quarter the amount owed to Britain by Germany and France; if Germany and France would pay America that sum, Britain would write off the rest of its debt.[3]

Under the circumstances, this was a reasonable offer, but France had no intention of paying either England or the United States from its own war-drained treasury when it was owed so much by Germany under the terms of the Versailles Treaty. France's new premier, Raymond Poincaré, upon taking office on January 12 of the new year, embarked upon a single-minded effort to extract every possible thing from Germany under its treaty obligations. Indeed, Poincaré was prepared to set aside all existing agreements and spoke as if he were entitled to rearrange international financial and territorial matters on a unilateral basis.[4] Payments to Britain and the United States would depend on what France could collect from Germany; in an interesting version of assigning a debt, Poincaré later in the year would suggest that the United States and Britain could pay themselves off by getting from the empty German coffers those sums they claimed were due them from France. At the same time, the French public, which had swooned when President Woodrow Wilson arrived in Paris after the war, began referring to the United States as Uncle Shylock.

The result was to place greater pressure on the Germans, who, ironically, were eager to keep the token American occupation force on their soil. With good reason, the Germans saw those few American battalions as a restraining influence upon Marshal Foch, who was always ready to march into the Ruhr.[5] For Poincaré, the sudden American insistence on fixing some scheme for payment was the perfect excuse for announcing that France reserved the right to take initiatives of its own choosing against Germany, whether or not they were sanctioned by the Versailles Treaty.

Across the Atlantic, the isolationist mood was strengthened by reports of the European tap dance over what Americans saw as straightforward financial matters that should be handled in a businesslike fashion. Senator James Reed of Missouri extended this thinking and came to the remarkable conclusion that Britain and France's various colonies around the world could be considered collateral for the loans. He rose in the United States Senate to say that if Britain and France did not agree on a scheme for repayment, American military forces had the right to occupy any of their colonies on twenty-four hours' notice.[6] Although far from being the official State Department view of the matter, Reed's speech was an indication of just how wide the Atlantic had once again become.

Bavaria was only a small part of this international picture, and the six thousand members of the Nazi Party were focusing their attention on matters closer to home as 1922 began. On January 12, the day that Poincaré came to power in France, the People's Court of Munich sentenced Hitler, Hermann Esser, and Oskar Körner to three months' imprisonment for the September disruption of Ballerstedt's Bavarian League meeting, when Ballerstedt received head wounds that required fourteen stitches. For the moment, the sentence was suspended.

Hitler immediately began using the suspended sentence as a form of political martyrdom; his language gave the impression that Nazis were being imprisoned for their beliefs. Addressing a crowd of 918 delegates at the first party congress, held on January 29 and 30 in Munich, Hitler said, "Our movement cannot be defeated by locking us up. We knew from the beginning that the leaders have to go through prison; it is in this way that our movement will become great. We go to prison as National Socialists and will come out again as National Socialists."[7]

This first congress was an entirely different gathering from the party's "annual meeting" of the year before. At that time, the NSDAP had been governed by true parliamentary procedures, despite Hitler's opposition to them, and Drexler's old guard had provided a counterweight to Hitler. The majority of members present on that occasion had been from Munich. Now all was changed. The loyalty of the Munich membership was in a sense taken for granted; although the great majority of the NSDAP's members lived in the city, only 200 of the 918 delegates came from the Munich local, while a great effort had been made to bring in 718 delegates representing the non-Munich locals.[8] The true purpose of the congress was twofold; both priorities were concerned with the Nazi groups from other cities and towns. The first was to strengthen them as Nazi missionaries, encouraging them to work diligently, and the second was to make them aware of the debt they owed to the party in Munich. "I would like to remind the local groups from outside Munich how much work is being done in Munich," Hitler told the gathering. "The whole movement was financed from Munich. Local groups from outside Munich should strive to stand on their own feet in future."[9]

Such exhortations had been met with a stony silence only a few months earlier, but now the leaders of the *Ortsgruppen*, the locals, accepted this readily. Indeed, the entire two-day assemblage was a collective stiffening of the spine, under the direction of Hitler. To put the leaders of the non-Munich locals in the right frame of mind for what was really to be a confrontation with their Führer the following day, on January 29 there was a *Festabend*. It was an evening that provided a speech by Hitler, the reading of patriotic poems by various members, and the singing of völkisch and military songs, along with satiric comic sketches. The entertainment was washed down with thousands of steins of beer in the Festival Hall of the Hofbräuhaus.[10]

The next afternoon, Hitler held a smaller meeting, attended by the top leaders from outside Munich. In effect, he laid down the law to them for two and a half hours at party headquarters. His message boiled down to a demand that the locals outside Munich support themselves financially, send a share of their revenues to headquarters, and accept full control of their political activities by the party leadership in Munich. Within minutes of his finishing this lengthy exhortation and demand, it became clear that Hitler had cemented his standing with yet another audience: those present, including the leaders of several locals in states outside Bavaria, unreservedly endorsed his claim on their obedience.[11]

That night, in another meeting, which lasted past midnight, Hitler presided over the culmination of yet one more personal victory. For this demonstration of fealty, Hitler had again brought the party faithful to the Festival Hall of the Hofbräuhaus; in addition to the 918 delegates, another 600 of the party's Munich membership were now present.[12] He produced a masterstroke for the Führerprinzip: the congress amended the NSDAP bylaws to empower Hitler to expel from the party not only individuals who displeased him — a privilege he already possessed through control of the subcommittee on investigation — but entire locals, as well.[13] Thus, in theory at least, der Führer had gained the authority to banish, without explanation, any combination of his six thousand followers. He was armed with a weapon that could strike down ideological deviation and chop off distant Ortsgruppe leaders who might become so popular as to pose a threat to his own leadership. As of this moment, the Nazi Party had in a sense lost its collective identity: it was defined by one man.

It had been a long two days for Hitler — a major speech the previous night, a two-and-a-half-hour speech to the Ortsgruppe leaders earlier in the day — and now, on the occasion of this victory, Hitler's principal gift failed him. "You will permit me to be brief," he said to the crowd. "I am quite worn out." A reporter noted, "His voice gives out. A cry: Spare your voice." Hitler nodded. "Quite right, take care of my voice."[14]

Emerging from the congress with ironclad dictatorial powers, Hitler not only showed his tactical strengths, but at times seemed to have a spatial sense of the party's position, progress, and deeds, almost as if he were perched on a height above the road that the NSDAP was traveling. In an information sheet circulated within the party early in the year, Hitler wrote in the tone of a man who is looking back a number of years, rather than just a few months. "The year 1921 found the young movement robustly moving forward as far as propaganda, agitation, etc., were concerned, but behind and undeveloped internally." From the same quasi-Olympian point of view, Hitler also said:

> The young movement was to supply what the others lacked: a
> völkisch movement with a strictly public base, including the
> broadest masses, welded together by iron-hard organization, filled
> with blind obedience and inspired with brutal determination, a
> party of battle and action.[15]

Hitler's behind-the-scenes story of some of the "battle and action," and an apparently unguarded and unreserved revelation of Hitler's innermost ideas, emerged in a private conversation Hitler had with Josef Hell. This Munich resident was an editor on the staff of the weekly magazine *Der Gerade Weg*, The Straight Path. He had been curious to meet Hitler, and Hitler apparently felt that the journalist might prove to be a political ally.

Meeting at the apartment of a mutual acquaintance, Hell said that Hitler first "outlined for me in a lively way" his earliest efforts to come to the attention of the newspapers.

> I decided to make the Bavarian love of fighting useful to me. I sought out some strong fellows among my followers and instructed them to spread themselves among the different tables [during beer hall speeches] and, on cue when I made provocative statements in my speeches, make interruptions, or, if the other side heckled me, to answer rudely, to bring about arguments. . . .
>
> As soon as the really serious fights began, the police, according to plan, were phoned for help. . . . Soon the word was "Hitler is surrounded by brawling!" and the curious and the pugnacious came in platoons and produced fights in all genuineness. . . . Naturally I kept the same content and form of my speeches, so that new substance for provocations was constantly produced, which . . . brought the Bavarian people's spirit to a boil.
>
> Now at last representatives of the press appeared, and the ice was broken.[16]

Hitler spoke to Hell with some pride about his ability to get bright red posters up quickly on the streets of Munich, responding to events in the news and announcing a Hitler speech using the news event as its departure point.

> It proved especially successful to put the posters up all at once in the whole city of Munich between ten and twelve so that knowledge of the text reached the public when they were out in force during the noon hour. That way, when they talked about it with family and friends, they were, whether they knew it or not, advertising my speech.

In recounting the conversation, Hell said, "Here I raised the question of the effective use of the forbidden fliers which repeatedly have rustled down like a local rain on the city of Munich."

Obviously pleased, Hitler replied, "The fliers were designed for the purpose of making completely unexpected events useful for an already announced meeting. The text of the flier can be in completed form in thirty minutes." Hitler explained that bundles of the little sheets were taken around the city by a "delivery car," which dropped them off at different corners where party members, alerted by "a single password announced by telephone," were waiting with their own cars. By arrangement, Hitler said, "on the exact minute, all the cars depart *simultaneously* and, taking into consideration the density of traffic, toss out the fliers into the streets." The police, he said, were powerless to react: "In about seven minutes the entire uproar is past and success is certain." He added that even if a policeman managed to note down a license number, nothing would come of it, because they used fake license plates for the operation.

After a minute, Hell came to the most serious of matters. "My next question concerned the entire problem of the persecution of the Jews. 'What do you plan to undertake, then, once you have full freedom of action against the Jews?' "

> While up until now Hitler had spoken comparatively calmly and moderately, his nature now changed completely. He no longer looked at me, rather above and beyond me into the distance and made his following statements with rising vocal effort, so that he fell into a kind of paroxysm and finally screamed at me as if I were an entire nationalist gathering:
>
> "When I really am in power, then the annihilation of the Jews will be my first and most important task. As soon as I have the power to do it I shall, for example, have erected in the Marienplatz in Munich gallows and more gallows, as many as can be fitted in without stopping the traffic. Then the Jews will be hanged, one after another, and they will stay hanging, until they stink. They will hang as long as the principles of hygiene permit. As soon as they have been taken down, the next ones will be strung up, and this will continue until the last Jew in Munich is destroyed. The same thing will happen in the other cities until Germany is cleansed of the last Jews."

Now it was Hell's turn. "When I raised the question, from what basis he felt driven to feel such hate against the Jews, and why he wanted to annihilate this unquestionably intelligent people, to whom the Germans and all other Aryans, even the entire world, are so enormously indebted in nearly all areas of art and science, of research and economics, Hitler suddenly became quiet again."

Assuming that Hell's account of what happened next is accurate, it is the only recorded instance in which Hitler spoke of his anti-Semitism in terms of being merely a useful tool that he had chosen as an instrument in his efforts to gain power. "It is clear and has proven itself in all revolutions through events and facts," Hitler said, "that a *battle for ideals*, for improvements of whatever kind, absolutely must be supplemented by a war against some kind of social class or caste." Hitler continued:

> In earlier revolutions — my goals are revolutionary goals of the first order, regardless of which methods I use and directions I take in the process — the battle was now against the peasants, now the nobility or clergy, now against princely houses and their many different followers. However, none of the revolutions has ever broken out without such a lightning rod through which the feeling of hate is conducted to the broad masses.
>
> Following this line of thought, I checked the details of revolutions in world history and then asked myself: Against which group in Germany can I employ my propaganda of hate with the greatest chance of success? . . . I have come to the conclusion that a battle against the Jews would be as popular as it would be successful.

Hell said that, as he listened, "icy-cold" shivers ran down his back. Hitler added:

> There are few Germans who are not angered here and there about the behavior of the Jews, or who have not been injured by Jews. In their relatively small number they control an enormous part of the German national wealth. That is money that you can confiscate and use for the state and the general public, just as was done with the property of the monasteries, the bishops, and the nobility.

Hitler concluded:

> Once the hate and the battle against the Jews is really fanned and stirred up, their resistance will collapse in the shortest possible time. They cannot even protect themselves, and no one else will provide protection for them.

Josef Hell apparently made notes soon after this conversation took place. When he decided to expand these notes, years later, he put at the head of his reminiscence: "How Adolf Hitler preached to me about himself, and converted me away from him forever."

II

On January 31, 1922, the day after the party congress in Munich closed, Chancellor Wirth announced in Berlin that Germany's new foreign minister was Walther Rathenau. The chancellor had appointed a man of exceptional stature and brilliance, a man of greater ability and vision than any other principal European or American diplomat of the day. In the eyes of many Germans there was, however, something that made Rathenau absolutely unfit to represent Germany to the world: he was a Jew. "Now we have it!" a völkisch newspaper screeched. "Germany has a Jewish foreign minister!"[17] *Wiking*, the publication that was subsidized by the secret Organization Consul and acted as its mouthpiece, said, "The appointment of the Jew Rathenau to be German foreign minister is the height of the politically grotesque. . . . But it will open the eyes of the German people as to who their true rulers are."[18] Hitler had already referred to him as "the internal organizer of the starvation of Germany during the war," and a right-wing ditty contained these two couplets:

> And Rathenau, old Walther,
> Shall have a timely halter!

> Shoot down Walther Rathenau,
> The Goddamned swine of a Jewish sow.[19]

Who was this villain, this alleged enemy of the people? He was in many ways a living contradiction, a phenomenally successful industrialist and financier who wrote sensitive philosophical treatises, a socialist sympathizer who wore fur-trimmed coats and fingered a gold chain around his neck, a man who abhorred war, yet had organized Germany's wartime supply of critical raw materials to remedy problems completely unforeseen by the General Staff. Originality in itself is not glorious — Adolf Hitler was proving that every day — but in Walther Rathenau Germany had a son of exceptional political ability, a rich bachelor who lived in an elegant little palace but preferred walks through the German countryside to the pleasures of Berlin. His life had been lived on the crest of the wave of Germany's industrialization, yet he constantly feared that mechanization would destroy the soul of modern man. Rathenau desired to free workers from industrial bondage and to secure for them a greater share of the nation's wealth, and to that end he was ready to abolish the right of inheritance and lay punitive taxes on fortunes such as his own. His was the examined life.

Walther Rathenau had been born in a veritable crucible of free enterprise. Connected to the house in which he lived as a child in Berlin's Chausseestrasse was his father's factory, which produced steam engines and other apparatus used by gas and water works. In 1881, when Walther was fourteen, his father experienced an industrial flash on the road to Damascus. The late nineteenth century was marked by great international trade exhibitions; at this one, in Paris, Thomas Edison was for the first time showing Europeans his incandescent light bulb. In that moment in Paris, Emil Rathenau, the builder of steam engines from Berlin, saw into the future; he bought Edison's European patents on the spot.

Thus began the stupendous German electrical giant that became known as A.E.G. Using an astonishing combination of the skills of the engineer, the salesman, the manufacturer, the distributor, and the financier, Emil Rathenau manufactured light bulbs, built power stations, constructed hydroelectric dams, marched power lines across Germany, and substituted electrical power for steam in the nation's factories and transportation system. Walther, who eventually succeeded his father, wrote, "Electricity in its present centralized form really originated in Germany, a country without any special qualifications for this so far as capital or geography is concerned."[20]

By the time Europe entered the mad years leading to the war, Walther Rathenau was an extraordinarily able and accomplished engineer, executive, and financier — at one time he served on the boards of eight-five German and twenty-one foreign corporations — yet he was also noted for a sensitivity that was unusual among his associates in banking and industry.[21] Surrounded by material goods, a tall, bald, slender bachelor who was aloof with women and seemed a figure of almost Proustian aesthetic sensibility, he enjoyed the comforts and advantages of wealth, education, travel, and brilliant society, yet could write with apparent sincerity: "We are not here for possessions, but for the glorification of the godly in the human spirit."[22]

The man who longed for a more spiritual world while living in privileged comfort in a competitive society had difficulties with his identity as a Jew in Germany. "In the youth of every German Jew," he wrote in 1911, "there comes a moment which he remembers with pain as long as he lives: when he becomes for the first time fully conscious of the fact that he has entered the world as a citizen of the second class, and that no amount of ability or merit can rid him of that status."[23] In Rathenau's case, converting to Christianity — something that had been done by a considerable number of prominent Jews in prewar Germany — would have smoothed his path. Since he already moved in circles that included members of the Kaiser's court, becoming a Christian would not have improved his social status, but it would have enabled him to be appointed to government positions not open to him in a nation whose prewar army accepted no Jews as officers. Rathenau was not a believer in Judaism; his objection to an otherwise convenient conversion was that "then I would, I am convinced, have been condoning the breach of justice committed by the ruling classes."[24] Despite the evidence that he was considered by German Gentiles to be different from them, a sort of Disraeli at the Prussian court, Rathenau believed that he was as German as any man in the empire. "I am a German of Jewish descent," he wrote. "My people is the German people, my fatherland is Germany, my religion that Germanic faith which is above all religions."[25] Trying to heal the division within himself, he also wrote: "I have no blood other than German, no other tribe and no other people."[26]

As the saber rattling reached a crescendo in the summer of 1914, Rathenau was one of the few prominent Germans who did not succumb to the lust for war that swept the populations of Europe. Right to the last moment, after the Austrian Archduke Franz Ferdinand had been assassinated by Serbian nationalists at Sarajevo, but before the declarations of war, Rathenau tried to inject a note of sober common sense into the thinking of his countrymen. On July 31, four days before Germany declared war on France, the readers of the *Berliner Tagblatt* were reading an article in which he urged the government not to plunge the nation into war simply because its ally Austria was determined to avenge the death of its archduke by attacking Serbia, whose ally was Russia. Rathenau pointed out to the *Tagblatt*'s readers that Austria would not be taking Europe to the brink of war without Germany's endorsement of her aggressive diplomatic maneuvers. The article reminded Germans that the final absurdity was that the Foreign Ministry in Berlin did not even know the contents of some of the correspondence pouring out of Vienna that might determine Germany's future. "The government and people of Germany have the right to know both what Russia has asked and what Austria has rejected. Such a question as the participation of Austrian officials in investigating the Serbian plot is no reason for an international war."[27]

The armies marched; having done what he could to avoid bloodshed, and feeling sick at heart at what he felt lay in store for Germany, Rathenau went to war in his own unique way. On August 8, four days after Britain entered, he went to the Ministry of War to see what plans involving strategic materials the General Staff had developed, and to offer his services in helping to implement them. To his dismay, Rathenau discovered that the General Staff was basing its war plans on an anticipated quick victory over France. Beyond what supplies of metals, chemicals, rubber, and other materials were on hand for a campaign of a few months, there was no stockpile, and no effective plan for amassing one.

The mere fact that Rathenau was upset about these deficiencies was persuasive, and the minister of war gave him a free hand. Under Rathenau, the War Raw Materials Department started with five workers and soon employed two thousand. The department established control over the nation's supplies of more than a hundred commodities and products, and Rathenau quickly bought materials available in Scandinavia and Switzerland.[28]

Despite his swift and immensely effective efforts to strengthen his nation's capacity to make war, Rathenau was nonetheless yearning for peace and thinking of humane and reasonable settlements to the conflict. Two months after the war began, when Germany was in the flush of her victories in Belgium, Rathenau wrote to one of his aristocratic friends, a diplomat attached to the offices of the chancellor, in terms that were most un-Prussian.

Dear Friend,
Now that Antwerp has fallen, I should like to think that the time had come for a declaration of a reassuring nature about the future of Belgium. This would help, I feel, to make the eventual peace negotiations more easy. . . . What I should most like to see would be the conclusion of a peace with France which would transform our enemy into an ally. . . . By building up a central European economic system, we should gain an internal victory far surpassing all external achievements.[29]

Rathenau's was indeed a voice in the wilderness; the German dream of conquest had no place for such ideas. Having organized the entire German stockpile and the method for delivering it to the factories, Rathenau resigned in 1915, and on his father's death assumed the chairmanship of the A. E. G. complex. In 1917, he unsuccessfully tried to persuade Ludendorff against the continuation of Germany's policy of unrestricted submarine warfare, but his disappointment with Ludendorff then was much less than what he felt a year later.

In 1918, when Ludendorff suddenly demanded that an armistice be reached overnight, Rathenau's long experience as a negotiator in business matters warned him that Germany must not throw away all its bargaining chips by rushing into a unilateral surrender that would inevitably result in harsh peace terms dictated by the other side. Rathenau had seen defeat coming for a long time, but now that it had overtaken those close-cropped Prussian generals with whom he was so disenchanted, Rathenau understood the final irony: Germany must fight on a little longer and give her diplomats room to negotiate, or the only peace they could achieve would result in future wars. He later referred to Ludendorff's insistence on an instant armistice as "the most disastrous piece of stupidity in history," and he was right.[30] On October 7, 1918, the *Vossische Zeitung* published Rathenau's appeal to the German people, in which he urged a final effort. Accurately foreseeing that Germany's appeal for real negotiations was about to be undermined by the Allied knowledge that Ludendorff had lost his nerve, Rathenau exhorted the authorities and the populace to send to the front every man capable of bearing arms. There must be a final group of volunteers who had not previously served; everyone on leave, no matter how well-earned his furlough, must return to the front; in the rear, able-bodied soldiers "must be combed out of the offices, the guard-rooms and depots, in East and West, at the bases and at home. . . . At this moment we have hardly half of the total available troops on the Western Front. Our front is worn out; restore it, and we shall be offered different terms. It is peace we want, not war — but not a peace of surrender."[31]

The hour was late; Germany was collapsing. As the cannon stopped firing, Rathenau found himself hated by those on both ends of the political spectrum. To the right, he was a leftist Jew who welcomed the end of the military's role as dictators; in the view of the völkisch elements, a Jew had no business tinkering with the German soul in philosophical pronouncements about Germany's future society and its ideal values. In the eyes of the left, Rathenau was a hypocritical capitalist who mouthed his vision of a socialist future while riding in his chauffeur-driven open car with a fur lap robe tucked around him. The workers did not see him as a statesman trying desperately to give his nation a chance for something better than humiliation and dismemberment at the peace table; they reviled him as an industrialist who wanted to "prolong the war."[32]

With no official part to play in the creation of the infant Weimar Republic, Rathenau still continued to use his vast international prestige to plead for justice for Germany. As the peace conference that was to result in the Versailles Treaty began to assemble in Paris, he sent a letter to Colonel House, the confidant and principal adviser to President Woodrow Wilson. In an appeal for compassion for Germany and a workable future for all Europe, he wrote:

> Never since history began has so much power been entrusted to any one body of men as to Wilson, Clemenceau and Lloyd George today. . . . As a humble member of a people wounded to the heart, struggling simultaneously for its new-found freedom and its very existence, I appeal to you, the representative of the most progressive of all nations. . . . Today we stand on the verge of annihiliation; a fate which cannot be avoided if Germany is to be crippled as those who hate us wish. For this fact must be stated clearly and insistently, so that all may understand its terrible significance, all nations and their peoples, the present generation and those to come: what we are threatened with, what the policy of hate proposes, is our annihilation, the annihilation of German life now and forever more.[33]

Colonel House was said to have been "deeply shocked" by this letter and to have drawn Wilson's attention to it, but the ineptitude of the American president at Paris in the face of Clemenceau's desire for revenge and future military and economic superiority over Germany left Rathenau as ineffective on the international scene as he was in his own land.[34]

Only after the failure of the Kapp Putsch in late March 1920 did Rathenau begin to resume a place of prominence in German affairs. He was a member of the delegation that went to confer with the Allies at Spa on the subjects of Germany's disarmament and reparations, the emphasis in the latter area being on deliveries of German coal. Rathenau sat composed but inwardly aghast as the German industrial titan Hugo Stinnes defied and insulted the representatives of the Allied powers. When the German delegation members met among themselves, Rathenau politely but firmly and convincingly criticized Stinnes, to his face. Defiance was a dead end, he said. The door must be kept open: "Once negotiations are possible, anything is possible."[35]

Rathenau's words did not fall on deaf ears. Joseph Wirth of the Center Party, the future chancellor who was attending Spa in his capacity as minister of finance, saw Rathenau as a man whose abilities must not be lost to the struggling young republic. When he became chancellor in May of 1921, Wirth appointed Rathenau minister of reconstruction. At the age of fifty-three, this Jew who was the ablest man in German public affairs had at last been invited to hold a cabinet position. In his maiden speech in the Reichstag, he told the nation's legislators, "I have entered a cabinet of fulfillment. We must discover some way of linking ourselves up with the world again."[36]

Across the next eleven months, Rathenau worked ceaselessly for a peace that would be fair to Germany and beneficial for Europe. He took part in the drafting of the separate peace treaty signed with the United States in November of 1921, and met with French officials to hammer out the Wiesbaden Agreement, an arrangement about reparations payments that for a time reduced friction with France. Forced to retire from the cabinet when the Social Democrats withdrew their ministers in protest over the settlement in Upper Silesia, Rathenau subsequently acted as Germany's emissary in economic discussions held in England with Prime Minister Lloyd George. These talks led to the "Chequers scheme," which envisioned a consortium, sometimes referred to as a United States of Europe, that would reconstruct Russia by harnessing the combined economic forces of both Germany and the Allies. Rathenau's candor, vision, and enthusiastic idealism stimulated discussions that embraced possible plans for canceling the various debts the Allies owed to each other, and for a peace pact designed to stabilize the troubled Rhine frontier.

It was on his return from an economic conference at Cannes in the south of France that Rathenau was named by Chancellor Wirth as Germany's foreign minister. Commenting on the significance of the appointment, Count Harry Kessler later wrote, "For the first time since the war a German statesman had forced the world to take him seriously and to glimpse behind the picture of Germany distorted by war and post-war propaganda another Germany, industrious, honest, peaceful, and ready to fulfill her obligations."[37] What Walther Rathenau was telling other nations, and Germany itself, was that Germany's only effective army was, and should be, its army of workers and thinkers, and that Germany's policy was, and should be, to use the nation's energy and intelligence to achieve a peaceful economic recovery that would of itself reduce the tensions between Germany and her neighbors.

III

For right-wing Germans, the new foreign minister was a marked man. Speaking to a Munich crowd two days after Rathenau's appointment was announced, Hitler said, "Making one Walther Rathenau foreign minister really is going too far." The crowd then shouted, "Rathenau, Judensau!" — Rathenau, Jewish pig! The four thousand Bavarians present in this gathering at the Zirkus Krone heard Hitler once again articulate his racial-sexual fantasy: "Our young girls are being seduced by the Jews and thus our people is being contaminated. Every Jew who is caught with a blond girl should be . . . ." Hitler paused, knowing that the crowd would have some suggestions. "Hanged!" came the shout. Hitler went on, "I don't want to say hanged; but there should be a court which condemns these Jews to death."[38] Soon thereafter, at a meeting of the SA, Hitler commented on what he claimed was the growth of anti-Semitism in the nation. "All middle class parties now promise to concern themselves with the Jewish question. For me that is too little."[39] As Hitler saw it, anti-Semitism must become the nation's overriding political issue. Suiting the action to the word, Hitler spoke about this topic in detail for another ninety minutes.

As for the members of the SA, their numbers were growing; in the months ahead, they would be organized into *Hundertschaften*, units of a hundred men apiece. Under the aegis of the SA, a Nazi youth group was planned. Announcing the creation of the "Jugendbund of the NSDAP," the *Völkischer Beobachter* said on March 8 that its purpose "is to gather together and organize all young supporters of our cause who as a consequence of their age are not allowed to belong to the Sturmabteilung as a political organization." This appeal for recruits under seventeen years old was directed to German youths "who are deeply concerned about the misery and suffering of our Fatherland and who later want to join the ranks of our party and the SA as fighters against the Jewish enemy, the sole creator of the present day disgrace and misery." The *Beobachter* announcement ended, "Hail to all young warriors!"

Just when the party appeared to be in a period of unhindered growth, with sufficient income to have thirteen full-time employees working on behalf of the six thousand members, a mountainous obstacle suddenly confronted Hitler.[40] On February 18, the People's Court of Munich once again confirmed the sentence of three months' imprisonment that Hitler must sooner or later serve for his role in the attack on Ballerstedt.[41] In addition, he was to be on probation for four years. On March 10, in answer to a question from the floor of the Bavarian parliament, Minister of the Interior Franz Schweyer said that deporting Hitler to his native Austria was being considered.

Here at last was the opportunity for liberal Germans to place the nation's most inflammatory anti-Semitic orator outside their border. The government headed by Lerchenfeld had none of Kahr's right-wing tendencies. Presumably Lerchenfeld had not been pleased by a recent Hitler speech that referred to him as a "clod" and accused him of lying to the people about the true causes of the post-Armistice leftist revolution in Bavaria.[42] In the view of the Lerchenfeld government, the activities of the NSDAP were a constant threat to law and order in Bavaria.

Hitler's style was not to lie low while his fate was under discussion by the authorities. The *Beobachter* soon came out with a tirade that was not signed by Hitler but was probably written by him. In any case, it could not have appeared without his approval.

> So this is what it has come to! Hundreds of thousands of Jews can immigrate from Galicia and spew out their poison in all the news-papers, but for the "German" government, a man immediately becomes a "foreigner" if he was born a few kilometers on the other side of the Bavarian boundary posts and is scraping to-gether all the forces which have any character left to combat the parasites. A man who, in addition, served and shed blood for the German Fatherland for four and one-half years in the most forward trenches, who, as a simple soldier, was awarded the Iron Cross, First and Second Class; who, in the final analysis, defended the jelly-bellies who now do the talking.[43]

Hitler's vulnerability was that his army service had not gained him German citizenship. Having just been convicted of a crime against public law and order, Hitler had furnished the Bavarian government with an excuse to deport him as a criminal without having to debate the merits of his party's program. The decision on issuing an "expulsion order'" rested in the hands of a meeting of leaders of the principal political parties active in Bavaria. As the discussion on Hitler's case began, the sentiment was overwhelmingly in favor of deportation.

One man, Erhard Auer, the leader of Bavaria's Social Democrats, disagreed. It was Auer who was shot at during the past October as he walked home after a political meeting; it was widely believed that the attempted assassination was an effort by Hitler's SA. The leftist Erhard Auer Guards frequently fought the Storm Troops in the streets. Auer now told the other political leaders that "democratic and libertarian principles" demanded that Hitler be accorded his right of free speech in a constitutional democracy, no matter how odious his religious slurs and abusive attacks upon the government might be.[44] After all, Auer told his fellow legislative colleagues, Hitler was *"nur eine komische figur,"* only a clown.[45]

This high-minded appeal turned the meeting around; if the Social Democrats would not throw Hitler out, none of the other parties wanted to initiate the action. So, said an Independent Socialist named Ernst Niekisch who was there, "the Social Democrats won the 'honor' of preserving Adolf Hitler for the German people."[46]

21

IN APRIL there came a diplomatic bombshell: during an international economic conference in progress at Genoa, Foreign Minister
Walther Rathenau had slipped off to the nearby Italian seaport and
resort of Rapallo. There he had met with Georgi Vasilievich Chicherin,
the Soviet foreign minister, who was also attending the conference at
Genoa. Without the knowledge of the delegations of the other twenty-
seven nations represented at Genoa, by evening Chicherin and Rathenau
had concluded their secret negotiations and initialed an agreement
that came to be known as the Treaty of Rapallo.[1]

The news of this pact caused a sensation. The conference had been
called into being partly as a result of Rathenau's suggestion to Lloyd
George that there be a resumption of relations with Russia on the part
of all the nations that had been boycotting the new and suspect communist state since the Revolution of 1917. Both the Soviets and Germany had been invited to attend as equal partners, but the assumption
had been that the two outcasts of Europe would arrive hat in hand.
Instead, under the noses of those who expected to manipulate them,
the two pariahs had agreed to resume diplomatic relations, and to
cancel any debts and claims that each might have in relation to the
other. Each granted the other "most favored nation" status in foreign
trade, and it was assumed by the other participants that the treaty
also included secret military agreements.

For the German right, this was the last straw. Chicherin was not a
Jew, Lenin was not a Jew, President Ebert and Chancellor Wirth and
the great majority of the Reichstag legislators were not Jews, but
völkisch thought hewed to its line. Rathenau *was* a Jew: commenting
on the pact three days after it was made, the *Völkischer Beobachter*
said, "In our eyes, the agreement of the German money market Jews

with the Soviet Jews means the following: Germany will be allowed to use her technology, her work, and her sweat to build up the bankrupt exploitive government of Soviet Russia so that the stock market Jews from all over the world can take over without danger to themselves."[2] Two days later, Hitler pronounced in a speech: "The annihilation of the two national states, Germany and Russia, has been achieved; the Jewish state is already established. . . . Genoa means the continuing enslavement of Germany. . . . Who is representing Germany in Genoa? Her destroyers!"

As Hitler put it, the excursion away from Genoa to Rapallo was nothing but the consummation of another Jewish-Marxist plot, another proof of "the Jewish world threat."[3]

Whatever else Rapallo was, and its circumstances and significance were to be studied and debated by scholars for decades, it was certainly no Jewish plot, nor did it have much to do with political ideology. Germany's right-wingers would have been startled to learn that the pact was strongly although silently endorsed by General von Seeckt, who thought that the agreement with Russia was well worth the muddled collapse of the rest of the conference. There were in fact no secret clauses in the Rapallo Treaty establishing a military alliance; none was necessary, because a few of the Reichswehr's leaders had such a secret agreement already worked out in practice.[4]

Here was an illuminating lesson in national self-interest as practiced in terms of *Realpolitik*, freed from the slogans of either right or left. Within a few months of the war's close, German industrialists saw that any resumption of their prewar trade in the West would be subject to myriad vindictive restrictions and penalties. By contrast, in the East were the markets of Russia, now controlled by a regime with which the Allies would not even establish diplomatic relations. It was a small and war-crippled market for German exports, but its potential was enormous. From the Soviet point of view, Germany not only possessed the factories that could produce goods needed by Russia, but also innumerable engineers who could assist it in building its own factories and systems of power supply so that it too could become a modern industrial state.

The Reichswehr's approach to this confluence of interest was determined both by general strategic interests and by those clauses of the Versailles Treaty which virtually banned Germany's possession of the three types of weapons that had emerged from the war as being incontestably the keys to future military survival and success: planes, tanks, and submarines. Within the borders of Germany, the Inter-

Allied Military Control Commission would have an excellent chance of discovering secret training grounds for tank warfare or airfields at which flyers were being trained, no matter how they might be concealed, and it would be difficult to build something like a submarine in secrecy. In the Soviet Union, however, there were no Allied inspectors prowling about; in return for teaching aspirant aviators of the Red Army to fly in the tradition of Baron von Richthofen, the Soviets might permit Germany to construct factories that would build planes of the latest design for the future use of both nations.

And so, by fits and starts, a series of industrial and military arrangements came into being, most of the latter shrouded in secrecy. From the time that Seeckt was put in charge of the *Truppenamt*, or troops office — the cover under which the Reichswehr continued the activities of the General Staff, which had been abolished by the Versailles Treaty — German policy toward Russia was aimed at rebuilding German armed forces and those German industries upon which the army must rely.[5] Eventually, within the cover group for the General Staff, Seeckt created the even more secret Special Group R, which continued sending envoys to Russia and receiving representatives of the Soviet military and of her defense industries.[6] On May 6, 1921, there had been a public signing of a German-Russian commercial agreement, which did in fact pertain to many nonmilitary matters, but also dealt with products that could be useful in warfare.[7] In September of 1921, Russia's chairman of the Council for Foreign Trade, Leonid Krasin, accompanied by Trotsky's friend and colleague Victor Kopp, entered into detailed negotiations with Reichswehr officers. The meetings took place in the Berlin apartment of the brilliant Major Kurt von Schleicher; Seeckt stayed at a discreet distance, but was kept informed of the proceedings.[8]

To this point, Seeckt and what was in effect a group of General Staff conspirators had been negotiating with a foreign state without the permission or knowledge of Chancellor Wirth and his cabinet. Now, however, when the Soviets had fully opened the door for German rearmament to take place on Russian soil, large sums of money were required, and Seeckt had no choice but to disclose the plan to the chancellor. Wirth was in no way dismayed; on the contrary, he thought the Reichswehr was moving in precisely the right direction. "Whenever our policy in the West has run aground," he said, "it has always been wise to try something in the East."[9] As for the Soviets, their highest councils had long been aware of these efforts to achieve economic and military cooperation. "I am not fond of the Germans by any means," Lenin said, "but at the present time it is more advantageous to use them than to challenge them. . . . Everything teaches us to look upon Germany as our most reliable ally. Germany wants revenge, and we want revolution. For the moment our aims are the same." The farsighted Soviet leader added, "When our ways part, they will be our most ferocious and our great enemies. Time will tell whether a German hegemony or a Communist federation is to arise out of the ruins of Europe."[10]

With Wirth's approval, another cover was created: the Company to Promote Industrial Enterprises, a supposedly private trading corporation, known as GEFU, which had offices in Berlin and Moscow, and an initial capital of 75 million marks, supplied by the government. GEFU was ordered to proceed with the placement of a Junkers aircraft production line near Moscow, at Fili; its task was to produce six hundred all-metal planes a year. There was also to be formed a joint venture with the Soviets at Troitsk, which would manufacture poison gas; three hundred thousand artillery shells were to be turned out at arms works in three other cities.[11] Plans were also put in motion for a tank factory to be built near Kazan, with training grounds for German armor officers. There would be facilities for training both German and Russian flying personnel.[12] Much of this came to pass; however, the poison gas production never became a reality, and an effort to build submarines in Russia was soon supplanted by a devious scheme in which submarines were constructed in Holland, Sweden, Finland, and Spain under the guidance of German naval officers, with some of the submarines being sent to the Soviet navy.[13]

Just how much Walther Rathenau knew about such plans when he arrived at the Genoa conference is uncertain. Ironically, considering that Hitler and the entire völkisch camp were to portray him as the Jewish traitor who had delivered Germany into the arms of Lenin and Red Russia, it was two Gentiles, Rathenau's friend Chancellor Wirth and Baron Ago von Maltzan of the Foreign Ministry, who literally maneuvered Rathenau into believing that if the German delegation did not immediately drive to Rapallo and conclude a pact with the Soviets, the Russians would within hours sign a treaty with France and England that would complete the encirclement of German interests in the East. There were reasons for Rathenau to think this might be true — the last three times he had attempted to communicate with Lloyd George at the villa the British prime minister was using, he had been put off, and the Russian foreign minister Chicherin was making a great show of being open to approaches by one and all.[14] Nonetheless, Rathenau's decision to go to Rapallo was based solely on a conviction that Germany must forestall even the possibility of the restoration of the prewar British-French-Russian alliance. Hitler would have been shocked to learn that Seeckt welcomed the Treaty of Rapallo, seeing it as the perfect way in which to place Poland in a vise between the Reichswehr and the Red Army, thus setting the stage for a hoped-for obliteration of the newly re-created Polish nation and the restoration of the 1914 boundary between Germany and Russia that ran down its center.[15] Equally astonishing to Hitler would have been the knowledge that Rathenau's treaty, far from selling out Germany to communism, was causing the greatest difficulty for the German Communist Party. Karl Radek, the Comintern's principal emissary to German communists, was making it clear that Moscow wanted to limit revolutionary activity against a German government in whose stability the Soviet Union now had a vested interest.[16]

II

In contrast to Rathenau's policy of creating balances and readjustments, Hitler was preaching undistilled vengeance. On May 10, addressing a crowd at the Bürgerbräu on the topic "The Unknown Soldier," he shouted, "We do not want to awaken peace and insight and harmony, but rather hate!"

By this time in the spring of 1922, a Nazi public meeting was apt to have a certain theatrical quality, designed to enhance the effect of the speaker and speech. Swastika banners were placed about the hall; a brass band played a combination of marches and German folk songs, often including "Ich hatt' einen Kameraden," the immensely popular song, moving to all Germans, that recalled a soldier's buddy who had been killed in the war. Before and during the meeting, the beer hall waitresses passed out steins right and left, so that, with the combination of alcohol, sentimental songs, and warlike marches, the audience was emotionally off balance before the speaker appeared.

This evening, Hitler had more hate to share with his audience:

Hate for the criminals who rendered meaningless the death of our heroes and who are still our "leaders" today. We also want to incite hate for those who deserve no mercy, those who are still selling out and betraying us, who still want to lead us to the slaughter; not to liberation, but to bled-to-death ruin. We want to forge a sword of revenge.[17]

The Jew was of course the principal target, and in another speech Hitler's frantic anti-Semitism led him into some singularly ugly characterizations of Germany's Jews, all of which were apparently received with enthusiasm by his audience. Speaking when the German mark was known as the "pfennig mark" because it had dropped to a hundredth of its prewar value, Hitler said:

> The Jew has not become poorer. He is gradually puffing up. And if you don't believe that, I ask you to look at our health resorts. There you'll find two types of people: the German who goes there for the first time in a long time to get some fresh air and to recuperate, and the Jew, who goes there to lose his fat. And go into our mountains. Whom do you find there in brand-new, splendid yellow hiking boots with pretty backpacks in which there is usually nothing useful? And why should there be? The Jews go up there to the hotel, usually as far as the railway goes, and where the train stops, they stop too. Then they just sit around within a kilometer of the hotel, like blowflies around a corpse.

By contrast, Hitler pictured true German workers as hiking up the slopes, but said that these real Germans would not go into the hotel, "because they are ashamed to enter this perfumed atmosphere in their old clothes dating from 1913 and 1914."[18] He then made a swift oratorical saber stroke at all of the left and most of the right: "And the right has further completely forgotten that democracy is fundamentally not German: it is Jewish."[19]

Now Hitler compared himself to Christ.

> Count Lerchenfeld said in the last session of parliament that his feeling "as a human being and a Christian" would prevent him from being an anti-Semite. I say: my Christian feeling tells me that my lord and savior is a warrior. It calls my attention to the man who, lonely and surrounded by only a few supporters, recognized the Jews for what they were, and called for a battle against them, and who, by God, was not the greatest *sufferer*, but the greatest *warrior*. . . .
>
> As a human being it is my duty to see to it that humanity will not suffer the same catastrophic collapse as did that old civilization two thousand years ago, a civilization which was driven to its ruin by the Jews. . . . I am convinced that I am really a devil and not a Christian if I do not feel compassion and do not wage war,

as Christ did two thousand years ago, against those who are stealing from and exploiting these poverty-striken people.

Two thousand years ago a man was similarly denounced by this particular race which today denounces and blasphemes all over the place. . . . That man was dragged before a court and they said: he is arousing the people! So he, too, was an agitator![20]

Four days after this outburst, an entirely different point of view was heard, from a man who was becoming increasingly worried about the political health of his nation. In the pages of the *Frankfurter Zeitung*, Thomas Mann said in a review of the new German translation of Walt Whitman's works that these poems from America had reinforced his conviction that democracy was "nothing other than that which we call, in our old-fashioned way, 'humanity.' " Mann added, "I am convinced that there is no more pressing task for Germany than to fulfill this word."[21]

It was a noble thought, but many Germans felt that terms such as "humanity" and "democracy" had an empty sound to them at a time when the mark's value fell from week to week and Germany's leaders were apparently throwing her into the arms of the Russian Bolsheviks. In Munich, the party's membership began to grow rapidly. Party theoretician Alfred Rosenberg said, "Letters containing suggestions, programs, poems, arrived constantly in an endless stream. They probably weren't kept. Occasionally all this turned our offices into a sort of spiritual torture chamber — and yet, what a wealth of suppressed love was there, that merely could not express itself! How much need and despair, anxious to find something to cling to!"[22]

Hitler was orchestrating everything in a skillful fashion. By now, he could almost count on being able to exploit the inflationary spiral. On February 11, the *Beobachter*'s price had gone from 50 to 60 pfennigs; on April 1, the price had been raised to one mark; on June 17, it would go from one mark to two. In an effort to keep up the influx of new members, Hitler used a party information sheet to point out to the leadership the desirability of making a strong first impression.

The careful preparation of gatherings is . . . one of the uppermost tasks of the leadership of individual local groups. Munich can be regarded as a perfect example in this respect.

Although we have repeatedly requested that the first meetings of the local group never take place in a hall that is too large . . . one of our local groups — Mannheim — held its first major public gathering in a room which was much too large and suffered a fiasco.[23]

There were now almost fifty Ortsgruppen, and on May 17 the *Völkischer Beobachter* sent out the news of the founding meeting of the Nazi youth group, which had previously been organized on paper. At this gathering, Hitler used a new technique: he deliberately arrived late, striding in while another of the party's leaders was speaking — an arrival that prompted the speaker to stop and the audience to erupt with applause at the mere appearance of der Führer. The *Beobachter* fulsomely reported Hitler's address to these boys under seventeen years of age.

He described in breathtaking words what had made Germany great: the systematic education of German males to physical fitness, the spirit of most loyal comradeship, the will to unconditionally obey the recognized leader. . . . The speaker closed with an appeal to the Jugendbund to practice obedience and discipline in their relationship with the Führer.[24]

CHAPTER

22

DURING THE COURSE of this spring, an unusual future recruit for the Nazi Party returned to his native Germany. Like most Germans, he had never heard of Hitler; if someone had told him that within a few months he would be representing something called the Nazi Party as its envoy to Benito Mussolini and his blackshirted Fascists, he would have scratched his elegantly barbered head. Thus far the Nazi Party had a Bavarian café luminary in Dietrich Eckart, but nothing in the way of an international playboy and sometime entrepreneur.

In a nation whose men vied with each other in their tales of wartime soldierly exploits, Kurt Ludecke was a refreshing exception. His entire military career had been a combination of a comedy of manners, and, literally, the madhouse. Doing a year's prewar compulsory military service in 1908, Ludecke soon demonstrated that he was proficient at his military duties, but, as he put it, "I was scornful of minor regulations that seemed to me senseless." This led him into trouble.

> Civilian clothes were forbidden us at all times, but having become attached to a young lady who had rejected an officer of my company, I put on a dinner-jacket and took her to the theatre — and in the foyer during the intermission we ran into the officer in question.
> After three days of "Mittelarrest," I emerged a black sheep, and a tough sergeant was put over me to see that I broke no more rules. By the time my enlistment was over, I had lost all desire for an army career and had gained a deep-rooted hatred for top-sergeants.[1]

Leaving Germany at the age of nineteen, Ludecke soon found, at race tracks in England and casinos in France, that he was one of the very few men destined to win more than they lose at gambling. "Some of the money I invested; much of it I spent in travel — the Balearic Isles, Italy, the Dalmatian coast, Egypt, India. There was no passport nuisance in those days." As 1914 approached, Kurt Ludecke was cutting quite a figure for a man in his early twenties.

I wore London clothes; my own chauffeur sat at the wheel of my big car; I had more money than I knew what to do with. And now I had Dolores, perhaps the one real person in my shallow world. She was the wife of another man, but we lived together.

Except for Dolores, the aimless and futile life of winning and spending would have become my routine. Every day in the year a man might kiss a countess, shake hands with a grand duke, have cocktails with an American millionaire; the only requisities were a clean face, a dinner-jacket, and some pocket-change. Repeat the formula three hundred and sixty-five days in succession and you've had a dull year.

The same mind that enabled Ludecke to survive at the gaming table made him an excellent chess player. In the summer of 1914, he and Dolores were in his chauffeur-driven car, traveling to an international chess tournament at Mannheim, near Heidelberg, when they learned that Germany was at war. The prewar party was over, snapped off almost in midsentence: René, his French chauffeur, was interned, and Ludecke enlisted and received mobilization orders. "I tried to persuade Dolores, an American, to leave Germany, but she refused."

Then began the absurdities. "Spy hysteria was gripping the nation." Ludecke's English suits and luggage caused him to be detained twice by the civilian police, and to be arrested twice by military authorities, before he could even take up his military duties at the headquarters of a regiment in Baden. He had received permission to live comfortably at a hotel while awaiting further assignment, and then "Dolores arrived, wearing Paris clothes and talking eagerly in French. Apprehensively I got her upstairs."

As the German armies crashed into Belgium, Private Kurt Ludecke was assisting the top sergeant of the first reserve company with clerical duties at the barracks while hiding his foreign mistress at the hotel. For three days Ludecke managed to keep Dolores out of sight, taking his meals with her in their rooms, and hoping that no one would arrest them as spies. "On the third afternoon we had just finished lunch when a gun-butt crashed on the door. It was [Lieutenant] Stroffel, with a military escort." Protected by her American passport and the fact that the United States was a neutral nation, Dolores was allowed to leave town; Private Kurt Ludecke was put under arrest.

Then began one of those sad persecutions. Lieutenant Stroffel was not only Ludecke's immediate superior, but also the regiment's judicial officer, empowered to mete out punishments as he pleased. First came two weeks of solitary confinement, with "one thick slice of bread and a pitcher of water" for three days, and a slender meal on the fourth. Then came ten weeks of every kind of company punishment. Finally, "I reported sick, and then broke down in the presence of the doctor; if he couldn't have me sent somewhere, anywhere, I should either have to desert or shoot myself. He was very gentle with me. Next day they had me up for examination again." This resulted in what Private Ludecke assumed was a routine transfer to Freiburg, but once the door was closed behind him in his new quarters, he found that he was in a psychiatric ward. As months passed and hundreds of thousands perished in Flanders, Ludecke discovered that there were doctors who thought there were other destinies for a young German than to die gloriously at the front. It was put to Kurt Ludecke that he was indeed sane but that it might be better to remain among the springtime blooms of Freiburg. "As we were allowed to enter the town whenever we pleased, and were required only to sleep at the hospital, I sent for Dolores." At last, after Dolores left for her native United States, which was becoming increasingly less neutral, Ludecke received an assignment to work as a clerk at a military hospital in Heidelberg. Looking around the office, he asked what sort of hospital it was, and was informed, "Didn't you know? It's for the insane."

In the late autumn of 1916, by which time a million young Germans had died in the war, Kurt Ludecke was quietly discharged from the army. Everyone — his military confidants and various doctors — urged him not to apply for service at the front, because such a request would reveal his record and simply get him into more trouble.

At the age of twenty-six, Kurt Ludecke found that he was something more than a gambler and a lover and a military misfit.

> From a small beginning as broker for the sale of several hundred head of sheep . . . in a few months I was buying agent for a group of large industries and municipalities, going to Copenhagen, Amsterdam, Zurich, with the satisfaction of knowing that I was procuring needed supplies for my country — an interesting work which

exempted me from further military service. . . . On one of my trips to Copenhagen I was given an opportunity by the intelligence service to report on the activities of two German agents suspected of serving both sides. In the Danish capital, spies were trailing spies, and they in turn were being shadowed by superspies, all under cover of a life of exaggerated brilliance and gaiety.

With the defeat of Germany, Kurt Ludecke began to accelerate his activities as an entrepreneur. In the immediate postwar situation, there were vast and varied stocks of surplus war supplies sitting in many countries; for a time, at least, there were few rules governing their purchase and sale. Some ideas worked, and some did not. At the age of twenty-eight, Ludecke almost pulled off a deal in which scores of German freighters and tankers would have been put beyond the reach of the Allies by transfer to a Danish-Mexican company that would have had them sail under the Mexican flag. According to Ludecke, the German shipping executives simply did not move fast enough: when the Versailles Treaty terms were announced, every German vessel over sixteen hundred tons was confiscated, both those in German ports and those in neutral nations.

Then there was Ludecke's scheme to sell German planes to Argentina. He went to Buenos Aires, where "General José Francisco Uriburu, later President of the Argentine Republic, willingly granted me space at the flying field and the use of a hangar. . . . The planes were practically sold, unseen."

Once again it was a matter of timing.

At length came a cable saying that they could not be shipped before November. Well before that date, a French mission arrived bringing forty planes, the whole paraphernalia of an air fleet, and an Argentine flyer who had fought in the Lafayette Escadrille and now wore the insignia of the Légion d'Honneur in his buttonhole. My prospects vanished.

Undaunted, Ludecke made his way to Mexico, where he became embroiled in the Mexican Revolution. Finding himself aboard a train taking President Venustiano Carranza from Mexico City to Vera Cruz, Ludecke drew the appropriate conclusions when the revolutionaries rammed a locomotive into the train full of government soldiers that was just ahead of him. "Certain that I was marked for death where I was, I got my bag out of the train and struck out into the country." Carranza stayed aboard, and by the time he and two hundred of his followers took to the hills, he was trapped and killed.

Ludecke crossed into the United States at San Antonio and made his way north in the first of two trips to the United States in his wanderings during the years just after the war. On his second visit, he talked at great length with William J. Cameron, the editor of Henry Ford's *Dearborn Independent*. On May 22, 1920, the *Independent* had started a series of ninety-one anti-Semitic articles, the first of which was "The International Jew: The World's Problem."[2] Among the others, which were eventually published as a book, *The International Jew*, were "The Jewish Associates of Benedict Arnold," "The Gentle Art of Changing Jewish Names," and "The All-Jewish Mark on Red Russia." The Jews, according to Ford's perception, had been involved in a lengthy conspiracy to create an "international super-capitalist government." The *Independent* stated that the world's movie industry was "exclusively under the control, moral and financial, of the Jewish manipulators of the public mind."[3] Hollywood and Broadway Jews were bombarding the American public with sexuality, vulgarity, and glorified immorality that was sure to poison American life.

Those sentiments struck a chord in Kurt Ludecke. As a clerk at the psychiatric hospital in Heidelberg, he had come under the influence of Professor Alfred von Domaszewski of Heidelberg University, a philosopher and historian. "From our first meeting I regarded him with a respect that ended in veneration. . . . I went steadily to his lectures and upon occasion was admitted to the circle of his friends."[4] Domaszewski and some of his colleagues frequented wine cellars where they discussed an idealized Aryan people whose splendid racial characteristics were in grave danger of being diluted by lesser breeds. This led Ludecke to a study of such anti-Semitic writers as Joseph-Arthur de Gobineau, Houston Stewart Chamberlain, and Paul Anton de Lagarde. His combination of listening and reading left him with a view of the Jews as enemies of what he called the "folk-soul" of the German people; in the United States, he took good note that a newspaper in the American heartland of Michigan, backed by Henry Ford's millions, was saying something akin to what he had heard in Germany.

Along with his adventures and imaginative business failures, there were moments of the Midas touch. The boom town on the Baltic was the port of Revel, later Tallinn, the capital of the new Republic of Estonia, which had split off from the Soviet Union. It was a trader's paradise, a doorway to the newly opened markets of Lenin's Russia. The tread tire for automobiles and trucks had just been developed; although it was preferable to the treadless tire, the old type was still usable. Ludecke knew of a firm in Frankfurt that still had what he described as an "enormous stock" of the treadless tires; he arranged to become the company's sales manager in the Baltic area.

> The Bolsheviks were buying avidly with the Czar's gold and being victimized, paying spot cash for carloads of rusty nails and American Army bacon too rancid for the soldiers. Granted that my tyres lacked a tread, they still were good tyres and I sold them with a will. . . .
> Once more I was in the money, determined now to keep it. The mark, still falling, was sixty to the dollar and I was putting my earnings into dollars and banking them in Amsterdam and Zurich. But life in Revel wore down the nerves, starved the spirit. I had made enough.[5]

In an effort to stave off boredom Ludecke went to visit some of his old playboy haunts.

> London was dismal; Paris, depressing and vulgarized now, had lost its magic. I journeyed through Switzerland to Vienna, once so beautiful, now sombre and terrible; on through Italy to Rome. Everywhere the picture was the same — Europe was gloomy, unsettled, unreal. . . . I began to listen to an inner voice I had been stifling all these restless years. Go home, it said, and stay there. Whatever the future of your country may be, your own is bound up with it.[6]

And so, in 1922, Kurt Ludecke returned to his native land. He was well off indeed, with bank accounts in foreign capitals that gave him access to hard currencies; with the mark at a hundred to the dollar and still slipping, he would cash checks for amounts that were just enough to meet his immediate needs, because he knew that his foreign-based dollars and pounds would provide him with an even better rate of exchange in a few days' time. He was torn by his reentry into German life in 1922. "Spring in Berlin, trees in full bloom, fragrance pervading Unter den Linden, the Pariserplatz, the Tiergarten, Potsdam and its beautiful park of Sans Souci. And yet even the birds did not seem to sing so lustily as in the old days." Kurt Ludecke had ample money in his own pockets, but everywhere he looked, there were either unemployed people or men and women who were throwing themselves into the frantic nightlife of postwar Berlin. "Everything I saw seemed sad or crazy."

At the age of thirty-two, Kurt Ludecke felt a great frustration as he witnessed the plight of his nation. The food he ate in Berlin's best restaurants seemed tasteless in his mouth. He was vigorous and able, and he was looking for something. "At last I had to face the truth I had been dodging: so long as Germany was sick, there would be no happiness for me until I lent my hand to those who were trying to work out a cure."[7]

II

During the first half of 1922, the terrorists of Organization Consul were rolling along from one violent act to another. A daring raid in January freed from prison a former naval lieutenant who was one of the tiny handful of German military men who were actually convicted and sent to prison under the "war criminal" provision of the Versailles Treaty. Across a span of weeks, the Hamburg cell of the O.C. set off a series of five bombs in the homes and offices of left-wing activists in that city. On June 4, as the Weimar Republic's first chancellor, Philipp Scheidemann, walked through the woods near Kassel, accompanied by his daughter and granddaughter, an O.C. operative leapt at him from behind some bushes. The would-be assassin squeezed a rubber bulb containing the form of cyanide known as prussic acid, and lethal amounts squirted through the nozzle at Scheidemann's face. A gust of wind diffused the deadly fluid, and Scheidemann's thick mustache kept the fatal drops from reaching the inside of his nose.

For Adolf Hitler, who read the reports of these right-wing attacks in the Munich newspapers, this form of terrorism seemed too selective. He shared the hatred of the O.C. assassins for their various targets, and rejoiced when any leftist leader was struck down, but at this point he felt that the objectives of the Nazi Party were not to be achieved by clandestine killings. Terror, yes, but those terrified must be the Erhard Auer Guards, as they faced the party's Storm Troops. Audiences must be fearful even of attending leftist gatherings, because they might at any moment be invaded by the Sturmabteilung. A number of NSDAP members were involved with the O.C. on their own initiative, but Hitler saw little practical use for conspiracies involving what he called "dagger and poison and pistol." The weapons he wanted were "a hundred thousand, and again a hundred thousand, fanatical fighters for our view of life. The work must be done not in secret conventicles, but in overwhelming mass demonstrations . . . in the conquest of the streets."[8] Hitler would, however, have sympathized with the emotional and political motivation for these attacks, as expressed by a young Freikorps veteran who was deeply involved in the O.C.'s current campaign:

> We believed that it was we who were meant to have the power and no one else, for Germany's sake. For we felt that we embodied Germany. We believed that we were entitled to have that power. The people at the head of affairs in Berlin had no such right. For we did not believe that they were working solely for the good of Germany, as we were, who felt that we *were* Germany.[9]

The young member of the Frankfurt cell of the O.C. underground who wrote these words was Ernst von Salomon, who at the age of eighteen had laid waste Latvian villages as the Iron Division retreated during its Baltic adventure. Now he was waging war right in his own country, working at odd jobs during the day and serving the O.C. at night. In the weeks after the attack on Scheidemann he was summoned to Berlin by one of his heroes, former naval lieutenant Erwin Kern. Twenty-five years old, Kern was a veteran of the Ehrhardt Brigade; in appearance, he was the personification of the blue-eyed, fair-haired Nordic type. During the first half of 1922, he seemed to be everywhere at once in Germany, running guns in East Prussia, abducting a separatist leader near Munich, organizing the Ditmarsch peasants into right-wing guerrilla bands. A contemporary characterized Kern this way:

> Handsome, narrow-minded, easily deceived, rash, obstinate, the born fanatic, fanned by Nationalist agitation into a fervour of hatred against Jews and the Republic; apart from this, not devoid of charm, a young Hotspur, who exercised a mysterious and irresistible attraction on men younger than himself. In these years after the war, when the older generation had lost all its authority, such gatherings of small groups of boys and youths about someone only a little older than themselves were by no means uncommon.[10]

Arriving in Berlin, Salomon found Kern in "a small secluded boarding house."[11] With Kern was another twenty-five-year-old, Hermann Fischer, a quiet, thoughtful engineer. Salomon enthusiastically plunged into the various schemes being developed by Kern, traveling around Germany to pass on the leader's instructions, but it seemed to him that Kern was becoming frustrated and irritable. Funds were drying up, and it seemed that only the operations under Kern's direct control were succeeding. There was evidence of betrayal in several matters, and a sense that police spies were closing in. The Berlin cell changed its place of residence every few days, which may have thrown off surveillance, but being on the run within Berlin was destroying the cell's efficiency, as well as making it almost impossible for the members to receive messages, and visits from individuals, that were necessary to the conduct of operations. Kern obviously had made a decision to concentrate on a single operation that would eclipse the others, but for the moment he would tell Salomon nothing. All that was known was that a high-powered car would soon be put at their disposal.

On the evening of one of the following days, Kern, Fischer, and I were sitting on a bench in the Zoological Gardens, waiting for the car which was due to arrive from Saxony. . . . Kern said: "If this final act is not attempted now, it may be impossible for decades. We want a revolution. We are free from the hindrance of plans, methods, and systems. Therefore it is our duty to take the first step, to storm the breach. We must retire the moment our task is done. For our task is attack, not government."
Fischer sat motionless. A policeman passed slowly and looked us up and down. Night came on. Kern said: "The desire for change is here, everywhere. . . . What we have done up to now has strengthened the position but it is not enough. . . . We have destroyed limbs but not the head and not the heart. I intend to shoot the man who is greater than all those who surround him."
My throat grew dry. "Rathenau?" I asked.
"Rathenau," said Kern and stood up.[12]

Soon after, Kern and Fischer went to the Reichstag at a time when Rathenau was speaking, and, entering the visitors' gallery, silently studied the man they intended to kill. Walking back to their temporary lodgings, they were joined by Salomon. As they made their way along the Unter den Linden, they passed the window of a photographer's studio in which was displayed a portrait of Rathenau. Kern stood in front of it for a long time. "The strange, dark, eager yet self-possessed eyes looked at us out of the narrow aristocratic face almost searchingly. Fischer after a long scrutiny said: 'He looks a decent sort.' "[13]

III

At some point during these first weeks of summer — the exact date will never be known, because Chancellor Wirth never specified the moment at which it occurred — a troubled priest presented himself at the Chancellery. Admitted into Wirth's presence, he said that, while hearing confessions, he had heard something of such gravity that he intended to break his vow to keep forever secret those things heard in the confessional. The priest then told the chancellor that a plot was afoot to kill Rathenau. "I could not question him," Wirth said, and it was never determined whether what the priest had heard was from the lips of one of the additional conspirators Kern recruited as the plot developed.[14] Indeed, with many right-wingers thinking of suitable ways to mark June 28, the impending third anniversary of the signing of the Treaty of Versailles, the priest might have been hearing of some entirely different scheme to do away with Germany's foreign minister.

"I immediately understood how serious was the warning," Chancellor Wirth later said, "and myself passed on the information to my officials." Rapidly, the republic's principal officials responsible for security arrived in the chancellor's office. Wirth briefly reviewed the situation; it was known that Rathenau had refused the recommendation that he have bodyguards with him at all times.

> Then Rathenau himself was called in. I implored him with all
> my might to give up his resistance to increased police protection
> for his person. In his well-known manner, with which many of
> his friends were familiar, he stubbornly refused. Thereupon I
> informed him of what had happened, and asked him whether
> he did not see that the step taken by the Catholic priest was a
> very serious affair.

The atmosphere in the chancellor's office was electric.

> My words impressed Rathenau deeply. He stood motionless
> and pale for about two minutes. None of us dared break the
> silence or speak a single word. Rathenau seemed to be gazing
> on some distant land. He was visibly struggling with his own
> feelings. Suddenly his face and his eyes took on an expression
> of infinite benevolence and gentleness. With a calm such as I
> had never witnessed in him, although I had gauged the measure
> of his self-control in many a discussion on difficult political and
> personal questions, he stepped up to me, and putting both his
> hands on my shoulders said: "Dear friend, it is nothing. Who
> would do me any harm?"[15]

By June 18, in addition to Kern, Fischer, and Salomon, the last of whom Kern had told that he would not be part of the final attack, there were four other young Germans in on the plot. One was Hans Stubenrauch, a seventeen-year-old schoolboy who was the son of a general; another was his fellow student, a boy named Günther. There was also the son of a Berlin magistrate, Ernst-Werner Techow, and his younger brother, Gerd, who had joined the O.C. at the age of fifteen.[16] During a meeting of the conspirators on the evening of June 18, Kern decided that the best way to kill Walther Rathenau was to drive their car alongside the open car in which Rathenau was driven to the Foreign Ministry each morning, and shoot him dead as he sat in the back seat. Leaving nothing to chance, Kern held a rehearsal on the twenty-first. Using the handsome dark grey six-seater touring car sent from Saxony, he had Ernst-Werner Techow drive it along the ambush route, practicing quick accelerations on the Königsallee in the residential suburb of Grünewald, where Rathenau lived. As a professional killer trained by the navy, the Ehrhardt Brigade, and the Organization Consul, Kern decided that a conventional pistol fired from one car to another when both might be veering could not guarantee a kill. He procured a secretly stored British weapon, a Lewis submachine gun, which could empty its forty-seven-round magazine in a few seconds.[17]

While Erwin Kern was practicing for his biggest operation, Adolf Hitler was preparing to go to prison. The Bavarian authorities had at last ordered him to begin serving a month-long sentence for breaking up Ballerstedt's Bavarian League meeting the previous autumn. Speaking of the Nazi leader's impending incarceration, on June 22 the *Beobachter* noted that the decision to imprison him could be considered a form of "protective custody" that would get him off the scene just before the rightist demonstrations that might be expected on June 28. "The imprisonment of Adolf Hitler . . . is, objectively viewed, a slap in the face of all the true Germans in Bavaria," the paper said.[18]

Walther Rathenau continued to refuse added police protection, although he did not object to the two plainclothes policemen who were already stationed at his house. On his morning drive to the office, however, he was accompanied only by his unarmed chauffeur. Chancellor Wirth, whose teeth had been chattering, according to one account, when he told Rathenau about the assassination plot, said that even then Rathenau "left the room with an expression of incomprehensible security on his face."[19] Count Harry Kessler, who had known Rathenau for decades, said, "He believed in Fate, and he did not really believe in Death."[20] All that may have been true, but the impression given by Rathenau's actions was that of a man who was, as usual, bent on serving Germany and was too busy to worry for long about anything else. On June 21, he rose in the Reichstag to condemn the international governing commission that, under the Versailles Treaty, held power in the German mining and industrial region, the Saar. Concluding his criticism of the Saar arrangement that had been forced upon Germany by the Allies through the League of Nations, Rathenau said: "But as Germans we can point with pride to the fact that in these difficult years of alien domination, of which only a few have passed as yet, the population of the Saar area have held together as never before, in order to preserve that which they regard as their most precious possession, their German nationality and culture."[21]

Rathenau's reward for this speech, which was patriotic by any standards, was to have his words completely misrepresented two days later in a speech by the Nationalist Party leader Karl Helfferich, a man who had in his youth been befriended by Rathenau's parents. Starting with jibes at some of the phrases Rathenau had used in parts of his speech, Helfferich went on to claim that Rathenau and his colleagues in Wirth's cabinet were responsible for "the pulverization of our middle class."[22] Speaking as if Rathenau was principally to blame, Helfferich said that "the policy of fulfillment has brought poverty and misery on countless families, it has driven countless people to suicide and despair, it has sent abroad large and valuable portions of our national capital, and it has shaken our industrial and social order to its very foundations!"[23]

Rathenau found it particularly upsetting to have such scorn heaped upon him by Helfferich at just this time. Only two evenings earlier, Helfferich and another Nationalist Party leader had been his guests for dinner at his house. Rathenau had spent the entire evening in what he thought was a useful dialogue with the two right-wingers; the conversation was friendly, and as they parted Helfferich had assured him that he would not undermine Rathenau's ability to conduct foreign policy.

Putting aside his annoyance with Helfferich, Rathenau went ahead with his plans to attend a dinner that evening at the United States embassy in Berlin. Here there were also differences of opinion, but they were discussed constructively. The talk turned to Germany's problems in delivering to the Allies the shipments of coal that were required under the reparations agreements. Rathenau suggested to his host, Ambassador Alanson B. Houghton, that Hugo Stinnes be invited to join in the after-dinner discussion. Stinnes arrived at about ten o'clock, and after some conversation about the technical aspects of the coal deliveries, the conservative Stinnes, who had so incensed the Allied representatives at the Spa Conference, swung his conversational guns around and began attacking Rathenau's foreign policy. As Rathenau had shown at Spa, where he and Stinnes had been the expert representatives of German industry, he could hold his own against Stinnes in a quiet and gentlemanly way, and Ambassador Houghton's other guests witnessed a lively debate that went on until well past midnight. Listening to the points of view set forth by Germany's two greatest businessmen of the era, one sympathetic to socialism and the other a believer in largely unrestricted free enterprise, Ambassador Houghton had the impression that the two men were more in agreement than was generally believed.

Always ready to discuss matters further in the hope of shedding light and reaching useful compromises, Rathenau accompanied Stinnes to the Esplanade Hotel, where the "merchant from Mülheim" was staying, and there the two men continued their discussion until almost four in the morning. Rathenau was then driven to Grünewald.[24] There were no longer any policemen guarding his house; annoyed that a friend had been stopped and asked to identify himself when he came to call a couple of days previously, Rathenau had used his governmental authority to insist that all his police protection be ended.[25]

Another conversation was taking place in the early hours of Saturday, June 24. Erwin Kern and the other Organization Consul conspirators were drinking various quantities of beer, wine, and cognac, and discussing once more the man they intended to kill when daylight came. Kern's reason for the assassination attempt was an expression of pure nihilism: Rathenau was, he granted, "the finest and ripest fruit of his age. He unites in himself everything in this age that is of value in thought, in honor, and in spirituality." Such a civilized being must be destroyed in order to make it possible to start all over again. "I couldn't bear it if again something great were to rise out of the chaotic, the insane age in which we live. . . . We are not fighting to make the nation happy — we are fighting to make it walk in the path of its destiny."[26]

At ten-thirty in the morning, the dark grey open touring car was in a side street off the route that Rathenau's car would pass. The three men who would make the attack — Kern, Fischer, and Ernst-Werner Techow, who would drive — were wearing handsome leather coats and soft brown leather aviator's helmets, with their straps buckled under the chin. Fischer was at the corner where the street opened into the Königsallee, watching for Rathenau's car.

Although Salomon was not to participate in the attack, he was waiting with them until the last moment: "I was trembling to such an extent that I felt as if the engine against which I was leaning had already started." Kern got into the front seat beside Techow, giving last-minute instructions to Salomon. He pulled the Lewis gun from where he had hidden it under the seat, and got it ready beside him. His last words to Salomon, as he leaned forward and tugged at the lapel of Salomon's coat, were "You can't think how thankful I am that everything is behind me."[27]

Some bricklayers were at work along the Königsallee. One of them, a man named Krischbin, noticed that at about a quarter to eleven two cars came down the Königsallee, a small one more or less in the middle of the road, and a grey touring car somewhat behind it and to the side.

> The big car overtook the smaller one. . . . When the big car had got about half a length ahead . . . one of the men in the leather coats leant forward, seized a large revolver, whose butt he put in his armpit, and pointed it at the gentleman in the other car. He did not even need to aim, they were so close. I looked him straight in the eye, so to speak. It was a healthy, open face; what we call "an officer's face."

Realizing that he was in the line of fire, the bricklayer leapt for cover.

> The shots came quickly, as quickly as a machine-gun. When the one man had finished shooting, the other one stood up, pulled the pin out of an egg-bomb and threw it into the small car. The gentleman had already collapsed in his seat and was lying on his side.

As the assassins' car "leapt forward at full speed" and tore down a side street, "the car with the dead man in it stood by the curb. At that moment there was a crash as the bomb exploded. The gentleman in the tonneau was actually lifted up into the air — and the car itself seemed to give a jump. We all ran up and found nine empty cartridge cases on the pavement and the pin from the bomb."[28] The chauffeur had escaped harm; Rathenau was still alive, but he soon died.

Count Harry Kessler, who was in Berlin that day, said of the killing, "Not since the assassination of Abraham Lincoln has the death of a statesman so shaken a whole nation."[29] Kessler wrote of the immediate public reaction:

> Meanwhile by noon on the day of the murder the news had spread, and the workers began swarming from the factories and shops to form countless processions. These soon merged into one and moved solidly and irresistibly through the streets. . . . Four deep they marched in their hundred thousands beneath their mourning banners, the red of Socialism and the black-red-gold of the Republic, in one endless disciplined procession, passing like a portent silently along the great thoroughfares lined by immense crowds, wave after wave, from the early afternoon till late into the June sunset.[30]

The Reichstag met at three o'clock. Rathenau's empty seat on the government bench was draped in black crepe, a bouquet of white roses on the table in front of it. When Nationalist Party leader Helfferich appeared, there were shouts of "Murderer! Murderer! Out with the murderers!"[31] The shouting stopped only when Helfferich retreated from the chamber. It was the beginning of scenes of immense drama. The following day Chancellor Wirth rose in the Reichstag to condemn the purveyors of völkisch propaganda that incited young men to think that they were serving Germany by committing murder. Once again, Kessler was present and reported Wirth's words, and their results.

> "The real enemies of our country are those who instill this poison into our people. We know where we have to seek them. *The Enemy stands on the Right!*" he exclaimed, pointing at the empty benches of the Nationalists, only a few of whom had dared retain their seats, sitting there ill at ease and pale as death, while three-quarters of the House rose and faced them. The effect was tremendous.[32]

Throughout Germany there were public processions that eclipsed anything in the nation's history. A million marched in Berlin; one hundred fifty thousand marched in Munich and in Chemnitz; a hundred thousand marched in tributes in Hamburg, Breslau, Elberfeld, and Essen. It was by far the greatest spontaneous outpouring ever accorded a German. The funeral was on Tuesday, June 27. Rathenau's coffin lay in state in the Reichstag; in the former royal box "sat Rathenau's mother, deadly pale and as if turned to stone, never moving her eyes from the coffin beneath."[33] The assassins would eventually be hunted down — Kern was killed by a police bullet; Fischer committed suicide next to him as the chase ended; Techow was arrested separately — but in his funeral address President Ebert spoke to them as if they were present in the hushed legislative chamber.

> What have you done? You have lain in cowardly ambush and murdered the noblest of men. You have laid a terrible blood-guiltiness upon the People whom this man always served with every fibre of his being. It is the nation itself whom you have shot through the heart. . . . Deluded fools — you have slain one man but you have wounded sixty millions. . . . In this man you have betrayed the fate of our people. You have shaken the foundation of all communal life — confidence. You have struck at Bismarck's work and the future of Germany.[34]

In Munich, the news of Rathenau's murder became known early in the afternoon of the day he was killed. General Ludendorff and Crown Prince Rupprecht of the former Bavarian royal House of Wittelsbach had both attended a ceremony at the University of Munich and were dining near each other when a telegram was delivered to the crown prince. He read the news of Rathenau's murder and stared at Ludendorff with cold contempt.[35] Ludendorff later wrote that he knew nothing of the murder, and disapproved of political killings for any reason, but added that he sympathized with the grievances felt by the killers. He said that they were correct in thinking that these wrongs against Germany were visited upon them by Rathenau, whom he characterized in the following words:

> The Jew Walther Rathenau, the Red Prophet of world revolution. Consciously he wanted to Bolshevise the German people with the help of the German intelligentsia. The Germans who executed the people's judgment on Walther Rathenau have acted with the thought that they have freed the German nation from vermin.[36]

Within hours of the killing, the police arrested Hitler and took him to Stadelheim prison in Munich, to begin serving his sentence. Before being taken away, he had an opportunity to address a few of his followers. Once again he likened himself to Christ: "Two thousand years ago the mob of Jerusalem dragged a man to execution in just this way."[37]

The battle lines were drawn; in the convulsive aftermath of Rathenau's murder, the republic would try to strike down its sworn enemies of the right. An ever-deeper chasm was opening between Munich and Berlin.

CHAPTER

23

D URING THE EARLY summer weeks leading to the death of Rathenau, the returned playboy and entrepreneur Kurt Ludecke
had, as he put it, "set about looking for a leader and a cause." The
going was not easy.

I made the rounds, going from place to place, from group to
group, confused, bewildered, diving now and again into the mad
scramble for diversion that surrounded me, but unhappy always
with a nostalgia for the proud Germany of my youth. I was looking for the German soul, or rather for the leader who would
know how to reanimate it, and I was resolved not to desert
again.[1]

After an encounter with a small völkisch group whose leader Ludecke referred to as a "thirsty mentor" who evidently used Ludecke's
donations to pay his liquor bills, he fell in with one of Bavaria's most
violent anti-Semites.[2] He was Julius Streicher, the DSP leader in Nuremberg, from whom Hitler had demanded, and received, a letter of
"clarification" in the wake of the stormy arguments following the merger
talks with the DSP — the same struggle that had given Hitler the
opportunity for his final showdown with his party's old guard. Streicher
was a thirty-seven-year-old veteran who, like Hitler, had won the Iron
Cross, First Class.[3] He had eventually been commissioned as a lieutenant, despite a stipulation entered in his prewar military service
record that he was not to be commissioned under any circumstances.
Shaven-headed, he had coarse and brutal features, and a psyche to
match. Like Hitler, Streicher was given to striding around with a whip
in his hand; unlike him, he was a womanizer, and a collector of por-
nography. In one respect, he and Hitler shared a nearly identical

fantasy, that of dark Jews seducing and raping blond Aryan women. A man with sufficient formal education to be qualified for his occupation as a schoolteacher, his obsessive anti-Semitism nonetheless enabled him to believe, as well as to write:

> The male sperm in cohabitation is partially or completely absorbed by the female and thus enters her bloodstream. One single cohabitation of a Jew with an Aryan woman is sufficient to poison her blood forever. Never again will she be able to bear purely Aryan children, even when married to an Aryan. They will all be bastards.
>
> Now we know why the Jew uses every artifice of seduction in order to ravish German girls at as early an age as possible; why the Jewish doctor rapes his female patients while they are under anesthetic.[4]

The Streicher whom Ludecke met was apparently successful in concealing some of the cruder side of his nature, although Ludecke noted that "Streicher was then already fanatically intent on the Jewish problem, and there was a vast amount of reading on the subject lying more or less undigested in his immature mind." Apparently Streicher had been studying the Bible to discover what the Jews believed, and "certain Old Testament seeds had sprouted in his brain. There was, for example, the wonderful principle of the fast as a means of renewing a man in body and spirit. Fasting would make us hard and fit for the struggle to save Germany."

Ludecke had met maharajahs and ballerinas, but "this man was an entirely new type to me, and soon I found his enthusiasm infectious. What could we fast on?"

The answer was not long in coming.

> We were in Nuremberg, and all round us in that lovely Frankenland country, cherries were hanging ripe on the trees. Why not try cherries? Jesus Christ had given cherries to his disciples, Streicher said.
>
> Excellent! But where? Streicher knew of a place that would be ideal. So off we went.
>
> Our regimen was to be nothing but cherries for two or three weeks, then a week of nothing but water. When that was over, we would be new beings.

Ludecke had imagined that their rebirth would take place in an idyllic landscape, some cherry orchard perfect for meditation. In reality, he found himself sharing a room with Streicher in a nondescript village, with the cherries being supplied, in boxes, by a farmer who came in from the countryside. Ludecke was paying for the room and the cherries, and Streicher was gone most of the time.

The dénouement was not long in coming. During the second day, Ludecke discovered that Streicher's long and frequent absences were to visit a woman he knew in the village. Only one more discovery remained to be made.

> On the third day I spied him in a little restaurant tucking away
> a huge "bauern" omelet. Cherries, quite understandably, had
> been insufficiently sustaining fare.
> There was nothing to do but laugh at ourselves. In all good will
> we parted, and I went on to Munich.[5]

The Bavarian capital made Ludecke forget this comic interlude. In these July days the political and economic effects of Rathenau's assassination were evident at every turn. At the time of the murder, the already shaky mark was fixed at 272 to the dollar. Seven days later the rate was 410 to the dollar, and in another week and a half it was at 550. By the end of July, it would take 670 marks to equal a dollar in value. In the Reichstag's efforts to put some teeth into the concept of law and order in Germany, membership in monarchist organizations had been made a criminal offense, and several German states, including Prussia, Baden, and Thuringia, had also banned the Nazi Party from operating within their borders.

The great turmoil, however, was caused by the Reichstag's swiftly passed Law for the Protection of the Republic, national legislation that was clearly aimed at curbing the excesses of the right. The initial decree, and the constitutional amendment making it a law, which quickly followed, resulted in new restrictions and penalties to be invoked against those who in any way planned or encouraged violence against the republican form of government, or any of its members. The parliaments of the German states were given the authority to ban public meetings that were deemed subversive; this was a discretionary power that undercut the new republic's hard-won right to the freedom of assembly, and it brought protests from a number of liberals, as well as from all the conservatives. From the völkisch point of view, as Ludecke put it, the law would make "Bavaria, like the rest of Germany, a hunting-ground for Berlin police seeking the extradition of National activists."[6]

No sooner had this package of provisions been published, on July 21, than the Bavarian government struck back at Berlin. Even under the moderate Count Lerchenfeld, the Bavarian legislature was unwilling to accept that part of the new law which would require trials for treason, political murder, and other acts against the state, to be tried at the Special Court in Leipzig. This would in effect wrest from Bavaria the extraordinary powers possessed by its People's Courts. These local tribunals were established in July of 1919, at a time when the right had shattered the immediate postwar power of the left in Bavaria. Supposedly a temporary measure, they had been operating for three years, dispensing justice that invariably favored defendants of nationalist and völkisch persuasion. What had developed in these tribunals was a politically oriented criminal law in which the rights of defendants were not protected unless the judges wanted them to be, and there was no means of appeal from their often arbitrary judgments and sentences.

To protect this questionable institution, on July 24 the Bavarian government set forth its own Decree for the Protection of the Republic, which, it claimed, could legally "replace the national law" as it applied to Bavaria.[7] It was in fact an entirely unconstitutional maneuver, destined to disappear in a welter of compromises with Berlin, but at the climax of this rift between Bavaria and Berlin, Munich witnessed its greatest mass demonstration, and it was here that something happened to Kurt Ludecke.

The day chosen for this immense outpouring of feeling against the national government was August 16, 1922, less than eight weeks after Rathenau's death. The protest was organized by the Fatherland Front, "which was," Ludecke said, "in effect, a holding company loosely coordinating all the patriotic societies, large and small."[8] The crowds were to gather at the Königsplatz, Munich's largest square. At the time this meeting was announced, Ludecke had been in Munich for about a month, busily talking with the leaders of the rightist Bund Bayern und Reich; he had joined it, but felt that it lacked the spirit for effective action. Moving as he did in right-wing circles, Ludecke heard of the Nazi Party, but had yet to catch a glimpse of its leader. Ludecke felt that Hitler was not well known to the general population of Bavaria, but, "because of his growing local importance and for the sake of a united front, he had been invited to appear as one of two speakers on a program in which all were taking part."[9]

Released only on July 27 from Stadelheim prison, where he had been given a cell with a private toilet and treated with deference by the guards, Hitler was eager to make the most of this opportunity to address the largest audience that had ever been made available to him. Ludecke said, "It needed no clairvoyance to see that here was a man who knew how to seize his opportunity. Red placards announced in huge black letters that he was to appear. Many who read them had never even heard his name."[10]

The enormous protest meeting took place on a bright summer day. Estimates of the crowd's size ranged from fifty to seventy thousand.[11] All the other nationalist groups, whatever their combinations of uniforms and insignia, had simply filed into place in the great square. The Nazi Storm Troops, who had yet to appear, now totaled some six hundred men. The SA's color was grey, but there was every sort of costume, including alpine hats and lederhosen. Some men wore grey shirts, some wore their old army tunics, some had straight trousers, and others had breeches and wrap-around leggings, but all wore the swastika armband on their left sleeve. Whenever the SA men marched, many swastika flags were in evidence, and two military brass bands had been formed to play the marches Germans loved so well. On this day, as the column of Storm Troops made its way through the city toward the Königsplatz, leftists attempted to break up their line of march. The men of the Sturmabteilung repulsed the attackers, sending them running down side streets, some bearing the marks of Nazi fists and blackjacks. Thus it was as victors in a series of minor skirmishes that the party's militant arm came on the scene. Ludecke knew nothing of the fighting that had immediately preceded their appearance.

The "patriotic societies" had assembled without bands and without flags. But when the Nazis marched into the Königsplatz with banners flying, their bands playing stirring German marches, they were greeted with tremendous cheers. An excited, expectant crowd was now filling the beautiful square to the last inch and overflowing into surrounding streets.[12]

One of Ludecke's latest völkisch counselors, Count Ernst zu Reventlow, had arranged for them to be next to the speakers' stand. The first orator gave what Ludecke felt was an uninspiring political harangue. Then it was Adolf Hitler's turn.

When the man stepped forward on the platform, there was almost no applause. He stood silent for a moment. Then he began to speak, quietly and ingratiatingly at first. Before long his voice had risen to a hoarse shriek that gave an extraordinary effect of an intensity of feeling. There were many high-pitched, rasping notes — Reventlow had told me that his throat had been affected by war-gas — but despite its strident tone, his diction had a distinctly Austrian turn, softer and pleasanter than the German.

Critically I studied this slight, pale man, his brown hair parted on one side and falling again and again over his sweating brow. Threatening and beseeching, with . . . flaming, steel-blue eyes, he had the look of a fanatic.

Presently my critical faculty was swept away. Leaning from the tribune as if he were trying to impel his inner self into the consciousness of all these thousands, he was holding the masses, and me with them, under a hypnotic spell by the sheer force of his conviction.[13]

Hitler invoked the ideas of German manhood and honor, and told these Bavarians what they wanted to hear: "Bavaria is now the most German land in Germany!" Then he repeated the claim that leftists had stabbed Germany in the back in November of 1918. "Plunging into sarcasm, he indicted the leaders in Berlin as 'November Criminals,' daring to put into words thoughts that Germans were now almost afraid to think and certainly to voice."[14]

Ludecke was staring at Adolf Hitler from a few feet away.

It was clear that Hitler was feeling the exaltation of the emotional response now surging up toward him from his thousands of hearers. His voice rising to passionate climaxes, he finished his speech with an anthem of hate against the "Novemberlings" and a pledge of undying love for the Fatherland. "Germany must be free!" was his final defiant slogan. Then two last words that were like the sting of a lash:

"Deutschland Erwache!" Awake Germany! There was thunderous applause. Then the masses took a solemn oath "to save Germany in Bavaria from Bolshevism."

Even many years later, Kurt Ludecke felt at a loss for words as he recalled that hour in the sunlit Königsplatz. The soldier who had never gone to the front said:

I do not know how to describe the emotions that swept over me as I heard this man. His words were like a scourge. When he spoke of the disgrace of Germany, I felt ready to spring on any enemy. His appeal to German manhood was like a call to arms, the gospel he preached a sacred truth. . . . I forgot everything but the man; then glancing round, I saw that his magnetism was holding these thousands as one.

Of course I was ripe for this experience. I was a man of thirty-two, weary of disgust and disillusionment, a wanderer seeking a cause; a patriot without a channel for his patriotism, a yearner after the heroic without a hero. The intense will of the man, the passion of his sincerity seemed to flow from him into me. I experienced an exaltation that could be likened only to religious conversion. . . .

The bands struck up, the thousands began to move away. I knew my search was ended. I had found myself, my leader, and my cause.[15]

As Ludecke had understood even before he saw Hitler, the party's Führer was indeed a man who knew how to exploit a situation; he had already arranged to follow up his appearance before the masses in the Königsplatz with a party meeting in the Zirkus Krone the following night.[16] Once again, Ludecke was with Reventlow, and they were shown to reserved seats at the very front. In a few minutes, Ludecke was caught up in an even more powerful performance than the one of the previous afternoon.

Standing under his own banners, addressing his own followers, Hitler was even more outspoken. . . . Again his power was inescapable, gripping and swaying me as it did every one within those walls. Again I had the sensation of surrendering my being to his leadership. When he stopped speaking, his chest still heaving with emotion, there was a moment of dead silence, then a storm of cheers.

As the crowd broke up, Reventlow introduced Ludecke to Hitler, who was still sweating and pale from the effort of his lengthy speech. "Looking closely at him for a long moment, I did not need to wonder where he found the reserves of character and courage that were enabling him to forge ahead of the other leaders. Everything dwelt behind his eyes." When Ludecke and Hitler parted a little later, it was arranged that they would continue their conversation the following afternoon at the Nazi Party headquarters in the Corneliusstrasse. As Ludecke entered, this is what he saw and experienced: "There was a show-window displaying Nazi literature, a large room with a reception corner barred off by a wooden rail, a counter where members paid their dues, a few tables and chairs. That was all, except for two smaller rooms beyond. Hitler took me into one of these and closed the door behind us."

Once he was alone with this man who was nine months older than he, Ludecke said, "I offered myself to him and to his cause without reservation." He told Hitler about his life, stressing the frustration he had felt as he tried to find a purpose in life during the past several years. "Hitler listened closely, studying me keenly, now and then rising from his chair and pacing the floor. I was impressed again by his obvious indifference to his personal appearance; but again I saw that the whole man was concentrated in his eyes."

Only once did Hitler frown: that was when Ludecke mentioned his affiliation with the Bund Bayern und Reich, which regarded him as an unpaid ambassador to the völkisch groups in the northern German states. After some discussion, Hitler agreed with Ludecke's suggestion that he maintain his connection with the Bund for a time, so as to keep abreast of what it was doing.

> When I rose to leave, it was after seven; we had been talking for over four hours. Solemnly clasping hands, we sealed the pact.
> I had given him my soul.[17]

II

The party that Kurt Ludecke joined in August of 1922 was experiencing dramatic growth and an extension of its activities, both public and covert. While Hitler spent his thirty-three days in jail, the party had been deprived of its greatest asset — his speeches and his energizing presence at party headquarters — but many activities rolled along on their own. At this time, when Bavaria felt its limited sovereignty being challenged and threatened by Berlin, there was talk of an impending right-wing coup in Munich that would displace the Lerchenfeld government and face Berlin with a regime determined to maintain Bavaria as a völkisch stronghold. Just where the Nazi Party was to fit in no one knew, but during the year its membership had risen from three to seven thousand, and the six Storm Troop companies of a hundred men each that had so excited the vast crowd in the Königsplatz would soon have two more Hundertschaften added to their number. The party's regular activities included recruiting trips to towns all over Bavaria: three or four trucks loaded with Storm Troops and festooned with swastika banners would arrive, and the inhabitants would be treated to a combination of political harangues, sometimes delivered from the back of one of the trucks. Afterward, the SA men would put up various posters throughout the community, all the while engaging the residents in conversations that were meant to impress and persuade them. These trucks were equipped with loudspeakers; even rolling past tiny hamlets, the propaganda cadres aboard the vehicles would shout through their microphones a few slogans that could be heard by peasants in the fields.

Hitler's greatest support was coming from the middle class; in his speeches, Hitler pictured the small tradesman as the victim of a Jewish-inflated manipulation of the mark, assisted by the Berlin government, and on one occasion he concluded with, "The middle class must fight for its existence, for its fate is the fate of our people and our race."[18] Nonetheless, Hitler maintained the party's stated position of being a workers' party, and it was here that the party's Führer initiated a number of devious activities. Because he sought the support of "large numbers of the better elements of the working classes," he "saw to it that all the initiates of the movement came to meetings without stiff collars and without ties, adopting the free-and-easy style so as to get the workers into their confidence."[19] This was only one of several misrepresentations. "I disorganized the meetings of other parties by sending members of our party in the guise of ushers to maintain order, but in reality with instructions to riot and break up the meeting." Opposition parties were also penetrated on another level: "I sent a few of our own people to take a course in public speaking in the schools organized by the other parties. Thanks to this, we obtained a good insight into the arguments which would be used by those sent to heckle at our meetings, and we were thus in a position to silence them the moment they opened their mouths."

The hecklers were dealt with according to their sex. Along the lines that Hitler had explained to Josef Hell, the Storm Troops were instructed to throw out male leftists with such violence that the socialist press, which Hitler said would otherwise have ignored the Nazi speeches, was compelled to call attention to them by indignantly reporting the injuries their adherents received. There was an entirely different technique for handling women who uttered leftist slogans:

> I dealt with the women from the Marxist camp who took part in the discussions by making them look ridiculous, by drawing attention either to the holes in their stockings or to the fact that their children were filthy. To convince women by reasoned argument is always impossible; to have had them roughly handled by the ushers of the meeting would have aroused public indignation, and so our best plan was to have recourse to ridicule, and this produced excellent results.

The women of the Nazi Party were given a special role in handling the situations that arose when the leftists called the police to come to a Nazi Party meeting from which socialists were being ejected.

> If the police intervened, women of our party were given the task of drawing their attention either to opponents or to completely unknown people who happened to find themselves near the entrance to the hall. In cases like this, the police invariably go about their job quite blindly, like a pack of hounds, and we found that this method was most efficacious, both for ridding ourselves of undesirable elements of the audience and for getting rid of the police themselves.

Although there was no doubt that Hitler in his speeches constantly struck responsive chords in his audiences, he did not leave the timing of the applause to chance. "I had . . . a number of party members in the audience, with orders to interrupt along lines carefully prepared to give the impression of a spontaneous expression of public opinion, and these interruptions greatly strengthened the force of my own arguments."

Immediately accepted into the party's inner councils at this time of tension and turmoil, Kurt Ludecke found his days filled with "conferences, speeches, the writing of editorials, membership drives, and money troubles" — the financial problems being the party's, not his, since his foreign investments were prospering.[20] The first really important assignment, however, came from the Bund Bayern und Reich, with which Ludecke remained intimately involved, in accord with Hitler's belief that it was vital to know what other parties were doing. The Bund's leader, Dr. Otto Pittinger, was planning a coup in which all the different nationalist organizations belonging to the umbrella organization, the Fatherland Front, were to join. At his own expense — no one ever offered to reimburse him — Ludecke was to alert sympathizers in the other German states to ready themselves for the opportunity to act in concert with the Bavarian groups, including the Nazi Party. The plan was to topple the Lerchenfeld government in Munich, and instantly replace it with an extreme right-wing regime. The hope was that the Bavarian example would set off a countrywide nationalist revolt that would bring down the government in Berlin, succeeding where the Kapp Putsch had failed.

Ludecke rushed to Berlin, briefing a worried Count Reventlow about the impending attempt, and sped north through other Prussian cities and towns. "Reaching Stettin late at night, I roused from his

bed Baron von Dewitz, leader of the Pomeranian Landbund. . . .
Tearing along by motor through a sleepless night, I expected at every
stop to hear that the great plan was accomplished."[21] Bewildered at
the silence from Munich, Ludecke returned to Berlin. As far as he
could determine, nothing had occurred. "Riding back to Munich in
the train, angry and baffled, I saw no humor in my shattered dream
of German destiny in the balance, and of myself as the German Paul
Revere."

As he stepped from the train in Munich, Ludecke had only one
idea, which was to find out what had gone wrong with this supposedly
life-or-death revolutionary effort.

> Driving directly to Pittinger's headquarters, I met the great
> man at the door. He was just getting into a gorgeous motor-coat
> and looked very haughty in his goggles — ready to speed away in
> his big Mercedes for his well-earned vacation in the Alps. "Is *this*
> the *coup d'état*?" I asked him, but he swept magnificently by.
> Every one I met was either sheepish, disgusted, or filled with
> rage. Hitler's men had been the only ones ready to march, I was
> told. But nobody knew where Hitler was now.

These first reports that Ludecke received were more or less accurate. On August 25, Hitler and Pittinger had assembled approximately
five thousand völkisch enthusiasts for a street demonstration that was
supposed to trigger the popular uprising against the Lerchenfeld government. The Munich police had told them that their open-air meeting
was banned, and the demonstrators had marched to the Kindlkeller;
in front of that beer hall, they had found a thousand or more leftists
waiting to fight them. The police had, however, managed to disperse
those in the streets, the potential fighters for both left and right. All
that then remained of this popular uprising against the Bavarian government was a lackluster speechmaking session within the beer hall,
participated in by several of the right-wing leaders. Hitler, seeing that
the whole thing was hopeless, had told everyone, at about eleven in
the evening, that the demonstration was over and that they should go
home quietly.

Hitler was hiding from the police in a bare attic room, where Ludecke found him.

> With him were only his faithful guard, Ulrich Graf, and a great
> police-dog. All the late newspapers were scattered about the
> small table and the floor. . . . When I reported my bootless jour-
> ney, ending with the encounter with Pittinger, he began to rave.

"I was ready — my men were ready!" he cried, spreading his arms in a wide gesture and letting them fall despairingly to his sides. Then his eyes narrowed. "I have learned," he said. "From now on I go my way alone. Resolutely alone. Even if not a soul follows. These cowards! I shall do it if no one else dares."

Partly to calm Hitler, Ludecke began to talk of events in the world outside Munich. It was easy for Ludecke, a much-traveled man, to think of the different nations of Europe as easily accessible places where support might be found for the party. In the headlines of the newspapers scattered about Hitler's hideout was the news that Benito Mussolini and his Blackshirts were occupying the entire city of Turin as part of their effort to take over Italy. Kurt Ludecke had no hesitation about seeking out famous men; in his mind there was forming the idea of an exploratory trip to make contact with the Italian Fascists.

For the time being, Hitler was not ready for this venture in unofficial right-wing diplomacy; indeed, the headlines reminded him that this man Mussolini had managed to take over a major Italian city, while he, Hitler, had failed in Munich and was holed up in an attic eluding the authorities. Ludecke was to swing back and forth in his estimate of the degree to which Hitler saw himself as a national leader, but, rather than discuss Mussolini, Hitler came out with this memorable statement:

No more Pittingers, no more Fatherland societies! One party. One single party. These *gentlemen* — these counts and generals — they won't do anything. *I* shall. *I alone.*

Ludecke drew this conclusion from that outburst:

Gone was Hitler's conception of himself as the advance agent, the drummer-boy. On that day of disappointment he became the Fuehrer. . . . This failure also altered his entire regard for the "great" people toward whom he had previously shown a certain deference and humility. But his demeanour did not change. He had found that it worked to be naïf and simple in a *salon*, to assume shyness. It was a useful pose, but now it covered scorn.[22]

Although the coup had fizzled, Bavaria once again, on balance, moved to the right. Because of widespread dissatisfaction with the compromise reached between Berlin and Munich concerning the status of the Bavarian courts under the Law for the Protection of the Republic, Count Lerchenfeld and his cabinet would soon resign. It was a measure of right-wing strength that even a compromise that really amounted to Berlin's retreating in the face of illegal Bavarian moves would not be enough to save a moderate Bavarian leader. The man who would be the new Bavarian minister-president, Eugen von Knilling, was little more than a front man for the former leader, Gustav von Kahr, a monarchist who was not to Hitler's liking, but who was for practical reasons allying himself with all elements of the völkisch camp.

The immediate result of Lerchenfeld's tottering position was that Hitler could emerge from hiding, and now Ludecke found him willing to listen to the idea of a reconnaissance trip to Italy. "I persisted in telling him that Count Reventlow seconded my suggestion that it might be well to find out more about Benito Mussolini." After all, Ludecke told Hitler, the Italian Fascists were an authoritarian right-wing party, just as the Nazi Party was, and they were going places. "To have an ally who was succeeding, even though the alliance were merely one of mutual sympathy, would be encouraging."

Hitler was at last listening, and listening carefully. Now Ludecke, as always undaunted by the names of the famous, said that it would be even better if he could first try to get an endorsement for this unofficial international contact from "General Ludendorff, whose name would be a passport into any political sanctum."

Hitler gave the whole idea his blessing, and promptly turned to other matters; as Ludecke contemplated the possibilities opening for him in his work for a party whose name he had not known a few weeks before, he suddenly realized that the most important part of what he was proposing might prove to be not Ludendorff's approval of a right-wing approach to Mussolini, but Ludendorff's endorsement of Hitler. Thus far Ludendorff had given no völkisch group his special approval. Ludecke quickly came to see the possibilities in these terms:

> The German movement that won the backing of Ludendorff's world prestige would find its fight for recognition accelerated beyond the power of any other single influence to speed it. . . .
> What a combination — Ludendorff, the General, with all that name implied of caste and authority, and Hitler, the dynamic corporal coming from the people![23]

Count Reventlow arranged the meeting, and Ludecke and Reventlow were soon seated in the study of Ludendorff's secluded villa in the Munich suburb of Ludwigshöhe, waiting for the general to come into the room. Ludecke was looking at an oil painting on the wall opposite him; it was the original of a widely distributed picture that showed Ludendorff and Field Marshal von Hindenburg bending over military maps spread across a table. Just for an instant, awaiting the entrance of the legendary figure who had been Germany's wartime dictator, Ludecke felt his confident sophistication vanish; recalling that moment, all he could remember thinking was "What was I doing here?" Then the door opened.

> The great Feldherr entered the room. Tall and blue-eyed, massive and powerful, calm but alert and determined, he seemed a tower that defies the world.
> After exchanging greetings with the Count, he welcomed me in a natural and simple manner. Seating us with a friendly gesture and a winning smile, offering cigars, he made us feel at ease.

Reventlow quickly brought Ludendorff up to date on anything he might not know about the event that Ludecke thought of as "the Pittinger fiasco." In a reaction that Ludecke was not expecting, Germany's most famous right-wing figure expressed satisfaction that this particular bid for power had failed, because there were too many Bavarian Catholics involved in it to suit his own Prussian Protestant tastes.

Ludecke and Reventlow had "decided to do our utmost to sell Hitler to the General," and this they attempted to do. Ludendorff expressed interest, but gave no commitment. When it came to Ludecke's proposed visit to Mussolini, Ludendorff "saw potential benefits from an understanding with Mussolini — or *of* Mussolini — and considered an overture wise, even though the Italian's future, like ours, was problematical." In closing the interview, Ludendorff said to Ludecke, concerning Mussolini, "And you may use my name."[24]

Feeling greatly pleased with himself, Ludecke returned to his lodgings in Munich to find a telegram from his old love, Dolores. They had met a few times since the war, both recognizing that their relationship was not what it once had been, but both reluctant to give it up altogether. Her message said that she was arriving that very night, from Paris. Because Ludecke was eager to head for Italy as soon as possible, he decided to take Dolores to hear Hitler address a mass meeting at the Zirkus Krone that evening, then travel with her to Paris before going on by himself to Milan.

The reunion with Dolores in Munich was not a success, starting with the Nazi meeting.

> Exquisitely dressed, with beautiful pearls at her perfect throat, Dolores walked bewildered beside me through the crowd, led re-

spectfully by sturdy Storm-Troopers to a box near the platform where Hitler was to speak. When he began, I kindled immediately. But Dolores, who understood not one word of German, saw only a slight figure with an absurd moustache, who waved his arms and shouted. When the arena rocked with applause, I was almost annoyed that she did not rise to her feet with the rest.

At the end of the meeting, Ludecke, accompanied by Dolores, drove Hitler to his lodgings, where they were to drop him off.

The fire-eater of the platform sat modest and exhausted in the corner of the car. It is hard for a man to be winning toward a strange lady who doesn't speak his language, especially if her lover is along — and Hitler succeeded no better than I in making a Nazi of Dolores. Worse, she definitely disliked him, and refused to understand my devotion. Her antipathy was so positive that she even warned me not to trust him, to leave him.[25]

After his farewell to Dolores in Paris — "It was our final parting" — Ludecke took the train for Milan, where he telephoned the Fascist newspaper, *Popolo d'Italia*. In his halting Italian, he asked to speak to Signor Mussolini, saying that he was an emissary representing influential people in Munich. "A moment later Mussolini was on the wire, expressing his pleasure and readiness to receive me. Would I come at three that very afternoon? I was amazed and gratified at the ease by which it was arranged."

The meeting took place at the office of the newspaper, which had been founded by Mussolini and edited by him for a time. Ludecke was struck by the fact that this Fascist headquarters occupied a large building, in contrast to the few rooms the Nazis had in Munich. A man in the black Fascist uniform sent him up to the second floor, and there another black-uniformed man took him to Mussolini's office. Ludecke noted that the party leader's desk was in the most distant corner, so that a visitor had to present himself by walking the entire length of the large room.

At the desk sat a square-cut man, in a dark shabby suit and untidy shirt, with a high dome of bald forehead and powerful, almost frightening eyes. He welcomed me in a pleasant, resonant voice. I conveyed the greetings of General Ludendorff and of Adolf Hitler.

Ludecke soon exhausted his limited Italian vocabulary, and Mussolini could do no better in German. "Laughing, we discovered that we did best in French, which we both spoke fluently." At last Ludecke could begin to observe this man whose powerful party wanted absolute control of Italy.

> I noticed his hands. They were small and showed how over-strung he was, for the nails were bitten not merely to the quick but almost to the moons. They shocked me slightly. He looked anything but healthy, his face sallow, his lips tired. But his strong gaze and his power of organizing his thoughts in forceful, rapid speech impressed me. . . .
>
> In fact, the longer we talked, the more I liked him — his swing, his allures, his pose, the marvelous acting that was part and parcel of the man. . . . I could see that this was an indomitable man; yet now he revealed such *esprit* and cultivation, such grace of gesture and phrase, that I completely forgot his iron core, his shabby clothes, his mutilated finger-nails.

Ludecke soon made a discovery: "Mussolini had never heard of Hitler." Starting from the beginning, Ludecke presented his account of how things were in Germany; describing the Nazi Party — it was the first time Mussolini had heard its name — he explained it as a movement that inevitably had to come into existence, one that was moving toward clear-cut objectives. As he spoke, it was obvious to Ludecke that he was striking a responsive chord in Mussolini. The Italian asked questions that were to the point, and agreed that Germany had been put in an "impossible" situation by the Treaty of Versailles; indeed, Mussolini was of the opinion that the arrangements for peace made at Versailles were bound to fail. They exchanged views on their aversion to Marxism, but when Ludecke raised the subject of the Jews, he found Mussolini giving the entire topic a low priority. The temperature dropped at only one moment — when Ludecke mentioned that part of the German-speaking Austrian Tyrol which had been captured by Italy during the war and confirmed at the peace table as being Italian territory. " 'No discussion about that — ever!' Now the suavity was gone, the force showed through. 'The Alto-Adige is Italian and must remain so. But even if it were not, military reasons alone make it imperative not to revert to the impossible old border.' "

After some discussion about German domestic politics, during which Ludecke did not hesitate to tell Mussolini that he had some wrong impressions of the situation, they turned at last to the question that much of Europe was asking: Was this man who was sitting across the table from Ludecke about to seize power in Italy?

The most interesting revelation to me was the extent to which matters in Italy had developed, not merely in plan but in fact. From the definiteness with which Mussolini seemed able to answer all questions, and from his air of complete preparedness to assume the burdens of government, I was sure that an Italian crisis was imminent; the next several months or perhaps even weeks would decide the fate of his movement. It was clear that he was staking everything on one play.

The subject of armed revolution and of bloodshed had not been raised, and now Ludecke asked that ultimate question. "Signor Mussolini, in case the Government does not yield, are you prepared to resort to force?"

With what Ludecke called "superb assurance," Mussolini replied, "*Nous serons l'état, parce que nous le voulons!*" — We shall be the state because we will it to be so.

"That is an answer," Ludecke replied, and Mussolini bowed.[26]

III

As soon as he got back from Milan, Ludecke telephoned Hitler at party headquarters. Hitler immediately went to the boardinghouse where Ludecke was living in Munich.

What then ensued was the first conversation ever recorded in which Hitler grappled with the possibilities of a realistic future Nazi-oriented German foreign policy. To this point, apart from slogans indicting the Versailles Treaty and a vision of international relations as a them-against-us conspiracy of Jewish financiers somehow manipulating all nations to encircle and bleed Germany, there had been no such thing as a coherent NSDAP statement concerning Germany's international future. Hitler had made various pronouncements concerning revenge upon the French, and had verbally lusted for German annexation of lands to the east, and he had listened as Alfred Rosenberg told him of the Red threat in the Baltic regions, but this discussion was far more practical. Ludecke said, "Hitler knew absolutely nothing about the Italian situation — the real situation, as distinct from what the papers printed." Now the Nazi Party's first real ambassador went to work on what he termed Hitler's "ignorance" about the non-German-speaking world.

It was easy to convert him to my opinion that, within a few weeks or months, Italy might mean — Mussolini. I emphasized the fortunate similarity between Nazism and Fascism: both fervently nationalistic, anti-Marxist, anti-Parliamentarian; in short, both dedicated to a radically new order. And I pointed out the similarity between the two leaders: both were men of the people, veterans, self-made and therefore original in their thinking; both were striking political speakers, with an appeal to the emotion and imagination of the masses.

What suggested itself was a future alliance: "If we had any hope of understanding among the major powers, we should find it in Italy — if Mussolini came to power. . . . In short, on Mussolini and his goodwill might depend the reshaping of the European constellation for our benefit."

As they talked, Ludecke felt that "for the first time, Hitler was really considering the ultimate possibilities of his programme in relation to the rest of Europe, and trying to see the international problem from a practical standpoint." They agreed that a future alliance with England would be desirable, but that, "with France holding a military trump-card, and Germany isolated politically and economically, we were in no position to bargain with England." From the Nazi point of view, the thought of any rapprochement with Soviet Russia was inconceivable; word of General von Seeckt's clandestine arrangements for military cooperation had not reached the NSDAP, and presumably would have been severely criticized if known. Italy, however, was providing an example from which Hitler was willing to learn.

Hitler paid the closest attention when I told him of Mussolini's direct challenge to the weak government at Rome, and how his organization of Blackshirts was taking active steps to break strikes and was waging stern warfare against the Soviet councils already entrenched in several northern cities. His eyes grew thoughtful when he heard how the Blackshirts marched into Bolshevized towns and took possession, while the garrisons kept benevolently neutral or, in some cases, even quartered the Fascisti. Mussolini was proving how much could be achieved by sheer nerve and initiative in dealing with a vacillating government.

Hitler had a landlocked mind, formed far from the salt water. This Middle European had been out of German-speaking areas only twice, and that was when, among German soldiers, he fought on the soil of Belgium and France.

298 ∎

Hitler was disturbed and pleased, both at once, by the new en-
largement of our outlook which resulted from the journey to
Milan. His thanks were profuse, however. For a long time, he
said, he had felt that he needed an assistant who was independent, a man of the world, speaking foreign languages, with vision
enough to see beyond the suburbs of Munich.[27]

No sooner had Hitler said that than he turned around and asked
Ludecke to carry out the purely domestic assignment of trying to gain
the support of influential nationalist figures. Ludecke immediately
sought out Ernst Pöhner, the former Munich police commissioner
who had answered, when asked whether he knew that political murders were being committed in Bavaria, "Yes, yes, but too few!"[28]

Pöhner was impressed when Ludecke mentioned his interviews
with Ludendorff and Mussolini, and Ludecke went on to say that Hitler
was undoubtedly the coming man of the right. The confidence that
emanated from the pages of the *Beobachter* was fully shared by Kurt
Ludecke; like other NSDAP activists, he talked as if he were referring not to a party that had fewer than ten thousand members, but
of an enormous force that was at the gates of national power. The
thrust of Ludecke's remarks was that there was just time enough to
jump on the bandwagon, and that Pöhner should meet with Hitler,
soon.

Hitler was duly invited to Pöhner's modest home, along with Ludecke, who described the meeting.

> All through the conference Hitler sat in his cheap raincoat,
> wearing impossible shoes, his felt hat crushed shapeless in his
> hands. Talking in his softest, most winning voice, with his slur-
> ring Austrian accent, he seemed anything but the fire-eater of the
> platform.[29]

When Hitler stood to go, he had a strong ally. Under the moderate
Lerchenfeld government, Pöhner had been out of favor, but with the
impending installation of Eugen von Knilling as Bavaria's new minister-president, nationalist-racist views would be much more acceptable. Hitler was far to the right of Knilling, and Pöhner understood
that, if Hitler prevailed, Ernst Pöhner would once again be deciding
what was legal and illegal in Munich, and perhaps beyond.

In the midst of these productive but essentially behind-the-scenes
activities, there suddenly arose a situation that, in both Nazi lore and
the public eye, was to eclipse the Saalschlacht of the previous autumn,

and become a milestone in the party's history. It was, as Ludecke put it, an opportunity that "was manufactured by Hitler out of the slimmest materials."[30] Through party business manager Max Amann, Hitler was handed an invitation from a völkisch leader named Hans Dietrich. A right-wing patriotic festival billed as a German Day would be held in Dietrich's northern Bavarian town of Coburg, 140 miles north of Munich, on the weekend of October 14 and 15. If Hitler agreed to participate, the invitation said, he might also bring along "some gentlemen of his company."[31]

The town of twenty-four thousand from which this invitation had come was an all-too-good example of Germany's political polarization. The previous year, after the assassination of Matthias Erzberger, the socialist parties and workers' councils of Coburg had protested a Bavarian governmental emergency decree prohibiting public demonstrations to mourn and honor the fallen Reichstag deputy. When Coburg's conservative authorities specifically forbade a planned parade, the workers defied them and marched; as a crowd threatened to overpower the police, two hand grenades were thrown by policemen into the assemblage, sending to the hospital six leftists, one of whom subsequently died. Now, a year later, it was the right that wished to parade on German Day, and the supporters of the left were negotiating with the still-conservative authorities in the hope of forcing the völkisch gatherings to be restricted to indoor meeting places.

This was the stormy background of the invitation to Hitler. There was reason to think that the Coburg rightist leader Dietrich, in suggesting he bring "some gentlemen of his company," was urging Hitler to bring some of his Storm Troops, but Hitler immediately leapt beyond any previously considered idea of what a political party might do in response to such an invitation. The rank and file of the Nazi Party became aware of what der Führer had in mind when they read the *Völkischer Beobachter* of Wednesday, October 11, three days before a Nazi delegation was expected in Coburg.

> On Saturday, October 14, at 8 A.M., a special train for members of the NSDAP will depart from the Munich train station for Coburg. All members of the SA as well as other male party members are requested to take part in the trip. . . .
>
> Quarters in Coburg will be taken care of. . . . Local groups are to bring along their flags.
>
> The meeting will certainly be an unforgettable memory for every participant.

As for costs, party members were told that there would be "voluntary contributions," but it was made clear that any male Nazi could have a free trip to Coburg. One piece of information had it that Dietrich Eckart was underwriting the cost of chartering the special train.[32] Perhaps in an effort to discourage women members of the party from participating in a potentially violent excursion, or perhaps to be consistent in regard to their second-class status within the party, the *Beobachter* stated: "Female party members who wish to participate in this trip at their own cost should report this by Thursday to the main office. The cost of the round trip is 190 Reichmarks."

News of these plans swiftly reached Coburg. For the socialists of that area, who were radical to the point of wanting to separate Coburg and the neighboring Bavarian area of Franconia from the rest of Bavaria in hopes of creating a small socialist state of their own, the impending arrival of a special Nazi train was virtually a declaration of war. The leftist *Coburg Volksblatt* immediately attacked the entire upcoming German Day, saying that it was nothing but a provocation of workers who were loyal to the constitution of the Weimar Republic. Even more pointedly, the *Volksblatt* published a list of the times and places of the impending German Day activities, as well as the exact time of arrival of the train bringing the Nazis from Munich on Saturday morning.[33]

None of this was lost on the authorities. The police commissioner met with the völkisch organizers and extracted from them an agreement that there would be no parades through the cobblestone streets of the ancient city. If the Nazis, or any other nationalist group, moved from one place to another, there was to be no music playing, no flags flying, no closed ranks, no marching in step. Everyone must stroll from one event to the next. In return, a union leader named Voye, who was also a member of the Bavarian parliament, told a Coburg police inspector that nothing would be done to disrupt the meetings of the nationalist-racists in their indoor meetings, but that the workers would be strongly represented on the streets, and would be at the train station on Saturday to see who arrived.[34] Underlying these stipulations was the fact that, despite Bavaria's predominantly anti-Berlin attitude, the Law for the Protection of the Republic was in force. Under it, a police official had no business permitting any political party to display itself in a provocative manner, particularly in outdoor areas that belonged to the public as a whole.

*

Although Hitler was scheduled to speak at Coburg, it was obvious from the outset that he intended the Sturmabteilung to be the centerpiece of the party's two days and one night in Coburg. There would be leadership, but the results of this bold move, and the effect produced on everyone — opponents, sympathizers, and those who were thus far uncommitted — depended on the Storm Troops in the ranks.

One such SA man was Gottfried Schmitt of the Third Company, who said of his orders for this occasion, "We were to assemble early at the Central Station and bring along rations for two days."[35] Schmitt was a workingman who lived in one room in Giesing, Munich's poorest district. His background and conversion to Nazism were entirely different from those of Kurt Ludecke. The events of November 1918 had propelled Gottfried Schmitt into the Communist Party. He may never have read a single paragraph of Marxist dialectic; as he described his motivation, "I couldn't see any other way to bring the sort of Socialism about that we wanted."[36] Schmitt was interested in results, and displays of force impressed him. In 1921, quite possibly after the SA's victory over the leftist intruders in the Saalschlacht, Schmitt had an experience, his account of which, in an English translation appearing in a British publication, made him sound like a navvy.

> One day some of our chaps turned up in the factory with their heads in bandages. At first they wouldn't let on what had happened, only mumbled something, and turned aside. But it must have been pretty lively, that scrap, the way them chaps seemed to have got it in the neck! It all came out, of course, sooner or later. A hundred or more of them had made it up together to go to one of this new Party's meetings and smash it up. . . .
> I couldn't rightly believe my ears when I heard as it was only a handful of fellows at the meeting as had chucked them out. . . . I thought I'd go and have a look in at the next meeting of these here Nationalists.

Schmitt stood well off to one side in a corner and looked around. He found it reassuring that there were many "plain folk like myself, working men and petty shopkeepers."

The speaker was Hitler.

> I saw at once this wasn't no common or garden tub-thumper, no gas bag like most of them. Everything he said was just common sense and sound. . . .
> I went to every one of his meetings after that. Bit by bit he won me round. . . . In the spring of 1922 I joined Hitler's Party.

They shoved me into the guard straight away, the Storm Troops
they were called, whose job it was to keep order at the meetings.

Schmitt's first close contact with Hitler came during what he called
a "propaganda outing" to Tölz, a town forty miles south of Munich.
In the first of the two trucks filled with SA men, "Hitler rode in front,
as usual in his old trench coat and black velours hat."

As soon as they arrived at the meeting in a small hotel in Tölz,
Hitler scented trouble. Before he started speaking, he turned and
quietly gave Schmitt some instructions. If anyone started trouble,
Schmitt was to grab the heckler by the collar, and the SA man beside
Schmitt was to shove the offender along from behind as they threw
him out the door. They were not to act, however, until Hitler gave
the order.

Soon after Hitler began speaking, a heckler stood up and started
shouting. Hitler was patient for a minute or two, but, "when the fellow
showed no sign of shutting up, he at last signalled with his hand to
me."

Schmitt and his Third Company comrade went into action.

> In a trice we'd nabbed the chap and run him to the door. A
> good one on the backside sent him flying down the steps. . . .
> We didn't have to repeat the lesson, Hitler finished what he had
> to say to the good folks of Tölz without further interruption.
> That, of course, was what we was for.

On the morning of Saturday, October 14, with the permission of
the Munich police, several of the eight Munich SA companies marched
from the party headquarters in Corneliusstrasse to the Central Station.
A number of new flags had been made for the occasion. At the station,
the forty-two-piece Peupus Band played cheerful marching songs; this
assemblage of musicians was going along to Coburg, in addition to the
two bands of the SA. In all, approximately 650 Storm Troops boarded
the train, and they were on their way.

Kurt Ludecke was in the compartment with Hitler and several of the
party leaders. "This was the first Nazi special train to run in Germany,"
he recalled, remarking on "the magnificent bluff of that special train,
when we scarcely had money enough to hire a horse!" The coaches
were draped in swastika banners, in itself an act of defiance against
the new national legislation prohibiting provocative political activity.
As the train went on, picking up small contingents of Nazis along the
way, "wherever it halted the sensation was terrific."[37] At Nuremberg

there was a thirty-minute stop. Among those boarding was Julius Streicher, who had just come over to the Nazi Party from the DSP; he was accompanied by about fifteen of his followers. Before the Nazi train was scheduled to leave, an express going from Munich to Berlin stopped on the other side of the platform, and a number of Jews got off. What they saw a few yards away from them was a group of Storm Troops handing out anti-Semitic and antirepublic leaflets. No one handed them to the Jews, but the Storm Troops began singing, "Throw them out, the gang of Jews."[38] When some of the Jews protested, Hitler's sometime chauffeur Julius Schreck waded into them with his fists flying.[39] Other SA men moved over to the express and began drawing swastikas on its side, while one of the bands, in Hitler's coach, started playing "The Watch on the Rhine."[40]

As the train continued toward Coburg, Ludecke took the opportunity to study the men who were sharing Hitler's compartment. Because Ludecke had joined the party so recently and spent time away from Munich, they were all still new to him. As he remembered it, there were six of them, in addition to Hitler and himself: Hermann Esser, Max Amann, Hitler's bodyguards Christian Weber and Ulrich Graf, Dietrich Eckart, and Alfred Rosenberg.

> Dietrich Eckart, a writer of long standing, outshone all the others with his wit and common sense. He spoke in a rumbling, blustering bass, looking positively benign with good humour; but his great, round head, powerful forehead, strong nose and chin, and piercing little eyes, indeed his whole person and carriage, revealed a dominating personality. . . . When he slipped his shell-rimmed glasses up to his forehead in a characteristic gesture and peered at you, there was a depth of joviality behind his fierce front.

Alfred Rosenberg offered a great contrast. "A block of ice! . . . His pale lacklustre eyes looked toward you but not at you, as though you were not there at all. . . . Rosenberg's aloof and chilly irony frightened people away, making them feel small and uncomfortable in his presence."[41] Kurt Ludecke had no idea that he was looking at the man who would prove to be his most faithful friend within the party, nor did he realize that the Nazi theoretician had a pistol in his pocket.

At 2:45 P.M., nearly seven hours after it left Munich, the banner-bedecked Nazi train pulled into Coburg. The various contingents picked up along the way gave the Sturmabteilung a strength of approximately 750 men. Many were carrying concealed knives and blackjacks, and in all probability a number of secreted pistols as well. However, what was visible was a great number of sturdy alpenstocks, the wooden staves used by climbers in the lower Alps.

SA-man Schmitt said of the arrival, "There was a deputation of the big-wigs in Coburg awaiting us at the station, all very solemn and proper in frock coats and top hats."[42] Ludecke noted that these men of the German Day committee had "a uniformed police-captain in tow."[43] Hitler remembered his meeting on the train platform with Hans Dietrich, who had issued the invitation.

> Dietrich came hobbling over to tell me that he'd made an agreement with the Trades Unions, by the terms of which we undertook not to march in ranks, with flags and music in front of us. I pointed out that he had no authority to give undertakings in my name, and that I would pay no attention to them. I ordered the flags and music to go in front, and the procession was formed.[44]

By virtue of being next to Hitler on the platform, Ludecke was in the center of activity.

> The band struck up. With flying banners, preceded by eight stalwart Bavarians, huge roughnecks from the Chiemgau, in leather shorts, who carried alpenstocks, but kept their rubber clubs and knives hidden, we moved forward. Hitler and the seven of us in his entourage followed the standard-bearers, and behind us moved the seven hundred men.
> We swept along the platform, through the undercut and out upon the station square. There we met a great storm of insults from a crowd collected by the Reds to hoot us. Disappointed by our success in flouting the order, they hurled every sort of name at us. We were "murderers, bandits, criminals, hoodlums."[45]

Schmitt and his comrades of the Third Company were not carrying weapons, not even a walking stick like the one Hitler had with him.

> At the fire station they were ready to turn the hoses onto us but just didn't — at the critical moment. Stones, however, began to fly around. Then things got hotter. The Reds set upon us with iron rods and cudgels. That was going a bit too far. Hitler swung round, flourished his walking-stick (that was the signal), and we flung ourselves upon our assailants. We were unarmed save for our fists, but we put up so good a fight that within fifteen minutes not a Red was left to be seen.[46]

Until then, the opposition had consisted of individual leftist workingmen who had spit at the marching Nazis and charged into the ranks in random fashion. Whether through an oversight, or by design of the police, the Nazi column was not led directly to the large shooting gallery on the edge of Coburg where they were to make their quarters, but were guided into the Coburg Hofbräuhaus in Mohrenstrasse, which was to be the scene of that evening's meeting. There was a courtyard in front of the beer hall, and as the SA companies marched through the gates of this fenced-off area, hundreds of leftist demonstrators came right to the iron railings, shouting at them. As the last man of the last company turned into the courtyard, the police quickly locked the gates and began putting up a barricade — whether to protect the Nazis from the workers or to keep the Nazis from emerging once again into Coburg, no one quite knew. Hitler explained what happened next.

> A policeman came and told me we were forbidden to leave the building, since the police declared itself unable to guarantee our protection. I replied that this protection of theirs was no concern of mine, that we were capable of protecting ourselves, and that I ordered him to open the gate. This he did, but explaining that I was compelling him to bow to force.[47]

Readying to move out and march across town to the shooting gallery quarters, where they should have been taken in the first place, the Nazis could see that this was developing into a serious matter. Ludecke said that Hitler addressed the SA men nearest him "in a few fiery words." There was no chance that music was going to be played under these circumstances; all the musicians, except the drummers, grasped their instruments as if they were weapons, and the drummers began a thunderous quick march. Banners still flying, the column moved forward. "We who were in the forefront with Hitler were exposed to very real danger," Ludecke said, "for cobblestones were fairly raining upon us."[48] Schmitt described his experience as the column moved through the narrow streets: "They rained tiles on us from the roof and windows and tore up the cobblestones for missiles. I got a thundering blow on the head which had to be attended to before I could carry on. I only found out afterwards how serious the wound was."[49] Alfred Rosenberg was feeling "slightly naïve" that he had not brought a stick, since it was clear that to fire his pistol might start some leftist gunfire that so far had been withheld. Moving just a few yards away from Ludecke, he saw that "those who were waiting for us with lead pipes and nail-studded, heavy sticks, were not strong enough to break up our parade. On the contrary, whenever they attacked, they were beaten back without mercy. Hitler himself left the ranks several times and used his stick."[50]

Ludecke's observations were:

Sometimes a man's muscles do his thinking. I sprang from the ranks toward a fellow who was lunging at me with his club uplifted . . . but at the same moment, our entire column had turned on our assailants.

For nearly a quarter of an hour it was an outright battle, man to man. At first the police took no sides, striking at everyone with impartial vigour. But soon, probably because they shared our enthusiastic dislike for the street rabble, most of them took our side, and before long we were masters of the field. . . .

When the fracas was over, I would not have exchanged my own bruises for medals. I had felt until then that the rank and file did not quite accept me. Now I was one of them. Seeing that one brawls as well in an English suit as in shoddy clothes, they forgave me my tailor.[51]

It was in this fashion that the Nazi Party arrived in Coburg, and settled into its quarters in the building on the far side of town that housed the shooting gallery. Several SA men had been hurt so badly that they were sent to the hospital, but the great majority of the Storm Troops were feeling pleased with themselves and were ready for more fighting if it developed. Stories of individual experiences were exchanged: even the music stands carried by some of the bandsmen had been used as weapons, and Hitler later said that "our musicians' trumpets came out of the affray twisted and dented."[52]

At 8:00 P.M. the official "welcoming evening" of the German Day festivities began at the Hofbräuhaus. Inside, the völkisch crowd was orderly and undisturbed by hecklers, but in the Mohrenstrasse, sporadic fights between workers and a strong contingent of SA men went on before the meeting and all during the evening. Inside, there were performances by artists from the Coburg State Theater and speeches by various representatives of the right-wing organizations.[53] Employing his new technique of never appearing before his moment to speak, Hitler remained offstage until after a "theatrical intermezzo."[54] The former Duke Carl Eduard of Coburg-Gotha and his wife were in attendance and on full display, but Hitler remained out of sight, aware of the immense curiosity building up in the audience about the man whose private army had swept the leftists from the streets during the afternoon. "Now Hitler himself arrives," a contemporary account stated, "and cries of 'Heil' sprang from a thousand throats. It seemed as if they made no impression on the man on the podium. He stood motionless."⁵⁵

Against the backdrop of the day's events, Hitler scarcely needed to make a particularly strong speech: the entire audience, including the duke and duchess, were already enthusiastic supporters of right-wing thought and action. Nonetheless, in front of a crowd that had tasted blood as they saw, and heard of, the successful Nazi invasion of Coburg, Hitler uncorked one of his best speeches. It was devoid of anti-Semitic remarks; once again, over the heads of those who were wedded to various political philosophies, Hitler offered the hand of friendship to Germany's workers. "We must fight against the insanity of class structure," Hitler told his audience. "We must demand respect for the handworker, because contempt for him was the breeding ground for this disease."

The main thrust of the speech was toward a völkisch spiritual regeneration.

> Today there are complaints about general misery. It is severe and pressing, but perhaps it has been given to us by Fate as a bit of good fortune. For peoples who lose their character and honor deserve no good fortune, no happy existence. Today, so-called prosperity would be a misfortune. We would forget all humiliation: there would be no more complaining about France if things were going well for us. Our people does not yet deserve earthly goods.

Pursuing the theme, Hitler told his audience that "the slogan that says that the economy as such could elevate us must be dropped. It is not the economy which builds a state, but rather a people creates its own economy. Day after day we must preach to all Germans a change of character." There were not many true völkisch activists, but "as long as the world has existed, history has been made by minorities." Hitler then modestly offered the Nazi Party as the answer to every problem.

> Germany and Europe will collapse unless a force arises which stands up for truth and conscience. Scientific knowledge does us no good today, but faith instead. Our [swastika] symbol is not the identification of an organization, but rather a victory banner. It will and must fly above the palace in Berlin and the peasant's hut alike. . . . Resurrection through readiness to act is our answer for the great German Fatherland which is coming!⁵⁶

*

During the night, the Storm Troops were bivouacked in the shooting gallery. There were several bloody encounters between Nazi patrols and small teams of Reds who were attempting to surprise them. In the morning leaflets were distributed throughout Coburg, condemning the Nazis as criminals who shattered law and order. A leftist counterdemonstration had been called for two o'clock that afternoon in the marketplace. Word came that truckloads of leftist sympathizers from other areas were rolling into town; one estimate was that as many as ten thousand might be assembled within a few hours.[57]

In the original German Day program, time had been left for a "noncompulsory walk" up to Coburg Castle, which stood above the Itz River.[58] Hitler decided that the noncompulsory walk, for the Nazi Party, would consist of a military parade to the castle, with bands playing and flags flying, and that the route would be right through the medieval marketplace where the leftist opposition was said to be gathering. The parade set off; by this time additional Nazi contingents had also reached Coburg, and hundreds of other rightist participants in the German Day activities fell in, so that two thousand men, marching behind swastika banners, entered the marketplace some time after noon. Instead of the thousands of opponents who were expected, there were about 150 workers, some of whom began shouting at them. A few individuals and groups charged into the Nazi column, but, as on the previous day, they were thrown back or chased down alleys.[59]

That march was the end of the battle for control of the streets of Coburg. The great leftist demonstration that was supposed to take place at two o'clock never occurred. At Coburg Castle, Hitler held a march-past of his Storm Troop companies, and everyone joined in singing "Deutschland über alles."[60]

When the Nazi column marched back through the city in midafternoon, the effects of their forcible occupation of Coburg became visible. According to Ludecke, "The town was alive with old Imperial flags," and Hitler said, "We were greeted with cheers from all the windows."[61] While Gottfried Schmitt and his comrades were waiting outside the Hofbräuhaus, where the final gathering of German Day was to take place, a number of workers, some with bandaged heads, diffidently approached them. "Then one of them came forward and said, 'Look here, you fellows — what's all the trouble about? You're workmen like us. Why are we at each other's throats?'" This led to an informal discussion in which more and more of the previous day's leftist opponents joined. Schmitt said that the situation developed in the following manner:

We laid ourselves out to explain things and make them see
what we were standing for. Lots of them felt like joining us. By
evening, when we were to march off again to the station, quite a
few came along too. . . . People cheered us, and flowers was
thrown.[62]

At the station there was a final show of socialist opposition. Hitler
recalled:

For our return to Munich, the Railwaymen's Trade Union told
us that it refused to give us transport. "Very well," I said to their
delegates, "I'll start by taking *you* as hostages, and I'll have a
round-up of all your people who fall into our hands. I have locomotive drivers amongst my men; they'll drive us. And I'll take
you all on board with us. If anything at all happens, you'll accompany us into the Other World!"[63]

The railroad men quickly capitulated, and, with swastikas flying,
the Nazi special train rumbled into the night.

The Nazi occupation of Coburg was news in many papers throughout
Germany. The interpretation of the events there differed little from
that of the socialist *Coburg Volksblatt*, whose headline ran, COBURG
UNDER THE CONTROL OF HITLER. CAPITULATION OF THE STATE TO
THE HITLER GUARDSMEN.[64]

Within the party, the Saturday and Sunday in Coburg were immediately perceived as the greatest event in the movement's history.
As a result of the temporary but impressive capture of Coburg, members of the public who had not previously committed themselves to
active membership in a political party made their way to the Nazi
Party office; every week, five hundred people joined the NSDAP. The
eight SA companies rapidly increased to twelve full-strength units of
a hundred men each; the twelfth was formed by Rudolf Hess from
students at the University of Munich. In Coburg, after the Nazi occupation, there was a distinct swing to the right among all levels of
the population.[65]

For Hitler, the message was clear: the public wanted to be on the
side of the winners. More and more he saw that his speeches, his
newspaper, placards and posters, leaflets, must work in tandem with
teams of harsh men who would unhesitatingly attack and thrash every
opponent who showed himself in the streets. There was persuasion,
but there was also intimidation. Riding the wave of confidence in the
party, within a week after the return from Coburg Hitler issued a

memorandum to the membership entitled "Expansion of the NSDAP."
It was in effect a shopping list of things that Hitler deemed to be
essential, for which money must be found. There must be "immediate
acquisition of trucks to transport [SA] companies to threatened areas."
The party should hire "four traveling speakers"; the *Völkischer Beobachter* must be enlarged to the point that it had its own offices in at
least twelve to fifteen good-size German cities. Hitler was specific
about the threat that these measures were intended to counter: "The
Bolshevization of Germany . . . means the annihilation of the entire
Western culture of Christendom."[66]

Exactly two weeks after the Nazi train returned from Coburg, Benito
Mussolini entered Rome aboard a train. This was the climax of the
Fascist Party "march on Rome," and by evening Mussolini was the
de facto leader of Italy. For Hitler, it was Coburg on a gigantic scale,
a confirmation that his party, like the Italian Blackshirts, must win
the battle of the streets in city after city.

In Germany, both right and left regarded Mussolini's assumption
of power as an event of great significance. Count Harry Kessler wrote
in his diary, "This may turn out to be a black day for Italy and for
Europe."[67] Hermann Esser, addressing an NSDAP meeting, cried out,
"We have no need to imitate an Italian Mussolini. We already have
our own. His name is Adolf Hitler!"[68]

24

FOR GERMANS who thought they had seen enough of postwar madness, the fall of the German mark in the closing months of 1922 was a revelation. The murder of Rathenau had destroyed all foreign confidence in Germany and its currency. This was accompanied by similar German self-doubt, resulting in a situation in which Germans were in effect saying to each other: "I don't think those pieces of paper are worth as much as they are supposed to be. You'll have to give me more of them to buy what I have for sale." On the day of Rathenau's murder in June, it took 350 marks to buy a dollar; now, at the beginning of November, the figure was 4,500 — a decline of 92 percent in four months.

On November 2, the Allied Reparations Commission, led by the French political leader Louis Barthou, convened yet another of its meetings, this time in Berlin. To bolster its repeated pleas for a moratorium on payments to the Allies, the German government had invited a number of prominent non-German economic experts, including John Maynard Keynes, who had been saying for more than three years that the financial demands of the Versailles Treaty would prove ruinous to all of Europe.

Once again, the negotiations failed. The mark continued its slide; by the end of the year it would momentarily be pegged at 12,000 to the dollar, an almost unthinkable loss for a unit of currency that had stood at 200 to the dollar as 1922 began. An immediate result of the failure of the economic conference in Berlin was the resignation of Chancellor Joseph Wirth. He was replaced by Wilhelm Cuno, the director of the Hamburg-American shipping line. Cuno had held positions of authority high in the government, as well as in business, and it was hoped that the "business ministry" he now formed would put Germany on a better economic footing both at home and abroad. He was, however, to prove of considerably less substance than his predecessor, Wirth. A man who looked every inch the statesman, Cuno was bringing true the prediction of Walther Rathenau, who said to his friends not long before his death, "We shall have to smoke even that cigar — if only because of its excellent wrapper."[1] Worse than Cuno's limitations were the actions of the Social Democrats, who for factional reasons chose not to participate in the new cabinet. As a result, there was no element of leadership from the party that represented the largest single bloc of voters in the nation.

The rain of inflation fell on the just and the unjust alike. In Berlin, Count Harry Kessler noted in his diary on November 7: "Nine thousand marks to the dollar. The daily rate of exchange shows the progress of our decline like the temperature chart of a very sick patient."[2] In Bavaria, where the rightist government of Eugen von Knilling had replaced that of Count Lerchenfeld, the price of the *Völkischer Beobachter* revealed the same monetary erosion that affected every other salable item. Having started the year at the price of 50 pfennigs — half a mark — by August it was at 2 marks, by September, 4 marks, and with the beginning of November its price began a dramatic rise, going from 10 marks to 30 marks by the end of the year. The one-mark fee charged the public for admission to NSDAP meetings, a startling innovation when Hitler introduced it in 1920, had remained constant, but it, too, was raised in November, to 5 marks, a change that could have come about only with the approval of the party's leader.

Soon after the victory at Coburg and the excitement caused by Mussolini's seizure of power came news of yet another bold and decisive move. During the first weeks of November, Mustafa Kemal, the founder and leader of the Turkish nationalist movement, overthrew Sultan Mohammed VI of Turkey, and drove him into exile. Kemal, later known as Atatürk, thus ended seven centuries of rule by the House of Osman and became dictator of the nation whose forces he had led in expelling the Greek armies from its soil.

For the Nazis, certain parallels to their own aspirations were apparent. Kemal, a military man who, like Hitler, was the son of a customs official, had developed his power base in the city of Ankara, from which he had challenged the sultan's government in the capital city, Constantinople, soon to be known as Istanbul. Mussolini had marched on Rome; Mustafa Kemal had, from a city distant from his capital, offered his people a vigorous program calculated to remove foreign control and restore national pride. Munich could be for Hitler what Ankara had been for the new dictator of Turkey.

The increasing power of the Nazis led to widespread talk in Bavaria of a Putsch. Even the most ardent Nazis saw no shortcut to Berlin; most of the German states had outlawed the NSDAP after Rathenau's murder, so it was only in right-wing Bavaria that a Nazi state could first become possible. If Hitler, or a Hitler-led coalition, could pull off a coup in Bavaria, then, immediately or later, the rest of Germany might follow suit.

Hitler was summoned by the Bavarian minister of the interior, Dr. Franz Schweyer. As the cabinet official responsible for security, Schweyer told Hitler that if he and his party were thinking of a Putsch, they should have no doubt that the Bavarian State Police and the Munich police would have orders to fire upon anyone attempting an armed overthrow of the Bavarian government.

According to one account, Schweyer's words produced this reaction: "Hitler jumped up from his chair, beat his breast with his right hand, and cried: 'Herr Minister, I give you my word of honor, never as long as I live will I make a *Putsch!*' "[3]

II

During November of 1922 the Nazi Party acquired an extraordinary new member whose cosmopolitan background in many ways outshone that of Kurt Ludecke. He was Ernst F. Sedgwick Hanfstaengl, who on his father's side was descended from a prominent family whose members had been privy councilors to the dukes of Saxe-Coburg-Gotha and were known as enthusiastic, knowledgeable, and generous patrons of the arts. Ernst Hanfstaengl's grandfather had founded one of the first and best firms specializing in the photographic reproduction of paintings and other works of art; the principal office and studio was in Munich, but there were branches in Rome, Paris, Berlin, London, and New York.

These antecedents and connections were interesting in themselves, but what made this thirty-five-year-old German particularly unusual was his connection with the United States. Nearly seventy-five years earlier, after the liberal revolution of 1848, his maternal grandfather, Wilhelm Heine, an architect from Dresden, had fled to the United States. In short order, Heine changed his first name to William, became a well-known illustrator, and was appointed the official artist to accompany Commodore Matthew Perry on the 1853 naval expedition that opened Japan's modern era of international relations and technical development. Heine married a young woman from a prominent New England family, the Sedgwicks, and went on to become a general during the Civil War. William Heine was one of the generals who were pallbearers at Abraham Lincoln's funeral; Heine's daughter, then six, remembered the sight of her father carrying the assassinated president's coffin long after the family returned to Germany, where she eventually met and married Edgar Hanfstaengl.

Their son Ernst very nearly died in childhood; at the age of two he caught diphtheria and was saved only by the constant ministrations of a family retainer, an old peasant woman who fed him constantly, cooing, "Putzi, eat this now, Putzi." Putzi, a term of endearment meaning "little fellow," became a singularly inappropriate nickname when the toddler grew to a height of six feet four inches, but to his German friends and acquaintances, Putzi he remained.[4]

As was the case in many families with business interests in several countries, a son was especially trained to become effective in a particular nation, and it was decided that Ernst would eventually take over the shop on Fifth Avenue in New York that his father had set up in the 1880s. Putzi had grown up speaking English as well as German, and it was also decided that, before entering on his business career, he would attend Harvard College, to which he had some ties through his New England grandmother. Arriving in the autumn of 1905, he immediately found himself a popular figure among his classmates, none of whom could pronounce his last name; he was promptly dubbed Hanfy. Immensely tall and very strong, he was soon pulling an oar in one of Harvard's crews on the Charles River, and his gifts and splendid training as a pianist made him a great attraction at parties.

Among his many friends were some destined for future fame: the poet T. S. Eliot, the political essayist and editor Walter Lippmann, the humorist Robert Benchley, and the journalist and leftist-radical leader John Reed. Through his friend Theodore Roosevelt, Jr., son of the president, Hanfy was invited to a stag party in the White House basement, where his huge hands managed to break seven bass strings on a Steinway grand as he played the piano with even more than his usual enthusiasm during the small hours of the morning.

Taking over the Fifth Avenue shop after his graduation, Hanfstaengl found it to be "a delightful combination of business and pleasure." Among those who went there to buy reproductions or simply to talk were the financier and bibliophile Pierpont Morgan, Arturo Toscanini,

Henry Ford, Enrico Caruso, and Charlie Chaplin. At the Harvard Club, where he usually took lunch, Hanfstaengl made friends with a young and politically promising New York state senator, Franklin D. Roosevelt.

This pleasant existence changed with the onset of the war and America's entrance into it in 1917. Hanfstaengl's shop windows were broken in a display of anti-German sentiment. The Custodian of Enemy Property took over the firm's assets, worth half a million dollars, and sold them at auction for eight thousand. Hanfstaengl was subject to internment as an enemy alien, but his Harvard connections proved useful: "I was fortunate in having Senator Elihu Root, who had been Theodore Roosevelt's Secretary of State, as my lawyer." In return for his pledge not to engage in activities that would hamper the American war effort, he was not confined, although he could not travel outside Manhattan.

Two years after the war, in 1920, Hanfstaengl married the daughter of a German businessman from Bremen who had settled in the United States, and in the following year their son, Egon, was born. Having been away from Germany for many years, Putzi felt a desire to return to his native land and sold his interest in the New York branch to his partner.

In July 1921, Ernst Hanfstaengl and his wife and son returned to Germany aboard the S.S. *America*.

> I found a Germany riven by faction and near destitution. . . .
> Even the bracing malt-laden air of Munich could not compensate
> for the unpainted look of the houses and the peeling facade of the
> great Court Theatre. . . . Almost the first political event which
> greeted my return was the murder of Matthias Erzberger, who
> had signed the 1918 Armistice, by a couple of young right-wing
> radicals. Counter threats, reports of separatism, putschism and
> terrorism filled the columns of the newspapers. The tone of the
> press increased daily in violence and abuse. It became evident to
> me that Germany, politically speaking, was a madhouse, with a
> thousand opinions and no saving idea. . . . I had been spared the
> misery of the previous decade and wanted in a confused way to
> help, but could find no outlet.

Kurt Ludecke, at this stage of his homecoming, had started the search for a solution to Germany's problems that led him to Hitler. Putzi had a different approach: "To get my bearings I decided to study German history." He was soon working on a book, with hopes of also making it into a film, about the American Loyalist Benjamin Thompson, Count Rumford, who in the 1790s had reorganized Bavaria's army, police, and civil administration and introduced revolutionary innovations for kindly and productive treatment of beggars and criminals. There were parallels between the situation that Thompson had faced and the disarray of the Weimar Republic, but for Putzi his research and writing offered a certain buffer; even after Coburg, although he was living in Munich, he had not heard the name Adolf Hitler. Well supplied with American dollars, which were commanding increasingly immense numbers of marks, he and his beautiful wife and little son lived a privileged life. His mother and sister Erna and brother Edgar had continued to live in Munich while he was away; every door was open to a member of a family that in the past had entertained not only all of Bavaria's nobility and cultural elite, but also numbered among their friends Mark Twain and the Norwegian explorer, scientist, and statesman Fridtjof Nansen.

This relative serenity was soon to be changed as the result of a long distance telephone call from Berlin, during the second week of November. The man on the other end of the line was Warren Robbins, a senior official in the American embassy. As Harvard undergraduates, he and Putzi had acted in a Hasty Pudding Club show called *Fake Fakirs*, in which the massive Hanfstaengl was costumed as a Dutch girl named Gretchen Spootsfeiffer.

> "Listen, Hanfy," he said. "What are you Bavarians up to?" I had to tell him that in all conscience I did not know. The whole country was a hotbed of political agitation in those troubled postwar years and I had not really been trying to keep the thread of events in my head. "Well, we are sending our young military attaché, Captain Truman Smith, down to have a look round," Robbins went on. "Look after him and introduce him to a few people, will you?"

Truman Smith was a Yale man who had fought with exceptional distinction during the war in the Fourth Infantry Regiment, and had chosen to remain in the service. Fluent in German, he had served with the American occupation forces in Coblenz, and had since 1920 been a military observer with the American diplomatic mission in Berlin, which had recently been reestablished as a full-fledged embassy. The six-foot-four Smith, who wore civilian clothes, and the equally tall Hanfstaengl got along immediately: entertaining the visitor who had graduated from Harvard's traditional rival, Putzi lightly said that, although Smith had a Yale degree, "I was nice to him. I gave him a letter to Paul Nikolaus Cossmann, editor of the *Münchner Neueste Nachrichten*, and told him to drop in to lunch at my flat whenever he felt like it. I must say he worked like a beaver."

Smith worked hard indeed. Arriving on November 15, he consulted with Robert Murphy of the consulate, and within a few days had seen Ludendorff, Crown Prince Rupprecht, Kahr, Count von Lerchenfeld, and several cabinet-level officials of the Bavarian government. He had been told to make a particular effort to acquaint himself with the facts concerning Hitler and his party, as well as their probable potential. Smith received greatly varying estimates of NSDAP membership figures, but soon began to understand the unique Bavarian political climate. On the one hand, Hitler might be warned not to attempt an armed revolt; on the other, he and the Bavarian government looked at the national government in Berlin as a common enemy. Smith's notes said:

> Bavaria is openly flouting the Reich (federal) law for the Defense of the Republic. The Bavarian minister of the interior just laughed when asked if the federal criminal police had yet been organized in his jurisdiction. The Bavarian government permits the National Socialists to do what they want. Police do not interfere if the Hitler people break up a Socialist meeting.[5]

After three days in Munich, Smith had a discussion with one of the most shadowy figures in the early Nazi Party. The small, neatly dressed man with pince-nez who talked with him was Max Erwin von Scheubner-Richter, a Baltic adventurer who had been a spy in Turkey during the war — one account had it that he was a Russian agent who subsequently defected to the Germans. His title "Doctor," supposedly of engineering, was suspect, as was the aristocratic "von" preceding his surname. He had been one of the intriguers involved in the Kapp Putsch, and in Munich's political half-light he occupied a special place as liaison between the White Russian and Ukrainian refugee communities in the city and the entire spectrum of nationalist-racist parties. Scheubner-Richter had connections with the House of Wittelsbach, and had persuaded the Duchess of Coburg to use him as the conduit through which funds were channeled to Munich's völkisch groups. He apparently was able to raise funds from industrialists for right-wing activities, and it was said that he was on good terms with leading churchmen. On this occasion he was accompanied by the Nazi propaganda writer, Alfred Rosenberg, another Balt — Hitler joked that the *Völkischer Beobachter* should carry near its title "Baltic Edition" — and the two men, Smith said, "talked to me in some detail about the movement."[6] Scheubner-Richter told him that there were thirty-five thousand party members in Munich, a number three and a half times larger than the figure being used by the Munich police, who were usually accurate in these matters.[7] "Richter told me that Hitler had reached a secret compromise with the Bavarian government, regarding what the party could and couldn't do within Bavaria. He also told me about the National Socialist invasion of Coburg." In what was surely one of the most stupendous lies told by a member since the party was founded, Scheubner-Richter "stated that the anti-Semitism of the party was purely for propaganda."[8]

On the afternoon of November 20, Smith met Hitler. The notes he made immediately afterward began, "A marvelous demagogue. I have rarely listened to such a logical and fanatical man. His power over the mob must be immense." In the course of an interview that lasted several hours, Hitler barely mentioned the subject of anti-Semitism to this representative of the United States of America. Hitler ran through his program; among the points he made, as Smith reported in his notes, were "Only a dictatorship can bring Germany to its feet" and "It is much better for America and England that the decisive struggle between our civilization and Marxism be fought out on German soil rather than on American or English soil." On two matters, Hitler claimed to hold positions that were directly contrary to everything he had been saying to his fellow Germans: he told Smith that he was in favor of paying reparations to the Allies and that he wanted an understanding with France.[9]

Smith later wrote that Hitler looked like a middle-class German shopkeeper, except for his eyes, which were "gleaming with fanaticism, intense and unceasing."[10] As for the conditions in which Hitler operated, Smith said, "It must ever and again be remembered that Germany is a sick nation, sick financially and economically, but still more sick intellectually and morally."[11]

Hitler was continuing to make remarks about being merely "a drummer" who was preparing the way for some greater leader, but to Smith he made a declaration that went beyond anything he had said to a German audience: "Hitler emphasizes that his movement is a federal one and that he seeks control of the Reich, not merely of Bavaria."[12] Certainly this was implied repeatedly in all that Hitler had said and that he and his party had done, but never had he so nakedly put himself forward as intending to become Germany's dictator. This statement of Hitler's was duly included in the full report that Smith sent to the Division of Military Intelligence of the War Department in Washington on November 25, 1922. There it lay. In contrast to Smith's discerning description and analysis, another foreign diplomat in Germany at the time dismissed Hitler as simply "an uneducated madman."[13]

On the last day of his visit to Munich, Smith was having lunch with Putzi Hanfstaengl. The embassy had asked him to return to Berlin on the evening train, and he was summing up some impressions. Speaking of his most memorable interview, he said, "I met a most remarkable fellow . . ." Putzi recounted the rest of the conversation.

> "Really," I replied. "What's his name?"
> "Adolf Hitler."
> "You must have the name wrong," I said. "Don't you mean Hilpert, the German nationalist fellow, although I can't say I see anything particularly remarkable in him."
> "No, no," Truman Smith insisted. "Hitler. There are quite a lot of placards up announcing a meeting this evening. . . . I have the impression he is going to play a big part and whether you like him or not he certainly knows what he wants. . . . He really seems to have a sense of direction which none of the others have. They gave me a press ticket for this meeting this evening, and now I shall not be able to go. Could you possibly have a look at him for me and let me know your impression?"[14]

Entering the packed Kindlkeller that night, Hanfstaengl was struck by the fact that the audience represented a cross section of the populace. "There seemed to be a lot of people of the concierge or small-shopkeeper class, a sprinkling of the former officer and minor-civil-servant type, a tremendous number of young people and the rest artisans, with a high proportion of the spectators in Bavarian national costume." He pushed his way through to the press table on the right side of the platform. This evening, Hitler was not staging one of his last-minute entrances, and Putzi soon had his first look at the party leader, who was standing with Max Amann and Anton Drexler, waiting for the meeting to begin.

> In his heavy boots, dark suit and leather waistcoat, semi-stiff white collar and odd little moustache, he really did not look very impressive. . . . However, when Drexler introduced him to a roar of applause, Hitler straightened up and walked past the press table with a swift, controlled step, the unmistakable soldier in mufti.

Putzi noted that "the atmosphere in the hall was electric." He was no more than eight feet away from Hitler and studied him carefully. Speaking quietly and standing rigidly, Hitler devoted the first ten minutes of his speech to a review of Germany's postwar history, stressing the Versailles Treaty and the way in which Marxist ideas of class war were creating a "hopeless stalemate" between workers and their employers.

As he felt the audience becoming increasingly interested in what he had to say, he gently moved his left foot to one side, like a soldier standing at ease, and started to use his hands and arms in gestures, of which he had an expressive and extensive repertoire. . . . He had an ingenious, mocking humor which was telling without being offensive.

A widely traveled man who could easily have been a professional musician, Putzi Hanfstaengl had a particular feeling for voices, as well as what they had to say. Listening to Hitler, he observed, "There was almost a note of Viennese coffeehouse conversation in the grace of some of his phrases and the sly malice of his insinuations. There was no doubt of his Austrian origin." As for content:

He scored his points all round the compass. First he would criticize the Kaiser as a weakling and then he rounded on the Weimar republicans for conforming with the victors' demands, which were stripping Germany of everything but the graves of her war dead. There was a strong note of appeal to the ex-servicemen in his audience. . . . He dwelt at length on patriotism and national pride.

There were attacks on the Jews, and "he thundered at the Communists and Socialists for desiring the disruption of German traditions." Problem after problem, Hitler assured his audience, could be solved by his approach.

As he warmed to his subject he started to speak more rapidly, his hands tellingly suggesting the highlights of thesis and antithesis, symbolizing the rise and fall of his cadences, emphasizing the magnitude of problems and the fleeting pizzicato of his ideas.

Hecklers occasionally interrupted. When they did, this was the response:

Then Hitler would raise his right hand, as if catching a ball, or would fold his arms and with one or two words bring the audience over to his side. His technique resembled the thrusts and parries of a fencer, or the perfect balance of a tightrope walker. Sometimes he reminded me of a skilled violinist, who, never coming to the end of his bow, always left just the faint anticipation of a tone — a thought spared the indelicacy of utterance.

Hitler had been talking for sixty minutes.

I looked round at the audience. Where was the nondescript crowd I had seen only an hour before? What was suddenly holding these people, who on the hopeless incline of the falling mark were engaged in a daily struggle to keep themselves within the line of decency? The hubbub and chattering had stopped and they were drinking in every word. Only a few yards away there was a young woman, her eyes fastened on the speaker. Transfigured as though in some devotional ecstasy, she had ceased to be herself, and was completely under the spell of Hitler's despotic faith in Germany's future greatness.

Hitler's final oratorical crescendo was met, Putzi said, with "frenzied cheering." Sitting at their tables in the beer hall, many of the audience held empty beer steins, with which they began "a cannonade of table-pounding. It sounded like the demoniacal rattle of thousands of hailstones rebounding on the surface of a giant drum."

As the audience began to leave, Ernst Hanfstaengl took stock of his own reaction to what he had just witnessed.

I was really impressed beyond measure by Hitler. . . . With his incredible gifts as an orator he was clearly going to go far, and from what I had seen of his entourage there seemed no one likely to bring home to him the picture of the outside world he manifestly lacked, and in this I felt I might be able to help.

A tall, physically powerful son of a prominent Bavarian family, a man who had chatted with Theodore Roosevelt and Charlie Chaplin, would have no hesitation about introducing himself to anyone he wished to meet, and Putzi walked over to where Hitler was standing on the platform, spent from his exertions.

Naive and yet forceful, obliging and yet uncompromising, he stood, face and hair soaked in perspiration, his semi-stiff collar, fastened with a square, imitation gold safetypin, melted to nothing. While talking he dabbed his face with a handkerchief, glancing worriedly at the many open exits through which came the draughts of a cold November night.

Putzi introduced himself, explaining that he had come at the request of Captain Smith, and added that he was most impressed by what he had just heard. He told Hitler that he agreed with 95 percent of his speech, "and would very much like to talk to [him] about the rest some time."

"Why yes, of course," Hitler said. "I am sure we shall not have to quarrel about the odd five percent." He made a very pleasant impression, modest and friendly.

Kurt Ludecke was also at this meeting, trying to bring yet another convert, "one of the richest princes in Germany," into the party ranks. As Ludecke described it, this particular recruiting effort was a fiasco.

The fellow turned out to be an exquisite young man who suffered tortures at such intimate contact with the rough masses. Attending incognito, of course, he received such a jostling . . . that he became almost ill; the close air overwhelmed him, and possibly he was frightened to learn that the lower classes could think and talk. I gave him up as a possible Nazi fighter. Nearly in tears, he fled outside to his Mercedes.

Before Ludecke and the prince got into the chauffeur-driven car, "Ernst Hanfstaengl of Harvard fame, who was hearing Hitler for the first time and was enthralled by the sheer artistry of his show, saw me leaving. Taking advantage of our slight acquaintance, he edged up for an introduction and drove away with us." When the prince's car dropped Ludecke off at his hotel, Putzi also got out. "Up and down the street we walked, discussing Hitler. In the flush of enthusiasm, I was eloquent. His interest became less detached."[15]

What began that night was an often spiteful rivalry between the two most worldly of the men attracted thus far by Hitler. They might have done better to become allies; each was destined to serve the party far better than it served him, and both were ultimately betrayed or humiliated by men who had seen little salt water. In different years, each would flee the party, and Germany, believing that it was necessary to save his life.

For the moment, however, all was discovery and hope. At home, Putzi could not get to sleep. "My mind still raced with the impressions of the evening. Where all our conservative politicians were failing abysmally to establish any contact with the ordinary people, this self-made man, Hitler, was clearly succeeding in presenting a non-Communist program to exactly those people whose support we needed."[16]

III

Through the last weeks of 1922, Hitler was making special efforts. On November 30, the citizens of Munich saw the battle for public opinion being fought before their eyes; endeavoring to offset a carefully orchestrated series of speeches at which the Social Democratic leader Erhard Auer had spoken to large audiences, Hitler gave five speeches in one evening. For him to accomplish this feat, NSDAP meetings were held in five beer halls; at each site, a program of Nazi speakers was arranged, and interrupted for Hitler when he arrived; for once, the audiences heard something much shorter than the usual two-and-a-half-hour harangue.[17] This proved so successful that on December 13, between 8:30 P.M. and midnight, Hitler spoke at ten NSDAP meetings throughout Munich.[18]

Near the end of December, in a conversation with Eduard August Scharrer, the co-owner of the daily *Münchner Neueste Nachrichten*, Hitler went into some of his ideas about Germany's future. By agreement, his interview was recorded by a stenographer; what is not known is whether Hitler realized that his views would be sent by Scharrer to Chancellor Wilhelm Cuno in Berlin. Labeled a "secret report," it paraphrased some of Hitler's remarks, but his characteristic thrust, and impatience with democratic niceties, were present in every line. Only a dictatorship could save Germany, Hitler said, and a dictator must be found immediately. There were thirteen mentions of this unnamed dictator, or his future regime. What was needed was "a man who would, if need be, walk through blood and corpse-strewn fields."[19] Always a grudging admirer of the British, Hitler envisioned a situation in which there would be a German-British alliance, and said that "the destruction of Russia with the help of England would have to be attempted. Russia would give Germany sufficient land for German settlers and a wide field of activity for German industry." In Hitler's view, this alliance would somehow guarantee Britain's neutrality during what would follow: "Then England would not interrupt us in our reckoning with France."[20]

Whatever Hitler's intentions toward France might be, France's intentions toward Germany were becoming more hostile than at any time since the guns stopped firing in 1918. After the German failure to negotiate successfully with the French-led reparations commission in Berlin in November, the premiers of France, Italy, and Belgium met in London on December 9 with the new British prime minister, Andrew Bonar Law. The Germans were not invited; the purpose of the meeting was to try to arrange a comprehensive workable solution to the twin problems of Germany's debts to the Allies and the huge wartime debts that France owed to Britain and the United States.

This new London Conference took up as its first order of business a proposal sent to it by Chancellor Cuno, which expressed the determination of the German government to make every effort to stabilize the mark even if no other nation should offer Germany the international loans it so desperately needed. In order to do this, however, Cuno said, the Allies should extend not only the moratorium that had been belatedly granted concerning money payments, but should, for a period of two years, cease requiring Germany to make its shipments of coal, timber, and other commodities.

Chancellor Cuno's plan had no appeal for France. The French premier, Raymond Poincaré, brought the entire conference to a standstill by taking the position that, unless Britain and the United States simply wrote off the tremendous debts owed them by France, he would insist on German payment of full reparations.

The situation came to a head on December 26, 1922, when the Allied Reparations Commission met in Paris. Poincaré was determined to collect his debt from Germany one way or another, with or without the assistance, or even the agreement, of his former allies. The Treaty of Versailles provided, in somewhat ambiguous language using terms such as "sanctions" and "measures," for forcible collection of reparations, in money or in kind. For years the French had been threatening to go into the unoccupied territory of the Ruhr, a move that would have been equivalent to taking over the Pittsburgh–Ohio Valley area and Detroit of that day. Then, under French bayonets, such enormous enterprises as the Krupp works in Essen would be working for France, on French terms.

To do this, however, the reparations commission had to find that there was in fact a German "default," which in view of the moratorium on money payments, had to consist of a failure to deliver required shipments of various raw materials and products, the "payments in kind." Germany was behind in its coal shipments, but the French singled out this statistic: with the end of the year a few days away, Germany had shipped only 100,000 of the 200,000 telephone poles that France was to have received by the close of 1922.

France was using these telephone poles as a pretext for taking action, but the fact remained that Germany was in default, and the reparations commission duly noted it. Then the chairman, Louis Barthou, recommended that the delinquency be classified as a punishable violation of the Versailles Treaty. That produced an eloquent protest on the part of the British member of the commission, Sir John Bradbury. With his sense of fair play outraged, he cried out that history had not recorded such a devious use of wood since the Greeks had used their wooden horse to sneak men inside the walls of Troy.[21] The only difference, he pointed out, was that this time French soldiers were to be placed in Essen. The Belgian and Italian representatives, unmoved by Sir John's indignation, joined France in finding Germany subject to extraordinary methods of collection. There the fragile matter rested.

IV

In the last part of 1922, Ernst Hanfstaengl quickly became a favorite of Adolf Hitler's. Putzi described the beginning of the relationship, starting with an evening when he took his wife to hear Hitler speak and introduced them after the meeting.

> He was delighted with my wife, who was blond and beautiful and American. He accepted very readily when she said how pleased we would be if he would come to coffee or dinner at the flat. Soon he was visiting us frequently, pleasant and unassuming in his too-small blue serge suit. He was respectful, even diffident and very careful to adhere to the forms of address still *de rigueur* in Germany between — what shall I say? — people of lower rank when speaking to those of better education, title or academic attainment. The only striking things about him were an extraordinary luminous quality in his blue eyes and his sensitive hands, plus of course very definite gifts of expression in conversation.[22]

With Hitler spending much of his limited spare time at the Hanfstaengls' — he won the approval of little Egon by his uncanny imitation of a steam engine, whistle, bells, and all — Putzi began his efforts to broaden Hitler's horizons. He tried to explain that the United States was "an absolutely new factor in European politics." Putzi pointed out that he had been in the United States in 1917 and 1918 and seen what the spirit and industrial might of that nation could do: "The Americans mobilized two and a half million soldiers out of nowhere and sent over 150,000 a month to hold the front. If there is another war it must inevitably be won by the side which America joins."

According to Putzi, Hitler greeted this with "Yes, yes, you must be right," but the idea of the necessity for having good relations with the United States was simply outside his frame of reference. The only time that Hitler appeared fascinated was when Putzi described the architectural features of skyscrapers or talked about American assembly lines. Hitler was somewhat interested in Henry Ford, not as a pioneering industrialist but as an anti-Semite who might be a source of funds, and he appeared to think that the Ku Klux Klan was a political party with which he might be able to form an alliance.

While Hanfstaengl was finding it uphill work to bring the world beyond Central Europe to Hitler's attention, Hitler was developing a great appreciation of Hanfstaengl's musical talent. There was an upright piano in the hall of Hitler's lodgings, and the first time Hanfstaengl played it was the night before Hitler had to appear as a witness in a political trial. He was extremely nervous and asked Putzi to play something to calm him.

> I played a Bach fugue, to which he sat listening in a chair, nodding his head in vague non-interest. Then I started the prelude to the *Meistersinger*. This was it. This was Hitler's meat. He knew the thing absolutely by heart and could whistle every note of it in a curious penetrating vibrato, but completely in tune. He started to march up and down the hall, waving his arms as if he were conducting an orchestra. He really had an excellent feeling for the spirit of the music, certainly as good as many a conductor. This music affected him physically and by the time I had crashed through the finale he was in splendid spirits, all his worries gone, and eager to get to grips with the public prosecutor.

Although Putzi did not realize it, his fate was sealed: his real function in the life of Adolf Hitler was to play the piano for him, not to be an instructor in international reality.

> After that we had innumerable sessions together. . . . In the end it always had to be Wagner, *Meistersinger, Tristan und Isolde* and *Lohengrin*. I must have played them hundreds of times and he never grew tired of listening. He had a very genuine knowledge and appreciation of Wagner's music which he had picked up somewhere, probably in his Vienna days, long before I knew him.

Soon enough, in addition to playing the piano for Hitler and introducing him to Munich society and making sure that he met various distinguished foreigners who happened to be in the city, Ernst Hanfstaengl became the party's official representative to the foreign press.

Of all the men close to Hitler at the time, Putzi made the closest study of the enigmatic party leader, and he later set down some vivid descriptions and interpretations of Hitler's behavior.

He could sprawl for hours like a crocodile dozing in the Nile mud or a spider immobile in the center of its web. He would chew his nails, look boredly into space and sometimes whistle. As soon as some person of interest — and there was no one he did not find interesting for a time — joined his company, you could almost see him mobilizing his internal machinery. The sonar pings of inquiry would go out and within a short time he had a clear image of the secret yearnings and emotions of his partner. The pendulum of conversation would start to move faster, and the person would be hypnotized into believing that there lay in Hitler immense depths of sympathy and understanding. He had the most formidable power of persuasion of any man or woman I have ever met, and it was almost impossible to avoid being enveloped by him.[23]

V

During 1922 the party had gained thousands of new members, including such unusual men as Kurt Ludecke and Putzi Hanfstaengl, but near the end of the year the NSDAP acquired its prize recruit. He was Captain Hermann Goering, the famous fighter pilot who had commanded the Flying Circus during the closing months of the war. Goering simply walked into party headquarters, asked for an application form, and filled it out. When the man to whom he handed it realized that this was the legendary soldier of the Pour le Mérite — equivalent to the Victoria Cross or the Congressional Medal of Honor — he was asked to wait. "Anyway," Goering said later, "somebody tells me that Hitler would like to see me immediately."[24] The meeting was cordial: "I liked him," Hitler later said.[25] Goering recalled, "He told me that it was a stroke of fate that I should come to him just as he was looking for somebody to take charge of the SA." They decided that he would eventually replace Klintzsch, and it was understood that Goering would immediately begin to familiarize himself with the Storm Troop organization. Ludecke asked Hitler about the new member.

"Oh! Goering!" Hitler exclaimed, laughing and slapping his knee with satisfaction. "Splendid, a war ace with the Pour le

Mérite — imagine it! Excellent propaganda! Moreover, he has money and doesn't cost me a cent."

In Hermann Goering, the party was getting a headstrong man of action whose psyche was formed in a turbulent background. At the time of his birth, his father had been a fifty-three-year-old official of the German consular service, married to a young woman who was twenty-seven. Three months after Hermann was born, his mother left him in a Bavarian town while she went to Haiti to rejoin her husband, who was stationed there and had their older children with him. Because the tropical climate was deemed to be quite possibly fatal to infants, the baby was left with a family in the Bavarian town of Fürth and brought up with their two young daughters, who recalled that he spent the three years of his mother's absence in loneliness, punctuated by alternating tantrums and tears, despite every kind gesture on the part of those charged with his care.

"It is the cruelest thing that can happen to a child," Goering later said, "to be torn from his mother in his formative years."[26] When his mother and father returned from their posting to the Caribbean and he was taken to the railroad station to meet the train, the little boy ostentatiously turned his back to the train as it clanked in. As his mother swept him into her arms, he started hitting her face and chest with his fists, and burst into tears.

Hermann Goering's later childhood had yet another complication. With his father's tacit consent, his mother became the mistress of the flamboyant and able Hermann Ritter von Epenstein, a physician whose title of nobility had been granted by the Kaiser. Although young Goering did not know it, Epenstein was the son of a Jewish doctor who had converted to Catholicism before marrying the daughter of a Gentile banker. On the birth of Hermann Goering's younger brother Albert, who grew up to bear a strong resemblance to Epenstein, the rich physician adopted all five Goering children as his godchildren. In the Germany of the day it was a very special form of protection, and *Pate*, the word for godfather by which they addressed him, was used by the children as a term of profound respect for their benefactor.

While Hermann Goering's real father, retired from the diplomatic service, sank into a civil drunken silence, Epenstein became the boy's idol. He established the family, including the thoroughly cuckolded Heinrich Goering, in a castle twenty-five miles north of Nuremberg. There were also long visits to another castle owned by Epenstein, at Mauterndorf in the Austrian mountains on the Bavarian frontier. Here there was pageantry and excitement enough for even the boldest boy: footmen in livery and powdered wigs, gamekeepers in garments that had changed little from medieval times, and days spent hunting chamois in the mountains with Hermann's idolized godfather. Meals at Mauterndorf were announced by the sharp wail of a hunting horn, and on special occasions there were minstrels and musicians, sometimes in medieval costume. On Sundays Ritter von Epenstein would lead his godchildren and his guests into the Catholic church in the village, where special pews were held in his name. For Hermann his godfather — on at least one occasion his tongue slipped and he called him his father — could not conceivably have been one of the Jews portrayed in the anti-Semitic stereotypes of the day: an indoor people, miserly and given to wearing dark clothes.

Hermann's discovery of the truth about his godfather's parentage came at a boarding school in Ansbach when he was eleven. Assigned the topic of writing an essay about "the man I admire most in the world," he promptly wrote a glowing description of his generous, colorful, sports-loving, and professionally successful godfather. The next day Hermann was called in by the headmaster and told that boys at this school were not meant to write papers praising Jews — Frederick the Great, Bismarck, or the Kaiser was acceptable, and some boys wrote about their fathers, who were of course Gentiles. When Hermann indignantly identified his godfather as a Catholic, the headmaster showed him a copy of a type of German Social Register in which titled German families of Jewish origin were listed, and there was Epenstein's name. Hermann was then told to go and write out, one hundred times, "I shall not write essays in praise of Jews," after which he was to copy, from the listing he had been shown, all the names from A to E. The report of the incident went through the school like wildfire, resulting in a fight in which Hermann took on three boys, lost, and was forced to march around the school grounds with a placard around his neck saying, "My Godfather Is a Jew." His response was to run away from school the next day, but not before shattering the violin that he had been forced to practice on, as well as cutting the strings of all the other instruments in the school orchestra's string section.[27]

None of that changed Goering's devotion to his godfather, but his experience at school turned him more and more to the outdoor life. He became increasingly interested in mountain climbing and horseback riding, and he developed an intense desire to become a soldier. Hermann first went to a military school at Karlsruhe, where he did well, then to the elite cadet college at Gross Lichterfelde, on the outskirts of Berlin. Posted to an infantry regiment, he was twenty-one years old when the war began. He conducted his first patrols against the French with an awesome disregard for conventional military ideas of oblique approaches or leaving open possible lines of retreat. On one of these missions he managed to capture four French infantrymen who had no idea that any Germans were behind them, and was mentioned in dispatches for the first time.

A bout of rheumatic fever took young Lieutenant Goering out of the trenches and began for him an entirely different career. A friend had become a pilot, and, after talking with him, Goering simply could not resist an opportunity to slip away from the hospital and start flying as an observer in the back seat of his friend's plane. Lieutenant Goering and the authorities soon found themselves in an unusual situation: technically a deserter from his infantry regiment, which wanted him back, he was spending his days rendering extremely valuable service as a cameraman-observer with an aerial reconnaissance unit flying over the front lines. The situation was eventually regularized, not without some behind-the-scenes assistance from his godfather.

From that moment forward, Goering managed to move into the front seat, literally and figuratively. After pilot training, he went on to become one of Germany's leading combat pilots, knocking down twenty-two Allied planes and taking charge of the Flying Circus in July of 1918, after the death of its commander, Manfred von Richthofen. It was a moment that would have presented special problems to any commander. When the Red Baron was shot down, several sub-unit commanders in the fifty-plane fighter group assumed that the next commanding officer would surely come from within their small and eminently elite number. Here was this man being brought in from the outside and placed over their heads. The resentment was stony, and Goering met it head on. His first orders were that, on the next day's mission, each of the sub-unit commanders was to hand over his command to his number two man; the sub-unit commanders were to fly in formation with him.

It proved to be a memorable day. Goering was flinging down the gauntlet; they were to get up there with him, and then everyone would see whether one of them, or he, deserved to be Richthofen's successor. He started the day by shooting down a British Spad, then spent the rest of the time performing maneuvers which set up shots for kills that were duly executed by his subordinate leaders. Having held them out of the main show, Goering then gave them the signal to cut loose on their own. He had shown these men his tremendous skill, and convinced them that they would fly either under his orders or not at all. Finally, to close the day's demonstration of who was who within the Flying Circus, he picked another Spad and, like a cat playing with a mouse, chased it all over the sky in a series of maneuvers, countering every effort the British pilot made to escape, before shooting down his second plane of the day and waving to everybody that it was time to go home and have a few drinks at the mess.

At the war's close, Goering and his pilots deliberately smashed their planes so that they would be of no use to the Allies. On the night the Flying Circus was disbanded, its survivors gathered in a restaurant in a town near Frankfurt, where the final paperwork for processing out of service had been done. Some had already been insulted by enlisted men with red armbands. One of his fellow pilots remembered the officers' party that night.

> At one point in the evening Hermann climbed onto the little bandstand with a glass in his hand, and though everyone was shouting and roystering there was something in his manner that made us all suddenly silent. He began to speak. He hardly raised his voice at all, but there was a strange quality to it, an emotional underbeat, that seemed to slip through the chinks in your flesh and reach right into your heart. He spoke of the Richthofen Squadron and what it had done, of how its achievements, the skill and bravery of its pilots, had made it famous the world over. "Only in Germany today is its name now dragged in the mud, its record forgotten, its officers jeered at."
>
> He began to inveigh against the revolutionary forces that were sweeping through Germany, and of the shame they were bringing upon the armed forces and upon Germany itself. "But the forces of freedom and right and morality will win through in the end," he said. "We will fight against these forces which are seeking to enslave us, and we will win through. Those same qualities which made the Richthofen Squadron great will prevail in peacetime as well as in war. Our time will come again." Then he raised his glass and said: "Gentlemen, I give you a toast — to the Fatherland and to the Richthofen Squadron." He drank and then smashed his glass down at his feet, and we all did likewise. Many of us were weeping, Hermann among them.[28]

This was the essence of the man who had joined the Nazi Party. In the intervening years he had worked as a charter pilot in Scandinavia, where he also represented the Dutch Fokker airplane manufacturing concern. He sometimes publicized Fokker aircraft by performing hazardous stunts in various aerial shows. Before going to Scandinavia, Goering had briefly visited Munich, where his mother was living. During the time of the Munich Soviet, he had been saved from capture by Red patrols through the kind protection of a British pilot, a captain serving on an Allied commission, whom Goering had entertained at his mess after the pilot was shot down behind German lines.

One winter evening in 1920, lost while flying a charter passenger through bad weather in the Swedish countryside, he brought his plane skidding to a halt on the surface of the frozen waters of Lake Baven, stopping just under the ramparts of Rockelstadt Castle. He had in fact arrived at the destination for which he had been looking, for his passenger was Count Eric von Rosen, who had missed his train and was attempting to get back to his home, which was this castle.

It was as if the twenty-seven-year-old Hermann Goering had come upon a scene that was a dream from his childhood castles. He was soon standing in Rockelstadt's great hall, which was hung with old weapons, armor, hunting trophies that included a huge stuffed bear which had been killed with a spear, numerous family portraits, and tapestries decorated with Nordic hunting and battle scenes. A guest left an account of what happened next.

> Hermann Goering stood before the open fire staring into the flames. Two great swastikas of wrought iron hung on either side of the bars on which the logs were burning. . . . Suddenly from the stairs above a woman began to descend, a woman of noble, queenly bearing. It was Carin, sister of the chatelaine of the household. Her deep blue eyes met Hermann Goering's searching glance. . . . He stood there, tongue-tied and in awe.[29]

Whatever was happening to the young war hero was also happening to this woman, who was five years older than he. In that same instant, she had fallen in love with him. "He is the man I have always dreamed about," she later said to her sister. There was just one problem: Carin was married to Nils von Kantzow, a Swedish army officer, by whom she had an eight-year-old son. What developed was a clandestine affair, but eventually Goering decided to leave Sweden and return to Germany. He went to Munich, largely because his mother was there, and began a fitful and superficial study of history and political science at the University of Munich. Carin could not stand the separation; she asked her husband for a divorce, which he agreed to with deep regret. Then the notably beautiful Carin von Kantzow went to Munich, where she and Goering were married in February of 1922.

Unlike the majority of those who joined the Nazi Party, Hermann Goering had not been hypnotized by one of Hitler's speeches. On the contrary, he first saw Hitler on an occasion when the NSDAP leader chose not to speak. In October of 1922 there had been a mass meeting at the Königsplatz protesting an Allied requirement that certain alleged war criminals be turned over to their custody. Any number of speakers from the various nationalist parties were holding forth, and the crowd began shouting, "Hitler! Hitler! Hitler!" By chance, Goering and Carin were standing near Hitler and heard him say that there was no point wasting time talking to "these tame bourgeois pirates." Something about Hitler's resolute demeanor as he said this impressed Goering, and he later attended a small Nazi Party meeting held at the Café Neumann.

> I just sat unobtrusively in the background. I remember Rosenberg was there. Hitler explained why he hadn't spoken. No Frenchman is going to lose sleep over that kind of harmless talk, he said. You've got to have bayonets to back up your threats. Well, *that* was what I wanted to hear. He wanted to build up a party that would make Germany strong and smash the Treaty of Versailles. "Well," I said to myself, "*that's* the party for me! Down with the Treaty of Versailles, God damn it! That's my meat."[30]

As 1923 began, Hermann Goering began his work with the Storm Troops. Since Coburg they had gradually been improving their uniforms; cheap grey ski caps were worn by nearly all the men, and a number of grey ski jackets were being seen, along with the grey wartime tunics and the many grey shirts. It was by now common knowledge that a Storm Troop member, in addition to carrying a blackjack, would probably have a pistol somewhere on him. Goering brought not only the type of discipline that he had exercised over the pilots of the Flying Circus, but also the Prussian parade ground methods that were stamped into every cadet at Gross Lichterfelde. He was a handsome young man, just thirty, with penetrating blue eyes, blond hair, and red cheeks that were beginning to get chubby. When he gave orders, men jumped. "Military!" Goering said of these early days. "I'll tell the world it was military!"[31]

Although it was clear that Goering was an important new addition to the party, various members saw him in different ways. Kurt Ludecke was not impressed, but Putzi Hanfstaengl took a broader view.

> Goering was a complete condottiere, the pure soldier of fortune, who saw in the Nazi Party a possible outlet for his vitality and vanity. Nevertheless, he had a jovial, extrovert manner and I found myself very much at home with him. . . . Goering had a certain humorous contempt for the little squad of Bavarians around Hitler, whom he regarded as a bunch of beer-swillers and rucksackers with a limited, provincial horizon.[32]

Goering was never to say how he reconciled his continuing devotion to his half-Jewish godfather with the anti-Semitism of the Nazi Party. At one point, when a subordinate voiced an implied criticism of Goering for having Jews as guests in his house, he snapped, "I'll decide who is and is not a Jew!"[33] He fell in with the party line on this and other matters, and considered Hitler as Germany's savior, but Putzi was right in seeing him as a man who lusted for action and was impatient with ideas. When asked about the party's platform, Goering responded that the National Socialist program was written on the faces of the marching Storm Troops, and he cut off another conversation with the blunt remark, "We are not here to make National Socialism. We are here to make history!"[34]

CHAPTER

25

IN THE MIDST of all this — the party's development, the jockeying for position, the hostility between Bavaria and Berlin, the constant struggle between Germany's socialists and right-wingers — France decided to carve out her pound of flesh.

As 1923 began, the Allies met again in Paris to consider new German proposals that were intended to postpone the penalties that the reparations commission had ruled could be levied against Germany because of her failure to deliver the hundred thousand telephone poles. The request for an extension, the German government said, was being put forward as "the last effort of an exhausted people."[1] The German representatives set forth their case on January 9, and on the same day were informed that Germany was considered to be in "voluntary default" of the reparations clauses of the Versailles Treaty.[2] France, Belgium, and Italy voted for sanctions against Germany; Sir John Bradbury voted against reprisals, and the American unofficial representative, who had no vote, nonetheless advised against the French-inspired action.

Although the Allied Reparations Commission's authority extended to many areas of the German economy, the target at which France and Belgium were aiming was the one that had always been uppermost in their minds. The Ruhr Valley, named for the river which wound through it from the east to join the Rhine in the west, contained Germany's industrial heart: the area, sixty miles long and thirty miles wide, contained 85 percent of the nation's coal. Literally above these mines — in some places coal was brought to the surface within a few yards of the furnaces that converted it to coke — were the mills that produced 80 percent of Germany's steel and iron. Packed into the area were hundreds of other factories that put forth a high percentage of Germany's metal products. Such giant enterprises as the Krupp works, which had traditionally manufactured everything from cannon to locomotives, were based in the city of Essen. In all, there were two million workers in the Ruhr Basin.

On January 10, a joint Franco-Belgian note informed the German government that in order to ensure strict German compliance with the production and delivery of coal as stipulated by the reparations commission, a control commission composed of engineers would be sent into the Ruhr. The note added that some French and Belgian soldiers would accompany this commission, but that "only such troops as are necessary to protect the commission and guarantee the execution of its duties are being sent into the Ruhr."[3]

What the French meant was clear to a West Pointer, Major General Henry T. Allen, commander of the small collection of occupation units known as American Forces in Germany. The American zone headquarters was at Ehrenbreitstein Fortress, on the Rhine at Coblenz, some seventy miles south of the Ruhr River. Allen, an able battlefield commander who had shown statesmanlike qualities in his successful administration of the American occupation, was perhaps the nearest thing to a neutral observer of the growing crisis. Although his son was married to a Frenchwoman and he had a half-French grandchild, Allen nonetheless had sympathy for the Germans who were under his control, and admiration for the energetic manner in which they were attempting to recover from the war. His diary for January 9 noted, in connection with French military movements through his area, "Up to ten o'clock to-night seventeen military trains have passed through Coblenz and nine more are scheduled to pass through by the same hour to-morrow night."[4] By General Allen's calculations, 22,500 French troops were moving through his area to join 30,000 additional French soldiers who were already poised on the edge of the northern French zone of occupation, ready to march into the Ruhr. Including the Belgian contingents, more than 60,000 soldiers were prepared to move into unoccupied Germany. As for the notion that all these men were simply a military escort to protect a cadre of civilian engineers, General Allen wrote: "However pacifically expressed or however carefully the phrases of the Treaty may have been employed, such a move could not be other than a military seizure."[5]

General Allen was as busy as any man in Europe. Just five days earlier, President Harding had stated in Washington that his administration was in favor of bringing home the last units of the American occupation forces; the president had added that not only the Allies but the Germans were desirous that they be kept in place on the Rhine, both sides believing that the Americans were a beneficial buffer force that could act to stabilize the deteriorating situation. Two days later, the United States Senate, determined that a few thousand Americans should not become engulfed in what appeared to be an impending French invasion of hitherto unoccupied areas of Germany, passed a resolution in favor of an immediate American withdrawal. On the day after he made his diary entry about French troops, General Allen received a telegram from Paris stating that President Harding had ordered the American troops home.[6]

The general's diary had become a witness to the intensifying crisis. On January 8 he had noted that a German newspaper, presumably with the government's blessing, had indicated that "the German government will consider the advance of the French into the Ruhr as a violation of the Versailles Treaty, which will thereafter be considered null and void."[7] On January 10 he duly noted this proclamation from Germany's President Ebert:

> Compatriots! Based upon military power a foreign nation is
> about to violate the right of self-determination of the German
> people. Again one of Germany's adversaries invades German ter-
> ritory. The policy of might and force, which since the conclusion
> of peace has been violating the treaties and trampling on human
> rights, threatens the principal German economic district, the
> main source of Germany's labor, the bread of German industry
> and the entire working classes. . . . The French move is a contin-
> uation of wrong and violence and a violation of the treaty aimed
> at a disarmed and defenseless nation.[8]

The proclamation from the German head of state was also note-worthy for what it did not say. There was no appeal to the populace to remain calm, and there was emphasis on the German government's intention to shorten, by unspecified means, any period of enemy occupation. It closed with an appeal for loyalty to the Fatherland. Even-handedly balancing the German view against French opinion, General Allen quoted from a leading French newspaper: "France has the profound conviction that she is right, that treaties are made to be executed, debts to be paid, pledges to be carried out, and conquerors to be indemnified."

On the morning of Thursday, January 11, 1923, the first French and Belgian columns of infantry marched into the Ruhr. They were accompanied by armored cars and artillery; military planes flew overhead. They were met by immense crowds of angry Germans who stood beside the roads and streets, staring at them with hatred and singing "The Watch on the Rhine."

While the unarmed Germans thundered their defiance, in Paris, on the same day, the Chamber of Deputies endorsed Premier Poincaré's move by giving him a vote of confidence, 452 to 72. On the following day, the French and Belgian ambassadors in Berlin were summoned to the Foreign Ministry and handed a note stating that "the mask would be torn from the face of the French government," and that France's actions were an invasion of Germany and a violation of the Versailles Treaty.[9] Germany's counterthreat was contained in its announcement that Germany would cease to make reparations payments of any kind, either monetary or in raw materials, to France and Belgium while the illegal occupation continued. The British view was expressed in a note of protest to their wartime allies, stating that the "Franco-Belgian action . . . was not a sanction authorized by the treaty itself."[10]

Undeterred by either German or British reaction, the Allied Reparations Commission declared that the German government was in a state of general voluntary default. On January 13, the Reichstag unanimously approved the German government's protest, and two days later the branch of the German government concerned with coal production ordered all Germans, either as individuals or as members of business concerns, to halt shipments of coal and coke to France and Belgium. The French instantly ordered German mine owners to continue deliveries, but, on January 19, the German government instructed its officials in the Ruhr to refuse to obey orders given by French and Belgian authorities regarding the takeover of any financial profits, or goods and materials, from mines, forests, and customs duties. An official German policy of "passive resistance" was thus declared, and France immediately responded by starting to remove German officials from their posts in the Ruhr and expelling them from the newly occupied area to fend for themselves elsewhere in Germany; eventually five thousand officials and their families, most of them natives of the Ruhr, would be summarily shipped out.

Classifying the Ruhr as being in a state of siege, the French and Belgian generals instituted the strictest form of martial law, and German civilians were tried by military courts. French soldiers took over the various branches of the Reichsbank, while German workers enforced their government's policy of boycott by walking off the job by the hundreds of thousands. For refusing to deliver shipments of coal, the owners and directors of such great corporations as Thyssen, Spindler, and Kestin were arrested by French soldiers and held in jail. The French quickly created a customs frontier that cut off the Ruhr from unoccupied Germany, thus controlling all exports and imports involving Germany's largest industrial area.

For a few days, Europe held its breath, wondering whether Germany might be goaded into some form of outnumbered and doomed counterattack. Despite the soothing language that the French had initially used — the French general Degoutte described his role as "assuring the security of the economic mission" — the Ruhr was already filled with seventy thousand French and Belgian soldiers, and European chancelleries had to consider the possibility that the French might move even farther into Germany.[11] General von Seeckt made it clear that the Germans would fight if the French advanced another yard; talking to the British ambassador about the French-occupied Ruhr city nearest to Berlin, the Reichswehr commander's voice shook with anger as he said, "The road from Dortmund to Berlin is not very long, but it passes through streams of blood."[12]

Germany was convulsed with rage at the French action, and the nation was united as it had not been since early in the war, but Germany had enemies other than France. The Poles instantly demanded a "rectification" of the still-disputed border of Germany, the new boundary to cede more German land. Sensing that both Germany and France were distracted, four days after the French marched into the Ruhr the Lithuanians seized the French-garrisoned former German Baltic city of Memel. It was the French who had to surrender and evacuate, but, in German eyes, this was proof that even the weakest nations on Germany's borders could seize and effectively annex a city whose population was predominantly German.

With this and the Ruhr crisis threatening the German republic, the government in Berlin once again felt forced to seek the aid of its bitterest domestic enemies. Having dispersed and outlawed the Freikorps units throughout the country, the socialist government asked these private armies to reconstitute their ranks of right-wing freebooters, but to stay in the shadows. A quick series of conspiratorial meetings among top government officials and General von Seeckt resulted in a secret understanding that the Reichswehr was to be augmented by a hidden reserve army that would far exceed the hundred-thousand-man limit set by the Versailles Treaty. These units were to be camouflaged as "labor associations," "sport societies," and other groups that would appear to be legal. As an overall force, they would be called *Arbeitstruppen,* or Labor Troops. This was the beginning of the infamous secret army known as the Black Reichswehr.[13]

The situation in the Ruhr rapidly turned into a stand-off. The contemporary novelist Lion Feuchtwanger wrote of it:

> Germany was an industrial country, and the Ruhr the heart of its industry. Whoever held the Ruhr held the heart of Germany in the hollow of his hand.
> But to have possession of that heart was only profitable so long as it beat.[14]

At his post in Coblenz, General Allen was uniquely equipped to study the situation as it developed. Faced with mass strikes and walk-outs, the French were putting their own foot soldiers to work mining coal, in an effort to make good the shipments of coal due France as reparations. The unskilled poilus fell hopelessly behind in production. General Allen observed, "It is no more possible to dig coal successfully with bayonets than it is to fell forests with sabers."[15] With the experience of a senior military commander, General Allen was aware of the problems confronting the French in transporting to France whatever they could take from the Ruhr. As Feuchtwanger put it, "A dense and intricate network of railways" honeycombed the Ruhr Valley.[16] It was a maze of trestles, tunnels, and switching points normally manned by workers of the German state railways. Now these locomotive engineers and signal tower operators and maintenance men had all walked off the job on government orders, and French soldiers attempted to replace the veteran railroad men. On January 27, sixteen days after the French marched in, General Allen wrote in his diary:

> A British staff official just returned from Düsseldorf reports that yesterday the French general commanding the line of communications ordered a locomotive and one car to be placed at this British official's service to take him from Düsseldorf to Neuss, but that, while there were many locomotives and cars idle, no one was available competent to operate the complicated switch and signal system through the Düsseldorf yards; that after two hours of hard work French engineer troops had managed to get the locomotive past five switch points, but that, since there were eight more to pass before the train could get on to the main line, the effort was abandoned as futile.
> This illustrates how hopeless must be the effort to operate the complicated agencies of a highly organized industrial area against

resistance even of the passive sort. It would appear that the effort cannot succeed until the Germans become worn down and hungry and succumb to siege tactics.[17]

As General Allen wrote these words, his troops were already on the way home; the American flag had been lowered from its staff high above the Rhine atop the tower of the Ehrenbreitstein Fortress. Two weeks later, while he prepared for his own departure, Allen noted that the French were now able to move out of the Ruhr "one-fifth of one day's normal output," but in the meantime there had been railroad collisions in which trains run by French soldiers had run into each other head on, causing the loss of lives, and there were acts of sabotage against the French and Belgians.[18]

The end of the American presence on the Rhine was a development overshadowed by the French measures and German countermeasures in the Ruhr, but its significance was not lost on General Allen. At a time when Chancellor Cuno took the extraordinary step of sending General Allen a letter that praised his wise, just, and humane conduct of the American occupation, Allen saw only trouble ahead for Europe, and he was not inclined to judge the United States innocent in the postwar settlement. Commenting in his diary on a letter he had received from a friend who was serving as the unofficial American representative on the reparations commission, Allen wrote: "One must go farther back than he does in laying great responsibility and much blame on the United States for present European conditions." In Allen's view, the United States could have insisted upon a treaty whose terms and arrangements would have thwarted the revenge seekers of both sides. Then the United States Senate should have ratified it, which it had not done with the Versailles Treaty, and the United States would have had a real voice in a reasonable postwar solution. If the United States had done those things, Allen said, "unquestionably much of the present European chaos would have been avoided."[19]

Leaving the American buffer zone, which was instantly filled with French soldiers, General Allen remarked that "the ancient enemies east and west of the Rhine were left face to face to settle the debts and punishments of the last war."[20] In a letter to Secretary of State Charles Evans Hughes, written shortly before leaving, Allen said of the French march into the Ruhr, "The movement actually under way is creating implacable passions. The prairie has been set on fire and the wind of hate is fanning it."[21] Packing up, Allen wrote, "For me these days represent the closing act in the Great War Drama as an active participator. But that does not imply that the war begun in 1914 is over in 1923."[22]

In the Ruhr, the passive resistance initially produced results that gave Germans a grim satisfaction. The French were being defied and thwarted. The British estimate of the situation was the same: speaking to the House of Lords, the foreign secretary, Lord Curzon, said that France was receiving from Germany only a fraction of the materials and payments that Germany had been sending under its treaty obligations before the French troops occupied the Ruhr.

There was, however, an obverse side to the coin, and it rapidly became visible. With many hundreds of thousands of German workers on strike in the Ruhr Basin, either in compliance with the government's wishes or on their own initiative, an immense welfare problem was immediately at hand. The German government assumed the responsibility for feeding and caring for these workmen and their families, but the cost was prodigious. French sentries, meanwhile, were stopping trains that were attempting to take raw materials and manufactured goods from the Ruhr into unoccupied Germany. The French message was not subtle: give us what we want, and you can resume these other shipments into the rest of your own nation.

The already dizzy German currency began wild gyrations. During late January, General Allen noted in his diary, "The mark has dropped two thousand points in twenty minutes — probably due to strike news."[23]

Whatever satisfaction the French may have received from this, they were soon to be startled by seeing the mark grow stronger. Committing a substantial portion of its gold reserves, the Reichsbank intervened by buying huge numbers of marks in Berlin and abroad, causing the mark to regain three fifths of its pre-Ruhr occupation value in ten days' time. Additionally, the blockage of goods from the Ruhr gave a great stimulus to the industries in the nonoccupied territory. Indeed, a certain manic vitality energized various levels of consumers. If the marks in one's hand, or in one's company's vaults, might be worth less tomorrow than today, then obviously the thing to do was to buy something with them, so that at least some value might be realized. Watching the German scene, Kurt Ludecke described that aspect of the inflationary phenomenon:

> The people, buying frantically in their flight from the mark, dared not retain currency for an hour. That explains the false prosperity which kept industry humming during the inflation years. There was little unemployed labour at a time when En-

gland already had millions out of work. Owners of buildings and homes, not knowing what to do with their marks, would order perhaps a new annex or general repairs — anything to get some value out of the tumbling currency.[24]

II

In Bavaria, the agony of the Ruhr and the reeling path of the mark affected every segment of society. At the Platzl, the famous Munich music hall that faced the Hofbräuhaus, the nationally known Bavarian comedian Weiss Ferdl was singing a plaintive song, "It Can't Go On Like This." Thomas Mann wrote to his brother Heinrich, "Our Frenchmen are behaving brilliantly. They seem determined to give the lie to everyone in Germany who urges moderation. . . . The anger is terrible — deeper and more united than that which brought on Napoleon's fall. There is no predicting the outcome."[25] To the scholarly author Ernst Bertram he wrote, "It is as though everyone else sees Germany not at all as a republic like any other, but rather as a leaderless land, an unfeeling torso with which one may do as he pleases."[26]

The French seizure of the Ruhr created a tidal wave of support for the völkisch parties, and Adolf Hitler took a unique position amidst the outpouring of enraged patriotism. By nightfall of the day the French marched, Hitler was shouting to an overflow crowd of nine thousand at the Zirkus Krone: "France thinks less of Germany than it does of a nigger state!"[27] There were other blasts directly at France, but Hitler quickly drew the crowd's attention to the real thesis of his speech. None of this would be happening, he said, if it were not for the treacherous and supine Marxist-Jewish government in Berlin, which had stabbed Germany in the back and had been selling it out to the French ever since. The German public must not waste its time cursing Paris, but must drive out the scoundrels in Berlin. "Not 'Down with France!' but rather, 'Down with the Betrayers of the Fatherland!' 'Down with the November Criminals!' must be our cry."[28]

Virtually alone among German politicians, Hitler insisted on this priority. Three evenings later, he restated what he wished to be the party line. Speaking to yet another crowd, he shouted "Down with the November Criminals! and then Down with France!"[29] In conversation with his party colleagues, he made it clear that he had no intention of submerging the Nazi Party in the "United Front" against France, of which so many politicians were speaking. It was a bold stand, unpopular with many in the party, and led to rumors that Hitler was in the pay of the French. The party leader remained adamant: speaking of his fellow Nazis who felt that the French must become the primary target of the party's propaganda, Hitler said, "If they haven't caught on that this idiocy about a common front is fatal for us, they're beyond help."[30]

As for what Hitler really thought should happen in the Ruhr, his words on the subject rendered Putzi Hanfstaengl momentarily speechless. Until then, Putzi's principal concern about Hitler had revolved around der Führer's landlocked ignorance of the non-German world. Now, as they walked through the night past Munich's monument to the poet Schiller, Hitler suddenly raised his voice to its speechmaking volume as he shouted that the Ruhr should explode with full-scale guerrilla warfare; only that would stop the French. "What does it matter," he shouted rhetorically, "if a couple of dozen of our Rhineland cities go up in flames! A hundred thousand dead would mean nothing, providing Germany's future is assured."[31] Hanfstaengl silently noted "this pyromaniac aspect of Hitler's character," but increasing numbers of Bavarians had no difficulty with any of Hitler's views.[32] During the early weeks of 1923 the party business office had to be closed for a time because it was overwhelmed by the daily crowds applying for membership.

For Hitler, there were crises far nearer and more personal than those in the Ruhr. This year's annual meeting was to be called a Parteitag, a Party Day, but it was planned as a three-day rally that was intended to eclipse all previous gatherings of the membership. Scheduled to run through the weekend of January 27–28 and end after a final Hitler speech on Monday night, it was expected to bring together about twenty thousand members, including delegations from other parts of Germany, most of whom were from areas where the party was officially prohibited. There would also be representatives from the National Socialist groups in Austria and Czechoslovakia. A special event would be the parade of approximately two thousand Storm Troops on Munich's Marsfeld, or Field of Mars, on Sunday, during which Hitler would perform the ceremony of dedicating and presenting new swastika banners to the assembled units.[33] To enliven the proceedings in other ways, the party had hired additional bands and troupes of folk dancers, and would have appearances by Weiss Ferdl. The propaganda tour de force was to take place on Saturday night; in an effort to reach as much of the public as possible, and to demonstrate the party's local strength, twelve of Munich's largest beer halls had been hired for the evening. In each there would be a full program of speeches and entertainment, and Hitler was to speed from one to another of these meetings, addressing the crowd in each hall for about fifteen minutes in a schedule that would have him making his last speech after midnight at the Hackerbräukeller. It was expected that more than forty thousand people would hear him that night.

These plans were making the Bavarian authorities nervous. Not by coincidence, the Social Democrats had announced a large demonstration of their own, to take place on the eve of the three-day Nazi rally. With all segments of the public inflamed by the events in the Ruhr, the government that had once warned Hitler against attempting a coup wanted to head off violence of any kind, and could think of no better way of starting that effort than to cancel both the rally of the Social Democrats and the Nazi extravaganza. The news of the government ban reached party headquarters on the afternoon of Thursday, January 25, less than forty-eight hours before the NSDAP events were to begin. Hitler was not to be found, so Max Amann, the party's business manager, rushed to the headquarters of the Munich police, in company with a Nazi named Dingeldey. They were granted an interview with Eduard Nortz, the police commissioner, and were still arguing their case for a removal of the ban when Hitler arrived at 7:00 P.M.; Dingeldey said that he was "obviously extremely upset."[34]

Addressing this audience of three, Hitler launched into a speech in which he praised the patriotism of his followers, his party, and, by implication, himself; only petty little men, he said, did not recognize that the NSDAP was the bearer of Germany's destiny. When Nortz suggested that Hitler put the entire matter before Minister of the Interior Schweyer for reconsideration, Hitler, in Nortz's words,

> rejected this flatly and said, no, he would in no case do that. . . .
> He was going to do nothing more in the matter. . . . Up until
> now he had kept his people, especially the Storm Troops, under
> control. Now they could do whatever they wanted and then the
> government could just see what would develop. . . . The govern-
> ment could shoot; he'd place himself at the head of the group,
> and they could shoot him down, but he could tell them that the
> first shot would unleash a red flood and what would come then
> they would see, and two hours after the first shot, the govern-
> ment would be finished.[35]

The answer to Hitler's tirade came on the following day, when the Bavarian Council of Ministers canvassed the various political leaders of the right, discovering that none of them intended to go down fighting with Hitler on this matter. The Bavarian government promptly declared a state of emergency, during which no political meetings could be held, and sent for state police and Reichswehr reinforcements.

In the meantime, Hitler was trying to outmaneuver those who intended to hem him in. His liaison with the Reichswehr was his scarfaced friend Captain Ernst Röhm, the early party member who had been Hitler's first strong link with the Bavarian Reichswehr headquarters in Munich. Röhm had never ceased to protect the interests of the party whenever it was possible for him to be of assistance. He had recently been transferred from the staff of General Franz Ritter von Epp, the ardent nationalist and supporter of militant right-wing activity, to the staff of General Otto von Lossow, who had been sent from Berlin specifically to counterbalance Epp, and to make certain that the regular army garrison in Munich remembered that its orders came from the national government in Berlin.

Although Röhm had found it exceedingly easy to work with his fellow völkisch extremist Epp, his new assignment with Lossow was a stroke of fortune for the Nazis, as Röhm was about to prove. First he asked Epp to intercede on Hitler's behalf to gain an audience with Lossow, who was the ranking regular army officer in Bavaria. This having been done, Röhm promptly took Hitler around to see Lossow, who did not care for Hitler's eccentric personality. Nonetheless, after Hitler promised that he would report directly to him immediately after the planned ceremonies involving the Storm Troop banners, Lossow agreed to take the whole matter under consideration. Röhm then popped Hitler into a car and drove off to see Bavaria's former minister-president, Gustav von Kahr, who was now the provincial president of Oberbayern, Upper Bavaria, the region in which Munich is located. The völkisch Kahr did not trust Hitler, but in his perpetual efforts to achieve some sort of balance of power on the right, he agreed to ask that the emergency decree be reconsidered.

Hitler had softened some of the forces that had suddenly locked him in, but, with twenty-four hours to go until the scheduled beginning of the Parteitag events, he was in the greatest crisis of his three-year-old political career. The emergency edict was still in force; even those in the government who were sympathetic to Hitler's views could not countenance such arrogant and open defiance of governmental authority. It appeared that Hitler must either cancel this highly publicized party rally and accept a tremendous and perhaps politically fatal loss of prestige, or proceed as planned and risk certain arrest and possibly an armed confrontation with the Reichswehr, the Bavarian State Police, and the Munich police.

It was time for new tactics. Toward evening Eduard Nortz received in his office at police headquarters an Adolf Hitler who bore no resemblance to the contemptuous fire-eater of the previous night. Hitler humbly assured the commissioner that he, Adolf Hitler, would vouch for the orderly behavior of every single Nazi in Munich during the next three days. As the commissioner undoubtedly could see, Nazis from all over Bavaria and beyond were pouring into Munich on the eve of the gathering; it was "technically impossible" to head off the crowds who were expecting to see the dedication of the flags and other scheduled events.[36] Surely it would be better to have orderly crowds attending patriotic speeches than to have disappointed masses out on the streets?

Nortz began working out a tentative compromise, to be ratified after he consulted with Minister of the Interior Schweyer. It was possible that the twelve beer hall meetings might go on as planned if the dedication of the SA banners was held indoors, at the Zirkus Krone, and not outdoors, where it could be interpreted as a provocation to the Social Democrats, whose rally had, after all, been canceled entirely.

Hitler agreed to abide by Schweyer's decision and said that his men would not march to the Zirkus Krone, but would assemble there in small groups for an indoor ceremony. By noon the next day, just an hour before the rally had first been planned to begin, yet a different Adolf Hitler was back in Nortz's office. Playing the role of a man who was simply swept away by events beyond his control, Hitler said that thousands of Nazis were moving around the city, relying on the schedules they had first been given, and there was no realistic chance of changing a single item of the original plans. Nortz insisted on cutting the twelve meetings down to six; Hitler went through the motions of telephoning printers and poster makers to see whether notices of the change could be printed at this late hour, and convinced the police commissioner that it was impossible. Much as the government disliked it, the twelve meetings were allowed to go forward.[37] So, too, was the scheduled dedication of SA banners on the Marsfeld; as Hitler vanished from the office, the Bavarian government was left only with a promise that no Nazi columns would march within a mile of the center of the city.

It was an astonishing victory for Adolf Hitler. Backed by a party that was assembling about twenty thousand members in Munich, of whom no more than two thousand were scheduled to parade on the Marsfeld, he had outmaneuvered a government that had responsibility for seven million Bavarians, and had wrung tacit concessions from a Reichswehr commander whose reinforced units could easily have obliterated the Sturmabteilung.

Hitler's cause was of course helped by his allies in high places, and the Bavarian government was to a considerable degree in sympathy with his views, but still it was a triumph of one man's reckless and determined personality over an established pyramid of authority. A stranger to Bavaria, hearing of such a feat, might well have expected to see a man of impressive bearing and presence, but here is what the off-platform Hitler looked like to Putzi's wife, Helene.

> He was at the time a slim, shy young man, with a far-away look in his very blue eyes. He was dressed almost shabbily — a cheap white shirt, black tie, a worn dark blue suit, with which he wore an incongruous dark brown leather vest, a beige-colored trench coat, much the worse for wear, cheap black shoes and a soft, old greyish hat. His appearance was quite pathetic.[38]

This odd fellow was about to be seen, in his hour of triumph, by a man with a unique perspective, Professor Karl Alexander von Müller, who had first noticed the awkward but eloquent Lance Corporal Hitler haranguing his fellow soldiers in the spring of 1919. Himself a conservative, Müller had been aware of Hitler's rise to local right-wing prominence, and he had seen Hitler at one or two informal gatherings at the houses of völkisch sympathizers, but he had never attended a meeting of the Nazi Party. On Saturday evening, January 27, just hours after the emergency decree was lifted, Müller arrived at the Löwenbräukeller, where the largest of the twelve meetings was to be held. Recalling the evening, and the notes he made during its course, the professor wrote:

> How many political meetings had I attended here in this hall. But neither during the war nor during the revolution had a scorching breath carried such a hypnotic mass excitement toward me when entering. It was not only the special tension of these weeks, of this day. "Special battle songs, special flags, special symbols, a special greeting," I put down.[39]

The "special greeting" had recently been adopted by the party: as they said "Heil!" the party members accompanied the salutation by stiffly raising their arms. Storm Troops were everywhere; Müller described the hall and the crowd: "A forest of fiery red flags with a black swastika on white ground; the strangest mixture of military discipline and revolution, of nationalism and socialism — even in the audience: the majority are the sinking middle class, with all its layers — will it be fused together?"

In making his rounds of the halls, Hitler was leaving the Löwenbräu until late in the evening. For hours, there was a series of short speeches by lesser Nazi figures. Then, at some point after ten that night,

> suddenly, at the entrance at the back, movement. Shouts of command. The speaker at the podium stops in the middle of a sentence. Everybody jumps up shouting "Heil." And through the shouting crowd and through the screaming flags comes the expected Hitler to the platform with his followers at a brisk pace, his right arm rigidly raised. He passed me very closely and I saw: that man was different from the person I had occasionally met in private homes: the sharp pale features as if contorted by an obsessed wrath, with cold flames leaping from his bulging eyes, which seemed to look to the right and left for enemies so as to overwhelm them.

Müller was a forty-year-old man of the world, a Rhodes scholar from the days before Britain's wartime suspension of those prestigious grants to Germans, but he had never sensed what he felt now in this hall. As Hitler spoke and the audience reacted, it prompted these thoughts in Müller: "Was it the crowd, which inspired him with this mysterious power? Was it floating from him to them?" His note said, "Fantasizing hysterical romanticism, with a brutal core of will."

Far from being grateful for the lifting of the ban on the party rally activities that were under way, Hitler heaped scorn upon the Bavarian government in his short and fiery speech. Ignoring the government's responsibility for keeping order, and conveniently forgetting the threats he had made to the police commissioner as to what would happen if the rally was prohibited, Hitler spoke as if the notion of an armed revolt was a figment of the collective imagination of the Council of Ministers. As Müller jotted it down, complete with the tone in which various things were said, Hitler carried out this imaginary rhetorical monologue: "Well, Herr Minister, how do you know that we National Socialists want to stage a Putsch? Yes (scornfully) the milk maid said so! A street car conductor said so, and a telephone operator heard something of the sort!"

Taunting the government, Hitler said that when the day came, the Nazi Party would not have to stage a Putsch. It was growing steadily stronger, the government was growing weaker, and all that would be needed when the right time came would be a little "horn-blowing," and the Bavarian government would fall. Casting the government in the role of villains who might still intervene in the NSDAP rally, Hitler gave everyone in the hall the opportunity to consider themselves martyrs.

> We won't stage a Putsch, we won't bring along any weapons, we'll come unarmed — *but we will come!* (frenzied applause). And then you can shoot into our midst, if you can find German soldiers who will shoot German men who want nothing more than to confess to being Germans on German soil! (frenzied applause).

Having, for a change, criticized the Bavarian government as much as the national government in Berlin, Hitler turned his guns on the French occupation of the Ruhr. Pointing out that the present membership, which he placed at forty thousand, was ten times the number of a year earlier, he quickly painted for his audience a picture of a movement whose eventual success was inevitable.

> We know that later generations will say: The National Socialists of 1919–1923, or perhaps 1924, established the basis for the re-strengthening of Germany, out of which the lightning emerged that annihilated France! (with an impassioned crescendo — raging applause).

Later that night, at home working on his notes, Müller reflected on what he called Hitler's "fanaticism for its own sake." Thinking of the manner in which Hitler was putting forward only himself and his party at a time when Germany was engulfed by the crisis in the Ruhr and the failure of the mark, he later observed, "What blatant selfishness, what brutal simplification! . . . Hitler is only interested in the future of his party, the future of his own will for power: but he succeeds in convincing his listeners that that is the only thing that matters, for the future of Germany." The professor was worried about the "unpredictable political consequences" that Hitler might produce, but his curiosity was piqued; he was ready to hear him speak again.

Another person was taking notes in Munich that night. The American journalist and author Ludwell Denny was at one of the twelve meetings. For an article that was soon to appear in *The Nation*, he wrote:

> Hitler going from meeting to meeting, is received with enthusiasm. He is an extraordinary person. An artist turned popular

prophet and savior, is the way members of the audience described him to me as we awaited for him to appear. A young man stepped on the platform and acknowledged the long applause. His speech was intense and brief; he constantly clenched and unclenched his hands. When I was alone with him for a few moments, he seemed hardly normal; queer eyes, nervous hands, and a strange movement of the head. He would not give an interview — said he had no use for Americans.[40]

III

At eleven the next morning, despite the strain of racing to and through a dozen separate speeches the previous night, Hitler was back in form as he reviewed his Storm Troops on the Marsfeld. About two thousand men were on the field, and another three or four thousand party members gathered near Hitler at the edge of the parade ground. A reporter for the *New York Tribune* said that "Hitler, surrounded by his staff, addressed his army, calling upon them to hold themselves in readiness for the 'final, decisive conflict.' "[41] Wearing a dark coat and giving a good demonstration of what Putzi Hanfstaengl called his "flaming personality," Hitler shouted through the snowflakes that had begun falling on the plain, "Either the National Socialist German Workers' Party is the coming movement in Germany, in which case not even the Devil himself can stop it, or it is not, and deserves to be destroyed!"[42]

Hitler then turned to the purpose of this gathering in what was turning out to be a snowstorm: the dedication of the flags to be presented to the two SA regiments from Munich, the regiment from Landshut in which many Oberlanders were wearing alpine costume complete with lederhosen, and the regiment from Nuremberg. Hitler had designed these standards, ceremonial banners that hung on richly embroidered loops from a horizontal bar at the top of a vertical staff. On each banner, beneath a swastika, were the words "Deutschland Erwache." This slogan — Germany, Awake! — had been coined by Dietrich Eckart, who wrote a poem with that refrain. The words had been set to music as a marching song for the Storm Troops.

The German word for this ceremony could be variously understood as meaning dedication, blessing, or consecration. In his exhortation accompanying the presentation of the standards, Hitler said, "No member of that race which is our foe and which has led us into this most abject misery, no Jew shall ever touch this flag. It shall wave before us throughout all of Germany in the march to victory, and pave the way for the flag of our new German Reich."[43] The *New York Tribune* reporter, whose readers across the Atlantic would be looking at this story the next day, said that Hitler concluded the ceremonies by ordering his troops "to take a solemn oath to carry the flag to victory, 'both in Berlin and on the Rhine.' "[44]

The emphasis on the Storm Troops during this party meeting was a logical extension of Hitler's combative personality and his fondness for military trappings, but it was also symptomatic of the need to arm themselves that was felt by many groups across the political spectrum. With the French in the Ruhr and no guarantee that they might not advance farther, with the mark lurching and the government in Berlin being perceived by many as having only tenuous control of the nation, both left and right were arming themselves to strike for national power should a complete collapse occur. On the very day that Hitler was presenting new banners to his Storm Troop units, the German Communist Party was holding its annual congress in the eastern city of Leipzig. It was forming what were known as Action Committees Against Fascism; the cutting edge of these committees was to be the newly organized Proletarian Hundreds (sometimes referred to as Red Hundreds). These were hundred-man units similar to the SA's Hundertschaften.

Under the command of Hans Ulrich Klintzsch — Hermann Goering had not yet taken over — the Sturmabteilung was becoming increasingly uniform in its appearance. Although many of the Oberland men still dressed in the full alpine costume, wearing only swastika armbands on the left sleeve of their loden jackets, virtually all the other Storm Troops now wore grey ski caps. An old wartime uniform was still a fully accepted and honored form of dress at SA turnouts, but more and more men were appearing in double-breasted grey canvas jackets, midthigh in length. The ideal uniform, at this stage, also included grey military breeches and puttees wound from above low military boots to a point just below the knee. However, any number of men on the Marsfeld were wearing regular-length civilian overcoats, plain long trousers and civilian shoes, and other variations in dress.

Looking at the strength of the party as a whole, observers found its exact size difficult to determine. At the end of 1922, the Munich police had placed it at approximately ten thousand; Hitler was now claiming forty thousand, and no one could doubt that the membership applications were pouring in.[45] One estimate had it that a thousand a week were joining. While an outsider like Professor von Müller could see the irrationality in both Hitler and his audiences, those audiences spent their days in what all Germans considered to be a never-never land. At the beginning of 1923, with the French in the Ruhr, every German saw foreign nations either as predators or as unfeeling strangers who cared nothing for the fate of the Fatherland. At a time when the government in Berlin could not protect the nation's borders or control the value of its money, the indictments and promises of Adolf Hitler made as much sense as the day's headlines, and were far more satisfying. As Hitler first spoke to two meetings of party delegates on the last day of the extended meeting, then addressed a large crowd in the Zirkus Krone that evening, he had in fact moved from being first chairman of a political party to being "honored leader" of a large, militant, excitable action group. Sacrifices were expected, and they were made. Special collections were constantly being taken up among the faithful; good contributors belonged to a "sacrificial ring" that received preferred seating at Hitler's speeches, and the party continued to sell bonds that were illegal because they bore no interest; printed on these securities was the statement that they would not be paid off if presented for redemption by a Jew.[46]

As Hitler led the NSDAP into 1923, there were still cracks in organizational solidarity — in Nuremberg, Julius Streicher and a Nazi named Walther Kellerbauer were in a public struggle for control of the local Nazi branch, and in spite of two visits in early 1923, Hitler was unable to resolve the feud — but none of the second-level backbiting and rivalries in Munich and elsewhere challenged Hitler's role as Führer.[47] Indeed, to many party members he had become a demigod. Heinrich Hoffmann, Munich's leading portrait photographer, recalled the wedding breakfast that he gave for Hitler's subordinate Hermann Esser. This was Hoffmann's effort to get into the good graces of Hitler, who at that time resolutely refused to have his photograph taken, on the grounds that the absence of a picture added an air of mystery to him, and that people would come out to see him in person instead. When the wedding cake was produced, to Hoffmann's surprise its center proved to have "an effigy of Adolf Hitler, made of marzipan and surrounded by sugar roses!" The Nazis acted as if it would be sacrilege to cut that part of the cake bearing der Führer's image; a few timidly cut themselves "a small morsel, taking great pains to avoid defacing the effigy." Asked to say a few words on the occasion, Hitler refused, explaining, "I must have a crowd when I speak. In a small, intimate circle I never know what to say. I should only disappoint you all, and that is a thing I should hate to do. As a speaker either at a family gathering or a funeral, I'm no use at all."[48]

At the beer halls, there continued to be large crowds and long speeches, and in the audience at one of these Nazi gatherings sat Professor von Müller, drawn back by curiosity. In watching Hitler the first time, he had been struck by an impression of "fanaticism for its own sake," and, although the party was increasing its influence in Bavaria and the German states beyond, these 1923 meetings also had about them an aura of spectacle for its own sake. It was politics as theater — long vertical red, white, and black swastika banners hanging from balconies in beer halls, bands playing, uniformed Storm Troops strutting up and down the aisles among the expectant audience, and then the new touch — Hitler suddenly there, walking through the audience from the back of the hall, his outstretched arm giving the new Nazi salute as he moved through waves of cheers to present the party's ultimate piece of theater — a speech by Adolf Hitler.

After attending several of these performances, Müller found that the original impression made on him was somewhat weakened but that "the hypnotic power of the speaker over the crowd remained the same." He saw two or three different Hitlers: "Sometimes he seemed like an actor, sometimes he seemed hysterical, sometimes he was like a maniac." Occasionally, Müller reported, "it took him a long time to screw himself up to the usual excitement. But there would never fail to be the orgiastic outbreak, and the orgiastic reply." Müller closed this part of his musings on what he saw at these Nazi meetings by giving, not a Germanic analysis and summation, but simply a word picture of how Hitler moved at least one of his audience. He described the fifty-four-year-old Dietrich Eckart's reaction: "After one of Hitler's orgiastic cascades he jumped onto the table with a fiery red face screaming his song, 'Deutschland Erwache!' frantically . . . while a brass band performed the music roaringly: it was the picture of a lunatic raging with frenzy."[49]

CHAPTER

26

THE COMING OF SPRING found Germany and France still dead-locked in, and over, the Ruhr. Both nations were spending fortunes to maintain their positions and policies. Germany's "passive resistance" was denying raw materials to the French, but it was also depriving the German economy of those commodities, as well as depleting the supply of products that were not being manufactured in idled Ruhr plants. The German government was having to support hundreds of thousands of striking workers and their families, and the Reichsbank was running through its gold reserves and foreign credits in its effort to shore up the mark and prove to France that Germany could survive the attempted stranglehold in the Ruhr.

For France, there was the embarrassing and costly loss of the greater revenue that had been flowing from Germany to France under the reparations agreements before French troops attempted to run Germany's industrial machinery. In addition, the population in the long-held French and Belgian occupation zones in the Rhineland had launched a wave of strikes, acts of civil disobedience, and incidents of sabotage, as a protest against the treatment of their countrymen in the newly occupied territory. On top of the enormous cost of the new occupation in the Ruhr, France had to reinforce its garrisons in a score of Rhineland cities.

If there were private second thoughts in France concerning the military adventure in the Ruhr, they were not shared by Premier Poincaré, who summed up his government's official view: "Germany will wait in vain for us to vacillate even a moment. . . . France will walk this road to its end."[1]

*

It was against this background that General Hans von Seeckt came from Berlin to Munich on March 12, for an inspection of his Reichswehr units. The Prussian Seeckt was now fifty-six; describing him, the British ambassador, Lord d'Abernon, remarked, "In appearance he is emaciated and severe. His face reminds one of a death's head, or, as somebody said, 'General into Fox.' . . . Those who criticise him say that his principal fault is that he is too intelligent to be a general."[2] Known as "the Sphinx with a monocle," the brilliant army commander spent most of his time circumventing Allied efforts to keep Germany militarily prostrate. He was one of the principal architects of the clandestine military mutual-aid arrangements with the Soviet Union; among his secret responses to the French march into the Ruhr was the government agreement to organize the covert reserve forces known as the Black Reichswehr and the creation of a special fund that financed sabotage operations in the Ruhr.[3] Seeckt saw that the Reichswehr would be destroyed in an open confrontation with the French army, yet he believed that Germany itself would be destroyed if the French cut any farther into the Fatherland. No one could say that, in the course of 1923, the Reichswehr might not have to fight French troops or put down an uprising within Germany's borders by armed leftists. To that end, the latest weaponry was being bought in neutral countries by Reichswehr representatives, then smuggled into Germany; among other purchases approved by Seeckt was the acquisition of a hundred Fokker fighter planes, bought in Holland.

In his contingency plans, Seeckt could not rule out the possibility of having to cope with armed takeover attempts by the extreme nationalists, the armed radicals of the right, such as the SA. Seeckt had warned that he would tolerate no armed interference in the affairs of the Berlin government from that direction, but nonetheless, in his shopping around for experienced units that could act as Reichswehr reserves, he was having to deal with Freikorps types who detested those in power. Three weeks before his trip to Munich, a conference between Seeckt and the leaders of a number of national right-wing organizations had shown him the gap between a conservative professional soldier like himself, who expected troops to obey orders that might not be to their political liking, and political activists who were indeed combat veterans, but wanted to specify the groups they would and would not be called upon to attack.

Bavaria was of course the home of the most extreme right-wing thinking in Germany, and the Reichswehr personnel bureau in Berlin almost routinely transferred out of Bavaria those regular army officers who were considered to have become too "blue and white," the colors of the Bavarian flag.[4] This suspicion was now beginning to attach itself to General Otto von Lossow, who had been in charge of the Bavarian Reichswehr for less than three months. Although Lossow was himself a Bavarian, his service since the war's end had been principally in northern Germany, and he had been viewed as an apolitical officer who did not share the ever-present Bavarian impulse for secession from Berlin. Indeed, Lossow had been sent to Munich to counterbalance the right-wing General Ritter von Epp, and to replace General Arnold Ritter von Möhl, who had begun to act as if orders from Berlin were an unwarranted nuisance.

The chain of command involving the Bavarian Reichswehr leader was a complicated one, and, from the outset, Lossow had fallen under the influence of those surrounding him in Munich, including some who admired Hitler. As commander of the Bavarian Military District and the Seventh (Bavarian) Division, Lossow was responsible to Berlin, but as *Landeskommandant*, commander of the forces of the state of Bavaria, he was a subordinate of Bavaria's minister-president, Eugen von Knilling, and his cabinet. All these individuals inevitably put Bavaria first, viewing the Reichswehr units in Bavaria as if they were the separate Bavarian army of prewar and wartime days, rather than a part of the national postwar army. They saw the troops under Lossow primarily as instruments of Bavarian domestic policy, available to protect Bavaria's borders and to put down civil unrest.

Confronted with a purely military situation, Lossow had always been an efficient soldier, but in the unremitting "blue and white" atmosphere of his discussions with Bavaria's leaders, he was becoming confused as to what his true role was. Whatever the civilians said to him was greatly augmented by the presence on his staff of such men as Captain Ernst Röhm, who saw the Reichswehr as the force that could free Germany from the government in Berlin.

Lossow had become increasingly convinced that Hitler could not be ignored, and he now arranged a meeting between the Nazi leader and Seeckt, who had never heard of the former lance corporal. On the morning of March 12, during his official visit to Munich, Seeckt turned to his aide, First Lieutenant Hans-Harald von Selchow, and said, "We must go again to the Military District Headquarters at twelve o'clock. There is a Bavarian prophet here named Hitler, whom General von Lossow wishes me to meet. He is supposed to be or to become an influential person."[5]

Five people were present at the meeting: Hitler, Seeckt, Selchow, and Lossow and his aide, a young officer named Oxner who was much under Hitler's spell.[6] It was the first time that Hitler had sat down with a member of Germany's postwar national leadership. Undaunted, he launched straight into a speech that lasted for one and a half hours, during which General von Seeckt sat without saying a word. Hitler covered all the familiar ground, suggested that Germany might disintegrate at any moment, and finally put forward a plan for a government that was to consist of a right-wing coalition, supported in power by an expanded Reichswehr and a huge militia under SA control. Once this government and armed force were in place, the French would be driven out of the Ruhr, and the Versailles Treaty would be but a memory.

At the end of his harangue, Hitler gazed at the silent Seeckt and said, "Herr General, I offer you the leadership of the whole German working-class movement."

The commander of the German army finally spoke, curtly. "Herr Hitler, what is your attitude to the soldier's oath of allegiance?"

Hitler leapt from his chair and said:

Herr General, my offer was not intended to conflict with your present duty of loyalty. It is self-evident that you cannot break your oath to the Weimar government. We National-Socialists will see to it that the members of the present Marxist regime in Berlin will hang from the lampposts. We will send the Reichstag up in flames and when all is in flux we will turn to you, Herr General, to assume the leadership of all German workers.

At this point Seeckt rose. "In that case you and I, Herr Hitler, have nothing more to say to each other."

While Hitler was being ushered out, Oxner went over to Selchow and whispered, almost as if conjuring up the assassination of Rathenau, "From now on Seeckt is a dead man." Even as an aside between two young officers, it was a staggering lapse in military propriety, and a demonstration of the influence Hitler was able to project into the Munich headquarters of the nation's army.

That night, in his compartment on the train back to Berlin, Seeckt talked for hours to Selchow. The meeting with Hitler had in some way stirred him; he spoke of his own life, of Germany's plight, of Hitler's open threat to bring down the government. "Come what may," he said to his young aide, "General von Lossow has assured me that

Hitler cannot make a Putsch without the Reichswehr, and that suffices for the time being. I simply do not believe that the Reichswehr could be brought to fire on other Reichswehr units."[7]

II

On the morning of Easter Saturday, March 31, a short and hitherto insignificant French army lieutenant was about to have his awful moment in history.[8] His name was Durieux, and he was in charge of an eleven-man detail of the 160th Infantry, a unit of the Ruhr occupation forces that had been assigned to control the industrial city of Essen.

Durieux and his men had the task of compiling a list of the vehicles kept in the central garage of the huge Krupp steel works. It seemed a routine matter, but going into the Krupp buildings was something the French had not done previously. Arriving at seven in the morning, the dozen Frenchmen had to wait until nine before someone appeared and unlocked the garage, which was on a public street.

Until then, it had appeared to be an uneventful morning in Essen. Despite the passive resistance, many thousands of the Krupp workers were still on the job; in the company's massive headquarters building, across the street from the central garage, Gustav Krupp himself was working at his desk near the bay window of his office.

Suddenly the siren of the company fire department, next to the garage, began its wail. A moment later the whistle of the headquarters building began sharp blasts. In a short time, no fewer than five thousand alarm signals of various kinds were rending the air throughout the enormous manufacturing complex.

Durieux asked the superintendent of the garage what all the screaming and tooting was about, and was told that it was the signal for "Down tools."

To this point the young lieutenant had not associated the uproar in these vast mills with himself and his eleven men. Now, going to the door of the garage, he saw a river of workers coming up the Altendorferstrasse toward him. Durieux had no way of knowing that it had been understood, among Krupp workers, that every alarm would go off if French troops entered any Krupp building.

The thousands of mechanics and laborers pouring out of their mills and shops had no plan at all, only the shouted information that the French were up by the headquarters building, but Durieux had no way of knowing that, either. The garage was surrounded by thousands of tough-looking steelworkers; some threw stones and pieces of coal, and one or two let the French see that they had pistols. Durieux ordered his men to move across the way to a smaller garage opposite the fire station. He felt that there was less chance that the mob could storm this building than the larger garage with its several entrances. His squad had a machine gun, and he ordered the men to set it up in the entrance to the smaller garage.

The crowd fell back some yards. The sirens were still screaming, and the dozen French foot soldiers with their rifles and machine gun stood silently confronting the thousands of equally silent men in their working clothes. The sound of the sirens seemed to hold everyone suspended, soot-faced German workingmen glaring at the tiny line of their wartime enemies in their pale blue uniforms.

One person had the power to end this confrontation. Short, portly Gustav Krupp could see the whole motionless stand-off from his office window above the street. He could have walked out there and told his men to go back to work; he could have sent any one of his subordinates, who would have been obeyed. Gustav Krupp did nothing to defuse the situation, although a union leader tried and was shouted down.

The tableau in the street — the dozen armed soldiers, the many thousand unarmed workers — remained frozen until the sirens finally died. Then the crowd began inching forward, minute by minute. Lieutenant Durieux was holding his ground in the doorway of the garage, feeling that he still had the situation under control, when he became aware of a sudden rush of steam, filling the building at his back. Unbeknown to the lieutenant, the smaller garage contained steam jets for scalding the dirt off vehicles; their controls were on the roof, and two Krupp employees had sneaked up there and turned them on. Now the twelve French soldiers had the angry crowd a few yards in front of them and clouds of steam behind them. With sweat suddenly pouring down his face and obscuring his vision, Durieux ordered his men to fire over the heads of the crowd, to drive them back so that the squad could step out into the street and away from the steam.

The rifles went off, but, possibly pushed from behind, the front of the crowd pressed closer, right up against the frantic Frenchmen.

Durieux ordered his men to aim their rifles straight at the Krupp workers and told his machine gunner to be ready to fire in earnest if the Germans would not fall back. Seeing nothing but fists and livid faces still on top of him, Lieutenant Durieux shouted, "Commence firing!"

The machine gun did most of it. The crowd dispersed in seconds, leaving thirteen men dead in the street and fifty-two wounded.

The effect in Germany was profound. Editorials throughout Europe condemned the French, but in Germany the deaths caused the largest public outpouring since the assassination of Walther Rathenau. On the day of the funeral, the bells in every church and town hall started to toll soon after sunrise; every flag in the nation was at half-mast, and the Reichstag met to pray for the dead workers. Forty delegations, representing the large German cities, political parties, and trade unions, converged on Essen.

Gustav Krupp produced and directed the spectacular funeral. In the huge marble lobby of the Krupp headquarters the thirteen coffins lay in a row, each draped in the old imperial red, white, and black. The great hall was lit only by candles, and in the shadows of a vast balcony a choir of five hundred Krupp workers sang during ceremonies presided over by a Catholic bishop and a Protestant pastor.

The men were to be buried in the Ehrenfried Cemetery, in a plot where only those who had performed acts of heroism were interred. It was four miles from the Krupp plants, and more than three hundred thousand people marched in the procession. First came a column of four hundred German flags, followed by the coffins, borne on horse-drawn caissons. Gustav Krupp walked behind them, bareheaded and alone; at a considerable interval behind him came the relatives of the slain workers. It took twenty minutes for all the wreaths that had been sent to be carried past. In reporting the speech made by the Catholic bishop at the cemetery, the *New York Times* said, "The word *murder* was used."[9]

The French thought they knew how to handle the situation. They arrested Gustav Krupp for "inciting a riot" on the day his workers were killed, and tried him before a military court that barred German reporters from covering the proceedings. Germany's leading industrialist was led away to spend seven months in prison.

III

Although Munich remained the focus of Hitler's activity and the seat of growing Nazi power, the party was constantly short of money; to remedy the situation, Hitler decided to take Putzi Hanfstaengl with him on a fund-raising trip to Berlin.[10] The only account of this junket was given by Putzi, who placed it as being "about the beginning of April" and said that he was along because "Hitler seemed to think that I would give an air of respectability to his begging expeditions." Four people set off on a spring morning in a rickety green Selve automobile — Hitler and Putzi, a youth named Fritz Laubőck, whom Hitler was trying to train to be his secretary, and Emil Maurice, Hitler's party associate and chauffeur, who had started what became the SA.

Putzi was by this time a close confidant of Hitler's, not on party matters, but on Hitler's view of the world. Although Hitler was invariably locked inside his own opinions, he would run his ideas on a variety of subjects past the towering Hanfstaengl, as if hoping for the approval of this educated member of a distinguished family. With Putzi, he would come out with such things as "Ah, Cromwell, that's my man. He and Henry VIII are the only two positive figures in English history."[11] On this trip he was to say, matter-of-factly, speaking of Czechoslovakia, "We shall have to get those Skoda works in Pilsen under German control one of these days." As if referring to the seizure of a famous armament works in another sovereign nation was not quite an aggressive enough sentiment, he also dropped this thought into the conversation: "The most important thing in the next war will be to make sure that we control the grain and food supplies of western Russia."

The route along which the old Selve was making its way to Berlin was a risky one for Hitler. They soon were going through Saxony, the German state in which the leftists had their greatest influence and power. In contrast to the sympathy felt for Hitler's views in Bavaria, in Saxony there was a standing warrant for his arrest if he should be found within its borders, and there was even a reward for his capture. Putzi described something that brought the random conversation to a halt.

> We were just coming up to Delitzsch, traveling fairly fast
> around a curve, when we saw the road was blocked by a unit of
> Communist militia. I don't think any of us said anything, there
> was no time. But I saw Hitler tense and his hand take a firm
> grip on his heavy whip, as we came to a stop. "Leave it to me,"
> I muttered as the militia came up and asked to see our identity
> documents. I got out of the car and produced the impressive
> Swiss passport on which I had traveled back from the United
> States. "I am Mr. Hanfstaengl," I said, in the most atrocious Ger-
> man-American accent I could muster. "I am a paper manufacturer

and printer and I am visiting the Leipzig Fair. This is my valet,"
pointing to Hitler, "my chauffeur and the other gentleman is the
son of a German business associate." It worked. My papers were
written in English and they made no attempt to look at the documents of the others, but waved us on in surly fashion. I jumped
in and we tore off.

Hitler fairly babbled his thanks: "Hanfstaengl, you really carried that off well. They would have had my head. You have saved
my life." . . . Even so, I think he resented having been called
my valet, even as a ruse.

As a fund-raising venture, this trip to Berlin was an unqualified
failure, and resulted in more time spent sightseeing than in talking to
prospective donors. It did, however, give Putzi some further insights
into the attitudes and behavior of the party's Führer. If there was one
thing Putzi knew about, besides music, it was art: for three generations
the family business had been the making and selling of photographic
reproductions of masterpieces. Now, at the national gallery in Berlin,
he had to endure Hitler's cocksure and frequently inaccurate running
lecture on the contents of one room after another. The climax came
when Hitler halted his three companions in front of Caravaggio's *St.
Matthew the Apostle,* a work that Putzi felt was "a somewhat florid
and not particularly successful composition." Hitler announced that
it was a Michelangelo. "There you are, Fritzl," he said grandly to
young Laubōck. "There was no end to his genius."

A different side of Hitler emerged at an amusement area within
Luna Park.

We looked around the side shows and found that one of the
main attractions was a group of women boxers. This seemed to
appeal to him, so in we went and watched several matches. It
was, I suppose, quite daring stuff for its day, with the women in
abbreviated trunks and shirts, mincing around and landing an
occasional tap. It was all pure circus, but Hitler was riveted. He
managed to keep his face expressionless and made a few superior
comments. . . . But we had to stay until the show was over. . . .
I could see he was taking good care not to show how much he
had enjoyed the unedifying spectacle.

The only donation that Hitler received during his fund-raising
trip to Berlin was a hat. Hitler and Putzi dined at the mansion of
the piano-manufacturing Bechsteins, with whom he had previously
stayed. On this occasion the Bechsteins were not inclined to part with

their money. Putzi described the final scene of their "begging trip" to Berlin.

> All we got as we were ushered out was a hat. When we came
> into the cloakroom Hitler could not find the broad-brimmed black
> gangster affair in which he usually went around. In its place there
> hung a very expensive grayish yellow fedora. "It is one of my
> husband's," said Frau Bechstein, "and he would like you to ac-
> cept it as a present." Hitler took it and thanked his hostess pro-
> fusely.

IV

Returning to Munich, Hitler was swept into a series of events that brought him and the Nazi Party into a sharply escalating conflict with the Bavarian government. The initial intention was simply to oppose the May Day plans of Munich's Marxists, rather than to challenge the authority of the state.[12] The parties of the left had indicated their intention of parading; Hitler pledged his opposition to any such demonstration. In Munich, the first of May was not only the traditional celebration of the left; for the right, it would mark the fourth anniversary of the day that Freikorps units had smashed into Munich and bloodily ended the postwar Bavarian Soviet Republic. To the more extreme nationalists, it was unthinkable that leftists should be allowed to parade on the anniversary of their extinction as the ruling power in Bavaria.

By the end of the first week in April, the impending confrontation between right and left was only a war of words, but on Saturday, April 7, Hitler appeared at a meeting of right-wing leaders who controlled substantial numbers of men and weapons, in addition to those possessed by the SA. This working committee was known as the Task Force of the Patriotic Combat Groups. Among these extremist units were the Bund Oberland, which had Freikorps antecedents and had repeatedly stood by the Nazis, and the Reichsflagge, or Flag of the Realm, in which Hitler's supporter Ernst Röhm played a key role, despite his being a captain in the regular army. A nonvoting member of the Task Force was a leader of Bund Wiking, the successor unit to Ehrhardt's feared secret Organization Consul, which had killed both Matthias Erzberger and Walther Rathenau. A self-proclaimed "powerful striking force," this alliance had as its military coordinator Hermann Kriebel, a wartime lieutenant colonel with much subsequent experience in running right-wing paramilitary organizations.

Urged on by Hitler, the leaders of the Task Force decided that on May 1 they would march through the "Banned Mile," the area of downtown Munich that the Bavarian government had declared to be off-limits for all organized political street demonstrations. What they envisioned was a several-faceted right-wing celebration, involving a parade, "military excercises" to be held in one of the city's large parks, some beer drinking, and speechmaking. The object was to block, scare off, counter, or outdo anything that the left might plan or attempt to execute.

This in itself added a certain excitement to Munich's April days of blooming flowers and the new brews of spring beer, but on April 12 the Supreme Court for the Defense of the Republic, in Leipzig — that special national tribunal, far from Bavaria, whose jurisdiction many in Bavaria questioned and resented — ordered the arrest of Dietrich Eckart and Hermann Esser for failing to appear before it. The charge was that they had libeled President Ebert in the pages of the *Völkischer Beobachter*.[13]

The Nazis had no intention of surrendering two of their most prominent figures. What happened to Esser is not clear — he certainly was not arrested, and seems to have vanished for a time — but Eckart became the central figure in a little drama that was half spy story and half comedy. No one was harder to hide than this compulsively extroverted burly beer drinker, for whom a day without a long session at a café, cheerfully trading witticisms, was a day wasted. The manner in which the Nazis were nonetheless able to keep Eckart out of the hands of the authorities demonstrates some of the ways in which they had penetrated the government, and helps to explain the Nazi belief that, one way or another, they could always accomplish what they set out to do. To begin with, Hitler had an early warning system: "There was a special branch man in the police headquarters who was a secret Nazi," Putzi Hanfstaengl said, "and used to come along and tell him whether there were any warrants being issued in connection with his political activities or what cases were coming up that might affect him."[14]

Warned, the Nazis had hidden Eckart with Fritz Lauböck's family. "But he couldn't resist the temptation to telephone right and left," Hitler recalled. "Already by the second day, he was clamouring that his girl-friend Anna should go and visit him. 'I'm incapable of hiding,' he used to say."[15]

The Nazis started to make plans to spirit Eckart out of town. Hitler recounted what happened next.

> One day Röhm telephoned me, asking me to go and see him immediately at the office of our military administration. There was a "wanted persons" service there that functioned in parallel with the civil police. Röhm told me that an attempt would be made to arrest Eckart during the night, and he advised me to take him elsewhere. A little later in the day I learnt from Röhm that all the roads round Munich had been barred. "Take him to the English Garden," he told me. "There you'll find a Reichswehr vehicle that I'm putting at his disposal."

That part of the solution was perfect — the police would not dream of stopping an army vehicle that was presumably on official business — but there was the willful and gregarious fugitive to consider.

> I commented to Röhm that Eckart would not consent to depart by himself. "So much the better," said Röhm. "It will be excellent if the vehicle is full." I went to see Drexler, and asked him if he would like to go off for a few weeks with Dietrich Eckart. He was enthusiastic at the proposal. Eckart began by jibbing at the idea, but in the evening he let himself be led off.[16]

The destination was a boardinghouse in the mountains near Berchtesgaden, a small alpine market town in the strongly pro-Nazi Obersalzburg area, seventy-five miles southeast of Munich. It lies in the salient of the Bavarian Alps that juts into Austria at Germany's southeastern corner.

The official army car that Captain Ernst Röhm produced for Eckart's escape was only the merest hint of the personal power, and Reichswehr equipment, that this staunch Hitler supporter had accumulated.[17] A combination of adroit staff work and relentless behind-the-scenes right-wing zeal had left him in charge of huge amounts of military supplies of all kinds that the Reichswehr and the Bavarian government wished to conceal from the Allied inspection teams that sometimes descended on them. A simple method for getting rifles out of government armories was to lend them to selected paramilitary organizations; Röhm did the selecting. Other supplies of arms were stored and kept in repair by Röhm's secret administrative fiefdom, and checked out to paramilitary groups for specific training exercises and maneuvers.

There was an impressive degree of sophistication in some of these subterfuges. To take masses of military equipment off the official rolls, the Reichswehr and the Bavarian government created two publicly owned corporations. The first, a secret entity staffed by Röhm and known as FZ, was the parent body for all the ordnance department transactions. The other, and more visible, corporation was the Faber Motor Vehicle Rental Service, run by a retired major of that name who was a civilian employee of the army and a Röhm protégé. Although this looked like a profit-making civilian enterprise, all its vehicles were military ones. Some were used by the Bavarian Reichswehr for official purposes, but Faber was in effect running a government-funded motor pool used by right-wing paramilitary units.

At the top in Bavaria, neither Minister-President von Knilling nor General von Lossow realized the extent to which really large numbers of army weapons and vehicles were at the disposal of one army captain whose loyalty to Adolf Hitler was greater than any feeling he had for the army chain of command. Thus far, the völkisch cronyism between the Reichswehr and the free-lance paramilitary units of the right had obscured an interesting question: How would these rifles, machine guns, and ammunition be used, if units like the Storm Troops were suddenly on one side, and the army on the other?

V

On April 20, with the impending May Day confrontation with Munich's leftists eleven days off, Hitler's inner circle paused to celebrate his thirty-fourth birthday. Hanfstaengl was one of the early well-wishers.

> I went along during the morning to congratulate him and found him alone, although the grubby little flat was stacked from floor to ceiling with flowers and cakes. Yet Hitler was in one of his curiously wary moods and had not touched a single one of the cakes. There they were, with swastikas and eagles in whipped cream all over them, looking like the baker's booth at a village fair. It was not much to my taste, I am a beer-and-sausages man myself, but even my mouth watered.
> "Well, Herr Hitler," I said, "now you can really have a feast."
> "I am not at all sure they are not poisoned," he replied.
> "But they are all from your friends and admirers," I told him.
> "Yes I know," he replied. "But this house belongs to a Jew and these days you can drip slow poison down the walls and kill your enemies."[18]

The man who thought his Jewish landlord might be dripping slow poison down his walls closed out his thirty-fourth birthday by addressing nine thousand people in the Zirkus Krone on the topic "Politics and Race: Why Are We Anti-Semites?"[19]

On April 26, a delegation of Task Force leaders went to see Minister-President von Knilling. Being of the opinion that General von Lossow would not use his regular army units to stop them, the Task Force leaders presented the government with their decision to hold "the Great German May Celebration" on May 1. The Task Force units would march, they told Knilling; they expected the government to ban the parades planned by the left.

Knilling was somewhat more tractable than they had previously found him to be, not because of their adamant attitude, but because he had no liking for the impending parade of leftist trade unions and Social Democrats through the streets of Munich. At this meeting, the real stone wall was erected by Interior Minister Schweyer, who had painful memories of Hitler's tap dance in January, that series of artful maneuvers which had kept the government off balance until it was too late to stop the Nazi Party rally. Schweyer told the Task Force leaders that any "national demonstration" by Task Force units would be considered a threat to public safety and order.[20] Since Knilling said nothing to overrule his interior minister, who had at his disposal Bavaria's state police, the heavily armed and well-trained Landespolizei, the Task Force delegation went off empty-handed.

On the next day, the Communist Party in Munich announced that all its members were being called out to take part in the leftists' May Day parade. Here was something more than the government had bargained for. Until this, the authorities had felt that they were dealing with a manageable aggregation of leftist groups, but the die-hard Marxist revolutionaries of the KPD were a different matter. They were sure to infiltrate the other groups; they added an unpredictable, inflammatory element to the proceedings. Bavaria had banned the Communist paramilitary "Proletarian Hundreds," and yet they might suddenly appear. The government decided that a massive Marxist march which included the Communists was unacceptable. The leftists were told that they could split their activities into seven smaller parades.

As far as Adolf Hitler was concerned, one parade or seven, it was all the same enemy. Speaking to a crowd at the Zirkus Krone on the evening of April 27, he was not quite prepared to say that the SA and other Task Force units were ready to confront the Reds with firearms on May Day, but he did say, of Nazi activities, "I am announcing that we will ruthlessly protect every meeting with weapons," a statement that released "roaring applause."[21] In this April of 1923, something new had entered the Nazi repertoire: in addition to the "Heil!" greeting among Nazis, the tumultuous cheering sometimes turned into cries of "Heil Hitler!"[22]

VI

On April 30, the moment of truth was at last upon the Nazis and their Task Force allies. With twenty-four hours to go before the seven government-sanctioned leftist May Day parades, the Task Force met to decide what it was going to do. Among the eleven men who gathered for this discussion of shared responsibility were Hitler, Goering, Röhm, and Kriebel, the Task Force military leader.

Kriebel, who was to coordinate the actual movements the following day, finally hammered out a consensus. The Task Force units were to be mobilized overnight and would assemble at several locations in Munich in the morning, with their weapons. If the Reds marched, their parades were to be attacked, but firearms were to be used only if the Marxists used them first. One of the restrictions the police had put on the leftists was that they were not to unfurl their red banners while on the march; if this happened, those flags were to be a focal point of attack. It was agreed that there must be one last round of calls on selected high Bavarian officials, informing them of these decisions and trying once again to compel the government to cancel the Red parades.

Hitler and Röhm went off to see General von Lossow. They asked the commander of regular army units in Bavaria to intervene in the impending confrontation, on their side. Furthermore, they said, they wanted the stores of weapons in the government armories that were designated for the use of the paramilitary organizations belonging to the Task Force.

There were conflicting reports of what happened at this meeting. Röhm pictured Lossow as admitting that the army had in the past led the militant right to believe that it could count on its support and weapons supply at such an hour, but that it would not be forthcoming. Lossow's operations officer said that Hitler kept repeating that there would be bloodshed if the army did not, one way or another, stop the march of the Reds; according to this account, Lossow kept trying to soothe Hitler, but in any event, Hitler and Röhm were informed that they would receive no weapons and no Reichswehr support of any kind.[23]

That Captain Ernst Röhm could be playing such a role in such an interview was in itself a commentary on the Bavarian political situation in the spring of 1923. Here was a regular army officer, on the staff of the commanding general in Bavaria, who at the same time was a key figure in a freelance armed military coalition that was embarking on a course of action opposed by the Bavarian government. In a less confused and conflicted time and place, Röhm would have left the room a military prisoner, bound for a court-martial.

While Hitler and Röhm were departing the scene of their fruitless discussion with the army commander, Goering and Kriebel were meeting with other government officials, demanding that they declare a state of emergency, under which all political gatherings would be banned. Kriebel had a particularly acid exchange with Eduard Nortz, who had acquired a profound mistrust of Adolf Hitler in January. If there was shooting the next day, Nortz told the Task Force military leader, the forces of the right would not be favored over those of the left; the Munich police would "fire in both directions."[24] Kriebel's answer: "I can no longer turn back; it is too late . . . whether or not blood flows."[25] Efforts to sway Colonel Hans Ritter von Seisser, the brilliant and ambitious young commander of the Bavarian State Police, also came to naught. The final possibility for a government reversal of position was at a cabinet meeting that evening, but the members simply reiterated that the seven leftist parades scheduled for the next morning were legal.

Realizing that they were on their own, Hitler and his Task Force allies of all ranks hurled themselves into mobilization and the business of trying to acquire more weapons, by any and all means. As the evening of April 30 progressed, some of the Storm Troops simply opened up a Nazi cache of arms hidden in a house on the Schellingstrasse. Other units of the SA were able to draw a large stock of weapons and ammunition from a government storage area near a dirigible hangar outside the city, one of Röhm's secret FZ depots. Some army trucks from the Faber Motor Vehicle Rental Service were also driven off into the night, along with an armored car, but by the time Goering arrived in an effort to tow away several cannon, the Reichswehr had at last stopped that particular unauthorized flow of weapons into the darkness. At the barracks of engineer troops, Task Force units had great success in collecting arms that had previously been issued to them for military exercises and maneuvers; the government, they told the supply sergeants, was worried about Red activity the next day and wanted good loyal völkisch volunteers under arms. The same tactics nearly worked at the barracks of the Nineteenth Infantry Regiment. Showing their training passes and a requisition slip made out by one of Röhm's subordinates, the Task Force men were nearly out the gate with their newly issued weapons when a Reichswehr lieutenant confronted them. The ubiquitous Hermann Goering was on the scene, but his vehement protestations, his Pour le Mérite around his neck, and his towering wartime reputation left the lieutenant unmoved: the weapons went back to the FZ storage shed.[26]

While this was going on in Munich, telephones were ringing throughout Bavaria. In the town of Landshut, forty-two miles northwest of Munich, a twenty-five-year-old decorated wartime lieutenant, Otto Strasser, was in the pharmacy run by his older brother Gregor, who was commander of the Sturmabteilung's Lower Bavarian Regiment. Otto was not a party member, but he wanted to be in on whatever happened. SA troopers in grey army uniforms filled the small store. Strasser remembered:

> An almost electric tension held the members present. Cigarettes were smoked incessantly in a nervous, jerky fashion; tempers were short under the strain. It was unlike any other gathering here preparatory to a political rally — and it differed in another way, too. In addition to wearing their field-gray uniforms, the men tonight had their steel helmets and their rifles. They were in earnest.
>
> When the telephone shrilled, every member gave a start and every eye became riveted on the instrument.

It was the order from Munich, telling them to come ahead for whatever May Day might bring.

> The tension was broken; only anticipation was present now and the ex-soldiers were like schoolboys in their horseplay as they trooped through the darkness.
>
> A number of old lorries had been offered for the use of the insurgents, and these we manned now to drive about the town of Landshut and pick up our cohorts. . . . Our ramshackle conveyances, lighted only by lanterns, rolled up and down the streets, pausing here and there to pick up a member. It was never neces-

sary to send in a summons. No sooner had we come to a halt than the door of the house would open and a dark figure would come running to climb aboard.

Soon the trucks were full. Otto was to remember it as being a much larger convoy, but there were about two hundred men in these trucks, equipped with 140 rifles and several light machine guns.[27] Once on the road to Munich, the men "sang lusty barrack-room ballads to express their surging sense of power and indomitability."[28]

In the first hours of May 1 the armed units of the Task Force began assembling at various locations in the still-sleeping city. "At three o'clock in the morning," Hitler said, "after taking possession of our weapons, we occupied Oberwiesenfeld according to plan."[29] This was the large parade ground on Munich's northwestern outskirts. Over the next few hours, Hitler was to be joined there by contingents of the SA, Reichsflagge, Bund Blucher, and Bund Wiking. In addition to rifles and machine guns, some horse-drawn cannon, a battery from a unit known as Organization Lembert, eventually arrived.[30] With Hitler were Goering, Hess, Julius Streicher with men from Nuremberg, and Gerhard Rossbach, whose Freikorps was now merged into the Munich SA regiment. Various estimates put their numbers at between twelve hundred and two thousand; including contingents of Bund Oberland assembling downtown, at least two to three thousand armed men of the right were moving into place to stop the leftists' May Day parades.[31] "At six o'clock," Hitler said, "gangs of Reds gathered to meet us. I sent some men to provoke them, but they didn't react."[32]

Others, however, were reacting. All night the Munich police had been trying to keep track of the armored car that had been spirited away from the dirigible barracks area by the SA; in this era before city patrol cars and portable radio units, the armored vehicle was being trailed by policemen on bicycles, who occasionally leapt off to report to headquarters by telephone.[33] With dawn, those at the Reichswehr headquarters were piecing together the various reports of attempts, successful or not, to gain control of weapons that had been under government control.

The atmosphere at Reichswehr headquarters was businesslike, but in no way panicky. By contrast, at 8:30 A.M. there was a call from Nortz, who demanded that the army move at once against the Task Force units on the Oberwiesenfeld and scatter them, firing if necessary. The call from the police commissioner was taken by a cool-headed lieutenant colonel, Theodor Endres, who asked if Nortz had talked to the state police before calling the army. When Nortz said that he had not, Endres explained that the army was not trained in crowd control tactics of the sort practiced by the state police; the army would shoot, and shoot to kill, if necessary, but the Reichswehr units should be held in reserve.

A subsequent conversation between Nortz and another army officer convinced the police commissioner to try the state police, and these Landespolizei units soon proved more effective than Hitler would have wanted them to be.[34] They took up positions on the side of the Oberwiesenfeld that led into the city, blocking the avenues that led to the Theresienwiese, where some of the Reds' May Day marching and celebrating would soon occur. Other state police units hemmed in the Bund Oberland downtown; before the Oberland leaders realized it, they had entered into an agreement to stay where they were, as long as they were permitted to keep their weapons.[35]

With the sun up, it was turning out to be a hot day. On the Oberwiesenfeld, Hitler was pacing back and forth in the midst of his heavily armed encampment, which had machine guns pointed toward the state police. This morning he was wearing a steel helmet and his Iron Cross, First Class. According to Otto Strasser, Hitler was waiting for some signal from Captain Ernst Röhm. Uncertain as to what to do next, the Task Force leadership had different units deploy around the vast parade ground in various military exercises. Otto Strasser pictured the scene this way:

> The sun climbed into the sky — eight o'clock . . . nine . . .
> ten . . . eleven. . . . Adolf Hitler paced a jittery path before his
> lieutenants, occasionally removing his steel helmet to wipe the rivulets of perspiration from his face and forehead, gazing long and
> often toward Munich, the scene-to-be of his great triumph.[36]

From the distance came the sounds of the leftists' May Day parades. At the edge of the Oberwiesenfeld, their weapons pointing at the Task Force, was the screen of Green Police, Bavarian State Police known by the color of their uniforms. Hitler later said that this was not to be simply a blow against Red parades in Munich, but that there was to be a coup against the national government, "here and there all over Germany," and that he was waiting for news of action in other cities.[37] There was nothing to support this claim, and nothing except Otto

Strasser's account, and circumstantial evidence, to suggest that he was waiting for a message from Röhm. Nonetheless, Hitler waited, and waited.

Captain Ernst Röhm was standing at attention in front of General von Lossow.[38] Within seventy-two hours, Röhm would be dismissed from his prestigious staff position and sent as a line officer to a rifle company, with Lossow characterizing Röhm's actions as "responsible in part for the grave derelictions [and] misuse of the offices . . . contrary to discipline."[39] For the moment, however, Lossow was determined to find out what was going on, and he intended to use Captain Röhm to stop it. The results were soon apparent to Otto Strasser, who was standing on the Oberwiesenfeld near his brother Gregor, Lieutenant Colonel Kriebel, and Hitler.[40]

> Then, shortly after eleven, a strong Reichswehr detachment swung into view, flanked right and left by the green-uniformed forces of the police. At sight of them Hitler's face contorted with rage; his body crouched forward, as though he would spring at these men who interfered with his destiny and whip them single-handed. For a moment I thought he was on the point of an hysterical fit, and then he saw Captain Ernst Roehm. . . .
>
> A soft cry sounded behind Hitler's clenched teeth and he leaped toward Roehm like a maniac, seizing him by the tunic with trembling hands. "Have you betrayed us?" he screamed in a frenzy. "Explain! Why are you with these traitors? What has happened?"
>
> By that time the demonstrators of the Oberwiesenfeld had been surrounded by the military; the situation was already hopeless, and Roehm seemed unimpressed with Hitler's fury. He looked at him coldly, and took his time before he said in a superior manner:
>
> "Control yourself. The time is not yet ripe."
>
> The two men gazed into each other's eyes, and Hitler was the one to give way. Perhaps the ingrained military training of years, his subconscious acceptance of their corporal-and-captain relationship, had something to do with it. In a moment his hands fell from Roehm's uniform and Hitler dropped his eyes. He turned away.[41]

In seconds, Kriebel and Gregor Strasser were arguing with Hitler, urging him not to accept this humiliating round-up of the Task Force, but to fight; as Otto Strasser put it, "They were all for firing upon the

Reichswehr and starting a pitched battle, but Hitler was adamant in his surly refusal. . . . He sulked, taciturn and glowering, but he wouldn't listen to those of his leaders who favored a pitched battle."[42]

Near noon, with his forces still armed, but surrounded by units of the regular army and state police, Hitler made a speech to his bewildered and frustrated Storm Troops. As if announcing some sort of victory, he said that the government had forbidden the communists to march through Munich's victory arch. Trying to portray the Task Force's intentions as protecting Munich's population, rather than the previously announced plan to attack the Red parades that were only too clearly in progress, Hitler said that in the city everything was "very peaceful," so there was no need for further action.

"No man should hang his head," Hitler said, "if the order is given that the weapons are to be surrendered. In the city everything is calm; the weapons are not there for the purpose of provocation. Should there, however, be confrontations" — Hitler did not specify whether they might occur later in the day, or in the future — "then we will manage somehow." Standing in the ashes of the defeat of all his plans for a great Nazi victory over Bavaria's leftists on May Day, he finished with the notably limp "Our day will probably come soon."[43]

It was as if the clock had stopped ticking for Adolf Hitler in the hot noon hour of May 1, 1923. Some Task Force units throughout Munich were forced to surrender their weapons on the spot, and march away in small groups. Others were marched under guard to Reichswehr barracks, where they handed over their rifles and machine guns, not a single bullet having been fired. There were a few scuffles between Task Force men and leftists during the afternoon, and that night Hitler tried to bluster his way through a speech in the Zirkus Krone, but what had happened was clear to all Bavaria: "He failed miserably on the first day of May," the famous Freikorps commander Hermann Ehrhardt would soon say, "and he will always fail."[44] Gregor Strasser and his two hundred men, who had come singing to Munich the previous night, returned to Landshut without their rifles and machine guns; Otto Strasser said of Hitler's May Day, "He could have known no more bitter humiliation, and he drank his cup of defeat to its bitter dregs."[45]

CHAPTER

27

HITLER was not the only one who had to digest the events of May Day; in rightist Bavaria, it was as if some ghastly feud had erupted in a family whose members still wished to believe that blood was thicker than water. The result was ambivalence; General von Lossow removed Captain Ernst Röhm from his position of influence, censured him, and went so far as to write Röhm a letter accusing him of being insane, but no court-martial action was taken.[1] As a direct result of the Task Force provocations on May Day, the Bavarian government enacted state-of-emergency legislation on May 11, but these restrictions on public demonstrations were used to suppress leftist organizations, while the Reichsflagge, the Task Force unit in which Röhm had held a key position, was allowed to hold machine-gun firing practice near the town of Feucht.[2] Eduard Nortz was given a transfer that was really a demotion: it was the government's way of saying that Munich's police commissioner had been too ready to compromise with the Task Force.

Within the Task Force, two of the "fighting units" withdrew from the alliance with the Nazis as a result of the fiasco, and a third floated into a friendly informal relationship with the party. The left tried to make political capital out of the Task Force's May Day threats and impotence, but encountered either indifference or a feeling that the racist-nationalist movement still represented Germany's salvation, but might be in irresponsible hands. Some newspapers that had been sympathetic to the Nazis began to reappraise their positions.[3]

Hitler was again at a critical point in his career. He was called in for questioning by the police, in the first step of a process that would in time lead to an indictment against him, with the possibility that he would be ruled as having broken the parole on which he was released from jail after serving part of his sentence in the Ballerstedt case. That could lead to his finally being deported from Germany.

Although he was depressed by his failure on May 1, on May 8 he went on the offensive, telling the police official who was questioning him, "I insist that I be interrogated in the matter by the public prosecutor himself, and not by the police."[4] It was pure Hitler; if he was forced into the criminal justice process, he wanted to speak to the top man, and get as much publicity out of it as he could. Hitler sensed that the Bavarian government's heart was not really in the prospective prosecution of Adolf Hitler as a revolutionary; up the line, between him and his critic Interior Minister Schweyer, was Minister of Justice Franz Gürtner, a völkisch sympathizer who had referred to the Nazis as "flesh of our flesh."[5] Hitler also let it be known that, if pushed, he would publicize various earlier agreements between the government and the Reichswehr, on the one hand, and rightist paramilitary organizations on the other, concerning the ownership of weapons and contingency plans for jointly opposing Marxist uprisings. Hitler's threat was clear: in light of such past discussions, the public might find it hard to believe that the Nazis had not in fact been trying to support the government against the left on May Day. Try it out, Hitler was saying; see if the public wants you to punish me for opposing a Communist parade on May Day.

Hitler's tactics worked — the indictment was eventually quashed, probably by Gürtner — but his political balance sheet in May of 1923 was dismal, and Hitler knew it. He had lost ground with the Reichswehr; he had lost ground with the Bavarian government; he had lost his position of primacy with the other Bavarian nationalist leaders and parties; and he had lost heavily with the public. A leader must lead; a revolutionary must not be seen as impotent, led away under guard with his men surrendering their arms. Indeed, it was the public perception of Hitler that was at this moment his greatest weakness, for the party was actually in good working order, with a momentum of its own, and key leaders of the nationalist movement in northern Germany were still seeking out Hitler during their trips to Bavaria.

It was time for the man who thrived on crowds to become less visible, to let the public forget that springtime sequence of brave words and abject surrender. Hitler's public appearances in Munich trailed off almost to nothing; when he did appear, he was the same strident orator, but most of his few speeches were at Nazi meetings held at other sites in Bavaria.

There was a new place in Hitler's life in the early summer of 1923. His wounded spirit, and his sense of tactics, led him to Berchtesgaden, where Dietrich Eckart was hiding, in comfort, from the police. The town had thirty-five hundred inhabitants, many of whom worked either in the local toy-making industry or in the nearby salt mines, which had been started 750 years earlier.

Above the town is an area of mountains known as the Obersalzberg, or Upper Salt Mountain, a hiker's paradise with panoramic views of snow-covered peaks. There, at the large boardinghouse known as the Pension Moritz, Hitler was reunited with the booming-voiced Eckart. The fifty-five-year-old was in failing health, although he looked well. His eighteen-year-old mistress, Annerl Obster, was with him, and much of his natural exuberance, and unsuitability for the role of inconspicuous fugitive from justice, remained. In a half-hearted attempt to avoid the police, he had assumed the alias Dr. Hoffman, but Hitler immediately saw that everyone knew his real identity.

By contrast, despite his many appearances before thousands in Munich, no one recognized the slender, pale, thirty-four-year-old man who was with the flamboyant Eckart. "He introduced me to the Buchners [proprietors of the Pension Moritz]: 'This is my young friend Herr Wolf.' Nobody could think of forming any connection between this person and that crazy monster Adolf Hitler."[6]

So began a summer in which, Hitler said, "every time I had a few free days, I used to return up there. . . . I'd fallen in love with the landscape." Compared to his usual frantic pace in Munich, his time in the mountains was relatively peaceful, but, like courtiers seeking out their king in his self-imposed exile, some of Hitler's inner circle visited him at the boardinghouse in the mountains. Even then, his anonymity remained intact — Hitler said, "It was very amusing to hear what people said at table about Hitler" — but it could not go on forever. He was scheduled to address a Nazi Party meeting at Passau, a town on the Austrian border where he had lived for two years as a child. A self-important man who had been sitting at the table with him and knew him as Herr Wolf suddenly announced, "I've come from Holstein as far as Berchtesgaden. I refuse to miss the opportunity of seeing this man Hitler. So I'm going to Passau."

Hitler decided that he might as well offer his loud table companion a ride, so off the man went in a touring car, unaware that his companions were Adolf Hitler, Hermann Goering, Emil Maurice, and Julius Schreck, the bodyguard who also served as a chauffeur. Arriving at Passau, Hitler separated from his guest in the car, "telling him I'd join him in the hall."

Then, as Hitler was introduced to his audience,

> I immediately recognised my man by his stupidly scarred face, lost in the confused uproar of the hall. When he saw me mount the platform and begin to speak, he fixed his eyes upon me as if I were a ghost. The meeting ended in a terrible brawl, in the course of which Schreck was arrested. I took my companion back to Obersalzberg. He was dumbfounded. I begged him to keep my secret.

The shaken man kept his promise not to reveal Hitler's identity, but Hitler was soon to be unmasked before all his fellow guests at the Pension Moritz.

> For a long time a meeting had been arranged at Berchtesgaden. The moment came when it was no longer possible to avoid it. "German Day at Berchtesgaden. Present: Comrade Adolf Hitler." Great sensation at Obersalzberg. The whole boarding-house, forty to fifty people in all, came down into the valley to see the phenomenon. . . .
> I came down by motor-cycle. At the Crown Inn, I was welcomed by a formidable ovation. All my boarding-house was gathered in front of the door — but the good people were in no way surprised, being convinced that every new arrival was greeted in this vociferous fashion. When I climbed on the platform, they stared at me as if I'd gone mad. When they became aware of the reality, I saw that it was driving them out of their minds.
> When Wolf returned to the boarding-house, the atmosphere there was poisoned. Those who had spoken ill of Adolf Hitler in my hearing were horribly embarrassed. What a pity![7]

Someone else was speaking ill of Hitler in June of 1923. Putzi Hanfstaengl had gone up to Berchtesgaden to put some ideas before Hitler; because the Pension Moritz was crowded, Putzi shared Eckart's room.

> Eckart unburdened himself for hours about Hitler; "You know, Hanfstaengl," I remember him saying, "something has gone completely wrong with Adolf. The man is developing an incurable case of *folie de grandeur*. Last week he was striding up and down

in the courtyard here with that damned whip of his and shouting, 'I must enter Berlin like Christ in the Temple at Jerusalem and drive out the moneylenders,' and more nonsense of that sort. I tell you if he lets this Messiah complex run away with him he will ruin us all."[8]

II

At the same time that Hitler was losing the confidence of Eckart — the man who had flown with him to Berlin at the time of the Kapp Putsch, who had been with him at Coburg, who had brought off the eleventh-hour deal that garnered the *Völkischer Beobachter* for the Nazi Party — a new and infinitely more prominent personage was starting to give Hitler his support. Since the war's end, General Erich Ludendorff had been the hero of the right, the "national commander" who had no job and no official position but whose name was an echo of wartime victories and the "stab in the back" legend that so many Germans cherished as an explanation for their nation's defeat. Living quietly in his villa in Ludwigshöhe, he filled his hours with gardening, answering letters, and setting down in writing his anti-Semitic, anti-Masonic, anti-Catholic prejudices. When invited, he would sally forth, past the Freikorps veterans who acted as armed sentries outside the walls of his villa, to attend the meetings of various right-wing veterans' organizations.

Occasionally a certain unwelcome light forced itself into the mind of the man who had been Germany's wartime dictator. His vision of himself usually blocked out the fact that he had been, at the very least, first among equals in plunging Germany into chaos in 1918, but early in 1923 he had experienced a troubling thought. The day before the French marched into the Ruhr he had been visiting the town of Wesel, which was about to be occupied. A regiment to which Ludendorff had been assigned in the earlier part of his military career had once been garrisoned in this town, and he was apparently there for a reunion of its veterans.

> The mood was depressed. One was waiting for the enemy to march in. But it was something else besides: something difficult to define was in the air. In this Catholic town, with comrades who should have been proud that I was once in their regiment, I felt rejected, as if I had been truly responsible for the outcome of the world war.[9]

At his villa near Munich, Ludendorff received visitors who represented the various völkisch groups. With all of them, he took a stance that was essentially unchanged from his attitude when he had presided over the bustling right-wing salon in his apartment in Berlin during the months leading to the failed Kapp Putsch in 1920. His politically minded guests found a big, dignified, impressive, coy Prussian bear. He would listen, he would nod, he would approve of this or that nationalist-racist remark, but he would throw in his lot with no one. As at the time of the Kapp Putsch, he still wanted a fait accompli, a successful coup whose leaders would turn to him to lead the nation. His position of being above the clouds, of waiting for destiny, was buttressed by a reputation that was truly international, although sometimes fantastically expressed: *Time* magazine, which had started publishing on March 3, 1923, gave an early example of its adjectival addiction when it described Ludendorff as "a solitary phantom striding the earth with noiseless, slippery, dreadful steps."[10]

Through the guarded gates at Ludwigshöhe, one May evening, came Rudolf Hess. Always able to make a favorable impression on those of higher rank, the polite and earnest Hess secured the general's agreement to receive Adolf Hitler. A few evenings later, Hitler came and sat in Ludendorff's study, talking to him beneath the famous painting of Ludendorff and Hindenburg poring over a map at the Eastern Headquarters of the wartime army. As usual, Hitler went on at length, giving his views on Germany's plight and what was necessary for Germany's future. Ludendorff liked what he heard and was impressed by what he called Hitler's "driving determination."[11] No one could doubt that it was a time of crisis for Germany. The French were still in the Ruhr, successfully wearing down Germany's "passive resistance," while the mark was disintegrating: pegged at 46,000 to the dollar on May 13, it would take 70,000 marks to equal a dollar on June 1. By the time of their meeting, Ludendorff, along with everyone else in and near Munich, must have been aware of Hitler's failure on May Day, but neither Hitler's armed defiance nor the fiasco that followed seemed to trouble him.

Until then, Ludendorff had refused to endorse any one leader of the right. In an interview with an American journalist some days after meeting with Hitler, the general said that the Task Force led by Hitler struck him as being the best example of "the growing aims which I follow."[12] Thus, without committing himself to the Nazis or even mentioning the NSDAP, Ludendorff sounded ready to anoint Hitler. That he had singled out for approval the split Task Force, which was discredited even in some rightist circles, confirmed the fact that Ludendorff wanted action, not ideas. The "growing aims" could only be those of forceful action, backed by weapons, bent upon the capture, redistribution, and redirection of Germany's political power.

While Ludendorff could apparently afford the luxury of waiting for others to bring him plots and schemes and plans, many prominent right-wing sympathizers in Munich were trying to position themselves to take advantage of the convulsions that they felt lay immediately ahead for Germany. As the summer moved on, the radical right in Munich was less interested in its relations with the Bavarian government, unsatisfactory as those might in some respects be, than in what could be expected to take place in Berlin. Great hopes were placed in the idea that the Reichswehr, in company with North German nationalists and fully supported by Bavaria, might simply close down the existing leadership and legislature of the national government, and substitute for it a directorate. This partnership of right-wing leaders would renounce the Versailles Treaty, stabilize the mark, strengthen the Reichswehr, strangle the left, throw the French out of the Ruhr, and march Germany into a glorious future.

III

Despite Hitler's sharp reduction of his speechmaking appearances in Munich during the summer of 1923, what happened on July 14 demonstrated that neither the Nazi Party nor the police had forgotten the May Day confrontation.[13] Munich was playing host to the Deutsches Turnfest, a large assemblage of Germany's gymnastic organizations, and the party announced a meeting at the Zirkus Krone. The program was scheduled to begin at ten in the evening, which gave völkisch-minded gymnasts and their newfound Nazi friends an opportunity to drink many gallons of the city's beers before going to hear Hitler.

Before the crowd gathered, a Munich police official appeared in the swastika-draped interior of the Zirkus Krone and informed Hitler that, pursuant to a police regulation set forth five days earlier, the flags of political parties could not be unfurled in the vast hall.

The prohibition against political banners may well have been aimed specifically at the Nazi Party; in any event, this was the police official's report of the party leader's reaction: "Hitler replied to me that he had rented the Zirkus and could do in the Zirkus whatever he wanted."[14] The evening began, with the hall festooned with swastika banners, and no police interference. Hitler was scheduled to speak on "The Curse of the November Revolution," and he did so, but with an extemporaneous excursion into the subject of flags. An account of the speech said that Hitler "released a tempest of uncontrolled passions with the cry: We want to have a symbol of a coming, growing, free Germany."[15]

At the close of Hitler's speech, some of the audience, a few complete SA detachments among them, decided to defy the authorities further; with swastika flags unfurled, they marched into the "Banned Mile." Alerted police units were lined up near the railroad station, and the Nazi column charged into them. Hand-to-hand struggles took place, with hundreds of participants, but there was no gun play. Wielding their heavy batons, the police beat back the Nazis and their gymnast sympathizers, and it was soon over, with no serious injuries. The police had won. The Nazis dispersed, but the evening was a perfect example of the growing truculence of Hitler and his followers. The police were sending a message, too: We intend to keep order in this city.

The immediate result of the July 14 battle with the police was that the *Völkischer Beobachter* was ordered to cease publication from July 17 through July 24 as a result of its post-riot story headlined PROVOCATION OF GERMAN GYMNASTS BY THE GOVERNMENT. . . . THE POLICE WITH COLD STEEL AGAINST THE GYMNASTS, but by now the party was advancing on so many fronts that the suspension of its official newspaper was nothing more than an inconvenience.[16] Spurred by the accelerating pace of inflation, more and more Bavarians were looking to Hitler and the party as an answer to their longing for a workable society. The Nazis even had a martyr to offer the public: Albert Leo Schlageter, a young Freikorps veteran and NSDAP member, had been executed by the French for blowing up a railway bridge in the Ruhr. Schlageter instantly became a national hero; although his act of sabotage had nothing to do with the party, the Nazis were quick to capitalize on their brief association with him.[17]

The party's numbers were growing, and so were its activities. The *Beobachter* might be suspended in Munich, but in Nuremberg Julius Streicher was publishing an ugly little sheet called *Der Stürmer*, which eclipsed all other völkisch publications in the matter of fantastic anti-Semitic tales and accusations. Party headquarters was strengthening its control over the growing number of SA units outside Munich.[18] Hans Ulrich Klintzsch had resigned as the SA's commander on May 11; Goering, already actively working with the Storm Troops, became their leader.[19]

There was one enigmatic development, apparent only to those who were close to the military side of the NSDAP. During this summer, in an action that must have been approved by Hitler and may have been initiated by him, Hitler's chauffeur Julius Schreck selected a group of tough young Nazis to form the nucleus of a hundred-man elite unit known as Stosstrupp Adolf Hitler, Shock Troop Adolf Hitler. This company was turned over to a former army lieutenant, Josef Berchtold, a Nazi who made his living as a tobacconist but threw himself into the job of giving these men special training.

The full story of the origin and purpose of this company has never been clear; whether first conceived by Schreck or by Hitler, it appears to have been intended as der Führer's personal military unit, trained and equipped to carry out special, unspecified missions, and to act as a bodyguard. Stosstrupp Adolf Hitler existed outside the SA chain of command, and immediately became the object of a resentful, envious suspicion on the part of the SA's Munich Regiment. The supposition is that Hitler, always ready to place counterweights to anything that might threaten his supremacy within the NSDAP, may have felt that the rapid growth of the SA regiments under Goering was escaping his control. Hence this highly disciplined company of men, more heavily armed than any SA unit, who were to be immediately responsive to Hitler's personally delivered orders. Indeed, the Stosstrupp may have been Hitler's answer to the SA's Stabswache, or Staff Guard, a special unit first formed by Lieutenant Klintzsch when he was SA commander, and continued by Goering. Attached to SA headquarters, these Staff Guard troops wore black ski caps instead of the grey ski caps worn by all other SA personnel. On the front of each black cap was a skull-and-crossbones insignia.[20]

The men of Stosstrupp Adolf Hitler were soon fully equipped with infantry combat gear; loaded on party-owned trucks and wearing steel helmets, they were indistinguishable from soldiers of the Reichswehr, except for their swastika armbands. Both Hitler and Goering were opening a new dimension in Nazi reality: the concept of a smaller, harder, more brutal armed force that was to exist within the larger phalanx of Hitler's uniformed followers.

In addition to the actual capacity for fighting, an obvious added purpose of the party's intensive military activity was to intimidate its targeted enemies, and in this it was succeeding. Elsewhere in Germany during the summer of 1923, the leftist paramilitary Proletarian Hundreds were experiencing a sharp growth — a hundred thousand men would soon be in their ranks, and in many cities they led parades during the Anti-Fascist Day demonstrations on July 29 — but in Bavaria the socialist Erhard Auer Guards did not challenge the Nazis' SA detachments as they moved about the streets of Munich.[21] In the case of the Jews of Bavaria, the combination of stated Nazi attitudes and the existence of Hitler's own private army of Storm Troops led them to fear for their lives. In a story filed from Munich some months earlier, *New York Times* foreign correspondent Cyril Brown characterized the Nazis as a "reactionary Nationalistic anti-Semitic movement," and described Hitler's speechmaking evenings as "patriotic revival meetings." He went on: "So violent are Hitler's fulminations against the Jews that a number of prominent Jewish citizens are reported to have sought safe asylums in the Bavarian highlands, easily reached by fast motor cars, whence they could hurry their women and children when forewarned of an anti-Semitic St. Bartholomew's night."[22]

IV

In the last week of July, when the mark was plummeting and more and more Bavarians were talking seriously of a "march on Berlin," a letter to Hitler was being prepared by the old guard of the Nazi Party. Young as the party was, it already had a past and milestones; two years earlier, Hitler had confronted the party's leaders, threatened his resignation, and destroyed the last vestiges of democratic thinking and parliamentary procedure within the NSDAP. Anton Drexler had been deposed as first chairman, and the party's statutes had been revised to give Hitler the powers that had resided in the executive committee. The capitulation of the old guard had been complete; as a sop, Hitler retained Drexler as a figurehead chairman who still occasionally appeared at speechmaking evenings, and Gottfried Feder was allowed to reiterate his interest-slavery ideas as a fuzzy concession to those who still wanted some socialism along with their anti-Semitic nationalism.

It was Feder who now spoke from the recesses of the Nazi past in an effort to turn Hitler from what the frustrated survivors of the party's old guard saw as a disastrous perversion of their original association. Feder's letter to Hitler was the voice of an informal committee of the party's founders, still hoping to regain a measure of their former influence. Hitler was requested to create a "spiritual general staff" to preserve the original workingman's ideals of the party. This demand was a reflection of the diehard ideas of Anton Drexler. Still holding down his job as a toolmaker at the shops of the Bavarian national railways in Munich, Drexler continued to believe that the highest priority of the NSDAP was to give the skilled worker a purely German form of socialism that would be more attractive than international communism.

Feder's letter spoke critically of Hitler's appearances in the upper reaches of Munich society; even at that, the wording was a mild reflection of the old guard's private references to Hitler as *"Arbeit-führer bei Sekt und schönen Frauen"* — champagne-and-pretty-women workers' leader. There was criticism of Hitler's chaotic and unpredictable daily schedule, which Feder called "the anarchy in the allocation of your time." This could be solved, Feder told Hitler, by acquiring a deputy who would properly handle Hitler's priorities and schedule, the implication being that this key aide should represent the old guard, rather than any of Hitler's more recent appointees.

In an echo of the lost battle over open debate and parliamentary procedure, Hitler was urged to have the party run candidates for office in the upcoming national and state elections. In flattering words, it was put to Hitler that he would be a most effective candidate, and that an election campaign would provide him with an effective forum in which his words would ring throughout Germany. In thus urging Hitler to run, the old guard knew full well that they were addressing a man who, at the moment, felt that the party should not send its representatives into legislatures where they would be treated as mere equals. They also must have known that, without German citizenship, Hitler was ineligible to run for office.

The letter closed with an appeal to Hitler to be less of a dictator in running the party: "We gladly yield first place to you, but for tyrannical tendencies we have no understanding."[23]

There is no record of this letter's being answered, or even of its receipt being acknowledged. As for the man to whom the appeal for some measure of moderation was addressed, a guest at a party he attended that summer left this description of his behavior:

> Hitler had sent word to his hostess that he had to attend an important meeting and would not arrive until late: I think it was about eleven o'clock. He came, none the less, in a very decent blue suit and with an extravagantly large bouquet of roses, which he presented to his hostess as he kissed her hand. While he was

being introduced, he wore the expression of a public prosecutor at an execution. I remember being struck by his voice when he thanked the lady of the house for tea or cakes, of which, incidentally, he ate an amazing quantity. It was a remarkably emotional voice, and yet it made no impression of conviviality or intimacy but rather of harshness. However, he said hardly anything but sat there in silence for about an hour; apparently he was tired. Not until the hostess was so incautious as to let fall a remark about the Jews, whom she defended in a jesting tone, did he begin to speak and then he spoke without ceasing. After a while he thrust back his chair and stood up, still speaking, or rather yelling, in such a powerful penetrating voice as I have never heard from anyone else. In the next room a child woke up and began to cry. After he had for more than half an hour delivered a quite witty but very one-sided oration on the Jews, he suddenly broke off, went up to his hostess, begged to be excused and kissed her hand as he took his leave. The rest of the company, who apparently had not pleased him, were only vouchsafed a curt bow from the doorway.[24]

If that was the private Hitler, the public man could hardly be less obsessed. Although the Nazi Party was making gains in membership and in its internal organization and strength, Hitler was still experiencing the results of his abysmal failure in his confrontation with the authorities. His losses with other nationalist leaders, and with the broad Bavarian public, were twofold: there was the May Day fiasco itself, and there was his confusing withdrawal to Berchtesgaden and the great reduction in the number of his appearances in Munich. Although it was desirable, for Hitler, to have the public forget May Day, visibility was credibility with the audience this politician needed to reach and to sway. His partial absence had created a partial vacuum; now, in an effort to reclaim his entire share of the right-wing position and to capitalize on the financial and political turmoil throughout Germany, on the first of August Hitler gave one of his most blazing speeches to date, to a crowd of eighty-five hundred at the Zirkus Krone. First he characterized the threat from the left, in these terms:

What is the Soviet star? The symbol of a race which is preparing to assume control from Vladivostok to Western Europe. The sickle is a sign of brutality; the hammer, the sign of Freemasonry. The rule by the Soviet star will only be a paradise for Jews; a slave colony for all others. The goal of the Communists is not the salvation, but rather the destruction of Germany.[25]

Having lashed out at the left, the Jews, and the Masons, Hitler turned to the Allies, with special reference to the continuing French presence in the Ruhr.

> The day must come when a German government will have the courage to proclaim to the Foreign Powers, "The Treaty of Versailles is founded on a monstrous lie, and we hereby dissolve it! Do what you will! If you want war, you can have it! Then we'll see whether you can turn seventy million Germans into serfs and slaves![26]

Pungent and calculating as some of these words were, in essence this much of Hitler's speech had been heard before. He then turned to the subject of whether the NSDAP should enter the forthcoming national and state elections.

> Our Movement was not formed with any election in view, but in order to spring to the rescue of this people as its last help in the hour of greatest need, at the moment when in fear and despair it sees the approach of the Red Monster. The task of our Movement is not to prepare ourselves for any coming election but to prepare for the coming collapse of the Reich, so that when the old trunk falls the young fir-trees may be already standing.[27]

Hitler became explicit about his alternatives to the democratic elections of the Weimar Republic. "We want to be the supporters of the dictatorship of national reason, of national energy, of national brutality and resolution."[28] He also demanded: "Fanatic national character in every form must be fostered."[29]

Throughout his speechmaking career, Hitler had vehemently attacked the government in Berlin, and had indeed coined the term "November Criminals" to describe the Weimar leaders. Now he went a step further. In tune with rightist talk in Bavaria and völkisch hopes in the north, Hitler intensified his call to arms. With a few words he seized the high ground on the right, taking a position so extreme that it was impossible for any völkisch leader to exceed it. "Either Berlin marches and ends up in Munich," he shouted at the roaring crowd, "or Munich marches and ends up in Berlin!"[30]

CHAPTER

28

I N AUGUST of 1923, the sick German mark began to die a violent
death. Although the slide to disaster had begun years earlier, the
Reichstag that reassembled in Berlin at the beginning of August had
to contend with problems that were guaranteed to produce a final
erosion in the public's confidence in its government and the currency
issued by the government. In Saxony and Thuringia, Social Democrats
were allying themselves with the German Communist Party to oppose
the national government, while the French-sponsored separatist movement in the Rhineland continued its attempt to pry that area loose
from Germany. All this unrest, coupled with the unceasing drumfire
from the right and Bavaria's widening split with Berlin, added to the
continued crushing presence of the French in the Ruhr, set the stage
for slashing criticism of Chancellor Cuno's government within the
national legislature itself. The Reichstag agreed with Cuno's proposal
that taxes be raised, but of what use were taxes if Cuno and his cabinet
were unable to rally a significant part of the nation in support of a
recognizable solution to Germany's problems? In fact, there was no
coherent government program; Cuno had experienced several nervous
breakdowns from the stress of trying to run Germany amidst pressure
from France and from domestic political extremists. He had no solid
base, and he told his associates that he could not continue to serve
under such circumstances. Cuno's despair was not offset by his foreign
minister, Dr. F. H. von Rosenberg, who told the British ambassador
that there was no solution to Germany's problems, and that the nation
would simply have to lie where it fell.[1]

Predictably, the Cuno government was unable to gain a vote of
confidence in the Reichstag, and on August 13 Gustav Stresemann

became Germany's seventh chancellor in five years. A seasoned politician and an able leader who simultaneously took on the post of foreign minister, Stresemann offered the nation a realistic but unpopular program — an end to the futile and costly "passive resistance" to the French in the Ruhr, coupled with the raising of taxes and a start to anti-inflationary fiscal reform. At a saner moment, this might have reversed the rush to chaos, but Stresemann was coming to the helm of a ship that was in a typhoon, with 80 percent of its crew terrified, and the remaining fifth openly mutinous. He could expect an armed revolt at any time, from either left or right, or both. Stresemann was a man of character, a statesman who did not fear to do his duty as he saw it, but soon he was saying privately to a caucus of his German People's Party, "I am sick of this dog's life, with treason on every side. If the nationalists come marching into Berlin I am not going to run off. . . . If they come, they can shoot me down right here, in the place where I have every right to sit."[2]

If that was the frame of mind of Germany's chancellor, the people in the street could scarcely be expected to have a higher degree of confidence in the nation's immediate future. Germany's runaway inflation was caused by much more than mere public perception and reaction, but a nation living in bewildered fear did not trust the value of the mark to hold for even an hour, and to that extent these fears became self-fulfilling prophecies. Until mid-1923 Germany's teachers had been paid their salaries once a month; now, with the purchasing power of their salaries dwindling daily, the teachers were paid once a week, so that they could rush out and get something for their marks before there was a further loss in their value. Soon they were being paid daily.

Inflation took on a life of its own. The numbers ceased to make any kind of sense, and soon the strings of zeros became arbitrary — millions, billions, it began to make no difference how many marks one had, because if one mark was worthless, a billion of them were no better. This was a crash in monetary value so profound, so sweeping, that it could not be judged in terms of any previous inflation in any nation. Nothing like it had been seen before.

Here and there, one might spot certain washed-away bridges in the river of marks heading over the waterfall. The *Völkischer Beobachter*, always eager to publicize any weakness that could be attributed to the Berlin government, had for some months been running a little box, usually on the front page, that featured the latest rate of exchange of the mark against the dollar. On May 4 it had taken 40,000 marks to equal a dollar; on May 22, it took 51,000 marks to equal a dollar in the morning, but by afternoon it required 52,500. On June 13 it required just under 100,000 marks to equal a dollar, but by June 28 the mark had lost one third that value in two weeks, and it required 152,617 marks to equal a dollar.

In July the bottom dropped out of the mark; by August 1, it took one million marks to equal a dollar, and a week after that, the figure was 3.5 million. The next day, a German would have needed 6 million marks to procure an American dollar. Germans were in panic over the fact that the mark had lost 99.3 percent of its purchasing power in three months, but even then, no one could have imagined that this tiny, emaciated splinter of a mark was about to lose another 93.3 percent of its purchasing power within a month, and go on down from there.

The rate of exchange was only a yardstick for measuring the disintegration of the mark; the true significance was of course in its effect on the lives of Germans. For those who lacked economic sophistication, the answer seemed to lie in just one direction: if the mark is buying less, then we must have more marks. The solution lay in an entirely different direction — Stresemann and his minister of finance, Dr. Rudolf Hilferding, knew that inflation would end only when this dead mark was buried and a new unit of currency put in its place, issued in conservative amounts and coupled with taxation that would bring all the nation's governmental budgets into balance.

Sadly, the knowledge possessed by Stresemann and Hilferding was not shared or believed in by a number of influential figures in Germany. Foremost among these economic dissenters was Rudolf Havenstein, an old-school civil servant who was president of the Reichsbank. During the war, Havenstein had done a good job of managing large-scale governmental loans, but his reaction to the inflationary crisis was to blame it on Germany's trade deficit, and on the undoubted lack of cooperation with government policy shown by some of Germany's industrialists, who dumped billions of marks on foreign exchange markets in an effort to get more stable currencies for their own use, at virtually any price.[3] Trotting out some of his own economic theories, Havenstein attacked the idea that Germany was experiencing what he described as "so-called inflation"; ignoring the fact that nothing would save the German mark if Germany flooded itself with paper money, Havenstein declared that there was no possibility of stabilizing the mark until there was a settlement of the reparations question with the Allies.[4]

What this boiled down to was that the president of the Reichsbank was having a reaction to Germany's monetary crisis that was in practice identical with that of the broad German public. Havenstein, too, believed that the answer lay in printing more money, and he was in a unique position: he controlled the printing presses, and, because of the independent postwar status of the Reichsbank, he could not be removed from his office by the chancellor. Feeling that his duty to the nation lay in supplying the public with the additional marks for which it was clamoring, he went right to work. During the August plunge of the mark Havenstein proudly reported to the Reichsrat, the Council of the Reich, that the Reichsbank was printing new bills night and day, and was able to issue 46 billion new marks every twenty-four hours.

This was of course fueling the inflation; with the bit in his teeth, Havenstein was in charge of an enterprise that was soon using 30 paper factories, 133 printing offices, and 1,783 printing presses. The denominations printed on the bills became larger, and then the decision was made to save time in rushing out the bills by printing them on only one side. Eventually, even these bills, which had been quite handsomely engraved despite the furor surrounding them, were simply run off the presses and then passed through a stamping machine that printed a higher number in black across the center of the note: a million-mark bill would have TEN MILLION across it, in big letters.

Watching this rising tide of paper, Lord d'Abernon was aghast at the idea that not a single member of the Reichsrat, one of Germany's two highest deliberative bodies, was challenging Havenstein's mass production of money. "It appears almost impossible," said the British ambassador, "to hope for the recovery of a country where such things are possible."[5] In private, he observed that a country which understood anything about the nature of money would take Havenstein out and hang him.

For once, Hitler was thinking along lines parallel to those of a representative of the Allies. "The country," he said, "is on the brink of a hellish abyss." He added, "The people are like a lot of children. You can only press million-mark notes into the hands of a childish public!"[6]

II

In mid-August, as the financial and political crisis within Germany heightened, Hitler left the country for a few days to attend the Inter-State Congress of National Socialists in Salzburg. Three years earlier, attending this meeting with the representatives of the National Socialist parties of Austria and the Sudetenland, Hitler had been a minor figure. Then it was Anton Drexler, as first chairman of the NSDAP, who was photographed with the other prominent figures at the meeting, while Hitler peered forth glumly from an inconspicuous place in a group photograph. Now Drexler was not even part of the Nazi delegation from Munich, which included Hermann Goering, Hermann Esser, and Max Amann.

Hitler swiftly took charge of the congress, serving as chairman of the Leaders' Council and making it clear to the Austrian and Sudeten National Socialists that he represented a far more powerful and dynamic party than theirs.[7] The principal item on the agenda of this meeting was the question of whether the Austrian National Socialists should enter into a coalition with the Greater German People's Party, a bourgeois Austrian Pan-German group with a strong völkisch position. Dr. Walter Riehl, the chairman of the Austrian National Socialists, believed that his party's only hope of achieving a real propaganda voice, and seats in the Austrian parliament, lay in forging the proposed bond with the Greater German People's Party.

This was by definition contrary to the thinking of Hitler, who had consistently rejected every suggestion that his own National Socialists merge with other parties. In the Leaders' Council, composed of the chiefs of the various National Socialist groups, Riehl was defeated by a margin of seven to one, his being the only vote for his own proposal. The other determining vote was cast by the delegates to the congress as a whole; led by a group of new Austrian National Socialist leaders who were described by Riehl as "young fanatics," the delegates also voted down the proposal.[8] This precipitated the resignation of Riehl, a lawyer who had been his party's moving spirit for fifteen years.

Thus, as had happened in the NSDAP two years earlier, the old guard of the Austrian Nazis was struck down by a younger and more militant faction, but none of the Austrian delegates understood Hitler's true attitude toward them. They assumed that he demanded that they subordinate themselves to him and to the NSDAP in Munich because his was the more formidable National Socialist entity; in reality, Hitler had contempt for the very idea of an independent Austrian nation, believing that it belonged within Germany's borders, and his contempt automatically extended to the notion of a separate Austrian Nazi Party. All should be under German rule.[9]

At the Salzburg meeting, there was one member of the NSDAP who had not come there from Munich with the delegation of German Nazis led by Hitler. This was Kurt Ludecke, who arrived from Budapest; strange things had happened to him since he had parted from his rich and elegant American mistress, Dolores, a year earlier. After the Storm Troop victory at Coburg, Kurt Ludecke had spent much of his time recruiting and outfitting a hundred-man military company. His intention was to present this trained unit to Hitler for incorporation into the SA on January 30, 1923, during the dedication of Storm Troop banners on the Marsfeld.

Kurt Ludecke was a generous soul; sophisticated in the ways of the fashionable world, he was naïve when it came to the vindictive jealousies of little men. To him it had seemed natural to lavish his bank accounts on the feeding and training of this company of unpaid volunteers. When he was arrested a few hours before the ceremony, with the police scattering his unit and confiscating the cache of contraband weapons in his apartment, it did not occur to him that the police were tipped off by SA officers who wanted to discredit him.

Kurt Ludecke spent ten weeks in jail.[10] At first he was under the impression that he was one of many Nazis imprisoned as part of a general round-up. Eventually he was charged with having unregistered weapons — a charge that was used selectively, because the Bavarian government knew that there were scores of thousands of weapons in that category — and with possession of foreign currencies. There had indeed been French francs in his apartment, left over from his travels, and the socialist newspapers seized on this to claim that the Nazis were in the pay of France.

Finally, the Bavarian authorities concluded that the man they were holding was not a spy and was not planning to overthrow the state with his own personal military company. When he was about to be released, Ludecke had a fascinating conversation with the chief prosecutor who had been in charge of this investigation, a man whom he described in these terms: "Kriminal-Kommissar Rupprecht was a rather gentle old man whose good manners set him apart from the rest of the police so sharply that I mistrusted him all the more at first, though he gave every sign of friendly feeling toward me."[11] As Ludecke recounted their talk, "He was conveying to me clearly enough that denunciations against me had come from Nazis as well as from our antagonists." Rupprecht put it to Ludecke this way:

> I am not permitted to tell you what is in the record, but those whom you have so warmly defended in each of our interviews have not always done the same for you. If you will take an old-timer's advice, you will think twice before you decide what to do after you are out of here.[12]

On his release, Ludecke learned that the party's administrative offices were still in Corneliusstrasse but that SA headquarters and the *Beobachter*'s editorial offices were now both at 39 Schellingstrasse, where he found Hitler, Eckart, and Rosenberg. They asked him many questions about his jail experience, and sympathized with him about his arrest. Back among those he considered comrades, Ludecke said, "I still believed that our enemies had engineered the whole thing by lodging false information with the police."[13] It still did not occur to him that some leaders of the SA had risked the party's reputation in a personal vendetta. Whether Hitler knew that Nazis had betrayed Ludecke was never clear, but the tales told him about Ludecke by Klintzsch and others kept him from using even indirect influence to protect Ludecke when he was arrested. Hitler did nothing for the man who had fought beside him at Coburg, had gone as his first emissary to Ludendorff, had been his ambassador to Mussolini. There had been no effort to supply Ludecke with a lawyer, no effort to inquire about or improve his conditions in jail, no effort to have anyone visit him during his confinement. Indeed, Hitler had awaited the outcome of the police investigation with great suspicion and concern.

In the days that followed, Hitler and Eckart both suggested to Ludecke that his own, and the party's, best interests would be served if he did not sue the government for false arrest. Hitler pointed out that the police had not prosecuted him for owning hundreds of illegal military weapons — it would be best to let the matter lie where it was. When Ludecke suggested that perhaps he should take a vacation before resuming his work for the party, Hitler and Eckart warmly endorsed the idea. "It was obvious that for the moment they would be embarrassed to have me in the public eye."[14]

Kurt Ludecke's lengthy vacation had begun in April; now, arriving at Salzburg in mid-August for the National Socialist Inter-State Congress, Ludecke was ending a trip that had taken him to Spain, Italy,

Austria, Hungary, and Austria again. On his travels he had acted as an unofficial representative of the NSDAP, observing the international political climate and talking to scores of European right-wingers who expressed varying degrees of support for the Nazi cause. Ludecke was not a man to dwell on his misfortunes. He was sure that the SA's Klintzsch had spoken against him within the party, but he could not believe that any Nazi had denounced him to the police.

From Salzburg, Hitler was going on to Linz, an important trade and transportation center a hundred miles to the northeast. As a boy, Hitler had lived in the area of this port on the Danube River, both in nearby Leonding and in Linz itself. He was nine when he moved there, and he had left Linz at the age of eighteen to make his way in Vienna. In a sense, the last time he had lived a normal life was in Linz; although he left in the months that marked the final illness and death of his mother, it was a place where he had gone to school, lived a life within a family, and tramped the countryside with his friend August Kubizek. After that had come hardship, disappointment, and bitterness in Vienna and prewar Munich, his years at the front during the war, and his singular experience as the speechmaking leader of a militant political movement.

Hitler had no official business in Linz; he simply wanted to visit again the scenes of his youth. Hermann Esser and Max Amann were accompanying him, and, interested in learning what Ludecke had seen and done in his recent travels, Hitler invited him to join them. After the first day in Linz the others left, and Kurt Ludecke, who thought of Linz as a small town despite its population of a hundred thousand, had Adolf Hitler to himself for a day in this peaceful Austrian city, at a time when Germany was entering the terminal phase of its inflationary convulsions.

"On the second day," Ludecke wrote, "Hitler and I had long talks alone."[15] Hitler described the crisis in which Germany found itself, and the opportunity that the situation presented to the Nazi Party. Ludecke recorded Hitler's view:

> The nation was poised for a drastic change; whoever pulled the first prop from under Berlin might very well succeed because all Germany would spring up to topple the Government. It was chiefly a question of finding the right moment to jump — and the right people to jump with us.

The talk shifted to the situation of the other nations of Europe, and Ludecke gave Hitler his report, based on his travels. It was agreed that Ludecke should go again to Italy: he was to talk with Mussolini, try to influence the Italian press in favor of the NSDAP, lobby for the Nazis in all influential circles, and try to raise funds for the party.

That night we decided to celebrate the new venture in advance. Linz was only a little town, but it was German, which is to say that it boasted the usual quota of beer-gardens and restaurants. To the largest and gaudiest we made our way. . . .

The big restaurant to which he led me enclosed what seemed like acres of Linz within its walls of abominably painted panels and gilt plaster. We had scarcely sat down before his architect's eye focused on the decorations of the room.

"Baroque," he explained needlessly, pointing at the bulbous cupids and fruity garlands. "*Bad* baroque. Has it ever occurred to you that there's no such thing as merely poor baroque? The style has no middle quality; when it is not perfect, it's impossible. And, of course, the very spirit of the style, its lush intimacy, makes it dangerous to splash baroque elements over a hall of such dimensions. One might as well gild a barn. But heavens, what a magnificent place this would be for a rally! Why, in this one room alone, I could swing all Linz!"

It was a cheerful evening; Ludecke found Hitler "in a gay mood," with his face "vividly expressive. . . . Each shade of thought or feeling was instantly reflected there, an entertaining study because his mind is kaleidoscopic. He loves nothing so much as to pour out his knowledge and opinions into a friendly ear."

The next afternoon was their last in Linz; the following day Hitler would return to the turmoil in Munich, and Ludecke was to meet with the right-wing leader Julius Goemboes in Hungary before going on to his assignment in Rome. Hitler asked Ludecke to walk with him to the top of the Poestlingberg, the great landmark of the Linz area, a tall solitary peak rising from the plains. In his teens Hitler had hiked through this countryside, wearing simple clothes, but that day he was wearing his ever-present dark blue suit.

When we reached the crest, a thrilling view unrolled below us. The Danube made a great loop into the distance and back again; and as far as the eye could reach, the farms and villages lay upon the flat lowland — modest, placid and peaceful, the broad, pleasant face of ancient Germania.

We sat for a while in silence. Hitler gazed over the vast landscape with love in his eyes; this was the scene he had known in his childhood. . . . He was just a smallish man sitting there in a neat, cheap, blue-serge suit, his head bare, his eyes shining — and I realized that he was peering backward through the mists of Time, and not forward into his own future.

When he next spoke, Hitler told Ludecke some of the history of the landscape that stretched away to the horizon, but Ludecke wanted to know of Hitler's young life in this place and asked him, "How do you remember all this?"

The floodgates of his memory opened. With that broad view spread out below, he spoke of his own boyhood. . . . I saw him through his own eyes, as he searched out the significance of those early years. He told me of the dreams which had impelled him to fight his way up from poverty and nothingness; he spoke without sentimentality, as though he had reasoned the matter through and had no doubt how the story would end. . . .

Finally he said, in a voice vibrant with intensity and with a hard gleam in his eyes, "Day after day, night after night, for four years, I have been animated by the burning desire to act. Now, at last, the hour of action is near!"

I experienced something like a second conversion. The sincerity of his conviction redoubled my loyalty. In the face of every difficulty this man would lead us forward, because in his soul he believed that circumstance had laid upon his shoulders the burden of Germany's salvation.

On this peak, in broad daylight, Hitler had an audience of only one, and that audience was a man who might well have been asking himself why his Führer had sent not a single underling to breathe a word of encouragement to him during his ordeal in jail, but Kurt Ludecke was as rapt as any beer hall crowd. Together, the leader and the follower walked down the mountainside.

I felt that I would see him next time either victorious or in prison — or perhaps read some morning in Rome that he had lost his life for his ideals. . . .

When we took leave of each other that night, I still felt the glow of self-sacrifice which his words had kindled. We said an affectionate farewell.

Just as I turned away, emotionalized almost beyond speech, Hitler flung after me a final injunction so brutally practical that I jumped.

"*Fetzen Sie aus Mussolini heraus, was Sie koennen!*" "Rip out of Mussolini whatever you can!"

III

Hitler returned from Austria to a Germany that was being sucked deeper into the whirlpool of inflation. Some men who understood money were making fortunes by paying debts with depreciated marks, but few others could really comprehend what was happening. The theatrical director Berthold Viertel had a smash hit running in Berlin, a production of *The Merchant of Venice*, with Fritz Kortner as Shylock and modern sets designed by two students from the Bauhaus. Night after night the theater was sold out, and box office receipts poured in, but the value of the previous night's stacks of brown thousand-mark notes had evaporated so much by dawn, said Salka Viertel, the director's wife, that they could "see in the morning paper that we were just as broke as ever."[16]

Those who had foreign currencies were living like kings. The American literary critic Malcolm Cowley visited Matthew Josephson, who with his friend Harold Loeb was publishing their magazine *Broom* in Germany because it was cheaper to produce it there and mail it to its English-speaking readership. Cowley found that

> for a salary of a hundred dollars a month in American currency, Josephson lived in a duplex apartment with two maids, riding lessons for his wife, dinners only in the most expensive restaurants, tips to the orchestra, pictures collected, charities to struggling German writers — it was an insane life for foreigners in Berlin.[17]

The mark kept weakening. An English girl in Cologne who was interested in taking singing lessons found that the leading soprano of the city's opera was eager to give her lessons for one British sixpence for each session. When the girl said that she would feel more comfortable in doubling the price and paying a shilling each time, the desperate opera star burst into tears of gratitude.[18] As the daily slide of the mark accelerated, thousands of city shops began a sideline as *bureaux de change*, offering the highest rates of exchange in hopes of acquiring even small amounts of the foreign currencies carried by tourists and foreign businessmen. For many a tobacconist or barber, just one such transaction might leave him in possession of foreign money that was worth more than a week's receipts of marks from his regular business. Stopping at a city in the Ruhr, an English traveler went into one of these places and asked for change in marks for a pound note, which was then worth just under five American dollars. The German proprietor was so thrilled at the prospect of getting his hands on an English pound, so certain that he could not lose on the transaction, that he pointed to his stacks of German marks of all denominations and told the visitor that he was welcome to take as many marks as he could carry out of the shop.[19]

In this swiftly deteriorating environment, in which it would soon be possible to buy a row of houses on a fashionable street in Berlin for fifty dollars, the views of Adolf Hitler sounded no wilder than the facts being reported in the morning papers. Everyone in Germany felt that something had to be done; as usual, Hitler was right there with his solution. Soon after his return to Munich from Salzburg, he had his first interview with an American newspaper, New York's *World*. Hitler referred to the chaos in Germany, and added:

> Germany's hope lies in a Fascist dictatorship, and she is going to get it. . . .
> What Germany needs is a revolution — not reform. The printing presses must stop; officialdom must be reduced to a minimum. This can only be effected by a Government not bound by republican slogans. This Government must rule by force.[20]

The inflationary madness continued. As the increasingly valueless marks turned out by the Reichsbank flooded the nation, anything of intrinsic value gave its possessor hitherto undreamed-of leverage. Working at a book publishing house in Munich, the gifted young liberal Franz Schoenberner, future editor of Munich's famous satirical political weekly magazine *Simplicissimus*, offered an example from his own experience.

> The smaller family fortunes invested in the safest securities, such as state bonds or mortgages, melted away like snow. But, on the other hand, friends of mine, finding among all sorts of rubbish in the attic the old, partly golden denture of their long since deceased grandmother, lived from this windfall for many weeks in a fashionable hotel.[21]

Those who needed money, and had something to sell, sold it — heirlooms, furniture, rugs, the family silver — and soon found that the money they were paid left them paupers again. Many had no jobs and nothing to sell: a man in Berlin who was about to buy a box of matches glanced at the banknote he was paying with, and saw on it, in a girl's handwriting, "For these . . . marks I sold my virtue."[22] Some who understood the worthlessness of money began to live by barter; certain theaters charged two eggs as the price of admission to the cheapest seats, with the best seats going for several ounces of butter. A number of cities and industries began issuing their own scrip, some of it redeemable for specific items, such as a pair of shoes, which could be worn or traded for other necessary articles.[23]

The vast majority of Germans, however, clung to the habit of working for wages. Hitler's socialist critic Konrad Heiden described these dismal paydays.

> On Friday afternoons in 1923, long lines of manual and white-collar workers waited outside the pay-windows of the big German factories, department stores, banks, offices: dead-tired working-men in grimy shirts open at the neck; gentlemen in shiny blue suits, saved from before the war, in mended white collars, too big for their shrunken necks; young girls, some with the new bobbed heads; young men in puttees and gray jackets, from which the tailor had removed the red seams and regimentals. . . .
>
> They all stood in lines outside the pay-windows, staring impatiently at the electric wall clock, slowly advancing until at last they reached the window and received a bag full of paper notes. According to the figures inscribed on them, the paper notes amounted to seven hundred thousand or five hundred million, or three hundred and eighty billion, or eighteen trillion marks. . . .
>
> With their bags the people moved quickly to the doors, all in haste, the younger ones running. They dashed to the nearest food store, where a line had already formed. Again they moved slowly, oh, how slowly, forward. When you reached the store, a pound of sugar might have been obtainable for two millions; but, by the time you came to the counter, all you could get for two millions was half a pound, and the saleswoman said that the dollar had just gone up again. With the millions or billions you bought sardines, sausages, sugar, perhaps even a little butter, but as a rule the cheaper margarine.[24]

With the mark dropping so much daily, employers who had begun to pay employees once a day, giving them time off to scramble to stores before their pay lost more value, found it necessary to pay them twice a day. It began to take so many bills to pay even a laborer half a day's wages that workingmen lined up with wheelbarrows, into which the packages of marks were dumped.

The handling of money became a physical problem, attended by any number of bizarre contrasts and ironies. Banks advertised for bookkeepers who were "good with zeros."[25] Even in the world of meticulous German bookkeeping, the need to push the paper money through the banks to the clamoring public necessitated drastic measures; tellers kept scales beside them and paid out stacks of bills by their weight, because there were too many to count individually. When the expedient was taken of issuing bills printed on only one side, clerks started using them for scratch paper, because they were cheaper than the pads offered in stationery stores. It required a load of paper to do any kind of shopping; Otto Strasser said, "Baskets were used now instead of wallets."[26] The story was told of a woman who took a wicker basket full of marks to buy some food; putting her basket down while waiting in line to make her purchase, she turned her back on her supply of marks. When she looked again, the marks had been dumped on the ground, and the basket stolen.[27]

Although aspects of the inflation had a zany quality, this march to monetary nothingness was a nationwide tragedy. There was poverty itself, accompanied by hunger and disease, but even for those who still had food and clothing and shelter, the sense of helplessness and impending personal disaster drove people beyond their psychological limits. There were hundreds of suicides in Munich. Irrational acts abounded. George Grosz had this to say about his section of Berlin:

> Barbarism prevailed. The streets became dangerous. . . . We kept ducking in and out of doorways because restless people, unable to remain in their houses, would go up on the rooftops and shoot indiscriminately at anything they saw. Once, when one of these snipers was caught and faced with a man he had shot in the arm, his only explanation was, "But I thought it was a big pigeon."[28]

There were those who never understood any part of what was happening to them. Millions of silent domestic horror stories were captured by Hans Fallada in his novel *Little Man, What Now?* Fallada, who lived through it all, portrayed a conversation between a young couple named Pinneberg and a widow who for some years had taken in lodgers to make ends meet. The widow had been crying.

> "Young people," she said, "before the war we had a comfortable fifty thousand marks. And now the money is all gone. How can money go?" she asked anxiously. "An old woman can't spend all that?"
> "The inflation," Pinneberg made the mild suggestion.
> "It can't all be gone," said the old woman, unheeding. "I sit

here and add. I've always put everything down. I sit and add. There it stands: a pound of butter, three thousand marks. Can a pound of butter cost three thousand marks?"

"In the inflation," began Bunny on her own account.

"I will tell you. I know now that my money was stolen. Someone who lodged here stole it. I sit and wonder who it was. But I cannot remember names, and so many have lived here since the war. I sit and rack my brains. His name will come back to me. He must have been very clever to falsify my accounts without my noticing. He changed three into three thousand, and I never noticed."

Bunny looked despairingly at Pinneberg. Pinneberg did not look up. . . .

"But it was the depreciation of money," Bunny said in a fresh attempt.

"He robbed me," said the old woman. The bright tears trickled from her eyes. "I will show you the books. I noticed that the figures became quite different after a while — so many noughts."[29]

In contrast to those who were bewildered, or those who understood what was happening but viewed it as they would an act of nature, an earthquake over which they had no control, other Germans were calling for action. Protest marches began to be seen in the cities of Germany, calling on the government for help. A witness to this phase of Germany's crisis was a twenty-six-year-old writer, Erich Paul Remark, a veteran of trench warfare; five years into the future, under the pen name Erich Maria Remarque, he would rocket to fame with his international best seller, the antiwar novel *All Quiet on the Western Front.* He was a man who felt deeply the sufferings of his people and the injustices visited upon those who could not help themselves, and in his novel *The Black Obelisk* he left this picture of Germany in its hour of madness:

A protest parade is slowly pushing its way toward me from the market place. Like sea gulls fluttering before a dark cloud, the brightly clad Sunday picnickers, with their children, lunch baskets, bicycles, and colorful knickknacks, scatter before it — then it is here and blocks the street.

The parade Remarque portrayed was of disabled veterans, protesting the insufficiency of the shrinking pittance given them by the government. Heading the procession is a man with only one arm, pulling a "board on rollers" on which sits a man who has lost both arms and legs. Behind them came ranks of one-legged men on crutches. "Then follow the blind and the one-eyed. You can hear the white canes tapping the pavement." Some carry placards, one of which says, "We are Starving." Remarque comments, as the column continues to limp past,

> These are the saddest victims of the inflation. Their pensions are so worthless practically nothing can be done with them. From time to time the government grants them an increase — much too late, for on the day the increase is granted, it is already far too low.

At the end of the slow-moving column, like wraiths, come the war widows, shepherding along children, who are "thin, hungry, woebegone." Because the parade of wounded men moves so slowly,

> behind it the cars of the Sunday excursionists are piling up. It is a strange contrast — the gray, almost anonymous mass of the silent victims of war, dragging themselves along — and behind them . . . in the cars are all the colors of summer in linen and silk — full cheeks, round arms, and round faces, the latter showing some embarrassment at being caught in so disagreeable a situation. . . .
>   I follow the procession to St. Mary's. There stand two National Socialists in uniform, with a big sign: "Come to Us, Comrades! Adolf Hitler Will Help You!"[30]

IV

At the beginning of September, a parade of a different sort took place, in Nuremberg. It, too, was part of a protest against the government, but it took the form of militant nationalist pageantry that conjured up memories of a triumphant imperial Germany, and a vision of a once-again invincible German military machine.

The occasion was a right-wing patriotic celebration whose weekend-long activities marked the anniversary of the Battle of Sedan on September 1, 1870. During that great victory, German columns had inflicted upon the French the decisive defeat of the Franco-Prussian War, forcing the surrender of Napoleon III, and a large part of his army, on the following day. Now, fifty-three years later and fifty-eight months after the bitter defeat of 1918, some two hundred thousand ardent nationalists from all over Germany converged upon the ancient walled city with its medieval Gothic castle, proud old bastions, and picturesque towers. Against this backdrop of massive stone gates, turrets, gabled houses, and narrow crooked streets, workmen had erected countless banners and yards of bunting that carried the long red, white, and black stripes of the imperial colors that had waved over Germany until the close of the World War.

On Sunday, September 2, before the parade began, a crowd of 150,000 members of veterans' organizations and völkisch paramilitary units assembled for an enormous outdoor mass that was a memorial to those of the army and navy who died between 1914 and 1918. The front-page *New York Times* story of the events in Nuremberg said that the huge congregation was addressed by both a Protestant clergyman and a Catholic priest; the latter led the crowd in taking a solemn oath "never to rest" until the French and Belgians were thrown out of the Ruhr and "the work of the old German army is finished."[31] This was followed by the entire congregation singing "Ich hatt' einen Kameraden," the ballad that touched all Germans, about a soldier's loss of his friend in battle. After a silence, there was an overwhelming eruption of sound: 150,000 voices fervently singing "Deutschland über alles."

Then the parade began. The *Times* estimated that two hundred thousand were in the line of march through the city. They were wildly applauded by an immense crowd. Trumpets and drums echoed through the old squares; thousands of military boots stamped out their cadence on the cobblestone streets, and forests of banners passed through the ancient arches. Leading the parade were a thousand students, "clad in uniforms of every color of the rainbow, representing a duelling corps. . . . They dragged tremendous sabres, rattled huge swords and carried great banners."[32]

Soon after the students passed, a tremendous ovation rang out as the crowd caught sight of a marching detachment of veterans of the Franco-Prussian War. These men of 1870, now in their seventies, were wearing the bright dress uniforms of that era, with medals glittering on their chests. They represented the memory of a different Versailles, not the hated recent treaty, but the day of January 18, 1871, when Wilhelm I, King of Prussia, stood in the Hall of Mirrors of the palace of the kings of France at Versailles and read aloud the proclamation that created him German emperor, ruling over a reestablished German Empire. It was war, and success in war, that had enabled Chancellor Bismarck to unify the German kingdoms and princely states into the greatest force in Europe. German columns paraded through conquered Paris; all of the French province of Alsace, and much of Lorraine, became parts of Germany; huge reparations were required of France. For the shouting völkisch crowds in the streets of Nuremberg fifty years later, these honored old warriors were the living link to the days of Bismarck's policies of "blood and iron."

Next in the endless column pouring through the city were the organizations of veterans of 1914–1918, with thousands of men in their ranks. The official police report, noting that in the line of march were battle flags of some of the regiments that had fought during the war, said of the crowd's reaction that such public patriotic frenzy had not been seen since the German army paraded through cities on its way to the front in 1914.

Following the veterans' associations came the units of the right-wing paramilitary organizations. The SA regiments had already gone past; the *Times* report said of them, "Herr Hitler's gray shirts followed in blue-gray caps, colored armbands, carrying banners."[33] Among the units now passing were the Nazis' old Task Force allies of May Day. Bund Oberland, led by Dr. Friedrich Weber, a decorated combat soldier who was a veterinarian from Munich, had thousands of men in the line of march, many wearing the Bavarian national dress of Tyrolean hats, lederhosen, and hiking boots. Also striding by were the uniformed ranks of the Reichsflagge, the organization in which Captain Ernst Röhm was one of the two principal commanders.

The martial music and endless ranks created an overpowering sense of a resurgent Germany, able to defy its enemies. The hundreds of thousands of enthusiastic spectators jammed against the buildings were ready to believe that, in this hour of national crisis, columns of marching men held the answer: for its future, the Fatherland must bring back its military and authoritarian past. The police reports of right-wing activities usually depended for any eloquence on a simple quoting or paraphrasing of the words of Hitler and other leaders, but the police reporter at Nuremberg was clearly excited by what he saw unfolding:

> Roaring cries of *"Heil!"* swirled around the guests of honor and
> their entourage. Countless arms with waving handkerchiefs
> reached out for them; flowers and bouquets rained on them from
> all sides. It was like the jubilant outcry of hundreds of thousands
> of despairing, beaten, downtrodden human beings suddenly
> glimpsing a ray of hope, a way out of their bondage and distress.
> Many, men and women both, stood and wept.[34]

Among those on the reviewing platforms, the focus of adulation, was General Erich Ludendorff, wearing a dress uniform of dark blue with red trim and gold buttons, with Adolf Hitler beside him. The long evolution of the nationalist movement had at last produced this combination: the world-famous Prussian general who had been Germany's wartime dictator standing beside and openly endorsing the lance corporal from the trenches who was the most effective political speaker in Germany.

Despite the prominence of his position beside Ludendorff on the reviewing stand during the great parade, despite the fact that he was scheduled to make four speeches during the coming evening, Hitler was still a question mark in the minds of many right-wing leaders. On this day, Bund Oberland and the Reichsflagge were entering into an alliance with the Nazis that was known as the *Kampfbund*, or Battle League, which all three groups considered the successor organization to the past spring's ill-fated Task Force. Still remembering Hitler's failure on May Day, Oberland and the Reichsflagge were not ready to grant him control of this new coalition of paramilitary forces, and other right-wing units were declining to join.[35] By agreeing to enter the partnership as a mere equal, Hitler tacitly admitted that there was not a consensus on his leadership role among the völkisch chiefs.

As a speaker, however, Hitler still had primacy. At six that evening, in Nuremberg's Festhalle, he launched into what the *Times* called "a firebrand oration," giving a speech that cast him in the part of revolutionary leader and spokesman. Once again, he took a position so militantly committed that no position could exceed it. Before twenty-five thousand nationalists, he called for "a nationalist revolution today to restore Germany's might and greatness. We can save Germany from internal and foreign foes only through blood and sword. We need a revolution, bloodshed and a dictatorship."

This was treason: an open call for an armed insurrection against the Berlin government. In case anyone did not understand that he wanted immediate, violent, bloody change, he closed his speech with these words: "We must have a new dictatorship. We need no Parliament, no Government like the present. We cannot expect Germany's salvation from the present condition, but only through a dictatorship brought through the sword."[36]

CHAPTER

29

SCORES OF TRAINS pulled out of Nuremberg, taking the great concentration of right-wingers back to their homes throughout Germany, but the thoughts expressed there, and ideas in opposition to them, were in the minds of many millions who felt that a decisive hour was at hand. ALL GERMANY TALKS OF CIVIL WAR DANGER was the headline of a *New York Times* story by Cyril Brown; the subhead read, PRINCIPAL CITIES EXPECT EARLY CLASHES OF REDS AND REACTIONARIES.

Writing at a moment in early September when the German public was experiencing ever-wilder inflation, passionate debate over the policies to be followed by the new Stresemann government in dealing with the French occupation of the Ruhr, and the increasingly militant mobilization of the forces of both right and left, Brown said: "All Germany is buzzing today about the 'Buergerkrieg,' or civil war, in a most matter-of-fact way. My personal reports from the principal parts of Germany indicate that the war is fatalistically considered as coming, and the sooner the better."

Referring to the German Communist Party's newspaper, the *Rote Fahne,* published in Berlin, Brown reported:

> Today's *Rote Fahne*'s entire front page features an appeal to proletarians to start civil war. For this it will undoubtedly be suppressed by the Prussian government tomorrow. Meanwhile the Communist fighting organ concludes: "The time is not far off when Germany's exploited workers, wage-earners, employees, officials, peasants, shopkeepers and middle-class generally must make up their minds whether they want to fight for what they need, namely:

"First, control of production; second, confiscation of wealth; third, a revolutionary government of workers and peasants.

"Up and at them! Forward to battle, then certain victory!"[1]

This sort of language was not new to the German Communist Party. It reflected the tensions that were acted out in factories around Nuremberg, where, in the wake of the right-wing rally, Marxist workers who had been thwarted in their efforts to challenge the giant gathering now beat up and threw out of the plants those workers who were known to belong to the Nazi Party or its allies. What was interesting about this particular home-grown communist exhortation was that it was coupled in this issue with a statement by one of the most powerful figures in Moscow, Grigory Yevseyevitch Zinoviev, the president of the Communist International, or Comintern. He told the readers of *Rote Fahne* that they would soon see the "impending last act of the German tragedy in the German revolution, which will be the beginning of a European revolution."[2]

It was of course the job of the president of the Comintern to export revolution, but during September of 1923 other prominent leaders in Moscow were beginning to overcome what had been a cautious approach to calling for a nationwide armed workers' revolt in Germany. In 1919, Rosa Luxemburg had warned Karl Liebknecht and other prominent German communists against going to the barricades prematurely, and with uncertain strength; they had done so anyway, Luxemburg and Liebknecht had been brutally murdered, and the uprising crushed. The Bavarian Soviet Republic of 1919 had ended in a slaughter conducted in Munich by Freikorps columns; a workers' uprising in Essen in 1920 had been similarly crushed by Reichswehr troops. Every subsequent attempt to ignite a revolution had failed.

In Moscow the predominant conclusion drawn from these setbacks had been that, since time was perceived to be on the side of communism, the German Communist Party had no need to gamble. It should preach revolution, strengthen its numbers, enter elections, agitate and engage in strikes and confront the right, but not try to topple the Berlin government unless victory was assured. On the other hand, the various clandestine armament arrangements with the Reichswehr should not stand in the way of a successful revolution, because even better schemes could be worked out with a communist German government.

The events of 1923 had slowly nourished the thought that this might be the year of destiny. Before the occupation of the Ruhr by the

French, Leon Trotsky had said to a group of foreign correspondents, "They talk of Bolshevist propaganda, but if M. Poincaré invades the Ruhr he will be a revolutionary propagandist a thousandfold more effective than we."[3]

The French had done just what Trotsky had hoped they would; when their columns marched into the Ruhr, complete with armored cars, artillery, and airplanes flying overhead, hundreds of thousands of leftist factory workers had been as infuriated as were the Nazis. The death of their coworkers at the Krupp works in Essen had solidified their anger, not only at the French, but at the government in Berlin that had neither the will nor the strength to eject the French army from German soil. There lay the seeds of revolution. Many a worker came to the conclusion that the government was spineless: what was needed was a shift to the left, to the far left, to an authoritarian communist regime, a disciplined populace, and a powerful Marxist Germany that could deal with France's army while converting France's workers to international communism.

Still cautious, despite the propaganda advantages and increase of interest in the German Communist Party that were created by the French entrance into the Ruhr, Moscow sent a team of twenty-four "civil war" specialists to Germany. They arrived in secret, and evidently restricted themselves to the role of underground observers for several months. By September, however, watching the way in which inflation was destabilizing Germany and fanning public willingness to look in almost any direction for a solution to the crisis, the leaders of the Soviet Union began to talk among themselves of a "German October."[4] This reference, sometimes worded as a "second October," was to October 1917, the climactic month of the Russian Revolution that brought the Bolsheviks to power, with Lenin installed as chairman of the Council of People's Commissars. The Soviet leadership and German Communist Party leaders found themselves in the same position that had been enunciated by Adolf Hitler to Kurt Ludecke in Linz: "The nation was poised for a drastic change; whoever pulled the first prop out from under Berlin might very well succeed, because all Germany would spring up to topple the government."[5]

The signal for the real change in the Russian commitment to creating a communist revolution in Germany came with the clandestine arrival in Berlin of "Rose," the code name for Alexis Skoblevsky, one of the early Red Army generals who had served in the civil war against the forces of the White Russians. An underground general staff of German communists was rapidly assembled. A command structure for the revolution was set up which duplicated the Reichswehr's division of Germany into seven military districts; a communist regional military-political commander was assigned to be the revolutionary warfare opposite number, and future opponent, of the Reichswehr general commanding each district. Each of these shadow generals was a German but had as his adviser a Russian military officer. The same guerrilla warfare duplication of the Reichswehr command structure was copied on the lower levels of the military districts and subdistricts. Special units were created: one was known as T, for *Terror*, and Z, for *Zersetzung*, infiltration and subversion. There was also WUMBA, the acronym for the German words for Office for the Procurement of Weapons and Ammunition.

Much of General Skoblevsky's underground army was funded by American dollars, sent into Germany from Moscow and, in the maelstrom of inflation, capable of giving the German Communist Party enormous buying power. The dollars arrived from Moscow in the diplomatic pouch sent to the Soviet embassy in Berlin and were distributed by a man who was nominally a press attaché in the embassy, but was in fact the agent in Germany of the Comintern's Department for International Liaison.[6]

The nationwide strategy called for the armed Proletarian Hundreds to go into action as soon as the signal was given. They were already stealing dynamite to fashion homemade bombs and grenades and had lists of the secret locations of right-wing arms caches, which they intended to raid in the first hours of the revolution. The plan envisaged action all over Germany, with two exceptions. The first exception was to avoid an armed confrontation within Bavaria, where the SA and other nationalist-racist paramilitary units were so strong, and simply to seal off Bavaria and prevent the völkisch forces from coming to the aid of their allies elsewhere in Germany. The second was the Ruhr, where the workers were to form columns and march out of the French-occupied territory; the objective was not to fight the French army, but to destroy the forces of the Berlin government. Indeed, the crucial battle was expected to be for Berlin itself, and the plan called for all available units from southwestern and central Germany to converge on the nation's capital as soon as they had secured their own areas.[7]

The communists had put into place a far more sophisticated and thorough plan than anything contemplated by the forces of the right. Hitler's Storm Troops and their allies in the Kampfbund were conducting their drills and maneuvers and parades, and talking about a "march on Berlin," but none of the nationalist-racist groups had a real plan of action. What the right did have, however, was a much greater number of men actually under arms, equipped and trained and in a state of discipline. The nationalist gathering in Nuremberg had proved that the right had two hundred thousand men who were willing to come at their own expense from all over the nation to show their loyalty to their cause, and it was clear that there were scores of thousands more who, in this time of economic crisis, could not afford to travel to Nuremberg, but could be counted on for loyal service in the ranks of their local paramilitary units. By contrast, the German Communist Party's own estimates of its nationwide strength totaled 294,230, including women and older men who might not be physically fit for the house-to-house fighting that was anticipated in many cities.[8]

By itself, the disparity in armed strength between the forces of the left and the right did not diminish the ardor of the revolution's more enthusiastic organizers. Millions of German workers were clearly sympathetic to the left, and the assumption in the German Communist Party and the Kremlin was that, given a stark choice in Germany's hour of crisis, several hundred thousand German workers would arm themselves and fight. In addition, there was apprehension that the forces of the right had committed themselves to an armed bid for power, possibly within the next few weeks. If that nationalist uprising occurred and was successful, the chance for a communist Germany might be put off for a generation.

The last of the leaders of the Soviet Union to overcome his skepticism about the "second October" was Joseph Stalin. The forty-three-year-old general secretary of the Communist Party had become, since Lenin had slipped into what would prove to be his terminal illness, the most powerful man in Russia. His and the Soviet Union's final endorsement of the impending uprising came with this letter to the readers of the *Rote Fahne:*

> The approaching revolution in Germany is the most important world event in our time. The victory of the revolution will have a greater importance for the proletariat of Europe and America than the victory of the Russian Revolution six years ago. The victory of the German proletariat will undoubtedly shift the center of world revolution from Moscow to Berlin. . . . From the bottom of my heart I wish the *Rote Fahne* new, decisive successes in the struggles ahead, for the conquest of power by the proletariat, for the unity and independence of a Germany about to be born.
>
> J. Stalin[9]

If this was Stalin's appraisal of the enormous significance of coming events in Germany, here was Hitler's, delivered during a speech at the Zirkus Krone in Munich on September 12:

> In a few weeks, the dice will roll. . . . What is in the making today will be greater than the World War. It will be fought out on German soil for the whole world.[10]

In the weeks that followed every kind of crisis rocked Germany — on September 30 the leaders of the Freikorps-loaded auxiliary forces known as the Black Reichswehr attempted a Putsch that was swiftly quelled by the very Reichswehr they were seeking to install in power, and the Rhineland was twice convulsed by confrontations with the French-backed separatists — but communist actions eclipsed those events.[11] By mid-October the German Communist Party had installed its members in important positions in the governments of the adjoining leftist central German states of Saxony and Thuringia, and expressions of support for an armed revolt were being heard from the worker populations of major cities elsewhere in Germany. The Moscow-endorsed date for a nationwide leftist uprising had been set for early November: on October 14, the German Communist Party's Zentrale distributed throughout Germany a proclamation summoning the nation's workers to secure arms for themselves, and to be ready for "a battle to establish a government of all working people in the Reich and abroad."[12]

These events were taking place against a background of continuing economic disintegration. There was at last on the horizon a government plan that might rescue the economy, but it had not yet been implemented, and might never be if Germany could not achieve political stability.[13] At the beginning of October, the runaway mark was quoted at 2 billion to the dollar; two weeks later, the mark had lost 92 percent of even that microscopic value, and it took 25 billion marks to equal a dollar. In Bavaria, the price of the *Völkischer Beobachter* provided a dramatic example of the accelerating rate of inflation. On October 2, a copy sold at the newsstand for 4 million marks; by October 15, the price was 20 million, and the next day it had gone to 25 million.

From his desk in Berlin, General von Seeckt was monitoring the communist activities in Saxony and Thuringia. The first of Berlin's countermoves came on October 13, when the commander of the Fourth German Military District, General Alfred Müller, issued an order banning the armed leftist Proletarian Hundreds in Saxony. The

Saxon government reacted in defiance, which sped Berlin right along to its next step: after consulting with Minister of Defense Gessler and General von Seeckt, General Müller decreed that all police forces in Saxony henceforth were to be under the immediate control and supervision of the Reichswehr.

This intensification of pressure from Berlin brought about more Saxon defiance, which the national government dealt with in an uncharacteristically firm manner. On October 20, Saxony's minister-president Erich Zeigner received an official communication from General Müller, saying, "I have been instructed to restore constitutional and orderly conditions in the Free State of Saxony with those means of enforcement . . . at my disposal."[14] In short, the Reichswehr intended to march troops in and impose martial law.

General Müller had thrown down the gauntlet for a stark confrontation with the Moscow-backed plan for a German October. The communists had expected to have another two weeks in which to ready themselves for their uprising, but now their hand was forced. If the Reichswehr could march unopposed into the self-proclaimed center of Communist Party influence and activity in Germany, then the revolution would be dead before it started.

Aware that the hour for action was upon them, communists circulated 150,000 copies of a leaflet ordering all party members and sympathizers to arm themselves by stealing weapons and digging up hidden caches. The *Rote Fahne* appeared with an exhortation from the party's leader, Heinrich Brandler. Under the headline EVERYTHING IS AT STAKE, Brandler avowed that German workers throughout the nation "[would] not allow the Saxon proletariat to be struck down."[15] Having no time to convene a meeting of leaders of councils of factory workers from throughout the nation, which had been envisioned as the final step before the revolution, Brandler hastily presented himself on October 21 at a workers' conference at Chemnitz, a city of 330,000 that was the chief manufacturing center of Saxony. This conference, while sympathetic to the communists, had not been organized by them, nor was revolution on its agenda. The 446 delegates represented the broad spectrum of Saxon labor, including 122 sent by labor unions and 140 from factory councils. There were 66 German Communist Party delegates. Some form of resistance to the looming Reichswehr "military dictatorship" was under discussion, but a higher priority had been assigned to the severe food shortage in Saxony, as well as to rising unemployment and the nationwide inflation.[16]

At the first opportunity, Brandler rose and called for the immediate declaration of a general strike. Stampeded as the communists had been by General Müller and the columns poised to march into Saxony, they had forgotten the well-known tendency of German labor to insist on working through study committees and parliamentary procedure. The workers in this assembly were incensed by the measures being taken against them by Berlin, but they were not prepared to call an immediate strike as a first step to armed revolution. The assembly voted to enter a series of negotiations that could develop a consensus for a general strike, but Brandler's appeal for instant action fell on deaf ears. The net effect was that, in the heart of the leftist German state on which the communists were pinning their hopes for revolution, a truly representative body of German workers rejected the call to go to the barricades. Brandler and the Communist Party delegation were left facing a hall full of workers who still hoped for a bloodless solution to the crisis. As the prominent German communist August Thalheimer put it, Brandler's attempt to ignite the German October at Chemnitz had resulted in a "third-class funeral."[17]

The Reichswehr regiments under General Müller started marching into Saxony within a few hours of the time that the workers had rejected the summons for an immediate general strike. For some of the embittered leftists, it was the Ruhr all over again, except that this time the invading army was German: the field-grey columns of regular army troops came across the Saxon border marching in step, with bands playing, banners flying, and weapons loaded and ready to fire. Brandler and the other Communist Party leaders had planned to mobilize the left in Saxony and Thuringia first, and to send out the nationwide order to start the revolution immediately afterward. Faced with the "third-class funeral" and the advance of hardened regular army veterans armed with live ammunition, they quickly decided that if the uprising could not be started then in the stronghold where they planned for it to begin, there should be a delay in sending out a call to other areas.

While the Zentrale held off on giving further orders for revolution, the Communist Party organization in Hamburg, apparently on its own initiative, decided to replace Saxony as the fuse that was to detonate the German October. At 2:00 A.M. on October 23, teams of communist shock troops began cutting down trees to block the highways leading into the city. Other units succeeded in blowing up some of the railway lines and cutting many telephone cables and telegraph wires in a further effort to isolate Hamburg from effective military and police reinforcement. At 5:00 A.M. a concerted series of attacks on police

416 ▪

stations began: by midmorning, seventeen of the twenty-six targeted police stations were in communist hands.[18]

This was the moment envisioned by the revolution's planners — after such initial successes achieved by small units of dedicated communist fighters, Moscow expected that the general population of workers, seeing that control could be wrested from the authorities, would flock to the Red banner and arm themselves. Then the wider and final stage of the revolutionary battle would begin.

It did not happen. Even the traditionally militant leftist Hamburg dockworkers, embroiled in a strike for higher wages and angered by the Reichswehr invasion of Saxony, failed to rally to the communist shock troops. By the end of the day, while brave and determined bands of communists continued to fire from rooftops at the armored cars that were entering the city, it was obvious that Moscow's dream of millions of German workers producing another Russian Revolution was not materializing. The Berlin government, far from being the nest of communists portrayed by the völkisch polemicists of Bavaria, was pouring its forces into Hamburg to put down the Communist Party revolt. Among those firing at the communists were men of the Reichsbanner, the armed militia of the Social Democratic Party, frequently cast in a villainous Marxist role by the right. For two more days the communists held out, in various pockets of resistance, as government reinforcements rolled in. On Thursday, October 25, the last shot was fired.[19]

The communist effort to take Germany by force was over. Defiant calls for continued militant thinking and planning for future action were heard, but Moscow soon comprehended that the German Communist Party had suffered a defeat of stupendous magnitude. The communists had been backed down and militarily defeated by the government, and abandoned or rejected by the millions who were to have produced the German October.

II

During the weeks in which the communists' plans for revolution rushed ahead to their destruction, the Berlin government was facing additional crises, including the widening split with Bavaria, while in Bavaria itself Hitler and his Kampfbund allies became increasingly militant.

By mid-September, Chancellor Stresemann had reached the conclusion that Germany must give up its policy of passive resistance to the French occupation of the Ruhr. Eight months after the French and Belgian armies had marched into Germany's industrial heartland, it was clear that the occupying powers were able to maintain their occupation forces without dislocating their economies at home. The same could not be said of Germany. There was nothing further to be gained by keeping German workingmen out of their factories in the name of a patriotic strike. Common sense dictated that the hundreds of thousands of workers in the Ruhr be taken off a dole that the government could not afford and sent back to work making products that were needed at home as well as for export in return for the hard foreign currency that Germany so desperately needed.

Stresemann let it be known that he and his cabinet were moving toward a decision that would, in effect, give the French another military victory, five years after Germany's defeat on the battlefields in the autumn of 1918. The chancellor had no doubt that his announcement, when it came, would bring down on his head the wrath of millions who, although they knew that Germany had no alternative, would nonetheless blame him for doing what had to be done.

In the time of heightened crisis that was bound to follow his announcement, Stresemann knew that he would have to rely on the army to support the authority of the state, and here, as in so many areas of German political life, the view was opaque. Although the Weimar Constitution specified that the nation's armed forces were subordinate to the nation's civilian leaders and must obey their instructions, the professional soldiers of the officers corps, almost to a man, detested the postwar government they were sworn to serve. The key figure in what the Reichswehr might or might not do was of course General von Seeckt. "The Sphinx with a monocle" had carefully nurtured the elite force of a hundred thousand men to which he was limited by the Versailles Treaty; it was he more than any other man who circumvented every Allied effort to curb Germany's postwar military strength. Having watched Seeckt's role in hiding military equipment from Allied inspection teams, Chancellor Stresemann might well have asked himself what other invisible conspiracies and plans Seeckt had on his agenda.

Earlier in September, following an official visit to the Reichswehr camp at Döberitz, twenty miles west of Berlin, Stresemann and Seeckt had spent a long evening in the officers' mess at the installation. The chancellor had been unfailingly polite and gracious to the officers who were gathered about. By contrast, Seeckt had been condescending in

418 ▪

his treatment of the chancellor, who was his superior. Sitting among his fellow officers, Seeckt appeared to enjoy this chance to remind Stresemann that, in these chaotic times, the army was all that stood between the civilian government and anarchy. When the conversation swung around to the current situation in Germany and the course the nation should take, Seeckt said coolly, "The Reichswehr stands behind you if the German chancellor goes the German way!"[20]

If this was obedience, it was certainly conditional: General von Seeckt would judge what was the "German way"; the implication was that the army would defend the republic only if he liked what he saw.

Seeckt was a larger question mark than the suspicious chancellor knew. He was, in fact, sizing up his chances of becoming Germany's leader. Seeckt had given considerable thought, as many other right-wingers had, to the idea of a directorate, in which he would play the principal role. Other possibilities were for him to become chancellor or to be the supreme figure in a military dictatorship.

On September 23, Seeckt received two delegations from the German Nationalist Party, which represented a sentiment that was right-wing but far more moderate than the radical right represented by Hitler and the Kampfbund. The nationalist delegations stated that they did not think that Gustav Stresemann was an effective chancellor, and that they hoped that Seeckt would take the position. The Sphinx with a monocle responded by saying that he would accept the chancellorship if the offer was made to him under circumstances that did not make him disloyal in accepting it. In short, he was willing to take the position normally occupied by a civilian, but he did not want to reach it in a hail of bullets.[21]

While Seeckt toyed with the idea of supreme power as he went about his business at Reichswehr headquarters in Berlin, Ludendorff, whom the right had been calling the national commander since the war's close, was biding his time in Munich. Since he had endorsed Hitler and his National Socialists at the German Day in Nuremberg, an alliance had come about that Margarethe, Ludendorff's wife, described this way:

> Our house had become the rallying-point, one could almost
> have called it the political centre of the National Socialists. It was
> like the continual coming and going in a pigeon loft. Not merely
> every day, but every hour there were conferences.
>   In order to avoid all suspicion, Ludendorff, with masterly
> acuteness, made a point of busying himself in the garden before

the eyes of everybody. He pruned the roses, watered the flowers, and sprayed the lawns, as though he were the most harmless fellow in the world, remote from any thought of political upheavals.[22]

For some time, General Ludendorff had been waiting for the wave of right-wing activity that he hoped would sweep him into power as Germany's leader. Like Hitler, Ludendorff had no use for the idea of a separate Bavaria: he wanted a strong, unified nation in which all the German states were subject to a central authority in Berlin. It was the nature of that Berlin government that he wanted changed.

This idea of a unified and authoritarian state appealed to German industrialists. When the fifty-year-old Fritz Thyssen, Germany's largest steel manufacturer, came to visit Ludendorff that autumn, the conversation developed along these lines, as recounted by the industrialist.

> I deplored the fact that there were not at that time men in Germany whom an energetic national spirit would inspire to improve the situation.
> "There is but one hope," Ludendorff said to me, "and this hope is embodied in the national groups which desire our recovery." He recommended to me in particular the Oberland League and, above all, the National Socialist party of Adolf Hitler. All these were leagues of young people and World War veterans who were resolved to fight Socialism as the cause of all disorder. Ludendorff greatly admired Hitler. "He is the only man," he said, "who has any political sense."[23]

The result of this visit was that Thyssen soon afterward gave "about 100,000 gold marks . . . to Ludendorff whom I desired to use it as best he could."[24]

Hitler was indeed aching for action, but the direction his thrust must take was still not clear to him, nor could it be. If, as he suggested might happen, Berlin marched on Bavaria, he and his SA regiments would have no choice but to fight side by side with Bavarian separatists who wanted a secession of Bavaria from Germany, a possible restoration of the Wittelsbach monarchy in the person of Crown Prince Rupprecht, and even a possible union with Austria. If the Bavarian government decided to march on Berlin, Hitler would most certainly join in that march and attempt to control it. If the Bavarian government did not march on Berlin, but decided to secede from the Reich, Hitler might be faced with a need to seize power in Bavaria, simply to keep a base for his further plans to take over the rest of the Reich at a later date.

Finally, there was the possibility that the Bavarian government, although right-wing in sympathy, might come to consider him such a thorn in its side that it would attempt to destroy him and his party. In that case, Hitler and his Storm Troops would be fighting for their very existence.

In point of fact, what lay ahead of Hitler was a strange sequence of actions that was akin to walking through a house of mirrors. With each of the contending entities watching one another so closely, Berlin, or Bavaria — or Hitler — was prone to strike at something seen in the mirror, even before the maker of the image walked down the hall. The Bavarian government was already assuming that, in Berlin, Chancellor Stresemann would soon announce the end of passive resistance in the Ruhr. That would produce all sorts of howls among the right-wing public in Bavaria, but for Minister-President von Knilling and his cabinet the chief threat came not from Berlin, or the French in the Ruhr, but from Adolf Hitler.

As the Bavarian leaders saw it, Stresemann's announcement concerning the Ruhr would guarantee that Hitler's Kampfbund allies would name him as their leader, thereby giving him control of a large and potent private army. With the Bavarian public in a ferment about the end of passive resistance, Hitler might have a real chance to start a stampede that would result in the overthrow of the Bavarian government.

To thwart that, Knilling and his ministers were discussing the enactment of emergency measures that would keep the control of public order firmly in their hands. There was much talk in government circles, and among the leaders of the more moderate political parties, about naming a *Generalstaatskommissar*, a general state commissioner. This would involve vesting the Bavarian state's executive power in one individual, who would become a virtual dictator for as long as a period of emergency was deemed to last.

On September 22, Knilling sat down with Gustav von Kahr, the stooped and swarthy former minister-president. Also present was Crown Prince Rupprecht, who had no official standing in Bavaria but was a popular figure who represented the stability of the prewar years. The talk was exploratory in nature: Kahr was considered the most suitable choice for the new position because he combined executive experience with a strong personal right-wing stance. He was a monarchist, and he was in sufficiently good graces with the völkisch movement that he could be expected to take away some of Hitler's right-wing support. No offer of the position of general commissioner was made at this meeting, but the three men parted with the understanding that Kahr was ready to serve, if asked.[25]

III

BERLIN, Sept. 24 (Associated Press). — Chancellor Stresemann announced tonight that the Government had decided to abandon passive resistance immediately and unconditionally, and had ordered resumption at once in the Ruhr and Rhineland in all lines of industry.

This decision was reached after a conference at the Chancellor's palace attended by three hundred representative spokesmen from the Ruhr and Rhineland, at which it was unanimously agreed that further opposition to the Franco-Belgian occupation was futile and that passive resistance must be abandoned.[26]

France had won the test of national wills and resources in the Ruhr. German workmen would go back to work, under the surveillance of French bayonets; the hated reparations payments would be resumed by a bankrupt nation in which food strikes were becoming daily occurrences.

In Munich, Adolf Hitler was galvanized by this further evidence of the Fatherland's impotence and humiliation. On September 25, the day after Stresemann's announcement, he went into a private conference with the half-dozen men who represented the leadership of the Kampfbund. For two and a half hours Hitler passionately portrayed his vision of vengeance against Germany's enemies, without and within. To these men who had withheld from him the leadership of the Kampfbund because of their memories of May 1, he argued that this was the moment of great opportunity for the right, and begged to be given the post of political leader of the Kampfbund.

Hitler's eloquence swept all before him: the May Day disaster was forgotten, and at least three of the leadership were in tears as they shook hands and agreed that Hitler was to lead them forward. Describing the moment, Ernst Röhm said that he, too, was crying, and that his body shook with emotion. Röhm made up his mind to resign from the Reichswehr the next day so that he could devote all his time to serving Hitler's ends.[27]

Although Lieutenant Colonel Hermann Kriebel remained the military leader of the Kampfbund, Hitler immediately began issuing commands of every kind. He ordered that the Storm Troops be put on an emergency alert. Many members of the Nazi Party still maintained ties with paramilitary organizations that did not belong to the Kampfbund; Hitler called on these man to give up those affiliations and join the Kampfbund within ten days. All who did not do this, he said, "will be considered excluded from the Party and are to return their membership cards."[28] As part of a new offensive in what he termed "the endless battles of words," Hitler announced a plan to hold fourteen mass meetings on the evening of September 27, which would be the day after Berlin's formal proclamation of the end of resistance in the Ruhr. During the course of that evening, Hitler intended to move throughout Munich, speaking to each crowd.

On September 26, against a background of unrest throughout Germany and persistent reports that Hitler's fourteen meetings might be a prelude to a Hitler-Ludendorff grab for power, Gustav von Kahr was appointed as Bavaria's general state commissioner. As he sat down at an evening meeting with Minister-President von Knilling and the Bavarian cabinet, there were many questions as to the extent of Kahr's authority and, indeed, even of the legality of creating such a position. Kahr was assured that he "would have a free hand in the exercise of the executive power," but the question remained: By what right had this supragovernmental position of Generalstaatskommissar been created?[29]

In an effort to justify the action it had already taken, the cabinet decided to declare a state of emergency, and to do so not under the Bavarian Constitution, as it had a right to do, but to invoke Article 48 of the Weimar Constitution, which was reserved to the national government for use in emergencies. With one quick step, the Bavarian government had acted in such a way that, as the *New York Times* said the next day, "The German Constitution has been declared put aside as far as Bavaria is concerned."[30]

Now that he held all governmental power in Bavaria in his hands, Gustav von Kahr issued his first order: the fourteen mass meetings announced by Adolf Hitler for the following night were prohibited.

When the news reached Hitler, he went berserk. He had hoped to maneuver the Bavarian government into a march on Berlin, in which he would be a full partner. His intention was to parlay that situation into his gaining control of all the Bavarian forces, followed by a capture of national leadership for himself and the Nazis. Instead, Hitler and his party were being treated as if they were naughty boys who must sit quietly in a corner while the real statesmen of Bavaria handled every aspect of the reaction to the German surrender in the Ruhr.

As for Kahr, Hitler at various times had called him a "high collar politician," a "feeble pre-war politician," and, somewhat inconsistently, a "pure Hun."[31] The idea that Bavaria in this hour was to be guided by a man who wanted to put Crown Prince Rupprecht on the extinct Wittelsbach throne and live in the past was maddening. As Röhm, Scheubner-Richter, and former police commissioner Ernst Pöhner spent hours trying to reason with him, Hitler screamed and shouted, insisting that there was no alternative but an immediate armed uprising to capture power in Bavaria. Only with dawn did he subside.[32]

CHAPTER

30

B<small>Y THE TIME</small> Adolf Hitler stopped his ranting and quieted down in the early morning hours of Thursday, September 27, a great deal had happened in Berlin.

The previous evening, after President Ebert and Chancellor Stresemann issued the official proclamation ending the resistance in the Ruhr, the members of Stresemann's cabinet had gone their separate ways, hoping for a good night's sleep. During the night, the news of Bavaria's unilateral actions reached Berlin. While it was still dark, Stresemann sent out the word to his cabinet to reassemble in the chancellor's library. One of the first to arrive was President Ebert. As the night turned grey, other ministers came in; several had not shaved, and one was without his necktie. Everyone was terribly agitated. Criticism of the hours-old proclamation was pouring in from rightists all over the nation, and now here was Munich, Berlin's traditional rival and postwar opponent, naming a dictator who was a Bavarian monarchist and handing him full powers under Article 48 of the national constitution, which the government of an individual state was not allowed to invoke. For months these ministers had been hearing about a possible Bavarian march on Berlin. Perhaps this was it.

During the nervous discussion around the table in the library, every reaction was that of men who felt that the Bavarian move was aimed directly at the national government. No one appeared to consider the possibility that Bavaria's right-wing government was attempting to mobilize itself against an attack from those who were even further to the right, and that the move was a domestic precaution rather than the prelude to a treasonous uprising against the national government. However, the blindness of Stresemann's cabinet to this aspect of the situation was understandable: not only was it true that most of Bavaria wanted a clean sweep of the existing government in Berlin, but the timing of Bavaria's emergency decree was bound to be considered a swift and violent reaction to the government's proclamation.

The question now in ministers' minds was one of defending the state against armed attempts at revolution. Although the minister of defense, Otto Gessler, was present at this meeting, General von Seeckt had yet to appear. All these men had lived through the Kapp Putsch of 1920, in which Freikorps units had taken and held the capital's government buildings for several days. On that occasion the Reichswehr in the Berlin area had remained in its barracks, and only a combination of Kapp's ineptitude and a general strike coordinated by the left had brought the right-wing effort to naught.

The door to the library swung open, and, perfectly attired, with every grey hair in place and his monocle firmly fixed in his left eye, General Hans von Seeckt entered the room and took his place among the flustered political leaders. President Ebert came straight to the point. "Will the army stick to us, General?"

As everyone listened intently, the commander of the Reichswehr answered, *"Die Reichswehr, Herr Reichspräsident, steht hinter mir"* — The army, Mr. President, stands behind me.[1] Once again, there was an echo of Seeckt's remark to Stresemann earlier in the month: "The Reichswehr stands behind you if the German chancellor goes the German way!"[2] Nonetheless, under the circumstances it was a pledge of loyalty to the German state and its duly constituted leaders, even though the man who made it had contempt for the liberalism they represented.

Heartened by Seeckt's evident desire to hold the nation together at this critical hour, the leaders of Germany proceeded to take measures for strengthening the government's position. Under the emergency clauses of Article 48, the executive powers of the nation were now handed to Minister of Defense Otto Gessler, but no one in the room, nor in the rest of Germany when the action became known, doubted that Germany's de facto leader, created by a stroke of the pen, was General Hans von Seeckt. The reason for giving the powers to Gessler was to place authority nominally in the hands of a civilian cabinet minister, but only General von Seeckt could effectively send orders down the chain of command.

Seeckt's new authority was far-reaching. Under Article 48 he could empower his generals, as national officials operating under an emergency decree, to override all decisions made by even the highest officials of the individual German states, such as Bavaria. General Otto von Lossow, still Reichswehr commander in Bavaria, had the authority to act as military governor in a state in which, by the national government's action, civil rights could be suspended. Additionally, the army had the right to, and would, oversee currency regulations and inspect the working conditions of laborers everywhere in Germany. It would run soup kitchens for the growing number of Germans who were hungry and set up a network of other relief activities for the millions without jobs.[3]

During the dawn conference, there remained the specific question of how to apply this national authority in dealing with Bavaria. It was understood that federal law overrode state law; the cabinet agreed that Berlin had the right to request, or to order, Bavaria to withdraw its emergency decree, no matter what basis the Bavarians claimed for its validity. That still left the question of what course of action would be the wisest and most effective to take.

The day's discussions were interrupted by a telephone call from Munich: Bavaria's Minister-President von Knilling was on the line. In his effort to explain the Bavarian action to Stresemann, Knilling said that Bavaria was in such turmoil that he and his cabinet had needed all these powers, should "one side commit a stupid act."[4] When it was put to Knilling that Berlin had the right to require Bavaria to withdraw its emergency measures, Knilling said that he would resist any such effort.

There the matter rested. Rather than pour more gasoline on the fire, Stresemann and his cabinet decided to take the view that the national emergency decree, and Munich's own measures, could coexist in Bavaria.

If there was one man whose situation had been radically changed on the morning of September 27, it was Hans von Seeckt. He had toyed with the idea of becoming Germany's leader, either as chancellor or as the key figure in a directorate that would dispense with parliamentary procedure; now, in a totally legal fashion, he had been handed the executive powers of the German state. Going to his office at Reichswehr headquarters in the Bendlerstrasse, he sat down at his desk, where his adjutant found him smiling broadly. In answer to a question as to what there was to be so happy about in the midst of the crisis, Seeckt said that he believed he could come to some sort of reasonable accommodation with the forces of the right.[5] Presumably he meant that the völkisch movement would accord the commanding general of the Reichswehr the respect and cooperation that were rigidly withheld from the socialist civilian leaders, whom the nationalists despised. As Seeckt saw it, he was on the one hand a more acceptable German leader, and on the other, he had the force to keep the radical right within bounds.

Just hours after telling his adjutant that he felt he could come to a comfortable rapprochement with the right, Seeckt had his composure shattered by more news from Bavaria. On the front page of the day's *Völkischer Beobachter*, there was an article entitled "The Dictators Stresemann-Seeckt." In even-handed fashion, the September 27 issue of the Nazi paper attacked both men. "It is hardly necessary to say," the assault on Germany's chancellor began, "that for Herr Stresemann the 'internal' enemy is the Deutschvölkische group. . . . One cannot very well expect anything else from this man . . . except the mounting of an attack on patriots."

The piece then turned on the commander of the Reichswehr, saying that the other high-ranking generals were not sufficiently impressed by the fact that "Seeckt's wife like Stresemann's is a Jewess, and influences Seeckt politically." The conclusion to be drawn, the *Beobachter* implied, was that, by invoking Article 48, the nation's chancellor and its commanding general were clamping down on the forces of the right on orders from their Jewish wives and other Jews.

"In well-informed Reichstag circles," the story went on, "it is openly claimed that the government of the Reich, on the basis of agreements with the majority parties, has already firmly determined to establish a dictatorship, presumably under the firm of Ebert-Stresemann-Seeckt." President Ebert and Chancellor Stresemann should beware of such an arrangement: "In Reichswehr circles, the really sly ones (the higher ranking officers! The Editor) assumed that Seeckt would sooner or later shove his partners aside and they are therefore making propaganda especially zealously for Seeckt's dictatorship, inside as well as outside the Reichswehr."[6]

In a sense, this blast from the Nazis' newspaper was just another attack on Berlin by a sheet that had carried endless numbers of them. It was in no way an official statement from the Bavarian government, and in essence was a footnote to the new confrontation between Munich and Berlin. Furthermore, the Nazis were much more worried about the next moves to be expected from Kahr, the Bavarian government's new dictator, than they were about any edict coming out of Berlin.

There was, however, always the matter of timing, and the ability to strike a nerve. Frau von Seeckt's father was in fact Jewish, although there was nothing to suggest that she participated in her husband's formulation of policies, and the *Beobachter* had struck close to the mark with its statement that the army's commander would like to become Germany's real ruler.[7] On top of this, Seeckt was infuriated by the suggestion that he might push aside President Ebert and Chancellor Stresemann, even though that was exactly what a number of high-ranking generals wanted him to do.[8]

The Reichswehr commander had no intention of ignoring this affront. In his eyes, the *Beobachter* article was seditious in nature and calculated to inflame public opinion against the national government. An order was sent to General von Lossow in Munich. Under Article 48, which gave the Reichswehr commander in Bavaria primacy over all the officials of the Bavarian state, Lossow was instructed to suspend publication of the Nazi Party newspaper until further notice. If the Nazis should resist, the premises of their publication were to be occupied by military force.

The Munich in which General von Lossow received this order was turning into a political madhouse. Even before the order from Seeckt was received, the situation had been pictured and interpreted in a *Chicago Tribune* story:

> Bavaria tonight proclaimed itself a dictatorship. Gustav Von Kahr brushed Field Marshall Von Ludendorff [*sic*], Herr Hittler [*sic*], Premier Von Knilling and other candidates aside and became the first Dictator in Bavaria.
>
> The Constitution has been suspended. . . . Among the laws definitely announced suspended are all those guaranteeing freedom of speech, press, assembly, telephone, telegram, secrecy of mail, secrecy and sanctity of person, dwelling and property. Habeas corpus is declared non-existent.
>
> Herr Von Kahr is vested with powers to call troops and use troops, arrest anyone he chooses, keep prisoners without trial and seize the property of any one he declares an enemy of the nation.[9]

Given this view of Kahr's authority, General von Lossow understandably felt that it would be unwise to shut down the *Völkischer Beobachter* without consulting the new general commissioner. Off he went to see Kahr, hoping that something might be worked out.

Gustav von Kahr was trying to position himself in relation to his new powers. He was being forced to ask himself what he really did want, what really was possible. The fact was that Kahr, from a family that had been advisers to the kings of Bavaria for generations, cared first and foremost about Bavaria. At this point, a march on Berlin was only a phrase to Kahr; by the same token, if he could place Crown Prince Rupprecht on a restored Wittelsbach throne, and have a respectful Berlin grant Bavaria some of its prewar autonomy, he would not care about leading Bavaria in an act of secession from the republic.

What mattered to Gustav von Kahr was that his new office, and he as the holder of it, be perceived as having real strength. Lacking a specific program, and having no assurance that Crown Prince Rupprecht would agree to become king of Bavaria even if it could be arranged, Kahr threw himself into an all-out effort to lower the level of political turbulence in Bavaria, and he did so on his own terms. Despite the shrill protests from the Nazis, he had held firm concerning the fourteen mass meetings that Hitler had wished to hold on September 27; only one meeting, of the Kampfbund as a whole, had been held, although Hitler did speak at that.

As General von Lossow was ushered in to see the new Generalstaatskommissar about the order to shut down the *Völkischer Beobachter*, he was hoping to avoid a test case of the emergency powers being claimed by both the national government and the Bavarian state. If Kahr was willing to use his own authority, however derived, to suspend the Nazi newspaper, it would prevent Lossow from having to order him to do so, or from having to do it himself.

Kahr told Lossow that he had no intention of letting Berlin direct him to shut down any Bavarian newspaper, and went on to forbid Lossow to halt publication of the *Beobachter*.[10] The irony in Kahr's position was that Kahr had not the least desire to protect the newspaper of the Nazis, whom he saw as a threat to public safety; he was refusing solely on the grounds that he felt Berlin had no right to interfere in Bavarian affairs.

Otto von Lossow suddenly had a great deal to think about. As a soldier, he had his orders from Berlin. As a Bavarian, he was sympathetic to Kahr's regional patriotism and pride. Being a sensible man, he did not want to cause an unnecessary rupture in the fragile remaining relations between Berlin and Munich. Painfully aware that he had not heard the last of this, from anyone, he took his leave of Kahr and went back to his headquarters to think some more.

II

While Munich and Berlin eyed each other warily, Adolf Hitler was traveling to yet another German Day, a right-wing patriotic celebration like the one held at Nuremberg at the beginning of September. This one, taking place on September 30, was in Bayreuth, 160 miles north of Munich.

At Bayreuth, Hitler reviewed a parade of four thousand of his Storm Troops and gave a speech to a Nazi Party meeting held in the riding hall that had trained the cavalry of the margraves of Bayreuth, but the special significance to him of the visit to this town of thirty-five thousand was not the cheering crowds and the sounds of boots on cobblestones. Bayreuth was inseparably linked with the life and work of Hitler's hero, Richard Wagner. It was there, in 1872, that Wagner had laid the cornerstone of the Festival Theatre, dedicated to the performance of his works. For the last seven years of his life, Wagner had lived there, in a house called Wahnfried: his tomb was in the garden, and fifty years after his death, members of his family still lived in the house.

If there was a mecca for Hitler, it was the home of the composer of *Tannhäuser, Lohengrin, Tristan und Isolde, Parsifal,* and the other great works of Germany's leading operatic genius. He wanted to see the rooms once occupied by the man whose glorious musical work had been accompanied by the writing of anti-Semitic speeches and essays that confirmed Hitler's belief that everything worthwhile was to be found in Wagner.

Hitler made arrangements to call on the Wagner family, a varied and brilliant group whose matriarch was Cosima Wagner, the composer's eighty-six-year-old widow. Friedelind Wagner, Cosima's young granddaughter, described the first glimpse she and her brother Wolfgang had of Hitler:

> For a long time we waited. Mother was talking to father eagerly, telling him how wonderful the young man was. Presently Wolfgang and I grew impatient and went to the front door to watch for a car coming up the drive between the borders of the chestnut trees. At last one turned in from Richard Wagner Street. We called father and mother and all of us went to greet the visitor at the front door. A young man jumped out of the car and came toward us.[11]

Friedelind was struck by his appearance: "His sharp cheekbones stuck out over hollow, pasty cheeks, and above them was a pair of unnaturally-bright blue eyes. There was a half-starved look about him, but something else too, a sort of fanatical look."[12]

The Wagners greeted him warmly, but Hitler was awkward and ill at ease as they showed him through the rooms of the house. He paused before the master's piano, which was open as if Wagner were about to return and play it, and he was impressed by the large library, with its shelves of books on many subjects and reams of musical scores. Wanting to visit Wagner's tomb by himself, Hitler stepped through the French windows at the back of the house and went down the stone steps into the garden. Going down a well-kept path and passing through a high wrought-iron gate, he took a few more steps and was at the tomb of Richard Wagner. As Friedelind's mother, Winifred Wagner, recalled it, Hitler "came back in a state of great emotion, saying, 'Out of *Parsifal* I make a religion.' "[13]

After that, the family gathered in the garden with their guest. Hitler started telling them about his plans to change Germany. Friedelind remembered the moment: "His voice took on tone and color and grew deeper and deeper until we sat like a circle of little charmed birds listening to the music although we didn't pay any attention to a word he said."[14]

For Hitler, there was yet one more call to be made. He crossed the street to the house of Houston Stewart Chamberlain, the widower who had married Wagner's daughter, Eva. Now sixty-eight, partially paralyzed and in a wheelchair, the racist author of *The Foundations of the Nineteenth Century* was born in England, the son of an admiral in the Royal Navy. Although he was raised by relatives in France, he had become increasingly attracted to everything German. In time, his admiration for things German had turned him into a writer who explained human evolution in terms of this idea: "Physically and spiritually, the Aryans stand out among all men, hence they are by right the lords of the world."[15]

Chamberlain's racism was clothed in language far different from that of Adolf Hitler. Hitler's socialist opponent Konrad Heiden saw Chamberlain's work for the racist propaganda that it was, but nonetheless felt compelled to say, concerning what else might be found in his writing: "Chamberlain was one of the most astonishing talents in the history of the German mind, a mine of knowledge and profound ideas. He combined sensitivity, gentleness, and elegance with a great intellectual stubbornness."[16] The wreck of a man with whom Hitler now sat had for a time seized the admiration of many throughout the world. In Germany, a great part of the response to his work had been pure adulation: in 1897, when *The Foundations of the Nineteenth Century* was published, Kaiser Wilhelm II invited him to his court, and thus began a friendship and a correspondence that was still in existence at the time of Hitler's visit to Bayreuth. Early in their friendship, the Kaiser wrote Chamberlain, "It was God who sent your book to the German people and you personally to me."[17]

During Hitler's visit to Chamberlain the writer may not have been able to speak, but Hitler talked to him of his dreams for Germany, and it is clear that Chamberlain listened. Back in Munich, Hitler received a letter from him. "You have ahead of you tremendous things to be achieved," Chamberlain wrote, and told Hitler that their meeting had given him a new confidence in Germany's future, and a new serenity.

> Your giving me peace of mind has a lot to do with your eye
> and the gestures of your hands. Your eye is so to speak gifted
> with hands; it catches hold of a person and holds him tight. . . .
> As for your hands, they are so expressive in their movements that
> they can compete with your eyes — Such a man is well able to
> let a poor tormented mind find peace!

Chamberlain added:

> My belief in the Germans has always been strong, although —
> I confess — it had ebbed. With one stroke, you have changed the
> state of my soul. That Germany gives birth to a Hitler in a time
> of direst need is proof of her vitality. . . .
> What a marvelous endorsement that the splendid Ludendorff
> openly supports and acknowledges your movement! I could easily
> go to sleep and have no need to wake up again.
> > May God protect you.
> > Chamberlain[18]

CHAPTER
31

O N THE DAY that Hitler was musing at Wagner's grave, there were further cracks and crumbling in Germany. In Munich, twenty thousand veterans of the Leibregiment, a prestigious infantry unit that traditionally had been the bodyguard of the kings of Bavaria, held a reunion that was in fact a monarchist demonstration. Taking the salute as the veterans marched past was Crown Prince Rupprecht. He was cheered by the paraders and spectators as king, and his young wife, a Luxembourg princess, was hailed as queen. A *New York Times* dispatch said that Rupprecht was "playing the favorite son, receptive attitude game with his ear to the ground waiting until 'the people call him.' "[1] In the meantime, throughout Bavaria, the red, gold, and black colors of the republic ceased to be flown; only the blue and white Bavarian flag was seen.

On the other side of Germany, conditions produced this special cable to the *Times*.

THE HAGUE, Sept. 30 — Great anxiety prevails in Holland regarding recent political developments in Germany and the possibility of a revolution. Detachments of Dutch troops, especially companies of cyclists, have been sent to the German frontier to be ready for emergencies, as the bands of armed and destitute Germans and desperadoes roving about the frontier increase daily, looting and robbing lonely farm houses and residences, often killing the inhabitants.

All the Red Cross authorities have also received instructions to hold themselves in readiness.[2]

In Vienna, France's solidification of its hold on the Ruhr brought out a demonstration of sixty thousand German-speaking Austrians, with right-wing paramilitary units marching and the entire crowd singing patriotic German songs and applauding speeches denouncing the French.

Also on this day, Premier Poincaré was standing before the monument to the French war dead at Bois d'Ailly, which was near some ruins that had still not been rebuilt. Far from suggesting that the German action in ending resistance might present an opportunity for an improvement in relations, France's leader snarled, "The surly proclamation of an inevitable truce is nothing; it is the execution which is everything." France would expect every centime owed her under the Versailles Treaty; Germany must resume sending both money and manufactured goods to the victor. As for the defiant sounds coming from Germany, he called them "these mildewed thunderbolts." Clearly, Poincaré believed that actions such as the seizure and exploitation of the Ruhr would break Germany's will to make future wars. He spoke of "our desire to obtain what is due us and remove forever from Germany the desire and the means to begin again her criminal enterprise."

Theatrically, the French premier closed with: "Dead of Ailly Woods! France has not yet got the victory the treaties promised her but she will get it. We have sworn it to you and we shall keep our word."[3]

Even as France's premier spoke, the French-backed separatist movement in the Rhineland was holding a rally of thirty-five thousand of its supporters, in Düsseldorf. Before the afternoon of September 30 was out, the meeting was fired on by unidentified German right-wingers, and in the ensuing violence twenty were killed and two hundred wounded. As if all that were not enough for one day in the disintegrating Germany of 1923, in the evening there began the short-lived Black Reichswehr uprising that became known as the Küstrin Putsch.[4] General von Seeckt put it down with ease, but this attempt by Freikorps veterans to seize power, even though it was intended to set the stage for a military dictatorship run by the Reichswehr, instilled in Seeckt a new and bitter skepticism concerning what could be expected from the extremists of the right.

On October 2, the day after the Küstrin Putsch was quelled, Chancellor Stresemann found that the coalition cabinet he had formed when he assumed power only six weeks earlier appeared to be collapsing. His minister of economics, Dr. Hans von Raumer, a member of Stresemann's own German People's Party, was proving unacceptable to the Social Democrats, while Dr. Rudolf Hilferding, the radical Social Democrat who was finance minister, had become equally unacceptable to Stresemann's party. Both would have to go. Stresemann's party was demanding that the German Nationalist Party — the same group that had sent two delegations to General von Seeckt stating that they considered Stresemann a failure as chancellor — be given a cabinet seat. In a midnight session that went on into the early hours of October 3, the Social Democratic members of Stresemann's coalition government backed a demand of the radical left that the state of emergency declared under Article 48 be repealed. It appeared impossible that Stresemann could win a vote of confidence from the Reichstag under these conditions, and it seemed likely that he would be turned out of office.

To the generals, this simply confirmed that parliamentary government was falling apart during the crisis, and had no relevance to Germany's overwhelming need for stability. As these soldiers saw it, Seeckt was the logical man to extend and institutionalize the army's temporary control of the nation, but if he would not do so, some other general must step forward and proclaim a full-scale military dictatorship. The name was not revealed, but a "leading officer of the defense ministry" was quoted as saying of Seeckt, "If he does not seize power now he must be removed!"[5] As far as the generals on active service were concerned, such a removal would presumably consist of an ultimatum presented to Seeckt, but there was a greater threat: a group of ultraconservative retired officers and Freikorps veterans were deciding that he was too middle-of-the-road, and that the surest way to rid the army of his restraining influence was to kill him.[6]

II

In Munich, Hitler was feeling an almost irresistible urge to strike out physically. After a day in which some Storm Troops had clashed with the police, coming off second best, Putzi Hanfstaengl spent the next hours with him, and left this account of what happened:

> I was sitting in Hitler's office with him that evening and he became so restless that he decided that Goering, Ulrich Graf, and I should accompany him on a reconnaissance trip round the city to see if there were any new developments. This was typical of him, you could never keep him off the streets. We ended up in the Hofbräuhaus about eight o'clock at night and Hitler had the idea of getting the people out of the big court yard in the back to follow us in a protest march, just for the sake of raising hell. The

beer-drinkers would have none of it and after calling us all the names under the sun and telling us to get out, started bombarding us with their heavy mugs. One whistled past my nose and shattered against the wall, spraying beer all around. . . . We had to beat a hurried retreat.[7]

If Hitler was restless, so was General Otto von Lossow. At his Munich Reichswehr headquarters, he was still trying to deal with Seeckt's order to close down the *Völkischer Beobachter* and Kahr's adamant refusal to let it happen. In addition to Lossow's Bavarian and völkisch sympathies, there was a certain duality built into the situation of any Reichswehr commander in Bavaria. Even in untroubled times, the post not only made him commander of the regular army forces stationed within the state of Bavaria, but also gave him command of all of Bavaria's armed forces — the well-armed state police, or Green Police, whose standards of training and discipline were comparable to those of the regular army, and any other militia and auxiliary forces sworn in by the state. Thus there was at least some responsibility to consult with and try to accommodate the leading officials of the state whose forces he also commanded.

Lossow was an efficient soldier, a man who was politically naïve, and an impressionable person who was surrounded by fervent right-wing supporters, many of whom believed that Bavaria must make herself independent of a liberal national government that seemed unable to run the country. Nor was he devoid of the ambition that had in varying degrees seized Ludendorff, Hitler, Kahr, and Seeckt himself. If Bavaria should emerge from the current German chaos as the force that installed a new right-wing government in Berlin, there was no reason that he, Lossow, should be regarded as a man who had stood in the way of that move. Indeed, if there was to be a shakeup, there was no reason for him to be left behind.

While Lossow was pondering these matters, on October 3 the Social Democratic delegation in the Reichstag voted against supporting an "enabling act" that would give Stresemann and his cabinet authority to move quickly and arbitrarily in setting up new regulations to combat inflation and the other economic problems plaguing the nation. Because Stresemann had in effect made action on this bill a vote of confidence, his cabinet resigned as soon as the vote was known, leaving the nation without a cabinet for the second time since Chancellor Cuno had resigned only seven weeks earlier. President Ebert asked Stresemann to form another cabinet, and he set about trying to do so. It was against this background that Lossow sent one of his staff officers to Berlin, to explain to Seeckt and Minister of Defense Gessler that Kahr was firm in his refusal to have any Bavarian newspaper shut down on orders from Berlin, and that Lossow did not want to force a confrontation with the Bavarian dictator. At first, Gessler was convinced, and the officer started back to Munich with instructions for Lossow to avoid the confrontation he feared. While the messenger was en route, Gessler and Seeckt changed their minds, and Lossow received a telephone call giving him a direct order to close down the *Beobachter* forthwith.[8] Lossow still protested to Berlin against carrying out these instructions, and on October 9 he received a letter from Seeckt:

> I have raised no objection to the right claimed by Your Excellency to examine an order, to consider whether it can be carried out with regard to local political opinion, and to mention any doubts. . . .
> The new order, however, given after the examination of these doubts, had to be carried out immediately. The responsibility for the carrying out rested solely with Your Excellency as the possessor of executive authority, and could not be shifted by informing the *Generalstaatskommissar* [Kahr] of the order. . . .
> The refusal to obey the order of the minister of defense therefore amounts to an offense against military discipline and deliberate disobedience. . . . I therefore request your Excellency to draw your own conclusions concerning your own position.[9]

This was the language in which high-ranking Reichswehr officers were told that their commander expected them to resign from the service. That was not, however, the action taken by General Otto von Lossow. He handed Seeckt's letter to Kahr, who wrote to Berlin describing his different view of the situation. Lossow, he told the Berlin government, was, under Berlin's own invocation of Article 48, an official who had such wide powers that he was now playing what was primarily a political rather than a military role.[10] Hence, his duty to consult with the Bavarian government, and to cooperate with it, meant that he was no longer simply a soldier who had an absolute obligation to follow orders.

What had seemed a simple directive from Berlin to the Reichswehr commander in Bavaria to close down a völkisch newspaper that had insulted the nation's leaders now became, with the unforeseen insubordination of Lossow, the test case in the struggle between Bavaria and the German government. Ironically, while Berlin had been unable to shut down the Nazi Party newspaper, on October 5 Kahr had closed it down for ten days because of a recruiting announcement that it had run for the "artillery regiment of the Sturmabteilung." The exhortation that led to the ban read, "Artillerymen! Prepare to open fire! Soon the command to open fire will resound! None of you must be missing!"[11] Kahr, feeling that these words might just as easily suggest Nazi cannon being hauled out of hiding places and aimed at the Bavarian government rather than being used for a march on Berlin, promptly accomplished the suppression of the *Beobachter* that had eluded the national government.

Adolf Hitler was employing some quiet diplomacy in these early October days. He knew that Kahr's ban on the *Beobachter* would be lifted on October 15; he wanted to avoid having Seeckt's ban somehow come into force as soon as the Bavarian suspension was lifted. Hitler sent Max von Scheubner-Richter to Berlin to open negotiations on this one matter, keeping it separate from the rest of the Bavaria-Berlin feud. The mysterious Balt succeeded in his sensitive mission; he returned to Munich with an understanding that, once the Bavarian ban was lifted, the federal ban would also be lifted if an apology was published.[12]

Along with the behind-the-scenes maneuver came some tough public talk. Hitler saw Kahr's dilemma: the general commissioner was finding the Bavarian right wing so taken with the idea of a march on Berlin that he felt he had to go along with it for the time being, or lose significant support. Hitler, who was ready for any kind of showdown, told a United Press reporter, "The Bavarian population will stand by me if I come into conflict with Herr von Kahr." He went on to restate his opposition to the monarchist ideals espoused by Kahr: "I am not a monarchist and will resist monarchistic ventures, for the Hohenzollerns would, like the Wittelsbachs, only evoke separatist splits. Germany must first and foremost concentrate on its own tight unification and absorb Austria into the Reich. Our party platform is one of national dictatorship."[13]

While Hitler waited to see how the fast-moving political situation would turn out for him, and for Bavaria, and for Berlin, Minister of Defense Gessler was still trying to bridge the gap that was opening. Hitler's newspaper was no longer the issue; what had to be restored was the ability of General von Seeckt to have his orders obeyed. Parallel to this was the question of whether the nation could survive if an individual state was able to defy the orders given by the national government under the powers reserved to it by the German constitution. In the wings, of course, was France, readying for further demonstrations in the Rhineland aimed at creating a separate state and eager to move in and capitalize on the chaos that was sure to ensue if Berlin and Bavaria came to an armed confrontation.

Wishing to break the stalemate, Minister of Defense Gessler decided to travel from Berlin to Bavaria, but not to Munich itself. He arranged for a meeting on October 18 in Augsburg with a high-ranking Reichswehr officer who was stationed in Bavaria, General Friedrich Freiherr Kress von Kressenstein, commander of the regular army's artillery units on duty in the Bavarian state. This officer was loyal to Berlin, yet on good terms with those of his fellow officers who wished that Bavaria would secede from the German state or march on Berlin and seize national power. Gessler told Kress von Kressenstein that an indispensable step in reducing the level of conflict between Berlin and Bavaria was for General von Lossow to stop putting the Reichswehr and the national government in an untenable position. Lossow must be made to understand that his duty to the nation required that he resign from the army, quickly and quietly. A new Reichswehr commander for Bavaria would be appointed; because the government would choose someone acceptable to the Bavarians, Kress von Kressenstein might well be the choice. Also, an effort would be made by the Berlin government to avoid giving orders that produced such a confrontation.[14]

By the time Gessler went to Augsburg, Lossow had gone beyond the stage of simply refusing, on grounds that it was politically unwise, to carry out an order to close down one newspaper. Although he was not present, he could not have failed to be aware of a meeting held at the Rheinischen Hof in Munich on October 16. It was a conference attended by representatives of the regular army stationed in Bavaria, the Bavarian State Police, and a wide range of right-wing paramilitary associations, including the Kampfbund, of which Hitler was the political leader. Indeed, with the Bavarian ban on the *Beobachter* having run its course, Hitler and his party were back on speaking terms with Kahr and the Bavarian government, although each side remained suspicious of the other.

The purpose of this meeting was nothing less than to begin organizing the details of a march on Berlin if such an attack to the north was in fact launched. It was agreed that this expeditionary force, whose backbone was to be the Reichswehr's Seventh (Bavarian) Division, would be under army control. The plan was to use as a pretext for moving north the threat of the Communist Party activity then going on in neighboring Thuringia, prior to the communists' ill-fated attempt at a national revolution. The Bavarian idea was to make a preemptive strike against the armed Proletarian Hundreds in the small adjacent state, and quickly expand it into a drive that would go all the way to Berlin.[15]

There could be no doubt that Lossow knew of this conference. As a loyal officer of the nation's army, he was duty bound to apprehend those army officers, and all other leaders of armed forces, who had met to plot against the nation's government. Failing to do so was in itself a form of treason.

III

Returning to Berlin after his meeting with General Kress von Kressenstein, Gessler reviewed the situation with Seeckt. Nothing had been heard from Lossow; there was nothing to do but wait for a reaction to Kress von Kressenstein's efforts as an intermediary.

From Berlin, and from Seeckt's desk in particular, the view of Germany looked dark, but with some light on the horizon. Seeckt hoped that Bavaria might yet come to its senses; Lossow still had the opportunity to resign rather than be dismissed from the army. In the nation's capital, Chancellor Stresemann had taken only three days to form a new cabinet, and the government was again functioning. On October 13, the Reichstag had finally passed the enabling act that gave the government authority to bypass parliamentary debate in enacting emergency measures to attack the problem of inflation, and to give relief to the nation's hungry and unemployed.

The government also established the German Mortgage Bank, the Rentenbank, and prepared to issue a new form of mark, known as the Rentenmark, whose value was to be determined by the price of gold. It was to be backed by a national mortgage on land, which was also set up in terms of a return to the gold standard. Unlike the valueless paper marks that had been shot from the government presses in a year-long blizzard, the Rentenmarks could be redeemed for gold mortgage certificates that bore interest. Here at last was a gleam of sanity in the German fiscal madhouse, but the program was not scheduled to begin until November 15.[16] It would fail if it had to start in the middle of a revolution, and in the meantime soaring inflation was making the public receptive to desperate ventures.

While Gessler and Seeckt awaited word from General Kress von Kressenstein, the Nazis seemed to be living the bizarre existence of those who continue their normal routine while living on the slope of an active volcano. Putzi Hanfstaengl was the bemused witness of Hermann Goering's activities. "Goering himself was bone lazy," he wrote. "His car would arrive hours late for an appointment, with Carin sitting in the back with some titled woman friend. Before he could be put to work, they were off again to have lunch at one of the expensive restaurants."[17] Putzi was perhaps underestimating the energy occasionally expended by Goering, who was putting the disciplined aggressive edge on the Storm Troops, but in any case he rather liked him. Nonetheless, Putzi could be exasperated by the famous wartime successor to the Red Baron.

> I remember rebuking Goering once at one of the Munich cafés for screwing a monocle into his eye and then looking round with this stupid air of superiority that the wearers of such objects usually affect.
> "Mein lieber Hermann," I told him, "this is supposed to be a working-class party and if you go round looking like a Junker we shall never attract their support." Whereupon he looked rather deflated and stuffed the glass in his pocket.[18]

Hitler, too, had his moments of behaving as if he and his party were not trying to change Germany's history at the first opportunity. On October 16, writing to Fritz Seidl, a schoolmate from his days in Linz, he said lightheartedly, "As far as my family is concerned, it consists of one wonderful German Alsatian dog. I have not managed to get any further so far."[19]

IV

At some point on October 19 or 20, General Kress von Kressenstein made his report on his effort to find a solution to the Lossow impasse. He informed Seeckt and Gessler that Kahr considered this to be one more interference by Berlin in Bavaria's affairs, and that Kahr felt that the differences between Munich and Berlin were apparently irreconcilable.[20] In the meantime, nothing had been heard from Lossow;

it was obvious that he did not intend to resign from the Reichswehr.

Seeckt and Gessler had come to the end of the line with their insubordinate Bavarian general. On October 20, President Ebert, acting in his capacity as the nation's commander in chief, dismissed Lossow from his position as commander of the Bavarian Reichswehr. The next step was to be his dismissal from the army. General Kress von Kressenstein was appointed to succeed him.[21]

In Munich, Kahr exploded. He refused to accept Berlin's authority to remove Lossow; characterizing President Ebert's action as "an invasion of the police power of Bavaria," he said he would no longer accept communications from the Ministry of Defense.[22] The Bavarian leader issued a proclamation, telling the people of Bavaria what he had done and urging their support for his stand against Berlin.[23] Not only did Kahr retain Lossow as Bavaria's military commander; on October 21, he came up with the most startling government order to be issued anywhere in Germany since the close of the war. Although the Reichswehr's Seventh Division was stationed in Bavaria and was composed largely of Bavarians, its men, like those of the other divisions of the nation's regular army, had taken an oath to uphold the German constitution and the national government. Kahr ordered that the division take a new oath of allegiance to the Bavarian state, and on October 22 every unit in the division was duly sworn in, with words that made no mention of service to the nation as a whole. As the Bavarians who agreed with Kahr saw it, they now had their own army, with no relationship to Berlin.[24]

Whatever General von Lossow's precise views and intentions may have been to this point, he enthusiastically accepted his new role as general of Bavaria's private army. He made a formal appeal to General Ludendorff and to Hitler, asking for their support of his refusal to work further with the authorities in Berlin. In an absolutely unprecedented move, using the infant medium of radio for what may have been one of the first political speeches ever carried on the air, Lossow broadcast an appeal to the German nation, asking that the public back him rather than Seeckt.[25]

This swift succession of moves landed like a salvo in Berlin. Seeckt was appalled and infuriated; he promptly issued a proclamation to the entire army, indicating his intention to see this matter through to the end. In part, his words read:

Whoever responds to the action of the Bavarian government breaks his oath to the Reich and makes himself guilty of military disobedience. I solemnly enjoin the 7th (Bavarian) Division of the Reichswehr to remain true to its oath to the Reich and to submit unconditionally to the orders of its highest military commander.[26]

In an effort to isolate Lossow and to keep a bridge to his troops in Bavaria, Seeckt took the position that only Lossow was suspended from duty, and that all other Reichswehr soldiers in Bavaria, whether they had taken a new oath or not, were still in the service of the national government. Berlin continued to pay and supply its regular army units, in the hope that everyone would come to his senses.[27]

CHAPTER

32

BAVARIA did not calm down. On October 23, the day after the doomed communist uprising began in Hamburg and Lossow's soldiers had taken their oath of loyalty to Bavaria, Hitler addressed the leaders of the Kampfbund. He made it clear that he was not only thinking of a literal march on Berlin, but that this was linked to the creation of what he called a "national dictatorship" in Bavaria. Who was to lead this dictatorship was not specified in his remarks, but unity was to be achieved by welding together the Bavarian Reichswehr units, the Bavarian State Police, and the Storm Troops and other paramilitary organizations of the Kampfbund.[1] What remained uncertain in the minds of Hitler's militant audience was whether the proclamation of a "national dictatorship" in Munich was supposed to attract the immediate allegiance of the other German states, or whether the new regime's forces would take power by making the march to Berlin through enthusiastic crowds along the way.

As Hitler's meeting progressed, it was pointed out that Munich itself must be cleansed of opposition. Hermann Goering rose and recommended that blacklists be drawn up. He specified what he expected of the Sturmabteilung and its Kampfbund allies: "The most vigorous forms of terror must be employed; anyone who creates the slightest obstruction must be shot. It is essential that the leaders decide now which individuals must be eliminated. As soon as the decree is issued at least one person must be shot immediately as an example."[2]

That was the Nazi view of how things should go. The next day General von Lossow held a meeting, and the invitation list said a great deal. Present were his Reichswehr subordinates, representatives of the Bavarian government and state police, and the leaders of seven

■ 445

prominent right-wing paramilitary organizations. As military chief of the Kampfbund, Lieutenant Colonel Hermann Kriebel was invited, but the Kampfbund's political leader, Adolf Hitler, was pointedly not asked, nor were his SA leaders.[3]

At this gathering, Lossow spoke as a man who was well aware that he had crossed the Rubicon. Instead of simply hearing of a meeting about a march to Berlin, he was now conducting one. His code name for the march was Sunrise.[4] Having broken with the Reichswehr, he did not wish to fight his former comrades and hoped that a quick bold march to Berlin would cause the collapse of the civilian government there and create the opportunity for a new right-wing government, thus closing the recently formed chasm.

To this point there was a similarity to Hitler's view regarding a march and seizure of national power. There was, however, a great difference concerning what was to happen in Bavaria. Hitler wanted a new regime, whereas Lossow saw the key figures in the march to Berlin, or any other significant Bavarian move, as coming from within the existing Bavarian governmental structure. They were Kahr, himself, and Colonel Hans Ritter von Seisser, the brilliantly able and ambitious commander of the Bavarian State Police.

Predictably, Lossow appealed for a massive and united right-wing effort in mounting the proposed march. He said flatly that the paramilitary leaders, and he included Kriebel and the SA regiments within the Kampfbund, must subordinate themselves to his control. Any units that tried to go it alone were sure to "have their necks wrung" by the forces available to Berlin; only a combined effort could succeed. He concluded his admonition and plea by saying, "We sit in the same boat."[5]

Adolf Hitler understood that he had been assigned a secondary position in Lossow's boat. Lossow was not saying that he and Kahr and Seisser were going to emerge as Germany's rulers, but he was certainly claiming primacy for this triumvirate in any Bavarian effort to seize national power. As always, Hitler desperately wanted to avoid having himself and his party submerged in a coalition, and here was a lineup in which he was not even mentioned.

Hitler immediately sought a meeting with Lossow, which took place later in the day. He had already established the most persuasive argument for himself he could produce: ordering his SA units into the streets, he gave instructions for them to be highly visible. A witness said, "All over the city the beat of drums and peals of band music could be heard. . . . As the day wore on, one saw uniformed men everywhere with Hitler's swastika on their collars."[6]

It was in these circumstances that Hitler harangued Lossow for four hours, overwhelming him with his reasons that the Nazi Party must be allowed to play a major role in coming events, no matter what they might prove to be.[7] Lossow finally could not stand the torrent of words and cut off the Hitlerian filibuster. Nonetheless, Hitler always had some influence on Lossow; earlier in the month he had won from him a conditional support of his aims, and been accorded the right to address groups of officers. Now, exercising that right, he gave a talk to the young officers and cadets from around the nation, most of them strongly rightist in their sympathies, who were taking courses at the Reichswehr's Infantry School, located in Munich. Speaking to them of the oath they had originally taken to serve the national government, he said, to great applause, "Your highest obligation under your oath to the flag, gentlemen, is to break that oath."[8]

On the surface it seemed that an uneasy working relationship had been established between Hitler and the Kampfbund, on the one hand, and the Bavarian governmental triumvirate of Kahr, Lossow, and Seisser, on the other. Everyone was now planning to head north toward Berlin, but Putzi Hanfstaengl was struck by "the atmosphere of double- and triple-cross reigning in Bavaria."[9] On October 25, just one day after Lossow had given in to Hitler's demands for a more prominent role, Hitler was back in the general's office, meeting with both Lossow and Colonel von Seisser. Hitler argued that he and not Gustav von Kahr was the coming political leader; they should dump Kahr and create a Hitler-Lossow-Seisser triumvirate.[10]

Kahr was busily returning the favor. Putzi received a tip from a newspaperman who had been told by Kahr that he had no intention of sharing any measure of power with Hitler; not long thereafter, Putzi overheard former Bavarian minister-president Count Hugo von Lerchenfeld say to the same journalist, "No, no, we shall have no use for the National Socialists, they are far too radical for our purposes."[11]

Verbal knives were also flashing within the Hitler camp. Speaking to one of General von Lossow's high-ranking colleagues, Hitler revealed this opinion of his new ally Ludendorff, whose name carried so much weight with the German public: "In politics he will not interfere with me in the slightest. . . . Did you know that Napoleon also surrounded himself with insignificant men when he was setting himself up as consul?"[12]

A different view of Ludendorff's importance was conveyed by Goering, who for the moment detached himself from the Hitler cult of personality. To a member of Lossow's staff, Goering remarked that Ludendorff was obviously the right man to lead Germany in a new regime, and that "something or other" would be created to keep Herr Hitler occupied.[13] Another observation that was less than a ringing endorsement of Hitler's fitness for national leadership came from Hermann Kriebel, who told a visitor that Hitler could not possibly be allowed to take over the nation because his head was loaded with nationalist-racist slogans and nothing else.[14]

There was another element in the Bavarian political picture: emissaries from the north. At least three groups of conspirators representing right-wing constituencies were moving around Berlin, expecting Chancellor Stresemann's efforts at governing to collapse under the weight of Germany's problems. If that occurred, the moment would be ripe to install a directorate; for such an executive group to step in and run Germany, it would need the backing of the army, and the full support of Bavaria. Indeed, there was a certain you-go-first aspect to the relationship between these conspirators and the Bavarian triumvirate. The northerners wanted Bavaria to start its march on Berlin, which they felt would give the final push to Stresemann and trigger a right-wing uprising that would make the revolution a fait accompli; the triumvirate wanted the northerners to make their move first, upon which the Bavarians would swiftly come to their support with the march on Berlin.

If it were not for the fact that much blood might run as a result of all the machinations, the arrival of the different northern conspirators in Munich could have been viewed as a comedy in which suitors narrowly missed each other as they slipped in and out of back doors. On October 28, two such men were crisscrossing Munich; each courted the triumvirate, and then, hedging his bet, went to see Ludendorff.[15]

The North German conspirator whom the triumvirate found most appealing was Friedrich Minoux, who until recently had been the principal lieutenant of the industrialist Hugo Stinnes. Minoux was convinced that the Stresemann government was about to disintegrate; he foresaw a ruling directorate that would consist of himself, General von Seeckt, General Director Henrich of the gigantic Siemens electrical engineering and manufacturing corporation, and Dr. Otto Wiedfeldt, an experienced government administrator who was ambassador to the United States.[16] The arrangement was acceptable to the triumvirate, but Minoux could give them no assurances that he had a commitment from General von Seeckt, who was the key to any transformation of the government in Berlin.

Like a good salesman, Minoux went along for a meeting with Hitler and Ludendorff, a move endorsed by Lossow and Seisser, who perhaps felt that the tension in Munich might ease a bit if everyone could get behind the same North German conspirator. As with so many of these meetings, it soon became apparent that the parties were ill matched. Minoux was no warrior; he saw a Germany in which the mark was quoted at 25 billion to the dollar, and financial stability had to be restored, above all else. Coming from an industrial background, he viewed the problem as one of management. Germany's present form of parliamentary government was inefficient and divisive: the Reichstag had to be scrapped, and the new directorate, unhampered by debate among political parties, would act by fiat in leading the nation back to economic health.

Hitler and Ludendorff had no patience with this. They were men of 1914–1918; the war had given each of them unparalleled tastes of excitement. Ludendorff was a Prussian officer; in his caste it was common to find men who believed that war was life's highest experience, and that war was an end in itself. In Hitler's psyche there was the war, the roar of thousands in a beer hall, trumpets and drums and flags and Storm Troops marching. There were enemies to be slain, a Versailles Treaty to be avenged.

And here was this businessman from Berlin who was more interested in the health of the mark than in the armed strike for power and the feel of power. Ludendorff exploded first. "You are much too economic for me!" he shouted at Minoux, and the meeting was at an end.[17]

II

During the jockeying for position, Hitler never forgot that his speeches were the fuel on which the Nazi Party ran. The tempestuous events of October, and his incessant probing for openings to power, had given him time to deliver only five speeches in the first three and a half weeks of the month, but on October 30 he filled the Zirkus Krone and gave a speech with an eve-of-battle tone that produced what were described as "jubilant cheers."[18]

The Hitler who approached the podium was feeling great pressure to act, and the audience before him, as well as the German public beyond the walls, was frantically seeking answers to the nation's problems. The housewives waiting to hear Hitler were paying more than a billion marks for a loaf of bread. Anyone wanting a loan from a bank had to pay an interest rate in excess of 90 percent. The previous day, a copy of the *Völkischer Beobachter* had cost 500 million marks; overnight, the mark had fallen so much that this day the party was forced to charge triple the price — 1.5 billion marks — for a copy of the newspaper.

In this world which had become so unreal, both financially and politically, Hitler's instinct was to keep asserting and reasserting his positions. Earlier in the day, in a desperate effort to goad Kahr into some sort of action on which he might capitalize, Hitler had withdrawn his pledge not to undertake any unilateral move. Historically, it was a moment of impending drama for Germany. The communists had made their play for power and failed. No one doubted that something big was going to happen at the other end of the political configuration.

"You cannot imagine how silent it becomes as soon as this man speaks," a young Nazi woman wrote to her family about the speeches Hitler was making. She added that the audience became so intent upon Hitler that it was as if no one could breathe.[19]

On the night of October 30, Hitler lived up to what Kurt Ludecke meant when he wrote, "He was complete master of the rhetoric of abuse."[20] Attacking the state of affairs in Germany, Hitler said, "Formerly one little mistake was all it took, and a ministry, a chancellor, had to go." Suddenly raising his voice to a shout, he added, *"Today, a Ruhr can disappear, but Stresemann remains!"* Hitler went on, at the top of his voice: *"Germany can go to ruin and Stresemann does not go!"*[21]

Still pushing for the march on Berlin, Hitler scorned the idea of "a dictatorship for Bavaria alone" if it was to be led by Kahr; it would, he said, "capitulate to Berlin in five weeks."[22]

The answer, of course, was Hitler and the Nazis.

> For me, Germany's problems will not be solved until the black-white-red swastika banner flies from the palace in Berlin. . . . There is no turning back now — we can only go forward! We all feel that the hour has come, and we will not shirk its demands, but, like the soldier in the field, we will follow the order: ready yourselves, Germans, and forward march![23]

CHAPTER

33

HITLER GAVE his speech on a Tuesday night; during the next two days, Germany experienced tensions that put pressure on the entire nation and pushed both Kahr and Hitler closer to the moment when each had to act or see his hopes vanish. On Thursday, November 1, the mark lost 60 percent of its previous day's value; it would soon take nearly a trillion marks to equal a dollar.[1] Men offering bold solutions to a frantic public had to start making good on their promises or stand discredited. At the same time that the mark was losing the last of its value, the Social Democrats, by far the largest bloc in the Reichstag, were reaching the decision to withdraw support from Chancellor Stresemann and his cabinet. That set the stage for Stresemann to be unseated; if General von Seeckt or any other potential leaders of a directorate were to make their bid for national power, no moment could be better.

In this crucial hour, Adolf Hitler was in the position of a man running frantically through a railroad station, unsure of which train he was trying to catch; even if he chose the right one, it might not have room enough for him. Gustav von Kahr had a different but equally pressing set of problems. He might be forced to march upon Berlin immediately, if he could get there, in order to produce the restoration of the Bavarian monarchy. As Kurt Ludecke put it, "Having kindled a forest fire to roast one Wittelsbach chestnut, Kahr had to hurry."[2] A few days more, and if someone else pulled the coup that gained national power, no one would care about helping him with his Wittelsbachs. If someone in Berlin was about to move, Kahr needed to find out just who it was, what his chances were, and what was in it for Bavaria.

To discover what was really in the offing, Kahr decided to send Colonel von Seisser to Berlin. Presumably Seisser could have hopped on the train without consulting Adolf Hitler, but before he left, he met with Hitler on November 1 at the home of Bund Oberland's commander, Dr. Friedrich Weber. Backed by Weber, Hitler again tried to persuade Seisser to throw in his lot with Ludendorff and himself, or, at the least, to make them full partners with the triumvirate. Weber later said he felt that Seisser and Hitler had reached an agreement, while Seisser denied it. In effect, the position remained the same: the triumvirate did not want to share power with Hitler and Ludendorff in Bavaria, nor did they want them as part of any directorate that might be established in Berlin.[3]

What was never disputed about the November 1 meeting was that, speaking of Seisser's imminent departure for Berlin, Hitler said, "Colonel, I will wait until your return, but act then and persuade the Generalstaatskommissar [Kahr] to act. It is high time. Economic pressures drive our people so that we must either act or our followers will swing to the Communists."[4]

As Seisser went off to Berlin, the radical right's demand for a dramatic move continued to mount. Wilhelm Brückner, the giant of a man who was commander of the Munich SA regiment, knew both the temper of his Storm Troops and the feelings of the young officers at the Infantry School who had enthusiastically cast their lot with the Bavarian stand against the Berlin government. Remembering what he had to report to Hitler, Brückner said:

> I had the impression that the Reichswehr officers were dissatisfied too, because the march on Berlin was being held up. They were saying: Hitler is a fraud just like the rest of them. You are not attacking. It makes no difference to us who strikes first; we are going along. And I myself told Hitler: one of these days I will not be able to hold the men back. Unless something happens now, the men will take off on you.[5]

II

While Seisser was in Berlin, the Nazis cooked up a kidnap plot in Munich. Just which combination of the party leadership had the idea was never certain, but the target was clear. On November 4, the Day of Homage to the Dead, the leaders of Bavaria, Kahr and Lossow among them, were to participate in a cornerstone-laying ceremony for the monument to be erected in the Residenz Gardens as a memorial to the men from Munich who had died during the war. Crown Prince

Rupprecht was to attend, and other prominent figures, including Ludendorff, had been invited. There was also to be a parade that would pass before these official and unofficial leaders.

The plan was to have armed Nazis seize the group of dignitaries and coerce them into a commitment to support and participate in a national revolutionary government that would then be proclaimed by Hitler. When Putzi Hanfstaengl learned of what he called "this crazy plan for capturing Prince Rupprecht and his staff," he discovered that it had been "concocted," as he put it, by two of the less visible men in Hitler's circle.[6] One was Max von Scheubner-Richter, and the other was Alfred Rosenberg, who earlier in the year had taken over the editorship of the *Völkischer Beobachter* from the ailing and somewhat disaffected Dietrich Eckart.

After finding out the first details from Rosenberg, who said that this would be a "short and painless" Putsch, with the captives being compelled to endorse and work with the Nazis, Putzi looked around for an ally to assist him in getting this thing called off.[7]

> Hermann Esser and I managed to stop that by arguing that
> any attack on Rupprecht's person would inevitably bring out the
> Reichswehr in force against us. Ludendorff and Scheubner-
> Richter had also been behind this plan, which was a good indica-
> tion of how completely out of touch they were with the situation
> in Bavaria.[8]

For whatever reasons, the attempt was not made. One explanation had it that the plan was still on until the moment that Rosenberg, on a reconnaissance just before it was to be carried out, found that exceptionally strong detachments of police were surrounding the dignitaries and that an effort to seize them would be impossible.[9] Whatever the truth of the matter, the plan was in keeping with Hitler's growing conviction that something bold must be attempted, and soon. There was an amusing footnote to the incident, one that lent credence to the existence of this kidnap plot: Ludendorff, one of the most prominent guests of honor, failed to show up. He later explained that he had been in an automobile accident.[10]

III

Colonel von Seisser came back from his meetings in Berlin empty-handed, as far as impending revolutions were concerned. Stresemann's fall might well occur within days, but everything depended on General von Seeckt; Seisser's notes of his conversation with Seeckt emphasized this sentence: "The legal way must be followed."[11]

Seisser's return was followed by a letter to Kahr from Seeckt dated November 5. The Reichswehr commander expressed great sympathy for Kahr's political conservatism: referring to the Weimar Constitution, he said, "It is in its basic principles contrary to my political thinking. I therefore understand entirely your determination to fight it." He also held out the hope that there might soon be a government in Berlin that would be more to Kahr's liking.[12]

Seeckt then turned to the subject of the forces that Kahr had stationed on Bavaria's border with Thuringia. These two paramilitary regiments, sworn in by Kahr as emergency police, were understrength, but, positioned where they were, they could give him the lead, literally and in the public mind, in any march to Berlin. They also represented an additional counterweight to any Kampfbund military adventure within Bavaria. Kahr had given command of his paramilitary force to the deadly Lieutenant Commander Hermann Ehrhardt of Freikorps fame, who had expressed his dislike for Hitler and Ludendorff.[13] Seeckt blew the whistle on any march to Berlin in these words: "I must mention here the situation in the Thuring.-Bav. border. Indiscreet actions, which must have incalculable consequences, must be avoided here. I request you to exert your full influence in this direction."

Perhaps remembering the Küstrin Putsch, Seeckt added a sweeping view of his concerns for the Reichswehr, and his fear that any kind of miscalculation by the right would lead to a situation in which men who should be on the same side — the Reichswehr and the paramilitary units of the right — would end up firing at each other. He wrote:

> It must not be placed in a position where it must fight friends
> for an essentially alien government. On the other hand, it cannot
> permit attempts by irresponsible and intrusive parties to under-
> take a change by force. It will break in this struggle if it has to
> defend the authority of the state in two directions. Then we will
> have played France's game. Then Moscow Communism will be
> offered its last chance for success.[14]

Seeckt's letter, and Seisser's report that none of the Berlin conspiracies seemed ripe for action, convinced Kahr that the situation in Berlin must be given more time to develop. One of the Berlin emissaries later said that at just this juncture Kahr agreed to serve in one of the prospective directorates if it gained national power, but the triumvirate was cautious nonetheless.[15] The Bavarian government leaders had seen the effective action recently taken by the national government against the communist uprising in Hamburg, and realized that the same fate could be in store for a premature march to the north.

As the triumvirate saw it, they could wait for Berlin, but time might be running out in Bavaria. Every right-wing group expected and wanted something big to happen. There could be no time at all left if some combination of these groups — Ehrhardt with his units on the Thuringian border, or Hitler and his Kampfbund — brought off a bold move, inside or outside Bavaria.[16] Such a unilateral action could pull all the other paramilitary units, and the public, into line, and Bavaria might have a new government within a matter of hours.

To underscore their determination to set Bavaria's political course, on the evening of November 6, Kahr, Lossow, and Seisser met with the leadership of the different militant right-wing groups. The Kampfbund was represented, but again, Hitler was not invited.

By the standards of the usually long-winded Kahr, he got right down to business. He affirmed his commitment to a right-wing regime in Berlin, to hold sway without interference from a national legislature. It was preferable that the transformation in government come about in a legal way, but it was possible that it might have to be brought about in an "atypical" manner, that is, by force. "The atypical way must be prepared. Preparations have already been made. But if the atypical way must be taken, then everyone must cooperate. It must be accomplished according to a united, sufficiently prepared and thought-out plan."[17]

Some of this talk about "preparations" was in all probability a sop to the radical right. There was no sop to the extremists, however, in what Kahr said next. If it became necessary to create a new government with armed force, he, Generalstaatskommissar von Kahr, and no one else, would give the orders for mobilization and action. If any group — no one present doubted that he meant the Kampfbund — took action on its own, it would find itself in opposition to the forces of the Bavarian state.

These warnings were repeated by both General von Lossow and Colonel von Seisser.[18] As the meeting closed, it was clear that it had been less a planning session for combined action than a warning to the paramilitary units. Seeckt had obliquely warned Kahr not to send troops out of Bavaria; now Kahr was admonishing Hitler not to make a move unless he had the triumvirate's permission to do so.

CHAPTER

34

A REPORT of the meeting was swiftly brought to Hitler, who immediately called a small conference of his own. Hitler never revealed the identities of those attending; Scheubner-Richter was almost certainly present, along with Theodor von der Pfordten, a counselor to Bavaria's highest court who had drafted a proposed new Nazi constitution for Germany.[1]

Time had finally run out for Adolf Hitler. Five days earlier, when Seisser was on his way to Berlin, Hitler had said to the state police commander, "Colonel, I will wait until your return, but act then and persuade the Generalstaatskommissar to act."[2] Seisser was back, and Kahr had acted, but the action had not been the move against Berlin that Hitler wanted; on the contrary, Kahr was holding all his options open while threatening to throttle any initiatives taken by Hitler and his Kampfbund allies. Hitler either had to accept this unofficial but real decree, which tied his hands and placed him in the position of a mere political hanger-on in Bavaria, or act to capture the power that Kahr would not share.

In the evening hours of Tuesday, November 6, Hitler and his fellow Nazis made the decision to use armed force to strike for power in Bavaria. If the triumvirate could be faced down without actual gunfire and made to issue orders for the Reichswehr and state police to cooperate, that would be fine, but it was time for a takeover.

Previously, in talking to the Kampfbund leadership, Hitler had mentioned the creation of a "national dictatorship," but now the plan was spelled out: the armed takeover, the "national revolution," would automatically create a "German national government" which would be proclaimed in Bavaria and quickly moved to Berlin. Whatever the extent of Hitler's wishful thinking — it was true, after all, that Colonel von Seisser had not stalked out of the room when Hitler tried to enlist him as an ally — he believed that the triumvirate would accept roles in his "German national government" if they were presented with a fait accompli.

Everything must be mobilized immediately. The Putsch was planned for Sunday, November 11, the fifth anniversary of the day the guns stopped firing on the Western Front and the era of Germany's humiliation began. On Saturday evening, Storm Troop columns and their Kampfbund comrades would start full-scale night maneuvers just north of Munich. In the morning they would march back through the city.[3] Munich would be waking slowly on Sunday; everything would fit an earlier statement, when Hitler said to Putzi, "Hanfstaengl, the only time to launch a putsch is over a weekend. All the people in the administration are then away from their offices and the police are only at half strength. That is the time to strike."[4]

Having reached the decision to commit his followers and allies to an all-or-nothing grab for power, Hitler called for another secret meeting the following day. By dawn, Hitler and some of the other conspirators were thinking that it might be wise to strike sooner than November 11, even though that was only four days off. At any moment, the triumvirate could make a move that might upstage them. Kahr might declare the independence of Bavaria and the restoration of the Wittelsbach monarchy; Adolf Hitler might be forgotten in an orgy of Bavarian patriotism.

It was not only the triumvirate that might on any coming day bury Hitler from public view. On November 6, a singularly powerful voice in Catholic Bavaria had been heard. The archbishop of Munich, Michael, Cardinal von Faulhaber, had written an open letter to Chancellor Stresemann, emphasizing the need for peace and reconciliation among all Germans.

> How can we hope to master the economic crisis that already is so great and the miseries of the coming winter that widespread unemployment will bring unless all decent men work together, regardless of faith, position, or party? How else can we eradicate the blind, raging hatred for our fellow Jewish citizens and other ethnic groups, a hatred that flies through the land screaming "Guilty!" but never asking proof?
>
> And how else can we avoid a civil war, which would wreak new, untold desolation and seal the ruin of our poor nation in the blood of self-inflicted wounds?[5]

At this Wednesday meeting called by Hitler, Scheubner-Richter was again present, as were Goering, Kriebel, and Weber. Despite his later statement that he was somewhere else, General Ludendorff was almost certainly there, having withdrawn everything from his bank account the previous afternoon.[6] Ernst Röhm may also have attended.[7]

By the time these key figures assembled, there was news that Kahr was going to make a speech the following evening at the Bürgerbräu-keller, the enormous beer hall across the Isar River where Hitler had spoken dozens of times. All the right-wing groups were invited; Lossow, Seisser, and many ranking officials and other prominent Bavarians would be present.

The announced purpose of this hastily arranged gathering was to demonstrate support for the triumvirate; the official information was that Kahr would speak on the policies and programs that he was implementing as general commissioner, and the meeting was to end with an endorsement of Kahr and his goals.

The Nazis were startled and troubled by the idea of this gathering. Was Kahr going to announce that Bavaria was declaring its independence? Was he going to produce Crown Prince Rupprecht and proclaim that Rupprecht was about to mount the Bavarian throne?

In fact, Gustav von Kahr had prepared a long and dull review of his own past anti-Marxist statements, combined with criticism of the government in Berlin. Nothing new was going to be put forth; the meeting was an effort to rally influential Bavarians behind the triumvirate and promote the image of men firmly in charge.[8]

The Nazis could not know any of that. If Kahr was going to say something that hurt their chances for reaching power, they intended to stop him from saying it, but beyond that, they suddenly saw the forthcoming meeting as a golden opportunity for themselves. Lossow and Seisser were sure to be seated near Kahr on the bandstand in the great dining room of the beer hall. The plan to capture these men at the dedication of the war memorial had been foiled, but here was a better chance. The Kampfbund leaders were all invited: Hitler, Goering, Rudolf Hess, and other Nazis could be within a few yards of Kahr when he started speaking. The triumvirate could be confronted and coerced, at gunpoint if necessary.

In an instant, the plan to start the Putsch on Sunday morning was changed. It would begin as Kahr spoke on the evening of Thursday, November 8. The triumvirate must be seized and held at the Bürgerbräukeller; whether they cooperated or not, the "national revolution" would be proclaimed then and there. Hitler was to be Germany's chancellor, with dictatorial powers, and Ludendorff would be named the nation's chief administrator and military leader, also with dictatorial authority. Armed men would be in place throughout Bavaria: in cooperation with defecting Reichswehr units, the SA, Bund Oberland, and other paramilitary groups would take over Munich. Similar moves were planned for Augsburg, Nuremberg, Ingolstadt, Würzburg, and Regensburg. In all these places, Kampfbund men would occupy the police headquarters, city halls, telephone exchanges, and power plants. As radio stations were captured, the airwaves would fill with proclamations of the new regime, along with propaganda supporting the leadership of Hitler and Ludendorff. Communist Party and socialist leaders would be rounded up, along with trade union officials and shop stewards.[9]

Orders were passed along in the quietest possible manner. Before those who had agreed on the overall plan parted from Hitler, they accepted his injunction that a minimum number of people know the real purpose of the movements and preparations that must be made. In many cases, this was an easy policy to carry out: virtually every SA unit in Bavaria had been through a series of mobilization drills during the past weeks; to assemble once more would tell the Storm Troops nothing new, nor would it alert the police, who had seen them turn out countless times. If messages were sent by telephone, the speakers were to assume that the lines were tapped by the police, and use language so guarded that an outsider could learn little from the conversation. At the Infantry School and in the Reichswehr units that had shown a desire to follow Hitler and Ludendorff, there was to be no mention of the Putsch until as late as possible on Thursday; even then, the word would be passed only to those soldiers who were absolutely reliable and needed to make specific preparations.[10]

In conjunction with these efforts to ensure security, there was a campaign of deception. Hitler had been scheduled to speak on Thursday evening in the town of Freising; the party officials there would continue to believe that der Führer would be with them as planned. Printing presses rolled out thousands of copies of a false document — a proclamation purportedly signed by Lossow, in which he said that an armed uprising against Berlin was a true act of patriotism. This handbill was distributed throughout Bavaria and well beyond its borders. Another proclamation was prepared, stating that Kahr and Lossow were joining Hitler in the creation of a new national regime.[11]

II

Later on Wednesday, Hitler met with Ernst Pöhner, Munich's former police commissioner whom he wanted to serve as Bavaria's new minister-president, and Wilhelm Frick, Pöhner's former deputy, who was in charge of the internal security and political surveillance section of the Munich police.[12]

Frick had continually tipped off the Nazis to any impending arrests or other moves by the police, and Hitler wanted him to take over as police commissioner. His assignment during the Putsch was to direct the police in such a way that the Nazis met no opposition. Part of the scheme was for Frick to gain control of the telephones at police headquarters and to use them not only to keep the police from interfering with the Kampfbund, but also to coordinate his moves with those of like-minded Reichswehr officers who would have gained similar control of key military telephones. If General von Lossow could be won over, then this infiltration of the Reichswehr would not be necessary, but otherwise the Reichswehr, like the police, must be misdirected and neutralized.

The mobilization of men was going smoothly; it was time to think about equipment. There were caches of weapons all over Bavaria, but the problem was to get them into Munich and the other cities, and quickly. Christian Weber, the sometime horse trader who was part of Hitler's entourage of rough beer-drinking Bavarians, was in charge of the Nazi motor pool. Trucks owned by the party sped through the alpine landscape. Rented vehicles were thrown into the transportation campaign, along with cars owned and driven by party members.[13]

Captain Ernst Röhm came up with a simpler way of acquiring rifles and machine guns. Since October 11, he had been the sole commander of a new paramilitary organization, the Reichskriegsflagge, Battle Flag of the Realm, which had split off from its less militant predecessor, the Reichsflagge, Flag of the Realm. Now Röhm marched some of his two hundred men, a fledgling Nazi named Heinrich Himmler among them, to a Reichswehr armory. There he told the man on guard that he was taking his unit on a night exercise and needed arms for them.[14] Even after the fiasco of May 1, the paramilitary organizations still had the right to draw out certain weapons that were reserved for their use. Since Röhm was asking only for weapons and no ammunition, the request aroused no suspicion among the Reichswehr soldiers on duty, and arms were issued to all of them. What the Reichswehr did not know was that thirty-two hundred boxes of ammunition were hidden downtown in the vaults of the Dresdener Bank. Röhm was ahead of the game, and thinking even further ahead; he and other paramilitary leaders were planning to open recruiting stations for their organizations, in downtown Munich, as soon as the Putsch was under way.[15]

III

The putschists were off and running with their plans, but some of the Bavarian authorities were not asleep. General von Lossow had no knowledge of the putschists' target or timetable, but this same Wednesday that Hitler was deciding in favor of the Thursday evening showdown at the Bürgerbräukeller, Lossow assembled his senior commanders at Reichswehr headquarters. In line with the warnings that had been issued to the right-wing paramilitary organizations the previous day, he laid down his policy. If there should be any attempt to wrest power from the Bavarian authorities, the Reichswehr was to suppress it. Lossow went on to mention Hitler as the man who might start just such an uprising. This policy and warning, he told his principal lieutenants, was to be communicated as an order to all officers on duty in Bavaria.[16]

Having done that, Lossow did not put the Reichswehr units on an alert status. During the day he learned of the meeting scheduled for the following night at the Bürgerbräukeller and planned to attend it, but he did not think of it as a potentially explosive occasion. Apart from that, however, he did have a private talk with Ludendorff that lasted half an hour. Since Ludendorff had not been present at the triumvirate's meeting with the militant right-wing paramilitary commanders, Lossow wanted to make certain that Ludendorff understood that any move to overthrow the Bavarian government would be opposed by armed force. "I laid out everything for him," Lossow noted. "In this meeting, 'pressure on Berlin,' and not a 'march on Berlin,' was also discussed."[17]

This meeting between two renegade generals was a dazzlingly improbable situation, but these were improbable times. Here was Germany's wartime military leader, one of the Prussian caste that laid such stress on loyalty to fellow officers, conversing with a general whom he knew was marked to be taken into custody at gunpoint within thirty hours. As for Lossow, he was a general who was guilty of insubordination, mutiny, and possibly treason.

Ludendorff departed, ever the picture of the bluff and straightforward soldier, leaving Lossow to ponder the situation. Most Reichswehr generals had become disillusioned by what they learned of Ludendorff's conduct near the end of the war and since the peace, but Lossow still shared a measure of the admiration for Ludendorff that existed among the junior officers and the enlisted men. If Ludendorff was to appear on the side of the Kampfbund during an armed confrontation with the Reichswehr, it was not certain what course those young soldiers would take.

In the meantime, there was the question of how much force each side would really have should there be a Hitler-led Putsch such as the one Lossow had warned about. If one looked at the Reichswehr and Bavarian State Police units that were actually trained, equipped for combat, and in the city, and added 250 men who might be available from among Munich's police force, the government could oppose any uprising with approximately 2,600 men, assuming that they remained loyal. Given time, substantial reinforcements could be brought in from other places, if those were not under attack.

To confront the government forces, from which they hoped to gain substantial defections, Hitler and the Kampfbund leaders were assembling four thousand men. More units existed throughout Bavaria but had been assigned to seize the other targeted cities.[18] The ranks of the Kampfbund held some Freikorps veterans and hardened survivors of the Western Front, but as a body they were not nearly as well trained and equipped as the regular army and the state police. The Kampfbund units were strongly motivated and knew that much of the population was sympathetic to any attempt to create a national dictatorship and impose drastic solutions on Germany's turmoil. In the matter of reserves, the putschists would probably have to stand or fall in Munich with the forces that began the effort.

Behind the military equation, however, lay personal feeling. For years, some members of the Reichswehr and the state police had attended Hitler's speeches. The army enlisted men stationed in Bavaria were nearly all Bavarians, as were a substantial majority of the officers. They had been required, two weeks earlier, to take an oath to Bavaria, diminishing any sense of belonging to a national army or owing allegiance to the government in Berlin. Now, in the never-never land of Bavarian politics, they were about to confront a situation in which Adolf Hitler, the legendary leader Ludendorff, and their many right-wing friends and acquaintances would ask them to take up the blazing new torch of "national revolution."

As November 8 began, Hitler stayed up long past midnight talking animatedly with some of his Kampfbund conspirators at Scheubner-Richter's apartment. Five years earlier on this date, he had been lying in a military hospital, blinded by chlorine gas, a soldier who had served from 1914 through 1918 with singular bravery and devotion. Lance Corporal Hitler, already in physical agony, had been about to be engulfed by the news of the Kiel Mutiny, the leftist revolution throughout Germany, the abdication of the Kaiser, and the surrender on the Western Front. Adolf Hitler was then a penniless Austrian who had failed in school and failed as an artist, a sallow-skinned former resident of Vienna's shelters for homeless men, one of society's castoffs who was a faceless unknown during the year he lived in Munich before the war.

Now, on November 8, 1923, in partnership with General Erich Ludendorff, and backed by the fifty-five-thousand-member National Socialist German Workers' Party that he had created from a handful of timid men, Adolf Hitler was going to try to take over Germany.

In the early hours of the morning, Hitler's followers bade him good night and went their separate ways.

CHAPTER

35

As DAYLIGHT CAME to Munich on Thursday, November 8, the city was in the grip of clammy winds. To the south, in the direction of the nearby mountains, snow was falling. Everywhere, the sky was grey.

On this crucial day, Hitler had a toothache and a pounding headache. When his Nazi comrades recommended that he get his tooth pulled immediately, Hitler answered that there was no time; there was a revolution to be started. Replying to the question of what would happen to the revolution if his toothache should fell him with a serious infection, Hitler said if that happened and he became gravely ill or died, it would simply mean that his mission on earth had ended.

As the morning began, there was not the slightest indication in Munich's streets that this was to be a memorable day. When the *Völkischer Beobachter* arrived at the newsstands, its front page contained a hint, but in a form that could well have appeared in any recent issue. There was a large black-and-white portrait of Yorck von Wartenburg, the Prussian general who withdrew his army from Napoleon's support at Tauroggen in 1812. That insubordinate action, tremendously popular among Germans, had nonetheless left him open to court-martial charges, which evaporated when Prussia followed his lead in officially allying itself against the French. Beneath Yorck's picture, the *Beobachter* had the caption "Shall we find a second General Yorck in our hour of need?" It was, Putzi Hanfstaengl noted, "a desperate ogle in von Lossow's direction."[1]

At nine o'clock, Max von Scheubner-Richter had a brief conversation with his valet, Johann Aigner, and informed him that they would be going to hear Kahr speak at the Bürgerbräukeller that evening. Both men had served in the army and were entitled to wear their uniforms on occasions when representatives of the "patriotic associations" were in the audience, but Scheubner-Richter told Aigner that they would wear civilian clothing. They would also, Scheubner-Richter said without further explanation, take notebooks and their pistols.[2]

By midmorning, the knowledge of the Putsch was still restricted to a handful of men. Captain Ernst Röhm was of course in the inner circle of plotters, although, despite what Hanfstaengl called his "shooting mentality," he had his doubts as to whether the time was right for such a fateful gamble.[3] Röhm was in a position to be uniquely helpful to the Nazis: he had sent in his resignation from the Reichswehr so that he could devote himself to Hitler's aims, but was still on terminal leave. Thus, as an officer still technically on active status, he could penetrate any army command post, pass any sentry, use any government telephone. Röhm, too, was following Hitler's practice of making everything look as if it were business as usual. Before the Putsch plot had materialized, he had arranged for a large beer party to be held that night for the Reichskriegsflagge. His men and many hundreds of their Kampfbund comrades were scheduled to have their gathering at the Löwenbräukeller, another of the Nazis' favorite beer halls, and everyone was expecting Hitler to put in an appearance after his scheduled speech in Freising. Indeed, for Röhm's purposes, there was no better way to assemble his striking force in downtown Munich than under the guise of a cheerful uniformed celebration. Among those who would be present was Heinrich Himmler, of whom Otto Strasser later remarked, "If Hitler had given him a gun and said, 'Here, Himmler, is a gun; now shoot your mother,' he would have said, 'I will do it, and be proud.' "[4]

At 10:00 A.M., Rudolf Hess was summoned to Hitler's shabby apartment. Neither man revealed what was said, but, since Hess was not to see Hitler again until evening, this was probably the time that he received an unusual order. He was to wait until an hour before Kahr's meeting began, then reserve, for the evening, a small side room in the beer hall, near the podium where Kahr was to speak.

Rudolf Hess walked away from this meeting through a city that was destined to explode, a Munich that had no idea that the detonation was only ten hours away. In one of the catacomb-like basements beneath the Capuchins' St. Anna Monastery, within the city, was a secret cache of three thousand rifles that had belonged to a postwar rightist Home Guard organization that had been disbanded. The weapons had never been turned in to the authorities. As part of Hitler's scheme, some of these rifles were to be distributed during the early evening hours to the Third Battalion of the Munich SA Regiment; even now, these Storm Troops had no idea of the existence of the arms dump under the monastery, and had not even received orders to assemble that night.[5]

During the course of the morning, the government officials involved with security took one or two measures that indicated an awareness of the tension existing between the triumvirate and the Kampfbund, but the limited nature of these steps proved that the government had no idea that a national revolution was about to be proclaimed. Soon there was to be much talk about the "word of honor" of various individuals; Hitler had once withdrawn his pledge not to attempt an armed revolt, but Kahr and others were certain that his pledge had been renewed. Whatever he thought about Hitler, Colonel von Seisser trusted Ludendorff; himself a former Reichswehr officer, the state police commander silenced suspicions of Ludendorff with a curt "General Ludendorff does not lie."[6] As had been the case with Lossow and the Reichswehr the day before, Seisser informed his senior state police officials that some sort of antigovernment action could occur, but he failed to put any units on alert.[7] This omission left Munich vulnerable to the putschists, because Seisser's well-drilled large units of the Green Police, armed with rifles and machine guns, were the force that was trained to respond first in any kind of uprising.

As for the Blue Police, Munich's city force in blue uniforms, Kahr's office did not want a heavy police presence at the Bürgerbräukeller, for fear that it would look as if the general commissioner had to be guarded from the population. The purpose of the meeting was to show that Kahr had support, and although much of the response stemmed simply from curiosity about what he intended to say, requests for additional tickets were pouring in. Some three thousand of Bavaria's most prominent citizens would be converging on the Bürgerbräu-keller, and Kahr's staff wanted to present that gilt-edged audience with the picture of a confident leader. An initial proposal to have a state police detachment of forty-five men on the premises was vetoed, and it was decided to place them as a reserve force in the headquarters of the Munich mounted police, a quarter of a mile away. Including these men and a similar reserve force of the Blue Police, as well as those on duty at two nearby police stations and the men assigned to traffic control and keeping order inside the hall, there were approximately two hundred policemen in the area.[8] It was a force much more

The influential Bavarian anti-Semitic writer Dietrich Eckart befriended the young Hitler and said of him, "There is the man of whom all the world will one day speak!" He was later honored by the Nazis with tributes such as this statue (National Archives).

Hitler with Julius Streicher, whose anti-Semitic diatribes in *Der Stürmer* furthered the Nazi philosophy (National Archives)

Although blurred, this rare photograph of the audience at an early Hitler speech offers evidence of the backing he received from the middle class. Note the number of women supporters (National Archives).

Walther Rathenau, the brilliant industrialist and statesman who was appointed Germany's foreign minister in 1922. He was assassinated five months later by right-wingers who found it intolerable for Germany to be represented on the international scene by a Jew (Suddeutscher Verlag Bilderdienst).

The Fattening of Hermann Goering

The legendary fighter pilot in 1918
(Süddeutscher Verlag Bilderdienst)

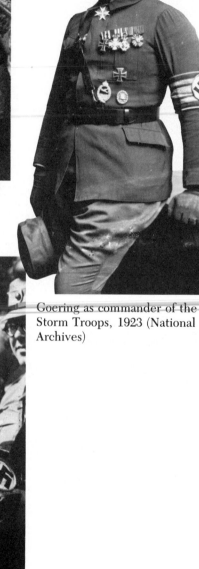

Goering as commander of the
Storm Troops, 1923 (National
Archives)

In 1928, Goering was already
the bloated figure the world
came to know after Hitler was
swept into power in 1930
(National Archives).

General Hans von Seeckt. The commander of the German army was known as "the Sphinx with a monocle."

Captain Ernst Röhm during the Beer Hall Putsch trial in early 1924. The photograph reveals his wartime wounds, including one to the bridge of his nose, which was shot away (National Archives).

Hitler in his cell at Landsberg Prison, where he began writing *Mein Kampf*
(National Archives)

Hitler on the day he left
Landsberg Prison,
December 20, 1924
(Library of Congress)

A cartoon in *Simplicissimus*, the Bavarian satirical
journal, showed Hitler hawking copies of his newly
published *Mein Kampf* in a Munich beer hall. One
of the *Bürgers* says to Hitler, "Twelve marks for
this book? Pretty expensive, my friend. You don't
happen to have any matches for sale, do you?"
(Süddeutscher Verlag Bilderdienst)

An unusual portrait conveys Hitler's sinister strength (National Archives)

than adequate for a normal gathering of this size, and woefully inadequate to counter the coup de main that Hitler planned.

II

By eleven o'clock on this raw morning, it seemed to be just another day in the modest tobacco shop run by Josef Berchtold in downtown Munich on a street named Im Tal, In the Valley. The twenty-six-year-old commander of Stosstrupp Adolf Hitler was dedicated to his 125-man strike force. With the rampant unemployment and inflation — the day's *Völkischer Beobachter* cost 5 billion marks, up from 2.5 billion three days earlier — jobless men of the Stosstrupp were always hanging around. One of them described Berchtold's establishment:

> The narrow store was more like a barracks. . . . Coats and pants were tried on, boots greased, steel helmets painted. . . .
> Josef Berchtold instead of selling his wares passed out cigarettes and tobacco to the chronically broke Stosstrupp men or stood in a corner composing [training] programs and orders.[9]

As Berchtold told it, his unit was indeed the Führer's special instrument.

> Hitler had his own method of attaching each and every man to himself. He would appear unannounced . . . on a drill night, and after a word or two with me, he would address the men in the most comradely way possible. Then he'd inspect the Company, but not so much like an officer as like a friend. He would shake each man's hand, and look him squarely in the eyes. It was this glance, more than anything, which made every trooper Hitler's man to the death![10]

This morning, when there were no more than the usual number of brawny young men on hand killing time, a messenger from Hitler suddenly appeared. Lieutenant Berchtold was to come immediately; the Führer wished to speak to him.

At about eleven-thirty, Putzi Hanfstaengl was sitting in the whitewashed office of Alfred Rosenberg at the *Beobachter*, discussing the possible effects of the morning edition's picture of Yorck von Wartenburg and the thinly disguised appeal to General von Lossow to throw in his lot with the Kampfbund. Remembering the scene as he looked over at Rosenberg, Putzi wrote:

> His desk was diagonally across the corner of the room, on it the pistol he always displayed. We could hear Hitler stomping up and down the corridor and heels clicking as he called out, "Where is Captain Goering?" It was all very military. Then he burst into our room, pallid with excitement, trench-coat tightly belted and carrying his riding whip. We both stood up. "Swear you will not mention this to a living soul," he said in a tone of suppressed urgency. "The hour has come. Tonight we act."

Hitler then told Rosenberg and Hanfstaengl that they were to be "part of my immediate escort. Rendez-vous outside the Bürgerbräu Keller at seven o'clock. Bring your pistols."[11] Looking down, Hitler saw the big picture of Yorck von Wartenburg on the front page of the newspaper. "After casting an approving glance at the copy on the table, Hitler said to me, as he turned to leave: 'I shall rely on you to look after the interests of the foreign press.' "[12]

Going out to the street, Putzi realized that the moment had come when there might be blood on the pavingstones of Munich.

> My first thought was to arrange for my wife, who had just become pregnant again, and my two-and-a-half-year-old son, Egon, to leave Munich. Walking quickly back to my flat in the Gentzstrasse, which I still retained as a pied-à-terre, I told them to pack up and go that afternoon to Uffing [Hanfstaengl's house in the country].[13]

Then Hanfstaengl turned his attention to the foreign correspondents who, in his words, "had come flocking to Munich in the expectation of exciting events." His task was to inform them "that they must under no circumstances fail to be at the Bürgerbräu Keller meeting that evening, although I could not tell them why."[14] It was an interesting group that had descended on Munich: Dorothy Thompson, the gifted thirty-year-old American freelance journalist; H. R. Knickerbocker of the *Baltimore Sun*, who was the best known of the American correspondents regularly covering Europe; Leo Negrelli of Rome's *Corriere Italiano*; Lincoln Eyre of the *New York Herald*; Larry Rue of the *Chicago Tribune*, who was not only a reporter but a skillful aviator who flew himself directly to the scene of fast-breaking stories all over Europe.[15] Either face to face, or by leaving notes at the hotels of these and other reporters, Putzi conveyed his message: Meet me outside the Bürgerbräukeller at seven this evening.

III

As Hanfstaengl was tracking down foreign correspondents, Hitler and Goering were holding a secret meeting at SA headquarters at Schellingstrasse. Paula Schleier, a young office worker at the *Völkischer Beobachter*, in the same building, found the atmosphere "electrifying, terrifyingly tense."[16]

Among those closeted with Hitler and Goering were Hermann Kriebel, military leader of the Kampfbund, Friedrich Weber of Bund Oberland, and the ever-conspiratorial Max von Scheubner-Richter. In light of Ludendorff's later claim that he had no idea that anything was going to happen on November 8, it is interesting to note that his stepson Heinz Pernet, who lived in his house, was at the meeting.

The group was completed by the arrival of a former Freikorps leader whose military reputation was second only to that of the legendary Lieutenant Commander Ehrhardt. First Lieutenant Gerhard Rossbach had been released from a federal prison some months earlier, when the prosecutors in Berlin were unable to find enough hard evidence to try him on charges of treason. A daring and efficient organizer and campaigner, this cheerful, open-faced, thirty-year-old hero of Germany's right-wing youth was the homosexual who later seduced Ernst Röhm. Arriving in Munich during the past summer, he had found that Edmund Heines, his military deputy and lover, who was also destined to become one of Röhm's sexual partners, had thrown in his lot with Hitler, taking with him the Bavarian Rossbach-Organization, which was now the SA Battalion Rossbach.[17]

Eager to strike a blow at Berlin, but unwilling to subordinate himself to Hitler, Rossbach had formed an alliance with Ludendorff. The two of them, working with Heinz Pernet, had won the allegiance of nearly a third of the 350 officer students and officer candidates at the Reichswehr Infantry School. Just four days earlier, on the day, Ludendorff said, an automobile accident caused him to miss the memorial service, he had entertained a large group of these disaffected young soldiers at his house. Ludendorff would have been happy to claim that the evening was a comradely gathering of young men who enjoyed hearing an old general tell of his experiences, but in fact Germany's wartime leader had used the occasion to put these already receptive infantrymen in the frame of mind to participate in a Putsch when it came.

Now the day of the Putsch was here. As they sat at this council of war with Hitler and the Kampfbund leaders, Rossbach and Pernet had commitments to act from twenty officers and eighty officer candidates, and their well-founded belief was that scores of the classmates of these men would turn out beside them when the signal was given. A man who had marched units to the Baltic and back could be counted on to attend to a few details: Rossbach had supplied the ringleaders at the Infantry School with swastika flags and hundreds of swastika armbands, which they were concealing until they received a message from the Bürgerbräukeller.[18]

The conspirators next decided on the core of the mobilization plan for the evening. Once again, Hitler was willing to risk waiting until the last instant rather than show his hand a moment before it was necessary to do so. The principal units of the Kampfbund were to assemble at 7:00 P.M. at four hotels and drinking places in downtown Munich. At about the same time, canvas-covered trucks loaded with weapons would be making their way quietly along back streets on the far side of the Isar River, near the Bürgerbräukeller. At designated dark street corners close to the beer hall, the Kampfbund troops, after grouping in downtown Munich and crossing the bridges over the river at intervals in small units, would line up and have weapons served to them from the backs of the trucks.

Only when Hitler's meeting at Schellingstrasse broke up, early in the cold grey afternoon, did the notices to the rank and file begin to flow through Munich. Storm Troops in civilian clothes acted as messengers, ringing doorbells or finding their comrades at their places of work. The notices were on white paper, which was used for orders to report for routine training drills, rather than red slips, which indicated a full-scale alert. The continuing security effort was mixed with deception: a number of Reichswehr soldiers who were to be off duty that evening were invited to a party by their Kampfbund friends — a party at which the hosts would not appear — in an effort to make certain that they were away from their barracks if their units were suddenly ordered out to oppose the Putsch.

Telephones rang all over Bavaria. Working at his new job as a laboratory assistant in a chemical fertilizer factory outside Munich, twenty-three-year-old Heinrich Himmler received a call telling him that attendance at the evening's Reichskriegsflagge beer party at the Löwenbräukeller was no longer optional — he was to be there, in uniform.[19] As early as noon, Julius Streicher had received a long distance call, in Nuremberg, from Max Amann, the party's business manager. Shouting over the static on the line from Munich, Amann told the Nuremberg party leader that it was "of the utmost *patriotic importance*" that he be at SA headquarters by 7:00 P.M. Always efficient, Amann had looked up the schedules and recommended that Streicher catch the 1:45 P.M. express.

Streicher was unimpressed; he had heard a lot of talk about patriotic duty in the past few years, and had harangued many a crowd in just those terms. He and three Nazi friends finally piled into an automobile at four in the afternoon and set off on the hundred-mile journey to Munich, wondering just what Adolf wanted them for this time.[20]

In addition to telephone calls of notification, there were others that might be described as intelligence-gathering. Dr. Weber of Bund Oberland, fully in on the plot, rang up Colonel von Seisser of the state police at noon. Under the guise of a cheery chat, he asked Seisser if he would be at the Bürgerbräukeller to hear Kahr speak, and received Seisser's assurances that he planned to attend.[21]

Others played a role by not saying anything at all. Lieutenant Colonel Ludwig Leupold, the deputy commander of the Infantry School, had been present at the meeting, more than twenty-four hours earlier, during which General von Lossow had issued his warning that Hitler might start a Putsch and instructed all in attendance to pass the order that the Reichswehr would put down any such Kampfbund attempt with gunfire if necessary. Lieutenant Colonel Leupold was a staunch supporter of the views and aims of Hitler and the Kampfbund; although he was not in on the plotting of Rossbach and Heinz Pernet, he had gone back to the Infantry School, which he knew was in political ferment, and said not a word about the anti-Putsch policy that Lossow expected his officers to adopt.[22]

While Lieutenant Colonel Leupold was maintaining his silence, Hitler was in a lengthy afternoon conference with Eduard Dietl, the captain of the First Company of the Nineteenth Infantry Regiment. The First Battalion of this regular army unit had three companies, including Dietl's, stationed at its barracks in Munich. Although these companies comprised only about three hundred men, Hitler, a former foot soldier, knew just how much effective firepower this highly professional force could bring to bear once it was committed to action. Captain Dietl's duties across the past year had included training the Storm Troops during the periods of cooperation between the Reichswehr and the right-wing paramilitary units. His contact with these men and their leaders had turned him into a strong supporter of Hitler's views, and like many junior officers, he had a great admiration for Ludendorff.

Hitler knew that a combat regiment of the line was entirely different from the Infantry School. The enlisted men, many of Bavarian peasant stock, did not spend their evening hours in political debate. There were occasional fistfights resulting from political arguments, and some of these troops attended Hitler's speeches and were convinced by them, but these were long-enlistment foot soldiers who, when it came down to it, would obey orders.

Thus it became a matter of who would be on hand that evening to give orders at the barracks of the Nineteenth Infantry Regiment, and what those orders would be. Because Lossow had not placed his Reichswehr units on alert, the evening promised to be the usual peacetime situation: half to three quarters of the enlisted men in Munich would be gone from the barracks with permission to amuse themselves in the city until midnight. Among the married sergeants and the officers, the ratio of those off post would be far higher; a senior officer cadet was usually the highest-ranking man on duty at the regiment's barracks in the evening.

When Captain Dietl left Hitler, the plan was for him to be the senior officer present when some three hundred SA and Oberland troops appeared at the barracks. Dietl was to help them take over the weapons-packed regimental armory and make the entire complex into a stronghold for the putschists. He was to use his authority with the enlisted men, and his influence with his brother officers, to bring as many Reichswehr personnel as possible into the ranks of the "national revolution."[23]

Having dealt with Captain Dietl, Hitler turned his attention to other details. It was shortly before three; Kahr's meeting at the Bürgerbräukeller was scheduled to begin at seven-thirty. Hitler intended to make his move at exactly eight-thirty. If it went as planned, *he* would be the real government of Bavaria the following day, with Ludendorff fobbed off in a largely titular military role; soon afterward Berlin would be his, and his "German national government" would be an established fact. They were going to require not only guns but paperwork, and Max Amann was planning, once they had control of Munich, to confiscate the offices of a bank on Kanalstrasse to house the interim government before the final move to Berlin.[24]

Always thinking in terms of propaganda, Hitler arranged to have three commercial printers keep their typesetters and pressmen on duty for as long into the night as they might be needed. It was too soon to let them know what they would be printing; when the hour struck, they would be rolling off tens of thousands of posters proclaiming the new "German national government," posters that would be distributed in Munich and also rushed to cities throughout the Reich.[25]

Finally, there were the propaganda and administrative resources belonging to the party itself. Rosenberg was ready to put out an extra edition of the *Völkischer Beobachter*, with a banner headline proclaiming the new era for Germany. A full crew of typists and secretaries had been told to be prepared to spend the night at Schellingstrasse, ready to work on anything that might be necessary.

Having done that, Hitler started out the door of the *Völkischer Beobachter*, accompanied by his heavyset bodyguard, Ulrich Graf. His new red Benz automobile, driver at the wheel, was waiting for him, but Hitler indicated that he would be back in a minute. He crossed the street and went up a few doors to the photographic studio of his friend Heinrich Hoffmann, who was becoming, in effect, the Nazi Party's official photographer. Hitler emerged a minute later with Hoffmann in tow. The driver of the Benz anticipated some vital mission, but when Hitler and Hoffmann got in, the Führer mentioned a tea shop in the Gärtnerplatz.

It was pure unpredictable Adolf Hitler. For four years he had expended enormous amounts of energy, and millions of words, to gain recognition, to gain power, to make real his particular vision of what Germany should be. Now, with his revolution scheduled to begin in five hours, he sat with Heinrich Hoffmann in a small tea shop, and, as Hoffmann put it, they began "talking about quite trivial matters."[26]

Hoffmann knew nothing of the Putsch; he was not planning to go to hear the long-winded General Commissioner von Kahr at the Bürgerbräukeller, and would later have his usual game of cards with Dietrich Eckart, once so prominent in Nazi affairs, at the Café Schelling-Salon. In the meantime, anyone looking in — a police detective, perhaps — could see a thin, ordinary-looking thirty-four-year-old man with a pale complexion chatting with a chubby friend who was four years older. In such circumstances, Hitler looked like the last person who could bring a crowd to its feet, howling for more of his thunderous oratory. A contemporary who sometimes saw him relaxing in Munich's tea-and-pastry establishments remarked that seeing Hitler away from the speaker's platform was like seeing a Stradivarius lying in its case.[27]

Hitler got up to leave. His half hour of relaxation was over, and he had to go to meet his destiny. Walking out of the tea shop with Hoffmann, a tired fedora hat on his head, he did not look like the sort of man who would move the essentially skeptical Otto Strasser to say "I would not be surprised if in his head he heard voices, like Joan of Arc."[28]

CHAPTER

36

IF HITLER'S DECISION to while away some time in a tea shop was surprising, Ludendorff's movements were positively startling. At 3:00 P.M. he met with Wolf Graf von Helldorff, a North German emissary who was one of the leaders of the powerful Stahlhelm veterans' organization. Helldorff, representing one of the prospective directorates, had no idea that the Putsch was about to begin. Ludendorff said nothing to enlighten him; they did, however, discuss a Putsch in hypothetical terms. As Helldorff remembered the conversation, "I asked Ludendorff whether he was certain of the Reichswehr in Bavaria and whether there was not a danger that the Reichswehr or at least portions of it would oppose the action. Ludendorff replied: 'The heavens will fall before the Bavarian Reichswehr turns against me!'"[1]

Then, telling Helldorff that he would return later, Ludendorff went off to an appointment that he had been seeking for twenty-four hours: a meeting with the triumvirate. At first he had requested the meeting for Hitler and himself; subsequently he asked for himself alone. At 4:00 P.M. he sat down with Kahr and Lossow and Seisser. Thus, Ludendorff was talking with three men who did not know that their capture was the scheduled first action of the "national revolution," and neither did Helldorff, waiting elsewhere in Munich for Ludendorff to return.

The triumvirate found the conversation, which lasted an hour and a half, baffling. Ludendorff repeatedly discussed the possibilities of a directorate being formed in Berlin, yet agreed with the triumvirate's contention that no one in Berlin was willing to seize power at this point. In retrospect, the picture that emerges is one of a proud man doing some last-minute shopping for power. Had the triumvirate offered to take him in as a full partner, with the promise of an important role in any future control they might have in Berlin, it seems entirely possible that Ludendorff would have betrayed Hitler and the Putsch then and there. As it was, he nearly gave the secret away. Kahr remembered one of the last exchanges of the meeting:

> Ludendorff replied that he, for his part, would get in touch with the North, but that the matter was very urgent, since danger was imminent. . . . The people might [initiate] the attack. Lossow asked: "What kind of people would do that? How do they see this thing? They certainly wouldn't battle with the Reichswehr. You will disappoint yourself if you believe the Reichswehr would desert its leaders and not obey their command." The conference was closed without further results.[2]

Ludendorff went straight back to Helldorff, who was planning to bring some associates with him from Berlin the following day. Ludendorff knew that a revolution was scheduled to intervene, but his own statement on what he then said was "[I] told Count Helldorff that nothing had changed and that he might look around for people in Berlin, and then drove home."[3]

At the Ludendorff villa the general's wife had found nothing unusual in his being in the city all day, but after his return, a certain electricity gripped the household. Margarethe Ludendorff, who knew nothing of what was going on, wrote:

> Towards evening, I saw our servant, Kurt Neubauer, hurrying out of the house in uniform. I was surprised and called after him, "Kurt, where are you off to in such a hurry and in uniform, too?" Without stopping, he turned round: "A meeting in the Bürgerbräu . . . detailed to guard the hall. I must catch the train," and he was gone. Half an hour later, shortly before the departure of the next train, I heard the clink of his spurs as my son Heinz went bounding downstairs. He also was going to the meeting. The only surprising thing was that, contrary to his habit, he was wearing his uniform. I wondered at that.
>
> Ludendorff was in his study. I heard him pacing restlessly up and down, instead of sitting, as usual, at work at his writing table.[4]

II

When Max von Scheubner-Richter and his valet Johann Aigner entered the SA headquarters shortly after six in the evening, they saw most of the Nazi high command. Hitler was there with Ulrich Graf.

Hermann Esser, Hitler's close associate and firebrand orator, was looking like the sick man he was. For weeks, Esser had been in bed with a bad case of jaundice. This afternoon, Hitler had stopped by his apartment on Bergmannstrasse and told him that he must pull himself together and get down to SA headquarters by evening. Hitler explained that he needed a speaker to stand in for him at the Reichskriegsflagge beer party. Everyone was expecting Hitler to speak, and he wanted to keep it that way as long as possible. As soon as Hitler accomplished what he intended to do at Kahr's meeting at the Bürgerbräukeller, Röhm and Esser would receive a message — "Safely delivered" — and the Reichskriegsflagge troops and their Kampfbund friends could put down their steins and go into action. Esser had struggled into his clothes, and there he stood, his face yellow, his body burning with fever, his muscles gripped with pain every time he took a step.[5]

Hitler was dressed for his great moment in an outfit that would have made Kurt Ludecke wince: he was wearing an ill-fitting morning coat, on the left breast of which he had pinned his Iron Cross, and baggy trousers. The effect was that of a headwaiter in a second-rate restaurant or a musician in a provincial orchestra.

By contrast, SA leader Hermann Goering, who was to make his entrance at the head of Lieutenant Berchtold's Shock Troop Adolf Hitler, was fully martial, wearing his captain's uniform with all his decorations, including the Pour le Mérite. On the left sleeve of his uniform he had a specially embroidered swastika armband, and on the Reichswehr helmet he had with him, a large white swastika, not tilted but sitting in an upright position, had been painted. A pistol and a ceremonial saber completed his equipment. Because it was, as one Nazi said, "a gloomy, rainy November evening," Goering intended to put a black rubber raincoat over his uniform, but only until he reached the beer hall.[6]

Among the men standing around nervously were Alfred Rosenberg and Max Amann. Goering and Hitler were even more nervous; Goering felt that Hitler was cutting it too fine by delaying the notices of mobilization as long as he had. Given the limited time, the SA messengers had been unable to track down some of the men. Other Storm Troops, seeing that the notices were the white ones indicating a routine drill rather than the red ones denoting an emergency, simply decided to stay home, out of the cold and rain. Hitler was now blaming Goering for the pace at which the mobilization was proceeding, but the SA commander had no time left to defend himself against the Führer's accusations.[7] He put on his black raincoat and, taking two men with him, went downstairs to a car that took them across the Isar River, to the place where many of the Storm Troops would soon have weapons issued to them in the darkness.

To this point in the day, Munich's very size and liveliness had provided a certain camouflage for the Kampfbund preparations. In a busy city of 620,000, sending out messages to some four thousand men was not an especially conspicuous thing to do, and most of the men were not to assemble until seven o'clock, by which time it would be fully dark. Munich was used to seeing men of the Kampfbund organizations walking around in uniform. The police knew that there would be a large crowd in the uniforms of several paramilitary units at the Reichskriegs-flagge party at the Löwenbräu; by coincidence, the men of the Völkische Rechtsblock — Nationalist-Racist Bloc — were having a large beer party at another huge hall often used by the Nazis, the Hofbräuhaus. This group had no connection with the Kampfbund and was in no way involved with the Putsch plans, but its party added to the police perception that a lot of tough young right-wingers were out on Munich's streets.

As the afternoon wore on, however, there were minor incidents taking place that, if added up, could have moved even the trusting Colonel von Seisser to put some of his state police forces on alert. Gottfried Feder, the Nazi Party's self-styled economic expert, strode into the Schneider & Münzing Bank soon after four o'clock, closed out his account, and abruptly demanded that he be given the stock certificates that the bank handled for him. When the manager explained that because some of the shares had not been validated, it would be impossible to give him his portfolio for another three days, Feder created a scene, to no avail. Compared to Ludendorff, who had cleaned out his bank holdings two days earlier, Feder was acting at the last minute, but he had his own claim to duplicity: in his pocket he had a decree, which he had written on Hitler's behalf, that would freeze all bank accounts as soon as Hitler's "German national government" seized power.[8]

There were other unusual occurrences. Captain Oskar Cantzler of the Reichswehr's Seventh Engineer Battalion was on a routine inspection of Engineer Barracks Number One on the Oberwiesenfeld when he came across several men of Bund Oberland who were fitting some of the Reichswehr's supply of live rounds of ammunition into machine gun belts, apparently with a view to leaving with as much ammunition as they could take. Although the Oberland troops had trained frequently at this installation, the unsupervised acquisition of live ammunition was completely unauthorized, and Captain Cantzler stopped it instantly.[9]

By six o'clock, with the city in November darkness and Kahr's meeting scheduled to start in ninety minutes, a number of people began to get suspicious. Plenty of people in downtown Munich were engaging in other things — the first ticket holders of what would be a large audience were arriving at the National Theater on Max-Josef Platz for a seven o'clock performance of Beethoven's *Fidelio* — but an unusual level of Kampfbund activity was becoming noticeable. At the English Garden Precinct station of the Munich police, a carpenter rushed out of the cold drizzle and said to the surprised desk sergeant, "I just saw a group of SA men, carrying a swastika flag, marching down Biedersteiner Strasse. They stopped off at a store, went in, and from inside I heard someone say, 'Alarm!' "[10]

There were other reports of detachments of Storm Troops moving around, and at least one member of the general public knew what was going on. A policeman was directing traffic at the square near the Isar River when a bicyclist called over his shoulder, as he pedaled by, "Haven't you heard yet? Tonight it starts."[11]

The report that should have been taken most seriously was phoned in to the Twelfth Precinct station by a patrolman who was at a call box near the Nazi Party administrative office in Corneliusstrasse. "A lot of passenger cars and trucks have been stopping in front of the building," he reported. "People in military uniforms have been hurrying inside, dashing out again after a few minutes, and driving off."[12]

These calls were duly noted in the police records, but the men making them were reminded by the precincts that there were reasons for all this activity. Some of the Kampfbund leadership had been invited to Kahr's meeting at the Bürgerbräukeller, where the audience was already pouring in, and then there was Captain Röhm's Reichskriegsflagge party, as well as the big right-wing gathering. It was going to be that kind of an evening.

Just what role was being played by Wilhelm Frick, the police department official who was a Nazi conspirator, is uncertain. He was ready to defuse police action as soon as he started receiving reports that something was going wrong at the Bürgerbräukeller; obviously, if an official at police headquarters brought him reports of a disturbing pattern of activity, Frick would give him the same comforting explanations that were going out to the patrolmen around the city.

One man who was ready to believe that there was trouble, and to act, was Erhard Auer, Bavaria's leading member of the Social Democratic Party, which was always a Nazi target. He was the man who, in 1919, had been severely wounded in the assassination attempt by an adherent of Kurt Eisner, who had been further to the left, and since then he had been shot at by Nazis. In 1922, he had successfully argued against the deportation of Adolf Hitler, on the grounds that Hitler, too, was entitled to freedom of speech.

Auer was sitting in his office at the left-wing *Münchener Post*. With him were Wilhelm Hoegner, an assistant district attorney who was one of the young leaders of the Social Democrats, and Hans Unterleitner, one of Bavaria's Social Democratic Party representatives in the Reichstag. A newspaper employee appeared, saying that a visitor needed to see Auer "urgently and privately."

The identity of the man who closeted himself with Auer was never known. He was in civilian clothes, said that he was a Reichswehr officer, and knew enough about the Kampfbund's plans to say "It could be tonight, it could be the weekend. I've heard both versions. But the Reich government and you, Herr Auer, are in very great danger."[13]

Auer knew that any massive Nazi action would include an attempt to take him into custody and perhaps execute him out of hand. He tried to telephone President Ebert in Berlin, with no success. Unterleitner was returning to Berlin on the nine o'clock train, and Auer hastily wrote a message to him to carry to Ebert. Then the three men started down the stairway of the newspaper building, only to hear the sound of boots coming down the street, in step, and voices bawling out a marching song. Auer turned off the lights, and they waited on the stairs, finally sticking their heads out the door into the courtyard in time to see a Storm Troop unit pass by. Auer decided not to sleep at his house that night.

III

All over Munich, people were moving toward Kahr's meeting at the Bürgerbräukeller. Professor Karl Alexander von Müller finished his last lecture in history for the day and walked from the university grounds to a trolley stop for the trip across the river to the beer hall. At about the same time, Robert Murphy, the twenty-eight-year-old American diplomat who was acting consul in Munich, also headed for the Bürgerbräukeller. Murphy had been sending detailed reports to

Washington on this man Hitler and his militant NSDAP following, but the State Department never displayed the slightest interest in what he was telling them. Minister-President Eugen von Knilling, somewhat eclipsed by the general commissioner whom he and his cabinet had appointed, set out for the meeting, where he was to sit at a table in the beer hall with cabinet officials, including Interior Minister Franz Schweyer.

The organizers of this meeting had felt that it would be useful to invite representatives of the large labor unions so that they could hear what Kahr did and did not think about Marxism. The trade unionists would be an exception, however, in a right-wing, or, as they termed themselves, "patriotic," audience. Count Josef von Soden, Crown Prince Rupprecht's principal deputy, would be present, as would Count Karl von Bothmer, the publicist and political leader in the Bavarian monarchist-separatist cause, who was strongly suspected of having received payments from the French. Former police commissioner Ernst Pöhner would be on hand, knowing that the evening was not going to proceed as expected.

A most interesting spectator, Admiral Paul von Hintze, would also be present. Hintze was a career naval officer whose assignments in the immediate prewar and wartime years had consisted of a succession of special diplomatic posts, as well as ambassadorial appointments. He had reluctantly agreed to serve as Germany's state secretary for foreign affairs at just the point in 1918 when the nation's war effort was about to collapse. In that capacity he had represented the foreign office at army headquarters. When, on the eve of what proved to be a disastrous last campaign, Hintze asked Ludendorff "whether he was *certain* of obtaining a final and decisive victory in his present offensive," Ludendorff's answer had been, "My reponse is a definite yes."[14] Hintze had gone on from there with Ludendorff, to be present at a final madness when Ludendorff suddenly reversed himself and insisted on an immediate armistice, thereby throwing away any residual German bargaining power, while Field Marshal von Hindenburg, at the same meeting, chimed in with the inanely unrealistic demand that a peace settlement must award Germany some French territory.[15] Whatever Paul von Hintze wanted for Germany, it could not be Erich Ludendorff.

At 7:00 P.M., the men of Stosstrupp Adolf Hitler assembled, in uniform, in the bowling alley of the Torbräu Hotel. This favorite gathering place was near Josef Berchtold's tobacco shop and opposite the Sterneckerbräu, the beer hall in which Lance Corporal Adolf Hitler had attended his first meeting of the little German Workers' Party, in 1919.

Berchtold spoke briefly to his men. "Any one of you," he said, "who isn't going into this thing heart and soul had better get out right now." No one moved. Berchtold continued, "It's our job, as Shock Troops, to bear the brunt of what's coming. We're going to run the government out." He may have believed what he said next: "Hitler and Kahr are united over this; they are going to set up another one."[16]

The men all shook hands. Dressed in battle gear identical with that of the Reichswehr — helmets, equipment harness, everything the same except for the swastika armbands — they moved out, to cross the river on foot. At the corner of Balan and St. Martin streets, they would find the trucks assigned to them. Inside the vehicles were their rifles, bayonets, hand grenades, and machine guns. They would wait beside the trucks, and wait, and wait, and wait, until they received the signal to mount for the swift short drive that would put them at the door of the Bürgerbräukeller at 8:30 P.M.

Only one more group needed to get under way. In the darkness, cars pulled away from SA headquarters. Wearing his worn light tan trench coat, Hitler left in the red Benz, with Rosenberg, Amann, and Ulrich Graf. Also in the car was Anton Drexler, a living reminder of the party's earliest days; he was under the impression that they were driving to Freising, where Hitler had been scheduled to speak. When he learned where his companions were going and what they intended to accomplish before the night was out, he perfunctorily wished them luck, made no offer to participate, and from that moment faded from the Nazi scene.[17]

C H A P T E R

37

THE BÜRGERBRÄUKELLER was a very large building, set inside its own grounds. Putzi Hanfstaengl thought of it as "an eminently respectable beer hall much frequented by a better class of people." It had a number of different-size bars and dining rooms, but its particular asset for occasions like this was its main hall. This room, the largest indoor public gathering place in Munich other than the Zirkus Krone, could hold three thousand people. Seated at roughhewn tables with eight chairs or stools at each, patrons could order beer and an assortment of dishes supplied by the huge kitchens.

When he arrived, Professor von Müller found that "the hall was packed and one had the impression that the whole event had got beyond the control of the organizers. Obviously, more people had come than was planned for. I got a seat opposite the platform . . . so that I could see the main events very clearly."[1]

On the rostrum from which Kahr was to give his speech, a band was playing lively thumping tunes. Waitresses were moving from table to table with beer and plates of food. Because of the overflow crowd, the police had closed the doors at seven-fifteen, and hundreds of disappointed people were milling around outside the building. The band was supposed to stop playing and leave the platform to the speakers so that the proceedings could begin at seven-thirty, but that hour came and went, and the band kept playing amidst the din of the huge crowd. A man entering the hall noticed "the vast pile of top hats, uniform coats and swords in the cloakroom. It was quite clear that the elite of the whole beer capital of Munich was there."[2]

Among those who were unable to get in was Putzi Hanfstaengl. By the time he found the various foreign correspondents he wanted to meet there, the police were refusing to let any more people in. Putzi and the journalists were, as he put it, "trying to bluff our way through and no sign whatsoever of Hitler."[3] Adding to Putzi's worries was the fact that he was carrying a concealed pistol, as Hitler had told him to. The handgun was so big that even the six-foot-four Hanfstaengl thought of it as a "cannon"; unaccustomed to firearms, Putzi felt that if called on to use it, "I would probably have maimed myself."[4]

Finally the meeting got under way. The triumvirate and other notables were seated on the bandstand. The tobacco merchant Eugen Zentz, who had organized the affair, introduced Kahr, striking the note of support for his policies by turning the podium over to the general commissioner with the words "Lead us, Excellency, we will all willingly follow you anywhere." The introduction produced "enthusiastic applause," but even this energetic audience, eager to hear words of hope in a time of national chaos, was soon bored by Kahr. The little general commissioner, his big head hunched down between his shoulders, peering through glasses as he read the text of his speech, was a disappointment. One member of the audience, seated only twenty-five feet from Kahr, felt that he was getting a history lecture, in language that was "so strawy" — political hot air, laden with clichés.[5]

Just after eight, Hitler and his companions drove up, followed by Scheubner-Richter and Aigner. Getting out of his car and looking around at the crowd still trying to get in, Hitler realized that this mass of people could block the Shock Troop trucks when they arrived for their foray into the hall. He suggested to the police that they clear the area, saying that all this commotion might disturb the audience inside, and perhaps even break up the meeting. The police, who knew Hitler and were under instructions to let him in when he appeared, followed his suggestion.[6] No sooner had they moved the crowd away than the first SA trucks came into sight, at ten past eight. The assignment of the men on these trucks was simply to remain in the vehicles, as inconspicuously as possible, until Goering and Berchtold's Stosstrupp roared in at eight-thirty. They were the ones who were going to break into the hall.

Hitler was on the sidewalk, with Rosenberg and Ulrich Graf beside him, when Hanfstaengl reached him and explained that he and the foreign correspondents were locked out.

> "These gentlemen are coming with me," [Hitler] said peremptorily to the police inspector on duty, and forward we all trotted at his heels.

I was bringing up the rear with an American woman journalist [presumably Dorothy Thompson], and although the others got through, the entrance door was then slammed in our faces. I stood outside, feeling uncommonly foolish, berating the police: "This lady represents an American newspaper," I said heatedly. "Herr von Kahr is giving an important speech and there will be a first-class scandal if reports are prevented from reaching the foreign press." What turned the tide was the fact that my companion was smoking an American cigarette, a scent so rare and luxurious in impoverished Germany that her bona fides was established. We were allowed to pass.[7]

Once inside, Hitler established himself next to a pillar, at the back of the vast hall. Gathered near him were some of the conspirators who had arrived with him, and others who had made their own way there: Rosenberg, Amann, Graf, Scheubner-Richter and Aigner, Kriebel, Pernet, and Weber. Rudolf Hess was there, having carried out Hitler's order to rent the room near the speakers' platform. Aigner kept going in and out of the hall, looking down the entrance hallway and through some of the tall windows. He recalled, "Hitler asked at various times, ironically, 'Doctor, do you understand what von Kahr is speaking about?' Doctor Scheubner-Richter would always say, 'No.'" Knowing what was coming, Aigner felt that "minutes seemed to be hours."[8]

Uncomfortably aware of the pistol he was carrying, and of the hour of eight-thirty fast approaching, Putzi Hanfstaengl was also beside Hitler.

Nobody seemed to notice us and we just stood there looking innocent. . . . Hitler, who had kept on his trench-coat, was chatting quietly to Amann, now and again biting a fingernail and occasionally looking sideways at the platform, where von Kahr, von Lossow and von Seisser sat.

Always a man with an eye to the social caliber of a gathering, Putzi looked around: "Sure enough, everyone was there, the Bavarian provincial Cabinet, leaders of society, newspaper editors, and officers." Ladies were there in long evening dresses.

Kahr was on his feet, droning away at some boring and incomprehensible speech. . . . I went over to the serving hatch and got three litre-jugs of beer. I remember they cost a billion marks apiece. I took a good swig at one myself and handed the others to our group. Hitler took a thoughtful draught. In Munich, I thought, no one will suspect a man with his nose in a stein of beer.[9]

Ulrich Graf was watching inside the front door of the building; his assignment was to hurry back to Hitler to tell him when the Stosstrupp rolled up. Aigner was near a checkroom when he saw and heard "a glaring headlight in the street, a short rumbling, and the Stosstrupp stormed in from the street." According to Aigner, the twenty to thirty Munich policemen in the entrance hallway started to confront the helmeted Shock Troops and were thrown aside so quickly and viciously, and were so impressed by the warnings barked at them and the expressions of the men who gave them, that they "walked into the street, silently weeping. In the meantime a heavy machine gun had been set up in firing position at the entrance to the hall." As for Aigner and Scheubner-Richter, Aigner said, "We laid our coats down, drew our pistols and into the hall we went."[10]

Three thousand people witnessed what happened next, but each had a particular vantage point, and, before long, each had an interpretation of what was going on. Kahr was saying, "And now I come to the consideration of — " when, Putzi said, "the door behind us flew open and in burst Goering, looking like Wallenstein on the march, with all his orders clinking." Goering was wearing his helmet and had drawn both his sword and his pistol. Berchtold and his Shock Troops brandished an assortment of weapons, including rifles with bayonets fixed on them. Putzi recalled the next moments. "What an uproar. Everything happened at once. Hitler began to plow his way towards the platform and the rest of us surged forward following him. Tables overturned with their jugs of beer. I saw Wutzlhofer, one of the members of the Bavarian Cabinet, crawl under a table for cover."[11]

The volume of human sound continued to rise. The plan called for Hitler, swept along by the Shock Troops, to move swiftly down the aisle, accompanied by a number of his pistol-carrying Nazi and Kampfbund comrades, to confront the triumvirate before they knew what had happened. Instead, the dense crowd was blocking the way. People were standing on benches and stools to get a better view; everywhere, dishes were falling off tables and breaking on the floor. "Women fainted," Berchtold said, and Aigner recalled, with some satisfaction, that "these pompous people almost suffered a nervous breakdown at the sight of the machine gun and the guns."[12] There was every kind of shouting. Women screamed at the sight of helmeted men in uniform using the butts of their rifles to clear a path through the audience. Some, recognizing Hitler and the swastika armbands, shouted an enthusiastic "Heil!"[13]

A few plainclothes police detectives in the audience were Nazi sympathizers; now they pulled out swastika armbands, put them on their sleeves, and produced their pistols, and in some cases hand grenades as well.[14] From where Professor von Müller was sitting, he first saw helmets, and then, "turning towards the podium, Adolf Hitler, pale, his dark strand of hair hanging into his face, to his right and left a member of the Storm Troop, wearing a red armband, pistols in their raised hands near their heads."[15]

Hitler, too, had a pistol in his hand. Major Franz Hunglinger of the state police, one hand in his pocket, stepped forward to intercept Hitler's progress down the aisle. Hitler remarked of this moment, "I had the feeling that he was drawing a pistol. I held my pistol against his forehead and said, 'Take your hand out.'"[16]

Kahr had a unique view.

I had been speaking for approximately a half an hour when, suddenly, shouting and commotion arose at the entrance to the hall. At first I believed it was the Communists. I saw a narrow path emerging through the crowd. A man wearing a dark suit and carrying a pistol was in the lead; I had the impression that he was pointing the pistol at me. Flanking him were men armed with pistols. The leader stopped a few steps in front of me, lowered his pistol, and began to speak. Only then did I recognize that the man was Hitler.[17]

Three thousand people were still yelling and talking excitedly; when Hitler tried to say something to Kahr, who was on a raised platform only two yards away from him, nothing could be heard. Finally, when Hitler said again in a loud voice that the action was not directed against Kahr, two men near Hitler tried to shout the same affirmation to the audience. That was when Hitler climbed up on a chair and faced the crowd, which showed no signs of stopping the tremendous racket. Suddenly a shot rang out. Even those physically closest to Hitler differed on just what happened. General von Lossow, who knew enough about firearms to recognize that Hitler was carrying a Browning pistol, said that Hitler raised it and fired it into the ceiling. Count von Bothmer said that it was fired by "one of his aides carrying a submachine gun."[18] Professor von Müller, too, said that Hitler "gave a signal to his companion on his right. A shot cracked out; one could see the hole which the bullet broke into the ceiling of the hall."[19]

Three thousand people were suddenly silent. Hitler climbed up on the platform and proclaimed, loudly and formally:

> I announce to those present that the national revolution has broken out in all Germany. Six hundred armed men are occupying this room, and no one can leave. The Reichswehr and the state police are marching from their barracks under our flags. A German national and Bavarian government is being formed, the Knilling government and the Reich government are deposed.

Hitler then called out, in what a witness described as "a harsh commanding tone," "His Excellency von Kahr, his Excellency von Lossow and Colonel von Seisser, I must ask these gentlemen to go with me. I guarantee their safety."[20]

While Hitler spoke, men with pistols were encircling Kahr, Lossow, and Seisser, who were standing at one edge of the platform. According to Lossow, "I dropped the remark, 'Put on an act!' during Hitler's first speech, and while we were being so disgracefully 'escorted' from the hall, unanimity of opinion was established between us. . . . We would have to carry out the charade until we had regained our freedom."[21] The triumvirate were duly marched off to the room that Rudolf Hess had reserved.

As the audience once again began to talk in wild excitement, Hanfstaengl, who had come forward to the platform behind Hitler, was reacting to what he had just seen. During Hitler's announcement, Putzi

> suddenly caught one glance from von Lossow at Hitler. There was such a furtive look of thinly veiled contempt on his monocled face, with its sabre cuts, that I knew he could not be trusted to go along with us. I turned to Goering and said: "Hermann, watch your step, Lossow is going to double-cross us."
>
> "How do you know that?" Goering asked me.
>
> "One look at his face is enough," I said. I felt in my fingertips that there was trouble brewing. Hitler and Lossow had been as thick as thieves for weeks, but I knew that no binding promises of assistance had been forthcoming from the army chief. He could never get over the fact that he was an aristocratic general and Hitler was an ex-corporal. There was still no room for self-made men in the Germany of those days.[22]

While Putzi had been having these thoughts, Admiral von Hintze was having his own reaction. Echoing Putzi's later statement that Hitler was wearing a "frightful tailcoat outfit" as he announced his new regime, Hintze subsequently said, "Hitler [was] dressed in a morning coat, that most difficult of all garments to wear, let alone a badly cut morning coat, and let alone a man with as bad a figure as

Hitler, with his short legs and his long torso. When I saw him jump up on the table in that ridiculous costume I thought, 'The poor little waiter!' "[23]

Just before Hitler entered the room to which the triumvirate had been taken, he turned to Scheubner-Richter. Hitler knew what the audience could not have known: the Reichswehr and state police were not marching to his support, and, whatever the night might bring to Munich and Bavaria, it was at this moment a lie to say "The national revolution has broken out in all Germany."[24] Hitler might not have the Reichswehr and state police, although he was about to enter the room where their commanders were sitting uneasily, but he had something else. "It is time," he whispered to Scheubner-Richter, "to get Ludendorff."[25]

Kahr, Lossow, and Seisser were being guarded by one man with a drawn pistol when Hitler walked into the bare cold room, waving his Browning automatic. "No one leaves this room alive without my permission!" he cried.[26] Then, trying to soften his manner: "Please forgive me for proceeding in this manner, but I had no other means. It is done now and cannot be undone."[27] Hitler was still waving his pistol around; the triumvirate saw that he was sweating and trembling.

Lowering his pistol, Hitler turned to Kahr. "The Reich government has been formed, the Bavarian government is deposed, Bavaria is the springboard for the Reich government. There must be a state administrator in Bavaria. Pöhner will be minister-president with dictatorial power." Pointing at Kahr, Hitler continued, "You will be the state administrator, Hitler will be in charge of the Reich government. Ludendorff is in charge of the national army, Lossow will be Reichswehr minister, and Seisser the minister of police."

While the triumvirate digested this, Hitler added, "I know that this step is difficult for you gentlemen, but the step must be taken. It must be made easier for you gentlemen to make the jump." No one said anything, and Hitler went on: "Each of you is to take his place; if he does not, then there is no justification for his existence. You must fight with me, be victorious with me, or die with me. If the undertaking fails, I have four bullets in my pistol, three for my collaborators if they leave me, and the last bullet is for me." Hitler still had the pistol in his hand; to emphasize his remarks about suicide, he put the pistol to his temple, then let his hand drop.

Kahr stared at Hitler, then said coldly, "You can arrest me, you can have me shot, you can shoot me yourself. To die or not to die is meaningless." Hitler petulantly turned to Seisser, who accused him of breaking his word of honor not to make a Putsch. Hitler shrugged his shoulders and said, "Yes, I did that, but in the interest of the Fatherland. Forgive me."

General von Lossow had risen and stepped toward a window that looked down into the garden of the beer hall grounds. He saw a group of Stosstrupp men looking at him from under the brims of their helmets, with their rifles pointed at the window. Seeing what Lossow was looking at, Hitler waved his hand at the men, indicating that they should fall back, and they disappeared into the shadows. Lossow then asked, "How does Ludendorff stand on this matter?"

"Ludendorff is available," Hitler replied, "and will be fetched immediately."[28] Then Hitler walked out of the room, leaving Rudolf Hess and Ulrich Graf, both of whose pistols were drawn, to guard the triumvirate.

While Hitler had been talking to the triumvirate, a thousand animated conversations were going on in the shocked audience in the main hall. The Hitler sympathizers were cheerful and optimistic. Others, not affiliated with the Kampfbund but yearning for some solution to the national crisis — it now took 2 trillion marks to equal a dollar — found themselves responding favorably to the bold show of force; for many, their right-wing sympathies led them to hope that a coalition could be formed by Hitler and the triumvirate. Still others found what they had witnessed to be offensive and absurd. Likening the action to one of the turnstile revolutions going on in Latin America, some shouted, "Banana Republic!" A few, feeling that the entire thing was some sort of hoax, hooted, "Theater!"[29] A number worried that if Hitler seized power, a war with France would be just days away. Hoping that the general commissioner could restrain whatever this turn of events represented, some said, "Thank God von Kahr is with them."[30]

Amid the clamor in the hall, Knilling and his cabinet ministers were huddled around a table in a worried discussion. Hitler was at least negotiating, even if at gunpoint, with Kahr, the general commissioner Knilling had appointed. By contrast, Hitler had just declared that Knilling and his colleagues were "deposed."

Other people had other problems. One man trying to leave the main hall to go to the men's room was roughly turned back by Storm Troops. Robert Murphy felt that the embassy in Berlin should know about this development at the earliest possible moment. Stating that a foreign diplomat could not be detained in this manner, he tried to talk his way past the Storm Troops, but was told to go back into the hall.[31]

The crowd was nearing hysteria when Hermann Goering appeared on the platform and shouted for silence in a voice he often used to command large formations of the SA. Silence returned, and Goering continued:

> This is not an assault on Herr von Kahr, the other two gentle-
> men, the police or the army, who are already marching out of
> their barracks with flags waving. It is directed solely against the
> Berlin government of Jews. It is merely the preliminary step of
> the national revolution desired by everyone in this auditorium.
> We have dared this step because we are convinced it will make it
> easier for the men who lead us to act.[32]

This last thought, perfectly in line with a remark of Hitler's, earlier in the autumn, that "we must compromise these people so they will march with us," struck a responsive chord in those in the audience who wanted to believe that all the elements of the right wing could work together.[33] "But until the step is completed," Goering added, "you must all stay seated and follow the orders and instructions of the guards." Then he shouted, "Long live the new Reich government — Hitler, Ludendorff, Pöhner, Kahr!"[34]

Somewhat to the surprise of those who disapproved and thought that no one could take it seriously, this exhortation brought rousing cheers from many people in every quarter of the hall. Then, as Hanfstaengl saw it, Goering made an unpardonable remark as he walked off the platform: " 'In any case there is beer to drink,' he said in the unmistakable tone of contempt of the northern Germans for the Bavarians, as if to suggest that as long as they had a stein in their hands there was little else that they needed."[35]

With his great height, Putzi was a visible figure, even in the tumult of this gathering; now, after Goering had spoken, all sorts of people were gathering around, pulling at Putzi's sleeves and asking questions.

> I, in my turn, climbed on a chair with a more peaceable and
> almost absurdly normal announcement that representatives of the
> foreign press should join me. Then I held an impromptu press
> conference, explaining that a new government had been formed,
> that all persons and property would be respected, that order and
> discipline would be restored in the country, and so on. All the
> things I truly believed at the time.[36]

Also while Hitler was talking to the triumvirate, telephone calls had gone out from the Bürgerbräukeller, giving the arranged signal "Safely delivered" — "delivered" not in the sense of a package delivered, but that of a baby, the new Germany, being born.[37] Kampfbund units all over Munich began to carry out their assignments. There was no turning back; if Hitler could gain the active cooperation of the triumvirate, it would be far better, but, either way, the strike for power was on. Men like Ernst Röhm knew that there was not a minute to lose. The Kampfbund had the element of surprise, but as the hours ticked by the possibilities of effective government resistance would increase.

For the moment, however, the putschists were virtually unopposed. The Reichskriegsflagge party at the Löwenbräukeller, which was being attended by more than eighteen hundred men of the different Kampf-bund organizations, broke up in delirious joy when the "safely delivered" message was announced and explained.[38] The men streamed out into the city and picked up their weapons at the prearranged locations that until then had been known to only a few of their leaders. Once armed, Röhm and his two hundred men made straight for Reichswehr headquarters. When they arrived there, demanding to be let in, the army sentries threatened to shoot. The officer in charge resolved the matter by stating that he was compelled to surrender to a greatly superior force, and the putschists took over. Röhm asked the officer who had been in charge to remain at his post; whether the triumvirate was coerced or agreed freely, Röhm expected that headquarters personnel would receive instructions to cooperate with the Kampfbund.

Aggressive action had started, and the sabotage of any prospective police response had also begun. Horrified by what he had seen at the beer hall, Police Inspector Philipp Kiefer managed to slip into the night and to the Weissenburger Platz Precinct station. Grabbing a telephone, he called police headquarters. At first the line was busy; then he was told that he would be called back. When the call did come, it was from Wilhelm Frick, the Nazi ally.

Kiefer poured out what he had seen. Frick responded in soothing tones, pointing out that he was not really the man in charge. Karl Mantel, chief of the Blue Police, was at the beer hall, along with many of the Bavarian authorities. Surely the whole thing could be worked out among the officials who were right there on the scene. In the meantime, of course, Kiefer should stay just where he was — at the Weissenburger station, not the beer hall — to await further instructions.[39]

II

Hitler, having failed to gain the cooperation of the triumvirate, returned to face the agitated and expectant audience. Leaving the stage after the initial seizure of the hall, Hitler had been heard to remark that the whole thing could be resolved between himself and the triumvirate within ten minutes. Professor von Müller described what happened next.

The ten minutes must have been just passed when Hitler returned — alone. He had not succeeded, as he had promised, in winning over the others. What would he say? A dangerous wave of excitement rolled up to him as he again climbed the podium. It did not subside as he began to speak. I still see clearly how he drew the Browning from his rear pocket and now himself fired a shot into the ceiling. "If you don't calm down," he shouted furiously, "I will order a machine gun placed in the balcony!"

What followed then was an oratorical masterpiece, which would have been to any actor's credit. He began quietly, in a completely matter-of-fact way. The enterprise was not directed against Kahr, in any sense. Kahr had his complete trust and would be regent in Bavaria. At the same time, however, a new government had to be formed: Ludendorff, Lossow, Seisser, and himself. I cannot remember in my entire life such a change in the attitude of a crowd in a few minutes, almost a few seconds. There were certainly many who were not converted yet. But the mood of the majority had abruptly changed. Hitler had turned them inside out, as one turns a glove inside out, with a few sentences. It had almost something of hocus-pocus, or magic about it. Loud approval roared forth; no further opposition was to be heard. Only then did he say, in deeply earnest, emotional tones: "Outside are Kahr, Lossow, and Seisser. They are struggling hard to reach a decision. May I say to them that you will stand behind them?" "Yes! Yes!" swelled out the roaring answer from all sides. "In a free Germany," he shouted passionately at the crowd, "there is also room for an autonomous Bavaria! I can say this to you: Either the German revolution begins tonight or we will all be dead by dawn!"[40]

The tumultuous applause continued well after Hitler disappeared, and the sound of it reached into the room where the triumvirate was being held, leaving no doubt in their minds that there had been a tremendous endorsement of what Hitler had just said.

Putzi Hanfstaengl had his own analysis of why Hitler "had the audience bawling its enthusiasm." Rather than picturing the triumvirate as opposed to his plan, Hitler had somehow managed to suggest that they wished to go along with it but lacked the courage that the audience could provide. Then there was the reference to Kahr as "regent," which suggested that the restoration of the Wittelsbach monarchy was part of the new arrangement the audience was being asked to approve. There may have been magic in Hitler's oratorical techniques, but Putzi felt that there was something else.

> For Hitler's words to achieve such an immediate effect, they needed to reach receptive ears. To a great many staid and established members of the audience he represented little more than an adventurer. Nevertheless, they had been tempted by the voluptuous picture of power that he had painted for them. Since Bismarck had founded the Second German Reich, Bavaria had been little more than a provincial vassal and here opportunity was being offered for Munich to assume the leadership of Germany and take it away from the despised Prussians in Berlin. There were a good many women in the audience, distinguished local matrons with heavy, provincial furs, and they had applauded the loudest.[41]

It was starting to snow, which did not make things easier for the grey Benz that had been sent to "fetch" General Ludendorff. A telephone call from the beer hall had alerted him, and he was waiting at the door of his villa, dressed not in his uniform, but in civilian clothes, so that he might claim that this was all most unexpected.[42] Now the car was tearing back to town: crammed in it, besides the large and portly general, were Ludendorff's valet, Kurt Neubauer, who had already been at the beer hall, as well as Scheubner-Richter and Aigner. The car was averaging speeds of fifty miles an hour; with a sense of history and some German efficiency, Aigner noted that the car made the fourteen-mile round trip through the snow in eighteen minutes.[43]

In the main hall of the Bürgerbräukeller, the crowd was once again becoming restless. Professor von Müller was making notes on what was happening. A few minutes earlier, most of the people in the hall had been cheering wildly for Hitler and the vision of glory that he had conjured up for them, but now, Müller wrote, "opinion is beginning to swing back in the other direction."

The crowd suddenly became quiet again. Rudolf Hess was standing on a chair in front of the platform, an armed Stosstrupp man beside him. He was holding a piece of paper Hitler had handed him. "The gentlemen whose names I am about to read are to go immediately to the main entrance of the hall," Hess said in a loud voice.

The audience knew instinctively that arrests were about to be made. "Some nationalist salvation this is!" one of the crowd yelled. "Hitler and his people are swine!"

Hess read from his paper. "Minister-President von Knilling."

"Here," Knilling answered, offering no resistance. Red with anger, he moved to the back of the hall, where the guards were waiting. Next came Interior Minister Schweyer. Seven more names were called out; two of the men were not in the hall, and a third tried to stay hidden in the crowd but was soon rounded up. The other four, including Minister of Agriculture Johann Wutzlhofer, gave themselves up.[44] The Storm Troops who were to guard them knew the agriculture minister as a declared opponent of Adolf Hitler and the NSDAP; they shoved him around in the hallway before taking him with the others to an upstairs room, and one putschist said, "He should be hanged."[45] The most unusual arrest made was that of Count von Soden, the chief aide to Crown Prince Rupprecht, who had been invited but was at his home in Berchtesgaden. At least some in the hall saw the inconsistency between that move and Hitler's statement that Kahr was to be regent in Bavaria.

Ludendorff appeared. He was brought in right through the crowd, coming down the same aisle that Hitler had, less than an hour earlier. Although in civilian clothes, he was immediately recognized, and received an ovation. Everyone present understood that Ludendorff would not be there, going to the room in which Hitler was negotiating with the triumvirate, unless he was in accord with the "national revolution" that Hitler had proclaimed. The appearance of the "national commander" was the greatest endorsement the highhanded Kampfbund action could receive, and the applause followed Ludendorff until he, too, disappeared from sight.

There were to be different versions, and several interpretations, of what happened next. Ludendorff walked in and greeted the triumvirate, whom he had last met that very afternoon.

"Gentlemen," he said in a trembling voice, "I am just as surprised as you are. But the step has been taken; it is a question of the Fatherland and the great national and racial cause, and I can only advise you, go with us and do the same."[46]

Before Ludendorff arrived, the pistols had disappeared. Weber came into the room, as did Pöhner. The tone was of friendly but urgent persuasion. General von Lossow was undoubtedly impressed by the appearance of Ludendorff, although he still had the gravest misgivings about this "national revolution." He knew that the pistols were still there, and was later to say that there was no true discussion: "They only wanted to hear a 'Yes' from us." Lossow felt that the only way to save the situation was to appear to go along. "After their efforts to persuade me had lasted for some time, I gave my consent, keeping in mind my decision arrived at some time before, with the dry words, 'Very well.' " Soon afterward Seisser also gave his consent.

Now everything was concentrated on the general commissioner. Lossow described the effort:

> It took longer to persuade Herr Kahr. Hitler, Weber, and Pöhner were involved here. Seisser and I were also commanded to join in the effort to persuade him. We did not give them an answer. I stood leaning against a table which was in the room. The reason for Kahr's hesitation was perfectly evident to me. From the start, he was as resolute as Seisser and I, but he tried to find the precise wording in which to couch a declaration of consent in the most neutral and vague terms.[47]

Lying about his intentions, Hitler told Kahr the regent idea he had mentioned to the crowd, although he had never previously discussed it with the general commissioner. Without specifying precisely what position the House of Wittelsbach was to occupy, Hitler indicated an immediate willingness to meet with Crown Prince Rupprecht, to assure him that this action tonight was to "make restitution" for the loss of the throne in 1918.[48] Kahr could never resist anything that seemed to reinvigorate the defunct Bavarian monarchy; he and Hitler agreed that he should be not a regent, a position whose existence implied that a monarch was absent, disabled, or too young to rule, but some form of royal governor, acting on behalf of Rupprecht. "I am prepared to assume the leadership of Bavaria as the viceroy of the monarchy," Kahr finally said. Hitler then urged him to repeat his statement in front of the waiting crowd, but Kahr answered that after the humiliating way in which he had been taken out of the hall at gunpoint, he did not want to reappear.

Hitler insisted: "If you do not join us, we will carry you in on our hands; you will be received with enthusiasm and people will kneel down before you."

"I set no great value in that," Kahr said, but he was moving toward the door.[49] Hitler repeated to the triumvirate, "There is no turning back now! The matter is already an historical event of universal importance!"[50] Kahr did not even look around, but he walked toward the main hall.

The scene that then took place was never forgotten by anyone who witnessed it, although, once again, there were different reactions. The crowd, some of them drunk by this time with beer as well as excitement, saw an extraordinary group coming toward the platform — Kahr in front, followed by Hitler, Ludendorff, General von Lossow, and Colonel von Seisser. Pöhner brought up the rear. There were no pistols in view; everyone appeared to be quietly determined. The group lined up in two rows on the platform, with Ludendorff in the middle of the front row, Kahr on his left, and Hitler on his right. The last sound of conversation died away in the vast hall.

Kahr stepped forward, his face devoid of expression. "In this hour of the Fatherland's greatest need," he said, "I have decided to accept the burden of steering Bavaria's destiny as governor on behalf of the monarchy —"[51]

One of the audience, standing right in front of Kahr, observed that these words "aroused frantic applause."[52] Professor von Müller was to agree that this was the largest single ovation of the evening.

"As governor representing the monarchy smashed by wanton criminal hands five years ago," Kahr continued when he could. "I do this with a heavy heart and, I hope, for the benefit of our beloved Bavarian homeland and our Great German Fatherland."[53] There was tremendous applause again, and Hitler stepped across in front of Ludendorff to grasp Kahr's hand and hold it, looking into his eyes as wave after wave of cheers came from the audience. "During this scene," Müller said, "Hitler was radiant with joy. One had the feeling that he was delighted to have succeeded in persuading Kahr to collaborate. There was in his demeanor, I would say, a kind of childlike joy, a very frank expression which I shall never forget."[54]

Then Hitler stepped back so that others could come forward to speak. Putzi Hanfstaengl was enthusiastic about what was happening, but did not see Hitler as a glamorous figure.

He could not have looked less like a revolutionary — a collector of taxes, rather. . . . This was the extraordinary thing about him, he still looked utterly mediocre in repose. . . . Just now he was quiet, looking like the slightly nervous sort of provincial bridegroom you could see in scores of pictures in the dusty windows of Bavarian village photographers.[55]

Then it was Ludendorff's turn. "Deeply moved by the momentousness of this occasion, although taken by surprise," he said, "I place myself in the service of the true nationalist government of Germany and will strive to restore to it the old black-white-and-red cockade stripped away by the infamous revolution."[56]

Watching from his seat near the platform, Müller was convinced that, if Hitler thought this was some sort of wonderful adventure, Ludendorff was approaching it as an overwhelming responsibility. "Excellency Ludendorff by comparison was extremely grave; when he came in he was pale with suppressed emotion. His appearance as well as his words were those of a man who knew it was a matter of life and death, probably death rather than life."[57]

Both Seisser and Lossow had practically to be dragged forward to say anything. Seisser appeared to be the most shaken of those on the platform, though he finally made some very brief statement that indicated that he was participating in this "national revolution."

Müller, like Putzi, had some doubts about just where Lossow stood. "Lossow's expression was very different; there was something detached, relaxed about his whole attitude. . . . It struck me that he made a slightly ironical fox face. A certain impenetrable smile never left his features."[58]

Then came Hitler's opportunity to say the last word.

> I am going to fulfill the vow I made to myself five years ago
> when I was a blind cripple in the military hospital: to know
> neither rest nor peace until the November criminals have been
> overthrown, until on the ruins of the wretched Germany of
> today there should have arisen once more a Germany of power
> and greatness, of freedom and splendor.[59]

These words were hardly out of Hitler's mouth before they were, Putzi said, "followed by the most impressive singing of 'Deutschland über alles' I have ever heard."[60]

At this point a man standing within ten yards of the platform turned and said to his neighbor, "Now only the psychiatrist is missing."[61]

The formal part of the meeting was over, but the members of the audience soon discovered that they were not free to walk out as they pleased. Storm Troops were at every exit, conducting "identity controls."[62] Every one of the three thousand people in the crowd was required to produce some kind of identification. Scores of Jews were pushed to one side and told that they would be spending the night in detention inside the beer hall. The trade unionists who had been invited to hear Kahr's views were similarly detained, as were a number of others who had incurred the displeasure of Hitler, Goering, and other members of the Kampfbund. Anyone who was thought to be a communist or socialist was held. Even those who were passed through were not necessarily out of trouble. One sixty-year-old man, on telling a couple of young Storm Troops that he had not liked being held in a building at gunpoint, was thrown up against the wall and punched.[63]

Hitler went upstairs to "apologize for the inconvenience" he was causing the high Bavarian officials who had been arrested. While telling them that Rudolf Hess would treat them well, he kept his eyes away from Schweyer, the minister of the interior, whom he had promised never to make a Putsch. Schweyer walked straight over to Hitler, causing the guards to bring their weapons up to a ready position. Poking Hitler's chest with a forefinger, Schweyer said, "I want to tell you something, Herr Hitler. Your promises do not mean very much. Let me ask whether you remember what you promised when you were in my office last year? Do you remember what you said then?"[64]

Hitler simply looked away and walked out the door.

Rejoining Ludendorff, Hitler attempted to make some sense of the information that was coming in. The triumvirate were on hand, no longer formally detained with pistols pointed at them, but surrounded by Kampfbund officials who had no intention of letting them leave.

As far as could be determined, the news of the "national revolution" was being hailed throughout Munich. Sick of both a national and a Bavarian government that seemed powerless to deal with inflation, unemployment, and food shortages, pedestrians were stopping to cheer every detachment that marched past with a swastika flag. The state police were not moving against Kampfbund units, and the Munich police appeared to be cooperating. Röhm and his force were in charge at Reichswehr headquarters, though many Reichswehr officers and men were scattered about the city, their loyalties unknown.

One report that came in made Hitler nervous. Something was going wrong at the Engineer Barracks, where Reichswehr Captain Cantzler had stopped the Bund Oberland men who were trying to steal ammunition. Some four hundred Oberland men had been sent to take the barracks and armory, where only a skeleton force of Reichswehr troops had been on hand. The securing of that key post was long overdue, and confusing versions of what was happening were being received. One, which seemed unlikely, was that the squad of regular army men had somehow managed to lock all four hundred Kampfbund troops inside the armory and were keeping them there. With no idea of what opposition might evolve, Hitler felt that there must not be any further delay in taking such an important objective, and that he must go to the barracks himself.

Hitler explained his intended action to Ludendorff. It was a classic example of previous conditioning. Lance Corporal Hitler, who had run forward through gunfire for four years to advance posts, finding out what was happening and bringing back the news to regimental headquarters, felt the need for a personal reconnaissance. General Ludendorff, accustomed to remaining at headquarters and sending out an able staff officer to ascertain the facts of a confused situation, had no intention of going himself.

After Hitler departed, a different mood settled on the four who were left — Ludendorff and Kahr, Lossow, and Seisser. Ludendorff began to feel uncomfortable as the captor of these men, who had, after all, given their word that they would cooperate in the venture. Kahr looked grey, completely drained from the evening, and perhaps sick. Lossow, a brother officer, had broken with Berlin weeks earlier. Seisser was a former general staff officer. For himself, Ludendorff wanted to stop leading a revolution from within a beer hall and move to the captured Reichswehr headquarters. It was twenty minutes to eleven, and many things needed to be done.

Addressing the triumvirate in the third person, Ludendorff put forward the idea that "it is time for the gentlemen to go to their respective posts." They would know, better than he, how to implement their roles in the formation of the new government and the march on Berlin.

Straight-faced, Kahr and Lossow and Seisser all bade Ludendorff good night and, disappeared through the door. Just then Scheubner-Richter reappeared in the room, having made a telephone call. Inquiring as to where in the building the triumvirate had been taken, he was horrified by Ludendorff's answer that they were on their way out, with his permission. "But, Excellency," Scheubner-Richter said, "you cannot just let them leave. Without a guard? Once they are out of this room, we have no means of holding them to their agreements."

Ludendorff looked down at Scheubner-Richter and gave him an imperial army answer: "They are officers, and they gave their word. I forbid you to doubt the word of a German officer."[65]

CHAPTER

38

O UT IN THE CITY, Hitler was moving impulsively, trying to get a
grip on his revolution. When he left the beer hall, unaware that
Ludendorff and the triumvirate would soon part company, his intention had been to go straight to the Engineer Barracks. Setting off with
what he called an "expeditionary force" — three truckloads of SA men
and, in two cars, Dr. Friedrich Weber, Ulrich Graf, and assorted
minor Kampfbund figures who were cocking submachine guns and
rifles — Hitler was driven across the Isar River via the Ludwig
Bridge.[1] Just after reaching the river's west bank, Hitler's mobile force
met a long column coming the other way, on foot. The leader, Gerhard
Rossbach, was followed by the 350 officers and cadets he had been
able to recruit from the Infantry School. Next in the column was the
Munich SA Regiment's Second Battalion, led by Edmund Heines.
Kurt Neubauer, having switched roles from servant to Kampfbund
soldier, was marching with them. They were on their way to the
Bürgerbräukeller, to report to Hitler.

Hitler ordered his driver to stop, and gave a short exhortation to
the excited soldiers. Then, as those troops passed across the river to
the beer hall, he decided to delay his reconnaissance of the barracks
in order to praise Ernst Röhm and his Reichskriegsflagge men for their
capture of Reichswehr headquarters. En route to the big stone structure on Schönfeldstrasse, Hitler passed through streets in which
crowds were cheering every marching group or vehicle that displayed
the swastika banner. Arriving at the army headquarters, Hitler was
exuberant as he greeted Röhm and the men who had bloodlessly
occupied the building. Röhm said of the moment:

> When I congratulated him on his success, he embraced me and
> said it was the most beautiful day of his life; he was beaming with

happiness and joy. "Now a better time will come," he said. "We all want to work night and day for the great goal: saving Germany from suffering and disgrace."[2]

Heartened by seeing with his own eyes that this vital objective was in the hands of a trusted and able subordinate who was ready to set up barbed wire entanglements around the building, Hitler moved across the city to the northwest, to the Engineer Barracks. There, he and Dr. Weber discovered that the seemingly impossible report was true: one Reichswehr officer and seven enlisted men had managed to lock four hundred Oberlanders into the drill hall. The Oberlanders could not shoot their way out, because they had counted on seizing arms and ammunition at the armory of this installation. The alert army officer who had neutralized this Kampfbund force was again Captain Cantzler. When the commander of the Oberland force had insisted that he had brought his men there only for a drill, Cantzler had stated that he would allow them to drill, all right, but only indoors. Once they were inside the drill hall, a confrontation had ensued, with the Oberland commander demanding, in the name of the new government, that his men be issued arms and ammunition. When Cantzler replied that he would comply only on orders from his superiors, and that he had no such orders, the Oberland commander ordered his men to arrest the tiny Reichswehr contingent, but the regular army men were too quick for them. The result was that four hundred Kampfbund soldiers were locked inside the drill hall, and Cantzler called for reinforcements that set up two machine guns outside to greet them if they were so foolish as to break down the door of the field house.[3]

This was the situation found by Hitler and his "expeditionary force." Although Hitler, before arriving there, had spoken wildly of breaking any impasse "with artillery if need be," he realized that these particular regular army troops were ready to fire if he interfered.[4] Believing that he had General von Lossow's pledge of cooperation, Hitler decided that it would be far better to return to the beer hall and have the Reichswehr commander straighten the matter out with a telephone call.

Returning to the Bürgerbräukeller, Hitler discovered that Ludendorff had allowed the triumvirate to leave, but for the moment he appeared to take little notice of that. Like Ludendorff, who was impassively present, Hitler was still convinced that General Commissioner von Kahr, General von Lossow, and Colonel von Seisser would honor the commitments of support they had made orally before the crowd.

What was disturbing Hitler was the lack of communication and the sense that things were not developing as rapidly as they should, although there appeared to be no danger at hand. Apart from the plight of the Oberlanders at the Engineer Barracks, the only other setback was the report that Captain Dietl of the Nineteenth Infantry Regiment had been thwarted by a superior and was unable to turn over the barracks of the First Battalion to SA and Oberland units. Kampfbund forces held all of Munich on the east side of the Isar River; on the west side, where the important government buildings were located, Röhm held the Reichswehr headquarters, and Pöhner and Frick appeared to be in control at police headquarters on Ettstrasse.

Although the Reichswehr had failed to hand over the infantry and engineer complexes, which were also on the west side of the river, there was no sign of any other move to hinder the "national revolution." Hitler sustained himself on the emotions of crowds, and every indication was that the people of Munich were applauding a bold move that they interpreted as being a start to the return of a proud and prosperous Germany.

Nevertheless, a vacuum was not what Hitler wanted. It was not enough to be able to say that no one — Reichswehr, state police, or Munich police — was moving against them. It was also true that Gregor Strasser and other able SA leaders were bringing limited numbers of reinforcements to Munich from different parts of Bavaria, but, looking around, Hitler saw SA men sitting at tables in the beer hall and his own leaders milling about aimlessly. Hitler was still wearing his "frightful tailcoat outfit," but he had on his trench coat, with a pistol in a holster on a belt, and carried his rhinoceros-hide whip. Striding back and forth in the entrance hall of the Bürgerbräukeller, Hitler began shouting orders to his subordinates.

Among those who were told to get out and start doing something were Goering, Berchtold, Weber, and two speechmakers — Hermann Esser, who was too excited to go back to bed, despite his jaundice, and Julius Streicher, who had arrived from Nuremberg during the course of the evening. Even Amann was ordered out with some armed men to take over the bank on Kanalstrasse that he had been eyeing as additional office space for the new government. With the rhythm of walking back and forth quickly in the vestibule, his voice rising as he gave orders, Hitler was soon in full oratorical flight, shouting, "Tomorrow either we are successful and masters of a united Germany, or we shall be hanging from the lampposts!"[5] Hermann Kriebel intruded on Hitler's pronouncements to tell him that the force from the Infantry School had lined up in formation on Rosenheimer Strasse, outside the beer hall, and wanted to salute Ludendorff and Hitler as they passed in review.

A moment earlier, Hitler had been urging everyone to get across the river and take further actions, like seizing government ministries. But any military ceremony was irresistible to Hitler and Ludendorff, so both men went out to the straight, broad street that ran down to the Ludwig Bridge. Lined up under the few street lights in the falling wet snow were the 350 men from the Infantry School. This was indeed an elite force, composed of outstanding officer candidates or promising young officers whose hasty wartime training was being reinforced by a far more extensive professional course, and Hitler and Ludendorff smiled happily as Gerhard Rossbach saluted and presented the unit. Rossbach had somewhere found a brass band that belonged neither to the military nor to the Kampfbund, and the musicians launched into strident flourishes of trumpets and beating of drums. Keeping one hand on his soft felt hat so it would not blow away in the wind, Ludendorff, wearing a brown loden overcoat, nodded approvingly as the high-spirited body of young men marched past in review. When the ceremony was completed, Hitler stepped forward and gave yet another short exhortation.

Soon after, Ludendorff left to join Röhm at Reichswehr headquarters. That, he felt, was the right place for the commander of the forces of the new "German national government" to be on the first night of the "national revolution." Hitler would soon join him there. It would be a much more suitable, and presumably more efficient, command post. Accompanied by his stepson and his valet, as well as Friedrich Weber and Hermann Kriebel, Ludendorff was driven to the big stone building. Once there, he sat waiting outside Lossow's office, indicating that he was certain that the commander of the Bavarian Reichswehr would arrive at any moment to use it himself.[6]

II

During this hour before midnight, the Putsch was at a stage that raised many more questions than it answered. The putschists had enjoyed the element of surprise, and judging by the public reaction, the momentum was still theirs. Dawn would come and with it a new day in which Hitler could make speeches, and the public could read the many posters proclaiming the new government that were being printed during the hours of darkness. Beyond Bavaria, there was the question of whether the spark struck in Munich might ignite significant action in Berlin. The groups of North Germans who had been in the wings, each cabal plotting to install its own directorate to lead the nation, might be forced into a desperate scramble to seize power. The Kampfbund move could have international implications: "The French are going to be marching before the night is over," a newspaper editor was saying privately in Munich.[7]

In contrast to the state of affairs at Coburg in October of 1922, when Hitler and a strong SA force had seized that far smaller city with the intention of holding it for two days and leaving, this situation was murky for all parties concerned. At Coburg, Hitler had arrived on a train filled with Storm Troops, fully aware of his objectives and his sole responsibility for achieving them. Now, in the slushy snow, an hour after the triumvirate had left the beer hall, no one in the Kampf-bund knew where those three leaders were or what they were doing. If Lossow intended to cooperate, or even to remain neutral, it would be folly to fire upon the Reichswehr — as it would be to take on Seisser and his even larger force of state police. No relationship was clear: some officers of the Kampfbund believed that they were acting as auxiliary police, supporting Kahr and the Bavarian government in a united cause. Many junior Reichswehr officers did not know what was expected of them. Were they to greet these marching Kampfbund columns as comrades, or were the Storm Troops to be regarded as enemies, even though they were rising against the Berlin government that so many in the Reichswehr also despised? Near midnight, the Kampfbund and the government were groping around Munich in a dangerous game of blindman's buff.

The events of the night were unfolding in a series of vignettes. The first senior officer of the Reichswehr to react decisively was Major General Jakob von Danner, the Munich city commandant. Sitting at home earlier in the evening, he had been alerted to the crisis by a call from a state police officer, and had rushed out in civilian clothes. Arriving at his office in a building three blocks from the captured Reichswehr headquarters, he gave a junior officer his opinion of what he had just heard about the events at the beer hall:

> Let me tell you something, Captain, Lossow cuts a sorry figure
> of a man. He has been meddling in politics and vacillating for
> months. But the least he could have done in the Bürgerbräu was
> to stand up to that little corporal and tell him, flatly, "No."[8]

Danner got on the telephone and started calling commanders of Reichswehr units throughout Bavaria. He told the startled officers, many of whom he was waking, to send reinforcements to Munich, and to disregard any orders coming from Lossow, since he might be issuing them under duress. Danner's orders were timely and wise, but it would take time to rouse these units from sleep, assemble and fully outfit them, and find sufficient vehicles to bring them to Munich. The nearest of the garrisons he had alerted was thirty miles away, and the farthest a hundred and twenty. What Danner could not know was that uprisings were planned in four of the cities whose garrison commanders he had just ordered to send troops to Munich. Moreover, the commander he had just talked to at Ingolstadt was in sympathy with the Putsch and let his men go on sleeping.[9]

Danner was still on the telephone issuing instructions to other distant units when General von Lossow walked in.[10] Having discovered that his own headquarters was in Kampfbund hands, the Reichswehr commander had come to the city commandant's office. It was a delicate moment. The others present were General Kress von Kressenstein, who had failed in his negotiations aimed at bringing the Bavarian Reichswehr back under Berlin's command after Kahr and Lossow broke with the national government, and General Adolf Ritter von Ruith, who had taken no part in Lossow's move to create a separate Bavarian army. Only Lossow had been at the hall; like Danner, the other two generals were in the civilian clothes they had been wearing when they learned of the emergency and rushed to help.

Lossow's high-ranking subordinates did not know where their commander stood. "Excellency," Danner said to Lossow concerning his pledge given at the beer hall, "surely that was all bluff?"[11]

Other than these four men, no one ever knew what was said next. The four generals went into an inner room and talked for half an hour. There was no doubt that Lossow had been impressed by Ludendorff's dramatic appearance at the beer hall and the role that Ludendorff was prepared to take in the "national revolution," and he may have been impressed by the pro-Kampfbund excitement being demonstrated by the crowds in the streets. However, the General von Lossow who emerged from this conference with his colleagues promptly announced to everyone present that because his commitment had been extracted at pistol point, he did not feel bound by it. He intended to move against the Putsch with everything at his disposal, but Hitler and Ludendorff were to be kept in the dark about his defection until he could organize effective countermoves.[12]

In the meantime, Colonel von Seisser had arrived. He expressed complete opposition to the Putsch and went out into the city again, trying to organize his state police units.[13] The generals decided to abandon this headquarters, which was deep in Kampfbund-controlled territory, and to set up an anti-Putsch command post at the headquarters of the Nineteenth Infantry Regiment, farther from the center of the city. Driving there, Lossow managed to get past a detachment of SA and Oberland men who were at the gates of the Infantry Barracks, uncertain of whether they should be blocking a general's staff car or saluting it.

Within minutes, Lossow was at a desk in the signals section of the regimental headquarters. Although the Oberlanders locked in the engineers' drill hall were less than two hundred yards away, this communications room was at the center of a strongly built complex that now had its troops on full alert.[14]

Testing their communications, Lossow and the signals officers discovered that they could still reach the switchboard of the Reichswehr headquarters downtown, despite its occupation by Röhm's men. Not only that: the man in charge of the switchboard was a Captain Daser, the same officer who had felt compelled to surrender the building to the Kampfbund's superior forces. Röhm had asked him to remain on duty, as a prelude to the cooperation, forced or voluntary, that he expected from Lossow, and then had forgotten about Captain Daser and his switchboard operators. The result was that Daser, under the noses of Hitler and Ludendorff, who were in the next room, was talking directly to Lossow's chief of staff at the Infantry Barracks. Daser was instructed to relay from his switchboard all the orders to bring in Reichswehr reinforcements from every corner of Bavaria. He proceeded to do so; a few yards away, Hitler and Ludendorff waited for Lossow to appear and honor his pledge to start working with them.[15]

With Lossow at the Infantry Barracks command post and Seisser moving around the city, the question remained: Where was General Commissioner von Kahr, and what was he doing?

After Ludendorff had allowed him to leave the beer hall, Gustav von Kahr was driven straight to his headquarters building, the Staatskommissariat. Intensely shaken by the evening's events, he was short of breath as he climbed the steps and barely greeted his daughter, who was waiting for him. He handed her his coat, asked her to prepare some tea, and walked to his office.[16]

In the next hour, Kahr puzzled one man and brilliantly deceived two others. The man puzzled was Franz Matt, Bavaria's minister of culture and a politician who had for years expressed his contempt for Kahr's bureaucratic maneuvers and infighting. That evening, having no intention of being bored by one of Gustav von Kahr's speeches, Matt had dined with Munich's Cardinal von Faulhaber and Bishop Eugenio Pacelli, the papal nuncio who later became Pope Pius XII. It was while he was with them that he learned of the Putsch, news that Cardinal von Faulhaber instantly deplored, remarking that he would work strongly against the uprising. When he heard that half the Bavarian cabinet had been taken into custody at the Bürgerbräu- keller by Hitler, Matt had promptly rounded up the remaining government ministers; he called Kahr from the apartment of a woman friend, where they all were anxiously waiting.

"What does Hitler want, anyway?" Matt inquired.

"The famous march on Berlin."[17]

Trying to ascertain just where Kahr stood, Matt spoke of Ernst Pöhner, whom Hitler had just named as Bavaria's new minister-president. In response to Matt's facetious question as to whether Pöhner was going to stop inflation by fixing the price of veal sausages, Kahr observed that setting the price ceiling for that particular item would be one of the hardest challenges that Pöhner would have to confront. Since Kahr was not noted for deadpan humor, his answer convinced Matt that the general commissioner was either in no condition to cope with the crisis or that he was going along with Hitler and Ludendorff. Hanging up the telephone, Matt told his cabinet colleagues that he was leading them to Regensburg, sixty-five miles north of Munich, where they could operate a loyal Bavarian government until the situation in Munich was resolved. Before they left, they wrote a proclamation that was intended to rally the Reichswehr, police, and all civil servants to the side of Bavaria's constitutional government, and to urge them to reject the Putsch. A particular verbal shot was aimed at "the Prussian Ludendorff, who has brought so much misfortune this night to the Bavarian people."[18]

Soon after his conversation with Matt, Kahr was informed that two men were waiting to see him. They were none other than Ernst Pöhner and Wilhelm Frick. The latter had just been named Munich's new police commissioner by Hitler.

Kahr's reaction was to keep the two men waiting outside his office for half an hour. Just what was racing or plodding through the general commissioner's mind during those thirty minutes was never clear. He had on the premises more than enough policemen to arrest the putschists, but he did not know where General von Lossow and Colonel von Seisser were, or what positions or actions they were taking. Separated from the other two members of the triumvirate, he apparently decided on a course of action identical with theirs: he was indeed defecting, but Hitler's forces must not know this until a counteroffensive could be mounted.

When the two men entered the office, Kahr greeted them with the excuse that he had been on the telephone all that time with Minister Matt. Pöhner and Frick said that they were there to discuss the manner in which state officials throughout Bavaria should be informed of the new government and its policies.

Kahr produced something that he had apparently written while keeping the putschists waiting. It was, he told them, the text of a telegram that he had already sent, informing the district prefects throughout Bavaria that he was assuming a new role as the representative of Crown Prince Rupprecht.[19]

The irony of this was twofold: an insincere concession to the Wittelsbach dynasty was not the part of the "national revolution" that the putschists wanted to stress, and there was never any indication that Kahr sent the message. It appears likely that he had spent some of the half hour in writing a telegram that he had no intention of sending, but that would convince Pöhner and Frick that he was acting in accordance with the agreement proclaimed by Hitler. Upset though he may have been, Kahr was justifying an earlier remark of Hitler's that he was a "cunning old rogue."[20]

Not questioning the document's authenticity, Pöhner asked whether he could show the telegram to the city's newspaper editors, whom he had summoned to meet with him at a midnight press conference. Kahr assured him that he could. Frick then said that they ought to issue some sort of joint proclamation to the residents of Munich, something that could be printed in the next few hours and distributed in the morning, but Kahr reminded them that Hitler had said, in their last conversations at the beer hall, that he was reserving the entire propaganda activity to himself. Frick agreed that that was true. The other topic that Kahr's visitors wanted to discuss was the matter of the appointments that Pöhner intended to make, creating new cabinet ministers.

Kahr assured Pöhner that he would be happy to discuss the matter with him at nine-thirty the following morning, and he jotted down the appointment on his desk calendar.

Believing that Gustav von Kahr was acting in accordance with the commitment he had given at the Bürgerbräukeller, Pöhner and Frick left the Generalstaatskommissariat. As they went out one door, Colonel von Seisser, unseen by them, was entering through another.[21]

It was shortly after midnight, and, out of the snow, the entire Infantry School column appeared in front of Kahr's headquarters. Rossbach's men were followed by a truck that was towing a loaded cannon. Within moments, the cannon was in place facing the building. Alongside it, machine guns were set up. On Rossbach's command, his men fixed bayonets on their rifles and, shoulder to shoulder, advanced toward the thin line of armed state police stationed in front of the building's east façade. In a moment, the young Reichswehr combat veterans were pushing right against the Green Police, many of them also combat veterans, who had loaded rifles at the ready across their chests.

At this juncture Lieutenant Colonel Otto Muxel of the state police arrived on the run, shouting that both sides must hold their fire. While Muxel parleyed with Rossbach, who repeated an earlier putschist request that Kampfbund forces take over guard duty on behalf of the new government, a runner from the Infantry School was dispatched to Ludendorff, who had ordered this takeover. At the same time, the state police quietly sent out an urgent call for reinforcements.

The Infantry School cadets had pulled back several yards during these negotiations, and during this phase of the stand-off Colonel von Seisser strode out of the building. According to one account, he went straight up to Rossbach and snapped, "There is no need for you where the state police are on guard. March off."

Rossbach's answer was also to the point: "I cannot, Excellency. I have specific orders from General Ludendorff to take over the guard here, by force if necessary."

"You heard what I said," Seisser flung over his shoulder as he strode back toward the building. "March your men away immediately or I will give orders to shoot."[22]

The runner returned with orders from Ludendorff: the building was to be taken at all costs. A few yards apart, the two forces looked at each other over the tips of their bayonets. With their newly arrived reinforcement, the state police numbered approximately one hundred men. Ready to come at them were 350 regular army soldiers who supported the Putsch, backed by machine guns and a cannon. Between the skirmish lines, some officers from both sides were still attempting to resolve the matter without bloodshed.

Suddenly Rossbach reappeared, shouting, "What? Still negotiating here? You know General Ludendorff's orders. Why the hesitation? Order your men to fire."[23]

In a desperate effort to prevent either side from firing, Lieutenant Colonel Muxel asked three Infantry School cadets, one of them a friend of his son's, to enter the building and discuss the matter in a calmer atmosphere. Other Infantry School officers agreed to this, but said that if their three comrades did not reappear within ten minutes, the attack would begin. In the meantime, the skirmish line from the Infantry School began edging toward the state police, who held their ground.

Then, for no reason that the state police could discern, the command "Companies withdraw!" was shouted down the Infantry School line, and within moments that force, with its machine guns and field artillery piece, had disappeared in the snow. The order that had broken the impasse had supposedly come from Ludendorff; in fact, Friedrich Weber of Oberland had sent it.[24]

As Rossbach led his column across the river to the beer hall for the second time, a dark green police staff car came tearing out of a side gate of the suddenly silent Generalstaatskommissariat, heading in the opposite direction from the withdrawing putschists. In the car were Colonel von Seisser and General Commissioner von Kahr, being driven to the barracks of the Nineteenth Infantry, where General von Lossow was organizing the government's resistance at the improvised command post in the regimental communications center. It was 1:00 A.M. — two and a half hours after they had been released from the Bürgerbräukeller by Ludendorff — and the triumvirate were once again together, behind the walls of a Reichswehr stronghold.

CHAPTER

39

W HILE EVENTS in Munich were unfolding tentatively, marked by periods of inertia and marching and countermarching through the snow in the darkness, the story of Hitler's move was flashing across the Atlantic. With the help of Putzi Hanfstaengl, the foreign correspondents at the beer hall had managed to avoid the lengthy "identity controls" and sneaked out through the kitchen. Rushing to their hotels, they had telephoned or cabled their stories out of Munich long before Bavarian government officials began trying to restrict communications outside the city to messages sent by the Reichswehr. With New York time six hours behind Munich's, it was only two-thirty in the afternoon when Adolf Hitler plunged toward Kahr in the Bürgerbräukeller to start the Putsch. During the evening the cables poured into the offices of New York's morning newspapers, giving the editors ample time to pull their planned front-page stories and put Munich in the headlines. By the time theatergoers emerged on Broadway street corners before midnight, they had a choice of headlines, most of them half right. BAVARIAN CAPITAL SEIZED, the *New York Tribune* declared, and went on to say, at an hour when Ludendorff was still sitting outside Lossow's office in Munich, waiting for him to appear, LUDENDORFF LEADS ROYALIST ARMY AGAINST BERLIN. The *New York Times* had MON-ARCHIST FORCES REPORTED MARCHING ON BERLIN, but was nearer the mark with BAVARIA IN REVOLT, PROCLAIMS LUDENDORFF DIC-TATOR. The *New York World* rushed in with BAVARIAN GOVERNMENT OVERTHROWN IN REVOLUTION; LUDENDORFF AND HITLER RULE.[1] In the Midwest, readers of the *Chicago Tribune* had the story by Larry Rue, who had taken at face value what he had seen in the beer hall. "Adolf Hitler overthrew Premier von Knilling of Bavaria tonight in collusion with Dictator von Kahr," Rue cabled from Munich.[2] A chilling note was struck in a dispatch from Paris, where the French government had put its army on full alert:

> France, acting individually but apparently as a preliminary to
> an Allied move to the same effect, has instructed its ambassador
> at Berlin to inform everyone interested, including Chancellor
> Stresemann, that it will not tolerate a military dictatorship
> as . . . such an action . . . would lead to a repudiation of the
> Treaty of Versailles and the beginning of a war of revenge.[3]

In Rome, where Kurt Ludecke had been sent by Hitler to cultivate a relationship with Mussolini's Fascist government, the sometime playboy and NSDAP fund-raiser was besieged by Italian journalists wanting to know what was going on and what it meant. Ludecke answered their questions, but decided to leave for Munich after an appointment the following morning to talk with Baron Russo, Italy's secretary of foreign affairs. As for his feelings, Ludecke wrote:

> Only to be there! I had told Hitler that it would break my
> heart to be out of Germany when things started going, that I
> wanted to be with them in the front line in Munich, and he had
> said, laughing: "You can fly here when it begins."[4]

It was one thing for the public in New York to read the misinformation that Ludendorff was leading a revolutionary army toward Berlin, but in Munich, at his midnight news conference with the editors of the city's papers, Ernst Pöhner confidently presented himself as the spokesman for a new regime that he claimed had the backing not only of Kahr but of Crown Prince Rupprecht. Taking the line that the press had a duty to assist the new government in calming any public doubts or unrest, Pöhner said that there would be no press censorship, but that he expected the Munich papers to publish the proclamations issued by Hitler and Ludendorff and to report the commitments of support that had been given by the triumvirate at the beer hall.[5]

Amidst the confusion, few of Munich's journalists felt like charging through the cold darkness, being challenged by armed sentries, to try to confirm Pöhner's assertions with government officials who could not be located. In the absence of any differing statements from the triumvirate, and not having received Minister Matt's proclamation issued before he led his rump government to Regensburg, the Munich papers went to press with stories that portrayed the Putsch as a fait accompli. When the hundreds of thousands of Müncheners who had gone to sleep knowing nothing awoke in the morning, the Nazis would have a great propaganda advantage in the public mind.

II

In Berlin, the government first learned of the Putsch from press sources at 11:30 P.M.

Chancellor Stresemann immediately called a cabinet meeting at his office. It was a repetition of the scene that had taken place on the September night when news came of Bavaria's action in naming Kahr as general commissioner, bringing to a crisis the confrontation between Munich and Berlin. As on that night, Germany's leaders converged on the chancellor's residence from all directions. The staff car bearing General von Seeckt also conveyed Minister of Defense Gessler, Seeckt's political adviser Lieutenant Colonel Kurt von Schleicher, and his aide, First Lieutenant Hans-Harald von Selchow.

At the meeting, Lieutenant von Selchow noted that the only two men in the room who seemed composed were President Ebert and General von Seeckt; the other ministers were unnerved, and Stresemann was "beside himself."[6] There was no reliable information from Bavaria, but in light of the events of the past six weeks, it was reasonable to assume that this was the start of the march on Berlin. The fragmentary press reports of Lossow's having thrown in his lot with Ludendorff and Hitler were perfectly in keeping with the recent record of a man who had presided over the Seventh Division as it took an oath of loyalty specifically to Bavaria, rather than to the Reich. There was also the fear that the French would start a large-scale march into Germany, claiming that they were occupying additional territory to avert a civil war.[7]

Agitated as some of these ministers were, they did not intend to repeat the behavior of 1920, when the government had run from Berlin during the Kapp Putsch, in which Ludendorff had also played a part. Reassured that Seeckt would use the Reichswehr to defend the nation's government against this "national revolution," the cabinet dug in its heels. It was agreed that strict press censorship would be imposed. Although there was still no communication with any Reichswehr office in Bavaria, all other army commands throughout the nation would be put on alert and their commanders informed that they were to regard the Ludendorff-Hitler venture as treason, to be opposed by armed force. During this midnight meeting, it was decided to isolate Bavaria, literally: passenger train and freight service was suspended, and all transfers of funds to and from Bavaria stopped.[8]

Now came the decisive move of the night. President Ebert, Minister of Defense Gessler, and General von Seeckt went off to one side for a talk of their own. Interestingly, Chancellor Stresemann received no nod to join them. As Seeckt stood saying nothing, Gessler suggested to President Ebert that the wide-ranging emergency powers invested in Gessler, but in practice used at the command of Seeckt, should be transferred directly to the Reichswehr leader. In short, Seeckt should assume the president's powers as commander in chief and become Germany's legal dictator, answerable only to Ebert. It was an unprecedented step, extending Seeckt's role as the prime strongman of Germany, and could be done with a stroke of the pen, under the emergency powers conferred upon the president of the republic by Article 48 of the constitution. Despite the profound differences in political philosophy that existed between Ebert and Seeckt, in this hour of crisis the president calmly replied to Gessler's proposal: "I have no reason to deny General von Seeckt this indication of my confidence."[9]

Not only was this step promptly taken, but Ebert, Chancellor Stresemann, and the cabinet went on to issue a proclamation that warned the people of the Reich against what they termed "the mad beginning made in Munich."[10] General von Seeckt issued his own proclamation: "Unauthorized interference with the order of the Reich and its states will be energetically suppressed by the Reichswehr under my command no matter from what side this attack may come."[11] Having just been created dictator of Germany by men who hated the idea of dictatorship but feared the reality of revolution, Seeckt decided that there was nothing more he could do then. After telling a lieutenant colonel to get on the telephone to try to establish communication with someone in the Reichswehr in Bavaria, the "Sphinx with a monocle" went home and to bed.

III

Whatever else could be said of the Putsch at this hour, it was demonstrating what a Nazi regime would mean if Hitler came to power. At the offices of the *Völkischer Beobachter*, where champagne and schnapps were flowing in celebration of the newly declared government, the paper that was coming out in the morning bore, on the front page:

THE FIRST DECREES OF THE NATIONAL GOVERNMENT

Announcement

For the judgment of those criminals who are a threat to the existence of the people and the state, a national state tribunal is herewith formed, to act as the highest court of the land.

The judgments of these courts are: guilty or not guilty.

Not guilty means dismissal; guilty means death.

Verdicts are rendered three hours after appearance.

There is no appeal.

The competence of the national state tribunals will be specially regulated.[12]

The implicit message — that political differences would be settled by the brutal application of force — was acted out as the night went on. On orders from Hermann Goering, Josef Berchtold rushed his Stosstrupp to the offices of the *Münchener Post*, the Social Democrats' newspaper that had so often criticized Hitler and the Nazis. "We forced open the doors of this place," Berchtold said, "ransacked the building and flung all the printed stuff we could lay hands on out into the street, where it was promptly burnt."[13]

Berchtold scarcely did justice, in this description, to the thoroughness with which he and his men carried out Goering's orders. When the *Bayerischer Kurier* got around to printing its stories of the night's events, it gave this picture of what was to be seen at the *Post*: "Not one window remains intact on the first and second floors. All doors smashed, chairs, closets, desks totally demolished. Type thrown all over the place in total chaos. Mailing lists destroyed."[14] Typewriters and other equipment were stolen by the Nazis.

For the Storm Troops, human targets were more interesting: a young Social Democrat, Engelbert Vallner, a schoolteacher who had dared to stand up to some SA men during a fight at a coffee house a few weeks earlier, was hustled from his house, taken to the Bürgerbräukeller, and kicked and beaten with truncheons until he was unconscious. Erhard Auer, the Social Democratic leader and editor of the *Münchener Post*, probably saved his life by his decision to spend the night at the apartment of his friend, the attorney Wilhelm Hoegner. Auer's family had to bear the brunt of the Nazis' frustration when they could not find their enemy at home. The Stosstrupp had been created for special missions; having broken 320 panes of glass as part of their destruction of the *Münchener Post*, fifteen of these men appeared at Auer's apartment. They were under the direction of one of Hitler's chauffeurs, Emil Maurice, the watchmaker by trade who had been the SA's first leader when it was a small organization known as the party's Sports Section. Auer's wife, Sophie, then fifty-five, recounted some of the details of this midnight visit.

> One of the first ones to enter the apartment was a tall, dark-haired man [Maurice] who pointed a pistol at my face and asked, "Where is your husband?" When I explained that he had gone away, I was asked when he had been here last and where he might be. I said I did not know.
>
> "Now we are the rulers and the government," he said. "If you won't tell us where your husband is but we find him anyway, you are done for." Just then my daughter Emilie Luber and her husband came out of their bedroom, and as the man said this to me, he gave me such a hard shove to the breast that I stumbled backward through their open door and would have fallen on the floor had I not been able to catch myself on their bed. Then he locked me into their room. . . .
>
> When [Maurice] went into the room of my daughter Sophie Fangler, she asked him not to make too much noise so as not to wake her baby, but he said that was not his concern. He asked her where the child's father was and whether she had any weapons. He wanted to open a sideboard in that room to which the lock happened to be broken. So he took his rifle and smashed the doors with the stock, to satisfy himself, apparently, that there were only dishes inside it. With the rifle he also knocked a brass tray from the sideboard to the floor. Then he went through her wardrobe, threw out the clothes and laundry, and trampled on them. He tore off the bedding and smashed with his rifle butt into a suitcase containing more dishes. When my daughter asked him not to do this, he said, "Keep your mouth shut."

Unable to find Auer or any incriminating documents, the Nazis left with a hostage — Auer's son-in-law, Dr. Karl Luber. "You'll do until we find your father-in-law," Maurice said as they bundled him off to join other prisoners of the new "German national government" who were being brought to the Bürgerbräukeller from different parts of Munich.[15]

While the hunt for Marxists went on, Edmund Heines, commander of the Second Battalion of the Munich SA Regiment, took an action, "because," as he later said, "I wanted to do something special for the revolution."[16] Marching his unit of some three hundred Storm Troops through Munich on the way to the Infantry School, Heines was struck by the thought that the Allied officers attached to the Allied control commission were billeted at the nearby fashionable Hotel Vier Jahreszeiten. Deciding that it would be a fine thing for the new, resurgent Germany if he were to capture some Allied officers, Heines had his battalion block every exit of the hotel while he led a detachment of twenty of his men across the thick rugs of the lobby to the reception desk. Drawing his pistol, he pointed it at the astounded night manager and ordered him to lead the way to the rooms of the Allied officers. On the floor where the French and Belgian officers had their rooms, the Storm Troops began shouting, "Open up! Out, out! Everybody into the corridor!" Even this did not produce an immediate result; the officers were asleep and had no idea of what had happened at the beer hall.

A Belgian major finally stuck his head out the door and said, "You Boches must be crazy to make so much racket so late at night." This produced a brandishing of Storm Troop pistols, and Heines told the hotel's night manager to inform the major that he was "under the arrest and custody of the new Reich government of Hitler and Ludendorff." The Belgian responded: "You really are crazy, but you are also armed and I am not. I am at your disposal. Do with me what you wish. Shoot me if you want. But remember that I am a Belgian officer and think of the consequences."

By this time, a French colonel down the corridor understood what was going on; from behind his bolted door, he shouted that he was armed and would fire at anybody who attempted to break into his room. This was more than the proud Storm Troop leader Heines could bear. He felt compelled, as he put it, "to teach the hated Frenchman a lesson," and to demonstrate "who gives the orders and who does not in the newly born Germany." At a command from Heines, one of his men lunged at the door with his rifle butt, breaking open a panel. On opposite sides of the shattered door, Heines and the French colonel faced each other, each with pistol raised.

The night manager, Christian Tauber, averted an international incident. Not for nothing had he soothed excitable guests from a dozen nations. Stepping between the pointed pistols, he first urged the French colonel not to resist and then suggested to Heines that the Allied officers on that floor might give their pledge not to leave the hotel.

Somehow this notion of a word of honor, given to him by his late enemies, seemed to soothe the Storm Troop battalion commander.

His intention had been to round up these Frenchmen and Belgians and march them across the river, under guard, to the beer hall. Now he left guards on this floor, strutted out of the hotel, and marched his battalion into the night.

Although socialists and Allied officers were good objects for vengeance, what the Nazis really wanted were Jews. In contrast to the Bavarian cabinet ministers who had been apprehended at the beer hall, but then were taken by Rudolf Hess to spend the night in the comfortable villa of the publisher Julius Lehmann, the sixty to seventy Jews who had been stopped by the "identity controls" when the audience was released were spending the night in discomfort at the Bürgerbräukeller, enduring the taunts and threats of Kampfbund men. Early on, an Oberland patrol was sent forth from the beer hall with orders to "search for Jews and other enemies of the people," and additional Oberland and SA men, moving around the city, took similar actions on their own initiative. A squad of Oberlanders charged into the café of the Fürstenhof Hotel, roaring, *"Alle Juden raus! — All Jews out!"* Finding no Jews there, and similarly frustrated at another restaurant down the street, they marched into the Excelsior Hotel. The concierge of the establishment, on being told by a man with a swastika on his sleeve that the new regime was rounding up Jews, replied, "We don't have any tonight."[17] This produced a demand to see the register of guests; try as the Oberlanders would, they could make none of the names seem Jewish.

Thrice disappointed, the squad went on to ransack once again the apartment of the Auers, who were Gentiles, and then began ringing the doorbells and entering the apartments of those whose doors bore Jewish-sounding names. Other units smashed the windows of shops whose proprietors were Jewish, in one case shooting at an owner who came out of a back bedroom to protect his property. Some of the looting and manhandling of Jews was the result of previous disputes — in one case, two brothers who were in the SA led an attack on the apartment of a family who had testified against them in a case of sexual molestation in which they had been convicted. Most of the break-ins and beatings, however, had a terrible impersonality about them. As the night went on, more patrols were sent from the Bürgerbräukeller, specifically ordered to spread terror among Jews. It was not a question of rich ones, or those known to sympathize with Marxist ideas — any Jew would do. Armed groups roamed Jewish neighborhoods, in one case prompting a couple whose apartment had been vandalized to make their way furtively to the Ostbahnhof, the railroad station on the city's eastern side, to wait for a train that would take them out of Germany to refuge in Vienna.

Fortunately for Munich's small Jewish population, the random searches during the night were inefficient and uncertain: some Storm Troops contented themselves with simply demanding any of the highly prized foreign currencies, and many patrols, when a door was not answered, just passed on. The height of impersonality was reached when at least one Storm Troop unit began looking through the telephone book, searching for the addresses of those whose names sounded as if they surely belonged to Jews.[18] By the time the entire abortive round-up sputtered out, fifty-eight people had been brought to the Bürgerbräukeller, where they joined those who had been detained there by the "identity controls."[19] Among those herded in during the night were several men in their seventies and others whose wives and daughters had insisted on going into captivity with them. A number of these men were badly beaten. Hermann Goering, passing through a room in which SA men were telling Jews that they might be executed, cut short those threats with this statement to his Storm Troops: "We do not have the right or authority to execute — yet."[20]

One special action that was carried out involved a Jewish firm, but the goal in this case was purely the acquisition of money, not the practice of anti-Semitism. The word was passed among the many hundreds of SA men who were spending the night in the beer hall, some asleep and some chafing for action, that bank employees were needed to volunteer for an unspecified task. Thirty-two men stepped forward and were placed aboard two trucks outside the beer hall.

Crossing the Isar River, the trucks headed into downtown Munich, stopping near the elegant Bayerischer Hof Hotel. Their destination was the printing plant owned by Parcus Brothers. Inside, the presses were feeding Germany's inflation with a night's production of 14 quadrillion marks. An indication of the limitless dimensions of the inflation was that the smallest bill being printed was a 50-billion mark note, worth about eight cents in American money. The freshly printed stacks of bills of all denominations were worth $22,200 in American currency — a stupendous fortune in terms of its buying power in Germany. The plan was to seize it and, later in the day, pay the Kampfbund troops handsomely for their work. Each man was to receive 2 trillion marks, or $3.17.

Striding into the plant with his makeshift unit of armed bank employees behind him, Karl Beggel of the First SA Battalion confronted the plant manager, who with a Reichsbank official was checking the latest press runs, and handed them a piece of paper signed "A. Hitler." The new government needed this money, Beggel declared; here was the document that would serve as a receipt. All that was necessary was for the plant manager to furnish the information about the number of marks on hand. Beggel would fill that out, and the firm could keep the receipt.

Neither the plant manager nor the Reichsbank official raised the slightest question about the legality of this proceeding. It is possible that they were intimidated by the sudden appearance of men in uniform, but many in Munich were under the impression that there was indeed a new national government, and that men with swastikas were authorized to conduct its business.[21]

CHAPTER

40

WHATEVER Hitler and Ludendorff may have been hearing or not hearing, believing or not wishing to believe, the triumvirate soon made their position clear. "Thus, a radiogram was drafted," Lossow said, "which would be broadcast by all German radio stations at 2:50 A.M." The text read:

> Generalstaatskommissar von Kahr, General von Lossow, and Colonel von Seisser repudiate the Hitler Putsch. The opinions expressed in the Bürgerbräukeller, extorted from us through armed force, are invalid. Caution against the misuse of the above names is urged. Signed: Kahr, Lossow, and Seisser.[1]

Sitting on a couch in the orderly room of the Nineteenth Infantry Regiment communications section, the heart of the command post, General Commissioner von Kahr was drafting a proclamation to be issued to the Bavarian public. There was a certain irony in the indignation Kahr expressed, since he had been hoping for a rightist overthrow in Berlin to replace President Ebert and Chancellor Stresemann, just the same sort of undercutting Kahr rightly felt that Hitler had attempted on him. A seizure of power in Berlin by a directorate would have been fully acceptable to Kahr, but he called Hitler's move in Bavaria "a repulsive act of terror." Kahr went on:

> The declarations extracted from me, General von Lossow, and Colonel von Seisser at the point of a pistol are null and void. Had this senseless and aimless attempt at overthrow succeeded, it would have plunged Germany, and Bavaria with it, into the abyss. . . .
> The guilty will be ruthlessly prosecuted and punished, and I hereby declare the National Socialist German Workers' Party, the Oberland League, and the Reichskriegsflagge Society disbanded and prohibited.[2]

Along with what was being heard at three in the morning, there were for the Nazis some alarming silences. Nothing was coming in from the Kampfbund leaders who were to have taken control of the Bavarian cities of Augsburg, Nuremberg, Regensburg, and Würzburg. At Regensburg, the SA battalion commander had been arrested at the very moment he demanded the surrender of the Reichswehr barracks, and his entire force had surrendered without firing a shot. The Putsch had similarly fizzled in each city where a seizure of power was attempted. Even before the triumvirate's radio message to the nation, informal reports that Lossow had "fallen away" were reaching the captured Reichswehr headquarters in Munich; shortly after 1:00 A.M., Ernst Röhm had finally discovered that Captain Daser was using the switchboard to call in Reichswehr reinforcements from outside Munich and arrested him.[3]

General Erich Ludendorff still believed that if he could only talk to General von Lossow, they could implement the commitments to cooperate that had been made at the beer hall. If Ludendorff sensed any turn of the tide, he gave no sign of it: impassive, he remained at Reichswehr headquarters, placing telephone calls to Lossow and being told that the general was not available. Ludendorff felt at home in a military headquarters; Hitler, after trying both the Reichswehr building and the Bürgerbräukeller, was more comfortable in the beer hall. Thus, in the midst of an already confused situation, the two principal figures in the "national revolution" were at times a mile apart.

Whatever Hitler might be saying to those around him, he sensed that failure was ready to grab him by the throat. Julius Streicher found him sitting sullenly at the beer hall, and, practically shaking him, urged him to go on the offensive with his best weapon: propaganda. The public must be reached. Streicher told Hitler that the Kampfbund must get into the streets, and Hitler must appeal directly to the Bavarian populace. As Streicher later described the scene, Hitler stared at him with a completely defeated expression, then wrote a note that transferred "the entire organization" to Streicher.[4] The document that Hitler scratched out in his angular handwriting has survived, complete with the almost certainly wrong date of November 8, which may give some indication of the stress Hitler was feeling well into the early morning of November 9. The words can be construed to mean that Hitler was turning the Nazi Party over to Streicher so that he could concentrate on being Germany's chancellor, but Hitler had always considered the party as his indispensable vehicle, and Streicher believed that he was witnessing an abdication.

For the Committee of the National Socialist German Workers' Party.
Munich, 8 Nov. 1923.
Comrade Julius Streicher:
In order to be equal to the great tasks of preventing the country
from ruin I must put the Party organization into your hands,
Comrade Streicher.
Everything for Germany.

Your Adolf Hitler.[5]

Perhaps a further indication of Hitler's frenetic state was the "clarification" that he placed right below this:

I, Adolf Hitler, place the position of Party Chairman into the hands
of the leader of the Franconian movement, Julius Streicher.
Done this 8th day of November, 1923, in Munich.

Adolf Hitler[6]

Having written his declaration, plus a directive empowering
Streicher to control party propaganda and requisition any vehicles that
might be necessary for the purpose, Hitler sank back for a few minutes
as if nothing that was going on around him was any of his affair. Then
he gave way to despair.

Streicher kept trying to encourage him, and, like a child, Hitler
allowed himself to be coaxed around. At first he was merely philosophical, in his own brutal way: "If it comes off, all's well; if not, we'll
hang ourselves."[7] A few minutes later, after someone reported to him
that the public mood, as far as it could be determined, was still running
in his favor, Hitler was suddenly the confident man of the speakers'
platform. "Propaganda, propaganda, now it all depends on propaganda!"[8] He ordered the planning for fourteen mass meetings to be
held at the end of that Friday, and on Saturday there was to be a
tremendous open-air meeting on the Königsplatz, with many, many
thousands saluting the new government with their cheers. Buoyed by
this vision of himself triumphant, past the present realities and once
again in the position of an orator in command of his audience, he
started thinking about the wording of the posters advertising the cel-
ebrations of victory.

II

In the hours between 3:00 A.M. and dawn, the putschists received
several more setbacks, but the Kampfbund's greatest difficulty con-

tinued to be its own failure of leadership. Everything had proceeded on one of two assumptions: either the triumvirate would agree to cooperate, or they would not. The idea that Kahr, Lossow, and Seisser would apparently agree and then renege had not entered the calculations of Hitler and Ludendorff; they both were befuddled by it, and Ludendorff simply refused to believe it.

Even now, there were key objectives to be had for the taking: the central railroad station, the telegraph building just across from it, and the central telephone exchange. The state police were slowly moving to guard some of these places, but in the hours after midnight they had been totally vulnerable. At Munich police headquarters at Ettstrasse, the Kampfbund was allowing to be perpetuated the dangerous fiction that everyone was working together, whereas they might have been safer had they secured the building with a heavy concentration of troops at an early hour.

The government was moving slowly, but with a specific plan. The objective was twofold: first, to recapture Reichswehr headquarters, then to mount an attack on the Kampfbund forces at the Bürgerbräukeller. By contrast, Hitler was still suggesting that SA patrols go throughout the residential quarters of the city shouting, "Put out your flags!" in the hope that, with dawn, a great display of swastikas and the old red, white, and black banners of Imperial Germany might help to turn the tide.[9]

Slowly — in some cases very slowly — the government was closing certain gaps. At 4:00 A.M., Berlin finally had some reliable information from Bavaria. After hours of trying, General von Seeckt's aide, Lieutenant von Selchow, finally got through to the Reichswehr commander in Stuttgart, near the Bavarian border, and that officer was able to pass on the information that the Seventh Division, at Munich, was firmly under Lossow's control and that Lossow was moving to put down the Putsch. For Berlin, this was the single most important piece of news: Selchow hung up the telephone thinking, "Now at least Reichswehr will not fire on Reichswehr."[10]

In one area, being slow meant losing: not until 4:00 A.M. did Kahr get around to giving an order to stop publication of Munich's morning papers, but by that time, the only one that was not already in the process of being printed and distributed was an afternoon paper. In the morning, the Munich public would be reading that there was indeed a new Hitler-Ludendorff government, and that the triumvirate was supporting it.[11]

In the darkness, only one part of the new contest could be called a draw at that hour. The government began placing detachments of state police on the west side of the bridges across the Isar. Hitler countered by seeing to it that Kampfbund units of equal size were placed at the east end of the bridges, and yet, in the snowy night, the mutual reluctance of both sides to take the final step toward bloodshed continued. While Ludendorff sat at Reichswehr headquarters, convinced that Lossow would still make his way to him and place the Seventh Division at his disposal, the bridges across the Isar remained open, with neither side trying to stop vehicles, no matter who or what they contained.

The string of Nazi tactical defeats that began at 3:00 A.M. started with what befell Wilhelm Frick, who had been working secretly for the Nazis within Munich police headquarters. In this never-never land of the Putsch, Frick was taking a nap in one room when, shortly after 3:00 A.M., a telephone call from Captain Karl Wild of the state police was being answered in another. The responder was Colonel Josef Banzer of the state police, whom Frick was allowing to continue his work at headquarters in the belief that the triumvirate was supporting Hitler and Ludendorff. Wild quickly told Banzer that he was transmitting a direct order from Kahr and Seisser to arrest Frick at the earliest opportunity.

That opportunity presented itself less than five seconds after Banzer hung up. Having finished his nap, Frick strolled into the room and suggested to Banzer that he go home and get some sleep. One account gave the following exchange:

COLONEL BANZER: Well, Herr Frick, I do have one more thing to do and also some information for you. You are under arrest.

FRICK: On whose orders?

COLONEL BANZER: The government's.

FRICK: But which government, Colonel?

COLONEL BANZER: Excellency von Kahr's. I am arresting you on the orders and in the name of the General State Commissioner.[12]

And so Wilhelm Frick, whom Hitler had named as Munich's new police commissioner, was locked up at the headquarters of the Munich police.

The next government action was taken at 4:40 A.M. Reacting to unconfirmed reports that Ludendorff intended to seek out Reichswehr units throughout the city and use his great personal prestige with the junior officers and enlisted men to urge them to back the "national revolution," the triumvirate issued an order that he was to be arrested on sight.[13] It was an almost unthinkable turn of events — conservative right-wing Bavarian leaders declaring their willingness to lock up the national commander who had for so long been a revered right-wing figure.

A few minutes later, one of the Putsch's many subplots began unfolding. This time the central figure was Ernst Pöhner, Hitler's choice to replace Eugen von Knilling as the new minister-president of Bavaria. Colonel Banzer quietly sent two captains and a detachment of state police to Pöhner's home to arrest him, but they failed to find him. In fact, Pöhner was with Scheubner-Richter at the captured Reichswehr headquarters. When he and Scheubner-Richter had arrived, the first thing they heard was the voice of Hitler, who had again crossed the Isar to the Putsch command post, where Ludendorff was still waiting to hear from General von Lossow. "Once the will of the masses is known," Hitler was saying in a loud, excited voice, "no one will dare to resist. It will be like a storm flood, and both the army and the police will be swept along with it. More propaganda, nothing but propaganda, that will turn the trick."[14] Seeing Pöhner, Hitler explained that he wanted to secure the headquarters of the Munich police with a large body of Oberlanders, and set that up as an advance post in the heart of the city, from which patrols could go forth to call "Put out your flags!" It would be both a military presence and a propaganda base near the large squares where he intended to have orators addressing crowds during the morning.

Pöhner set off on his new assignment, but decided not to take the proffered battalion of Oberlanders with him. Unaware of Frick's arrest, and feeling confident that the men of the Munich police, whom he had previously commanded as commissioner, would obey his instructions, he went along to the headquarters at Ettstrasse. As he walked into the headquarters building, he promptly encountered Colonel Banzer, who had just received the report from his two captains that Pöhner had not been at his house when they went to arrest him. Pöhner gave this account of what happened next:

> Colonel Banzer . . . answered my question as to whether he
> had seen Frick, by saying he had orders from the Generalstaats-
> kommissar to arrest me. That hit me like a hammer! I asked,

"Who ordered that? The Generalstaatskommissar personally?" He answered, "Yes, the order came to police headquarters from the Generalstaatskommissar."[15]

Thus, one of Hitler's most important appointees — the man who was to rule Bavaria in the new government — was locked up near his fellow putschist Wilhelm Frick. At about this time, in the government command post at the Infantry Barracks, the triumvirate was reaching yet another decision. Orders were to be sent to the appropriate authorities throughout Bavaria, ordering all the Kampfbund leaders to be arrested, wherever they might be found. The border police were told to watch closely, and to apprehend any putschists who might try to slip into Austria.[16]

In the background of these moves and countermoves were the women of Munich. Margarethe Ludendorff remembered the night this way:

> About nine that evening [my husband] came into my room and said: "I have to go into the town. I shall shortly be fetched by a car. My presence is required at a national assembly."
> Soon after this a motor dashed up at a tearing speed and stopped in front of the house. The horn sounded. Ludendorff left the house and stepped inside and the next moment it had gone. It had all happened as though in a dream and events had marched with such speed that I had not even recognized my son at the steering-wheel of the car. It was long past midnight and neither my husband, my son, nor our servant had returned. I waited until half-past three and then went to bed. Next morning I heard that none of the three had come home.[17]

As the night wore on, telephone calls from anxious wives, mothers, sweethearts, sisters, and daughters poured in to Nazi Party headquarters and the offices of the *Völkischer Beobachter*. Only the smallest handful of the thousands of Kampfbund men had known what this night might entail; some had guessed that the call to their units was the beginning of something big and dangerous, but many SA men, summoned by the white slip used to indicate a routine drill, had left their homes with only the most routine good-byes.

III

Somewhere between five and six in the morning, General Erich Ludendorff stopped waiting for General von Lossow. In an effort to satisfy himself as to what was really going on, Ludendorff had sent an emissary to Lieutenant Colonel Ludwig Leupold, the deputy commandant of the Infantry School. Leupold, yet another Reichswehr officer sympathetic to the Putsch, was taking no active role in it. Asked to come to see Ludendorff at the Kampfbund command post at the captured Reichswehr headquarters, he entered the room where Ludendorff and Hitler were waiting shortly after 5:00 A.M.

Ludendorff started off by saying, indignantly, that he had been waiting for Lossow at Reichswehr headquarters since 11:00 P.M. Leupold, who recounted the subsequent conversation in some detail, replied:

> "I can explain that. He will not come. . . ." Now [Ludendorff] stated that Lossow having been "forced" was out of the question; that as long as he had been [at the beer hall], no force had been used. I replied that I heard in conversations with General Hemmer regarding Seisser and Lossow that pistols were used quite a lot. Ludendorff replied that he did not know anything about it; nothing had happened in his presence.[18]

Later, Ludendorff said that during this part of the conversation, Hitler, who had himself pointed a pistol at the triumvirate, "did not say much."[19] It was true that the pistols had been put back in their holsters by the time that Ludendorff appeared in the back room in the Bürgerbräukeller where the triumvirate were being held, but even he could not have failed to notice the extreme pressure that was being put upon them. Not feeling inclined to debate with Ludendorff, and not having been in the room himself, Leupold went on to say to Ludendorff and Hitler:

> I had been told that [the triumvirate] were not supporting the affair and that troops had been sent to Munich. At that, Ludendorff asked, with great surprise, "What does [Lossow] want with that?" Then I said: "I do not know either; I think he wants to restore order."
> Now Ludendorff concluded that I was to ask Lossow once again about his views; that I was to tell him Ludendorff was counting on his word of honor; and that I should ask him to come there. The use of force would be out of the question. The National Movement was progressing beautifully and, if he were to oppose it, the entire Movement would be finished.
> I told him I did not believe Lossow would change his mind since orders had already gone out to the troops.

Then it was Hitler's turn. He told Leupold, "You know that I am an idealist," and went on to say that for four years he had done nothing but devote himself to the völkisch cause. Leupold's account closed in this fashion:

Hitler then continued: "If they destroy my work for which I have lived these four years, then I am also determined to fight for my cause. You know I am not a coward. I have the most enthusiastic people. I wish to impress that upon Lossow. I have expressed my regrets [for the manner in which Lossow's statement of support for the Putsch had been obtained] — but I do not believe a violent conflict will occur." Furthermore, he said, "If the gentlemen are going to destroy my work, they no longer have a reason for existence." I was to give them this message. I then took my leave and said I would return if I was ordered to do so.[20]

After Leupold had left, Hitler announced that he was going back to the beer hall; the way in which he spoke of carrying on the fight from there strongly implied that he felt that Ludendorff should come, too. If what they had just heard was true, their present command post might be attacked at any time. Ludendorff agreed that the leadership should move back across the Isar River; before going, he ordered Röhm to hold the captured Reichswehr headquarters building at all costs.

Hitler's apartment was on the west side of the Isar, so before crossing to the beer hall on the east bank, he went to his rooms and changed from his morning coat into a dark double-breasted suit. He did not stop to shave, but he did transfer his Iron Cross, First Class, to the left breast of the jacket in which he would face the day ahead.

CHAPTER

41

AT SIX in the morning a short column of trucks was making its way southward on Ismaninger Strasse, parallel to the east bank of the Isar. This was a reinforcement of 150 SA men of Gregor Strasser's Lower Bavarian Regiment, just arriving in Munich. Strasser was with the column.

A Storm Troop member, Paul Goebel, was in the cab with the driver of the lead truck. As they headed toward the Bürgerbräukeller, both of them were glancing inquisitively through the windows, trying to assess the state of affairs in the city. Finally, Goebel said to the driver, "What kind of a revolution do you call this? People are going to work as usual. Something's wrong."

At the beer hall, Gregor Strasser reported to Hermann Goering, who wasted no words in describing the situation. "Those fellows," Goering said, referring to the triumvirate, "didn't come over to our side after all. They broke their word to the Führer, but the people are with us. We're going to try the whole thing over again."[1] With that, Goering ordered Strasser to take his men down to the river and guard the Wittelsbach Bridge.

As the full early daylight came to Munich that Friday morning, the city was gripped in chilly dampness. Dark grey clouds hung low over its spires and towers, and the occasional snowflakes vanished as they hit the pavements. In keeping with Hitler's attempt to win the day by propaganda, a small Kampfbund detachment fanned out, putting up the freshly printed posters that proclaimed the "German national government" and asked for the public's support. Johann Aigner described the confusion that ensued: "In the meantime the Blue Police took down the appeals of the new government, something our troops didn't approve of; that's why they arrested some police patrols. On the other hand, the police arrested our patrols. The situation was not clear at all."[2]

Inside the beer hall, a thousand soldiers of the Putsch were at loose ends. Some were asleep, slumped over tables; others were cleaning their rifles. The inexperience of some of these young paramilitary men was manifested every few minutes when a shot rang out somewhere in the great hall because of careless handling of a weapon. The night before, the huge kitchens of the Bürgerbräukeller had been able to produce hundreds upon hundreds of plates of food; all those cooks and waitresses had gone home, and with dawn, the ovens were cold. There was no breakfast for the thousand unshaven men at the command post of the revolution. Some squads were sent out to requisition bread from bakeries. Individuals produced sausages and pieces of cheese that they had brought along the previous night and breakfasted in ad hoc fashion. Only the beer of the Bürgerbräukeller was still flowing, and many Storm Troops had it for breakfast.

The Putsch was at an ebb. The majority of these Kampfbund men were tired after their uncomfortable night — many of them had spent it tramping around the city with no firm results — but only a handful knew about the triumvirate's renunciation of their pledge. One lieutenant of the Infantry School who came to Gerhard Rossbach, saying that he had learned that the Putsch leaders were concealing the government's opposition to the "national revolution," was curtly told that he could leave the building and cross the river, but that he must not speak to anyone else. Even among those who had no idea that government forces were beginning to deploy against them, there was a nagging sense of self-doubt. They were supposed to be the saviors of Germany; they were warriors in uniform. Thus far, they had marched to the scenes of confrontations, then turned and marched away. In many men, there was stirring a desire to do something irrevocable.

The symbolism of this vast echoing beer hall, of men in uniform simply sitting about, was overwhelming. It was in beer halls that Hitler had created himself as a political force; it was in beer halls that he had threatened the government in Berlin and scorned the government of Bavaria. In this very hall he had repeatedly conjured up the vision of armed Nazi might. Now, in this morning hour, the question was there to haunt the leaders of the NSDAP: Was this the beginning of what their prophet had promised them, or was the movement spent and dead?

*

Around seven in the morning, Hitler and Ludendorff fell to arguing.[3] This was the surest sign of the desperation that Hitler was feeling: Otto Strasser said of Hitler's usual deference to Germany's wartime leader, "In the presence of Ludendorff, he made an impression closer to that of an orderly; he acted more like a waiter."[4] Hitler was at last pointing out to Ludendorff the folly of allowing Kahr, Lossow, and Seisser to walk out of the beer hall as free men; Ludendorff retorted that Hitler should never had drawn his pistol on Kahr, and that it was Hitler who had ruined everything by humiliating the triumvirate with a display of armed coercion in front of three thousand of Bavaria's most prominent citizens. Predictably, neither of these iron-willed egotists made the slightest impression on the other, and Ludendorff lapsed into granitic silence.

Hitler, on the other hand, walked over to Julius Streicher and urged him to get out into the city and begin the morning's speechmaking: he and Esser and other proven Nazi orators must start generating massive and highly visible support for the newly proclaimed regime. Then Hitler turned to Max Josef Neunzert, a wartime lieutenant who was a member of Röhm's Reichskriegsflagge. Neunzert was a friend of Crown Prince Rupprecht and accompanied him on cheerful hunting parties in Bavaria's mountainous forest areas. Hitler dispatched Neunzert to call on the crown prince at Berchtesgaden, in the hope of securing his endorsement of the Putsch. This mission was a tribute to the power of Hitler's wishful thinking; only a man with an idée fixe could have imagined that Rupprecht would smile on the men who had arrested his adviser, Count von Soden. The crown prince detested Ludendorff for his outspoken anti-Catholicism, considered Hitler and Ludendorff to be irresponsible extremists, and was to refer to Hitler's armed intrusion into the beer hall as a "mad act." Although Rupprecht did not make a public statement at the time, his views were known in the circles in which he had influence; all three of the principal organizations of retired Bavarian army officers were within hours of declaring themselves opposed to the Putsch.[5]

There was more formal government opposition to the Kampfbund. At the same time that Neunzert set off to see Crown Prince Rupprecht — 7:30 A.M. — a direct telephone link was at last established between the Reichswehr in Bavaria and General von Seeckt's headquarters in Berlin. Even then, the Bavarian end of the telephone connection was not in Munich; an officer in Regensburg succeeded in getting through to Seeckt's operations chief. Berlin now heard it directly from Bavaria: Lossow, in the midst of a full-scale mobilization of the Reichswehr forces at his command, was ready to use whatever force was necessary to parry the Kampfbund's strike for power.[6]

In addition to providing Berlin with specific and most welcome information, this call had a further significance: implicit in the fact that this conversation took place was the reestablishment of the chain of command as it had existed before Lossow had the Bavarian forces swear a separate oath of allegiance. Although the message was relayed, Munich was reporting to Berlin, and Berlin was ready to send reinforcements if needed. By coincidence, at 7:40 A.M., only ten minutes after the call was made, Lossow issued the orders in Munich that assigned to several Reichswehr units the mission of recapturing the Reichswehr headquarters still held by Röhm and his men. The operational order instructed the unit commanders to have their troops surround the building, after which its surrender was to be demanded.[7] The die was cast, but it would be four hours before the units were actually brought into place.

II

It was eight in the morning when Putzi Hanfstaengl arrived at the Bürgerbräukeller; he had had several hours' sleep at home. He soon found Hitler and Ludendorff.

They were no longer in the small room on the ground floor where Ludendorff had so misguidedly accepted his fellow general's word of honor, but had moved to a larger private room upstairs. The old Quartermaster General was sitting stony-faced and frightening in his unperturbed calm, sipping away at red wine, the only sustenance the conspirators had enjoyed. The air was thick with cigar and cigarette smoke. In the anteroom there was a little orchestra platform and on it, in a pile about five feet high, thousands of million and billion mark notes, in neat banker's bundles. . . .

Evidently none of the money was intended for the civilian brass band, which Brückner, Hitler's adjutant, had rustled up from somewhere. By this time there were about eight hundred uniformed men in and around the hall, all somewhat dispirited. It was an unlikely day for a Putsch, cold with flurries of snow, and most of the S.A. and Kampfbund men were in thin cotton shirts and had had nothing to eat since the night before. Anyway this morose and resentful brass band was produced but the men demanded breakfast and their wages in advance, neither of which they received. Brückner bawled them out, sent them up onto the platform and ordered them to play. We could hear them tootling away without any life in the music, even making a hash of Hitler's favorite Badenweiler march.

There was some desultory discussion about what to do next, but no conclusions were reached.

Hitler said he was relying on me to keep him informed about the general feeling in Munich and I spent most of the morning travelling by car between the Bürgerbräu and the *Beobachter*. I had to find some version to satisfy the suspicious foreign correspondents, who were more or less encamped at the newspaper, and the best I could do was to suggest that a few personal differences had arisen between the leaders of the conspiracy and that all would soon be settled. Rosenberg was under no illusions. "It is no good, the whole thing has failed," he said despairingly.[8]

At the beer hall, the Kampfbund leadership was examining a sample of the government's propaganda. A poster that had been printed overnight and placed on a kiosk by the Munich police was torn down and brought in for inspection. In heavy type it screamed HIGH TREASON. The attack was more upon Ludendorff than Hitler; denouncing "the Prussian Ludendorff" as a traitor, it urged all those who loved Bavaria to reject the adventures of this "ambitious character."[9]

Looking back on his feelings at this hour, Ludendorff was to say that he felt "*wehmütig*" — melancholy. The mood he was in, however, conjured up for him the memory of a night before victory: the sleepless hours he had spent on a hill above Liège, before the day in 1914 when that Belgian city surrendered, making him a German national hero.[10]

Hitler was about to use Ludendorff, the presence of Ludendorff, in an effort to stave off the possible defection of the Infantry School contingent, all of whom were in the beer hall at the moment. Increasing numbers of these young officers and cadets were becoming worried about the rumors they were hearing of a split between the triumvirate and the Kampfbund leadership. Gerhard Rossbach, who had handled this elite force without serious incident to this point, asked Hitler to speak to the young men.

Counting on the magic that Ludendorff's name still held for many of the Reichswehr's junior officers, Hitler said to the Infantry School men, "It is your patriotic duty to follow His Excellency General Ludendorff wherever he leads you. Those who doubt, those who question, are free now to leave this room!"

Hitler was back in oratorical stride. The master of timing stopped and looked around, waiting to see whether anyone would go. The ranks did not stir. He went on, "Now, I will call upon each of you to swear an oath of loyalty and obedience to the leader of Germany's new national army, to Ludendorff, the man who will guide us to renewed greatness!"[11]

And so Adolf Hitler administered to these young army officers an oath of personal allegiance to Ludendorff, the man of whom Hitler had recently said, concerning the new government he planned to bring out of the Putsch, "He will not interfere with me in the slightest."[12]

III

The foreign correspondents who had spent the night at the *Beobachter* kept demanding that Putzi Hanfstaengl escort them to the Bürgerbräukeller for an interview with Ludendorff and Hitler. Putzi was at last able to arrange this; even though state police platoons were stationed on the west side of every bridge across the Isar, traffic and pedestrians were still being allowed to pass freely throughout the city, and soon after 9:30 A.M. he brought the journalists onto the grounds surrounding the beer hall. The tempo of activity had risen as the morning went on. Larry Rue of the *Chicago Tribune* described his first glimpse of the Kampfbund's commandeered base as

> reminiscent of the early days of a war. Rations and equipment
> were being issued . . . youths were drilling in the garden and
> various courtyards. Recruits were being enlisted. The utmost op-
> timism and enthusiasm prevailed. Rows of lorries were drawn up
> which moved off at intervals with troops, munitions, or supplies.
> All thought that the movement was a success.[13]

As the reporters were ushered into their presence, Ludendorff and Hitler were studiously projecting the image of men who were in control of the situation. Conferring over a map of Munich, surrounded by written reports, here they were: the leaders of the "national revolution," planning the next stage of their campaign on the battlefield of the city.

The correspondent of the *New York Times* noted that Hitler received him and his colleagues politely, "but was obviously overwrought and dead tired." Hitler was a disappointment; the new self-proclaimed leader of Germany "scarcely seemed to fill the part — this little man in an old waterproof coat with a revolver at his hip, unshaven and with disordered hair, and so hoarse that he could scarcely speak."

As for Ludendorff, the *Times* man found that he was also "anxious and preoccupied [as] he talked with Hitler and some other political advisers." When Ludendorff turned to the journalist, his manner was "extremely friendly," and he spoke as if he were indeed a head of state: "My government is eager to have the approval of the United States and of England." The correspondent jotted down Ludendorff's words concerning the "future glory of the new Germany," then took up with him the subject of the problems he and his colleagues had encountered in sending their stories.[14] The correspondents told Ludendorff that, from midnight on, they had been unable to send cables, and long distance telephone service had also been shut down. Ludendorff assured them that he would see to it that they could transmit their stories freely. He apparently believed that the putschists were in control of Bavaria's telephone and telegraph systems, when in fact they could not even reach Ernst Röhm at the Reichswehr building.

IV

Across the river, the Nazi Party's semiofficial photographer, Heinrich Hoffmann, was in action. "Early in the morning on that memorable 9th November I was out with my camera. It was a dull day, and the light was very poor from the photographer's point of view."[15] Pedaling his old bicycle and performing something of a balancing act with his camera and case filled with glass photographic plates, Hoffmann stopped in front of the Reichswehr headquarters to take a picture of the Reichskriegsflagge men who were guarding it. The photograph he took caught the reality: Heinrich Himmler was standing behind a chest-high barbed wire entanglement that had been set up in the street some ten yards from the building's stone walls. Metal shutters had been rolled down over the ground-floor windows. Himmler, peering at the world through thick glasses, was holding a Reichskriegsflagge banner, the pole nestled in the crook of his arm. Men with rifles slung over their shoulders stood beside him, all looking out over the barbed wire. Some of them had expressions of curiosity, but the principal mood was that of soldiers, waiting.

Moving along on his bicycle, Hoffmann arrived at the Marienplatz to find the square packed to its edges by a crowd of thousands. It was so jammed that the blue and white Munich streetcars could not move; they sat like islands in the sea of people. The crowd was listening intently to Julius Streicher, who was speaking from a vantage point atop the base of St. Mary's Pillar, a monument in the center of the square. The shaven-headed anti-Semite from Nuremberg was having no trouble in whipping up support for the "national revolution." Dressed in a dark suit and turning from side to side so that he could look directly, for a moment at least, at every segment of the crowd that encircled him, Streicher was talking without notes, making vigorous gestures with his hands. As Hoffmann managed to get himself and his camera to a perch above Streicher at one side of the square, the man to whom Hitler had entrusted the Nazi Party the previous night was shouting: "Do you want to know what this new government will do? I will tell you what it is going to do. It will hang the Jewish profiteers from the lampposts. It will close the stock exchanges, those dirty Jewish dens of exploitation, and it will nationalize the banks!"

In his next remarks to the crowd, Streicher struck many of the chords that Hitler had found to be so effective.

> The new government will also give you bread. Adolf Hitler, our great leader, has already put behind bars those men who have robbed and plundered us. . . . It is a sign that the time of shame is over, that the time of freedom has begun. In the future there will be only two parties in Germany. You have your choice between them. One is the party of the poor, the hungry, the people, the other that of the usurers. The party of Christian Germans against that of the Jewish bloodsuckers. To which do you want to belong? Those who side with the Jews should go; those who want to be German should come to us. The flag of black-red-and-gold will no longer exist, and those who wear its colors of shame will be shot. Those who refuse to cooperate will be hanged, and those who join us shall look forward to a glorious German future.[16]

From a crowd that did not know that Pöhner had been arrested and was locked up at the nearby police headquarters, this produced a great rhythmic shout: "Heil Hitler, Heil Ludendorff, Heil Pöhner!" Then thousands of Müncheners spontaneously broke into "Deutschland über alles."[17]

*

The crowd in the Marienplatz soon had something more than a speech to capture its interest. After a raid on the police headquarters in Ettstrasse had been called off because the building was so heavily defended by government forces, the Stosstrupp was reassigned to make another raid. The target was Munich's Rathaus, the New City Hall, which, along with the Old City Hall, faced the square in which Streicher addressed the excited Kampfbund sympathizers.

At 10:30 A.M. the helmeted men of Shock Troop Adolf Hitler dashed into the New City Hall. Their commander, Josef Berchtold, gave his account:

> I was aware that a session was in progress. I flung open the doors and, cocking my revolver, informed the assembled Councillors . . . that they must consider themselves under arrest. Alarmed and startled, they sprang to their feet.

A few of the members of the city council were acceptable to the Nazis, and were not disturbed. Nine were immediately arrested. Sixty-two-year-old Mayor Eduard Schmid, a Social Democrat, was grabbed by the collar and thrown against the wall. Albert Nussbaum, another Social Democrat, had the barrel of a rifle slammed against the side of his head. Berchtold described what happened next:

> We shepherded them from the chamber, and the building, and down the wide flight of steps without.
>
> Here the rest of my men took charge. Each member, accompanied by two troopers, was assisted into a truck. Meanwhile enormous crowds had gathered on the Marienplatz who greeted the appearance of the Councillors with jeers and insults. As a matter of fact it was we Storm Troops who had to defend them from the onslaught of the people. Otherwise actual fatalities might have occurred. It was quite a job getting them safely loaded into the lorries. So we went on to the Bürgerbräu and locked up the whole lot.[18]

V

Although public opinion in Munich, as far as it could be judged, was behind the Putsch, the Kampfbund's military situation continued to deteriorate. Moving back and forth between the *Beobachter* and the Bürgerbräukeller, Putzi Hanfstaengl by 11:00 A.M. was experiencing "great difficulty with ominously increasing police cordons."[19] Government armored cars and trench mortars were being positioned at strategic intersections throughout the city. But everywhere were signs of an odd inconsistency. Kampfbund recruiting offices had been opened throughout the city, and young men were lining up to enlist to serve the "national revolution" while members of the Munich police looked on. Many Müncheners thought the whole thing was a *Gaudi*, an entertaining spectacle. On the east side of the Museum Bridge, a youthful-looking putschist, Hans Frank, was helping his Kampfbund comrades put a heavy machine gun in position. A group of tough workingmen stood by, laughing at their efforts. One asked Frank, "Does your Mommy know you're playing with such dangerous things right on the open street?"[20]

Arriving at the beer hall soon after eleven, Putzi Hanfstaengl came upon a scene that he described in these words:

> I found uncertainty and glum faces. No one was talking very much. Goering was all for retreating in the direction of Rosenheim and there collecting reinforcements for a fresh start. However, Ludendorff put a stop to that: "The movement cannot end in the ditch of some obscure country lane," he said tersely, and, sipping his red wine, froze them into submission.[21]

Hermann Goering was not the only man who felt that the Kampfbund needed to regroup in some area outside Munich that was supportive of Hitler's aims. Rosenheim was strongly loyal to National Socialism; the first Ortsgruppe, party local outside of Munich, had been founded there early in 1920. Lieutenant Colonel Hermann Kriebel, the military commander of the Kampfbund, was also in favor of a retreat to Rosenheim, or some similar safe base.

Ludendorff was unmoved. He did not intend to retreat from Munich. Something must be done. He said to the Kampfbund leaders, "We cannot just sit around here all day and wait — for what?"[22]

A new idea was put forward; according to Putzi, Ludendorff was the man "pressing firmly" for it.[23] All available Kampfbund forces would be assembled, and there would be a great march into the city. This was not to be an attack upon the government, but a demonstration that would bring into the streets crowds whose size would eclipse the tens of thousands who had turned out in various squares to hear Streicher and other Nazi orators during the course of the morning. The Reichswehr and state police could not just fire at random into huge crowds that were simply cheering a military parade. Such an enormous outpouring of popular support would have to modify whatever measures the government was moving to undertake. Perhaps the triumvirate would feel forced to come to some sort of accommodation with the "national revolution," after all.

Hitler was not so sure about any of this. He did not want to retreat from Munich, but he mistrusted what was a planless march in the direction of the strongest government positions and forces. This discussion, in various forms, had been going on for at least a couple of hours. Having given his opinion, Goering had gone, with Ulrich Graf, to inspect the situation at the bridges over the Isar. They now returned, reporting that there were strong concentrations of state police on the western side of every bridge across the river. At the Ludwig Bridge, nearest the beer hall, there was even a detachment of thirty state police on the eastern side, in what the putschists considered to be their territory.

Just before eleven-thirty, another report came in: large Reichswehr and state police columns had been seen moving to encircle Röhm and his men at the Reichswehr building, and might by now have them surrounded.

Here was the moment of crisis. No one could doubt that something must be done immediately. To wait in the beer hall was to wait for the same sort of siege that Röhm was obviously about to endure.

The man who spoke was Ludendorff, not Hitler. Germany's wartime dictator snapped out the command *"Wir marschieren!"* — We shall march![24]

Faced with the reality that they were going to march, Hitler began trying to see the favorable side of it. His whole political career consisted of taking positions so extreme, so impossible to surpass, that no one could eclipse him in the public mind. If there was to be a march, it could not be Ludendorff's march; at the very least, he must be at its head, beside the "national commander." Hitler was part actor, and he could see the possibilities of this role. Marching steadfastly at the head of thousands of Kampfbund men, he would be reunited with the great crowds across the river. They would be unable to resist the sight of Hitler and Ludendorff marching through the heart of Munich. Everyone would know that the true leadership of Germany was not in those great stone buildings downtown, but in the streets, receiving the acclaim of the German people. Then it would be Kahr and Lossow and Seisser who would be isolated in their Infantry Barracks command post.

Hitler still thought it was a gamble, but he was a gambler. It might be a fatal gamble, but something might be gained. He later spoke of it this way:

> We would go to the city to win the people to our side, to see how public opinion would react, and then to see how Kahr, Lossow, and Seisser would react to public opinion. After all, those gentlemen would hardly be foolish enough to use machine guns against a general uprising of the people. That's how the march into the city was decided on.[25]

VI

At the captured Reichswehr headquarters, Ernst Röhm was facing his hour of crisis, alone. There was no communication with the Bürgerbräukeller; there was no communication with anyone. At eleven in the morning, learning that he was soon to be surrounded by government forces, Röhm deployed his two hundred men in defensive positions throughout the large building. He described his preparations:

> I ordered the occupation of the designated places and expressly forbade all leaders to open fire on the Reichswehr.
> I spoke to the leaders: "The Reichswehr is nationalist-minded and will one day fight the freedom fight shoulder to shoulder with us."
> I reserved for myself alone the right to give the order to fire; a secure and speedy communication with all detachments was guaranteed by a reserve force of messengers.[26]

In the streets surrounding the large building, many civilian spectators were milling about, oblivious of the possibility that they might get hurt in the impending confrontation. The approaching government forces scattered these inquisitive Müncheners by firing blank cartridges as they converged on the captured Reichswehr headquarters from all sides. From the upper-story windows of the building, where they were waiting with rifles and machine guns, Röhm's men watched the professionals get ready for action. Government troops began appearing on roofs across the street. Cannon were wheeled into position below, and trench mortars were set up on their bipods. Machine guns were pointing at the building from side streets, roofs, and upper-story windows.

The force surrounding Röhm was overwhelmingly superior to his. It included two infantry battalions, three artillery batteries, a trench mortar company, eight armored cars, a battalion of engineers, and what Röhm described as "almost the entire Landespolizei [state police] of Munich, augmented by eight companies from elsewhere."[27] Now, under white flags of truce, several Reichswehr officers came into the building to persuade Röhm to surrender himself and his men. These army officers received a careful hearing from Röhm, because he knew that they were intensely sympathetic to the Putsch. Among them was Lieutenant Colonel Hans Georg Hofmann, the commander of the Reichswehr garrison in Ingolstadt; Hofmann was the officer who had let his troops sleep all night, giving the Putsch every chance to succeed, before alerting his command and bringing his units to Munich. Even more persuasive to Röhm was the appearance of Major General Franz Ritter von Epp, recently retired from the army, who had been relieved as a senior Reichswehr commander in Bavaria because he was judged to be an enthusiastic backer of the extreme right. Epp told Röhm flatly that his position was hopeless, and that resistance would mean only the slaughter of his men.

Hofmann made a telling point with Röhm when he described the new and fully dictatorial powers that had been granted General von Seeckt during the night. Billing this as being in fact the new right-wing government in Berlin that they had all wanted, Hofmann took the position that further struggle was senseless, since the ends of the Putsch had been achieved.

All of Röhm's visitors stressed that if the beleaguered defenders would simply cooperate, they would be allowed to march out, receiving the salutes of the Reichswehr and state police, in a fully honorable form of surrender. At last, Röhm agreed to a two-hour truce. At 11:45 A.M., he was taken to see General von Danner, the commandant of the Reichswehr's Munich garrison.[28]

No sooner had Röhm left the beleaguered building than the tight control he had maintained broke down. Two rifle shots cracked out from within the headquarters, wounding two Reichswehr soldiers who were part of the besieging units that had been placed on Kaulbachstrasse.

This flagrant violation of the truce brought an immediate response. A sergeant of the Nineteenth Infantry, in charge of a machine gun positioned atop a building from which he could cover part of the Reichswehr headquarters courtyard, had orders to fire if fired upon. He aimed at the first two putschists he could see, and let go with a burst. Reichskriegsflagge trooper Martin Faust was killed on the spot. One of his superiors, Lieutenant Theodor Casella, a former Reichswehr officer, had leapt to safety when the machine gun bullets started snapping. Now, exposing himself to fire in an effort to drag Faust to cover, he was also hit and fell beside Faust, bleeding from massive wounds. Heinrich Himmler and two other men dashed out into the courtyard to try to rescue their comrades, and the shooting stopped. Completely shaken, Himmler and others picked up the two casualties and carried them at the run to a neighboring hospital, the Josephinum. There, the doctors needed only one look to see that Faust was dead. Casella died an hour later.[29]

For those who learned of this bloodshed in the minutes before noon, Reichskriegsflagge men and civilians alike, the Putsch instantly lost its aura of a painless military adventure. Those who had seen the uprising as a Gaudi suddenly realized that this was no extension of the recent Oktoberfest, the Munich beer festival that also brought scores of thousands into the streets. Most of the putschists in Munich did not know what had happened, but sixteen hours after Adolf Hitler had approached General Commissioner von Kahr in the beer hall with a pistol in his hand, the message for the Kampfbund was clear. Government forces would shoot, and shoot to kill.

Even before the lethal firing, Alfred Rosenberg made the decision to leave the *Beobachter* offices and cross the river to the beer hall, where the march into the city was being organized. The *Beobachter's* printer, Adolf Müller, issued a succinct bit of advice: "Don't go along, Herr Rosenberg; this is pure suicide."[30]

CHAPTER

42

At NOON, the Kampfbund units milling around the Bürgerbräu-keller finally began lining up on Rosenheimer Strasse for the march across the river and into the heart of the city. Officers formed their units in columns four men wide. Then three of these columns were placed side by side, so that when they stepped off, the Kampfbund would be marching twelve abreast.

The putschists were to claim that the march was peaceful in its intent, a propaganda demonstration rather than a deployment for battle. It was true that Hitler went down the long column, ordering every unit to march with unloaded weapons, but, having given these instructions, he walked back to the front without seeing whether they were carried out. In fact, many of the Kampfbund, and perhaps most of them, carried loaded weapons. In one of the front lines, Streicher would march with a drawn pistol, and Hitler himself had his Browning in a holster on a belt around the waist of his trench coat. Down the length of the column, a number of troopers were carrying fully assembled machine guns — something exceedingly awkward for infantrymen to carry any distance, and done only if there is a desire to have the weapon ready for instant action.[1] Halfway down the column there was a truck, filled with armed men, with a machine gun mounted atop its cab.[2] A putschist later described an open car that accompanied the column, with a machine gun set up in it.[3]

Way at the end of the line, with a Red Cross flag on a staff on its side, was a bright yellow Opel. Two armed Nazis were in the front, and in the back sat Dr. Walter Schultze, a young physician who served in the Munich SA regiment.

Even at this last moment, while the cold winds whipped the banners in the column, there were different views among the marchers as to what this exercise was meant to accomplish, and what chances it had of succeeding. Hans Frank, who earlier had been the butt of workingmen's jokes, felt that these more than two thousand men gave the appearance of "a defeated army that hadn't fought anybody."[4] As for the objective, Josef Berchtold, whose Shock Troop Adolf Hitler was one of the three units lined up directly behind the leaders, knew that his men were marching with loaded weapons, but insisted that it was a propaganda march. "The appeal was to be to the streets, to the people, to Munich. No arms to be used. Everything was to be put to the test of popular feeling."[5]

While Berchtold and many other putschists were thinking in terms of stirring up massive civilian support, Johann Aigner felt that "the idea of this demonstration was to show the officers and troops of the Reichswehr that we were all fellow soldiers of German blood." Thinking of the Oberlanders still locked in at the Engineer Barracks, and of the triumvirate command post at the Infantry Barracks, Aigner said that "the Führer ordered that we would march peacefully to our locked up comrades and walk together to the armed power in the barracks."[6]

On orders from Goering, Josef Berchtold and some of his Shock Troops brought the captured mayor of Munich and the city councilors out of their place of confinement in the beer hall. Goering wanted them placed at the end of the line of march, as portable hostages. If the Kampfbund column encountered any resistance from the forces of the Bavarian government, the mayor and the councilors were to be shot.

Learning of this, Hitler countermanded Goering's order, and told him to have the hostages placed back under guard in the Bürgerbräukeller.[7] "I don't want any martyrs," he said.[8]

Ready to move out, these two to three thousand men and their impending march were a Nazi metaphor. The majority were very young men who saw their world in black and white; they believed in a Führer who claimed to have the answer to Germany's problems. Everything could be solved by quick, bold actions. Everything could be solved on the physical plane. For these Storm Troops, politics was force: political opponents were literally beaten; the domestic enemies of Germany must be physically destroyed; the foreign enemies of Versailles must be slaughtered on some future battlefield. There must be simple answers to inflation and food shortages. They would march; a march would set things right.

The men at the front of the column took their places. There were six men carrying flags positioned at the very front, then came the leaders. There was still some talking and gesturing. Ludendorff told Kurt Neubauer to go home. Johann Aigner was amused by this: "This order almost made me laugh, since I knew Kurt well and I was sure he would not carry out that order."[9] Aigner was right; his friend Neubauer and another man took up positions between the leading four color bearers and two who came after them. Ludendorff could not have avoided seeing this disobedience of his order, but said nothing.

Hitler was more animated than he had been earlier in the morning, but his expression was grim. Rosenberg, arriving at the last moment, shook hands with Scheubner-Richter and asked him how things were going.

"The situation stinks," Scheubner-Richter replied.[10] Lining up near him was Nazi Party member Theodor von der Pfordten, the counselor to the Bavarian Supreme Court who had spent many hours of his free time drafting a new authoritarian constitution for Germany. A copy of this Hitler-endorsed document, which included provisions for forced labor, concentration camps, and the death penalty for advocating democratic government, was in his inside jacket pocket.[11]

In the first line, Ludendorff stood as straight as the Prussian cadet he had once been, looking every inch the general despite the soft green felt hat and loose-fitting brown loden coat. To his right was Hitler, carrying his battered felt hat in one hand, the collar of his trench coat raised against the wind. Next to him was Scheubner-Richter; among those strung out to his right were Ulrich Graf, Hermann Kriebel, Friedrich Weber, Julius Streicher, and Hermann Goering. In the line behind the leaders were Lieutenant Heinz Pernet, Johann Aigner, Gottfried Feder, newly named economic chief of Hitler's "German national government," and some others.

A few of the men who had been close to Hitler in his long struggle toward this day were not present. Rudolf Hess was still at the suburban villa of the publisher Julius Lehmann, guarding the Bavarian cabinet ministers, and was unaware of what was happening in the city. Putzi Hanfstaengl was on the other side of the river. Apparently unaware of the impending march, and seeing the Reichswehr and state police buildup, as well as watching the Munich police tear down all the Kampfbund posters, he concluded that "the situation seemed hopeless and I decided to hurry home and prepare for a get-away."[12]

Fifty-five-year-old Dietrich Eckart had not even learned of the Putsch until hours after the drama at the beer hall. Aware that his relations with Hitler had cooled, but still hurt that he should be so thoroughly left out of the Nazi Party's greatest venture, the ailing Eckart had crossed the river earlier in the morning to be part of whatever might happen next in the movement to which he had made so many significant contributions. As the man who had given the SA its battle song with its refrain of "Germany, Awake!" waited outside a conference room, the door opened and Hitler walked out. According to Eckart, Hitler "looked very dark and said, 'Good day,' in a hard voice." Leaving the beer hall, Eckart encountered Ludendorff, who replied to his polite greeting with "an indifferent tip of the hat."[13] Eckart had gone back across the river, but was still mingling with the excited crowds.

The column started to march. Hitler said of this moment, "We set out convinced that this was the end, one way or another. I remember someone who said to me as we were coming down the steps, 'This finishes it!' Everyone had that same conviction."[14]

All down the moving column, men began to sing Eckart's song.

The first confrontation came only a quarter of a mile from where the march started, with the unit of the state police that had taken up a position on the east side of the Isar River, just where Rosenheimer Strasse opened onto the Ludwig Bridge. The scene was preposterous: thirty Green Police fanned out across the entrance to the bridge, preparing to block the advance of between two and three thousand men. A surreal touch was added by the normal traffic of passenger cars and trolleys still crossing the bridge.

The participants on both sides later agreed on the details of what happened next. The Shock Troop Adolf Hitler, under Berchtold, was sent forward. The commander confronting Berchtold was Lieutenant Georg Höfler of the state police. He wrote:

> The leader of this unit gave orders to walk on slowly, where-upon I explained to him that if he didn't stop walking I would give the order to shoot. I ordered my detachment, which was standing about ten steps behind me, to "load ball ammunition!" The Nationalist Socialists shouted, "Don't shoot at your comrades!"[15]

Johann Aigner, who was with the Shock Troop, gave this account:

> We raised our hands and shouted, "Don't shoot, Hitler is coming, Ludendorff is coming, comrades, don't shoot at your fellow Germans!" . . . We were approximately 10 meters away from

them, when the police officer in charge ordered them to take the safeties off their rifles. At about 5 meters' distance we raised our hands again, and repeated our statements to them.[16]

Shock Troop leader Berchtold described the transition to action.

We were within a stone's throw of them when they raised their rifles. Ulrich Graf, Hitler's bodyguard, shouted, "Don't fire; Ludendorff is with us," whereupon they lowered them again, and I sprang forward at the head of some ten of my fellows and promptly disarmed them.[17]

Berchtold may indeed have dashed at them, but far more than ten Kampfbund men were involved within seconds. A trumpet at the head of the Kampfbund column sounded, and the outnumbered state police were immediately surrounded. State Police Lieutenant Höfler said that his men were "spat at, beaten, their skins pierced by bayonet jabs, and everyone was threatened by at least five gun-barrels."[18] In the confusion, another state police officer, some distance off, was shot at by the putschists, but they missed. With their hands over their heads, the thirty surrendered state police men were told by the putschists that they were going to be put up against a wall and shot, but Berchtold and a detail of his men rushed them back to the beer hall, where they were added to the prisoners taken in Hitler's revolution.

The Kampfbund column swept on across the bridge, suddenly excited and confident as a result of this first capture of those who dared to oppose them. Dr. Weber put it this way: "Naturally we intended to march through the city and after the encounter at the Ludwig Bridge we did not even consider [the possibility of] being halted by the state police. There the state police had given way. . . . We assumed that this would happen elsewhere."[19]

Across the river, large and enthusiastic crowds were waiting for the putschists. Teams of National Socialist speakers had been haranguing the public in Munich's largest central squares all during the morning, and support for the "national revolution" was feverishly high. Many in the crowds were unaware of the rift between the Bavarian government and the Kampfbund, but for these many thousands of Müncheners, the forces led by Ludendorff and Hitler were the heroes of the hour. Whatever they wanted to do, the crowds wanted, too. Moving along the Tal, past Berchtold's tobacco shop, the Kampfbund column began to pick up spectators who marched alongside it, joining in the patriotic songs the putschists were singing lustily. Others in the crowd fell in at the end of the column and marched along.

On the sidewalk, Dietrich Eckart was standing by himself, watching the parade. Hitler spotted him and stared at him; Eckart felt that Hitler's expression said, despite the coldness of his greeting earlier in the morning, "The rest of us are here. Why aren't *you*?"[20] An open automobile was coming along beside the column; Max Amann was riding in it, as was Hermann Esser, who for the second day was out and about, despite his jaundice. Eckart stepped forward, and they let him in.

At the Marienplatz a tremendous crowd was waiting. The sight of the front line of swastika flags and other red, white, and black banners coming into the square through the arch of the Old City Hall brought forth an excited roar of approval.

Professor von Müller was standing there with a friend who was an official at the Ministry of Education. His feelings were to stay with him for a long time.

> Hitler and Ludendorff, in civilian clothes, were leading the march. I remember seeing Ludendorff with an emotion which can perhaps be understood only by people of my generation — it was one of the deepest shocks of my life. Ludendorff's overall behavior was repugnant to me; I never had any personal dealings with him. Nonetheless, there was the general of the war. Whatever one wanted to say, he was one of the great generals of the old German army, the planner and winner of glorious battles. There he was, walking at the head of a crowd of desperate revolutionaries, wearing a crumpled civilian coat, a shabby soft hat on his head.[21]

If ever there was a scene of apparent triumph, it was presented by the spectacle in the Marienplatz. In the wake of the earlier Shock Troop raid on the New City Hall, a swastika flag had been left flying from one of its balconies, and the red, white, and black stripes of the imperial flag were also in evidence. The Kampfbund column was stopped in the middle of the crowd, which thronged admiringly about the armed troopers. Here at the very heart of the city there was no sign of opposition; with the crowd and the Kampfbund soldiers all singing "Deutschland über alles," everyone present had an overwhelming conviction that Munich was theirs.

Effective as this scene was as propaganda, the truth was that no one in the Kampfbund line of march knew what to do next. Between songs, the crowd was cheering, "Heil! Heil! Heil! Ludendorff! Hitler!" but neither of the leaders gave a signal.[22] Lieutenant Colonel Kriebel had expected that this would be the climax of the march, and that the column would return to the Bürgerbräukeller. That was also what Dr. Weber expected.[23]

Hitler appeared to be in such a withdrawn state that nobody approached him. If the Führer had a plan for further action, he kept it to himself. It was Ludendorff who suddenly gave the signal to move north out of the Marienplatz, up Wienstrasse, in the direction of Ernst Röhm and his Reichskriegsflagge men at the besieged army headquarters.[24]

With this move, General Erich Ludendorff opened an entirely new dimension to the march. From the moment the Kampfbund column turned into Wienstrasse, they were twelve hundred yards from the captured building, and every step was taking them closer to the Reichswehr soldiers who were encircling it. Knowing that there were armed allies of the Reichskriegsflagge moving about the city, the Reichswehr commanders conducting the siege had no intention of allowing themselves to be surprised by an attack from their rear. The mission of providing a screening force in the area south of the siege had been assigned to the state police. Lieutenant Max Demmelmeyer of that force had been given the task of blocking off the Odeonsplatz, a square whose southern side, nearest the oncoming putschists, was only five hundred yards from Reichswehr headquarters.[25]

There was a jumble of little streets south of the Odeonsplatz, and Demmelmeyer had no way of seeing down to the Marienplatz, or of knowing that a column of two to three thousand men was soon to come into view. Two of these narrow streets to the south opened onto the Odeonsplatz — Theatinerstrasse and Residenzstrasse. Because the Theatinerstrasse was the straightest route from the Marienplatz, Demmelmeyer positioned most of his small force a short way down that street, leaving only a handful of men to cordon off the top of the Residenzstrasse. Small as these detachments were, they were all that stood between the advancing Kampfbund and a breakthrough into the rear of the Reichswehr troops. If Ludendorff could get through here, his column could attempt the rescue of Röhm and his men.

As for what Ludendorff was thinking, what caused him to lead the Kampfbund toward a large Reichswehr operation that he knew was in progress, he later wrote:

At certain moments in life, one acts instinctively and doesn't know why. I fought the battle of Tannenberg. When I ask myself why I fought it the way I did, I don't know. The reasons given in those splendid history books I only thought of afterward. We just wanted to get to Röhm and bring him back.[26]

And so Erich Ludendorff marched up the street, with Adolf Hitler on his right and two to three thousand men coming on behind him. Lieutenant Colonel Kriebel said of this new route, "If Ludendorff is marching that way, naturally we'll go with him."[27] Many of the spectators from the Marienplatz were coming right along with the column, some thinking that the Putsch had been a complete success and that this was the victory march.

At the point where Wienstrasse fed into Theatinerstrasse, Ludendorff saw Lieutenant Demmelmeyer's detachment of state police, far up the street, blocking the Odeonsplatz and the route to Reichswehr headquarters beyond. Taking a slight detour, Ludendorff led the Kampfbund column to the right for the few short yards of the Perusastrasse, then turned left into the Max-Joseph Platz. From there they moved north on the narrow street parallel to the Theatinerstrasse, the Residenzstrasse, on the right of which stood the two-hundred-yard-long west façade of the Residenz, the huge palace of the kings of Bavaria.[28] At the far end of this street, just before it opened onto the Odeonsplatz, was the Feldherrnhalle, the Hall of Generals. This stone structure, a copy of the Loggia dei Lanzi in Florence, was a monument to Bavarian generals of an earlier era. If the Kampfbund column got past the Feldherrnhalle, it would be hard to stop them in the open area of the Odeonsplatz, and after that they would be in the Ludwigstrasse, three hundred yards from the backs of the Reichswehr troops encircling the building defended by Röhm.

Lieutenant Demmelmeyer was spread thin. He had men positioned in the Theatinerstrasse, but almost none in the Residenzstrasse, up which the putschists were actually coming. Demmelmeyer was trying to be everywhere at once. He later wrote:

> I hurried over to the Residenzstrasse and saw an endless Hitler column, the front of which was already in the middle of the Residenzstrasse. I rushed into the Residenz and alerted [the state police battalion headquarters located there]. The Second Company came out in a short time. . . . The policemen advanced with rifle butts forward, with rifles held across their bodies, and with nightsticks against the column in order to halt it.[29]

Coming up the street at the head of the Kampfbund column, Johann Aigner saw the state police troops moving down the Residenzstrasse toward him: "As a soldier, I realized at once that these squads were not as nervous as those that had been at the Ludwig Bridge. I was sure: one order and the guns would shoot."[30] The Kampfbund column, still with enthusiastic spectators striding along on either side of it, was singing, "O Germany, High in Honor."[31] Seeing the Green Police coming toward them, Adolf Hitler locked his arm with that of Scheubner-Richter.

Aigner said, "Again we raised our arms, and mentioned the presence of Hitler and Ludendorff to the troops," but this time there was no effect.[32] Still trying to avoid bloodshed, but determined to stop the Kampfbund advance in this narrow street, the state police were using crowd-control tactics, coming forward slowly with their weapons held across their chests, rather than pointed to fire.

Despite their willingness to try to stop so many men, this state police unit was overwhelmed. The putschists at the front of the column kept coming, and the state police were shoved back. The Kampfbund men kept shouting that Ludendorff was with them, and the state police were shouting orders to halt. The policemen were wrestled off to one side, and the sea of Hitler and Ludendorff's followers simply washed over them. Back along the column, Kampfbund men were still singing "O Germany, High in Honor."

At the top of the street, the state police had placed a machine gun at the Feldherrnhalle, and in the Odeonsplatz, just beyond, a state police armored car was swinging its turret so that another machine gun was pointing down the Residenzstrasse.

Then Lieutenant Michael Freiherr von Godin of the state police brought to the scene a small but desperately needed reinforcement. He came, at the run, straight into a hand-to-hand situation, which he described:

> I dashed with my platoon [which was] in the Theatinerstrasse back around the Feldherrnhalle and realized that the counterattack of the Hitler troops, who were armed with every kind of weapon, had easily broken through the cordon in the Residenzstrasse. I went over to the counterattack against the successful breakthrough of the Hitler people, with the order: "Second Company, double time, march."
>
> I was received in their ranks with level bayonets, unlocked rifles, and leveled pistols. Some of my men were grabbed and had

pistols held against their chests. My men worked with rifle-butt and night-stick. I myself had taken a rifle so as to defend myself without going over too soon to the use of my pistol, and parried two bayonets with it, overturning the men behind them with rifle at high port. Suddenly a Hitler man who stood one step half left of me, fired a pistol at my head. The shot went by my head and killed Sergeant Hollweg behind me.

There was to be debate about whether this was the first shot, and which side fired first, but there was no question as to what happened next.

> Then, before I could give an order, my people opened fire, with the effect of a [volley]. At the same time the Hitler people commenced firing and for twenty or thirty seconds a regular fire-fight developed.[33]

"Everything happened in a flash," Ludendorff said of this eruption of gunfire at point-blank range.[34] In these moments, German history was in the balance: Scheubner-Richter, whose left arm was locked in Hitler's right, was hit by a bullet in the heart and died instantly, but Hitler, who had escaped death by inches so many times on the Western Front, was not touched. Tangled with Scheubner-Richter, and trying to throw himself flat on the pavement to escape the continuing state police gunfire, Hitler dislocated his shoulder and lay still. The American diplomat, Robert Murphy, watching from the side, said, "Both Ludendorff and Hitler behaved in identical manner, like the battle-hardened soldiers they were. Both fell flat to escape the hail of bullets."[35]

Johann Aigner, lying flat and firing back, experienced all this in seconds:

> An armored scout car opened its machine gun fire from the front; fortunately it jammed after 55 shots — as was found out later. When I fired my 4th shot I realized that Kurt Neubauer, my best comrade, Ludendorff's orderly, was dying. I crept to him, gave him my hand, wiped the foam off his mouth.[36]

As Kurt Neubauer died, Aigner felt warm blood all over the back of his neck and thought that he himself had been hit; turning, he saw blood spouting from the throat of a putschist next to him whose jugular vein had been torn open by a bullet.

When Hitler had gone down, his bodyguard had thrown himself on top of Hitler to protect him. Lying there, Ulrich Graf was hit by one bullet after another; in all, he received eleven wounds. He was saying to himself, "Ulrich Graf, now they've finally got you!"[37] Behind him was Alfred Rosenberg, who had been warned by the *Beobachter*'s printer that it was "pure suicide" to go on the march. Rosenberg had been in the second rank when the state police volley struck; throwing himself toward the pavement as quickly as he could, he landed on the body of a dead Kampfbund man. To his right he saw Hermann Goering, bleeding from wounds in the groin and thigh, crawling for cover under a stone lion in front of the Residenz. Suddenly Rosenberg became aware that a Kampfbund rifleman was using him, and the corpse beneath him, as sandbags, firing his rifle across Rosenberg's back at the state police. Rosenberg shouted at the man, "For God's sake, stop it! It's doing no good."[38]

The senior state police officer on the scene, Lieutenant Colonel Otto Muxel, was just coming out the gateway of the Residenz when the firing erupted. He saw that "our people of the Second Company were suddenly pushed back through the narrow main gate, where in one instant the wounded and dead were lying upon one another in two or three layers and blocking me from getting out to the street. A terrible shooting continued through the gate."[39]

Out in the street, Josef Berchtold had a different view:

> Everywhere people were going down, writhing on the ground in agony, dead and dying, while the guns still rattled death and murder into their stampeding midst. It was madness and slaughter.
>
> Goering and Graf fell, badly wounded; fourteen dead were trampled under people's feet throwing [tripping] the living down; blood flowed everywhere over the grey pavement. The whole thing was a ghastly debacle. Shrieks and cries rent the air, and ever that insane firing went on.[40]

Bystanders were caught in the gunfire. A young Englishwoman, Suzanne St. Barbe Baker, a tourist who had been visiting friends in Feldafing, twenty-five miles away, wrote of her experience:

> I had come to Munich to persuade the British Consul to grant me an extension of my permit, and was blissfully ignorant of any political trouble. Apparently it had just pleased Mr. Hittler [*sic*] . . . to arrange a miniature revolution and select the Odeon[s]-platz as the scene of war. Within half a minute the square was surrounded by troops and police and transformed into a battle-field, where the machine-gun bullets whizzed past my head, so

that I had to creep on all fours to cover. I found this in a café that could no longer boast of a single window-pane.[41]

The shooting stopped, but the cries of the wounded did not. The men of the Kampfbund were fleeing back down the Residenzstrasse, and Friedrich Weber was leaning against the wall of the palace of the kings of Bavaria, unscathed but weeping hysterically. Dr. Walter Schultze, the staff physician to the Munich SA Regiment, observed Hitler's next movements:

> I realized that Hitler was the first one who got up, and, apparently injured in his arm, moved to the rear. I hurried after Hitler and got one of our automobiles standing on the Max-Joseph Platz. Into this auto Hitler was brought and wanted to drive back to the Bürgerbräukeller through the Alten Hof via Marienplatz. Twelve to fifteen meters from the Marienplatz in the Burgstrasse we received heavy machine gun fire from Marienplatz and then drove . . . to the Isartorplatz and there received fire for the second time. During the entire time I was standing on the running board next to Hitler to show my red-cross band.[42]

While Hitler was fleeing the scene, someone else was behaving differently. As Lieutenant Demmelmeyer looked across the blood-stained area, he observed the following:

> I saw a civilian and a Hitler officer who had a bleeding nose come toward me. I recognized the civilian — it was General Ludendorff. I walked up to Ludendorff and told him, "Excellency, I must take you into protective custody." Ludendorff agreed, with the following words: "You have your orders, and I will follow you." I walked the two gentlemen to the Feldherrnhalle and ordered Sergeant-Major Kröhler to take Ludendorff to the Residenz. Then I walked back to my cordon.[43]

Having left his dead and wounded followers behind, Hitler was trying to make good his flight from the authorities. Dr. Schultze told more of their frantic ride through the city:

> After the Isartorplatz and the Ludwig Bridge were closed off, we were forced to make a detour in the direction of Sendlinger-Tor-Platz-Thalkirchner Strasse. At about the height of the southern cemetery we again were fired upon, at which point I decided to take Hitler, who was in bad pain, outside the city and possibly treat him there.

The men in the yellow Opel finally managed to get out of Munich and drove around back roads, trying to decide on a destination. Schultze

556 ∎

said, "During our aimless driving I had Hitler undress and established that he did not suffer a bullet wound but a severe shoulder dislocation. We decided to go to Uffing where a party friend by the name of Hanfstaengl lived." The yellow car sped through the quiet countryside; it reached the village of Uffing, thirty-five miles south of Munich, at about four in the afternoon. Putzi was not there, but, Schultze said, "Hitler was immediately taken in by Mrs. Hanfstaengl."[44]

II

Hitler had left a tragic shambles in Munich. Four state policemen were dead; including the two Reichskriegsflagge men shot in the court-yard of the Reichswehr headquarters, sixteen putschists had been killed. Among the dead lying in the street before the Feldherrnhalle was Oskar Körner, the toy shop owner who had been one of Hitler's earliest supporters. When the body of Theodor von der Pfordten was prepared for burial, a blood-soaked draft of his harsh new constitution for Germany was found in his jacket pocket. Scores were seriously wounded; at the teaching hospital of the University of Munich, the famous surgeon Ferdinand Sauerbruch and his colleagues set to work trying to save twenty-three critical cases that had been rushed to them, and the operating rooms of other hospitals were busy all afternoon and into the night.[45]

Some of the Kampfbund wounded, knowing that the police would arrest them if they turned themselves in for medical care, tried desperately to find help from other sources. Bleeding from the wounds to his groin and thigh, Hermann Goering crawled down Residenz-strasse and was helped by fellow Nazis through the doorway of the Ballin Furniture Company, whose owner was Jewish. Frau Ballin and her sister knew the anti-Semitic significance of his swastika armband; nonetheless, they dressed his wounds, called his wife, and managed to have him taken to a private clinic.[46]

The police had arrested twenty Kampfbund officers in the immediate area of the firing, but literally thousands of putschists were attempting to evade arrest. The gunfire had barely stopped echoing in the Residenzstrasse when a pastry shop, Rottenhöfer's Konditorei, suddenly had terrified young men hurtling through the doorway and dashing up to the bakery on the second floor. There they hid their weapons, shed their uniform caps and jackets, and attempted to slip farther away into the city.[47] At the Eiles Coffee Roasting Company, putschists hid their tunics in the back of the store and attempted to mix in with the customers. Some putschists borrowed the civilian coats of friends who worked in the area and quickly moved on.[48]

The Bavarian State Police were everywhere, rounding up all the Kampfbund men they could find, arresting some, and simply disarming others. Several SA men who still had their weapons, but were trying to run as far from the Feldherrnhalle as they could get, were suddenly cut off in the street by a truck filled with state police. As the Storm Troops laid down their arms and put up their hands, one of them, Alois Winderl, saw two waitresses in a coffee shop looking through the window and laughing at the scene. He remembered the contrast with his own feelings: referring to combat veterans by the German term "front soldiers," he said, "And among us, front soldiers were crying. We were all howling with rage inside. Then we went home, beaten."[49]

Many of the prominent putschists were arrested, including Weber of Bund Oberland and Wilhelm Brückner, commander of the Munich SA regiment. Dietrich Eckart, who had caught up to the march to the Marienplatz only at the last instant, was arrested and held on grounds of his past Nazi prominence.

Those who could, managed to flee to Austria. Among them were Hermann Goering; Rudolf Hess, who released his captured Bavarian cabinet ministers; the Freikorps leader Gerhard Rossbach, whose Infantry School contingent faced possible charges of mutiny; Hermann Kriebel of the Kampfbund; and Gottfried Feder. Hermann Esser went to Czechoslovakia. Putzi Hanfstaengl, sure that the police would pick him up if he went to his house at Uffing and never dreaming that his wife was hiding Adolf Hitler there, crossed the Austrian border.

At one-thirty in the afternoon of this day of violence, Ernst Röhm surrendered himself and his two hundred Reichskriegsflagge men. His troops were allowed to march out the back gate of the Reichswehr headquarters, but Röhm was taken to Stadelheim Prison and confined there, pending trial on charges of treason.[50] At two o'clock a large state police force — far larger than proved to be necessary — surrounded the Bürgerbräukeller. The small group of putschists who were still at the Kampfbund command post seemed in a daze and surrendered without resistance. On the premises, the police collected four truckloads of weapons, and set free the captured Jews whom Hitler's men had kept right to the end.[51]

*

Although angry pro-Hitler crowds would continue to roam the streets of Munich for another three days, these mobs of Nazi sympathizers were not armed. In the first hour after the shooting at the Feldherrnhalle, the city had been filled with rumors that both Ludendorff and Hitler were killed. The truth eventually became known, but these crowds now had völkisch martyrs for their cause. Röhm's men carried their dead comrade Martin Faust in a solemn procession through the streets, attracting a large crowd, and eventually delivered the corpse to the Faust home on Gollierstrasse by ringing the doorbell and presenting what was left of their son to his horrified parents.[52]

Despite the turmoil throughout the city, at 3:00 P.M. General von Lossow reported to General Commissioner von Kahr: "Excellency, the Ludendorff-Hitler Putsch has been broken."[53] A similar message was passed to Berlin.[54] Once again, the significance of a report from the government of Bavaria to the government in Berlin was not simply the information that was conveyed, but the very fact that the report was made. All thought of a march to Berlin vanished during the firing at the Feldherrnhalle; Bavaria was acknowledging the primacy and authority of the national government.

Inevitably, the French had something to say about the situation. Calling on Chancellor Stresemann, who had General von Seeckt's pleased assurances that the Bavarian Reichswehr had the situation fully under control, the French ambassador asked Stresemann whether the Putsch was not proof that there were, in unofficial hands, "far too many guns and cannon around the country."

Stresemann replied that governmental authorities had just demonstrated their ability to deal with an armed uprising. He continued, "Moreover, the Bavarians and the Putsch would never have got started had it not been for the fact that every Reich government since the war has been virtually driven from one disaster to the next by the intolerable conditions imposed upon it from abroad."[55]

After his initial dignified surrender, Ludendorff acted like a petulant child. Inside the Residenz, where he was taken by Sergeant-Major Kröhler of the state police, he was greeted politely by Lieutenant Colonel Muxel. When Muxel offered to telephone Ludendorff's house to inform his wife that he was unharmed and in no physical danger, Ludendorff shouted that he did not want any favors. He added:

> Do not call me "Excellency." From now on I am simply "Herr Ludendorff." The German officer lost his honor today. I am ashamed to have ever been a German officer. You are all revolt-

ing. I want to vomit before you. As long as you and others like you wear that uniform, I will never put mine on again.[56]

Even that was not all. Sergeant Wilhelm Baier said, as part of a formal statement: "In the battalion headquarters I heard Ludendorff shouting wildly. He continually shouted, 'Pfui!' and reviled my chief, Lieutenant Colonel Muxel." After a time, Ludendorff said that he needed to go to the bathroom. When First Lieutenant Oskar Erhard, into whose custody he had been placed, indicated the direction in which Ludendorff should go, the general insisted that since he was a common prisoner, he must be escorted to the bathroom by an armed guard. Lieutenant Erhard simply offered him the key, saying he had no intention of going with him to or from the bathroom, and Ludendorff refused to take it. Erhard, who was Muxel's adjutant, went on about his paperwork in his office, ignoring Ludendorff, who soon found that he could not maintain the position he had chosen to take. Ludendorff silently took the key and went down the hall.[57]

Later in the afternoon, Ludendorff was interviewed by an assistant prosecutor.[58] He was abusive, but began to picture himself in quite a different light from the one in which his fellow putschists had seen him only a few hours earlier. The man who had insisted "We shall march!" and had decided on, and led, the final fatal march from the Marienplatz to the Feldherrnhalle, now pictured himself as a retired soldier who was simply lending his name to others' efforts aimed at strengthening Germany. The general who had told Captain Ernst Röhm to hold the captured Reichswehr headquarters at all costs now denied having given any such order.[59]

After this first interrogation, Ludendorff was told that he was free to go home and await further proceedings there, if he would give his word of honor not to leave the environs of Munich. This elicited more churlish remarks. The offer was undoubtedly prompted by the triumvirate's realization that the radical right would gain propaganda advantages from every hour that this national hero was perceived to be behind bars. There would have to be a trial, but until then Ludendorff would be less trouble out of jail than in. With another string of invectives, General Erich Ludendorff marched out of the palace of the kings of Bavaria.[60]

The authorities had no inkling of where to begin looking for Adolf Hitler. The crowds in the streets were still cursing the authorities for destroying Hitler's revolution, but for some on the right, Hitler's flight from the Feldherrnhalle was insupportable. The idea that the Führer, the Leader, the combat veteran who held the Iron Cross, First Class, should abruptly turn his back on the Kampfbund's dead and wounded and drive off in an automobile, was not in the German military tradition he so constantly extolled in his speeches. The Freikorps leader Friedrich Wilhelm Heinz gave a scathing critique of the day's activities. "Hitler led his men into battle with absolutely no protection. He had no idea of what he wanted. Then when things got tough, Adolf the Swell-head took off . . . and left his men in the lurch. . . . Did you expect that he'd do anything else?"[61]

In newspapers around the world, the Putsch was seen as the climax to a type of German madness that had already been going on far too long. The *New York World* put it this way, under the headline MUNICH UPRISING FIZZLES OVERNIGHT. In part, the front-page story said:

> General von [*sic*] Ludendorff, the most dangerous man in Germany for the last four years, came to the end of his rope this afternoon when he was taken captive. . . . With his arrest the Bavarian revolution collapsed like a punctured balloon. . . .
>
> Driven mad by ambition and having lost all sense of proportion in his determination to reunite Teutonic peoples into a solid fighting force which yet would conquer the world, Ludendorff allied himself with Hitler. When Hitler went off half-cocked last night, declaring the Fascist revolution in Munich, Ludendorff was dragged down with him.[62]

As for Hitler's political future, the *New York Times* was succinct: "The Munich putsch definitely eliminates Hitler and his National Socialist followers."[63]

III

The occupants of Putzi Hanfstaengl's house in Uffing were electrified by Hitler's sudden secret arrival. They were a strange group to be concealing the most wanted fugitive in Germany. With Putzi fleeing to Austria, the household consisted of his wife, Helene, who was pregnant, their little son, Egon, and two maids who did not know whether to be elated or terrified by the presence of this explosive guest. For Egon, it was an adventure to have Uncle 'Dolf appear out of nowhere to stay with them, and to be told that he must not mention to anyone that he was there; for Helene Hanfstaengl, there was the certainty that the police would come looking for Putzi and find Hitler if he did not move on.

That night Hitler stayed in an attic bedroom, racked with pain. He was wearing a pair of Putzi's outsize white pajamas and was wrapped in two English traveling blankets that Putzi had taken with him when he went to Harvard in 1905.[64] This was his third night virtually without sleep. He had stayed up talking most of the night before the Putsch and had been in action all over Munich the night of the Putsch itself, and now the pain from his dislocated shoulder was reducing him to a sleepless wreck.

The next morning, Saturday, November 10, brought some measure of relief for Hitler. Dr. Walter Schultze returned with a colleague, and together they set Hitler's shoulder. Before Dr. Schultze returned to Munich, Hitler asked him to pass an urgent message to his friends the Bechsteins, the enthusiastic Nazi Party supporters who had often been willing to put some of the family piano-manufacturing fortune at Hitler's disposal. They lived in Berlin, but frequently visited Munich. What Hitler needed from them now was not money, but a car and a driver. Much as he hated the thought of leaving Germany, to hide for the time being in his native Austria, that prospect looked far better than the certainty of arrest and imprisonment if he stayed where he was.

During the afternoon, an unwelcome caller came to the front door. Hermann Goering's gardener from Munich told Helene Hanfstaengl that he wanted to talk to Hitler. Putzi had often thought the man was a police informer who had been slipped into the Goerings' employ, and Helene told him that Hitler was not there. But the man continued to insist that he must see Hitler. Reluctantly accepting the fact that he was not going to be allowed into the house, he finally left, not to return to Munich, but to stay for the night at the Hotel zur Post in Uffing.[65]

Despite that worrisome visitor, Hitler had a good night's sleep in this house beside the lake known as the Staffelsee. It was not until nearly noon that he came down on the morning of Sunday, November 11, the fifth anniversary of the day that the guns ceased firing on the Western Front. Although he was in somewhat better physical condition, Hitler became increasingly distraught as the afternoon wore on. His one hope lay with the arrival of a car from the Bechsteins; it was more than twenty-four hours since he had sent his desperate appeal via Schultze. What could be wrong? Had the police picked up Schultze? Had the police sealed off the city? Was Schultze unable to reach the Bechsteins?

The November afternoon turned dark over the snowy alpine landscape. Hitler asked Helene Hanfstaengl to close the curtains and shutters. It was as if the gloom of the dusk outside was beginning to alarm him.

According to a state police report, it was 4:20 P.M. when Colonel von Seisser's office in Munich called Senior Lieutenant Rudolf Belleville, who was in charge of the state police company at Weilheim, the headquarters of the district in which Uffing was located. The message to Belleville was short. Hitler was at the Hanfstaengls' house and was to be arrested immediately. Belleville was to take a contingent strong enough to ensure that no one could interfere with Hitler's arrest and subsequent transportation to the maximum-security fortress prison at Landsberg.[66]

In the tantalizingly uninformative words of the report, "It was of course difficult for Senior Lieutenant Belleville to carry out the order of arresting Hitler; in 1920 he had even worked in cooperation with him."[67] What form of right-wing activity this referred to was not specified, but at the war's end Belleville had served with Rudolf Hess as an observer and gunner in the planes Hess piloted.[68]

Orders were orders, and, though it was a Sunday afternoon, Belleville was soon on the way with eleven state policemen in a commandeered brewery truck. A detective had gone ahead by train to alert the local police.

When they arrived in the village beside the lake, Belleville at first surrounded the wrong Hanfstaengl house — the villa belonging to Putzi's mother. Believing that this was the house in which Hitler was hiding, he entered and began a thorough search. Just as he became convinced that there was no fugitive on the premises, the telephone rang, and the state police officer heard a maid saying softly into the phone, "The police are here searching."

Belleville snatched the phone and said into it, "Who is this speaking?"

Helene Hanfstaengl identified herself.

Belleville asked where her husband was, and Helene said that she had not seen him for three days. He then inquired when she had last seen Adolf Hitler, and Helene Hanfstaengl hesitantly said, "Today."[69]

Knowing that the police were on their way at last, Helene Hanfstaengl went up to the attic bedroom. Hitler was standing near the door, in Putzi's mammoth pajamas and a huge blue terry cloth bathrobe. What she had to tell him was simple enough — the police were sure to be there soon — but Hitler's reaction was not. He became hysterical, produced his pistol, and, waving it, said that he would shoot himself before he allowed the police to arrest him.

There was no doubt in his hostess's mind that he intended to kill himself within the next few minutes. Putzi had once taught Helene what he described as "one of the few jujitsu tricks I know: how to wrench a pistol out of someone's grasp." Helene put her training to the test, and, as Putzi later recounted it, "Hitler's movements were awkward with his dislocated shoulder and she managed to get the thing away from him and fling it into a two-hundredweight barrel of flour we kept up in the attic to combat the current shortages."[70]

The fit seemed to pass; Hitler dropped into a chair, holding his head in his hands. "What do you think you're doing?" Helene asked him. "How can you give up at the first reverses? Think of all your followers who believe in you, and who will lose all faith if you desert them now." Quietly, she added, "How can you leave all the people you have gotten interested in your idea of saving your country — and then take your own life?"[71] Then she told him that Hitler's subordinate leaders in the NSDAP would need some guidance as to what to do while he was in prison, and pointed out that he had only a few minutes to write instructions and leave them with her.

Hitler roused himself and was soon dictating one short message after another to Helene. The most remarkable was the one to Alfred Rosenberg: "Dear Rosenberg. From now on you will lead the movement."[72] This was Hitler at his most manipulative, producing a clever maneuver even while under extreme pressure. If he had to go to prison, he did not want some strong and able person to step in and become an effective leader of his movement during his enforced absence. (Rosenberg himself was to be startled by this decision: "I was rather surprised. Hitler had never taken me into his confidence as far as organizational matters were concerned and now I was to assume control at this critical moment!")[73]

Just as Helene was hiding Hitler's various instructions in the flour barrel, there was the sound of vehicles pulling up in the drive and the barking of police dogs. An official report described what happened next.

> After they had knocked, the door was opened. A lady came to meet Senior Lieutenant Belleville. After he had introduced himself the lady asked if Senior Lieutenant Belleville was the leader. When Belleville said that he was, she said, "May I ask you to come in alone first."
> Senior Lieutenant Belleville considered that he might be about to walk into a dangerous trap, but he did as she asked. The detachment waited outside the house. Without saying a word, Frau

Hanfstaengl led him up to the door of a room, hesitated for a moment, looked at Senior Lieutenant Belleville for several seconds, opened the door, and said, "Please go in."

In the room stood Hitler in white pajamas, his arm in a sling. . . . Hitler stared at him quite absent-mindedly; when he learned that he had come to arrest him, Hitler gave him his hand and explained that he was at his disposal. . . .

Hitler was assisted in getting dressed by Frau Hanfstaengl and Senior Lieutenant Belleville. His Iron Cross, First Class, was pinned on, as this was his desire. The detachment cleared the street of curious bystanders and after a somber good-bye he climbed onto the truck.[74]

Adolf Hitler was a prisoner of the state, charged with high treason.

CHAPTER

43

To know Hitler, means to know him before he came to power.
— OTTO STRASSER

BY THE TIME Hitler's trial for treason began on February 24, 1924, profound changes had occurred in Germany. On November 15, 1923, four days after Hitler was arrested, the planned introduction of the new Rentenmark currency was begun. When the gold-backed marks were introduced, it took 4.2 trillion of the old marks to equal one American dollar. A nation desperate for stability responded to the monetary reform. Within days, the nightmare inflation was brought under control; under the chairmanship of Charles Dawes of Chicago, who would soon become vice president of the United States, an international commission set to work on a plan that would at last give Germany the opportunity for a measure of economic recovery free from French obstructions.

On the domestic political scene, Chancellor Gustav Stresemann and his cabinet did indeed fall, as so many rightist conspirators had predicted, but they were not replaced by any of the prospective directorates that had maneuvered so frantically during the autumn. On November 30, Wilhelm Marx of the Center Party assumed power as chancellor. In an uninspired but effective manner, Marx brought about a rapprochement with the Social Democrats and presided over a program of sixty-six emergency decrees enacted under enabling legislation passed on December 8.

Thus, as Germany entered 1924, there was greatly increased financial and political stability coupled with a sharply reduced opportunity for the French to have their way unchallenged in German affairs. Both Britain and the United States were determined to end the series of crises that had marked the German postwar era. The separatist movements lost their strength, and the presence on the Dawes Commission of such internationally respected financiers as Owen D. Young of New York, and the German willingness to cooperate with such men and their recommendations, produced an entirely new and more favorable international climate. Although nothing could satisfy the demands of the right, Chancellor Marx strengthened the effectiveness of the rest of the political spectrum, and Germany's international position, by appointing former Chancellor Stresemann as foreign minister. In an act of unrepentant madness, a cabal of ex-officers, all members of right-wing organizations, put into action their plot to assassinate General von Seeckt. In the view of the radical right, the army chief had forfeited his right to live when he failed to seize power as a right-wing dictator, and then condemned the Putsch in Munich. Soon after midnight on January 15, 1924, the would-be assassins were arrested in Berlin, just hours before they intended to shoot the "Sphinx with a monocle" as he took his morning walk in the Tiergarten.[1]

Outwardly, Germany had passed through a great convulsion, yet, ironically, it was the new stability that afforded many Germans the luxury of admiring what Hitler and Ludendorff had endeavored to do in Munich. Knowing that a revolt had been put down and that there was no prospect of a similar attempt in the foreseeable future, conservatives throughout Germany could simultaneously enjoy a sane economy and indulge themselves in "what if?" daydreams of a völkisch triumph. Hitler had acted out the fantasies of millions of more timid men who also wanted to replace the type and nature of government in Berlin. He was behind bars awaiting trial, but the Putsch had catapulted his name into the national consciousness — every German who could read a newspaper knew of Adolf Hitler.

As always, what might be a ripple of rightist feeling in other parts of Germany was a powerful current in Bavaria. Although the Nazi Party was outlawed and its remnants were in disarray, the Nazi photographer Heinrich Hoffmann gave an indication of the feeling for Hitler that was still present in Munich. Speaking of the weeks just after Hitler's arrest, he recounted this incident:

> The artists in the Hitler movement planned to celebrate Christmas at the Blüte Café in the Blütestrasse with a *tableau vivant*, entitled, "Adolf Hitler in prison."

I was given the task of finding a suitable double for Hitler. As it happened I came across a man who bore a most striking resemblance to him. I asked him if he would take part in this *tableau vivant,* and he agreed to do so.

The great hall of the Blüte Café was filled with people. A reverent hush fell as the curtain went up and a prison cell became visible on the half-darkened stage. Behind the small barred window, snowflakes could be seen falling. At a small table, his back to the audience, his face buried in his hands, sat a man. An invisible male choir sang, "Stille Nacht, heilige Nacht."

As the strains of the last note died away, a tiny angel came into the cell, carrying an illuminated Christmas tree, which was placed gently on the table of the lonely man.

Slowly "Hitler" turned until he was face to face with the audience. Many thought that it was indeed Hitler himself, and a half-sob went through the hall.

The lights went up, and all around me I saw men and women with moist eyes, handkerchiefs hastily disappearing.[2]

With the Nazi Party proscribed, the "Hitler movement" was fragmented. The men who had borne arms against the Bavarian government, and those like Wilhelm Frick who had worked to subvert Bavaria's forces during the Putsch, were under arrest, but those who had been the party's journalists and speechmakers found that arrest orders were never issued for them or were soon rescinded. Alfred Rosenberg, Hitler's inspired choice as a leader who was sure to accomplish little, gathered as many Nazis as he could in a new Munich-based cover group known as the Greater German People's Community. His rival claimants for Hitler's followers were Julius Streicher, who was also in possession of a piece of paper handing the movement over to him, and his ally Hermann Esser, who had returned from his post-Putsch flight to Czechoslovakia. Streicher founded the Bavarian Nationalist-Racist Bloc; aided by Max Amann, Streicher and Esser began plotting to seize and absorb Rosenberg's group. A third contender was the National Socialist Freedom Party. Among its organizers were Ludendorff and Gregor Strasser, and it was attracting the Nazis who lived outside Bavaria.[3]

Forgotten amidst the turmoil of the dissolution of the Nazi Party was the fate of Dietrich Eckart. Arrested four days after the Putsch, on December 13 he was sent to the maximum-security fortress at Landsberg where Hitler was incarcerated, probably because General Commissioner von Kahr thought that Eckart was still a prominent Nazi. Prison life proved to be hard on Eckart, who was suffering from a heart condition. Putzi Hanfstaengl, who was no longer wanted by the police, was back in Bavaria; according to him, Eckart suffered a heart attack at Landsberg when a machine gun was fired without warning during the night as part of a drill against escapes.[4] Eckart petitioned Kahr, whom he had attacked so scathingly in the past, begging to be released. Three days before Christmas, friends took him from Landsberg to Berchtesgaden, where he was reunited with his young mistress. He died on December 26.[5]

During the time he was imprisoned awaiting his trial, Hitler added a great deal of drama to life at Landsberg. The prison was built in 1909 and housed only ordinary convicts until 1920. It was then, in the violent postwar period, that a wing was set aside for political prisoners and referred to as the *Festung*, or Fortress.

Until the arrival of Hitler, the sole long-term occupant of this political wing was Count Arco-Valley, who had assassinated the leftist Bavarian minister-president Kurt Eisner in 1919. The entire prison complex of grey-white buildings existed in a setting that was both beautiful and remote. Situated on a wooded alpine height above a valley through which ran the stream known as the Lech, the prison overlooked the town of Landsberg, which then had fewer than five thousand inhabitants. Located fifty miles west of Munich, the town was described by a visitor:

> It remains unspoilt to this day, one of the most beautiful survivals of the Middle Ages in Germany. The houses have preserved their old-world character. Modern times have failed to make any impression upon Landsberg: the little old town might have fallen asleep five hundred years ago, and never since waked up.[6]

That was about to change. Franz Hemmrich, then the warder in charge of the Fortress, later detailed his sudden involvement with the man who had, overnight, become Germany's most famous political prisoner.

> Then, on November 11, 1923, I remember, there was a real storm raging. The wind howled and shrieked round the place and tore at the barred windows. Rain dashed against the panes as if it would break them. At that time I had a room within the prison. It was night, and I'd gone to bed. All was still save for the muffled tread of an officer going the rounds, or for the ticking when he clocked in.

Hemmrich was suddenly wakened and ordered to report immediately to the warden, who in the German prison system held the title "Governor." Throwing on his warder's uniform, he was soon facing Herr Oberregierungsrat Leybold.

"See here," he said, and his face was as serious as his voice, "Hitler's coming here to-night. He has been arrested at last, and he'll certainly be sent along to us. We'll have to be prepared for anything. His followers may make an attempt at rescue —"
While we were speaking the telephone rang, and word came through that a strong detachment of the local Reichswehr had been detailed to take over guard in the prison. I received the order to get ready a cell for Hitler in the fortress division.

Realizing that the regular army soldiers would want to control a room in the political wing through which everything and everyone would have to pass before entering the cell in which Hitler would be confined, Hemmrich roused Count Arco-Valley, who occupied the only cell with an anteroom sufficiently large for the purpose. After the prisoner was transferred to another cell, Hemmrich continued working on the arrangements for Hitler. A bell connected to the guard post at the huge nail-studded, iron-sheathed wooden entrance gate rang in his upstairs corridor.

I hastened down and soon met a strange enough group of men coming through the halls, with their shadows flickering and dancing in the darkness before them. First I recognized the governor, accompanied by the superintendents of police, one of whom led a dog on a leash. Between these came Hitler, very upright, the Iron Cross on his breast. Over his shoulder was slung the grey trenchcoat he had been wearing in the Odeonsplatz. His left arm hung in a sling. Bareheaded, white and worn in the face, he marched thus to the place we had prepared.

The other officials left, and Hemmrich "stayed to give him a hand with his undressing. He was just about all in. He refused food or soup, but lay down on the cot." Hemmrich took special care in locking Hitler's cell and then withdrew.
The Reichswehr detachment soon arrived and set up elaborate security arrangements. "Helmets and rifles glittered everywhere," Hemmrich said. Sentries were placed on guard outside Hitler's cell, machine guns were mounted in the yard, and additional telephone lines were installed.
Perhaps because of the presence of regular army troops, Hitler

thought that he was going to be summarily executed by a firing squad. The following morning, however, the appearance of an assistant prosecutor from Munich gave him reason to believe that he would be the defendant in a trial. Accompanied by a stenographer, the man who had come to question him was Hans Ehard, who had interrogated Ludendorff during the hours of his brief period of arrest immediately after the Putsch. When Ehard and the stenographer entered Hitler's cell, Hitler simply turned away and faced the wall. Ehard's memory of the occasion was that Hitler "was going to eat me, he was so angry." Hitler said only one thing, but said it repeatedly: he was not going to talk. "I am not going to jeopardize my political career by giving you a statement."[7]

This went on for more than an hour. Finally Ehard decided to try a less official approach. What he knew, and Hitler did not, was that he had an astonishing ability to reconstruct every significant word of a conversation, hours after it took place. Ehard offered to send the stenographer out of the room and began to flatter Hitler. He told Hitler that he had always been fascinated by his political views, and that he simply could not go back to Munich without giving himself the opportunity to hear them directly from the Nazi Party leader, simply for his own enlightenment about the great issues facing Germany.

Hitler agreed; no sooner had the stenographer walked out of the cell than he launched into the sort of monologue with which he had favored Seeckt, Kahr, and Lossow in the months leading up to the Putsch. Gradually he switched to his full beer hall oratorical style. On this day his supply of sentences was truly inexhaustible: not stopping to eat, never going to the bathroom, Hitler spoke from early morning until early evening. The sole moments when he was not excitedly speaking were those when Ehard slipped in an admiringly worded request for clarification of some point, each time successfully bringing out Hitler's full complicity in an array of acts of high treason.

After spending twelve hours with Hitler, Ehard thanked him profusely for "the illuminating interview."[8] Then he moved quickly out of Hitler's cell to an office in the prison, where he promptly sat down to re-create verbatim the incriminating parts of the marathon conversation. Before dawn he left for Munich; under his arm was Hitler's inadvertent confession that he was guilty as charged.

The next act of the celebrated prisoner in Cell 7 was to go on a hunger strike. There were to be different accounts of the length and severity of this action. Anton Drexler still had hope for Hitler and the Nazi Party, despite his disapproval of the Putsch, and was able to visit him because the authorities quite rightly had no charges against Drexler for revolutionary activity. He recalled the moment when he was allowed in to see the prisoner: "I found him sitting like a frozen thing at the barred window of his cell." Consulting with the prison physician, a Dr. Brinsteiner, Drexler learned that Hitler had not eaten for two weeks; the doctor added that Hitler would die if he did not stop his fast. Drexler, who had been removed from any real power in the Nazi Party when Hitler confronted and defeated the old guard in the summer of 1921, returned to Hitler's cell, intent on preserving the man who had taken from him the party that he and Karl Harrer had started in 1919.

> I said he'd no right to give up all for lost, however bad things seemed. The party would look to him to start it all up again someday. But I couldn't make any impression. He was utterly in despair, so I nearly fell into despair myself, but at last I said how we'd all rather die than go on without him.[9]

Drexler kept repeating this sentiment for close to two hours, and finally felt that he had made some progress with Hitler. Another visitor, Hans Knirsch of the Pan-German group of National Socialists in Czechoslovakia, encountered a man who was still fasting and was severely depressed. When Knirsch began to speak encouragingly, Hitler repeatedly shook his head, but eventually he "timidly asked who would continue to follow a man with such a fiasco behind him."[10] Knirsch pointed out that the Putsch had focused on Hitler national and international attention that completely eclipsed any previous interest in him. He went on to say that this was no time to falter; great men climbed over their failures to reach their ultimate goals. According to Knirsch, this did the trick; Hitler decided to end his fast, and the prison doctor recommended that his first food be a bowl of rice.

Hitler soon resumed thinking about the future. Apparently content to let the Nazi Party remain fragmented until he could resume active leadership and supervision of it, even in this dark hour of his fortunes he was thinking of new sources of funds for his movement. At a conference in Vienna of some of the Nazis who had fled to Austria after the Putsch, it was suggested to Kurt Ludecke, who had arrived from Italy, that he go to the United States to raise money there for the party's aims. When he learned of this, Hitler strongly endorsed the idea by smuggling out of Landsberg a letter to Ludecke, written on the letterhead of Lorenz Roder, Hitler's defense lawyer. The letter carefully avoided mention of the party by name. It said in part:

> First expressing my heartiest thanks for your representation of the movement in Italy, I ask you to solicit in the interest of the Germany Liberty Movement in North America and especially to assemble financial means for it.
>
> I ask you to receive these means personally, and, if possible, to bring them over in person.[11]

Thus, Hitler was already collecting funds for his future war chest, to be put at his disposal when the moment was ripe. On January 8, four days after the date on the letter to Ludecke, the prison doctor submitted a report to the warden concerning Hitler's physical and mental capacity for standing trial. Hitler's dislocated shoulder was still giving him discomfort, but was no obstacle to his being able to understand the nature of the case being prepared against him. Dr. Brinsteiner stated specifically that Hitler had exhibited no symptoms of mental disorder, and that no psychopathic tendencies were evident. During his observations, the doctor said, "Hitler was at all times in control of himself, and his will and his mental capacity were not impaired by any illness, even if the aims and purposes of the Putsch are interpreted as being faulty."[12]

II

The trial that began on February 24, 1924, was truly a sensation.[13] There were ten defendants, but the presence of Ludendorff by itself guaranteed that this would not be a factual adjudication of the events in Munich on November 8 and 9, 1923. That the leading general of the war could, five years later, head an armed column that was shot down by government authority, raised the entire matter to the level of a national debate. For millions of Germans, the question at issue was not Ludendorff's conduct, but the nature and policies of a national government whose attitudes had driven Ludendorff to such desperate measures. Depending on how one looked at it, the entire right-wing movement was on trial, or, conversely, the entire succession of postwar German chancellors and their cabinets was under examination.

None of the courtrooms in Munich was large enough to stage what the German press was calling "the trial of the age."[14] The press alone, with a solid phalanx of German newspapermen, and correspondents from five continents, would have cramped any of the existing venues. The site chosen was a large lecture hall in the Infantry School, which had recently been closed down by General von Seeckt. (Enraged by the defection of its young Reichswehr officers and cadets during the Putsch, Seeckt had moved the school out of Bavaria.)

Outside the great brick building, an excited crowd of thousands milled about, knowing that they had no chance of being admitted to the high-ceilinged courtroom. Two battalions of Colonel von Seisser's state police were on duty to control the crowds, using barbed wire entanglements to hold them back. Of the triumvirate, Seisser was the only man still holding the position in which he had served at the time of the Putsch: six days before the trial began, Gustav von Kahr had resigned his post as general commissioner, and General von Lossow had recently been allowed to resign from the Reichswehr, under the darkest of clouds.

Even as this trial was beginning, one German thinker was demonstrating that he did not understand that Hitler had already managed to place military spectacle and mindless cheering at the center of the German political stage. In one of his lectures, Oswald Spengler derided the Nazi use of banners, parades, and hate-laden chants. "These things undoubtedly satisfy feelings," said the man who had earlier given trappings of intellectual respectability to certain völkisch attitudes, "but politics are something else."[15]

The ten defendants in the dock included the Kampfbund leaders Ernst Röhm and Friedrich Weber, but from the outset the focus was entirely on Ludendorff and Hitler. In the case of Ludendorff, the atmosphere was rather that of a right-wing testimonial dinner than a trial in which he was accused of the crime of high treason. The tribunal was one of those known as People's Courts, odd relics of Bavaria's postwar history. Created after the leftist defeat in 1919, each of these courts was composed of only two professional jurists, with the other three judges drawn from entirely different occupations. Therefore, in this trial, which was being held without a jury, Ludendorff's fate lay in the hands of two experienced judges, two insurance salesmen, and the owner of a stationery store.[16] These local courts had an unbroken record of favoritism toward defendants of völkisch persuasion; the three laymen on this one could scarcely restrain themselves from applauding whenever Ludendorff spoke. The presiding judge was Georg Neithardt of Nuremberg. Although he had a reputation as an enthusiastic right-winger, only he, of the five men on the bench, made an effort to apply the law to the facts of the case.

Ludendorff appeared in uniform, despite his angry vow, on his arrest, never to wear it again. His approach to the proceedings was to berate everyone except his fellow defendants and their lawyers. G. Ward Price, the famous English correspondent, could scarcely believe that he was covering a trial. In describing Ludendorff's behavior he wrote that Ludendorff would

> bark at the court in *Kommandostimme*, the tone of the parade ground, every syllable clipped harsh, and when his imperious voice rose, the little Chief Justice in the middle of the bench would quiver until his white goatee would flicker so badly he had to seize it to keep it quiet.[17]

Although it was obvious from the beginning that Ludendorff would receive nothing more than a suspended sentence, and perhaps not even that, the case of Adolf Hitler was somewhat different. Thousands of his supporters in the excited crowds were being held back by the state police in the streets outside, but he did not have the sacrosanct status of the victor of Liège and Tannenberg. Such prosecution witnesses as Lossow and Seisser intended to say every damning thing they could to substantiate the facts and to picture Hitler as a moving spirit in an armed uprising against the legally established government.

There was still another card that could be played against Hitler. A provision of the Law for the Protection of the Republic automatically required that any foreigner convicted of high treason be deported from Germany. The Austrian-born Hitler was still not a German citizen, despite his wartime military service; by convicting him and sending him out of the country, the Bavarian Ministry of Justice could rid the state of its worst troublemaker and avoid having Hitler stay on at Landsberg, a political martyr on Bavarian soil.

Hitler fully understood the stakes. In the first instance, he was fighting simply to keep from being shackled by a long prison term or deportation from the nation that was his political arena. Only a great and daring egotist could have seen beyond this goal and identified the full opportunity offered by the trial. Daring as it might be, here was his chance to stand before the German nation and offer himself as its leader. With a hundred reporters eager to seize on each memorable phrase and counteraccusation, Hitler turned the lecture hall of a dingy red brick structure in a dull Munich suburb into the scene of the greatest oratorical performances he had yet given.

At the first opportunity, Hitler went on the offensive. His moment came at 2:30 P.M. of the trial's first day, when the presiding judge opened the afternoon session by asking Hitler if he wished to explain how he became involved in the Putsch. Almost immediately, Hitler was taking the court back to the war years and reconstructing the formation of his own version of the stab-in-the-back theory of why Germany had lost the war. Speaking of his time in a field hospital with a thigh wound, in the winter of 1917, Hitler said:

> While we at the front still believed in absolute obedience at that time, it was practically nonexistent in the field hospitals. I was reading a book on military science in the hospital when the head doctor slammed the book shut and took it from me. Afterward a Dr. Stettiner asked me, "What are you reading here? I thought you were smarter than that." I was completely dumbfounded. Of course, Dr. Stettiner was a Jew. [18]

Hitler then turned to his discovery of the evils of Marxism. As he portrayed it, the worst crime of Marxism was that it tried to divide pure Aryan Germans along class lines, suggesting that a German worker had more in common with, for example, a Polish worker than he did with his own German employer.

> And so it becomes possible that a German considers his own blood brother a mortal enemy while he considers a racial alien — let us say a Hottentot — his brother. . . . Either Marxism will poison the people, or this poison will be bled off. Then Germany can recover, but not before. As far as we're concerned, Germany will be rescued when the last Marxist has been converted or annihilated. [19]

Another few minutes, and Hitler was saying, "France's objective is to reduce Germany to a number of small states." [20] Invoking the French occupation of the Ruhr, Hitler claimed that only he and his National Socialists had taken a sufficiently determined stand against the French move. Speaking in lower tones, but using the same phrases that brought his beer hall audiences to their feet, Hitler said, "Policy is made not with the palm branch, but with the sword." [21]

Having established his credentials as a wounded combat veteran, an anti-Semite, an enemy of Marxism, and an implacable foe of the French — personifications cherished by the great majority in the room — Hitler turned at last to his relations with the triumvirate.

Alluding to additional German problems, such as inflation and the separatist movement in the Rhineland, he portrayed himself as a man sympathetic to the triumvirate's plans to steer Bavaria out of trouble in an authoritarian manner. It soon became clear that this was to be the heart of Hitler's argument: he and Ludendorff had wanted for Germany precisely what Kahr and Lossow and Seisser had wanted for Germany. They had all wanted the same thing; they had all agreed on the desirability of doing whatever they could to create a new government in Berlin.

Soon enough, in the minds of the judges, and the spectators, there occurred the question that Hitler wanted them to ask themselves: If all these right-wing German patriots, the triumvirate and Hitler and Ludendorff, wanted the same thing and consulted with each other so often, was it really possible that two of them should be guilty of high treason and the other three be innocent, wronged parties?

Hitler was acting out the proposition that the best defense is a good offense. As the days in court went on, he was in effect putting the triumvirate on trial. The previous autumn, with Lossow ordering the Seventh Division to take a separate oath of allegiance to Bavaria, and with Reichswehr officers meeting with the Kampfbund's military leadership to discuss the outline of a march to Berlin, why should Hitler have doubted that a bold shove in the same direction would not give the triumvirate the pretext for doing what they so clearly wished to do? Either they should all be in the prisoners' dock together, or they should all be freed.

The interpretation begged the question of whether Hitler had committed criminal acts on November 8 and 9. When confronted at last with the facts of his own actions, Hitler immediately transposed them into his own context.

> I cannot declare myself guilty. True, I confess to the deed, but
> I do not confess to the crime of high treason. There can be no
> question of treason in an action which aims to undo the betrayal
> of this country in 1918. . . . I consider myself not a traitor, but a
> German who desired what was best for his people.[22]

As Hitler accepted responsibility for his actions, albeit on his own terms, so Ludendorff was willingly being upstaged by the Nazi leader. Convinced that he had somehow walked at the last minute into a Putsch with whose planning he had nothing to do, Ludendorff managed to make the entire courtroom feel that it was somehow a national disgrace for him to be asked to appear. Though Heinz Pernet had acted as a constant go-between for Ludendorff and the Kampfbund leaders and was also a defendant, Ludendorff later spoke as if he had been victimized. "Hitler misled me," he said to Hans Frank. "He lied to me. He told me on the evening of his mad Putsch that the army was behind it to a man. . . . He is only a speechmaker and adventurer."[23]

Although presiding Judge Neithardt appeared to be unwilling or unable to stop Hitler's flow of words, General von Lossow struck out at Hitler with all the indignation of an aristocratic general expressing his scorn for an upstart lance corporal. Alone among the many figures who spoke during the trial, Lossow said for the record that Hitler was a liar: "No matter how often Herr Hitler says so, it is not true." He went on to describe Adolf Hitler as "tactless, limited, boring, sometimes brutal, sometimes sentimental, and unquestionably inferior."[24]

Hitler was dominating the proceedings during the days of this crucial courtroom appearance, and the judges were doing much to assist him. Even the two senior prosecutors, one of whom had been threatened by violence from a students' group for agreeing to present the case against Hitler, were diffident in presenting the case against him. Only Hans Ehard pushed forward with a systematic approach to the case. A German reporter who covered the trial later reflected on it:

> I never can think without melancholy and bitterness about this monstrous trial. What went on there reminded me of a Munich political carnival. A court which time after time gave the accused the opportunity to make lengthy propaganda speeches; a lay judge who after Hitler's first speech, declared (I heard it myself), "But he's a colossal fellow, this man Hitler"; a presiding judge who let one man ridicule the highest officials in the Reich . . . an officer who shouted to an American journalist who was chatting in English with a colleague, "speak German in my presence!"; a presiding judge who banished a newspaper cartoonist from the courtroom because one of the accused felt that he had been the subject of a cartoon — doesn't all this belong in the Munich picture book of a great political carnival?[25]

Much of the twenty-five days that this trial consumed happened to coincide with Fasching, Munich's equivalent of the Mardi Gras pre-Lenten festivities. In Munich's streets and beer halls, the spirit was that of a Gaudi filled with practical jokes and jests. Ludwig Hümmert, a freshman law student at the University of Munich, managed to get into several sessions of the trial, and was disgusted by it: "The biggest jest in town was the one in that courtroom." He also characterized the proceedings as "a travesty of justice, a farce that made Bavaria the laughingstock of the world."[26]

A number of German newspapers began expressing concerns and objections as to the manner in which the trial was being conducted. Some of the foreign correspondents filed dispatches in which they said they found it hard to believe that this was really a trial. On March 4, a meeting of the Bavarian cabinet was devoted exclusively to expressing indignation about what was going on in the courtroom at the Infantry School. Interior Minister Franz Schweyer, to whom Hitler had sworn never to make a Putsch, still was considering the possibility of deporting Hitler. He told his colleagues that the kind of abuse Justice Neithardt was allowing the defendants to heap upon the Reichswehr and the Bavarian State Police was bound to undermine public confidence in those arms of government; the trial itself was proving to be a threat to the security of the state. Another minister spoke up and said that he doubted that Neithardt was competent to conduct such a trial; yet another minister said that government circles in Berlin were viewing the trial as a crisis only somewhat less severe than the Putsch itself.

These questions and criticisms were typified by the report of a minister who had taken it on himself to ask Justice Neithardt point-blank whether he thought it proper to allow Hitler to answer a single prosecutorial question by speaking for as long as four hours at a time. According to this cabinet minister, all that Neithardt could summon up in answer was "It is impossible to keep Hitler from talking."[27]

In a sense, the richly justified criticism was mere infighting. What was happening, in terms of history, was that Adolf Hitler was winning a tremendous propaganda victory, no matter what his sentence might prove to be. Perhaps the shrewdest assessment of what went on during those twenty-five days in the courtroom was provided by Konrad Heiden, a socialist who never fell into the trap of underestimating Adolf Hitler. He saw the long shadows that were being cast.

The unknown stood up and proclaimed to the world: Make no mistake. I am the Leader.

Many times in the course of the trial he was asked directly and indirectly by what right he, a man without origins, title, or virtually any education, arrogated to himself the right to govern Germany, sweeping aside all the generals, presidents, and excellencies. Hitler replied: "This was not overweening or immodest of me. On the contrary, I am of the opinion that when a man

■ 579

knows he can do a thing, he has no right to be modest. . . . In such questions there are no experts. The art of statecraft is — well, an art, and you've got to be born to it. . . .

"My standpoint is that the bird must sing because he is a bird. And a man who is born for politics must engage in politics whether free or in prison, whether he sits in a silken chair or must content himself with a hard bench. . . . The man who is born to be a dictator is not compelled; he wills; he is not driven forward; he drives himself forward. . . . The man who feels called upon to govern a people has [a] duty to step forward."[28]

Having let Hitler speak for himself, Heiden finished by saying of this part of Hitler's presentation of himself at the trial, "In conclusion, he informed the judges that despite everything that had happened they must honor the future state power in him."[29]

By the time the defendants made their closing arguments at the morning session on March 27, the force of Hitler's personality had beaten down virtually everyone in the courtroom. Only Assistant Prosecutor Hans Ehard remained unbowed, ignoring Hitler's jibes, the judges' caprice, and the rumbling reactions of the courtroom spectators, while he calmly and efficiently put on the record the evidence against the defendants.

Hitler was never again to have quite the same kind of showcase for his talents as a speaker and actor. It was almost as if by declaring that this was a morality play, he had made it one. He cast himself in the role of the poor patriot, the wounded veteran, whose love for the Fatherland was destined to conquer little men and evil forces. He spoke to the judges, but the judges heard the approving murmurs of the courtroom audience. Do not be deceived, Hitler was telling the judges and the journalists: the power is not in these government buildings; it is in the crowds outside, it is in the beer halls where I speak, it is in the paramilitary columns, singing as they march through the streets.

The man attracting the attention of many millions of Germans was described by Ferdinand Jahn, a United Press correspondent who had interviewed Hitler two days before the Putsch. His perception of Hitler was later given by Jahn, when he was asked to mention what particularly struck him about Hitler's physical appearance.

Mr. Jahn observed no indications of unusual nervousness or of tension. The things that impressed him most about Hitler were his eyes and his hands. His eyes he described as a bright blue with an extraordinary quality. He failed, however, to observe any of the hypnotic qualities which so many people have commented upon. The hands he described as most extraordinary. They seemed to him to be about medium in size with long fingers and very finely structured. He commented upon the extraordinary dexterity with which Hitler used them while speaking.[30]

On the morning of Thursday, March 27, the defendants had their opportunity to make closing statements to the court. Hitler was scheduled to speak last; immediately before him came Ludendorff.

The legendary quartermaster general of the Kaiser's army displayed a wistful desire to be considered not as a relic of the past, but as a colleague of the younger activists of the radical right.

> I am generally seen as the man of Tannenberg, of great battles and brilliant campaigns, as the representative of the old Army. You see me as the representative of a great era, a representative who now witnesses a period of deterioration. What you don't see, however, is my life's work: the struggle of the German people for its future.[31]

With this, Ludendorff briefly recounted his efforts during the war, emphasizing that he had foreseen a need for even greater sacrifices and dedication than the German people had proved willing to make. He blamed the nation's political leaders for failing to educate the population as to what was required of them.

> Now the disaster is here. I think that every German ought to put himself at the service of his country with twice, or three times the determination. Then it would be different. Only in the German Freedom Movement, in the Völkische Movement, did I meet men who were willing to serve. These men, who are now accused, wanted nothing else than to call attention to this struggle. The defendants stand before Your Honor, but also before the judge of world history. And world history will not send those men who have fought for their Fatherland to prison; they will be sent to Valhalla.[32]

There was a certain eloquence in the old soldier's pleading that his younger comrades were guilty of nothing but patriotism, but once again there was no attempt to refute the fact that the leaders of the Kampfbund had participated in an armed and bloody uprising against the authority of the state.

At last it was Hitler's turn. In any other court in the world he would by then have received a number of citations for contempt, but as he rose there was an atmosphere of expectation, as if he would make everything clear, once and for all. He began with a simple enough proposition: "Power is never identical with law."[33] Referring admiringly to Mussolini's seizure of power in Italy in October of 1922, Hitler said, "Mussolini's action became legal through an overwhelming cleanup. The march to Rome was finally legitimated on the day Rome was cleansed of those same signs of deterioration which mark our political life."[34]

Hitler then laid at the door of the successive postwar governments in Berlin the responsibility for the Versailles Treaty and the manufacture of paper marks that fueled the inflation. Once again, as in so many beer hall speeches, Hitler expressed the need for a moral resurgency: "Today's legislators have established laws without any consideration being given to ethics, morals, and decency."[35] Only right-thinking, völkisch-thinking Germans could set matters straight, by coming to power.

> Only then will a different court be set up, only then will the law be respected again. Only then will a prosecutor stand up in court and say: "I hereby accuse Ebert, Scheidemann, and friends of treason and high treason. I accuse them of having destroyed a people of seventy million."[36]

This produced one of Justice Neithardt's few remonstrances: "You are going too far when you accuse Ebert, Scheidemann, and friends of high treason."[37]

Hitler continued, simply brushing aside the reproof. Like Ludendorff, he had no intention of talking about the Putsch, except as a symptom of the plight of Germans who thought as he did. Now it was France's turn to be brought into his summation — not a summation of his case, but of Germany's situation in 1924 as seen by Adolf Hitler. "No matter what kind of a government there is in France, France's foremost goal will be to destroy Germany, to annihilate twenty million Germans and break up Germany into single states."[38]

Finally coming to the events of the Putsch, Hitler noted that the state police, rather than the army, had stopped the Kampfbund march by the firefight at the Feldherrnhalle.

> When I heard that it was the Green Police who had fired the shots, I was happy. At least it had not been the Reichswehr. The army has not become tarnished; it is as stable as it was before. The day will come when the Reichswehr will be on our side — both the officers and the troops.

The presiding judge once again protested: "Herr Hitler, you have just accused the Green Police of having been disgraced; I must object to that."[39]

Again, Hitler went on as if the judges were not there. He was the orator; the hall was his. In eloquent cadences, he closed his justifications of himself, his fellow defendants, and the Hitler movement.

> The army which we have formed grows from day to day, hour by hour. Even now I have the proud hope that one day these raw units will grow to battalions, the battalions to regiments and the regiments to divisions, when the old cockade will be raised from the mud, when the old banners will once again wave before us; and the reconciliation will come in that eternal last court of judgment, the Court of God, before which we are ready to appear. Then from our bones, from our graves, will sound the voice of the only tribunal that has the right to sit in judgment upon us.

The courtroom was still except for Hitler's voice, which was solemn, with no tinge of beer hall rhetoric.

> Gentlemen, judgment will not be passed on us by you; judgment will be passed on us by the Eternal Court of History. The verdict that you will pass I know. But that other Court will not ask of us, "Did you or did you not commit high treason?" That Court will pass judgment on us, on the quartermaster general of the World War and his officers, who as Germans wanted the best for their people and their country, and were willing to fight for it. You may say "Guilty" a thousand times, but the Goddess who presides over the Eternal Court of History will with a smile tear up the indictment of the public prosecutor and the verdict of this court, for *she* acquits us.[40]

III

The handing down of the sentences took place on April 1. Arriving early at the courtroom, Assistant Prosecuter Ehard found dozens of women already there, carrying bouquets for Adolf Hitler. Ehard had the bailiffs remove the flowers.[41] Other women were wearing rosettes made of red, black, and white ribbons, the imperial colors adopted by the nationalists.[42] A number of the women spectators asked Ehard whether, now that the trial was almost over, they could take baths in the tub that Hitler had used in the guardhouse area, where the defendants had been held during the course of the trial. Ehard said he did not think that would be possible.[43]

At 10:00 A.M. the defendants posed for a picture on the curb just below the steps to an entrance to the Infantry School building. In a sense there had been two classes of defendants, both in the same trial. The lesser lights were Ernst Röhm, Wilhelm Brückner, Heinz Pernet, Wilhelm Frick, and Lieutenant Robert Wagner, who had played a leading role in getting the young officers and cadets of the Infantry School to join the Putsch.

In the photograph, the principal defendants stand in the center, flanked by these lesser prisoners. This group consisted of Ernst Pöhner, Friedrich Weber, Lieutenant Colonel Hermann Kriebel, who had returned from hiding in Austria to surrender himself, and Ludendorff and Hitler. The men looking into the camera wear solemn expressions, with a gleam of triumph in their eyes. They had gone into the lion's den of a treason trial, and found it a surprisingly hospitable place. Lieutenant Wagner found that the judge would allow him to heap insults upon General von Lossow. When Lossow complained, Justice Neithardt reproved Wagner so mildly that Lossow stalked out of the trial and refused to take any further part in the proceedings, thus earning a citation for contempt of court. In the photograph, Ludendorff and Kriebel, equal in height, are in the center, wearing the highly polished, spike-tipped helmets of the Kaiser's army. Their faces exude self-righteousness. Hitler, wearing a single-breasted raincoat over a dark suit, his left hand tightly gripping a felt hat, has his hair brushed neatly to the side, not falling down into his eyes, as it so often did. His face is somewhat pudgy. Despite his prison fast three months earlier, the records showed him weighing 170 pounds, the heaviest he had ever been.[44]

The picture-taking session over, the group went inside to be sentenced. To no one's surprise, everyone soon heard: "Ludendorff is acquitted of the crime of high treason. The costs incurred for his trial will be borne by the public treasury." Brückner, Röhm, Pernet, Wagner, and Frick were convicted for "abetting the crime of high treason" and sentenced to fifteen months' imprisonment. However, they were immediately paroled, and were free to walk out of the court.

This left Hitler, Weber, Kriebel, and Pöhner. Each of the four was sentenced to five years' imprisonment for "the crime of high treason," but would be eligible for parole after serving six months.[45]

The sentence was no shock to Hitler, but what he needed to hear was whether the Bavarian authorities were going to deport him to

Austria. For that piece of information, he had to wait more than an hour, while the Justification of the Verdict was read. At least some indication of the way the decision might go came when Justice Neithardt said, as part of the justification:

> The Court has also become convinced that the motives of the defendants were genuinely patriotic, noble, and selfless. [They] believed most conscientiously that they had to act in order to save the Fatherland. They thought they were complying with the earlier intentions of [the triumvirate]. This does not justify their plans, but it does provide the key to understanding their actions.[46]

Several minutes later, Neithardt came to the question of whether Hitler would be deported, as required by law under these circumstances.

> Hitler is German-Austrian. He considers himself to be a German. He is a man who thinks and feels as a German. He fought in the German army for four and one-half years. He received high honors for outstanding courage in action. He was wounded and his health has suffered in other ways. . . . For these reasons, it is the Court's opinion that it is both meaningless and without purpose to apply the provision of Article 9, paragraph II, of the law for the protection of the republic.[47]

That brought the trial to an end, but General Ludendorff was not quite finished. Feeling that he should have been convicted with the others, he rose to say "I think this acquittal is an affront to my uniform, the medals I wear, and to my comrades." This produced shouts of "Heil!" throughout the courtroom.

Amidst the turmoil, Justice Neithardt, who had been intimidated by Ludendorff for the five weeks of the trial, said, "I call His Excellency Ludendorff to order. I consider his remark quite improper. It is also improper for the spectators to applaud in this manner."[48] Neithardt instructed the bailiffs and additional police guards to arrest those they could identify as having just shouted, and ordered that they be jailed for three days. Perhaps the policemen were looking the other way; they could not identify a single person who had cheered for Ludendorff.

The judges filed out. As soon as they had left the room, the newly freed Wilhelm Brückner shouted to his fellow right-wingers, "It's up to us now!"[49] The crowd outside the building cheered for the defendants. Hitler was allowed to appear at a window of the building to receive the wild applause of those below. Now that the trial was over, flowers from admirers were allowed to be brought into the building, and as Hitler and the others who were to serve their time at Landsberg sat in a guard room waiting for transportation, bouquets surrounded them.

At Landsberg, Hitler began writing the book that he called *Mein Kampf — My Struggle*. When he first began working on it, he intended to write the story of his political career, starting when he first discovered and joined the tiny German Workers' Party. The idea was to bring it through to the Putsch and his trial, and to call it *Four and a Half Years of Struggle Against Lies, Stupidity, and Cowardice*. As the book developed, it expanded in every sense and became a remarkable document — part self-promotional autobiography, part reflections on lessons learned, and part blueprint for future action. In these unevenly written pages, the threads appear in various combinations. There were pages that purported to be valid science and history but were hogwash, and pages that were sentimental tripe, but underlying the harsh evaluation of life was a body of primitive thought with a skeleton of steel. The Bavarian authorities had unwittingly given Hitler the opportunity to sit down and sort out the total experience of his life and thought. Years later, when he had the power of which he then dreamed, Hitler said of those who had imprisoned him, "They would have been far wiser to let me make speeches all the time, without giving me respite!"[50]

Just as Hitler had devoured the libraries of Linz and Vienna in his youth, so he now threw his concentrated energies into placing on paper his Weltanschauungg. Rudolf Hess, who had returned from Austria and surrendered himself, was one of the forty Nazis convicted on lesser Putsch-related charges who were imprisoned at Landsberg with Hitler. Sometimes Hitler dictated passages to Hess, who discussed ideas with him and tried to edit his ornate but energetic prose; Hess rattled on the typewriter deep into the night. Sometimes Hitler dictated parts of the book to Emil Maurice, who had also been sent to Landsberg as a result of one of the less-publicized trials. In the evening, all the Nazi prisoners would gather around their leader. Franz Hemmrich said, "As he finished one section of the book after another he would read it aloud to the others in their evening assemblies."[51]

The book on which Hitler was working would remain largely unread by Nazis, and it would be ignored by those opponents who so consistently underestimated Hitler, but it was a key not only to Hitler, but to the history that he would make. On the very first page of his book, Hitler revealed the little German-speaking boy, born in Austria, with his nose pressed to the store window looking in at what he conceived to be the treasures of Germany.

> Today it seems to me providential that fate should have chosen Braunau on the Inn as my birthplace. For this little town lies on the boundary between two German states which we of the younger generation at least have made it our life work to reunite by every means at our disposal.
>
> German-Austria must return to the great German mother country, and not because of any economic considerations. No, and again no! Even if such a union were unimportant from an economic point of view; yes, even if it were harmful, it must nevertheless take place. One blood demands one Reich. Never will the German nation possess the moral right to engage in colonial politics until, at least, it embraces its own sons within a single state. Only when the Reich borders include the very last German, but can no longer guarantee his daily bread, will the moral right to acquire foreign soil arise from the distress of our own people.[52]

It was all there, frightening in the prosaic manner in which it was said. The little boy was looking straight through history to the Anschluss, the annexation of Austria that this convict would bring about in fourteen more years. "One blood demands one Reich." All the bogus Aryan racial philosophy was there, all the misunderstood Darwinism, all the might-makes-right that would cause agony and death for millions. Germany would again be "colonial"; Hitler was already looking eastward, positing a "moral right to acquire foreign soil."

Even those who had watched, with whatever reaction, Hitler's meteoric rise from nobody to most-talked-of German should not have been expected to understand that this was a man who could make the future happen. Hitler had that weird combination of talents: the ability to reorder the world in his dreams, and the practical skills and magnetic qualities of leadership that could cause men and nations to do his bidding. Hitler defined it himself, halfway through the first of the two volumes that became *Mein Kampf* as the world knew it:

> For if the art of the politician is really the art of the possible, the theoretician is one of those of whom it can be said that they are pleasing to the gods only if they demand and want the impos-

sible. . . . In long periods of humanity, it may happen once that the politician is wedded to the theoretician.[53]

The man who could both dream and do: Captain Ahab in *Moby-Dick*, saying to and of himself, "Now, then, be the prophet and the fulfiller one." Hitler knew things that had to be understood about human beings if they were to play the subservient roles in which he cast them. No man on earth was better equipped to write on the subject of propaganda; Hitler had been its foremost practitioner, without stopping to analyze what it was that he knew about audiences that made him so successful. Now he marshaled his observations in a manner that made Machiavelli seem reticent.

> The art of propaganda lies in understanding the emotional ideas of the great masses and finding, through a psychologically correct form, the way to the attention and then to the heart of the broad masses. . . . The receptivity of the great masses is very limited, their intelligence is small, but their power of forgetting is enormous. In consequence of these facts, all effective propaganda must be limited to a very few points and must harp on these in slogans until the last member of the public understands what you want him to understand by your slogan.[54]

Speaking of "the primitive sentiments of the broad masses," Hitler laid down for propaganda the maxim that he had been practicing in the hundreds of beer hall speeches he had given since early 1920: "It must confine itself to a few points and repeat them over and over. Here, as so often in this world, persistence is the first and most important requirement for success."[55]

And so the months passed for Adolf Hitler, busy writing down what he was to unleash upon the world. His life at Landsberg was comfortable. Putzi Hanfstaengl, free to move about since the order to arrest him had been rescinded, told of what he found when he went to visit Hitler.

> The ascendancy he gained over the officials and guards at Landsberg was quite extraordinary. The jailers even used to say "Heil Hitler" when they came into his cell. This was partly due to the extraordinary magnetism of his personality, and to his political martyrdom, which found a wide acclaim across many and varied sections of the community. He received favored treatment, which included freedom to accept gifts of food from outside, and this again gave him a further hold over his warders. It was very

easy to say "Take this box of chocolates home to your wife" when he had almost unlimited quantities available. He and Hess had not so much cells as a small suite of rooms forming an apartment. The place looked like a delicatessen store. You could have opened up a flower and fruit and wine shop with all the stuff stacked there. People were sending presents from all over Germany and Hitler had grown visibly fatter on the proceeds.[56]

Putzi decided that Hitler was unaware of how pudgy he was getting, and how bad for his health it was to lead a completely sedentary life.

"You really must take part in some of the gymnastic exercises and prison sports," I told him.
"No," he said, and the reply was very typical of his mentality. "I keep away from them. It would be bad for discipline if I took part in physical training. A leader cannot afford to be beaten at games."[57]

With the Nazi Party members who were imprisoned with him, Hitler maintained a friendly but strict observance of the Führerprinzip, the leader principle. Warder Hemmrich afforded a glimpse of how this worked at the Nazis' noon meal:

Shortly before twelve o'clock they would spread the cloth for dinner in the common room. This cloth didn't properly come under orders, but the convicts instituted it and we made no demur. They brought the meal in one large vessel and served it to the prisoners. As a rule the meal consisted of but one dish. Everyone waited for Hitler, each standing erect behind his own chair. When the leader appeared there was a cry of " 'tenshun!" and he strode to the top of the table, and remained standing, until every man in turn came forward with his table-greeting. Then all sat down and fell to.[58]

Although Hitler had virtual carte blanche at Landsberg, with permission to keep his lights on until midnight and to do nearly as he pleased, there were certain ways in which the prison authorities insisted on keeping up appearances. Hitler was allowed a stream of callers of both sexes, but the regulations required that a guard be present during each visit, and that it be completed within an allotted time. This gave Hemmrich the opportunity to observe Hitler as he dealt with a variety of individuals.

I used to "take" Hitler's visits in a room set apart for the purpose. . . . In the course of so many but so brief interviews Hitler developed an extraordinary terseness and fluidity of expression. It often went severely against the grain to me to bring these to a close. The moment, however, I made a sign that time was up, Hitler broke off, and withdrew. . . . It was really a wonderful experience to listen to Hitler in face-to-face conversation. I don't know anyone whose personality was so overwhelming. As a rule when I had to "take" one of these visits, I made a point of having a newspaper on hand, in which for appearance's sake I could appear to immerse myself. Very often, though, I just used it to screen the intense interest I myself was feeling in the conversation. Hitler's way of putting things was not mere talking: he made you feel the point come right home: you yourself *experienced* every word.[59]

It was also Hemmrich's duty to remain in the doorway of the common room of the political wing on evenings when Hitler and his followers gathered for political discussions, or to hear him read the latest chapter of *Mein Kampf*. Other prison guards would join Hemmrich to listen to Hitler, "but throughout his whole ten months [including pretrial confinement], Hitler never talked to us officers directly on the subject. Yet I don't think I should be off the mark if I were to say that before we saw the last of him everyone here, from the Governor to the furnace man, had become a convinced believer in his ideas."[60]

Even before Hitler started working on *Mein Kampf*, the nationwide elections on May 4 had produced some interesting results. Although the Nazi Party was officially dissolved, ten of its members, running as candidates on the tickets of either the National Socialist Freedom Party or the Bavarian Nationalist-Racist Bloc, won seats in the Reichstag. These two parties placed an additional twenty-two candidates in the Reichstag, giving Nazis and those who believed as they did thirty-two seats out of 472. Among those elected to the national legislature was Erich Ludendorff. While the total of two million votes was not large in a nation of seventy million, the result in Bavaria was to make the Nationalist-Racist Bloc the second strongest party in the Bavarian legislature.

It was against this background that Hitler spoke when he was visited by Kurt Ludecke, who had returned from a fruitless effort to raise funds in the United States. While there he had met with Henry Ford, who was known for his anti-Semitic views, but, Ludecke reported, as for contributing money to a racist party in Munich, Germany, "If I had been trying to sell Mr. Ford a wooden nutmeg, he couldn't have shown less interest in the proposition."[61] Although Ludecke wanted to hear details of the Putsch, which had failed while he was in Italy, Hitler simply guided the subject to other topics. He did, however, begin a line of conversation that made it clear that he had been drawing conclusions from the fiasco.

> "From now on," he said, "we must follow a new line of action. It is best to attempt no large reorganization until I am freed, which may be a matter of months rather than of years."
> I must have looked at him somewhat incredulously.
> "Oh, yes," he continued, "I am not going to stay here much longer. When I resume active work it will be necessary to pursue a new policy. Instead of working to achieve power by an armed *coup,* we shall have to hold our noses and enter the Reichstag against the Catholic and Marxist deputies. If outvoting them takes longer than outshooting them, at least the results will be guaranteed by their own Constitution!

Ludecke was surprised to hear this from the man who had spoken so openly of his contempt for majority votes and democratic procedures, but it was obvious that Hitler had decided to take the route to power through the ballot box. As Ludecke listened, Hitler continued:

> Any lawful process is slow. But already, as you know, we have thirty-two Reichstag deputies under this new program. . . . Sooner or later we shall have a majority — and after that, Germany. I am convinced this is our best line of action, now that conditions in the country have changed so radically.[62]

Both parts of the message were clear to Kurt Ludecke. They were going after the mass vote in future elections, and just as important, the translation of "it is best to attempt no large reorganization until I am freed" was "I don't want anyone to have the opportunity to replace me while I am locked up here."

While Hitler was writing about propaganda in *Mein Kampf,* among the adulatory letters from strangers that poured in for him at Landsberg was one from a twenty-six-year-old admirer named Joseph Goebbels, who had received a Ph.D. in philology from Heidelberg. Praising Hitler's closing statement at his trial, Goebbels wrote, "What you stated there is the catechism of a new political creed coming to birth in the middle of a collapsing, secularized world. . . . To you a god has given the tongue with which to express our sufferings. You formulated our agony in words that promise salvation."[63] Although Hitler was thinking intently about the future, this letter received no special treatment. He went on with his work, unaware that he had heard from the man who, in what Hitler would call the Third Reich, would hold the title Minister for Public Enlightenment and Propaganda.

Regarding the manipulation of the public, Hitler placed in *Mein Kampf* a classic passage, one that explained how and why he constantly wove together such different entities as the French, Marxism, the Berlin government, and the Jews.

> The art of all truly great national leaders has at all times primarily consisted of this: not to divide the attention of a people, but to concentrate that attention on a single enemy. . . . Therefore a great number of basically different enemies must always be described as belonging to the same group, so that as far as the mass of your followers is concerned, the battle is being waged against a single enemy.[64]

Within a few pages of this tactical doctrine, Hitler gave an example of substituting one enemy for another.

> It was and it is Jews who bring the Negroes into the Rhineland, always with the same secret thought and clear aim of ruining the hated white race by the necessarily resulting bastardization, throwing it down from its cultural and political height, and themselves rising to be its master.[65]

It was of course the French who had used their black colonial troops in the postwar occupation of the Rhineland; Jews had had no more to do with that decision than had Hindus. Hitler's anti-Semitic obsession enabled him to believe that the posting was part of a Jewish plot, and in a book filled with violent rhetoric and deceptive assertions, it is in the passages dealing with the Jews that a real sickness of mind makes itself particularly evident. Interspersed among otherwise reasonably worded autobiographical passages concerning his days as a young man in Vienna, there are the extraordinary reactions to his first encounters with the Jews of that city.

> By their very exterior you could tell that these were no lovers of water, and, to your distress, you often knew it with your eyes closed. Later I often grew sick to my stomach from the smell of these caftan-wearers. . . .
> Was there any form of filth or profligacy, particularly in cultural life, without at least one Jew involved in it?[66]
> When carefully cutting open such an abscess, you found, like a

maggot in a rotting corpse, a little Jew, blinking at the sudden light.[67] . . . This was pestilence, spiritual pestilence, worse than the Black Death of olden times, and the people were being infected with it![68]

Within a few paragraphs, Hitler says that "the deeper [he] probed," the more it became apparent to him that this was not solely a spiritual and intellectual problem.

The relation of the Jews to prostitution, and even more, to the white-slave traffic, could be studied in Vienna as perhaps no other city in Western Europe, with the possible exception of the southern French ports. If you walked at nights through the streets and alleys of Leopoldstadt, at every step you witnessed proceedings which remained concealed from the majority of the German people until the War gave the soldiers on the Eastern Front occasion to see similar things, or rather forced them to see them.[69]

In the cosmic and insanely false indictment of the Jews that Hitler was constructing, they were by implication also responsible for syphilis.

The cause lies, primarily, in our prostitution of love. Even if its result were not this frightful plague, it would nevertheless be profoundly injurious to man, since the moral devastations which accompany this degeneracy suffice to destroy a people slowly but surely. This Jewification of our spiritual life and mammonization of our mating instinct will sooner or later destroy our entire offspring.[70]

As a parallel, Hitler brought forward his equation that Jews were Marxists, Marxists were Jews. Again, the imagery suggested a view of the subject that had little to do with political debate or sociological observation. Of his verbal exchanges with Jewish leftists in Vienna, Hitler said, "Whenever you tried to attack one of these apostles, your hand closed on a jelly-like slime which divided up and poured through your fingers, but in the next moment collected again."[71] For Hitler, the Jew was the defiler of the nation's life, morally, culturally, politically, economically, and genetically.

With satanic joy in his face, the black-haired Jewish youth lurks in wait for the unsuspecting girl whom he defiles with his blood, thus stealing her from her people. With every means he tries to destroy the racial foundations of the people he has set out to subjugate. Just as he himself systematically ruins women and girls, he does not shrink back from pulling down the blood barriers.[72]

Hitler then reached a remarkable summation and conclusion. Believing himself to be on the side of nature, he saw nature's task as the preservation of its superior species. What he called "the aristocratic principle of Nature" was in his eyes the ability — given, intended, and sanctioned by Nature — of the strong to dominate the weak. In Hitler's cosmic view, as long as this principle obtained and operated effectively, humanity would continue to exist, and the Aryan people would enjoy their rightful supremacy.

In this construct, however, it was vital that Aryan blood remain undefiled. Enter the Jew attempting to destroy the Aryan, not by the pounce in the jungle or manly conflict in battle, but by defilement of the racial stock, corruption of the culture, devious manipulation of the economy, and the introduction of a Marxist political system that, Hitler said, "denies the value of personality in man, contests the significance of nationality and race, and thereby withdraws from humanity the premise of its existence and its culture." If the Jews succeeded, Hitler concluded, they "would bring about the end of any order intellectually conceivable to man." Physical chaos would follow close behind, with despair, lack of will, murder, and incessant warfare. There could be only one result: "destruction for the inhabitants of this planet." The Jew would literally have destroyed humanity, "and this planet will, as it did millions of years ago, move through the ether devoid of men."

Against this annihilation stood Adolf Hitler. He would save the future of mankind. "Hence today I believe that I am acting in accordance with the will of the Almighty Creator: *by defending myself against the Jew*, I am fighting for the work of the Lord."[73]

It was a supremely false redefinition of the human condition, but it was not stupidly written. Morality is different from the logic of argumentation. Again and again, Hitler's premises were wrong, in every sense of the word, but he argued from the false premise to the horrendously evil conclusion in a logical manner.

The call to arms was clear enough, but the clues to Hitler's formation of his attitudes lay in the autobiographical sections of the book, coupled with what else was known about him. Throughout *Mein Kampf*, Hitler revised the known facts of his life to enhance his image as a penniless, selfless young patriot who had a vocation to save the Fatherland. Nonetheless, even the Hitler-edited version of his life left a profile that could explain some of the basis for his attitudes, although nothing could explain the extraordinary gifts that enabled him to put his grandiose schemes into action.

Viewing what Hitler said about himself and what else is known about him, first came the boy who was beaten unmercifully by his father, creating within the wounded child the classic desire to repeat the action as an adult and to seek revenge against a yet unspecified enemy.[74] The sensitive boy grew up feeling that his German identity was constantly threatened by the other ethnic groups contending for power in the Austro-Hungarian Empire. After his move to Vienna, his own failures and insecurities, including a great shyness with young women, paralleled the time when, he later said in *Mein Kampf,* he was discovering that the true culprits in the world were the Jews.

Then came the war, an experience effectively and for the most part honestly recorded by Hitler. The young man is for the first time appreciated and honored in an authoritarian male society in which everyone has a position and a function, and the great purpose of warfare is carried on without democratic discussion. Hitler sees might-makes-right on the battlefield, so when German might begins to fail, there must be some sinister explanation for it.

Blinded and half dead, Hitler hears the news of Germany's defeat while in a hospital. Everywhere there are suddenly traitors. He reports for duty in Munich in time to see a Marxist revolution in which a number of the leaders are Jews.

He has his enemy; being Hitler, he also has his mandate, which is to destroy the Jews, return Germany to greatness, and punish the wartime enemies who laid upon the Fatherland the provisions of the Versailles Treaty. Not only must "racial purity" be preserved, but there must be more Germans, for the good of the world and to make it numerically impossible for inferior breeds to destroy the earth's finest race. The new German breeding grounds will be to the east: Poland and Russia. The inferior peoples of Eastern Europe exist only to serve this new German empire; if they oppose or hinder it, they must be destroyed.

Adolf Hitler completed the first volume of *Mein Kampf* at Landsberg in 1924. He was thirty-five and in excellent physical health. Vigorous in mind and body, ambitious as few men have ever been, he was a loner, a man who could best connect to his fellow human beings through shared hatred. For Hitler, there was no need for the world to have any fully autonomous person other than himself. The Germans were to do his bidding, and all would be well. He was pragmatically committed to gaining power through the ballot box, but the German state he envisioned had nothing to do with democracy. The German destiny was to be a racial evolution, a racial self-purification: in the name of a false and meaningless racial "science," Germany's mission was to breed more and better Aryans, and destroy or enslave the lesser breeds. For those not privy to this grotesque idea, it seemed impossible that a modern state should be devoted to such a quest; to the very end of Hitler's Germany, few of its enemies would understand that racism was not just a part of National Socialism, but its core.

The racial militancy must be coupled with martial ardor: as Hitler saw it, the state was a nation in arms, a place of national values and practices that moved Mirabeau to observe in an earlier era that "Prussia is not a nation with an army, but an army with a nation."

Goering's remark that the program of National Socialism was written on the faces of its marching Storm Troops was consonant with Hitler's love of military spectacle. The banners and music at a Hitler speech, the fact that the response of the crowd mattered more than what was said to it, prefigured a state in which one of the primary purposes of government was to organize and participate in large uniformed spectacles; the ultimate uniformed spectacle, of course, was war. But just as the strategic objectives set forth in *Mein Kampf* preceded the mobilization of the state to implement those objectives when Hitler reached power, so the marches themselves made the transition from uniformed political displays to the Wehrmacht columns marching into Poland in 1939. *Mein Kampf* looked into the future, foretold the wartime agony of Europe and the murder of the Jews, but nowhere in its pages was there a hint of the final shattering irony of the fate that this self-appointed savior of Germany would bring down upon his nation. Hitler would have shrieked in horror had he foreseen that his military adventures would result in the splitting of his nation into two Germanys, West Germany and East Germany, with nearly twenty million Germans living under a communist regime and the city of Chemnitz being renamed Karl-Marx-Stadt.

Hitler would have his Third Reich, his purge of those who opposed him on his way up, his vile and supremely bloody experiment in racism, and his war. National Socialism and Hitler were one; as a political philosophy, it did not outlive its prophet and leader by a single day. Like *Mein Kampf,* the Third Reich undeniably existed, but it was the culmination of the crazed dreams of one man who had an insatiable desire to be heard and to control.

IV

During the early autumn, the Bavarian authorities began sparring with each other about Hitler's possible release from prison. On October 1, he would become eligible for parole.

This prospect was in no way pleasing to the Bavarian State Police, who had not forgotten the four men of their ranks killed at the Feldherrnhalle. On September 22, the director of the state police sent to the Bavarian State Ministry of the Interior a report recommending that parole for Hitler "should not be considered." He added that if parole was granted, it would be desirable "to deport Hitler as the soul of the entire nationalistic and racial movement in order to avoid the immediate danger to the Bavarian State." The reasoning behind the recommendation rested on these observations:

> Hitler will resume his political activities, and the hope of the nationalists and racists that he will succeed in removing the present disunity among the officials of the paramilitary troops will be fulfilled. Hitler's influence on all who are nationalistically inclined — today he is more than before the soul of the entire movement — will again carry the entire movement forward. It will even absorb great masses of people who are now foreign to his ranks and convert them to the idea of the National Socialist German Workers' Party.[75]

On the same day a different estimate of Hitler, written four days earlier by the governor of Landsberg Prison, was forwarded to the Ministry of the Interior. This report also made the point that "Hitler will undoubtedly return to political life," but treated it as no threat to the state.

> He proposes to refound and reanimate his movement, but in the future he proposes not to run counter to the authorities. . . .
> During his ten months under detention while awaiting trial and while under sentence, he has undoubtedly become more mature and calmer. When he returns to freedom, he will do so without entertaining vengeful purposes against those in official positions who opposed him and frustrated him in November 1923.

In noting that "his behavior while under detention merits the grant of an early release," the governor of Landsberg Prison went on to praise Hitler. "He is amenable, unassuming, and modest. . . . He has no personal vanity, is content with the prison diet, neither smokes nor drinks, and has exercised a helpful authority over other prisoners." There was also this interesting touch: "He has no interest in women, and received the visits of women friends and followers without any particular enthusiasm but with the utmost politeness, and never allowed himself to be drawn into serious political discussions with them."[76]

The bureaucratic tilting began. The Ministry of the Interior was ready to grant parole, but the Ministry of Justice thwarted it by stating that Hitler's steady stream of visitors at Landsberg flagrantly broke the rules as to how many visitors he could have. Parole was denied, to Hitler's disgust. During the same period, the Bavarian Supreme Court recommended parole, but this recommendation was successfully opposed by the Office of the State Prosecutor. At the same time, deciding that it did not want Hitler, no matter what the Germans did with him, the Austrian government deprived him of citizenship so that he would no longer be eligible for deportation to Austria. Always ready to play any propaganda card, large or small, Hitler reacted by issuing a statement that he "never felt like an Austrian citizen, but always like a German."[77]

The second round of negotiations began in December. Once again, the prison governor wrote on Hitler's behalf, saying, among other things, "He is undoubtedly a political idealist."[78] Behind the scenes, the three lay judges who had been so impressed by Hitler during his trial for treason made it known that if he was not released forthwith, they would issue a public appeal that he be freed.

The consequences of the sparring became apparent to Heinrich Hoffmann on the morning of Saturday, December 20.

Adolf Müller, the proprietor of the Munich Publishing House [and printer of Nazi publications], came to see me. "Would you like to come on a little picnic with me," he asked, "to Landsberg?" I understood, of course, that he was going to visit Hitler. To be on the safe side, I took my camera with me. One never knows one's luck.

I was surprised to see that Müller did not take his chauffeur with him, but drove his big Daimler-Benz himself. As we settled in the car, he told me that he was going to fetch Hitler! "Very few people," he added, "know the exact date and time at which he will be released." . . .

Very soon the big Daimler-Benz drew up outside Landsberg Fortress. I got out and prepared my camera. Then I heard a grinding noise — the gates were being opened. The historic mo-

ment, apparently, was upon us! But in reality, it was not! It was
only the uniformed gatekeeper, who drew my attention to the
fact that all photography was forbidden. I retorted that he was ex-
ceeding his authority, which did not stretch beyond the confines
of the fortress itself; to which he replied quite calmly that if I
ignored his warning, he would confiscate my camera. . . . I
demanded to see the Director [governor]. The Director was
friendly, but quite firm. "Instructions from the government," he
said. "Hitler is not to be photographed as he leaves the fortress."
And that was that.[79]

Behind the prison gate that Hoffmann was watching, some emotional
good-byes were taking place. Hitler shook hands with the Nazis who
were not yet being released and gave them the 282 marks in his
possession.[80] According to Hitler, the guards were weeping as they
said good-bye to him, "but not I!"[81]

Just before leaving, Hitler shook hands with Warder Franz Hemmrich and thanked him for the good treatment he had received. Hitler
then bade good-bye to the governor and walked out to freedom. As
he left, the governor turned to Hemmrich and said, "Well, if it's in
any way possible to lift up this country again and set her on her feet,
that's the man to do it!"[82]

Hoffmann was still waiting outside.

With a terse greeting, [Hitler] stepped swiftly into the car, and
we drove off. . . . It seemed to me essential that a photograph to
mark the occasion should be taken in Landsberg itself; and if that
were not possible in front of the fortress, then I must take one
elsewhere. I suggested that we stop by the old city gates, where
we would still retain something of the fortress atmosphere. To
this Hitler agreed, and I took several pictures.

The same day, I sent the photographs to all the various home
and foreign newspapers, with the caption "Adolf Hitler leaves
Landsberg Fortress." As I anticipated, the picture was published
all over the world. But when I received my copies, I could not
help laughing. Not a single newspaper had used my caption. Instead: "The first step to freedom" — "The Fortress Gate has
opened" — "On to new deeds" — "Thoughtfully, Hitler stands in
front of his prison — what will he do now?"

What Hitler actually did was to say to me: "Get a move on,
Hoffmann, or we'll have a crowd collecting; and anyway, it's
bloody cold!"

We returned to the car, and I asked him what he intended to
do next. "I shall start again from the beginning," he said deci-

sively. "The first thing I want is office space. Do you know of anything in that line, Hoffmann?"

I told him that at 50 Schellingstrasse there were thirteen empty rooms to let.

"That's fine!" he answered gleefully. "I'll take twelve of them."

Hitler, among other things, was very superstitious.[83]

V

The man who was freed from Landsberg would soon begin rebuilding his political fortunes. As Hitler saw it, and as it came to pass, his Storm Troops would be used to intimidate and beat up political opponents in the streets, but not to attack the government. What lay ahead was an eight-year march to power, with its climax on January 30, 1933, when Hitler was appointed chancellor by a senile President Paul von Hindenburg. The appointment was part of a backstage deal in which, as usual, other political leaders underestimated Hitler and felt that they could control him.

In the immediate future, precisely such an underestimation was going to occur. On January 4, 1925, Hitler met with the new Bavarian minister-president, Dr. Heinrich Held. Hitler virtually prostrated himself at their meeting, stating that the Putsch was a grievous error. He told Held that he, too, was offended by Ludendorff's attacks on the Catholic Church, and assured the Bavarian leader that he intended to have nothing more to do with Ludendorff. Hitler promised that he would support the authority of the state in every way, and pleaded for the release of the Nazis still in prison at Landsberg.

As usual, Hitler wanted something in return for his cooperation. This time he wanted the ban on the Nazi Party lifted and sought permission for the *Völkischer Beobachter* to resume publication.

Minister-President Held agreed. That evening he said to Bavaria's minister of justice, "The wild beast is checked; we can afford to loosen the chain."[84]

Just what this meant to Hitler became clear when he delivered his first speech after his imprisonment. On February 27, with the National Socialist German Workers' Party once again legally sanctioned and the *Beobachter* beating the drums for Ludendorff, who had agreed to run as the Nazi Party candidate in the upcoming presidential election, Hitler chose an interesting place to resume his political speaking — the Bürgerbräukeller. Speaking of efforts to persuade him to dilute his authority as the party's leader, Hitler said words that went well beyond the immediate moment: "If anyone comes and wants to impose conditions on me, I shall say to him: 'Just wait, my little friend, and see what conditions I impose on you.' "[85]

All that lay ahead. A few hours after he returned to Munich, Hitler went to dinner at the Hanfstaengls' new house in Herzog Park. After more than a year behind bars, he was particularly sensitive to the atmosphere of a family home, and he was struck by the comforts of Putzi's new establishment. With Christmas five days off, there were decorations and a tree with presents beneath it, including some for Hitler. The dinner was to celebrate Hitler's freedom, and Putzi wrote:

> He arrived about half past six in the tight blue serge suit, of which he was so proud, straining at the buttons with the weight he had put on in Landsberg. Egon was with me to greet him at the door. "I am so glad to see you again, Uncle 'Dolf," he said and Hitler took his hand as we walked down the corridor. I had a big concert grand in the studio and before I could gather my wits or offer any hospitality, Hitler, who seemed tense and wound up, said, almost pleadingly: "Hanfstaengl, play me the *Liebestod*." . . . So down I sat and hammered out this tremendous thing from *Tristan und Isolde*, with Lisztian embellishments, and it seemed to work the trick. He relaxed.[86]

Helene Hanfstaengl entered the room. It was the first time Hitler had seen her since he had been arrested at the Hanfstaengls' country house at Uffing, thirteen months earlier. Hitler apologized for the turmoil he had caused, and then, Putzi said, made a particular point of being charming to Helene, as well as "crooning over our new little daughter, Hertha. In his curious frustrated way he was somehow jealous of me for having such a good-looking wife."

Before dinner, there was small talk.

> Suddenly he looked over his shoulder and stopped in mid-sentence. "I am sorry," he apologized ruefully; "that is the effect of prison. You always expect someone to be listening," and he launched into a graphic description of the psychological effect of the peephole in the prison door.

Later there occurred a moment that summoned up the past, prefigured the future, and showed Hitler, at this Christmas season, with his abilities and preoccupations, as he was at the beginning of his long final march to power. Hitler's apprenticeship was over; after prison and the work on his book, he had no new lessons to learn; he was a hardened and ruthless professional who needed only to apply what he knew, again and again.

After dinner he started warming up, striding up and down the room like a soldier, hands clasped behind his back. He was never much of a man for sitting down. Somehow he got back on to the subject of the war again, and we discovered that his powers of mimicry did not cover only the human voice. He was describing some recollection of the Western Front and started imitating an artillery barrage. He could reproduce the noise of every imaginable gun, German, French or English, the howitzers, the 75's, the machine guns, separately and all at once. With that tremendous voice of his we really went through about five minutes of the Battle of the Somme and what the neighbors must have thought I cannot imagine.

NOTES

BIBLIOGRAPHY

INDEX

NOTES

CHAPTER 1

1. Deuerlein, "Hitlers Eintritt," 177–227, gives details of this course, which was presented twice: June 5–12, 1919, and June 26–July 5, 1919. The program on pp. 191–192 lists Müller as a lecturer on June 5 and 6.
2. Müller, *Mars und Venus*, 338.
3. Ibid.
4. Hanser, 191.
5. Fishman, 249.
6. Hanser, 182.
7. Hitler, *Mein Kampf*, Manheim trans., 215.

CHAPTER 2

1. Toland, *Adolf Hitler*, 7.
2. Ibid., 9.
3. Ibid., 12–13. The number of lashes is from Maser, *Hitler*, 208. See also Waite, *Psychopathic God*, 132.
4. Ibid., 15.
5. Jetzinger, 71.
6. Kubizek, 79.
7. Maser, *Hitler*, 33.
8. Wildberg Castle and reaction to *Rienzi:* Kubizek, 91, 98–101.
9. Hitler, *Mein Kampf*, Manheim trans., 20.
10. Maser, *Hitler*, 41.
11. Kubizek, 152, 157, 158.
12. Hitler, *Mein Kampf*, Manheim trans., 76.
13. Ibid., 77.
14. The facts concerning Room 21 and numerous other details of Hitler's life in Vienna are from Jones, 129–134 et seq.
15. Bradley F. Smith, *Hitler*, 139.

16. Fest, *Hitler*, 56.
17. Hitler, *Mein Kampf*, Manheim trans., 37–38, 97, 121, 38.
18. This quotation from a translation of Hans Mend, *Adolf Hitler im Felde* (Munich: Eher, 1931), citing 16–17, is in Toland Papers, Container 48, labeled "Hitler, Adolf — World War I."
19. Heiden, *Der Fuehrer*, 74.
20. Mend translation, Toland Papers.
21. Jäckel and Kuhn, 67.
22. Westenkirchner interview, Toland Papers, Container 48.
23. Jäckel and Kuhn, 67.
24. Maser, *Hitler*, 81.
25. Ibid., 82.
26. Ibid.
27. This incident in "Shrewsbury Forest" is in the account of Ernst Schmidt, Toland Papers, Container 48; he identifies the area as "the forest in the shape of an axe." Engelhardt, later a major general, confirmed the incident (Payne, 112).
28. Maser, *Hitler*, 82.
29. Westenkirchner interview, Toland Papers.
30. Jäckel and Kuhn, 61.
31. Hitler, *Secret Conversations*, 12; Hitler, *Mein Kampf*, Manheim trans., 163; Toland, *Adolf Hitler*, 68.
32. Hanser, 86.
33. Mend translation, Toland Papers, citing p. 124.
34. Account of Hans Raab in Toland Papers, Container 48.
35. Schmidt statement, Toland Papers.
36. Westenkirchner interview, Toland Papers.
37. Mend translation, Toland Papers, 115, 156.
38. Westenkirchner interview, Toland Papers.
39. Statement of Heinrich Lugauer, Toland Papers, Container 48.
40. Mend translation, Toland Papers, citing pp. 113–114.
41. Payne, 114.
42. Supplementary statement by Westenkirchner, Toland Papers, Container 48.
43. Hanser, 87.
44. Toland, *Adolf Hitler*, 67.
45. Payne, 119. A photograph appears among the illustrations following p. 120.
46. Mend translation, Toland Papers, citing p. 115.
47. Westenkirchner interview, Toland Papers.
48. Mend translation, Toland Papers, citing p. 161.
49. Westenkirchner supplementary statement, Toland Papers.
50. Lugauer statement, Toland Papers.
51. Hitler, *Mein Kampf*, Manheim trans., 35.
52. Maser, *Hitler*, 52.
53. Westenkirchner interview, Toland Papers.
54. Hitler, *Mein Kampf*, Manheim trans., 181.
55. Ibid., 145.
56. Ibid., 180–185.

57. Mend translation, Toland Papers, citing p. 172.
58. Jäckel and Kuhn, 74. On pp. 36–37, under "Comments on Individual Sources," the editors say: "Poems. While it had not even been known up to now that Hitler wrote poems at all — apparently mainly during the First World War — this book is able to publish for the first time a rather lengthy series of them. This reproduction of the poems is undertaken without examination of the question as to whether the texts were composed or only copied by Hitler, or are partly based on poems by someone else."
59. Schmidt statement, Toland Papers.
60. Engelhardt quotation from Heiden, *Der Fuehrer*, 83; Baligand quotation is as remembered by Paul Bertelman, who spoke frequently with Baligand during the years 1925–1930. Bertelman's full statement is in Toland Papers, Container 48.
61. Maser, *Hitler*, 87–88.
62. Ibid., 88.
63. Toland, *Adolf Hitler*, 64.
64. Mend translation, Toland Papers, citing p. 37.
65. Hitler, *Mein Kampf*, Manheim trans., 202.
66. Raab account, Toland Papers.
67. Hitler, *Mein Kampf*, Manheim trans., 202.

CHAPTER 3

1. Hitler, *Mein Kampf*, Manheim trans., 203, 202.
2. Hitler, *Mein Kampf*, Eher ed., 222.
3. Watt, 160–161.
4. The shooting of the rebellious sailors at Kiel is based on the descriptions in ibid., 165.
5. Max of Baden, vol. 2, 188.
6. Ibid., 348–368, for Prince Max's account of the events of Nov. 9., 1918.
7. Watt, 196–197.
8. Ibid., 198.
9. Waite, *Vanguard*, 5.
10. Hitler, *Mein Kampf*, Manheim trans., 203–205.

CHAPTER 4

1. Mitchell, 35–74, gives extensive biographical information on Eisner.
2. Watt, 283.
3. Ibid., 287–288.
4. Hanser, 180.
5. Wheeler-Bennett, 33; Dorpalen, 27.
6. Watt, 247.
7. Waite, *Vanguard*, 16.
8. Romains, 434.

9. A detailed account of Freikorps involvement in the Baltic area is in Waite, *Vanguard*, 94–139.
10. Watt, 266.
11. Hanser, 152.
12. Watt, 272, 263.

CHAPTER 5

1. Jäckel and Kuhn, 1260.
2. Ibid.
3. Hitler, *Mein Kampf*, Manheim trans., 207.
4. Hanser, 183.
5. Voting results: Watt, 292.
6. Hanser, 161.
7. Ibid., 160.
8. Ibid., 162. There are differing accounts of the weapon used by Lindner and the manner in which he brought it into play.
9. Mitchell, 290.
10. Ibid., 299.
11. Ibid., 300.
12. Ibid., 311.
13. Hanser, 171.
14. Mitchell, 311–312.
15. Payne, 123.
16. Mitchell, 327–329. Levien and Leviné had resigned from the Vollzugsrat, the revolutionary ruling body, on Apr. 27, but Egelhofer, in a view endorsed by Leviné and other communists close to him, took the position that the revolution must run its course.
17. Hanser, 189.
18. Waite, *Vanguard*, 89.
19. Payne, 127.

CHAPTER 6

1. Watt, 407. For a latter-day historian's view that the treaty "was severe, but it is amazing that it was not more so," see Marks, 11; for a comment that the treaty "left Germany's potential strength virtually untouched," see Eubank, 12.
2. Snyder, 17. The quotation is from Article 87 of the Versailles Treaty.
3. Watt, 407.
4. The quotation is from the article "Versailles, Treaty of," *Encyclopaedia Britannica*, 14th ed., vol. 23, 94.
5. Mee, 218.
6. Mann, *Letters*, 94–95.
7. Kessler, *In the Twenties*, 117.
8. Hitler, *Mein Kampf*, Manheim trans., 632, 464.
9. Breucker, 68.

10. Dorpalen, 51.
11. Hitler, *Mein Kampf*, Manheim trans., 215–216.

CHAPTER 7

1. All documents quoted from or referred to are in Deuerlein, "Hitlers Eintritt," 193–199. The report from Lechfeld is dated July 19, 1919, and an endorsement of it, made in Munich, is dated the same day.
2. Toland, *Adolf Hitler*, 85.
3. Deuerlein, "Hitlers Eintritt," 199.
4. The early history of this paper, destined to become the *Völkischer Beobachter*, and to be bought by the Nazi Party, appears in Franz-Willing, 144–169, and in Phelps, "Before Hitler," 255–261. (Phelps, 256n, mentions the rejection of Hitler's offer.) Hanser, 255, tells of the paper's having been a trade journal for butchers.
5. Adolf Hitler to Adolf Gemlich, Munich, Sept. 19, 1919. Jäckel and Kuhn, 88–90.
6. Mann, *Diaries*, 65.
7. Hitler in civilian clothes: Deuerlein, *Hitler-Putsch*, 28–29. Hitler's inscription in register: Maser, *Hitler*, 113.
8. Occupations of those present: Maser, Hitler, 113.
9. "Financial crank": Hanfstaengl, 47; background on Feder and his ideas: Hale, 358–360; Hanfstaengl, 87–88; Heiden, *Der Fuehrer*, 90; Heiden, *History*, 9–10; Rosenberg, 40–41.
10. Feder's topic: Deuerlein, *Hitler-Putsch*, 28.
11. Hitler, *Mein Kampf*, Manheim trans., 219.
12. Franz-Willing, 66–67.
13. Hitler, *Mein Kampf*, Manheim trans., 219.
14. Ibid.
15. Payne, 137.
16. Heiden, *History*, 5–6.
17. For national socialism in Austria and the former Austro-Hungarian Empire, see Pauley, 24–33.
18. Hitler, *Mein Kampf*, Manheim trans., 220.
19. Hitler, *Mein Kampf*, Eher ed., 240.

CHAPTER 8

1. Hitler, *Mein Kampf*, Manheim trans., 221–222.
2. Ibid., 222–223.
3. Principal sources for völkisch origins of, and influences on, the German Workers' Party: Sebottendorff; Phelps, "Before Hitler"; Franz; Maser, *Hitler*, 109–113.
4. Phelps, "Before Hitler," 250, 251n.
5. For Thule activities during the Eisner regime and the first half of 1919, see Phelps, "Before Hitler"; Franz.

6. Harrer, Drexler, and the Circle: Phelps, "Hitler and *Deutsche Arbeiterpartei*"; Orlow, *History of Nazi Party*, vol. 1, 11–13.
7. Phelps, "Hitler and *Deutsche Arbeiterpartei*," 977; Fest, *Hitler*, 117; Toland, *Adolf Hitler*, 86; Hanser, 156–157.
8. Toland, *Adolf Hitler*, p. 86.
9. Jäckel and Kuhn, 91.
10. Hitler, *Mein Kampf*, Manheim trans., 354–355.
11. Jäckel and Kuhn, 91.
12. Hitler, *Mein Kampf*, Manheim trans., 355.
13. Jäckel and Kuhn, 91.
14. Toland, *Adolf Hitler*, 93.
15. Jäckel and Kuhn, 92.
16. Hitler, *Mein Kampf*, Manheim trans., 358.
17. Hanser, 209.
18. Toland, *Adolf Hitler*, 95.
19. Phelps, "Hitler and *Deutsche Arbeiterpartei*," 980–981.
20. Hitler, *Mein Kampf*, Manheim trans., 358, 354.
21. "Collection NSDAP Hauptarchiv," Reel 3, Folder 76. A text is in Jäckel and Kuhn, 95. See also Phelps, "Hitler and *Deutsche Arbeiterpartei*," 981.
22. Toland, *Adolf Hitler*, 95.
23. Ibid., 88.
24. Additional details on office are in Heiden, *Der Fuehrer*, 91; Hanser, 210; Phelps, "Hitler and *Deutsche Arbeiterpartei*," 981–982.
25. Toland, *Adolf Hitler*, 95.
26. Fest, *Hitler*, 120.
27. Harrer resigned on Jan. 5, 1920.
28. Phelps, "Hitler and *Deutsche Arbeiterpartei*," 982.
29. Toland, *Adolf Hitler*, 96.
30. Snyder, 23.
31. Noakes and Pridham, 38.
32. Payne, 143.
33. Snyder, 24–25.
34. Payne, 145.
35. Hitler, *Mein Kampf*, Manheim trans., 356.
36. Toland, *Adolf Hitler*, 96.

CHAPTER 9

1. Mee, 16.
2. Craig, *Germany*, 253.
3. Mann, *Diaries*, 84.
4. Totals and occupations of German Workers' Party members: Franz-Willing, 130; Hanser, 212.
5. Franz-Willing, 179.
6. *Völkischer Beobachter*, Jan. 3, 1920.
7. Ibid., Jan. 7, 1920.
8. Grill, 34.

9. *Völkischer Beobachter*, Nov. 7, 1920.
10. Franz-Willing, 71.
11. Phelps, "Hitler and *Deutsche Arbeiterpartei*," 982.
12. Hanser, 212–213; Rosenberg, 59.
13. Peter Hoffmann, 8–9.
14. Hitler, *Mein Kampf*, Manheim trans., 490.
15. Phelps, "Hitler and *Deutsche Arbeiterpartei*," 982; Douglas, 8.
16. Mann, *Diaries*, 84.

CHAPTER 10

1. De Jonge, 78.
2. Ibid., 79–85, for incidents concerning the Allied occupation of the Rhineland.
3. Allen, *Rhineland Occupation*, 319–324, contains extracts from this report. On p. 319 reference is made to "sixty-six cases of alleged rape," but the summary of dispositions on p. 320 totals sixty-eight. No reason for the discrepancy is given.
4. Ibid., 323–324; Morgan, 193–194, 246–247.
5. Mann, *Diaries*, 85 (entry of Feb. 10, 1920); Wheeler-Bennett, 70–71.
6. Seeckt's war plan: Wheeler-Bennett, 71.
7. A brief study of the reduction of the German army is in Gordon, *Reichswehr*, 78–81. Morgan, 111, gives additional figures.
8. The embittering experiences of the Freikorps officers are set forth in Waite, *Vanguard*, 94–139.
9. Morgan, 70.
10. Mann, *Diaries*, 85 (entry of Feb. 10, 1920).
11. A partial text of this speech of Jan. 23, 1920, is in Jäckel and Kuhn, 106.
12. Hanser, 223.
13. Mann, *Letters*, 261, 61, 62.
14. Gay, 85.
15. Ibid.
16. Ibid., 86.
17. Ibid.
18. Spengler, *Aphorisms*, 68.
19. Markham, 195.
20. Ibid., 207.
21. A study of the meeting of Feb. 24, 1920, and the discrepancy between Hitler's version and what actually occurred is in Phelps, "Hitler and *Deutsche Arbeiterpartei*," 983–986. Phelps, "Hitler als Parteiredner," 275–277, 286, 295, offers additional information and quotations concerning this meeting. A partial text of Hitler's remarks on this occasion, and the police reporter's observations, is in Jäckel and Kuhn, 109–111.
22. Franz-Willing, 179.
23. Ibid., 73.
24. Payne, 147.
25. Phelps, "Hitler and *Deutsche Arbeiterpartei*," 984.
26. Hanser, 214; Phelps, "Hitler als Parteiredner," 277.

27. Phelps, "Hitler and *Deutsche Arbeiterpartei*," 984.
28. Franz-Willing, 148.
29. Phelps, "Hitler and *Deutsche Arbeiterpartei*," 983.
30. Jäckel and Kuhn, 110.
31. Ibid.
32. Toland, *Adolf Hitler*, 97–98.
33. Phelps, "Hitler als Parteiredner," 277.
34. Jäckel and Kuhn, 110–111.
35. Phelps, "Hitler als Parteiredner," 277.
36. Phelps, "Hitler and *Deutsche Arbeiterpartei*," 985.
37. Douglas, 4.
38. Phelps, "Hitler and *Deutsche Arbeiterpartei*," 984.
39. Ibid., 984–985.
40. Hitler, *Mein Kampf*, Manheim trans., 370.

CHAPTER 11

1. Waite, *Vanguard*, 131.
2. De Jonge, 62.
3. Kaufmann, 91.
4. Gordon, *Reichswehr*, 75–78, sets forth the problems inherent in the ill-defined spheres of authority in the highest echelon of the Provisional Reichswehr.
5. Friedrich, 59.
6. Waite, *Vanguard*, 51.
7. Margarethe Ludendorff, 180. During the summer and early autumn of 1918, Ludendorff's condition was described in these terms by Colonel Max Bauer of his staff: "Ludendorff is deeply depressed and needs relief and recuperation" (Parkinson, 176). There were also frequent nervous outbursts. Ludendorff continued at his post, but underwent a four-week program of therapy as the patient of a Surgeon-Major Hochheimer, a psychiatrist. Details of Ludendorff's behavior, his staff's concern, and Hochheimer's treatment are in Foerster, 71–77, and Kaehler, 3–28.
8. Margarethe Ludendorff, 280.
9. Ibid., 177.
10. Waite, *Vanguard*, 151–152.
11. Morgan, 68–69.
12. Mann, *Diaries*, 88.
13. Morgan, 71.
14. Wheeler-Bennett, 74.
15. Gordon, *Reichswehr*, 114–115. I have repunctuated the translation.
16. Friedrich, 70–71.
17. Jäckel and Kuhn, 114.
18. Orlow, "Organizational History," 216.
19. *Völkischer Beobachter*, Mar. 10, 1920.
20. Franz-Willing, 149.
21. Mann, *Diaries*, 89 (entry of Mar. 13, 1920).
22. Although this appeal was signed by such figures as Ebert and Noske as

members of the Social Democratic Party rather than in their governmental capacity, it was perceived as an official government proclamation. See Waite, *Vanguard*, 174n.

23. Hauner, 20. Engelman, 165–166, says that the impetus for making this flight came from Captain Karl Mayr, who was still Hitler's immediate superior officer.
24. Gillespie, 17.
25. Peter Hoffmann, 18–19.
26. Toland, *Adolf Hitler*, 99.

CHAPTER 12

1. Peter Hoffmann, 18–19; Toland, *Adolf Hitler*, 99.
2. Gordon, *Reichswehr*, 116.
3. Ibid., 133–138, for a detailed study of the stances taken by various Reichswehr commanders during the Kapp Putsch.
4. Wheeler-Bennett, 77.
5. Waite, *Vanguard*, 159, 145n.
6. Friedrich, 69.
7. Hanser, 226.
8. Goodspeed, 228.
9. Parkinson, 200.
10. Gordon, *Reichswehr*, 123–124.
11. Wheeler-Bennett, 79
12. Ibid., 80.
13. Waite, *Vanguard*, 159.
14. Details of Trebitsch-Lincoln's life are in Lampe and Szenasi.
15. Toland, *Adolf Hitler*, 101.
16. Jäckel and Kuhn, 117, give this report of Mar. 29, 1920.
17. Waite, *Vanguard*, 164.
18. Ibid., 166.
19. Carsten, 85.
20. Waite, *Vanguard*, 142.
21. Hanser, 225.
22. Morgan, 92.
23. Engelman, 166.
24. Toland, *Adolf Hitler*, 101; Hanser, 230–231. Both these accounts have Hitler also meeting Helene Bechstein, wife of a piano manufacturer. Engelman, 207, refers to letters that indicate this introduction took place during a trip to Berlin that Eckart and Hitler made a year later.
25. Waite, *Vanguard*, 161–162; Goodspeed, 231; Parkinson, 200–202.
26. Jäckel and Kuhn, 120.
27. Waite, *Vanguard*, 177; pp. 172–182 give an account of the Ruhr campaign.
28. Ibid., 171.
29. Ibid., 182.
30. Manchester, 307. Waite, *Vanguard*, 176–177, speaks of what was evidently a similar defense made at this site or one like it in Essen, with

the roles reversed. Apparently occurring at the outset of the communist seizure of the Ruhr, the engagement is described by Waite: "The Essen watertower was the scene of a gallant defense made by the Weissenstein Volunteers. Forty of the men were killed and their leader shot with the white flag of surrender in his hand. The National Socialists later converted the watertower into a Nazi shrine."

31. Gordon, *Reichswehr*, 128.
32. Waite, *Vanguard*, 167.
33. Ibid., 161.
34. Hanser, 228.
35. Toland, *Adolf Hitler*, p. 101.
36. Hanfstaengl, 49.
37. Ibid., 50.
38. The figure 1,800 is from Payne, 151.
39. Jäckel and Kuhn, 119–120.
40. Ibid., 127–129.
41. The membership figure is arrived at by adding to the Jan. 1, 1920, total of 190 those who joined on various dates during the first four months of the year, as set forth in Douglas, 4–5.
42. "Cold as the tip": Ludecke, 90; "sallow" and "infuriating": Hanfstaengl, 33, 99.
43. *New York Times*, Aug. 7, 1987. Letter of Professor Jeffrey L. Sammons of Yale University.
44. Toland, *Adolf Hitler*, 103; *Encyclopaedia Britannica*, 14th ed., vol. 2, 78.
45. Hitler, *Mein Kampf*, Manheim trans., 307.
46. Dawidowicz, 61.
47. Jäckel and Kuhn, 152.
48. Ibid.
49. Ibid., 138.
50. Ibid., 148.
51. Ibid., 147.
52. Franz-Willing, 149–150.
53. Ibid., 149.
54. *Völkischer Beobachter* suspended from publication from Apr. 29 to May 5, 1920: Franz-Willing, 160; "He's the most artful": Hanser, 244.
55. Hanser, 279.
56. Hitler, *Mein Kampf*, Manheim trans., 494–495.
57. Fest, *Hitler*, 128.
58. Hitler, *Mein Kampf*, Manheim trans., 496.
59. Hitler, *Mein Kampf*, Eher ed., 556.
60. Hitler, *Mein Kampf*, Manheim trans., 496.
61. Ibid., 495.
62. Ibid., 496.
63. Ibid.
64. Waite, *Vanguard*, 118, gives this in German, with a slightly different translation at 118n.
65. Ibid., 203; Diehl, 107–108.
66. Diehl, 315.
67. Waite, *Vanguard*, 199.

68. Ibid., 162.
69. Parkinson, 201–202.
70. Stachura, *Strasser*, 17.
71. Hanser, 254.
72. Chamberlain to Hitler, Oct. 7, 1923: American Historical Association, Microcopy No. T-84, Roll 4, Folder 8, Frames 3715–3721.
73. Kessler, *In the Twenties*, 121–122.

CHAPTER 13

1. Stachura, *Strasser*, 21.
2. Schwarzwäller, 44.
3. For Hess's military service, see Schwarzwäller, 47–55. A record of his wounds is in Thomas, 28–30.
4. Schwarzwäller, 53–54.
5. Ibid., 55. Hess was discharged Dec. 13, 1918.
6. Ibid., 58–59.
7. Sebottendorff, 25.
8. Schwarzwäller, 66.
9. Ibid., 70.
10. Ibid., 73.
11. Jäckel and Kuhn, 131.
12. Conot, 44.
13. Jäckel and Kuhn, 131–132.
14. Craig, *Germany*, 438.
15. Eyck, vol. 1, 170.
16. Jäckel and Kuhn, 156–159.
17. Details concerning Hugo Stinnes: Craig, *Germany*, 438, 451–452; Eyck, vol. 1, 166–168; *Encyclopaedia Britannica*, 14th ed., vol. 21, 410.
18. Eyck, vol. 1, 166.
19. Ibid., 167.
20. The protocol also required of Germany the action resulting in the Disarmament Law, which took effect on Aug. 11, 1920. At Spa, agreement was also reached concerning the trial of war criminals.
21. Jäckel and Kuhn, 162.
22. Phelps, "Hitler als Parteiredner," 307. This incident is also noted briefly in Jäckel and Kuhn, 154n.
23. Phelps, "Hitler als Parteiredner," 307.
24. Ibid., 307; Jäckel and Kuhn, 162.
25. Hanfstaengl, 70–71.
26. Hermann Esser interview, Nov. 17, 1971, Toland Papers, Container 42; Hanfstaengl, 54.
27. Rosenberg, 61; Hanfstaengl interview, Sept. 16, 1971, Toland Papers, Container 45.
28. Ernst Hanfstaengl, an early supporter of Hitler, quotes him as saying in conversation: "Die Masse, das Volk, dass ist für mich eine Frau." Hanfstaengl interview, Oct. 14, 1970, Toland Papers, Container 45.
29. Jäckel and Kuhn, 776. It was published May 14, 1923.

30. Pool and Pool, 27.
31. Toland, *Adolf Hitler,* 198–199; Fest, *Hitler,* 135.
32. Waite, *Psychopathic God,* 54. My assumption is that Frau Hoffmann was one of the "three motherly old ladies" who presented him with whips.
33. Strasser and Stern, 48.
34. Fest, *Hitler,* 129.
35. Esser interview, Toland Papers; Ludecke, 94–95.
36. Kubizek, 114.

CHAPTER 14

1. Pauley, 32–35.
2. Engelman, 179, speaks of the cleavage between Hitler and Drexler at this meeting.
3. A complete text is in Jäckel and Kuhn, 173–180.
4. Hauner, 22–23; Jäckel and Kuhn, 182–183.
5. Diehl, 81. See also 70–73, 78–93.
6. Ibid., 92.
7. Eyck, vol. 1, 176.
8. Ibid., 177.
9. Speech of Aug. 6, 1920: Hauner, 22; Jäckel and Kuhn, 172.
10. Speech of July 27, 1920: Hauner, 22; Jäckel and Kuhn, 165.
11. Speech of Aug. 1, 1920: Hauner, 22; Jäckel and Kuhn, 169.
12. Speech of Aug. 1, 1920: Hauner, 22; Jäckel and Kuhn, 168.
13. Speech of Aug. 13, 1920: A complete text is in Jäckel and Kuhn, 184–204. This is the "basic" anti-Semitic Hitler speech studied in Phelps, "Hitlers 'Grundlegende' Rede."
14. Speech of Aug. 25, 1920: Hauner, 23.
15. Hanser, 260–261.
16. Howard Stern, 20–32; Diehl, 107–109, 112–113.
17. Howard Stern, 22–23; Diehl, 109, 113.
18. Waite, *Vanguard,* 214.
19. Diehl, 108.
20. Röhm, *Geschichte,* 131.

CHAPTER 15

1. Jäckel and Kuhn, 242.
2. Ibid., 245.
3. All quotations and descriptions of this incident are from Deuerlein, "Hitlers Eintritt," 219–222. Ruetz is sometimes spelled Ruez.
4. *Völkischer Beobachter,* Nov. 18, 1920.
5. Hitler, *Mein Kampf,* Reynal & Hitchcock ed., 517–518.
6. Jäckel and Kuhn, 265.
7. Deuerlein, "Hitlers Eintritt," 221–222.
8. The figure 190, from Franz-Willing, 130, represents membership in January 1920. Douglas, 4–5, gives a table of 1920 NSDAP recruitment in

Munich by month; that total is 1,322, giving the NSDAP an overall strength of 1,512 in Munich at year's end.

9. The figure 62,000 is from Hauner, 25, and refers to the eleven months ending Jan. 21, 1921. The total of public meetings is from Douglas, 4–5. Totals of Hitler's appearances are tabulated from their listing in Hauner, 18–24.
10. Orlow, "Organizational History," p. 215.
11. Hauner, 24. The DSP had gone out of existence for a time, but was enjoying a modest postwar renascence.
12. Accounts and records of the purchase of the *Völkischer Beobachter:* Sebottendorff, 191–196, with a list of shareholders and their holdings, 195; Franz-Willing, 181; Engelman, 184–187; Stachura, *Shaping of Nazi State,* 60; Phelps, "Before Hitler," 256; Pool and Pool, 32–33.
13. Jäckel and Kuhn, 277.
14. Feder and the relationship with Bothmer: Stachura, *Shaping of Nazi State,* 55–59. Bothmer's separatist activity: Kaufmann, 82–84; Engelman, 172–175.
15. Engelman, 186.
16. Orlow, "Organizational History," 212–213, points out that the newspaper automatically came within Hitler's jurisdiction.
17. Jäckel and Kuhn, 277–278.
18. Orlow, *History of Nazi Party,* 22.
19. *Völkischer Beobachter,* Nov. 7, 1920.
20. Stachura, *Shaping of Nazi State,* 60.
21. *Völkischer Beobachter,* Dec. 25, 1920.

CHAPTER 16

1. Hitler's articles and speeches in the first days of 1921: Jäckel and Kuhn, 279–294.
2. Hitler, *Mein Kampf,* Manheim trans., 367.
3. Hanfstaengl, 22.
4. Ludecke, 24–25.
5. Dodd, 64.
6. Mann, *Letters,* 124.
7. Hanfstaengl, 41.
8. Waite, *Hitler,* 8.
9. Hanfstaengl, 331.
10. Ludecke, 22.
11. Maser, *Hitler,* 210, quoting Ernst Hanfstaengl.
12. Ludendorff, *War Memories,* vol. 2, 769.
13. Grosshans, 28.
14. Ibid., 63.
15. Conway, 38–44.
16. Grosshans, 21–22. See also Pachter, 275–284.
17. Spengler, *Selected Essays,* 150.
18. Ibid., 16–17.
19. Waite, *Vanguard,* 23.

20. Ibid.
21. Ibid., 28.
22. Stirk, 92.
23. Wurgaft, 8. The manifesto was proclaimed in 1909, but Marinetti and his associates maintained their views during and after the war.
24. Horgan, 291.
25. Margarethe Ludendorff, 114.
26. Fest, *Hitler*, 130.
27. Speech of Jan. 4, 1921: Jäckel and Kuhn, 295.
28. Sackett, 121.
29. Hitler, *Mein Kampf*, Eher ed., 551.
30. *Völkischer Beobachter*, Jan. 6, 1921.
31. Jäckel and Kuhn, 303.
32. Ibid., 304.
33. Bracher, *German Dictatorship*, 87.
34. Ratio of women: Douglas, 16; women donating more per capita: Ludecke, 99.
35. Douglas, 8.
36. Kubizek, 343.
37. Hitler, *Speeches*, vol. 1, 528.
38. Maser, *Hitler*, 200.
39. Luehr, 238.
40. Hitler, *Mein Kampf*, Manheim trans., 498.
41. Ibid.
42. Hitler, *Mein Kampf*, Reynal & Hitchcock ed., 739. I have retained the German *Zirkus* throughout to avoid confusion.
43. Hitler, *Mein Kampf*, Manheim trans., 500.
44. Ibid., 499.
45. Ibid.
46. The figure 20,000 is from Hitler, *Speeches*, vol. 1, 130.
47. Hitler, *Mein Kampf*, Eher ed., 559–560.
48. Hitler, *Speeches*, vol. 1, 130.
49. Hitler, *Mein Kampf*, Manheim trans., 499.
50. Hitler, *Mein Kampf*, Reynal & Hitchcock ed., 741.
51. Ibid., 519–520.
52. Hitler, *Mein Kampf*, Manheim trans., 500.
53. Ibid.
54. Ibid., 500–501.
55. Ibid., 501.
56. Deuerlein, *Hitler-Putsch*, 45.

CHAPTER 17

1. Luehr, 239.
2. Eyck, vol. 1, 175.
3. Ibid., 179.
4. Nelson, 198–199. The same pages indicate Germany's continuing interest

in having the American forces remain, as a deterrent to French moves against Germany.

5. A balanced picture of friction and fraternization is presented in Cornebise. Nelson, 198, quotes from a note received by American sources on Mar. 29, 1922, in which Foreign Minister Walther Rathenau characterized the American force as being "distinguished by its impartiality and detachment." See also Allen, *My Rhineland Journal* and *Rhineland Occupation*.
6. Eyck, vol. 1, 179.
7. Craig, *Germany*, 440.
8. Ibid. A full-scale study of the German inflationary phenomenon is in Bresciani-Turroni.
9. Resurgent Freikorps activity: Waite, *Vanguard*, 227–232.
10. Jäckel and Kuhn, 320.
11. Hauner, 27.
12. Ibid.
13. Tyrell, 41. Tyrell believes that at this time Hitler had ambivalent feelings about assuming a clear-cut role as the party's leader. See pp. 12, 14, 38, 41–43, 106–107, 122, 165.
14. Ibid., 42, 106–107.
15. Ibid., 39. Drexler to Feder, Feb. 13, 1921.
16. Ibid., 106.
17. Ibid., 62.
18. Ibid., 40.
19. Heinz, 111. This source must be viewed with caution, in the sense that it is a fulsome and propagandistic praising of Hitler, published in England the year after he came to power. However, the author apparently did interview many of Hitler's early associates and acquaintances in Munich, and there appears to be no reason to question most of their anecdotes and descriptions.
20. Ibid., 276.
21. Hanfstaengl, 98.
22. Toland, *Adolf Hitler*, 107.
23. Ludecke, 96.
24. Toland, *Adolf Hitler*, 110, for "raging Austrian"; Hanser, 270, for second quotation.
25. Deuerlein, *Hitler-Putsch*, 40.
26. *Völkischer Beobachter*, May 14, 1921.
27. Ibid., Jan. 30, 1921. The quotation is from the second installment of a two-part article by Hitler. A complete text is in Jäckel and Kuhn, 298–302.
28. Speech of May 31, 1921: Jäckel and Kuhn, 426–427.
29. Hitler, *Secret Conversations*, 509.
30. *Völkischer Beobachter*, May 15, 1921.
31. Fest, *Hitler*, 154
32. Hanser, 231. For Eckart's relationship with the Bechsteins, see Engleman, 209.
33. Hanfstaengl, 65.
34. Hanser, 231; Hanfstaengl, 48.
35. *Wölfchen:* Hanser, 231; for Frau Bechstein's being "convinced that she

was going to be able to marry her daughter Lotte to him," see Hanfstaengl, 44.

36. Pool and Pool, 35.
37. Hanfstaengl, 58.
38. Engelman, 209.
39. Hitler, *Secret Conversations*, 509.
40. Pachter, 35. Einstein was not tall, but he seemed so to this young admirer.
41. Hanser, 233. See also Gay, 130–131; Laqueur, 140–154; Craig, *Germany*, 478.
42. Laqueur, 155 et seq.; Gay, 131.
43. Laqueur, 157.
44. Ibid., 160.
45. Friedrich, 73–74.
46. Pachter, 45.
47. Laqueur, 227–228. Laqueur's description of Grosz and Rudolf Leonhard is set in the Romanische Café, which later in 1921 replaced the des Westens as a gathering place for this group.
48. Friedrich, 84.
49. Hanser, 379.
50. De Jonge, 139.
51. Röhm, *Memoiren*, 201. Waite, *Vanguard*, 131n, speaks of Rossbach as "the notorious homosexual who, according to his own testimony, perverted Ernst Röhm."
52. Morgan, 52–53.
53. Hanser, 235.
54. De Jonge, 140.
55. Ibid.
56. Quotation: Hanser, 232; postcard: Jäckel and Kuhn, 435.
57. Hanser, 233.
58. Pachter, 87.
59. Craig, *Germany*, 478–479.
60. Hanser, 237.
61. *Völkischer Beobachter*, June 19, 1921.
62. Franz-Willing, 160. There is a possibility that this newspaper may already have existed as a party organ in Rosenheim, and that the *Völkischer Beobachter* staff in Munich used it or its name on behalf of the party as a whole.
63. Jäckel and Kuhn, 436–438.
64. Orlow, *History of Nazi Party*, 25–31.
65. Jäckel and Kuhn, 437.
66. Ibid.
67. Ibid., 436.
68. Ibid., 436–438.
69. Fest, *Hitler*, 141; Franz-Willing, 113.
70. Orlow, *History of Nazi Party*, 28. The figure 3,000 is from Hanser, 290.
71. Maser, *Hitler*, 9–10, identifies Ehrensperger.
72. Heiden, *History*, 49.
73. Fest, *Hitler*, 141.
74. Heiden, *History*, 52.

75. Ibid., 50. Although the translation here is "low hound," the German is presumably *gemeiner Hund*, which also translates as "son of a bitch."
76. Hitler, *Mein Kampf*, Reynal & Hitchcock ed., 534–536.
77. Orlow, *History of Nazi Party*, 29.
78. Jäckel and Kuhn, 445.
79. Hauner, 29.
80. Ibid.; Orlow, *History of Nazi Party*, 29.
81. Membership number: Maser, *Hitler*, 325; ultimatum: Jäckel and Kuhn, 445.
82. *Völkischer Beobachter*, July 31, 1921. See also Jäckel and Kuhn, 446.
83. Jäckel and Kuhn, 446–447.
84. Ibid., 447.
85. Hanser, 247, attributes "guttural thunder" to Konrad Heiden.
86. Jäckel and Kuhn, 448.
87. Orlow, *History of Nazi Party*, 30; Payne, 159, identifies Posch.
88. Jäckel and Kuhn, 450.

CHAPTER 18

1. Details of the party reorganization and efforts to win the endorsement of party members are in Orlow, *History of Nazi Party*, 30–36.
2. Heiden, *Der Fuehrer*, 114.
3. *Völkischer Beobachter*, Aug. 4, 1921.
4. Ibid.
5. Ibid., Aug. 11, 1921.
6. Hitler, *Mein Kampf*, Manheim trans., 344n.
7. Ibid., 346.
8. Jäckel and Kuhn, 481. This is from *Rundschreiben* Number 4, issued Sept. 10, 1921.
9. Hanfstaengl, 45–46.
10. Ludecke, 63.
11. Franz-Willing, 138.
12. The first official use of the term *Sturmabteilung* is in *Rundschreiben* Number 4, Sept. 10, 1921. See Jäckel and Kuhn, 481.
13. Franz-Willing, 141.
14. Ibid., 142.
15. Mee, 121.
16. For details of Erzberger's life, see Epstein.
17. Ibid., 202.
18. Ibid., 257–283, sets forth the chain of events that led to Erzberger's signing the Armistice agreement. On pages 272–274, Epstein points out that the military did not maneuver Erzberger into his position as head of the German Armistice Commission.
19. Ibid., 278.
20. Ibid., 281.
21. Jäckel and Kuhn, 211, 266, 364.
22. Ibid., 92, 370.
23. Ibid., 110.

24. Epstein, 385–386.
25. Ibid., 386–387.
26. Grill, 23.
27. Eyck, vol. 1, 189.
28. Epstein, 388.
29. Jäckel and Kuhn, 475. The term is found in Hitler's notes for his speech of Sept. 8, 1921.
30. *Völkischer Beobachter*, Sept. 1, 1921. Eckart wrote, "Er war ein Lump."
31. Various details of the flight and subsequent experiences of the killers: Waite, *Vanguard*, 217–218; Diehl, 112; Epstein, 389n; Hauner, 264.
32. Heiden, *Der Fuehrer*, 112.
33. Parkinson, 203.
34. Craig, *The Germans*, 136.
35. Mann, *Diaries*, 84 (entry of Jan. 21, 1919).
36. Brennan, 149–150.
37. Hitler, *Secret Conversations*, 214.
38. Noakes and Pridham, 48–49. Hitler's version of the meeting is in Jäckel and Kuhn, 492–493.
39. Jäckel and Kuhn, 493.
40. Noakes and Pridham, 49.
41. Jäckel and Kuhn, 493.
42. Crippen, 166 (letter of Ernst Toller, published in *Münchener Post*, Mar. 14, 1922); Payne, 160.
43. Noakes and Pridham, 49.
44. Heiden, *National Socialism*, 36.
45. Franz-Willing, 141, gives the Storm Troop statistic.
46. Ibid., 162.
47. Jäckel and Kuhn, 486.
48. Ibid., 483.
49. Ibid., 484–485.
50. Ibid., 486.
51. Ibid., 492. Communiqué Number 2 was issued on Sept. 24, 1921.
52. Ibid., 496. This was *Rundschreiben* Number 7, issued on or close to Oct. 1, 1921.
53. *Völkischer Beobachter*, Oct. 15, 1921.
54. Franz, 334n.
55. Parkinson, 206.

CHAPTER 19

1. Hitler, *Mein Kampf*, Reynal & Hitchcock ed., 542–544.
2. Jäckel and Kuhn, 505–506.
3. Ibid., 508.
4. Ibid., 508–509.
5. Ibid., 512.
6. Ibid., 513, for excerpts from this speech.
7. Hitler, *Mein Kampf*, Manheim trans., 502–503.
8. Ibid., 503.

9. Hitler, *Mein Kampf*, Reynal & Hitchcock ed., 745.
10. Ibid., 746.
11. Jäckel and Kuhn, 513.
12. Hitler, *Mein Kampf*, Manheim trans., 504.
13. Hitler, *Mein Kampf*, Eher ed., 565.
14. Heinz, 133. As previously noted, this source contains much unstinting praise of Hitler. Published in England in 1934, the year after Hitler became chancellor of Germany, *Germany's Hitler* definitely seems to be a propaganda effort. Nonetheless, it contains what appear to be authentic interviews with persons who are known to have associated with Hitler during the years of his rise to power. Regarding Frau Schweyer's account of the events of Nov. 4, 1921, she is obviously in error (Heinz, 134) in dating this event Feb. 24, 1920, the evening that Hitler first announced the party's program. Frau Schweyer's account also contains several descriptions that are virtually identical with the language used by Hitler in *Mein Kampf*.
15. Ibid., 134.
16. Ibid., 136.
17. Hitler, *Mein Kampf*, Manheim trans., 505.
18. Heinz, 136.
19. Jäckel and Kuhn, 513.
20. Hitler, *Mein Kampf*, Manheim trans., 505.
21. Heinz, 136.
22. Hitler, *Mein Kampf*, Manheim trans., 505.
23. Hitler, *Mein Kampf*, Eher ed., 566.
24. Heinz, 137. The language is as rendered in English by Heinz.
25. Hitler, *Mein Kampf*, Manheim trans., 505–506.
26. Ibid., 506.
27. Ibid.
28. Heinz, 137.
29. Hitler, *Mein Kampf*, Manheim trans., 506.
30. Heinz, 137–138.
31. Hitler, *Mein Kampf*, Manheim trans., 506.
32. Ibid.
33. Eight days after the event, in NSDAP Information Sheet Number 6, Hitler estimated that "there was a solid dispersal troop of 400–450 men in the hall" (Jäckel and Kuhn, 515). By 1924, when Hitler started to write *Mein Kampf*, he spoke of "our enemies, who must have numbered seven or eight hundred men" (*Mein Kampf*, Manheim trans., 506).
34. Jäckel and Kuhn, 514.
35. Ibid., 527.
36. Ibid.
37. Ibid., 470. The letter is dated Sept. 6, 1921.
38. Ibid., 532.
39. Eyck, vol. 1, 130–132.
40. Craig, *Germany*, 450.
41. Ibid.
42. Simon Taylor, 39 (quotation in photo caption).
43. Jäckel and Kuhn, 520.

44. Ibid.
45. Ibid., 537.
46. Franz-Willing, 179, gives the quotation and says that these notes were illegal; Fest, *Hitler*, 166, gives information on total sold and contains other facts on party finances.
47. Fest, *Hitler*, 145.
48. Jäckel and Kuhn, 530. The account here quoted, given by a member of the audience some time after Hitler came to power in 1933, implies but does not prove that Hitler used the German word for concentration camp. However, the term was already known to Europeans: in 1901, during the Boer War, the British confined some of the noncombatant Boer population in camps so named.
49. Mention of these persistent but unsubstantiated rumors can be found in Bullock, 39, and Maser, *Hitler*, 195. Jones, 284, states that Wasserman tests administered in 1940 "discount the possibility that Hitler suffered from syphilis," but points out that "it is still possible that he did contract some minor disease." Results of the relevant 1940 medical examination are in Irving, 288, and Heston, 151. It should be repeated that there is no evidence that Hitler ever contracted a venereal disease.
50. Jäckel and Kuhn, 531.
51. Ibid.
52. Hanser, 278.

CHAPTER 20

1. Trager, 813.
2. Troop strength is from Allen, *Rhineland Occupation*, 130.
3. *Encyclopaedia Britannica*, 14th ed., vol. 12, 462–467.
4. Eyck, vol. 1, 199–200, 208–209.
5. Nelson, 202–230; see p. 231 for the remarks of the German ambassador to the United States.
6. Allen, *Rhineland Journal*, 568.
7. Jäckel and Kuhn, 552.
8. Orlow, "Organizational History," 223.
9. Jäckel and Kuhn, 558.
10. Orlow, "Organizational History," 223.
11. Ibid.
12. Jäckel and Kuhn, 558, give 1,500 as the attendance figure.
13. Orlow, "Organizational History," 223.
14. Jäckel and Kuhn, 558.
15. Ibid., 542.
16. The quotations from this meeting are in the Josef Hell manuscript.
17. Craig, *The Germans*, 143.
18. Howard Stern, 28.
19. Hitler quotation: Jäckel and Kuhn, 433; couplets: Crippen, 162.
20. Kessler, *Rathenau*, 16.
21. Ibid., 117, for board memberships.
22. Davidson, 165.

23. Craig, *The Germans*, 141.
24. Ibid., 142.
25. Waite, *Vanguard*, 219.
26. Davidson, 163.
27. Kessler, *Rathenau*, 169.
28. Ibid., 172–173.
29. Ibid., 223.
30. Ibid., 244.
31. Ibid., 245.
32. Ibid., 246.
33. Ibid., 261–262.
34. Ibid., 262.
35. Ibid., 277.
36. Ibid., 291.
37. Ibid., 300.
38. Speech of Feb. 2, 1922: Jäckel and Kuhn, 565.
39. Ibid., 568.
40. Number of employees: Orlow, "Organizational History," 221.
41. Jäckel and Kuhn, 604.
42. Speech of Feb. 20, 1922: ibid., 579.
43. *Völkischer Beobachter*, Mar. 15, 1922.
44. Fest, *Hitler*, 155.
45. Hanser, 289.
46. Ibid.

CHAPTER 21

1. An overview of the Genoa Conference and the Treaty of Rapallo is in Eyck, vol. 1, 197–211. An intimate view of the conference is in Kessler, *In the Twenties*, 159–181.
2. *Völkischer Beobachter*, Apr. 19, 1922.
3. Jäckel and Kuhn, 629.
4. Useful studies of the various German-Soviet overtures, agreements, and activities of this period include Rosenbaum, 57–61; Edward Hallett Carr, 16–66; Wheeler-Bennett, 119–139; Carsten, 135–143; Gordon, *Reichswehr*, 179, 188–189, 344–345; Eyck, vol. 1, 204–205; Post, 110–125.
5. Gordon, *Reichswehr*, 178–179, questions the widely held view that the existence of the Truppenamt was a violation of the treaty terms. Certainly some of the purposes to which it was put were in direct opposition to the intentions of those who wrote the treaty.
6. Ibid., 179. Gordon states that this came into existence after 1921.
7. Eyck, vol. 1, 204–205; Wheeler-Bennett, 127.
8. Carsten, 136; Edward Hallett Carr, 58–59.
9. Eyck, vol. 1, 205.
10. Wheeler-Bennett, 126–127.
11. Ibid., 128. See also Carsten, 143.
12. Edward Hallett Carr, 60–61; Wheeler-Bennett, 128; Rosenbaum, 223.

13. Edward Hallett Carr, 61.
14. Kessler, *In the Twenties*, 169. See also Edward Hallett Carr, 64–65.
15. Rosenbaum, 42; Post, 122; Eyck, vol. 1, 204.
16. Angress, 235–239.
17. Jäckel and Kuhn, 640–641.
18. Speech of Apr. 12, 1922: ibid., 615.
19. Ibid., 620.
20. Ibid., 623–624.
21. Hamilton, 203. Bürgin, 56, dates the article Apr. 22, 1922.
22. Rosenberg, 65.
23. NSDAP Information Sheet Number 14, Apr. 26, 1922. Jäckel and Kuhn, 632.
24. *Völkischer Beobachter*, May 17, 1922.

CHAPTER 22

1. Ludecke, 27–28. The following quotations from Kurt Ludecke are from Ludecke, 29–44.
2. Pool and Pool, 87.
3. Ibid., 99.
4. Ludecke, 36.
5. Ibid., 45.
6. Ibid., 46.
7. Ibid., 11.
8. Hanser, 272.
9. Crippen, 170.
10. Kessler, *Rathenau*, 349.
11. Crippen, 172.
12. Ibid., 173.
13. Ibid.
14. Kessler, *Rathenau*, 343. See Kessler, *In the Twenties*, pp. 337–338, for Rathenau's telling a confidante that the priest received this information during a confession.
15. Kessler, *Rathenau*, 343.
16. Accounts of the conspiracy include Salomon's in Crippen, 171–173; Kessler, *Rathenau*, 347–351; Friedrich, 98–99, 104–107.
17. In Crippen, 178, Salomon identifies the weapon.
18. *Völkischer Beobachter*, June 22, 1922.
19. Wirth's teeth chattering: Kessler, *In the Twenties*, 337; quotation: Kessler, *Rathenau*, 343.
20. Kessler, *Rathenau*, 346.
21. Ibid., 353.
22. Eyck, vol. 1, 212.
23. Kessler, *Rathenau*, 354.
24. Ibid., 354–355.
25. Kessler, *In the Twenties*, 385.
26. Friedrich, 104–105.
27. Crippen, 174.

28. Ibid., 175.
29. Kessler, *Rathenau*, 359.
30. Ibid., 357.
31. Ibid., 358.
32. Ibid., 359.
33. Ibid.
34. Crippen, 176.
35. Parkinson, 206.
36. Ibid., 207.
37. Heiden, *Der Fuehrer*, 117.

CHAPTER 23

1. Ludecke, 17.
2. Ibid.
3. See Nicholls and Matthias, 129–159, for biographical data on Streicher.
4. Conot, 382.
5. Ludecke, 17–18.
6. Ibid., 20.
7. Eyck, vol. 1, 219.
8. Ludecke, 20. Ludecke is in error in giving the date as Aug. 11.
9. Ibid., 21.
10. Ibid.
11. Jäckel and Kuhn, 680. Ludecke, 21, makes the questionable claim that "there were well over a hundred thousand."
12. Ludecke, 21.
13. Ibid., 22.
14. Ibid. The same thought appears in Jäckel and Kuhn, 680, but in that source the partial text of this speech, pp. 679–681, does not indicate use of the term "November Criminals." The first officially recorded instance of Hitler's use of the term is on Sept. 18, 1922 (Jäckel and Kuhn, 692). Hitler had used the term "national criminal" as early as Mar. 15, 1921 (Jäckel and Kuhn, 348), and "state criminal" on Mar. 21, 1921 (Jäckel and Kuhn, 355).
15. Ludecke, 22–23.
16. Ludecke, 23, is in error in saying that the meeting in the Zirkus Krone was on the evening of the same day as the gathering in the Königsplatz. However, Hitler did give a speech in the Bürgerbräu on the evening of Aug. 16.
17. Ludecke, 24–25.
18. Speech of Sept. 28, 1922: Jäckel and Kuhn, 699.
19. This and Hitler's following remarks on the manipulation of meetings are from Hitler, *Secret Conversations*, 335–336.
20. Ludecke, 59.
21. Ibid., 59–61, for Ludecke's role in the Pittinger attempt.
22. Ibid., 61.
23. Ibid., 63–65.

24. Ibid., 66–70.
25. Ibid., 70–71.
26. Ibid., 71–74.
27. Ibid., 80–82.
28. Röhm, *Geschichte*, 131.
29. Ludecke, 84.
30. Ibid., 85.
31. Erdmann, 94.
32. Ibid., 95, for the comment "Dietrich Eckart was said to have financed the whole train."
33. Ibid., 96.
34. Ibid., 97–98.
35. Heinz, 151.
36. Ibid., 144–150, for this and the following quotations from Schmitt.
37. Ludecke, 85.
38. Erdmann, 99.
39. Hitler, *Secret Conversations*, 111.
40. Erdmann, 99.
41. Ludecke, 86.
42. Heinz, 151.
43. Ludecke, 88.
44. Hitler, *Secret Conversations*, 112.
45. Ludecke, 88–89.
46. Heinz, 152.
47. Hitler, *Secret Conversations*, 112.
48. Ludecke, 89.
49. Heinz, 152–153.
50. Rosenberg, 68.
51. Ludecke, 89–90.
52. Hitler, *Secret Conversations*, 112.
53. Erdmann, 95.
54. Jäckel and Kuhn, 700n.
55. Erdmann, 102.
56. Jäckel and Kuhn, 700–701.
57. Ludecke, 90–91; Heinz, 153–154; Hitler, *Secret Conversations*, 112; Hitler, *Mein Kampf*, Manheim trans., 550.
58. Erdmann, 95.
59. Ibid., 105; Hitler, *Mein Kampf*, Manheim trans., 550; Hitler, *Secret Conversations*, 112.
60. Erdmann, 105.
61. Ludecke, 91; Hitler, *Secret Conversations*, 112.
62. Heinz, 155.
63. Hitler, *Secret Conversations*, 113.
64. Erdmann, 107.
65. Fest, *Hitler*, 156, says "significantly, Coburg became one of the most reliable NSDAP bases."
66. Jäckel and Kuhn, 702–708.
67. Kessler, *In the Twenties*, 195.
68. Heiden, *History*, 97.

CHAPTER 24

1. Eyck, vol. 1, 227.
2. Kessler, *In the Twenties*, 196.
3. Heiden, *Der Fuehrer*, 155.
4. Biographical data and quotations concerning Ernst Hanfstaengl are from Hanfstaengl, 24–32.
5. Truman Smith, 50.
6. Ibid., 56.
7. The figure 10,000 is from Hanser, 313.
8. Truman Smith, 57.
9. Ibid., 60–61.
10. Hanser, 299.
11. Truman Smith, 70.
12. Ibid., 64.
13. Hanser, 299.
14. This and subsequent quotations of Ernst Hanfstaengl are from Hanfstaengl, 32–38.
15. Ludecke, 95.
16. Hanfstaengl, 38.
17. Jäckel and Kuhn, 743–752.
18. Ibid., 757–766.
19. Ibid., 772; for the complete transcript, see 770–775.
20. Stachura, *Shaping of Nazi State*, 34.
21. Eyck, vol. 1, 231.
22. Except for Egon Hanfstaengl's recollection of Hitler's imitation, Egon Hanfstaengl interview, March 18, 1971, Toland Papers, Container 45, this and subsequent quotations from Ernst Hanfstaengl's reminiscences are from Hanfstaengl, 40–52.
23. Hanfstaengl, 281.
24. Toland, *Adolf Hitler*, 123.
25. Hitler, *Secret Conversations*, 139.
26. Mosley, 3.
27. Ibid., 7–8.
28. Ibid., 45.
29. Ibid., 55.
30. Toland, *Adolf Hitler*, 123.
31. Ibid.
32. Hanfstaengl, 75.
33. Mosley, 219.
34. Remark on party program: Waite, *Vanguard*, 276; quotation: Strasser and Stern, 55.

CHAPTER 25

1. Allen, *Rhineland Occupation*, 271.
2. Ibid., 272.
3. Ibid., 273.

4. Allen, *Rhineland Journal*, 510.
5. Allen, *Rhineland Occupation*, 273.
6. Allen, *Rhineland Journal*, 513.
7. Ibid., 508.
8. Ibid., 510.
9. Allen, *Rhineland Occupation*, 280.
10. Eyck, vol. 1, 255. Although the note was not delivered until Aug. 11, 1923, this was the British position from the outset.
11. Allen, *Rhineland Journal*, 514.
12. Waite, *Vanguard*, 239.
13. Ibid., 240.
14. Feuchtwanger, 593.
15. Allen, *Rhineland Occupation*, 286.
16. Feuchtwanger, 593.
17. Allen, *Rhineland Journal*, 543.
18. Ibid., 562.
19. Ibid., 549.
20. Allen, *Rhineland Occupation*, 292.
21. Allen, *Rhineland Journal*, 523.
22. Ibid., 557.
23. Ibid., 534 (entry of Jan. 23, 1923).
24. Ludecke, 147.
25. Mann, *Letters*, 122 (letter dated Feb. 17, 1923).
26. Bürgin and Mayer, 58 (letter dated only as January 1923).
27. Jäckel and Kuhn, 783.
28. Ibid., 785.
29. Ibid., 791.
30. Fest, *Hitler*, 163.
31. Hanfstaengl, 83.
32. Ibid.
33. Estimates of NSDAP strength at the beginning of 1923 vary widely. Hanser, 313, cites a police estimate of 10,000 members in Munich at the end of 1922; on Jan. 27, 1923, Hitler was claiming a total of 40,000 party members (Jäckel and Kuhn, 813). Regarding SA strength in Munich, Captain Truman Smith reported that he saw 1,200 SA men from Munich parade in the city on Nov. 18, 1922 (Truman Smith, 57). There were of course additional units in other areas.

    Considering the dramatic growth of the party as a result of the Coburg success and in response to the French occupation of the Ruhr, figures of approximately 20,000 party members, of whom about 2,000 belonged to the SA, seem a reasonable estimate for the end of January 1923.
34. Jäckel and Kuhn, 802n.
35. Ibid., 802. Besides Jäckel and Kuhn, 802–805, other sources for Hitler's negotiations with the authorities are Gordon, *Putsch*, 186–191; Fest, *Hitler*, 161–162; Ludecke, 110–111.
36. Jäckel and Kuhn, 804.
37. Ibid., 805.
38. Toland, *Adolf Hitler*, 135.

39. This and the following quotations from Müller, including his rendering of what Hitler said, are from Müller, *Im Wandel*, 144–148.
40. Toland Papers, photocopy of typescript quotation cited as Ludwell Denny, "France and the German Counter Revolution," *The Nation* 116 (Mar. 14, 1923): 295.
41. Jäckel and Kuhn, 820, quoting *New York Tribune*, Jan. 29, 1923.
42. "Flaming personality": Ernst Hanfstaengl interview, Sept. 16, 1971, Toland Papers, Container 45; Hitler quotation: Fest, *Hitler*, 162.
43. Jäckel and Kuhn, 819.
44. Ibid., 820.
45. See note 33, above.
46. Pool and Pool, 76.
47. Streicher's feud: Nicholls and Matthias, 143–149.
48. Heinrich Hoffmann, 47.
49. Müller, *Im Wandel*, 149.

CHAPTER 26

1. Eyck, vol. 1, 243.
2. Carsten, 103.
3. Ibid., 154–155. For Seeckt's views and actions concerning Germany's situation in 1923, see Gordon, *Reichswehr*, 255–258; Wheeler-Bennett, 108–109; Carsten, 155–162.
4. Gordon, *Putsch*, 140–151, addresses the special situation of the Reichswehr in Bavaria.
5. Gordon, *Reichswehr*, 413.
6. Hanfstaengl, 89–90, gives the principal account of this meeting. It is a secondhand account, but, according to Hanfstaengl, is based on the diary entry made by Selchow a few hours after the meeting.
7. Ibid., 90.
8. Events at the Krupp works are from Manchester, 314–317, and *New York Times*, April 1, 2, 5, 9, 11, 1923.
9. *New York Times*, April 11, 1923.
10. The quotations concerning the fund-raising trip are from Hanfstaengl, 58–67.
11. Ibid., 69.
12. Gordon, *Putsch*, 191–209, presents a study of the events leading to and through the May Day confrontation. See also Diehl, 125–130.
13. Engelman, 225–226.
14. Hanfstaengl, 50.
15. Hitler, *Secret Conversations*, 173.
16. Ibid., 173–174.
17. Röhm's activities are detailed in Gordon, *Putsch*, 160–164.
18. Hanfstaengl, 69.
19. Jäckel and Kuhn, 906.
20. Gordon, *Putsch*, 194.

21. Jäckel and Kuhn, 914.
22. The first mention I found of the "Heil Hitler!" ovation and salutation is in Jäckel and Kuhn, 886, where the police report of a Hitler speech at the Zirkus Krone on Apr. 13, 1923, includes "prolonged applause and cries of 'Heil Hitler!' "
23. Gordon, *Putsch*, 196–197.
24. Ibid., 197.
25. Fest, *Hitler*, 170.
26. Gordon, *Putsch*, 197–199.
27. Strasser and Stern, 57–58. Otto Strasser is an unreliable source, but there is no reason to doubt that he accompanied his brother Gregor on the expedition. The weapons figures are from Bullock, 96.
28. Strasser and Stern, 58.
29. Hitler, *Secret Conversations*, 222.
30. Gordon, *Putsch*, 199.
31. Ibid., 199–200, places 1,200 to 1,300 men on the Oberwiesenfeld with Hitler, and refers to an unspecified number of Bund Oberland men at the Maximilianeum. Diehl, 130, puts the number with Hitler at 2,000, and estimates the Bund Oberland strength at 800. Diehl believes that the city-wide total of Task Force members assembled on May 1 reached 4,800.
32. Hitler, *Secret Conversations*, 222.
33. Gordon, *Putsch*, 197–198.
34. Ibid., 200.
35. Ibid., 199–200.
36. Strasser and Stern, 61.
37. Hitler, *Secret Conversations*, 222.
38. Bullock, 97.
39. Gordon, *Putsch*, 203.
40. Stachura, *Strasser*, 23–24, outlines some of Gregor Strasser's activities, Apr. 30–May 1, 1923.
41. Strasser and Stern, 61. Although Otto Strasser is sometimes unreliable, it seems thoroughly plausible that he would have been with Gregor, who was next to Hitler during these events.
42. Ibid., 62.
43. Jäckel and Kuhn, 917.
44. Waite, *Vanguard*, 261.
45. Strasser and Stern, 62.

CHAPTER 27

1. Gordon, *Putsch*, 202–203, 148.
2. Nicholls and Matthias, 148.
3. Gordon, *Putsch*, 204–209.
4. Jäckel and Kuhn, 926.
5. Fest, *Hitler*, 172.
6. Hitler, *Secret Conversations*, 174.
7. Ibid., 176.
8. Hanfstaengl, 86.

9. Parkinson, 208.
10. Hanser, 318.
11. Goodspeed, 233; Parkinson, 208–209. Some secondary sources have placed Hitler's first meeting with Ludendorff in Berlin at the time of the Kapp Putsch in 1920, but Hitler arrived in the capital only a few hours before a harried Ludendorff fled to Bavaria. Otto Strasser, in Strasser and Stern, 41–44, describes an informal meeting with both Hitler and Ludendorff at the house of his brother Gregor at a date earlier than the spring of 1923, but in Stachura, *Strasser*, 20–21, this is evaluated as a most unlikely possibility.
12. Parkinson, 209.
13. Gordon, *Putsch*, 210.
14. Jäckel and Kuhn, 948.
15. Ibid., 949.
16. *Völkischer Beobachter*, July 15/16, 1923; announcement of the suspension is in the issue of July 17.
17. Waite, *Vanguard*, 236–238, offers biographical information on Schlageter. This source is in error in stating (p. 237) that 70,000 SA men attended Schlageter's funeral; in the autumn of 1923, several months after this event, the entire NSDAP membership numbered approximately 55,000.
18. Nicholls and Matthias, 146–152, describes the early publication of *Der Stürmer* and gives details of the manner in which the Nuremberg SA was subordinated to SA headquarters in Munich.
19. Halcomb, 16.
20. The origin and composition of Stosstrupp Adolf Hitler and the Stabswache is given briefly in Gordon, *Putsch*, 63–64. Heiden, *History*, 96–97, says the Stosstrupp was formed in August 1923, and characterizes it as "this personal bodyguard of Hitler's."
21. Diehl, 133–135, 340–341, provides information on the growth of these units during 1923.
22. *New York Times*, Nov. 21, 1922.
23. Hale, 358–362.
24. Bullock, 102–103.
25. Jäckel and Kuhn, 955.
26. Ibid., 960–961.
27. Hitler, *My New Order*, 66.
28. Ibid.
29. Jäckel and Kuhn, 956.
30. Hitler, *My New Order*, 66.

CHAPTER 28

1. Eyck, vol. 1, 252.
2. Hanser, 323.
3. Eyck, vol. 1, 253, 256–259.
4. Bresciani-Turroni, 156; see also pp. 46, 63, 180.
5. Eyck, vol. 1, 257.
6. Pool and Pool, 75.

7. Pauley, 36–38, describes the congress.
8. Ibid., 38.
9. Ibid., 37, 223.
10. Ludecke, 111–118, gives the account of his arrest and imprisonment.
11. Ibid., 115.
12. Ibid., 117.
13. Ibid., 118.
14. Ibid., 122.
15. This and the following quotations concerning the stay in Linz are from Ludecke, 128–137.
16. Friedrich, 125–126.
17. Ibid., 125.
18. De Jonge, 98.
19. Ibid., 99.
20. Jäckel and Kuhn, 974–975, giving text from the *World*, Aug. 20, 1923.
21. Schoenberner, 147–148.
22. Craig, *Germany*, 451.
23. De Jonge, 96; Hanser, 308.
24. Heiden, *Der Fuehrer*, 126.
25. De Jonge, 96.
26. Strasser and Stern, 36.
27. This story, possibly apocryphal, is recounted in Hanser, 307, and in Pool and Pool, 67.
28. Friedrich, 126.
29. Fallada, 46.
30. Remarque, 260–263.
31. *New York Times*, Sept. 3, 1923.
32. Ibid.
33. Ibid.
34. Fest, *Hitler*, 172.
35. Ibid., 173.
36. *New York Times*, Sept. 3, 1923.

CHAPTER 29

1. *New York Times*, Sept. 3, 1923.
2. Ibid.
3. Ibid.
4. An excellent study of the abortive communist revolution of October 1923 is in Angress, 378–429.
5. Ludecke, 131.
6. Angress, 417–419.
7. Ibid., 420–421.
8. Ibid., 421.
9. Ibid., 428. The letter, although addressed to August Thalheimer, editor of the *Rote Fahne*, was clearly intended for publication.
10. Hanser, 321–322. This source cites these words as part of a speech given at Nuremberg during the events of Sept. 1–2; the small excerpts from

Hitler's speech of Sept. 2 in Jäckel and Kuhn, 990, do not include this, but Jäckel and Kuhn, 1013, have it in his speech of Sept. 12.

11. For the Black Reichswehr uprising, sometimes called the Küstrin Putsch, see Waite, *Vanguard*, 242–244, 248–253; Eyck, vol. 1, 262–263; Gordon, *Reichswehr*, 128n, 233–235; Carsten, 150, 158–159, 168; Wheeler-Bennett, 92, 92n, 95n, 111–112, 112n.

The first of the separatist crises came in Düsseldorf on Sept. 30, 1923. There were clashes between separatists, backed to some extent by the French military, and unidentified anti-separatist Germans, backed by the German state police, resulting in twenty deaths and the wounding of some two hundred people. Eyewitness accounts are in the *New York Times* of Oct. 1, 1923. The second crisis consisted of unsuccessful French-supported separatist attempts to seize power in the Rhineland during the last week of October. See Eyck, vol. 1, 278–279.

12. Angress, 433.
13. The reference is to the plan to introduce the Rentenmark. See Eyck, vol. 1, 258, 265–266.
14. Angress, 439.
15. Ibid., 440.
16. Ibid., 441.
17. Ibid.
18. Ibid., 449–450.
19. Ibid., 450.
20. Carsten, 165.
21. Ibid.
22. Margarethe Ludendorff, 245.
23. Thyssen, 79.
24. Ibid., 82. Thyssen's activities occurred during October 1923.
25. Gordon, *Putsch*, 215. That such an understanding existed can be inferred from Kahr's acceptance of the position when it was offered to him four days later.
26. *New York Morning Newspapers* (a combined format used during a newspaper strike), Sept. 25, 1923.
27. Fest, *Hitler*, 173.
28. Jäckel and Kuhn, 1014.
29. Gordon, *Putsch*, 216.
30. *New York Times*, Sept. 27, 1923.
31. The sources of the quotations are, in sequence: Hanser, 327; Fest, *Hitler*, 177; Hitler, *Secret Conversations*, 95.
32. Fest, *Hitler*, 174.

CHAPTER 30

1. Wheeler-Bennett, 109–110. The author gives the German quotation and translates it as "The army, Mr. President, will stick to me."
2. Carsten, 165.
3. Wheeler-Bennett, 110.
4. Eyck, vol. 1, 261.

5. Carsten, 166.
6. *Völkischer Beobachter*, Sept. 27, 1923.
7. Gordon, *Putsch*, 230n, confirms that one of Frau von Seeckt's parents was Jewish, but does not specify which. Assuming that the *Beobachter* article was correct in giving her maiden name as Jakobsohn, it was presumably her father.
8. Carsten, 166.
9. Datelined Berlin, Sept. 26, and carrying the *Chicago Tribune* copyright notice, the story appeared in the *New York Times*, Sept. 27, 1923.
10. Gordon, *Putsch*, 228–229.
11. Pool and Pool, 122.
12. Bullock, 80.
13. Grosshans, 20.
14. Toland, *Adolf Hitler*, 147.
15. Heiden, *Der Fuehrer*, 237.
16. Ibid., 233.
17. Ibid.
18. Chamberlain to Hitler, Oct. 7, 1923. American Historical Association, German Records Collection, Roll 4, Microcopy No. T-84, Folder 8, Frames 3715–3721.

CHAPTER 31

1. *New York Times*, Oct. 1, 1923.
2. Ibid.
3. Ibid.
4. Ibid.; see also note 11, Chap. 29.
5. Carsten, 170.
6. Wheeler-Bennett, 109.
7. Hanfstaengl, 93.
8. Gordon, *Putsch*, 229.
9. Carsten, 173–174.
10. Gordon, *Reichswehr*, 238.
11. *Völkischer Beobachter*, Oct. 4, 1923.
12. Gordon, *Putsch*, 239–240.
13. Jäckel and Kuhn, 120. The interview took place at Bayreuth on Sept. 30, 1923.
14. Deuerlein, *Hitler-Putsch*, 244–246, 234–236; Carsten, 174.
15. Deuerlein, *Hitler-Putsch*, 81–82.
16. Eyck, vol. 1, 265–266.
17. Hanfstaengl, 80.
18. Ibid., 76.
19. Hauner, 43.
20. Some form of report from Kress von Kressenstein to Seeckt and Gessler at this time can be inferred from the fact that Gessler met with him in Augsburg on Oct. 18, Kahr discussed the meeting and its implications

with the Bavarian cabinet on Oct. 19 (Deuerlein, *Hitler-Putsch*, 234–236), and Lossow was dismissed from his post on Oct. 20.
21. Wheeler-Bennett, 115.
22. Ibid.
23. Gordon, *Reichswehr*, 238.
24. Carsten, 175.
25. Gordon, *Reichswehr*, 239–240.
26. Ibid., 239.
27. Carsten, 179.

CHAPTER 32

1. Hauner, 43. For a Sept. 30 statement by Hitler that he intended to establish a "national dictatorship," see Jäckel and Kuhn, 1022. On the day here noted, Oct. 23, Hitler also spoke to a meeting of SA leaders (Jäckel and Kuhn, 1043).
2. Fest, *Hitler*, 178.
3. Carsten, 177–178; Deuerlein, *Hitler-Putsch*, 257–258.
4. Fest, *Hitler*, 178.
5. Carsten, 178.
6. Fest, *Hitler*, 178.
7. Gordon, *Putsch*, 252.
8. Fest, *Hitler*, 177.
9. Hanfstaengl, 97.
10. Gordon, *Putsch*, 254.
11. Hanfstaengl, 97.
12. Fest, *Hitler*, 177.
13. Heiden, *Der Fuehrer*, 181.
14. Fest, *Hitler*, 177.
15. Gordon, *Putsch*, 247, 250.
16. Ibid., 246.
17. Heiden, *Der Fuehrer*, 179. Heiden does not cite Hitler as being present, but presumably this was the meeting arranged by Lossow and Seisser mentioned in Gordon, *Putsch*, 254.
18. Jäckel and Kuhn, 1049.
19. Toland, *Adolf Hitler*, 149.
20. Ludecke, 221.
21. Jäckel and Kuhn, 1048.
22. Ibid., 1049–1050.
23. Ibid., 1050.

CHAPTER 33

1. Bresciani-Turroni, 222.
2. Ludecke, 151.
3. Gordon, *Putsch*, 255–257.

4. Ibid., 255.
5. Fest, *Hitler*, 179.
6. Hanfstaengl, 93.
7. Rosenberg quotation: Toland, *Adolf Hitler*, 150.
8. Hanfstaengl, 94.
9. Heiden, *Der Fuehrer*, 185.
10. Gordon, *Putsch*, 259. Gordon thinks that there was no kidnap plot and that it entered Nazi lore at a later date.
11. Carsten, 180.
12. Ibid., 117.
13. Gordon, *Reichswehr*, 235, 240; Gordon, *Putsch*, 407. For Ehrhardt's dislike of Hitler and Ludendorff, see Waite, *Vanguard*, 261, and dislike of Hitler as a result of a meeting with him, Gordon, *Putsch*, 386.
14. Gordon, *Reichswehr*, 242–243.
15. Gordon, *Putsch*, 249, says that Major Emil Vogts later stated that on Nov. 6 it was agreed that Kahr should be part of a directorate which would be a product of an alliance between the Alldeutscher Verband and the Landbund. This represented a shift away from Friedrich Minoux and his group, whom the triumvirate had previously favored.
16. Waite, *Vanguard*, 258n, says that one of Ehrhardt's lieutenants later stated that Ehrhardt was considering a march to Berlin, without Kahr's permission or backing.
17. Toland, *Adolf Hitler*, 152.
18. Gordon, *Putsch*, 256.

CHAPTER 34

1. Gordon, *Putsch*, 259. Von der Pfordten's position as Oberstlandesgerichtsrat is identified in Müller, *Im Wandel*, 151. For details of the proposed constitution, see Gordon, *Putsch*, 267; Hanser, 384.
2. Gordon, *Putsch*, 255.
3. Fest, *Hitler*, 182; Eyck, vol. 1, 273; Hanser, 332; Toland, *Adolf Hitler*, 152.
4. Hanfstaengl, 92.
5. Eyck, vol. 1, 271.
6. Gordon, *Putsch*, 263, mentions Ludendorff's bank account.
7. Ibid., 259–260, for those present and the possibility that Röhm was among them.
8. Ibid., 280–283, explains the origins, purposes, and planned program of this meeting.
9. Ibid., 260.
10. Ibid., 260–261.
11. Ibid., 263–264.
12. Toland, *Adolf Hitler*, 153.
13. Gordon, *Putsch*, 262.
14. Ibid. For Himmler's involvement, see Bradley F. Smith, *Himmler*, 132–

136. Aged twenty-three, Himmler had joined the NSDAP in August 1923, and held membership card No. 42404.

15. Gordon, *Putsch*, 263.
16. Ibid., 274.
17. Hitler, *Trial*, vol. 2, 146.
18. Gordon, *Putsch*, 270–273.

CHAPTER 35

1. Hanfstaengl, 99.
2. Aigner manuscript, 6.
3. Quotation: Ernst Hanfstaengl interview, Oct. 14, 1970, Toland Papers, Container 45.
4. Otto Strasser interview, Mar. 25, 1971, Toland Papers, Container 56.
5. Gordon, *Putsch*, 291–292.
6. Ibid., 275.
7. Ibid. Gordon says, "Seisser allegedly did warn his commanders," but suggests that such a warning would have been less definite than Lossow's.
8. Ibid., 281–282.
9. Typescript translation of document identified as: Kallenbach, Hans. *Mit Hitler auf Festung Landsberg* (Munich: Kress & Hornung, 1943), 15, Toland Papers.
10. Heinz, 173.
11. Hanfstaengl, 96.
12. Ibid., 99.
13. Ibid.
14. Ibid.
15. Dornberg, 93, lists these journalists as being at the Bürgerbräukeller during the Putsch. I have been unable to locate proof that Dorothy Thompson was there, but find persuasive the reference in Hanfstaengl, 100, to the entrance into the hall of "an American woman journalist."
16. Dornberg, 22.
17. Gordon, *Putsch*, 299–300. (For Rossbach's homosexuality, see Waite, *Vanguard*, 131n, 192n.)
18. Ibid., 299–301.
19. Dornberg, 12, 23.
20. Ibid., 24.
21. Gordon, *Putsch*, 275.
22. Ibid., 274n.
23. Ibid., 295, 339–340.
24. Dornberg, 109.
25. Ibid., 26–27. The text of one of these posters, and a draft of a different version, are in Jäckel and Kuhn, 1056–1057.
26. Heinrich Hoffmann, 54.
27. Toland, *Adolf Hitler*, 157–158, attributes this to Ernst Hanfstaengl.
28. Otto Strasser interview, Oct. 1, 1971, Toland Papers, Container 56.

CHAPTER 36

1. Gordon, *Putsch*, 351.
2. Hitler, *Trial*, vol. 2, 205.
3. Ibid., vol. 1, 246.
4. Margarethe Ludendorff, 247–248.
5. Dornberg, 25–26.
6. Quotation: *Völkischer Beobachter*, Nov. 9, 1923.
7. Dornberg, 49.
8. Gordon, *Putsch*, 263; Dornberg, 27–28.
9. Gordon, *Putsch*, 296.
10. Dornberg, 32.
11. Ibid.
12. Ibid.
13. Ibid., 33.
14. Eyck, vol. 1, 30.
15. Ibid., 32.
16. Heinz, 177.
17. Hanser, 337.

CHAPTER 37

1. Noakes and Pridham, 56.
2. The quotation is from Hanfstaengl, 100.
3. Ibid.
4. Ibid., 101.
5. Typescript translation of document identified only as "Bavarian gov't. document from Allegemeine Staatsarchiv," Toland Papers, Container 48.
6. Gordon, *Putsch*, 283–284.
7. Hanfstaengl, 100. Regarding Dorothy Thompson, see note 15, Chap. 35.
8. Aigner manuscript, 9.
9. Hanfstaengl, 100–101.
10. Aigner manuscript, 9–10.
11. Hanfstaengl, 101.
12. Berchtold quotation: Heinz, 178; Aigner quotation: Aigner manuscript, 10.
13. Dornberg, 68.
14. Ibid., 69.
15. Müller, *Im Wandel*, 161.
16. Gordon, *Putsch*, 286.
17. Hitler, *Trial*, vol. 2, 206.
18. Ibid., 25.
19. Müller, *Im Wandel*, 161.
20. Jäckel and Kuhn, 1052.
21. Hitler, *Trial*, vol. 2, 153.
22. Hanfstaengl, 102.
23. Ibid., 106; Ludecke, 175. Ludecke first gives the German *"Armes Kellnerlein,"* and then the translation, "The poor little waiter!"

24. Jäckel and Kuhn, 1052.
25. Dornberg, 71.
26. Ibid.
27. Gordon, *Putsch*, 286.
28. Jäckel and Kuhn, 1053.
29. Hitler, *Trial*, vol. 2, 30; testimony of Karl Alexander von Müller.
30. "Bavarian govt. document," Toland Papers.
31. Dornberg, 71.
32. Ibid., 72.
33. Hanfstaengl, 91.
34. Dornberg, 72.
35. Hanfstaengl, 103.
36. Ibid.
37. Gordon, *Putsch*, 291n, gives the message as "Glücklich entbunden!"
38. Ibid., 291.
39. Dornberg, 74–75; Gordon, *Putsch*, 303–304.
40. Müller, *Im Wandel*, 162–163.
41. Hanfstaengl, 102–103.
42. The reason for Ludendorff's wearing civilian clothes is subject to conjecture.
43. Aigner manuscript, 11–12. Aigner mentions the car's speed, not the distance.
44. Dornberg, 100–101.
45. Gordon, *Putsch*, 243.
46. Hitler, *Trial*, vol. 2, 293; testimony of Colonel von Seisser.
47. Ibid., 156–157; testimony of General von Lossow.
48. Dornberg, 104.
49. Hitler, *Trial*, vol. 2, 209–210; testimony of Gustav von Kahr.
50. Ibid., 157; testimony of General von Lossow.
51. Dornberg, 105.
52. "Bavarian govt. document," Toland Papers.
53. Dornberg, 105.
54. Noakes and Pridham, 60.
55. Hanfstaengl, 104.
56. Dornberg, 107.
57. Noakes and Pridham, 60.
58. Ibid.
59. Bullock, 109. A German text is in Jäckel and Kuhn, 1055.
60. Hanfstaengl, 105.
61. "Bavarian govt. document," Toland Papers.
62. Dornberg, 110.
63. Gordon, *Putsch*, 290.
64. Dornberg, 130.
65. Ibid., 133.

CHAPTER 38

1. Dornberg, 131.
2. Röhm, *Geschichte*, 212.

3. Gordon, *Putsch*, 296–297.
4. Dornberg, 131.
5. Hanfstaengl, 107.
6. Gordon, *Putsch*, 311.
7. Dornberg, 165.
8. Ibid., 124.
9. Ibid., 125.
10. Gordon, *Putsch*, 318; Dornberg, 150–151.
11. Hanser, 353.
12. Gordon, *Putsch*, 318–319.
13. Ibid.
14. Ibid., 319.
15. Ibid., 293–294, 325.
16. Dornberg, 146; Gordon, *Putsch*, 316–317.
17. Hitler, *Trial*, vol. 2, 211; testimony of Gustav von Kahr.
18. Dornberg, 149.
19. Ibid., 164.
20. Hanfstaengl, 97.
21. Dornberg, 164.
22. Ibid., 170.
23. Gordon, *Putsch*, 306–307.
24. Ibid., 307.

CHAPTER 39

1. Dornberg, 196.
2. Ibid., 128.
3. Ibid., 197. This dispatch was from the Paris bureau of the *New York Herald*.
4. Ludecke, 154.
5. Dornberg, 166–168.
6. Gordon, *Putsch*, 452.
7. Ibid., 453–454.
8. Ibid., 452.
9. Gordon, *Reichswehr*, 248.
10. Dornberg, 193.
11. Eyck, vol. 1, 275.
12. *Völkischer Beobachter*, Nov. 9, 1923.
13. Heinz, 180.
14. Typescript translation of *Bayerischer Kurier* of Nov. 10–11, 1923, Toland Papers, Container 48.
15. Dornberg, 177–179.
16. Ibid., 175–177, for this and subsequent quotations involving the Allied officers.
17. Ibid., 180.
18. Eyck, vol. 1, 276, says that twenty-four Jews whose names were selected in this fashion were taken into custody.
19. Dornberg, 187.

20. Ibid., 188.
21. Ibid., 234–235.

CHAPTER 40

1. Hitler, *Trial*, vol. 2, 163; testimony of General von Lossow.
2. Dornberg, 206.
3. Gordon, *Putsch*, 325.
4. Fest, *Hitler*, 187.
5. Jäckel and Kuhn, 1057.
6. Ibid., 1058.
7. Fest, *Hitler*, 187.
8. Ibid.
9. Hanser, 371; Dornberg, 225.
10. Gordon, *Reichswehr*, 248.
11. Ibid., 337–338.
12. Dornberg, 208–209. I have placed the quotations from this passage in dialogue form.
13. Gordon, *Putsch*, 337.
14. Dornberg, 224.
15. Hitler, *Trial*, vol. 1, 105; testimony of Ernst Pöhner.
16. Gordon, *Putsch*, 337.
17. Margarethe Ludendorff, 248.
18. Hitler, *Trial*, vol. 1, 366; testimony of Lieutenant Colonel Leupold.
19. Parkinson, 216.
20. Hitler, *Trial*, vol. 1, 366–367; testimony of Lieutenant Colonel Leupold.

CHAPTER 41

1. Hanser, 360–362.
2. Aigner manuscript, 19.
3. Dornberg, 232.
4. Otto Strasser interview, Mar. 25, 1971, Toland Papers, Container 56.
5. Gordon, *Putsch*, 446.
6. Dornberg, 258.
7. Gordon, *Putsch*, 343.
8. Hanfstaengl, 108–109.
9. Hanser, 368.
10. Ibid., 367–368.
11. Dornberg, 241.
12. Fest, *Hitler*, 177.
13. Dornberg, 265.
14. Ibid., p. 266.
15. Heinrich Hoffmann, 56.
16. Dornberg, 262–263.
17. Ibid., 263.
18. Heinz, 183.

19. Hanfstaengl, 109.
20. Hanser, 369.
21. Hanfstaengl, 109.
22. Dornberg, 273.
23. Hanfstaengl, 109.
24. Fest, *Hitler*, Ullstein ed., vol. 1, 268.
25. Toland, *Adolf Hitler*, 167.
26. Röhm, *Geschichte*, 215.
27. Ibid., 216.
28. Dornberg, 276–277; Gordon, *Putsch*, 346–347.
29. Dornberg, 279; Gordon, *Putsch*, 347.
30. Rosenberg, 72.

CHAPTER 42

1. Gordon, *Putsch*, 354.
2. Dornberg, 284.
3. Gordon, *Putsch*, 357.
4. Hanser, 373.
5. Heinz, 184.
6. Aigner manuscript, 22.
7. Gordon, *Putsch*, 354.
8. Dornberg, 283.
9. Aigner manuscript, 23.
10. Hanser, 375.
11. Hanser, 384; Gordon, *Putsch*, 267; von der Pfordten's position as Oberstlandesgerichtsrat: Müller, *Im Wandel*, 151.
12. Hanfstaengl, 110.
13. Toland, *Adolf Hitler*, 168.
14. Fest, *Hitler*, 188.
15. Deuerlein, *Hitler-Putsch*, 332.
16. Aigner manuscript, 24.
17. Heinz, 184.
18. Deuerlein, *Hitler-Putsch*, 332.
19. Gordon, *Putsch*, 360. Gordon uses *Landespolizei*, the German term for state police.
20. Hanser, 378.
21. Müller, *Im Wandel*, 166.
22. Dornberg, 289.
23. Hanser, 379.
24. Ibid.; Dornberg, 290; Toland, *Adolf Hitler*, 169.
25. Gordon, *Putsch*, 359–360.
26. Hanser, 379.
27. Toland, *Adolf Hitler*, 169.
28. Gordon, *Putsch*, 357.
29. Ibid., 359.
30. Aigner manuscript, 25.

31. Ibid.
32. Ibid., 26.
33. Gordon, *Putsch*, 360–361. A German text is in Deuerlein, *Hitler-Putsch*, 330–331.
34. Parkinson, 217.
35. Toland, *Adolf Hitler*, 170n.
36. Aigner manuscript, 26.
37. Ludecke, 166.
38. Hanser, 383.
39. Deuerlein, *Hitler-Putsch*, 366.
40. Heinz, 185.
41. Baker, 36.
42. Translation of document identified as: Hoegner, Wilhelm. *Hitler und Kahr. Die Bayerischen Napoleonsgrössen von 1923*. Ein im Untersuchungsausschuss des Bayerischen *Landtags aufgedecker Justizskandal*, II Teil Mai 1928. Vom Landesausschuss der S.P.D. in Bayern, München, 173, Toland Papers.
43. Deuerlein, *Hitler-Putsch*, 365.
44. Hoegner, Toland Papers.
45. Dornberg, 296.
46. Ibid., 297.
47. Hanser, 387.
48. Dornberg, 298.
49. Hanser, 387.
50. Dornberg, 304; Gordon, *Putsch*, 348.
51. Dornberg, 306; Gordon, *Putsch*, 350.
52. Dornberg, 304.
53. Hanser, 388.
54. Dornberg, 318.
55. Ibid., 318–319.
56. Ibid., 299.
57. Gordon, *Putsch*, 470.
58. Dornberg, 299.
59. Gordon, *Putsch*, 470.
60. My assumption is that Ludendorff was still fuming as he left; his wife said that when he arrived home, "his indignation knew no bounds" (Margarethe Ludendorff, 252).
61. Waite, *Vanguard*, 259.
62. Dornberg, 316–317.
63. Hanser, 391.
64. Hanfstaengl, 113; Dornberg, 323–324.
65. Dornberg, 324.
66. Ibid., 325.
67. Deuerlein, *Hitler-Putsch*, 372.
68. Dornberg, 325.
69. Ibid., 326.
70. Hanfstaengl, 113.
71. Toland, *Adolf Hitler*, 175.

72. Rosenberg, 73.
73. Ibid.
74. Deuerlein, *Hitler-Putsch*, 372.

CHAPTER 43

1. Wheeler-Bennett, 109.
2. Heinrich Hoffmann, 57.
3. Fest, *Hitler*, 222; Orlow, *History of Nazi Party*, vol. 1, 49–53; Rosenberg, 73–79. Rosenberg refers to the Grossdeutsche Volksgemeinschaft as the Greater German People's Union, and says (p. 73) that "it was the brain-child of one of the section leaders of the [Nazi] party."
4. Hanfstaengl, 116.
5. Engelman, 230–233.
6. This and the following quotations concerning Hitler's arrival at Landsberg are from Heinz, 192–196.
7. Dornberg, 328.
8. Ibid., 329.
9. Toland, *Adolf Hitler*, 182.
10. Ibid., 183.
11. Ludecke, facing p. 176. (The translation appears beneath a photograph of the letter.)
12. Toland, *Adolf Hitler*, 186.
13. For various aspects and circumstances of this trial, see Hitler, *Trial*, vol. 1, xxviii–xxxi, and Gordon, *Putsch*, 166, 455, 475–485, 533.
14. Dornberg, 333.
15. Toland, *Adolf Hitler*, 188.
16. Dornberg, 333–334.
17. Toland, *Adolf Hitler*, 189.
18. Hitler, *Trial*, vol. 1, 49.
19. Ibid., 50.
20. Ibid., 51.
21. Ibid., 52.
22. Fest, *Hitler*, 191.
23. Toland, *Adolf Hitler*, 189.
24. Fest, *Hitler*, 191–192.
25. Toland, *Adolf Hitler*, 191.
26. Dornberg, 335–336.
27. Toland, *Adolf Hitler*, 189.
28. Heiden, *Der Fuehrer*, 204–205.
29. Ibid., 205.
30. Photocopy of typescript identified as "Interview with Mr. Ferdinand Jahn, United Press, April 24, 1943," Toland Papers, Container 48.
31. Hitler, *Trial*, vol. 3, 350.
32. Ibid., 351.
33. Ibid., 352.
34. Ibid., 353.
35. Ibid., 357–358.

36. Ibid., 358.
37. Ibid.
38. Ibid., 359.
39. Ibid., 365.
40. Jäckel and Kuhn, 1215–1216.
41. Toland, *Adolf Hitler*, 192.
42. Wheeler-Bennett, 181.
43. Toland, *Adolf Hitler*, 192.
44. Ibid.
45. Hitler, *Trial*, vol. 3, 367.
46. Ibid., 393–394.
47. Ibid., 395.
48. Ibid., 396.
49. Fest, *Hitler*, 194.
50. Toland, *Adolf Hitler*, 197.
51. Ibid.
52. Hitler, *Mein Kampf*, Manheim trans., 3.
53. Ibid., 212.
54. Ibid., 180.
55. Ibid., 183–184.
56. Hanfstaengl, 119.
57. Ibid., 120.
58. Heinz, 201.
59. Ibid., 218.
60. Ibid., 223.
61. Ludecke, 186.
62. Ibid., 217–218.
63. Fest, *Hitler*, 200.
64. Payne, 199.
65. Hitler, *Mein Kampf*, Manheim trans., 325.
66. Ibid., 57.
67. Hitler, *Mein Kampf*, Eher ed., 61.
68. Hitler, *Mein Kampf*, Manheim trans., 58.
69. Ibid., 59.
70. Ibid., 247.
71. Ibid., 62.
72. Ibid., 325.
73. Ibid., 65.
74. In *Mein Kampf*, Hitler did not mention any beatings. For the evidence, see Toland, *Adolf Hitler*, 9, 12–13; Maser, *Hitler*, 208; Waite, *Psychopathic God*, 132.
75. Typescript translation of document identified as "Report to the Bavarian State Ministry of the Interior, Munich," Toland Papers, Container 48. Below the date, Sept. 24, 1924, is the designation IV a. Nr.: 2427.
76. Payne, 202–203.
77. Jäckel and Kuhn, 1246–1247.
78. Payne, 204.
79. Heinrich Hoffmann, 59–60.
80. Toland, *Adolf Hitler*, 202.

81. Hauner, 49.
82. Heinz, 224.
83. Heinrich Hoffmann, 61.
84. Hauner, 49–50.
85. Ibid., 50.
86. This and the following quotations are from Hanfstaengl, 125–126.

BIBLIOGRAPHY

MANUSCRIPTS AND MICROFILM COLLECTIONS

Aigner, Johann von. "Als Ordonanz bei Hochverrätern. Ein Beitrag zur Geschichte der nationalen Erhebung im November 1923." Typescript from the F. J. M. Rehse Collection in the German Captured Documents Collection, Manuscript Division, Library of Congress, Washington, D.C.
American Historical Association Committee for the Study of War Documents. Miscellaneous German Records Collection. Microfilm: National Archives Microcopy No. T-84, National Archives, Washington, D.C.
"Collection NSDAP Hauptarchiv." Microfilm Collection, Hoover Institution, Stanford, California.
Hell, Josef. "Wie mich Adolf Hitler über sich belehrte / Und für immer mich von seinem Ich bekehrte." ZS 640, Institut für Zeitgeschichte, Munich.
John Toland Papers, 1962–1983. Franklin D. Roosevelt Library, Hyde Park, N.Y.

PUBLICATIONS

Abel, Theodore. Why Hitler Came into Power: An Answer Based on the Original Life Stories of Six Hundred of His Followers. New York: Prentice-Hall, 1938.
Adolf Hitler: Faces of a Dictator. New York: Harcourt, Brace and World, 1969.
Allen, Henry T. My Rhineland Journal. Boston: Houghton Mifflin, 1923.
———. The Rhineland Occupation. Indianapolis: Bobbs-Merrill, 1927.
Angress, Werner T. Stillborn Revolution: The Communist Bid for Power in Germany, 1921–1923. Princeton: Princeton University Press, 1963.
Ansell, Florence Jean, and Frank Roy Fraprie. The Art of the Munich Galleries. Boston: L. C. Page, 1927.
Baden, Max of. The Memoirs of Prince Max of Baden. Trans. W. M. Calder

and C. W. H. Sutton. 2 vols. London: Constable, 1456–1461, 1928. Reprint. New York: Kraus, 1971.

Bailey, George, and the editors of Time-Life Books. *Munich.* Amsterdam: Time-Life Books, The Great Cities, 1980.

Baker, Suzanne St. Barbe. *A Wayfarer in Bavaria.* Boston: Houghton Mifflin, 1931.

Banuls, André. "Das völkische Blatt 'Der Scherer': ein Beitrag zu Hitlers Schulzeit." *Vierteljahrshefte für Zeitgeschichte* 18, 2 (1970): 196–203.

Barnes, James J., and Patience P. Barnes. *Hitler's "Mein Kampf" in Britain and America: A Publishing History 1930–1939.* Cambridge: Cambridge University Press, 1980.

Bracher, Karl Dietrich. *Die Auflösung der Weimarer Republik: eine Studie zum Problem des Machterfalls in der Demokratie.* Villingen/Schwarzwald: Ring-Verlag, 1971.

———. *The German Dictatorship: The Origins, Structure, and Effects of National Socialism.* Trans. Jean Steinberg. New York: Praeger Publishers, 1971.

Bradley, John. *The Illustrated History of the Third Reich.* New York: Grosset and Dunlap, 1978.

Brennan, Joseph Gerard. *Thomas Mann's World.* New York: Columbia University Press, 1942.

Bresciani-Turroni, Constantino. *The Economics of Inflation: A Study of Currency Depreciation in Post-war Germany.* [Great Britain:] Augustus M. Kelley, 1968.

Breucker, Wilhelm. *Die Tragik Ludendorffs: eine kritische Studie auf Grund persönlicher Erinnerungen an den General und seine Zeit.* Stollhamm (Oldb): Helmut Rauschenbusch Verlag, 1953.

Bruce, George. *The Nazis.* London: Hamlyn, 1974.

Bullock, Alan. *Hitler: A Study in Tyranny.* Rev. ed. New York: Harper and Row, 1962.

Bürgin, Hans, and Hans-Otto Mayer. *Thomas Mann: A Chronicle of His Life.* University: University of Alabama Press, 1969.

Carr, Edward Hallett. *German-Soviet Relations Between the Two World Wars, 1919–1939.* Baltimore: Johns Hopkins University Press, 1967.

Carr, William. *Hitler: Face of a Dictator.* New York: St. Martin's Press, 1979.

Carsten, F. L. *The Reichswehr and Politics, 1918 to 1933.* Oxford: Clarendon Press, 1966.

Conot, Robert E. *Justice at Nuremberg.* New York: Harper and Row, 1983.

Conway, John, trans. *The Path to Dictatorship, 1918–1933.* Garden City, N.Y.: Doubleday, 1966.

Cornebise, Alfred E. *The Amaroc News: The Daily Newspaper of the American Forces in Germany, 1919–1923.* Carbondale and Edwardsville: Southern Illinois University Press, 1981.

Craig, Gordon A. *The Germans.* New York: G. P. Putnam's Sons, 1982.

———. *Germany 1866–1945.* New York: Oxford University Press, 1978.

Crippen, Harlan R., ed. *Germany: A Self-Portrait; A Collection of German Writings from 1914 to 1943.* London: Oxford University Press, 1944.

Davidson, Eugene. *The Making of Adolf Hitler.* New York: Macmillan, 1977.

Dawidowicz, Lucy S. *The War Against the Jews, 1933–1945.* New York:

Holt, Rinehart and Winston, 1975. Reprint. New York: Bantam Books, 1976.

Deák, István. *Weimar Germany's Left-Wing Intellectuals: A Political History of the "Weltbühne" and Its Circle.* Berkeley and Los Angeles: University of California Press, 1968.

De Jonge, Alex. *The Weimar Chronicle: Prelude to Hitler.* New York: Paddington Press, 1978.

Deuerlein, Ernst, ed. *Der Hitler-Putsch: Bayerische Dokumente zum 8/9 November 1923.* Stuttgart: Deutsche Verlags-Anstalt, 1962.

———, ed. "Hitlers Eintritt in die Politik und die Reichswehr." *Vierteljahrshefte für Zeitgeschichte* 7, 2 (1959): 177–227.

Deutscher, Isaac. *Stalin: A Political Biography.* 2d ed. New York: Oxford University Press, 1966.

Diehl, James M. *Paramilitary Politics in Weimar Germany.* Bloomington: Indiana University Press, 1977.

Dodd, Martha. *Through German Eyes.* New York: Harcourt, Brace, 1939.

Dornberg, John. *Munich 1923: The Story of Hitler's First Grab for Power.* New York: Harper and Row, 1982.

Dorpalen, Andreas. *Hindenburg and the Weimar Republic.* Princeton: Princeton University Press, 1964.

Douglas, Donald M. "The Evangelist's Apprenticeship: Hitler's Effectiveness as a Public Speaker, 1919–1921." *Wichita State University Bulletin* 50, 1 (February 1974): 3–18.

Drexler, Anton. *Mein politisches Erwachen: Aus dem Tagebuch eines Deutschen sozialistischen Arbeiters.* Munich: Deutscher Volksverlag, 1923.

Encyclopaedia Britannica. 14th ed. 24 vols. London: Encyclopaedia Britannica Company, 1929.

Engelman, Ralph Max. *Dietrich Eckart and the Genesis of Nazism.* Ph.D. diss., Washington University, 1971. Ann Arbor: University Microfilms, 1984.

Epstein, Klaus. *Matthias Erzberger and the Dilemma of German Democracy.* New York: Howard Fertig, 1971.

Erdmann, Jurgen. *Coburg, Bayern und das Reich, 1918–1923.* Coburg: A. Rossteutscher, 1969.

Eubank, Keith. *The Origins of World War II.* Arlington Heights, Ill.: AHM Publishing, 1969.

Eyck, Erich. *A History of the Weimar Republic.* Trans. Harlan P. Hanson and Robert G. L. Waite. 2 vols. New York: John Wiley and Sons, 1962.

Fallada, Hans. *Little Man, What Now?* Trans. Eric Sutton. New York: Simon and Schuster, 1933.

Fest, Joachim C. *The Face of the Third Reich: Portraits of the Nazi Leadership.* New York: Pantheon Books, 1970.

———. *Hitler.* Trans. Richard and Clara Winston. New York: Harcourt Brace Jovanovich, 1974.

———. *Hitler: eine Biographie.* 2 vols. Frankfurt-am-main: Ullstein, 1978.

Feuchtwanger, Lion. *Success.* Trans. Willa and Edwin Muir. New York: Viking Press, 1930.

Fishman, Sterling. "The Rise of Hitler as a Beer Hall Orator." *Review of Politics* 26 (1964): 244–256.

Foerster, Wolfgang. *Der Feldherr im Unglück*. Wiesbaden: Limes Verlag, 1952.

Franz, Georg. "Munich: Birthplace and Center of the National Socialist German Workers' Party." *Journal of Modern History* 29, 4 (1957): 319–334.

Franz-Willing, Georg. *Die Hitlerbewegung, I: Der Ursprung, 1919–1922*. Hamburg: R. v. Decker's Verlag G. Schenck, 1962.

Frentz, Hans. *Der unbekannte Ludendorff: Der Feldherr in seiner Umwelt und Epoche*. Wiesbaden: Limes Verlag, 1972.

Friedrich, Otto. *Before the Deluge: A Portrait of Berlin in the 1920's*. New York: Harper and Row, 1972.

Gay, Peter. *Weimar Culture: The Outsider as Insider*. New York: Harper and Row, 1968.

German Cultural History from 1860 to the Present Day. Munich: Nymphenburger Verlagsbuchhandlung, 1983.

Gies, Joseph. *Crisis 1918: The Leading Actors, Strategies, and Events in the German Gamble for Total Victory on the Western Front*. New York: W. W. Norton, 1974.

Gillespie, William. *Dietrich Eckart: An Introduction for the English-Speaking Student*. 2nd ed. Houston: William Gillespie, 1976.

Goodspeed, D. J. *Ludendorff: Soldier, Dictator, Revolutionary*. London: Rupert Hart-Davis, 1966.

Gordon, Harold J., Jr. *Hitler and the Beer Hall Putsch*. Princeton: Princeton University Press, 1972.

———. *The Reichswehr and the German Republic, 1919–1926*. Princeton: Princeton University Press, 1957.

Gottfried, Paul. "Otto Strasser and National Socialism." *Modern Age* 13 (Spring 1969): 142–151.

Grill, Johnpeter Horst. *The Nazi Movement in Baden, 1920–1945*. Chapel Hill: University of North Carolina Press, 1983.

Grosshans, Henry. *Hitler and the Artists*. New York: Holmes and Meier, 1983.

Grunfeld, Frederic V. *The Hitler File*. New York: Random House, 1974.

Halcomb, Jill. *The SA: A Historical Perspective*. Overland Park, Kans.: Crown/Agincourt Publishers, 1985.

Hale, Oron James. "Gottfried Feder Calls Hitler to Order: An Unpublished Letter on Nazi Party Affairs." *Journal of Modern History* 30, 4 (1958): 358–362.

Hamilton, Nigel. *The Brothers Mann*. New Haven: Yale University Press, 1979.

Hanfstaengl, Ernst. *Unheard Witness*. Philadelphia: J. B. Lippincott, 1957.

Hanser, Richard. *Putsch! How Hitler Made Revolution*. New York: Peter H. Wyden, 1970.

Hauner, Milan. *Hitler, The Chronology of His Life and Time*. London: Macmillan, 1983.

Heiden, Konrad. *Der Fuehrer*. Trans. Ralph Manheim. New York: Lexington Press (distributed by Houghton Mifflin), 1944.

———. *A History of National Socialism*. New York: Alfred A. Knopf, 1935. Reprint. New York: Octagon Books, 1971.

Heinz, Heinz A. *Germany's Hitler*. London: Hurst and Blackett, 1934.

Held, Hans Ludwig, ed. *Munich*. Munich: Richard Pflaum Verlag, [1950].

Heston, Leonard L., and Renate Heston. *The Medical Casebook of Adolf Hitler*. New York: Stein and Day, 1980.

Hindenburg, Marshal [Paul] von. *Out of My Life*. 2d ed. Trans. F. A. Holt. London: Cassell and Company, 1933.

Hitler, Adolf. *Hitler's Secret Book*. Introduction by Telford Taylor. Trans. Salvator Attanasio. New York: Grove Press, 1961.

———. *Hitler's Secret Conversations, 1941–1944*. Introduction by H. R. Trevor-Roper. New York: Octagon Books (Farrar, Straus and Giroux), 1972.

———. *The Hitler Trial*. Ed. Harold J. Gordon, Jr. 3 vols. Arlington, Va.: University Publications of America, 1976.

———. *Mein Kampf*. Munich: Zentralverlag der NSDAP. Franz Eher, 1938.

———. *Mein Kampf*. New York: Reynal and Hitchcock, 1939.

———. *Mein Kampf*. Trans. Ralph Manheim. Boston: Houghton Mifflin, 1971.

———. *My New Order*. Ed. Raoul de Roussy de Sales. New York: Reynal and Hitchcock, 1941.

———. *The Speeches of Adolf Hitler, April 1922–August 1939: An English Translation of Representative Passages Arranged Under Subjects*. Ed. Norman H. Baynes. 2 vols. London: Oxford University Press, 1942.

Hoffmann, Heinrich. *Hitler Was My Friend*. Trans. Lt. Col. R. H. Stevens. London: Burke, 1955.

Hoffmann, Peter. *Hitler's Personal Security*. Cambridge, Mass., and London: MIT Press, 1979.

Höhne, Heinz. "Warten auf Hitler." *Der Spiegel*, January 3 and 10, 1983.

Horgan, Paul, ed. *Maurice Baring Restored*. New York: Farrar, Straus and Giroux, 1970.

Hughes, H. Stuart. *Oswald Spengler: A Critical Estimate*. New York: Charles Scribner's Sons, 1952.

Irving, David. *The Secret Diaries of Hitler's Doctor*. New York: Macmillan, 1983.

Jäckel, Eberhard, and Axel Kuhn. *Hitler: Sämtliche Aufzeichnungen, 1905–1924*. Stuttgart: Deutsche Verlags-Anstalt, 1980.

Jetzinger, Franz. *Hitler's Youth*. Trans. Lawrence Wilson. London: Hutchinson, 1958. Reprint. Westport, Conn.: Greenwood Press, 1976.

Jones, J. Sydney. *Hitler in Vienna, 1907–1913*. New York: Stein and Day, 1983.

Kaehler, Siegfried A. "Zur Beurteilung Ludendorffs im Sommer 1918." *Nachrichten der Akademie der Wissenschaften in Gottingen. Philologisch-Historische Klasse*. 1 (1953): 3–28.

Kater, Michael H. *The Nazi Party: A Social Profile of Members and Leaders, 1919–1945*. Cambridge: Harvard University Press, 1983.

Kaufmann, Walter H. *Monarchism in the Weimar Republic*. New York: Bookman Associates, 1953.

Kessler, Harry. *In the Twenties: The Diaries of Harry Kessler*. New York: Holt, Rinehart and Winston, 1976.

———. *Walther Rathenau: His Life and Work*. New York: Harcourt, Brace, 1930.

Kitchen, Martin. *The Silent Dictatorship: The Politics of the German High*

Command Under Hindenburg and Ludendorff, 1916–1918. New York: Holmes and Meier, 1976.

Kubizek, August. *The Young Hitler I Knew*. Boston: Houghton Mifflin, 1955. Reprint. Westport, Conn.: Greenwood Press, 1976.

Lampe, David, and Laszlo Szenasi. *The Self-made Villain: A Biography of I. T. Trebitsch-Lincoln*. London: Cassell, 1961.

Langer, Walter C. *The Mind of Adolf Hitler: The Secret Wartime Report*. New York: New American Library, 1972.

Laqueur, Walter. *Weimar: A Cultural History, 1918–1933*. New York: G. P. Putnam's Sons, 1974.

Ludecke, Kurt G. W. *I Knew Hitler: The Story of a Nazi Who Escaped the Blood Purge*. London: National Book Association (by arrangement with Jarrolds Publishers), 1938.

Ludendorff, [Erich]. *Auf dem Weg zur Feldherrnhalle: Lebenserinnerungen an die Zeit mit Dokumentum in 5 Unlagen*. Munich: Ludendorffsverlag, 1937.

————. *My War Memories, 1914–1918*. 2 vols. London: Hutchinson, n.d.

Ludendorff, Margarethe. *My Married Life with Ludendorff*. Trans. Raglan Somerset. London: Hutchinson, 1930.

————. *Urkunden der Obersten Heeresleitung über ihre Tatigkeit 1916–18*. Berlin: E. S. Mittler & Sohn, 1922.

Luehr, Elmer. *The New German Republic: The Reich in Transition*. New York: Minton, Balch, 1929.

Manchester, William. *The Arms of Krupp, 1587–1968*. Boston: Little, Brown, 1968.

Mann, Thomas. *Letters of Thomas Mann, 1889–1955*. Trans. Richard and Clara Winston. New York: Alfred A. Knopf, 1971.

————. *Past Masters and Other Papers*. Trans. H. T. Lowe-Porter. N.p.: Martin Secker, 1933. Reprint. Freeport, N.Y.: Books for Libraries Press, Essay Index Reprint Series, 1968.

————. *A Sketch of My Life*. Trans. H. T. Lowe-Porter. New York: Alfred A. Knopf, 1960.

————. *Thomas Mann Diaries 1918–1939: 1918–1921, 1933–1939*. Trans. Richard and Clara Winston. New York: Harry N. Abrams, 1982.

Markham, Violet R. *A Woman's Watch on the Rhine: Sketches of the Occupation*. London: Hodder and Stoughton, 1920.

Marks, Sally A. *The Illusion of Peace: International Relations in Europe, 1918–1933*. London: Macmillan, 1976.

Maser, Werner. *Hitler: Legend, Myth and Reality*. Trans. Peter and Betty Ross. New York: Harper and Row, 1973.

————, ed. *Hitler's Letters and Notes*. Trans. Arnold Pomerans. New York: Harper and Row, 1974. Reprint. New York: Bantam Books, 1976.

McBride, Robert Medill. *Towns and People of Modern Germany*. New York: Robert M. McBride, 1930.

McInnis, Raymond G. "Adolf Hitler's *Mein Kampf*: Origin, Impact, Criticism, and Sources." *Reference Services Review* (Spring 1985): 15–24.

McRandle, James H. *The Track of the Wolf*. Evanston, Ill.: Northwestern University Press, 1965.

Mee, Charles L., Jr. *The End of Order*. New York: E. P. Dutton, 1980.

Mitchell, Allan. *Revolution in Bavaria, 1918–1919: The Eisner Regime and the Soviet Republic.* Princeton: Princeton University Press, 1965.

Mommsen, Hans, ed. *Hitler and the Surrender of Political Realism, 1928–1933: The Crisis of the Weimar Republic and the Rise of National Socialism as Reflected in Contemporary Election and Documentary Films.* Munich: Goethe-Institut, 1981.

Morgan, J. H. *Assize of Arms: The Disarmament of Germany and Her Rearmament (1919–1939).* New York: Oxford University Press, 1946.

Mosley, Leonard. *The Reich Marshal: A Biography of Hermann Goering.* Garden City, N.Y.: Doubleday, 1974.

Müller, Karl Alexander von. *Im Wandel einer Welt: Erinnerungen 1919–1932.* Munich: Süddeutscher Verlag, 1966.

———. *Mars und Venus: Erinnerungen 1914–1918.* Munich: Süddeutscher Verlag, 1954.

Nelson, Keith L. *Victors Divided: America and the Allies in Germany, 1918–1923.* Berkeley and Los Angeles: University of California Press, 1975.

Nicholls, Anthony, and Erich Matthias, eds. *German Democracy and the Triumph of Hitler: Essays in Recent German History.* New York: St. Martin's Press, 1971.

Niewyk, Donald L. *The Jews in Weimar Germany.* Baton Rouge: Louisiana State University Press, 1980.

Noakes, Jeremy, and Geoffrey Pridham, eds. *Documents on Nazism, 1919–1945.* New York: Viking Press, 1975.

Orlow, Dietrich. *The History of the Nazi Party.* 2 vols. Pittsburgh: University of Pittsburgh Press, 1969.

———. "The Organizational History and Structure of the NSDAP." *Journal of Modern History* 37, 2 (1965): 208–226.

Pachter, Henry. *Weimar Etudes.* New York: Columbia University Press, 1982.

Parkinson, Roger. *Tormented Warrior — Ludendorff and the Supreme Command.* New York: Stein and Day, 1979.

Pauley, Bruce F. *Hitler and the Forgotten Nazis: A History of Austrian National Socialism.* Chapel Hill: University of North Carolina Press, 1981.

Payne, Robert. *The Life and Death of Adolf Hitler.* New York: Praeger, 1973.

Phelps, Reginald H. "Anton Drexler — der Grunder der NSDAP." *Deutsche Rundschau* 87, 12 (1961): 1134–1143.

———. " 'Before Hitler Came': Thule Society and Germanen Orden." *Journal of Modern History* 35, 3 (1963): 245–261.

———. "Hitler als Parteiredner im Jahre 1920." *Vierteljahrshefte für Zeitgeschichte* 11, 3 (1963): 274–330.

———. "Hitler and the *Deutsche Arbeiterpartei.*" *American Historical Review* 68, 4 (1963): 974–986.

———. "Hitlers 'Grundlegende' Rede über den Antisemitismus." *Vierteljahrshefte für Zeitgeschichte* 16, 4 (1968): 390–420.

Plewnia, Margarete. *Auf dem Weg zu Hitler: der "völkische" Publizist Dietrich Eckart.* Vol. 14 of the Bremer Reihe — Deutsche Presseforschung. Bremen: Schuenemann Universitaetsverlag, 1970.

Pool, James, and Suzanne Pool. *Who Financed Hitler?* New York: Dial Press, 1978.

Post, Gaines, Jr. *The Civil-Military Fabric of Weimar Foreign Policy.* Princeton: Princeton University Press, 1973.

Price, Billy F. *Adolf Hitler: The Unknown Artist.* Houston: Billy F. Price Publishing, 1984.

Remarque, Erich Maria. *The Black Obelisk.* Trans. Denver Lindley. New York: Harcourt, Brace, 1957.

Röhm, Ernst. *Die Geschichte eines Hochverätters.* Munich: Verlag Franz Eher Nachfolger, 1928.

———. *Die Memoiren des Stabschefs Röhm.* Saarbrucken: Uranus Verlag, 1934.

Romains, Jules. *Verdun.* Trans. Gerard Hopkins. New York: Alfred A. Knopf, 1939.

Rosenbaum, Kurt. *Community of Fate: German-Soviet Diplomatic Relations, 1922–1928.* Syracuse, N.Y.: Syracuse University Press, 1965.

Rosenberg, Alfred. *Memoirs of Alfred Rosenberg.* Trans. Eric Posselt. Chicago: Ziff-Davis Publishing, 1949.

Ryder, A. J. *Twentieth Century Germany: From Bismarck to Brandt.* New York: Columbia University Press, 1973.

Sackett, Robert Eben. *Popular Entertainment, Class, and Politics in Munich, 1900–1923.* Cambridge, Mass.: Harvard University Press, 1982.

Schoenberner, Franz. *Confessions of a European Intellectual.* New York: Macmillan, 1946.

Schoonmaker, Frank. *Come with Me Through Germany.* New York: Robert M. McBride, 1930.

Schmidt, Royal J. *Versailles and the Ruhr: Seedbed of World War II.* The Hague: Martinus Nijhoff, 1968.

Schwarzwäller, Wulf. *Rudolf Hess: Der Mann in Spandau.* Vienna: Verlag Fritz Molden, 1974.

Sebottendorff, Rudolf von. *Bevor Hitler kam: Urkundliches aus der Frühzeit der nationalsozialistischen Bewegung von Rudolf von Sebottendorff.* Munich: Deukula-Verlag Graffinger, 1933.

Showalter, Dennis E. *Little Man, What Now? "Der Sturmer" in the Weimar Republic.* Hamden, Conn.: Archon Books, 1982.

Smith, Bradley F. *Adolf Hitler: His Family, Childhood, and Youth.* Stanford: Hoover Institution, 1967.

———. *Heinrich Himmler: A Nazi in the Making, 1900–1926.* Stanford: Hoover Institution, 1971.

Smith, Denis Mack. *Mussolini.* New York: Alfred A. Knopf, 1982.

Smith, Truman. *Berlin Alert: The Memoirs and Reports of Truman Smith.* Ed. Robert Hessen. Stanford: Hoover Institution, 1984.

Snyder, Louis L., ed. *Hitler's Third Reich: A Documentary History.* Chicago: Nelson-Hall, 1981.

Spengler, Oswald. *Aphorisms.* Trans. Gisela Koch-Weser O'Brien. Chicago: Henry Regnery Company, 1967.

———. *The Decline of the West.* New York: Alfred A. Knopf, 1939.

———. *Letters of Oswald Spengler, 1913–1936.* Trans. Arthur Helps. New York: Alfred A. Knopf, 1966.

————. *Selected Essays*. Trans. Donald O. White. Chicago: Henry Regnery, 1967.

Stachura, Peter D. *Gregor Strasser and the Rise of Nazism*. London: George Allen and Unwin, 1983.

————, ed. *The Shaping of the Nazi State*. London: Croom Helm, 1978.

————. *The Weimar Era and Hitler, 1918–1933: A Critical Bibliography*. Oxford: Clio Press, 1977.

Staudinger, Hans. *The Inner Nazi: A Critical Analysis of "Mein Kampf."* Ed. Peter M. Rutkoff and William B. Scott. Baton Rouge: Louisiana State University Press, 1981.

Stern, Howard. "The *Organisation Consul*." *Journal of Modern History* 35, 1 (1963): 20–32.

Stern, J. P. *Hitler: The Führer and the People*. Berkeley and Los Angeles: University of California Press, 1975.

Stirk, S. D. *The Prussian Spirit: A Survey of German Literature and Politics, 1914–1940*. London: Faber and Faber, [1941].

Strasser, Otto, and Michael Stern. *Flight from Terror*. New York: National Travel Club (Robert M. McBride), 1943.

Taylor, A. J. P. *The Origins of the Second World War*. 2d ed. New York: Fawcett Premier, 1961.

Taylor, Simon. *The Rise of Hitler: Revolution and Counter-revolution in Germany, 1918–1933*. New York: Universe Books, 1983.

Thomas, W. Hugh. *The Murder of Rudolf Hess*. New York: Harper and Row, 1979.

Thyssen, Fritz. *I Paid Hitler*. New York: Farrar and Rinehart, 1941.

Toland, John. *Adolf Hitler*. Garden City, N.Y.: Doubleday, 1976.

————. *Hitler: The Pictorial Documentary of His Life*. Garden City, N.Y.: Doubleday, 1978.

Trager, James, ed. *The People's Chronology*. New York: Rinehart and Winston, 1979.

Tschuppik, Karl. *Ludendorff: The Tragedy of a Military Mind*. Trans. W. H. Johnston. (Reprint of *Ludendorff: The Tragedy of a Specialist*. London: Allen and Unwin, 1932.) Westport, Conn.: Greenwood Press, 1975.

Tucholsky, Kurt. *Deutschland, Deutschland über alles*. Amherst: University of Massachusetts Press, 1972.

Tyrell, Albrecht. *Vom 'Trommler' zum 'Führer': Der Wandel von Hitlers Selbstverständnis zwischen 1919 und 1924 und die Entwicklung der NSDAP*. Munich: Wilhelm Fink Verlag, 1975.

Völkischer Beobachter. (Munich: January 3, 1920–April 28, 1945.) Microfilm Collection, Library of Congress.

Waite, Robert G. L. *The Psychopathic God: Adolf Hitler*. New York: Basic Books, 1977.

————. *Vanguard of Nazism: The Free Corps Movement in Postwar Germany, 1918–1923*. Cambridge, Mass.: Harvard University Press, 1952.

Waldman, Eric. *The Spartacist Uprising of 1919*. Milwaukee: Marquette University Press, 1958.

Watt, Richard. *The Kings Depart. The Tragedy of Germany: Versailles and the German Revolution*. New York: Simon and Schuster, 1968.

■ 657

Wheeler-Bennett, John W. *The Nemesis of Power: The German Army in Politics, 1918–1945.* 2d ed. London: Macmillan, 1964.

Willett, John. *Art and Politics in the Weimar Period.* New York: Pantheon Books, 1978.

Wurgaft, Lewis D. "The Activists: Kurt Hiller and the Politics of Action on the German Left, 1914–1933." Philadelphia: Transactions of the American Philosophical Society 67, 8, 1977.

INDEX

Economics, 142–43
Economy, German, 40, 50, 59, 143, 234–35, 312, 336, 356, 414, 457, 566, 567; central European economic system plan, 249, 252. *See also* Inflation; Poverty; Unemployment
Eduard, Duke Carl, 307
Egelhofer, Rudolf, 54, 56, 57, 608n.16
Ehard, Hans, 571, 578, 580, 583, 584
Ehrenbreitstein Fortress, 337, 342
Ehrenfried Cemetery, 362
Ehrensperger, Ernst, 201
Ehrhardt, Lieutenant Commander Hermann, 55, 105, 106–7, 120, 121, 135, 158, 376, 454, 455, 638n.16
Ehrhardt Brigade, 55–56, 105–7, 110–11, 134–35; government payment of, 120, 126; in Kapp Putsch, 109, 111, 112, 118–19, 120, 121, 123–24, 125, 128; violence of, 123–24, 217, 274. *See also* Association of Former Ehrhardt Officers
Eichhorn, Emil, 33
Eichmann, Consul. *See* Ehrhardt, Lieutenant Commander Hermann
Einstein, Albert, 83, 193, 197, 620n.40
Einwohnerwehr. *See* Civil Guard
Eisner, Kurt, 37–38, 48, 49, 62, 101, 480, 569
Eitington, Max, 194
Ellendt, Andrea, 177
Enabling act, 437, 441, 566
Endres, Theodor, 374
Endziel (final goal), 114
Engelhardt, Lieutenant Colonel Philipp, 15, 16, 24

Engineer Barracks Number One, 478, 499, 501, 502, 546
Epenstein, Hermann Ritter von, 329–30
Epp, Franz Ritter von, 116, 166, 347, 358, 543
Erhard, First Lieutenant Oskar, 560

Faber Motor Vehicle Rental Service, 368, 371
Fallada, Hans, 403
Fangler, Sophie, 517
Fascism, 218–19
Fascists, Italian, 218, 264, 292, 293, 298, 311
Fatherland Front, 284, 290, 292
Fatherland Party, 107
Faulhaber, Michael, Cardinal von, 457, 508
Faust, Martin, 543, 544, 559
Feder, Gottfried, 66, 72, 74, 78, 81, 131, 139, 187, 386–87; in Hitler Putsch, 478, 547, 558; *Volkischer Beobachter* and, 165, 167
Fehrenbach, Konstantin, 128, 147, 184, 189
Feldherrnhalle (Hall of Generals), 57, 552, 553, 556, 557, 559, 560, 582, 597
Ferdinand, Archduke Franz Ferdinand, 248
Ferdl, Weiss, 344, 345
Festabend, 241
Festival Theatre, 431
Festung (Fortress). *See* Landsberg Prison
Feuchtwanger, Lion, 341
Fighter Squadron 35, 139
First Company of the Nineteenth Infantry Regiment, 471, 472
First Regiment of Foot Guards, 141

National socialism, 68, 73, 80, 98–99, 112

Patriotism, 173, 344; of Hitler and Nazi Party, 321, 346, 386; of right-wing groups, 72, 73, 284, 285, 407, 431, 481, 581; as sanction for anti-Semitism, 64, 133

Paulukun, Georg, 53

Pavlova, 195–96

Pension Moritz, 379, 380

People's Court of Munich, 240, 253, 574

People's Naval Division, 38, 39

Pernet, Lieutenant Heinz, 469, 470, 471, 476, 485, 547, 577, 584

"Pessimism?" (Spengler), 172

Piscator, Erwin, 193

Pittinger, Otto, 290, 291, 292, 294

Pius XII, 222, 508

Planck, Max, 194

Pogroms, 65, 130

Pöhner, Police Commissioner Ernst, 158, 159, 219, 221, 299, 424; in Hitler's "national government," 460, 489, 508, 513; in Hitler Putsch, 481, 496, 497, 503, 508–10, 527–28; on trial for role in Putsch, 584

Poincaré, Raymond, 239, 240, 325, 339, 356, 411, 435

Poland, 59; alliance with France, 96, 144, 185; conflicts with Germany, 42, 95, 96, 105, 144, 152, 185, 210, 224, 260, 340; German expansionism and, 191, 212, 595. *See also* Polish Corridor; Upper Silesia

Police, 33, 437, 440, 446, 454, 462; Hitler's encounters with, 377–78, 563, 564–65, 597; during Hitler Putsch, 460, 466–67, 479, 483, 484, 486, 487, 492, 499, 503, 510–11, 525, 526, 531, 539–40, 541, 548–49, 551, 552, 553–54, 557–58, 582; Hitler Putsch trial and, 574, 579, 583; May Day

(1923), 369, 371, 373, 374; Nazi confrontations with, 211, 227, 290, 314, 384, 436; right-wing and Nazi influence in, 158, 159, 217, 221, 227, 307, 318, 366, 371, 445, 460, 462, 479–80, 487, 492, 526; uprisings and, 33, 111, 113, 121, 231, 232, 291, 371, 373, 374, 415; *Völkischer Beobachter* shut down by, 133, 198–99, 222, 384

Polish Corridor, 59, 152

Political Theater, 193

Political Workers' Circle, 72, 73, 78, 79

Pölzl, Klara. *See* Hitler, Klara

Pomeranian Landbund, 291, 638n.15

Popolo d'Italia, 295

Popp, Arthur, 28

Posch, Rudolf, 203–4

Poverty, 197, 235, 403, 434

Press, the, 316; foreign coverage of Hitler, 512–14, 535, 536–37, 561, 573–74, 579, 599; Hitler's view of, 175, 191; right-wing bias of, 147, 377. *See also* Censorship

"Preussentum und Sozialismus" (Spengler), 98

Price, G. Ward, 575

Pröhl, Ilse, 141

Proletarian Hundreds (Red Hundreds), 353, 369, 385–86, 412, 414, 441

Propaganda, 114, 206–7, 535; Hitler's theories of, 21–22, 168, 523, 524, 588, 592; Nazi trucks, 179, 288–89. *See also* Indoctrination

Prostitution, 196, 197

Protocols of the Elders of Zion, The, 130–32

Prussia, 36, 59, 236

Prussia, West, 152

Prussian Diet, 115, 120

435, 576; German-Allied negotiations on, 144, 146, 185, 240, 325; industry in, 145, 336–37, 341, 343, 356

Ruhr Echo, 126

Ruith, General Adolf Ritter von, 506

Rumford, Count. *See* Thompson, Benjamin

Rundschreiben. *See* Circular Letter

Runge, Private Otto, 44

Rupprecht, Crown Prince, 91, 279, 318, 421, 434, 495, 533; movement to restore power of, 420, 424, 430, 496, 509; Nazi plot to kidnap, 452–53, 638n.10

Rupprecht, Kriminal-Kommissar, 395–96

Russia, 42, 52, 144, 252; communist revolution in Germany and, 410–12, 413, 415, 417; expansion of Germany and, 191, 595; German-Russian alliance, 156, 256–60, 298, 357; Hitler's views on, 324, 595; during World War I, 30, 59

Russian Revolution, 28, 31, 40, 51, 195, 256, 411, 413

Russo, Baron, 513

SA (Storm Troops), 210, 211, 253, 353, 355, 357, 363, 423, 445, 471, 546; Battle of the Hall, 227, 228–29, 231, 232–33; Berlin overthrow, plans for, 412–13, 446, 452; Coburg occupation, 300, 302, 303, 304–5, 307, 309; Goering, as head of, 328, 334, 442; in Hitler Putsch, 457, 459, 466, 470, 472, 477, 479, 484, 487, 490, 491, 495, 498–99, 501, 503, 505, 507, 516, 517, 518–19, 531, 534, 558; at Königsplatz demonstration (1922), 285; May

Day (1923), 371–73, 376; membership, 209–10, 211, 225, 226–27, 253, 288, 310, 384, 385; at Nuremberg right-wing rally (1923), 407; at Parteitag, 345, 346, 347, 348, 349, 352–53; police relations, 221, 226–27, 436; presence in Munich, 446–47; Sports Section (Sportabteilung), 176, 177, 198, 209, 517; Storm Section (Sturmabteilung), 210, 621n.12; violence of, 227, 254, 270, 274, 285, 289, 304, 386, 516, 518–19, 600; youth recruitment for, 225, 253. *See also* Hundertschaften

Saalschlacht. *See* Battle of the Hall

Saar Basin, 91–92, 113, 275

SA Battalion Rossbach, 469

Sachs, Hans, 194

Salomon, Ernst von, 105–6, 271–72, 273, 277

"Salon Communists," 194

Salzburg, 151–54

Sandmeier, Marie, 157, 159

Sarajevo, 248

Sauerbruch, Ferdinand, 557

Saxony, 155, 363, 390, 414, 415, 416

Scharrer, Eduard August, 324

Scheidemann, Philipp, 32, 45, 60, 108, 270, 582

Scheubner-Richter, Max Erwin von, 318–19, 439, 453; in Hitler Putsch, 456, 458, 463, 464–65, 476, 484, 485, 486, 489, 494, 500, 527, 547, 553, 554

Schiller, 47

Schilling, Alexander, 154

Schlageter, Albert Leo, 384, 633n.17

Schleicher, Lieutenant Colonel Kurt von, 258, 514